Praise for *The ESL/ELL Teacher's Survival Guide*

"An engaging, practical, and highly accessible book .... The authors share strategies that have been proven effective through research as well as their own practice. There is truly something valuable for any teacher, even those who have extensive experience with ESL classes."

—**PIA WONG**, professor, Bilingual/Multicultural Education, California State University, Sacramento

"This is an invaluable resource for all new and experienced teachers who desire to see their language learning students thrive and achieve at high levels."

—**DANA DUSBIBER**, classroom teacher with over 30 years of experience working with ELLs

The ESL/ELL Teacher's Survival Guide

SECOND EDITION

The ESL/ELL Teacher's Survival Guide

Ready-to-Use Strategies, Tools, & Activities for Teaching All Levels

LARRY FERLAZZO AND KATIE HULL SYPNIESKI

SECOND EDITION

JB JOSSEY-BASS™
A Wiley Brand

Library of Congress Cataloging-in-Publication Data is Available:

ISBN 9781119550389 (paperback)
ISBN 9781119550426 (ePDf)
ISBN 9781119550419 (ePub)

Cover Design: Wiley
Cover Image: © banyumilistudio/Shutterstock

SKY10045600_041123

About the Authors

Larry Ferlazzo teaches English and social studies to English language learners and English-proficient students at Luther Burbank High School in Sacramento, California. He has written, co-authored, or edited 12 books on education.

He has won numerous awards, including the Leadership for a Changing World Award from the Ford Foundation, and was the grand prize winner of the International Reading Association Award for Technology and Reading.

He writes a popular education blog at http://larryferlazzo.edublogs.org and writes a weekly teacher advice column for *Education Week*. His articles on education policy regularly appear in *The Washington Post*. In addition, his work has appeared in publications such as *The New York Times, ASCD Educational Leadership, Social Policy,* and *Language Magazine*.

Ferlazzo was a community organizer for 19 years prior to becoming a public school teacher. He is married and has three children and four grandchildren.

Katie Hull Sypnieski has taught English language learners of all proficiency levels and English-proficient students for 25 years in the Sacramento City Unified School District. She has served as a teaching consultant with the Area 3 Writing Project housed at University of California-Davis for the past 20 years.

She has co-authored three books on teaching ELLs and has co-edited three books on education. She has published articles and instructional videos for *Education Week*. In addition, she has co-authored articles for *Edutopia, The New York Times Learning Network,* and *ASCD Educational Leadership*.

Sypnieski currently teaches English to English language learners and English-proficient students at Arthur A. Benjamin Health Professions High School in Sacramento, California. She is married and has three children.

Larry and Katie have co-authored two other books on teaching English language learners, *The ELL Teacher's Toolbox* and *Navigating the Common Core with English Language Learners*, both from Jossey-Bass/Wiley.

Contents

About the Authors vii

Acknowledgments xv

About the Contributors xvii

Introduction xxi

PART ONE: GETTING STARTED WITH ENGLISH LANGUAGE LEARNERS 1

1. ELL Instruction: The Big Picture 3

ELL Population Growth 4

How Are English Language Learners Described? 5

Adolescent English Language Learners 7

A Primer on ELL Research 8

A Quick Tour of ELL Best Practices 12

2. ELL Classroom Basics: Building a Positive and Effective Learning Environment 17

The First R: Building *Relationships* 18

The Second R: *Resources* in the ELL Classroom 36

The Third R: Establishing *Routines* 43

PART TWO: TEACHING BEGINNING ENGLISH LANGUAGE LEARNERS 47

3. Key Elements of a Curriculum for Beginning ELLs 49

Key Elements of a Curriculum 50

4. Daily Instruction for Beginning ELLs 115

Picture Word Inductive Model Unit Plan 116

PART THREE: TEACHING INTERMEDIATE ENGLISH LANGUAGE LEARNERS 161

5. Key Elements of a Curriculum for Intermediate ELLs 163

Key Elements of a Curriculum 164

6. Daily Instruction for Intermediate ELLs 213

Designing Thematic Genre Units 213
A Sample Unit: Problem-Solution 215
Sample Lesson Plans 245
Inductive Lesson Plan 245
Using Text to Generate Analytical Writing Lesson Plan 251
A Sample Week in a Two-Period Intermediate ELL Class 258

PART FOUR: TEACHING ENGLISH LANGUAGE LEARNERS IN THE CONTENT AREAS 263

7. English Language Learners in the Mainstream Classroom 265

What Is the Organizing Cycle? 267

8. Teaching Social Studies 283

Building Relationships with Students 284

9. Teaching Science 301

Introduction: Science and Language 302

10. Teaching Math.. 315

Introduction.. 316
Challenge: Reading Mathematics Texts 317
Challenge: Knowledge of Appropriate Academic Vocabulary 319
Challenge: Participating in Mathematics Conversations................. 321
Challenge: Understanding Abstract Concepts......................... 324

PART FIVE: WORKING WITH SPECIFIC GROUPS OF ENGLISH LANGUAGE LEARNERS 327

11. Supporting Long-Term English Language Learners.............. 329

Who Are Long-Term English Language Learners? 330
How Can We Best Support LTELLs?................................... 330
How Did Larry and His School Try to Put These Recommendations into Action?.. 331

12. Working with Elementary ELLs 339

Who Are Elementary English Learners?.............................. 340
Do Elementary English Language Learners Have Different Needs?
Does Their Instruction Need to be Different from that of Older
English Learners? 342
Program Types in Elementary.................................... 342
The Core Elements of Supportive Instruction for
Elementary English Language Learners 345
What Does a Model Classroom that is Highly Supportive of
Elementary English Learners Look Like?.......................... 345
What Does a Model Classroom that is Highly Supportive of Elementary
English Learners Sound Like?................................... 347
What Does a Model Classroom that is Highly Supportive of Elementary
ELLs Feel Like?.. 349
Instructional Strategies that Support Elementary ELLs................. 352

13. Teaching Adult Ells.. 355

The Differences in Teaching English to Adults Versus Children.......... 356
How to Foster Success with Adult Learners......................... 362

14. Teaching ELLs with Learning Differences 371

Considerations for Further Investigation............................ 372

Considerations for Determining Services..373
Considerations for Placement/Scheduling..375
Resources...376

PART SIX: FURTHER STRATEGIES TO ENSURE SUCCESS 377

15. Culturally Responsive and Sustaining Teaching.....................379

What Is Culturally Responsive and Sustaining Teaching?....................380
The Organizing Cycle..381

16. Addressing Additional Opportunities and Challenges...393

Student Motivation...394
The Advantages of Being Bilingual or Multilingual Lesson Plan.........395
Social Emotional Learning...408
Textbook Integration...410
Error Correction...412
Limited Access to Educational Technology...414
Multilevel Classes..415
Co-Teaching and/or Working with an Aide/Paraprofessional..............419
Classroom Management...421
Book Selection..422
Supporting ELL Students with Limited or Interrupted Formal
Education (SLIFEs)..424

17. Home Language of ELLs...427

Seeing Home Language as an Asset..429
A Mini Lesson on the Value of Home Languages....................................430
Research on Home Languages in the Classroom......................................431
Turning Bloom's Taxonomy into a Home-Language Framework..........434
Abandoning English-Only Policies...440
Conclusion...442

18. Using Learning Games in the ELL Classroom........................445

Research Support..445
What Are the Qualities of a Good Learning Game?................................446

19. Assessing English Language Learners 461

Assessing ELLs: Key Principles...462

20. Reflective Teaching/Professional Development 487

The Bread in the Pond 487
Why Should We Have an Intentional, Formal Process for Reflecting? 488
Why I Began Filming Myself and Why I Continued..................................489
Adopting a Reflective Mindset 490

Afterword 497

Notes 499

Index... 539

Bonus Web Content

Companion papers are available online, at www.wiley.com/go/eslsurvivalguide2, on these topics related to teaching english online and around the world:

- Distance Learning
- Teaching English Internationally
- Non Native English Speakers Teaching English
- Teaching Science (from 1st edition)
- Teaching Math (from 1st edition)

Acknowledgments

Larry Ferlazzo. I'd like to thank my family—Stacia, Rich, Shea, Ava, Nik, Katie, Karli, Federico and especially, my wife, Jan—for their support. In addition, I need to express appreciation to my co-author, Katie Hull Sypnieski, who has also been a colleague and friend for eighteen years. I would like to thank my many colleagues at Luther Burbank High School, including Principal Jim Peterson, for their assistance over the years. And, probably most important, I'd like to thank the many English language learner students who have made me a better teacher—and a better person.

Katie Hull Sypnieski. I would like to thank all the students I've had over the years for their determination, their creative energy, and for helping me to grow as an educator and as a person. In addition, I am grateful for all of the support I have received from my colleagues, especially Larry Ferlazzo, my co-author, co-teacher, and friend. Finally, to all of my family members, especially my husband, David, and children Drew, Ryan, and Rachel, I want to thank you for supporting me in this process—you are the best!

There are also several people we would both like to thank:

We must offer a big thank-you to Amy Fandrei and Pete Gaughan at Jossey-Bass for their patience and guidance in preparing this book, and to David Powell for his assistance in formatting our manuscript submission.

And, of course, we have to thank the *10* other contributors to this second edition (you can see their complete biographies elsewhere in this book):

Laura Gibbs
Stephen Fleenor
Cindy Garcia
Valentina Gonzalez
Antoinette Perez
Jessica Bell
Tan Huynh
Carol Salva
Jenny Vo
Lorie Hammond

About the Contributors

Nine other educators have made sizable contributions to this second edition.

Laura Gibbs received her PhD in Comparative Literature from UC Berkeley in 1999. She joined the University of Oklahoma faculty where she taught online courses in folklore and mythology; she retired from teaching in 2021 in order to write full-time. She is the author of a translation of *Aesop's Fables* for Oxford University Press, and she is also the author of a free OER book series: *Tiny Tales*, which is available online at LauraGibbs.net.

Stephen Fleenor is an educational consultant in San Antonio, Texas with Seidlitz Education (www.seidlitzeducation.com). Stephen earned a PhD in Developmental Neurobiology from the University of Oxford before teaching high school science in a highly disadvantaged community in San Antonio. His pedagogy developed out of a passion to serve English learners and other at-risk students while spreading his love for science. As a facilitator of professional development and developer of educational materials, he advocates for a growth-minded approach to teaching and learning that encourages and strengthens learners' academic expression.

Cindy Garcia has been a bilingual educator for 15 years and is currently a districtwide specialist for P-6 bilingual/ESL mathematics. She is active on Twitter at @CindyGarciaTX and on her blog (https://teachingelementaryels.weebly.com/).

Valentina Gonzalez has more than 20 years of experience teaching and working with multilingual students from around the globe. Her personal experience as an immigrant from Yugoslavia and language learner fuel her desire to advocate for English learners and support teachers with the best research-based teaching methods. Her work's primary focuses have been on literacy, culture, and language. Valentina is the coauthor of *Reading & Writing with English Learners: A Framework for K-5.*

Antoinette Perez has more than 10 years of experience working with English Language Learners of all levels, including extensive experience with international and adult learners. She has worked in California and Georgia at schools with high percentages of ELs, which motivated her to obtain TEFL certification to teach English abroad. She currently serves as the English Co-Department Chair at Buena High School in Ventura, California where she runs the ELD program and teaches honors and AP English. In another capacity, she instructs online English classes for children and adults. Her dedication to students and ESL instruction has taken her around the world to enrich her ability to connect with students and enhance her professional practice.

Jessica Bell, M.Ed, taught English and ENL for 19 years, serving students from a diverse mix of backgrounds. A SIOP practitioner while in the classroom, she believes all students deserve equitable access to rigorous academic instruction. Jessica has transitioned from the classroom to the EdTech space, helping provide teachers with digitals tools to enhance instruction.

Tan Huynh (@TanKHuynh) is a career teacher specializing in language acquisition. He nerds out on all things related to multilingual students and shares what he has learned from experts, scholars, and master teachers through his writings, podcast, courses, conference, and workshops.

Carol Salva is an international education consultant with elementary, middle and high school teaching experience. She provides sheltered instruction workshops, coaching and modeling through Seidlitz Education. Carol is the co-author of *Boosting Achievement: Reaching Students with Interrupted or Minimal Education.*

Jenny Vo earned her B.A. in English from Rice University and her M.Ed in Educational Leadership from Lamar University. She has worked with English Learners during all of her 27 years in education, first in Houston Independent School District and then in Katy Independent School District. Jenny recently made the move to International Leadership of Texas and serves as the Houston area EL Coordinator. Jenny has served on the Board of TexTESOL IV for several years and was the 2020–2021 president. She works to advocate for all English learners and enjoys sharing her knowledge and passion with others at local and state conferences. She loves learning from her #PLN on Twitter so feel free to follow her @ JennyVo15.

Introduction

There was a great forest fire—everything was burning and all the animals were scared and didn't know what they could do. A hummingbird, though, went to a lake and got a drop of water. It flew to the fire and dropped the water there, and it kept on going back again. The other animals kept on telling the hummingbird that it was wasting its time, telling it there was no way a little water was going to make a difference. The hummingbird replied, "I'm doing the best I can."

—Modern ecological parable[1]

The hummingbird did its best in the face of many challenges and adversity, and nothing could stop it.

While it would have been ideal for the hummingbird to organize all the animals to join it in fighting the fire, always encouraging the use of that kind of strategy is not the main point of the story or this book. This book is primarily designed to help secondary-level ELL teachers do the best they can in their classrooms (though it does also include a chapter on how to help mainstream educators make their content more accessible to English language learners, too). In addition, the majority of approaches and strategies we discuss can be easily modified for younger ELLs.

This book is primarily written by two committed and experienced educators who have a rich family life outside of school, plan on continuing to teach for years to come, and who are always interested in providing high-quality education to their students without requiring enormous extra work for the teacher. In addition, nine—count 'em, *nine*—other very experienced educators have contributed towards making this book nearly twice the size of the first edition!

It is not written by or for teachers who lack awareness of their own limitations and what is needed to stay in education for the long haul.

This book is a careful distillation of selected instructional strategies that have been used successfully by us for years in the classroom.

It is not a laundry list of every ELL teaching method that's been discussed in the literature.

In addition to providing a selective review of ELL teaching methods, this book shares highly regarded research supporting just about everything we suggest.

It is not just speaking from our experience and what we think is good. This book shares numerous specific suggestions about how ELL teachers can use technology to bring a value-added benefit to their language-learning students.

It is not a treatise on how educational technology is the "magic bullet" that is always (or even often) superior to nontech strategies.

This book recognizes that teachers need to deal with standards (we discuss both Common Core and The Next Generation Science Standards), textbooks, and standardized tests. This book also recognizes that not everything always goes according to plan, and includes a lengthy chapter on how to deal with potential problems. This book understands the realities of what work in the classroom world actually is like.

It does not offer a pie-in-the-sky view assuming we operate in an ideal classroom world all the time.

This book emphasizes the importance of learners being co-creators of their education.

It does not encourage the teacher being the "sage on stage."

The point of this book is not to claim it is the be-all and end-all for ELL teacher professional development. We strongly encourage teachers and their schools to develop ongoing mentor relationships with experienced educator organizations, and we recommend three of them in the Afterword.

This book does not promote the idea that any teacher is an island and only needs a few books and informal professional relationships to reach his full potential.

We hope that you can gain from the second edition of this guide at least as much as we learned from writing it.

Bonus Web Content

The last five chapters are "web-only" and available without any registration required. These include the original chapters on teaching Science and Math that appeared in the first edition. This second edition contains entirely new chapters, but we still believe the original ones can be very helpful to teachers of ELLs. Two of the chapters relate to teaching internationally. We thought that putting them online would increase their accessibility to teachers outside of the United States. The final chapter is about distance learning, and Wiley graciously allowed us to put it freely online in the middle of the COVID-19 pandemic (though, we have made some minor changes since then). Numerous Tech Tools supporting the lessons and instructional strategies that we discuss are highlighted throughout this book. In addition, we have a lengthy web page listing links to all the tools we cite, as well as to many others that we did not have space to include. All Exhibits (primarily student handouts) in the book can also be downloaded. Readers can access these resources by going to www .wiley.com/go/eslsurvivalguide2.

PART ONE

Getting Started with English Language Learners

CHAPTER ONE

ELL Instruction: The Big Picture

Long ago a wise, old teacher lived in a village near a range of mountains. Climbing the highest of these mountains was considered an important accomplishment, and all the young boys of the village couldn't wait until they were old enough to make the climb on their own.

One night, the wise teacher gathered a group of boys together and said to them, "You have reached the age to take on the challenge. Tomorrow you may all go and climb that mountain with my blessings. Go as far as you can, and when you are tired, turn around and come home. Remember to bring back a twig from the place where you turned around."

The next morning, the boys began the long-awaited climb. A few hours later, one of the boys returned with a piece of buckthorn. The teacher smiled and said, "I can see you made it to the first rockslide. Wonderful!" Later in the afternoon, another boy arrived with a cedar frond. "You made it halfway up! Well done!" remarked the teacher. An hour later another boy returned with a branch of pine, and the teacher said, "Good job. It looks like you made it three-quarters of the way. If you keep trying, next year you will surely reach the top!"

As the sun began to set, the teacher began to worry about the last boy, who still had not returned. Just when the teacher was about to send out a search party, the boy finally returned. He ran to the teacher and held out his hand. His hand was empty, but his eyes sparkled with happiness as he said, "Teacher, there were no trees where I turned around. I saw no twigs, no living things at the very top of the peak, and far away I could see the majestic sun shining off the sea."

The teacher's eyes also sparkled with joy as he proclaimed, "I knew it! When I looked in your eyes I could see that you made it! You have been to the top! It shines in your eyes and sings in your voice! My son, you do not need twigs or branches as prizes of your victory. You have felt the prize in your spirit because you have seen the wonder of the mountain!"[1]

This tale describes the satisfaction and joy felt by the boy who reached the mountain's peak and witnessed the compelling view from the top. He didn't return with any physical "prizes" but instead carried the treasures of his journey within himself. The next time he climbs the mountain, he will be motivated from within, not because there are tokens or prizes to be collected.

As educators, we hope all of our students will "see the view from the peak" and will feel compelled to take on many more journeys as they learn and grow. Researcher Stephen Krashen explains how "compelling input" relates to language learning: Compelling means that the input is so interesting you forget that it is in another language. It means you are in a state of "flow."[2] In flow, the concerns of everyday life and even the sense of self disappear—our sense of time is altered and nothing but the activity itself seems to matter.[3]

This idea will be reflected throughout this book as we identify and describe research-based instructional strategies and approaches that "compel" students to want to learn English. Compelling input can help students "reach the peak" of acquiring language without seeking external rewards. However, it is ultimately important for students to come to their own conclusions about the value of "reaching the peak." Once students see the value of language learning and become intrinsically motivated to learn English, they will take the risk and climb that mountain over and over again. Sometimes they will need encouragement and support from us, especially when the peak is obscured by clouds along the way.

This book contains strategies and tools for teachers of English Language Learners to act as guides on this trek up the mountain. We hope it will help you feel prepared and excited about this journey. We know that everyone's trail will be different, and we hope this "survival guide" will serve as a compass rather than a direct map.

In the following subsections we will lay out a big picture of ELL instruction, including statistics on the English language learner population, research on language development, and several ELL instructional best practices. Later chapters will go into more detail on how to implement these big picture research findings and practices in your own classroom.

ELL Population Growth

It is hard to find a school district in this country that doesn't have an English Language Learner population. For teachers in states like Alaska, California, Colorado, Florida, Illinois, Massachusetts, Nevada, New Mexico, Texas, and Washington, it is sometimes hard to find a school or even a classroom without any English language learners. ELL enrollment in K–12 schools increased 28 percent between the 2000–2001 school year and the 2016–2017 school year.[4] In fact, the US Department of Education estimates that approximately five million English language learners are enrolled in public schools across the country—roughly 10 percent of all students enrolled in K–12 schools in the United States.[5]

While English learners in this country come from over 400 different language backgrounds, the majority (around 75 percent) of English Language Learners are Spanish speakers.[6] Arabic and Chinese are the second most common home languages spoken among ELLs (accounting for 2.7 percent and 2 percent, respectively, of the ELL population).[7] English is the fourth most common home language (spoken by about 2 percent of ELLs) and may reflect students raised in multilingual households as well as students adopted from other countries who were raised speaking a different language but who now live in an English-speaking household.[8]

US school districts in more urban areas have higher percentages of ELL students. ELLs make up 14 percent of students in city school districts, compared with just 4 percent in rural districts. Suburban districts and towns fall in the middle with ELLs making up 9 percent and 6 percent of total public school enrollees.[9]

In general, most ELLs are in the elementary school grades. In 2018, 15.1 percent of kindergarteners were ELL students, 8.9 percent of 6th-graders and 7.4 percent of 8th-graders were ELLs. Only 5.1 percent of 12th graders were ELL students. It is believed this pattern reflects, in part, students who were identified as ELLs when they entered elementary school but gained enough English Language Proficiency by the upper grades to be reclassified as proficient.[10] However, the majority of public school districts in the United States do have English Language Learners in their high schools. In fact, 62 percent of public high schools have at least some number of ELLs enrolled with around 800,000 high school ELL students nationwide.[11]

How Are English Language Learners Described?

ELLs are a diverse, dynamic group, which is evident in the variety of terms used to describe them. Here are several of the most common:

ELL, or English Language Learner. *ELL (or EL)* is the most common term currently used in the United States to describe students who are in various stages of acquiring English and who require different levels of language support and development in order to become fully proficient in English.

Emergent Bilingual. The term emergent bilingual, coined and popularized by Dr. Ofelia García, focuses on "an asset-based view of the capabilities of emergent bilingual students, who are simultaneously acquiring a new set of linguistic capabilities in school and building on the valuable knowledge of their first language."[12]

EMLL, or Emergent Multilingual Learner. *EMLL, or Multilingual Learner (MLL)*, further expands the term *emergent bilingual* to highlight students as speakers of multiple languages with many linguistic resources upon which they can build.[13]

DLL, or Dual language learner. A DLL is a child between the ages of zero and eight and who is in the process of learning English in addition to their home language(s) or who is learning two or more languages at the same time. DLLs may or may not be considered English language learners by their schools, depending on their performance on English language proficiency assessments.[14]

LEP, or limited English proficiency. *LEP* was used for many years by the US Department of Education for ELLs who had not yet demonstrated proficiency in English, according to state standards and assessments. When referring to students, the term LEP has been replaced by the term English Learner (EL) or ELL. However, when referring to parents of ELLs, the Department of Education still refers to them as LEP (Limited English Proficient) parents.[15]

ESL, or English as a Second Language. The term *ESL* was formerly used as a designation for ELL students, but is more commonly used as a general term for a program of instruction (e.g., the study of English in an English-speaking country) or a field of study.[16] ESL is sometimes still used at the postsecondary level to refer to multilingual students.

ELD, or English language development. *ELD* is often used to describe instruction and programs for ELL students that focus on specifically developing English language proficiency in the domains of reading, writing, listening, and speaking. ELD differs from *Sheltered Instruction* where instruction in a content area is being "adjusted" or scaffolded in order to help students learn content skills and knowledge while also supporting the learning of English. To put it simply, ELD instruction is mainly focused on developing proficiency in English, while Sheltered Instruction focuses on academic success in the content areas.[17]

TESOL, or Teaching English to speakers of other languages. *TESOL* is widely used to describe both TESL (teaching English as a Second Language) and TEFL (teaching English as a foreign language). In general, TESL tends to emphasize the needs of English language learners living in English-speaking countries who will need to use English in their daily lives, while TEFL involves teaching English as a foreign language in countries where English is not widely used.[18]

Many educators and researchers, including the authors of this book, prefer the term *ELL* because it emphasizes that students are active *learners* of English, as opposed to being limited or deficient in some way.

Adolescent English Language Learners

Adolescent ELL students are a fast-growing population and come from a variety of cultural, linguistic, and educational backgrounds.

Newcomer or refugee students represent a smaller, but highly vulnerable section of the adolescent English learner population. While it is difficult to know exactly how many newly arrived immigrant learners enroll in secondary schools each year, data suggests in 2015 around 42 percent of ELLs in US schools grades 6–12 were foreign-born.[19] More recently, there has been a sharp rise in unaccompanied minors at the Southern border of the United States. In fact, the Department of Homeland Security projects there will be 117,000 unaccompanied child migrants crossing the border in 2021, a large number of whom are teenagers.[20] In addition, increasing numbers of refugee students have been arriving from Afghanistan.

While some newcomer and refugee students come with high literacy skills and content knowledge, many arrive with limited or interrupted formal education and are described by researchers as Students with Limited or Interrupted Formal Education (SLIFE). A recent study found that 11.4 percent of foreign-born 10th-grade students have experienced school interruptions upon arrival in the United States.[21] SLIFE students face huge challenges as they enter US schools with limited educational experiences and lower levels of literacy in their home languages. Not only are they met with the academic demands of secondary school while adjusting to a new language and culture, but some are also dealing with poverty, the stresses of family separation and/or reunification, and trauma due to violence suffered in their home country or during migration.[22] See Chapter Sixteen for a more detailed discussion on working with this group of students.

A larger group of secondary ELL students have been described by researchers as Long-Term English Language Learners, or LTELLs. These are ELL students who have attended school for six years or more but who continue to require language support services. The population of LTELLs in US schools has been steadily increasing and has been estimated to represent one quarter to one half of the total ELL population.[23] In California, the number of LTELLs grew from 62 percent of all secondary school ELLs in 2008 to 82 percent in 2016.[24] Typically, these students have high levels of oral English proficiency, but may lack the academic language and literacy skills needed to master subject matter. Many are "stuck" at the intermediate level of proficiency and face disproportionately high drop-out rates.[25] Many of these students may not have received targeted language development, may have been placed with teachers lacking the professional development needed to meet specific language needs, and may have lived in particularly challenging socioeconomic conditions, including poverty.[26] See Chapter Eleven for more research and resources on LTELLs.

With such diversity among adolescent ELLs, it is important for teachers to learn as much as possible about their students and to have knowledge of strategies that directly address the needs of these students. Chapter Two contains ideas for getting to know students and for building relationships of trust with students and their families. It also outlines important resources for working with adolescent ELLs and gives ideas for establishing classroom routines that promote a positive learning environment. Chapters Three and Four present instructional strategies designed for newcomer and beginning students, and Chapters Five and Six offer numerous strategies designed for intermediate-level learners, including long-term ELLs.

While adolescent learners enter our classrooms with diverse needs and challenges, it is important to remember that they also possess creative minds capable of processing higher-order thinking and learning. The general public may often have the impression that language learning is easiest for young children and becomes harder and harder with age. However, recent research has shown that teens can learn a language as quickly as young children. One study found that the optimal window for language learning could be open a decade longer than previously thought—until the age of 17! [27]

A Primer on ELL Research

The following subsections present basic descriptions of research and concepts that are foundational components of ELL instruction. While this is not a comprehensive summary of all the research on language development, it is an introduction to several key concepts that are highly important for teachers of ELLs and can serve as launching points for further study.

L1 AND L2

Researchers and educators commonly use the term *L1* to refer to a student's home language (also called first language, native language, or heritage language) and *L2* to refer to the language a student is acquiring in addition to their home language, which in the United States is English. Children exposed to their first and second languages at the same time (usually prior to age three) are referred to as *simultaneous bilinguals*. Individuals who develop their second language after their first are known as *sequential bilinguals*. In general, if a child is exposed to their second language after the age of three, then they will become a sequential bilingual.[28]

The next subsection, on ELL best practices, will discuss the important link between L1 and L2 in language learning.

BICS AND CALP

Jim Cummins, a professor at the University of Toronto, first introduced the distinction between BICS (basic interpersonal communicative skills) and CALP (cognitive academic language proficiency).[29] His research has had a major impact on policy and practices in second language education. Figure 1.1 summarizes Cummins's distinctions.

More recent research has extended CALP to include the following three dimensions of academic English: linguistic (knowledge of word forms, functions, grammatical elements, and discourse patterns used in academic settings), cognitive (higher-order thinking involved in academic settings), and sociocultural-psychological (knowledge of social practices involved in academic settings).[30]

Instruction based on CALP is still widely accepted as best practice,[31] as many researchers agree upon the need to focus on academic language proficiency in order for ELLs to succeed in school.

ACQUISITION VERSUS LEARNING

Most researchers acknowledge a distinction between language acquisition and language learning. A simple explanation of the difference is that acquisition involves being able to easily use the language to communicate, while language learning might place more emphasis on filling out grammar worksheets correctly. This does not mean, however, that the two are mutually exclusive.

BICS	CALP
Listening and speaking skills that are acquired quickly in a new language in order to communicate in social situations	The academic language and more cognitively demanding skills required for academic success
Usually acquired within the first couple of years	Often takes longer to develop, between five and seven years, or longer for students with less proficiency in their home language
Context-embedded (meaning is accomplished with the assistance of contextual cues such as pictures, body language or intonation)	Context-reduced (meaning must be constructed without the benefit of contextual cues and literacy demands are high)
Example: Asking someone for directions or talking with friends on the soccer field	Example: Responding to an essay prompt or summarizing a chapter in a textbook

Figure 1.1. BICS and CALP

From L. Ferlazzo and K. H. Sypnieski, *Navigating the Common Core with English Language Learners* (San Francisco: Jossey-Bass, 2016), p. 6.

This distinction has led to much debate over the place of explicit grammar study in language development. Some linguists have argued for a more communicative approach, where the focus is on the message versus the form and fosters language acquisition, while others believe students need direct instruction in grammatical forms of the target language.[32]

Recent research has proposed a more balanced approach—that second language instruction can provide a combination of both *explicit* teaching focused on features of the second language such as grammar, vocabulary, and pronunciation, and *implicit* learning stemming from meaningful communication in the second language.[33] We agree that the best language instruction uses meaningful input and contexts to help students develop their English skills, but we also feel that teaching language features in context is also necessary for students to develop proficiency. Specific strategies for how to employ this kind of balanced approach in the classroom will be described in later chapters.

STAGES OF LANGUAGE DEVELOPMENT

While it is important to note that ELL students come with different cultural and educational experiences that can affect their language development, researchers, beginning with Stephen Krashen and Tracy Terrell,[34] have generally agreed on the following five stages of second language acquisition:

Preproduction. This phase is also called the "Silent or Receptive Stage" and is when the student is "taking in" the target language. The student may spend time learning vocabulary and may or may not practice pronouncing new words. The length of this phase is dependent on each individual learner and can last several hours or several months.

Early Production. In this phase, which may last about six months, the student begins to try speaking using words and short phrases, even though they may not be grammatically correct. A big focus is still on listening and absorbing the new language.

Speech Emergence or Production. By this stage, learners have typically acquired a few thousand words. Words and sentences are longer, but the student still relies heavily on context clues and familiar topics. This is an important stage where learners are developing greater comprehension and begin reading and writing in the new language.

Intermediate Fluency. In this stage, learners begin to communicate in complex sentences in speaking and writing. Learners also begin thinking in their second language which results in even more proficiency gains.

Advanced Fluency/Continued Language Development. As students reach advanced fluency they are able to communicate fluently and can maneuver successfully in new contexts and when exposed to new academic information. Learners need ongoing opportunities to further improve their accuracy and to maintain their fluency.

It is important to remember that not all students' experiences fall neatly into these categories, and that prior educational experiences, and literacy in their L1 can have a great impact on students' language acquisition processes. Researchers believe oral proficiency can take three to five years to develop and academic English proficiency can take four to seven years, or even longer for students with less proficiency in their first language.[35]

Knowing students' proficiency levels can help teachers differentiate their instruction and address the language needs of each student. For example, when working with students in preproduction and early production stages, it can be useful to ask yes-or-no questions. Students at the speech emergent level could be asked questions that require fairly short, literal answers, and students at the intermediate fluency stage could be asked if they agree or disagree with a statement and why.

ENGLISH LANGUAGE PROFICIENCY LEVELS

As described earlier, research has found that ELLs progress through several stages of language acquisition. These stages have traditionally been divided into five levels of English proficiency: Beginning, Early Intermediate, Intermediate, Early Advanced, and Advanced. Some states and organizations (like WIDA and ELPA21 which are consortiums comprised of states, territories and/or federal agencies) have developed their own terminology for these progressions. See Figure 1.2 for a chart illustrating how these different proficiency level labels correspond. Also, see the first chapter in our book *Navigating the Common Core with English Language Learners*[36] for an in-depth discussion on the various English Language Proficiency (ELP) Standards and ELP Assessments used nationwide.

Researchers have also discovered that students generally progress much more quickly from beginning to intermediate level (often taking two to three years) than from intermediate to advanced (often taking four or more years).[37] This is likely because the lower levels of proficiency require simpler vocabulary and sentence patterns and involve language situations that are highly contextualized (familiar, recurrent, and supported by nonlinguistic clues such as gestures and intonation). Full proficiency, on the other hand, means students must have command of more complex sentence structures and vocabulary. They must have the academic English to function well in less contextualized situations (for example, a classroom discussion or a prompted essay), where they must clearly communicate their ideas on higher-level, more abstract concepts.

Traditional Labels	Beginning	Early Intermediate	Intermediate	Early Advanced	Advanced	Proficient
WIDA	Entering	Emerging	Developing	Expanding	Bridging	Reaching
ELPA21	Level 1	Level 2	Level 3	Level 4	Level 5	Proficient
California	Emerging	→	Expanding	→	Bridging	Proficient/ Life Long Language Learning
New York	Entering	Emerging	Transitioning	Expanding	→	Commanding
Texas	Beginning	Intermediate	Advanced	→	Advanced High	→

Figure 1.2. English Proficiency Level "Labels"

Modified from L. Ferlazzo and K. H. Sypnieski, *Navigating the Common Core with English Language Learners* (San Francisco: Jossey-Bass, 2016), p. 7.

This research directly contradicts the argument that students who are immersed in all-English instruction will quickly become fluent, and it challenges the policies previously proposed and implemented in some states requiring students to move into mainstream classes after just one year of school.[38]

Of course, students' language acquisition often doesn't progress in a linear fashion within and across these proficiency levels. Students can demonstrate higher levels of proficiency in one domain versus another (e.g., speaking versus writing) and may even demonstrate different levels of proficiency within a domain, depending on the task.

It is also important to remember that a label of "Level 1" or "Beginner" doesn't identify the student's academic or social skills or potential, instead it only identifies what a student knows and can do at their current stage of English Language Development.

A Quick Tour of ELL Best Practices

The following are a few basic best practices in ELL instruction that will guide the strategies and activities presented in the following chapters. We have found that consistently using these practices makes our lessons more efficient and effective. We also feel it is important to include a few "worst" practices we have witnessed over the years in the hopes that they will not be repeated! The best practices outlined below, as well as others, will be explained in greater detail in subsequent chapters.

MODELING

Do model for students what they are expected to do or produce, especially for new skills or activities, by explaining and demonstrating the learning actions, sharing your thinking processes aloud and showing samples of good teacher and student work. Modeling (or demonstrating) is one way for teachers to provide students with "critical input" in order to help students process content more "deeply and comprehensively."[39] Effective modeling should make the expectations of a task clear (without providing the "answer") and remain available for student access throughout the activity.[40]

Teacher modeling can take a variety of forms including providing sentence starters or frames to support discussion and writing tasks, completing the first example in a set of questions/problems, or demonstrating a learning process step-by-step while "thinking aloud" about what the teacher is doing and why.

Don't just tell students what to do and expect them to do it.

RATE OF SPEECH AND WAIT TIME

Do speak slowly and clearly and provide students with enough time to formulate their responses, whether in speaking or in writing. Remember—they are thinking and producing in two or more languages! After asking a question, wait for a few seconds before calling on someone to respond. This wait time provides all students with an opportunity to think and process, and gives ELLs an especially needed period to formulate a response.[41] Research shows incorporating three to five seconds of wait time increases student participation, improves the quality of student responses, and develops learning while boosting confidence.[42] In addition, providing a few seconds of wait time *after* a student responds and the teacher has acknowledged this response can allow for further elaboration from the student. This additional wait time also gives the rest of the students time to consider the responses and to formulate their own.

Don't speak too fast, and if a student tells you they didn't understand what you said, never, ever repeat the same thing in a louder voice!

USE OF NONLINGUISTIC CUES

Do use visuals (such as pictures), sketches, gestures, intonation, and other nonverbal cues to make both language and content more accessible to students. Teaching with visual representations of concepts can be hugely helpful to ELLs.[43] Specific suggestions are included throughout this book.

Don't stand in front of the class and lecture or rely on a textbook as your only visual aid.

GIVING INSTRUCTIONS

Do give verbal *and* written instructions—this practice can help all learners, especially ELLs. In addition, it is far easier for a teacher to point to the board in response to the inevitable repeated question, "What are we supposed to do?"[44]

Don't act surprised if students are lost when you haven't clearly written and explained step-by-step directions.

CHECK FOR UNDERSTANDING

Do regularly check that students are understanding the lesson. After an explanation or lesson, a teacher could say, "Please put thumbs up, thumbs down, or sideways to let me know if this is clear, *and it's perfectly fine if you don't understand or are unsure—I just need to know.*" This last phrase is essential if you want students to respond honestly.

Teachers can also have students write answers to specific comprehension questions on a sticky note that they place on their desks or on mini-whiteboards. The teacher can then quickly circulate to check responses.

When teachers regularly check for understanding in the classroom, students become increasingly aware of monitoring their own understanding, which serves as a model of good study skills. It also helps ensure that students are learning, thinking, understanding, comprehending, and processing at high levels.[45]

Don't simply ask "Are there any questions?" This is not an effective way to gauge what all your students are thinking. Waiting until the end of class to see what people write in their learning log is not going to provide timely feedback. Also, don't assume that students are understanding because they are smiling and nodding their heads—sometimes they are just being polite!

ENCOURAGE DEVELOPMENT OF HOME LANGUAGE

Do encourage students to use their home language (L1) to support learning in your classroom. Research has found that learning to read in a home language can transfer to increased English acquisition. These transfers may include phonological awareness, comprehension skills, and background knowledge.[46]

Identify the home languages of your ELLs, make sure you have the appropriate bilingual dictionaries in your classroom, and allow students to access their smartphones to use for translation. Remember that validating students' home languages and encouraging them to continue reading and writing in their L1 has been identified as a best practice.[47]

While the research on transfer of L1 skills to L2 cannot be denied, it doesn't mean that we should not encourage the use of English in class and outside of the classroom. For ideas on how to balance the use of L1 and L2 in the classroom, see Chapter Seventeen.

Don't "ban" students from using their home language in the classroom. Forbidding students from using their home languages does not promote a positive learning environment where they feel safe to take risks and make mistakes. This practice can be harmful to the relationships between teachers and students, especially if teachers act more like language police than language coaches.

PROVIDE GRAPHIC ORGANIZERS AND LANGUAGE FRAMES

Do provide students with graphic organizers to help them organize their learning, make connections between new and prior knowledge, support demanding cognitive and linguistic tasks, and to promote active learning and engagement. Give students practice with a variety of organizers, ask them to reflect on which ones are more effective and why, and then encourage them to create their own.

Support student thinking, writing, and speaking by providing sentence stems, frames, and writing structures. These types of scaffolds can help ELLs build their language skills by providing a "push" to get started, reducing students' stress levels, and serving as models of the language features students are learning. See Chapter Five for information on Graphic Organizers, Writing Frames and Writing Structures.

Don't "hand out" graphic organizers without any instruction or modeling of how to use them and then expect them to be effective. Don't think of these kinds of scaffolds as a form of cheating! Scaffolds are meant to be temporary, but serve as a critical support in building students' English proficiency.

RECOGNIZE THE ASSETS ELLS POSSESS

Do remember the many assets that ELL students bring with them every day to your classroom, the school, and the community! The presence of immigrant students in a school has been shown to increase achievement for *all* students.[48]

Don't look at ELLs through a lens of deficits. Recognize and build upon what students *can do* and honor the resilience, perseverance, and many other powerful qualities demonstrated by these students and their families.

We hope you will keep this big picture of ELL demographics, research, and best practices in mind as you explore the rest of this book and as you teach in your classroom.

Additional resources, including ones on current ELL research and instructional strategies, can be found on our book's web site at www.wiley.com/go/eslsurvivalguide2 .

CHAPTER TWO

ELL Classroom Basics: Building a Positive and Effective Learning Environment

ong ago there was an old farmer who was dying. He had two lazy sons and he wanted them to care for the farm after his death. On this farm, they grew grapes. The dying man told his sons that there was gold treasure hidden on the farm.

The two sons spent many days looking for the treasure. They dug up the ground all over the farm, but never found any gold.

However, all the digging helped the grapevines. Many more grapes grew on the vines. Because of their hard work, the farm flourished and the sons were rich.

The two sons had learned a lesson from their father about the importance of hard work. From then on they were no longer lazy and took great care of the farm.[1]

The two sons in this fable learned that their hard work of turning over the soil resulted in a more fruitful harvest. The same holds true in the classroom. Doing the hard work of "preparing the ground"—developing relationships with students and parents, gathering resources, and establishing routines—will yield a fruitful learning experience for all.

There isn't a perfect formula for being an effective ELL teacher, but for growth to occur, students must feel comfortable taking risks, making mistakes, and assuming ownership of their learning. The teacher needs to take the lead in building relationships and fostering this kind of encouraging classroom environment.

Teachers can work tirelessly to develop a curriculum with well-thought-out strategies and engaging, relevant topics, but if they don't "prepare the ground" and create an atmosphere that facilitates student engagement and achievement, then the results will not be fruitful.

You will notice this chapter comes prior to our sharing more specific ideas for curriculum, instructional strategies, and assessment. It serves as a foundation upon which to build, mirroring the foundation that must be built in the classroom between teacher and students, students and students, and teacher and parents.

We have found that there are three primary components of creating a positive, effective learning environment. Most people have heard of the traditional three Rs—Reading, wRiting, and aRithmetic—but we will be describing the three Rs of a successful ELL class: relationships, resources, and routines.

The First R: Building *Relationships*

Building relationships with students is vital. Simply put, it is perhaps the most critical factor affecting student motivation and learning. This is especially true for students in an ELL class who are faced each day with the challenging and often scary experience of learning a new language and interacting in a new culture. In order for students to learn and thrive, they must be willing to take risks, make mistakes, and receive feedback. Research and overall human experience have taught us that these behaviors are more likely to occur when one feels safe and supported.

For students learning a new language, feeling safe is *required* for language acquisition to occur. When a student's "affective filter" is raised, a concept originated by Stephen Krashen,[2] language acquisition becomes difficult to achieve. Feelings of anxiety, fear, or embarrassment can raise a student's affective filter, essentially acting as an imaginary wall in the mind, blocking input and learning. On the other hand, when students feel safe and supported, the affective filter is lowered and language acquisition can occur more easily. Recent research also points to the negative effects of stress on learning and memory.[3]

A safe, supportive learning environment can be created when teachers build relationships of trust and mutual respect with students and their families. This section presents strategies to promote positive relationships between teachers and students, students and students, and teachers and parents.

Supporting Research

When students feel that they matter, their levels of motivation and achievement are more likely to increase. Joanne Yatvin[4] explains this idea in the context of the "Hawthorne effect." This effect was identified in a study that tested whether the level of worker productivity would change when the plant's lighting was dimmed or brightened. Results showed that productivity increased with *any* change in lighting. Yatvin explains that this study is often interpreted as illustrating "the fact that human subjects who know they are part of a scientific experiment may sabotage the study in their eagerness to make it succeed." However, she points out a deeper meaning that reflects the importance of students feeling valued in the classroom: "When people believe they are important in a project, anything works, and, conversely, when they don't believe they are important, nothing works." In other words, when students believe they are an important part of the educational process, then they will act like it!

Education researcher Robert J. Marzano also points to relationships as a key ingredient to a successful learning environment when he sums up, "If the relationship between the teacher and the students is good, then everything else that occurs in the classroom seems to be enhanced."[5]

TEACHER-STUDENT RELATIONSHIPS

Positive relationships are the foundation of a successful ELL classroom. Teachers must learn about their students' experiences and backgrounds in order to connect them to new learning. Teachers also need to know what their students are interested in and what their goals are in order to create lessons that engage students and are relevant to their lives. When teachers get to know their students, they can make better decisions about the curriculum, instructional strategies, classroom management, assessment, pacing, and so forth.

The simplest way for teachers to get to know their ELL students is by talking with them on a daily basis. This can easily be done by "checking in" with a few students each day either before class, while students are working at their desks, or after class. Taking this time to ask students about their experiences, both inside and outside of school, helps to build a genuine relationship, one where the students feel that their teacher takes an interest in their lives. We often have students who speak several different home languages in our beginning classes, so we often rely on translating apps on our phones, gestures, and a lot of care and concern to support our daily conversations with these students! See the Technology Connections for more on translation tools.

Using multilingual online survey tools, like Google Forms, is another strategy to learn about students' lives. It is critical however, for teachers to use a survey response as a springboard to a follow-up conversation with a student and not as an end in itself. See Chapter Sixteen for further details on how we use Google Forms for this kind of activity.

Another simple way for teachers to learn about their students is by reading what students write. Sometimes students feel more comfortable sharing through writing, and a quick note responding to a student can mean a lot. There have been many times we have learned about our students' feelings, problems, and successes by reading their weekly journals (see the homework sections in Chapters Three and Five).

This process can also be reversed and students can read what the teacher has written, especially when this writing is about the class and about the students. In today's world, many teachers already write about their teaching experiences online or on social media. However, they may not take the extra step of sharing this writing with their students. This can be powerful on a number of levels, but in terms of relationship building, it shows students that the teacher thinks about them outside of the classroom.[6] Of course, we only share positive experiences when discussing students (we feel very comfortable talking about our own mistakes) and never share names, images, or student work without written permission.

In addition, just as students are asked to write reflections to share with the class, teachers can do the same. Taking a few minutes to write about the class (whether it is a simple reflection on how a lesson went, how a student demonstrated an exceptional insight, or sharing a few successes and challenges from the week) and then sharing this writing with the class can increase trust and respect between the teacher and the students.

The simple activities described above serve to build positive, trusting relationships between students and the teacher. In addition, researchers Jenna Sethi and Peter C. Scales describe five key actions teachers can take to build these types of "developmental relationships":

- Show students that they matter
- Challenge students to regularly improve
- Provide support
- Share power with students in the classroom
- Introduce new ideas, concepts and possibilities.[7]

The strategies presented in the rest of this book are grounded in these student-centered approaches.

Supporting Research

Unfortunately, not all ELL students experience positive, supportive relationships at school. Some teachers and school administrators have diminished expectations for their newcomer and refugee students, despite the fact that these students tend to be more optimistic about school and their futures than students who have lived in the United States four or more years.[8] We know from experience that taking the time to get to know students and their dreams and goals is a crucial step in helping students meet these goals. In fact, research has shown that positive school-based relationships strongly contribute to both the academic engagement and the achievement of ELLs.[9]

High-quality teacher-student relationships can also help to minimize and prevent classroom management issues. A study conducted with high school students found that students in classes with teachers who focused on building relationships were more cooperative and engaged in class activities.[10]

STUDENT-STUDENT RELATIONSHIPS

In an effective ELL class, the students and teacher have developed positive, trusting relationships. It is also critical that ELL students develop the same kinds of relationships with each other. One of the best ways to facilitate strong relationships between students in an ELL class is through group learning activities. Students can gain valuable speaking practice while learning from each other and building leadership skills.

However, in order to serve these purposes, these activities must be thoughtfully structured. Simply telling students to work together or assigning them to groups does not always build relationships or constitute effective learning and, when it comes to group activities, we think it's important to distinguish between *collaborative learning and cooperative learning*.

In *collaborative learning* activities, students do their own thinking and writing *first* and then connect with peers to provide and receive feedback for improvement. This student interaction results in an end product to which everyone has contributed and is superior to what a student creates on his or her own. *Cooperative learning*, on the other hand, often involves students in a group completing individual parts of a task without peer feedback and then putting the pieces together to present as a final product. Of the two, a collaborative group process—one that provides both individual think/work time and group sharing and feedback—has been shown to produce the best results.[11]

Ideally, we try to facilitate collaborative learning as much as possible, but we also use cooperative learning activities and don't beat ourselves up over it. The group activities described throughout this book can be done both ways— cooperatively or collaboratively.

Considering the size and makeup of groups and whether the groups will be created by the teacher or by the students are other important elements of effective cooperation or collaboration. Research indicates that the biggest individual academic gains result from students working in groups of two to four students and that when the group is larger than four, academic *losses* can be the result.[12] Specific ELL research recommends that working in pairs is more effective for language activities because half the class is able to talk simultaneously, thus maximizing the amount of classroom language use, and all students leave class with more "miles on the tongue."[13]

At times, the teacher may also want to consider grouping students in a way to promote relationship building by grouping students of different language backgrounds together and creating different triads each time so students have a chance to work with everyone in the class (being mindful of proficiency levels and trying to evenly distribute students within each group). At other times, it may be more appropriate to group students who speak the same home language for learning support. The teacher can model positive behaviors expected when working in a group, including academic language that promotes interpersonal skills (such as how to respectfully disagree or ask someone to speak up or repeat what they've said).

Another strategy we have found helpful in supporting student collaboration and relationship-building is to establish *leadership teams* in each of our classes. During the first couple of weeks of classes, we identify students who seem to be taking leadership in group or class activities and ask them to stay after class for a few minutes. Then, we ask them if they would be part of a class leadership team where their responsibilities would include leading group activities, helping answer questions in their groups, and being welcoming to new students. We periodically ask student leaders to reflect on how it's going, to share with each other, and to discuss who else should be invited to join.

In addition to collaborative learning as a way to reinforce student relationships, we have students write weekly about two positive events that occurred in their lives and one not-so-positive event (along with what they could have done to make it better or what they learned from it). Students then share what they wrote in small groups. Research has shown that this kind of sharing results in "capitalization"—the building of social capital, also known as strengthening relationships.[14]

Supporting Research

Research on collaborative learning and adolescents has shown the importance of peer relationships in relation to learning and overall well-being. Research on adolescents in particular has confirmed that positive peer relationships can increase academic achievement.[15]

TEACHER-PARENT RELATIONSHIPS

Building relationships between teachers and parents is also key to increased student motivation and academic achievement. A trusting partnership relationship between teachers and parents can have a major impact on the level of parent participation in their child's academic development.[16] While we use the term "parent" in this section, we are conscious to use broader terms like *guardians, family, or caregivers* with our students as we recognize the many different living situations of our students.

When connecting with ELL parents it can be helpful to consider the distinction Larry Ferlazzo has made between *parent involvement* and *parent engagement*.[17] *Parent involvement* often starts with the *school* trying to "sell" their ideas to parents. The school staff might feel they know what the problems are and how to fix them. *Parent engagement*, on the other hand, begins with the *parents*. Ideas and needs are elicited from parents by the school staff in the context of building trusting, positive relationships. Providing opportunities for parents to shape the activities and programs that will directly help their families can result in them being more invested in seeing those efforts succeed.

Taking steps to reach out to parents of ELL students can be more challenging when the teacher doesn't speak the home language of the parents; however, this shouldn't be seen as a barrier. Many schools and districts have bilingual aides or staff members who can translate written communication, make phone calls, and translate during meetings. See the following Tech Tool for resources on translating.

When sending home notes or communicating with parents by phone or in-person, it is best not to assume the language they prefer. We make sure to ask, "Which language do you prefer?" so we can take the appropriate next steps. Another way to do this is by sending home a survey at the beginning of the year asking about preferred language and preferred communication method (e.g. text, phone call, note, email).

Contacting parents on a regular basis to give positive feedback about their children's achievements, behavior, and other areas of improvement serves to build trust between parents and the school. Frequent teacher-family communication has also been shown to increase student engagement.[18] These conversations are opportunities to let parents and students know that positive behaviors and successes are valued and recognized, which can increase student motivation to reproduce positive outcomes. Of course, this doesn't mean the teacher should never call home to discuss negative behaviors or academic problems, but these conversations will be better received and will be more productive if a genuine relationship has already been formed with both the parents and the student.

It is not uncommon for us to ask a student to translate when we call home with a quick positive commentary about how they are doing. However, it is never appropriate for a student to translate during more formal meetings or conversations. In those situations it is the legal responsibility of the school to provide an interpreter.[19] If students are asked to take on this role, especially in high-stakes situations, it is not surprising that they often experience feelings of pressure and anxiety.[20]

Home visits can be a powerful way to connect with parents and students. Some districts provide funding and training for teachers, counselors, and interpreters to conduct visits with families before the school year starts and periodically throughout the year. This is a valuable opportunity to learn more about the student's background experiences and educational strengths and challenges. Parents may share what has and has not worked with their child in the past and what goals they have for themselves and for their child. Many schools across the country work with the Parent-Teacher Home Visit Project (www.pthvp.org), which has developed a highly successful model of training teachers and other school staff to implement home visits as a key strategy in strengthening relationships with families and, in turn, increasing student academic success.

Building positive relationships with parents can also lead to shared learning between students and their families. An example of this is the Family Literacy Project at our school (Luther Burbank High School in Sacramento), which grew out of conversations between parents and teachers during home visits and on-campus meetings. Many new immigrant families faced the challenge of lack of access to technology and little proficiency in English. To address these issues, the Family Literacy Project (funded by a small private grant and then by the school district) distributed free home computers and Internet service to over 40 immigrant families who used the technology to read and learn together nightly. This project was powerful for the families and for the students, who showed four times greater improvement in English literacy than a control group without home computers.[21]

Just as we want to view our ELL students through a lens of assets instead of deficits, it is important to view parents through this same lens. For example, during one home visit, we learned that a student's father was an expert at making and repairing the traditional Hmong flute called the *qeej*. We invited him to visit our beginning ELL class, where he demonstrated how to make one and also performed. He didn't speak English, but we had prepared for his visit by learning new vocabulary, and then wrote and talked about it afterward using the Language Experience Approach (which is explained in full in Chapter Three). He later became one of the leaders of the effort to create the Family Literacy Project we described earlier. Forming these types of links between home and school can lead to stronger relationships between families and educators. When teachers validate the experiences and knowledge of parents, great learning experiences can take place while also strengthening the relationship between students, their families, and school.

Once these kinds of positive relationships have been established, it can be valuable to engage parents in conversations about the important link between primary language proficiency and second language development. Many parents, especially those with fewer formal schooling experiences, are unsure about how to support their children as they are acquiring a new language. Teachers can share suggestions for activities such as reading books together in their home language or parents asking their children what they learned that day. Chapter Seventeen on Home Language discusses more extensively how these activities can assist students' English language development. Chapter Twenty-One on Distance Learning (available online) offers bilingual graphics that explain multiple activities parents can do with their children at home.

More and more research is being published highlighting the increased benefits of being bilingual on brain-based activities like problem solving, learning, multitasking, and memory, and on increased earnings in the workplace.[22] We have found that sharing this research with parents often increases their self-confidence in supporting their children to develop English skills. A lesson plan highlighting these benefits can be found in Chapter Sixteen.

Supporting Research

A common misperception about parents of ELL students is that because they are sometimes less involved in school-based activities, they don't care about their children's education. However, research has indicated the opposite—that immigrant parents place a high value on education, but also face barriers to being involved in their child's education such as limited English proficiency, lack of formal education, time constraints (work and family responsibilities), and limited knowledge of mainstream American culture."[23] The suggestions we have shared, including phone calls, home visits, and making efforts to learn about the lives of parents, can all be effective responses to these challenges.

Recent research shows the harm teacher misperceptions of ELL parent engagement can have on students. A longitudinal study found teachers were less likely to see immigrant parents as "involved in their children's education" in comparison to native-born white parents. And, students whose teachers believed their parents were less engaged had lower grade point averages and were less likely to be recommended for honors or Advanced Placement courses.[24]

Tech Tool

Online Resources: Translating

It is not always possible to have translators and/or bilingual staff available to translate when needed. While translation technology tools available online and on smartphones aren't always 100 percent accurate and easy to use, they can at least show parents the teacher is making an effort to clearly communicate.

One free tool we like is Microsoft Translator (https://translator.microsoft .com/). The Translator lets you speak in your home language while others see it simultaneously (more-or-less) translated in the language of their choice. Another is the "Interpreter Mode" in the mobile Google Assistant app. Download the free app, say something similar to "Be my Spanish translator," and it will automatically translate in writing and in audio what you say in English to Spanish, and then what the other person says in Spanish into English. It can translate in 44 languages.

There are several online tools that allow teachers and parents to communicate multilingually through texts, including Remind (https://www.remind.com/) and TalkingPoints (https://talkingpts.org/).

To find the latest online tools that can help with simultaneous or almost-simultaneous translations, go to "The Best Sites For Learning About Google Translate & Other Forms Of Machine Translation" https://larryferlazzo.edublogs .org/2012/06/04/the-best-sites-for-learning-about-google-translate/.

ACTIVITIES TO BUILD AND STRENGTHEN RELATIONSHIPS IN THE ELL CLASSROOM

There are many activities that can be used both as introductory activities and throughout the year to build and maintain positive relationships in the classroom. Some activities that work well to introduce students to each other and to the teacher can be used again at later points in the year as students' interests change and as they gain new life experiences. While this is certainly not an exhaustive list, it contains several activities we have found successful and that can easily be adapted for use with different levels of students.

All About Me

This activity is sometimes called an All About Me Bag. Students choose a few objects that reveal things about themselves or are special in some way and bring them in to share with the class. The teacher models this activity first by bringing in items special in her life (for example, a photograph, a piece of sports equipment, or a paintbrush) and describing what the object is and what it represents or why it is important. Then the teacher can take a few minutes to answer any questions from students. Students can share their items in various ways—a few students can share each day or students can share in small groups or with a partner and take turns asking each other questions. Question and answer frames can be helpful for beginning students (e.g. Why did you bring _____? This is a _____. It is special to me because _____). It may also be helpful for the teacher to remind students not to bring very valuable items to school, but they can instead draw or take a picture of the item to share.

"All About Me" activities can also be structured as games to boost engagement and further build community. One gamified version of an "All About Me" activity that we like was introduced to us by educator Donna DeTommaso–Kleinert[25] and involves using the popular game-based learning platform Kahoot! (https:// kahoot.com/).

This activity involves the teacher creating a Kahoot! with information about themselves and their interests and having the class play it. In other words, students have to guess the "right" answers to questions about the teacher. Then, students can create their own Kahoots with information about themselves. The teacher can support this process by sharing simple written directions and modeling how to create a Kahoot! In addition, sentence starters or frames for the questions and answers can be given to students with less English proficiency.

Students can then play their classmates' Kahoots and the teacher can lead the class in a discussion about what the class has learned about each student. The teacher can again provide sentence frames to support student responses.

A final step that can be used with any All About Me activity—where students are sharing interesting facts about themselves—is having them write a short essay about the class using the information they've learned. For beginners, this might be a shared writing activity where the teacher provides sentence frames like "Students in our class like to eat lots of different foods. For example, _____." Intermediate or advanced students could be asked to work with a partner or on their own to describe what they've learned about the class. These writing pieces could then be shared in different ways—in small groups, whole class, or even recorded and posted on a class YouTube channel.

"I Am" Project

There are many variations of I Am activities. Students can create a poster, a poem, a slide show, a Top Ten list, a collage, or other item to describe themselves (you can find many examples by searching *"Who am I?"* or *"I am"* activities online). At the start of the year, it serves as a way for students and teachers to learn about each other's experiences and interests. It can be helpful to give students sentence starters to spur their thinking and writing. There are endless possibilities, but here are a few examples:[26]

> I love _____because_____.
>
> I wonder _____.
>
> I am happy when _____.
>
> I am scared when _____.
>
> I worry about _____because _____.
>
> I hope to _____.
>
> I am sad when _____.
>
> In the future, I will _____.

For newcomers, we modify the activity by encouraging them to complete it in their home language. They can also add drawings or pictures cut from magazines to represent their interests, feelings, and goals. We then have students share their projects in small groups and ask them to look for two similarities and two differences. Each group can then share their findings with the whole class.

Teacher-Student Letter Exchange

A good way for teachers to introduce themselves to students is by writing a brief letter to share during the first week. This letter can serve as a model for students to follow as they write back to the teacher. The teacher's letter can be simplified depending upon the level of the class, and the teacher can give beginning students sentence frames to scaffold their letter. (My name is _____. I am _____ years old. I was born in _____.) This activity helps teachers learn more about their students and also provides a quick sample of each student's writing. It can be helpful to keep copies of both the teacher letter and the instructions for the student letter on hand to give to new students as they enter the class later in the year. Students and teachers can also exchange letters at different points during the year. We've found it helpful to do at the end of a quarter or semester to reflect on the highs and lows of those months and the growth experienced during that time. See Exhibit 2.1 for a sample of a teacher letter used at the beginning of the school year.

EXHIBIT 2.1. Teacher Letter Sample

Dear Students,

Welcome back to school! I always feel nervous and excited about the first day of school. It is fun to see everyone and get back into a routine, but I will miss being able to stay up late and sleep in (when my kids let me)!

I've been teaching at Burbank for a while and I <u>love</u> this school! Most of the teachers are caring and funny, and the students are even smarter, kinder, and funnier than the teachers! Here are some things I love about school: students, lunch with my friends, good books, and clean floors. Here are some things I don't love about school: meetings at lunch, boring books, and dirty floors. What do you like about school? What don't you like about school?

My family is very important to me. I like them most of the time and I love them all of the time. I live near downtown Sacramento with my husband and our three kids. When you visit our house there is a good chance you might step on a Lego piece, a Star Wars action figure, a Hot Wheels car, a Barbie shoe, or a Dora necklace. You also might see lots of sports equipment because we like to play soccer, baseball, football, and golf. We are San Francisco Giants fans and we root for the 49ers. We also read books together, go on hikes, and play at the park. What is your family like? What do you like to do when you are not at school?

I am looking forward to our school year together. We will get to know each other better and will learn from each other. I expect you to try your best and be willing to make some mistakes because that is how we learn. What do you expect from me?

Here's to an awesome year together!!

Sincerely,

Ms. Hull

"Find Someone in this Class Who . . ." Scavenger Hunts

A scavenger hunt is an easy way to get students out of their seats, talking, and interacting within minutes. The teacher can easily create a sheet (there are many variations on the Web) listing several categories with a line next to each one. Then students circulate and must find someone who has experienced each category (for example,

"Has been to the ocean," "Has a brother and a sister," or "Has broken a bone"). The student must ask for their classmate's name and write it on the line next to the category. The teacher can collect the sheets, choose different items to share, and, depending upon the class and comfort level, ask students to share more details about a specific experience.

This type of activity can be varied by having students write one fact about themselves on a strip of paper. The teacher collects them and redistributes them throughout the class so each student receives one strip containing a fact about another classmate. Students then have to try and guess who the "fact" belongs to by circulating and asking each other questions.

Another twist on a scavenger hunt and a fun way to get students talking and learning about each other is playing "Sit down if. . ." or "Put a finger down if. . ." . The teacher says a statement and the students sit down if it applies to them (e.g. Sit down if you have more than three siblings, Sit down if you like soccer, Sit down if you like the rain). In the "Put a finger down if. . ." version, students start with all ten fingers up and then put one finger down each time a statement is true for them. The teacher can pause and ask students to share more about their responses or can give students an opportunity to ask their classmates questions. Students can even take turns leading the activity.

Two Truths and a Lie

This activity is commonly used as an icebreaker and works great with students who don't know a lot about each other. The teacher first models the activity by writing down three statements about herself on an index card and explaining that two of the statements are true, but one is a lie (for example, "I can play the guitar" or "I was born in New York City"). Students can talk in pairs and guess which statement is the lie. Then each student writes two truths and one lie on an index card. They can share their statements in pairs, small groups, or to the entire class and take turns guessing each other's lies. The teacher can facilitate a follow-up discussion by asking students to share more about their truths, either by speaking or in writing.

We have extended this activity into a version we call *Two Truths and a Lie-Plus*. For the plus version, we give students a piece of legal-size white paper or construction paper and explain that they will be making a mini-poster called "My Truths, No Lies!" We model how to take our two true statements from the first activity and add three more, so we have five written "truths" in total. We explain students will do the same by writing their five true statements on the mini-poster and adding illustrations or symbols to visually represent these statements. Students can then share their mini-posters in pairs or small groups. These discussions can support students in developing student-student relationships as they learn about each other and discover similarities and differences (which the teacher can ask each group to share with the class). This activity could also be done digitally in a slideshow, but we like hanging these mini-posters on our walls because they reflect the truths of all our students!

Tic Tac Toe

This activity comes from the Hands Up Project[27] and works well as an introductory exercise, but could easily be applied to reinforce vocabulary or content throughout the year. The teacher draws a "Tic Tac Toe" grid (nine squares) on the board or projected on a screen and in each square writes *an answer* to a personal question about himself (e.g. San Francisco—Where were you born?, Green—What's your favorite color? Three—How many children do you have?). Students can then work in pairs to discuss and write down what they think *the question* is for each square. The class is then divided into two teams and they take turns asking the teacher questions. If the answer is on the grid then their team gets to claim that square. The first team to make a line across the grid in any direction is the winner. The teacher can provide question stems to support beginning students. The game can be made more challenging for higher proficiency students by adding the stipulation that groups can only get a square if the question is asked accurately or written correctly on a mini-whiteboard.

Students can then create their own Tic Tac Toe grids and play the game in small groups or with a partner. This activity can also be used during the year as a way to reinforce vocabulary or content. The teacher or students can create grids containing vocabulary words from a unit of study and groups can take turns guessing the correct definitions or providing synonyms. Or, the teacher can write different *answers* to content questions in each box and student groups have to come up with the corresponding *questions*.

Four Squares

The Four Squares activity can help students get to know each other better, while promoting writing and speaking practice. The teacher models how to fold a piece of paper into four boxes and numbers them 1, 2, 3, and 4. Students then write a different category or topic next to the number at the top of each box. The categories could include family, what I like about school, what I don't like about school, places I've lived, my favorite movie (and why), and so forth. Students are given time to write about each category and then asked to stand up. The teacher then instructs students to share their Box Ones with a partner, their Box Twos with a different partner, and so on.

This activity can be varied in multiple ways—different topics to write about, the number of boxes, how they are shared, and so on. It can also be used at any point during the year. For example, it can be used at the end of the semester with a box for the student's biggest accomplishment, one for the biggest challenge, and one for goals for the next semester. See Figure 2.1 for one example of how to use the Four Squares activity.

Weekly Reflections

One way for teachers to stay connected to students is by having them write a weekly reflection. This reflection can simply be a journal or responses to questions. The teacher can structure the journal prompt or questions to invite

My family:	What I like about school:
What I don't like about school:	My favorites: Food: Movie: Music: After-school activity: Place:

Figure 2.1. Four Squares

students to share their feelings, concerns, and questions about the class and about their lives outside the classroom (What classroom activity did they like the best this week and why? What are their weekend plans?). Reading student reflections can help teachers take the pulse of the class—which activities are being enjoyed, areas of confusion, pacing issues, and so forth. Teachers can immediately make adjustments, offer feedback, and address any student concerns. Teachers also gain important information about what is going on in their students' lives and can use this information as talking points when they speak one-on-one with students. These reflections can also function as a formative assessment. See the section on reflection in Chapter Three for more ideas on incorporating reflection into the ELL classroom.

Daily Dedications

A practice we learned about from educator Henry Seton that fosters a positive learning environment is having students take turns "dedicating" that day of learning to someone who has inspired them.[28] This activity not only serves as a positive way to open class, but strengthens both teacher-student relationships and student-student relationships *and* fosters student motivation to learn.

In our version of the activity, we create a slideshow for each of our classes called "Daily Dedications." The first slide contains the directions, the second slide is where students sign up for a day to share their dedication slide with the class, and the third slide contains a teacher model of the activity. Students then add a slide of their own to the class slideshow with their own description of who they would like to dedicate their learning to and why. They can also include an image and can format their slide any way they'd like. A different student can present at the start of class each day or every other day. Once the slideshow is complete, we can periodically revisit it for reflective activities or when a dose of inspiration is needed! See Figure 2.2 for a teacher model.

Talking and Walking

Having one-on-one conversations with students about their goals, interests, struggles, and the like can be difficult to do during class time. One way to quickly connect with students is to take a brief walk around the school campus. This five-minute conversation can take place before or after school, or even during a teacher's prep period (if you make prior arrangements with the student's teacher for that time). These talks can strengthen the teacher-student relationship and can also be helpful when getting to know new students or when dealing with students who are having behavior challenges.

I'd like to dedicate my teaching and learning today to my father. He was an immigrant from Italy and became a college teacher. Though he left that position to work in business, he continued to teach English to new immigrants at night. He was kind to all and was a good man. He inspired me to want to leave the world a better place than it was when I entered it.

Mr. Ferlazzo

Figure 2.2. Teacher Model

Class and Teacher Evaluations

A teacher can build trust with students by asking them to anonymously evaluate her teaching and use the results to reflect on her practice. This can be done by distributing a quick survey or set of questions for students to answer about class activities, the teacher's style, the pace of the class, and so forth. These evaluations can also prompt students to consider their own learning strengths and challenges. They can take many different forms including multiple-choice, question-answer, fill-in-the-blank, and so on. See the next Tech Tool for more examples of class and teacher evaluations and see Exhibit 2.2 for an example of an evaluation we use with students at the end of the quarter.

EXHIBIT 2.2. End-of-Quarter Evaluation

Please read the sentences and circle the answer that best describes your feelings.

1. In this class this quarter I learned   *a lot   some   a little.*
2. My teacher talked   *too fast   just right   too slow.*
3. The work in this class was   *too hard   just right   too easy.*
4. My teacher cares about what is happening in my life   *a lot   some   a little.*
5. This quarter I tried my best   *all of the time   some of the time   not a lot.*

Please write your answers in the space below each question.

1. Which activities *helped you* learn English the most this quarter?

_____

_____

2. Which activities *did not really help you* learn English this quarter?

_____

_____

3. Which activities did you enjoy *the most* this quarter?

_____

_____

4. Which activities did you enjoy *the least* this quarter?

_____

_____

5. What could *your teacher* do differently or better to help you in this class?

_____

_____

6. What could *you* do differently or better to help yourself in this class?

_____

_____

7. What else would you like your teacher to know?

_____

_____

Source: Adapted from Ferlazzo, L. (2011). *Helping Students Motivate Themselves: Practical Answers to Classroom Challenges.* Larchmont, NY: Eye on Education, p. 99.

Tech Tool

Online Resources: Building and Strengthening Relationships in the ELL Classroom

For additional resources on building relationships and community in the classroom, see "The Best Resources on Developing a Sense of Community in the Classroom" at https://larryferlazzo.edublogs.org/2017/07/18/the-best-resources-on-developing-a-sense-of-community-in-the-classroom/. For specific ideas on building a positive learning environment at the beginning of the school year see "The Best Resources for Planning the First Days of School" at https://larryferlazzo.edublogs.org/2011/08/08/the-best-resources-for-planning-the-first-day-of-school/ .

For many examples of class and teacher evaluations, along with the results, visit "The Best Posts on Students Evaluating Classes (and Teachers)" at https://larryferlazzo.edublogs.org/2010/05/08/my-best-posts-on-students-evaluating-classes-and-teachers/.

The Second R: *Resources* in the ELL Classroom

Resources are an important factor in supporting effective instruction in any classroom. The following are several resources we have found vital to structuring an ELL class where students feel comfortable, challenged, and confident.

BASIC ART SUPPLIES

Having basic supplies like pens, pencils, markers, construction paper, glue, scissors, and highlighters can be useful for many different projects and activities. Having supplies on hand that are easily accessible also allows students to immediately focus on the content of the lesson and to immediately get to work.

While this book includes many ideas for using technology with ELL students to increase motivation and enhance language development, it is important to remember that paper, pens, and pencils still matter!

Recent research on the brain, learning, and handwriting shows that putting a pen or pencil to paper is important for new learning to occur, especially when learning a language. Studies have shown that both children and adults learn more and remember better when writing by hand.[29]

BINDERS AND FOLDERS

Even with many of our students now having laptops, there will likely always be a place for physical materials in class. The age-old debate of whether students should take their materials home every day or leave them in the classroom goes on in many schools. While it may be necessary for students to take some items home (such as a reading book, a laptop, or homework papers), it can be helpful to have a binder or folder for each student to leave in the classroom. A binder can be divided into sections (for example, homework, current unit, and reflections) and can easily be passed out and collected by students. Another option is to give each student a hanging file folder (with a name label) that can be stored in a file cabinet or a plastic file crate. This folder can hold other items (such as a current unit folder, student portfolio, and notebook) and can also easily be distributed or picked up by students as they enter the classroom.

Having students keep their materials in the classroom helps students and teachers keep track of papers and makes it easier for students to get to work immediately. To help with organization, students can keep a Table of Contents in the front of their folder or binder section with a running list of materials. Teachers may find this helpful because they can keep track of which activities they did and in what order—always helpful for the next school year!

BILINGUAL DICTIONARIES

Bilingual dictionaries and online translation sites and apps are important tools in an ELL classroom, and having dictionaries available in the languages spoken by students is obviously a good idea. However, many schools have bilingual dictionaries only in the most common languages. We have found bilingual dictionaries in many languages available for purchase online.

Even though online tools can provide instantaneous translation in most languages, we have still found that students enjoy and learn from bilingual hard-copy picture dictionaries.

There has been much discussion over the use of dictionaries and direct translation in the ELL classroom. Some have argued that direct translation (from L1 to L2 or vice versa), especially when reading, should be avoided because it can interrupt and slow down the reading process. However, more recent research has found bilingual dictionaries to be an important component of language learning.[30] As Professor Jim Cummins explains, there must be a balanced approach to direct translation—using context clues to decipher meaning should be encouraged, and "bilingual dictionary use can provide rapid access to the meaning of target language text and eliminate the frustration that derives from attempting unsuccessfully to infer meanings from context."[31]

Our experience is aligned with Cummins's findings. Of course, it is counterproductive for a student to look up every unfamiliar word or to directly translate their writing word for word. However, bilingual dictionaries can be very helpful, especially for assisting students to understand more complex words and concepts. So, just to be clear, we tell students "use dictionaries or your phone to look up individual words, but *please, please, please* don't write an entire sentence in your home language, use your phone to translate it into English, and then put the result in your essay."

It is also important for the teacher to *model* when and how students can best use dictionaries to increase language development. For example, the teacher can demonstrate trying to figure out the meaning of a word by "thinking aloud" as she looks for context clues in a piece of text. The teacher can then show students what to do if they can't figure out the meaning based on context by modeling how to look up the word in the dictionary. See Chapter Seventeen on Home Language for more ideas.

CLASSROOM LIBRARY

As you will see in later chapters, research clearly supports the practice of Free Voluntary Reading, which involves letting students choose reading materials based on their own interests. Having a well-stocked, well-organized library (hard copy and online) is a key way to build and sustain motivation for this kind of reading practice.

Some schools provide books for classroom libraries in English classes, but this isn't always the case. Teachers can build a library over time on their own—used book stores, garage sales, and the local library are great places to find low-cost or free books. It is also important to provide students access to a wide variety of books online. See the next Tech Tool for resources to obtain engaging virtual books for all English proficiency levels.

Building a classroom library, however, is not a matter of filling the shelves with just anything. Books should be culturally diverse, age-appropriate, of high interest, and in good condition. It has been our experience that students won't check out books with torn covers and tattered pages. While some high-quality children's books can be accessible for beginning-level students, there are also plenty of high-interest, language-accessible books geared toward older ELLs including graphic novels and graphic non-fiction books.

It is helpful if the classroom library is organized for accessibility, but not exclusivity. Organizing books by level (placing more accessible books in one area and more challenging ones in another) can be helpful to ELLs. However, it is very important that students not feel restricted when choosing books.

There is much debate about the effects of controlling the books that students are allowed to read. While some studies have found that student test scores increased after using an "accelerated reading" program,[33] other researchers question the validity of these studies. They claim that these "accelerated reader" programs, which are incentive-based and require that students read books only within their level until they "test out,: can actually decrease motivation for reading in the long-term.[33] In our experience we have found that it is best *not* to restrict student choice. However, we sometimes guide students toward choosing books at the appropriate level and that match their interests. See the section on Book Selection in Chapter Sixteen for more ideas on helping students find books.

Along with being divided by level, books can also be shelved according to genre or by simply dividing them into fiction and nonfiction. Some teachers have used colored stickers to indicate different types of books.

Because it is important for students to take books home to read (especially ELL students who may not have many English-language books at home), a checkout system can help keep track of books and prevent loss. Keeping a binder or clipboard near the classroom library makes it easy for students to "check out" a book by writing down their name, the title of the book, and the date checked out. Upon returning the book, students can cross off their name or enter the date the book was returned. It can be useful to stamp or label books with the teacher's name so they can be returned if left somewhere else on campus. There are also classroom library management tools available online, such as Booksource

Classroom (https://www.booksource.com/), for teachers to inventory and manage their libraries.

It is also important to help students build their own libraries at home. Research has shown that children with more books at home go further in their education, even if their parents aren't highly literate.[34] Many libraries have auxiliary groups that collect donations of books and sell them at a minimal cost. Some even distribute free books to teachers. For example, the Friends of the Library Program in Davis, California, has donated thousands of books to distribute to our students over the years. Taking a field trip to the local library and helping students to get a library card is another way to promote reading at home. Most libraries also provide access to online books as well and often don't even require students to register for accounts in person at their facility.

Tech Tool

Online Reading Resources

For many resources related to online reading for ELLs at different proficiency levels see "The Best Websites to Help Beginning Readers" at https://larryferlazzo.edublogs .org/2008/01/22/the-best-websites-to-help-beginning-readers/, "The Best Websites for Beginning Older Readers" at https://larryferlazzo.edublogs.org/2008/01/23/the-best-websites-for-beginning-older-readers/, and "The Best Websites for Intermediate Readers" at https://larryferlazzo.edublogs.org/2008/01/26/the-best-websites-for-intermediate-readers/.

PEER TUTORS

Peer tutors can be a very valuable resource in an ELL class, especially in a large class or a class with a range of proficiency levels. Many secondary schools give students the opportunity to take a period as a Teacher's Assistant. These are usually older students who have already met many of their graduation requirements. At diverse schools, many of these students are bilingual and can serve as excellent role models, translators, and classroom helpers. Patient English-only students can also do a great job as peer tutors. At our school, students receive credits for serving as peer tutors in ELL classes. They help our ELL students with assignments, offer advice, and even attend field trips with our class. In fact, in an effort to "accelerate learning" after the pandemic caused nearly a year of remote teaching, Larry's school quadrupled the number of peer tutors in his ELL classes. The effort proved so successful that nearby schools duplicated the program. Also, See the next Tech Tool box for peer tutor training resources and see Chapter Three for ideas on pairing ELL classes with mainstream English classes.

Recent research on the effects of peer tutoring on English language learners indicates a positive impact on learning for these students: "When peer tutors are used, the tutees have a live example to emulate and behavior to observe which helps to understand the language and culture more so than a textbook could display."[35] It has also been found that pairing younger arriving ELLs with older ELLs can enhance language development in both their native language and in their second language.[36]

Tech Tool
Peer Tutor Training

Resources to help train peer tutors working with ELLs can be found at "The Best Resources To Help Prepare Tutors & Volunteers In ELL Classes – And, Boy, Do I Need Suggestions!" https://larryferlazzo.edublogs.org/2021/08/29/the-best-resources-to-help-prepare-tutors-volunteers-in-ell-classes-and-boy-do-i-need-suggestions/.

CLASSROOM WALLS

The walls of the classroom can be another important resource for ELL students. Word walls, concept maps, academic sentence frames, posted classroom routines, and schedules are tools that become more accessible to students when posted on the classroom walls.

During a thematic unit, displaying a word wall with key vocabulary words along with their meanings and/or pictures allows students to easily access the spelling and meaning of the words as they read, write, and talk.

By taking words from the word wall and expanding the visual representation to show how they relate to one another and to key concepts, you can create a *concept map*. In other words, a visual demonstration of how the different types of knowledge connect to each other. For an example of a concept map used when teaching a problem-solution essay in an intermediate class, see Figure 2.3.

Academic sentence frames are also important to display on the classroom walls so that students can access them when writing and speaking—such as, "I agree (or disagree) because _____." It can be helpful to rotate different sentence frame posters that are based on the unit of study.

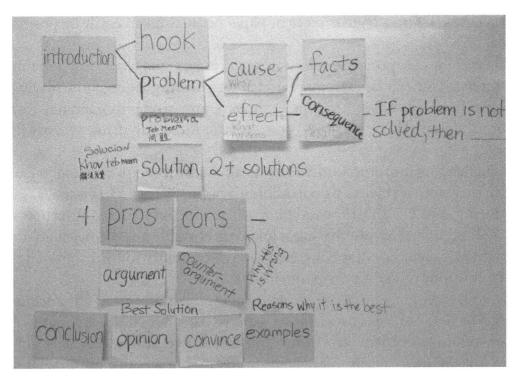

Figure 2.3. Sample Concept Map

When creating posters for the walls, teachers should pay attention to size (large enough for students to see from their desks) and amount of text (not too much). Involving students in the process can be fun, can reinforce learning, and can save teacher energy!

Of course, classroom walls are also a place to publish student work. Students often enjoy seeing their own work and their classmates' work displayed on the walls. Teachers can incorporate displayed student work into a lesson by conducting "gallery walks" where students can read, evaluate, and even add to student work posted on the wall. See Chapter Five for more ideas on gallery walks.

TECHNOLOGY BASICS

Document cameras, projectors, and having access to devices (laptops, smartphones, tablets) and the Internet can greatly enhance learning in an ELL class.

Document cameras open up many possibilities in the classroom. A document camera (attached to a computer projector) simply projects whatever you place underneath it onto a screen. It facilitates teacher modeling and makes it easy for teachers to show good student models, or even better, for students to come up and show the whole class. It also makes it possible for students to create a "poster" to share with the class on a regular piece of paper because it can easily be projected for all to see.

Using a computer projector allows you to project images from your computer onto a screen. This can be extremely useful for showing video clips, playing computer games as a class (see Chapter Eighteen), and student-generated computer projects (Chapters Three and Five give specific ideas for using video with ELL students).

It is challenging for some students to speak loudly when presenting in front of a class, whether due to shyness or natural low volume voices. This issue was exacerbated during the COVID-19 pandemic when students in many schools wore masks. We responded by purchasing a low-cost portable speaker with an attached microphone. Student use of it enhanced everyone's ability to hear so much that we expect to continue to use it post-pandemic.

This book will present many ideas for using technology to enhance student learning and that don't require a lot of work to use. Incorporating many of these activities requires student access to computers and to the Internet—in other words, a one-to-one computer laptop or tablet cart or a computer lab. Of course, since the COVID-19 pandemic began, many more students have school-issued laptops. See Chapter Sixteen for specific ways to maximize the use of technology when computer access is limited. Also see the upcoming Computer Routines section in this chapter for tips on using computers effectively in the ELL classroom.

As previously mentioned, students at our school who participated in a Family Literacy Project with home computers showed great improvements in their reading scores. We further found that students who participated in an after-school computer lab program, where they spent an hour on sites accessible to English language learners in a variety of content areas, scored a 50 percent greater gain on reading comprehension assessments than ELLs who did not come to the lab.[37]

Another study on the use of technology for teacher feedback (students recording oral assignments and the teacher responding to them) found that students enjoyed the learning process more and also met their learning goals. Other benefits included "ease of use" because the technology was easy to learn, "affordability" because students could use their phones to record, and "organizational" benefits such as assignments being easily archived.[38]

Tech Tool

Using Technology in the Classroom

For lots of ideas and resources on using technology in the classroom see "The Best Advice on Using Education Technology" at https://larryferlazzo.edublogs. org/2013/07/14/the-best-advice-on-using-education-technology/ .

Because so many schools use Google Classroom, we recommend visiting "A Beginning List of the Best Resources for Learning About Google Classroom" at https://larryferlazzo.edublogs.org/2016/09/11/a-beginning-list-of-the-best-resources-for-learning-about-google-classroom/ .

The Third R: Establishing *Routines*

Establishing routines is another way to support a positive and effective learning experience for all students. Having a system of procedures not only benefits the students, but preserves teacher sanity as well. For ELL students in particular, having routines frees them up to learn new concepts. Being consistently exposed to new routines *and* new concepts can be overwhelming, frustrating, and detrimental to the learning process. Students can put their focus on learning activities when they know what to expect and are familiar with classroom routines.[39]

This section will present several routines we have found successful. While these routines are crucial for creating an optimal learning environment for ELL students, it is also important to balance routines with novelty. In other words, procedures and routines are valuable for structuring and managing the time spent with students, but what the teacher does *within* this time is hugely important. Learning should never be "routine," and in order to keep students engaged, learning activities must be presented in different ways.

GREETING STUDENTS

Greeting students at the door can be challenging to adopt as a *daily* routine but, in our experience, it is well worth the effort. We try to greet all of our students at the door each day—with a smile and verbal welcome, a handshake, fist bump, or any other greeting students are most comfortable with. Letting them know we see them and are glad they are there, even if the interaction only lasts a few seconds, goes a long way in building positive relationships. Students often use this time to quickly tell us how they're doing that day (e.g. sick, excited, mad, tired, etc.). Once we are "tuned in" to students who may be having a particularly hard day, we can check in with them once the class is engaged in their warm-up activity. Of course, there are days when we can't make it to the door for individual greetings, but when this happens we always make sure to welcome the class as a whole.

One important note when it comes to greeting students by name—we make it a priority to correctly pronounce them! Making sure we are correctly pronouncing students' names and calling them by the name they want to be called (which may be different from the one on our roster), signals respect and a validation of who they are.

OPENING AND ENDING PROCEDURES

Having a walk-in procedure like Free Voluntary Reading, a warm-up question, or a journal topic is a good way to get students focused and learning from the minute they walk in even if the bell has not yet rung.

Using the last few minutes of class to do a brief closure activity each day is a routine that can serve many purposes. Teachers can quickly assess student learning by having students respond in writing to a question related to the lesson. Students can use this time to reflect on their learning, ask questions about something that is unclear, or set goals for themselves based on the day's lesson. The possibilities are endless, and it is important to keep "mixing it up" so students stay engaged. See the section on Reflection in Chapter Three for detailed suggestions.

PROCEDURES FOR DISTRIBUTING MATERIALS

Having procedures for distributing and collecting materials can reduce teacher stress and create smoother transitions from one activity to another. These procedures can simply consist of assigning "student jobs" for passing out binders, art supplies, collecting assignments, and so forth. In order to allow for a smooth distribution and collection process, classroom supplies need to be well organized and easy for students to access. Labeling plastic bins or trays is a way to keep supplies like glue, scissors, markers, and colored pencils organized. Binders can be stacked on bookshelves or stored in plastic crates. Some teachers have found it helpful to have a table dedicated solely to supplies that students can easily access. If students are seated at tables or grouped in pods, it can be helpful for each table to have a plastic pencil box that contains supplies like markers, highlighters, sticky notes, and such.

POSTING AGENDAS AND SCHEDULES

It is helpful to post the day's schedule on the board or document camera. Students can easily spend a couple of minutes copying the homework or day's activities. This helps familiarize students with classroom routines and following written directions. Posting basic information like the school bell schedule and classroom protocols (for example, how to check out a book) reinforces for students that the walls of the classroom are important resources.

MODELING ROUTINES AND MAKING MODELING A ROUTINE

Not only is it important to model routines for students so they know what is expected, but it is critical for teachers to make modeling a part of *their* daily routine in order to make input more comprehensible for students.

COMPUTER ROUTINES

Introducing new routines in a language classroom on a regular basis can be confusing and frustrating for students. The same holds true for technology—introducing new web sites or applications too often does not build success. When considering how to structure time using computers, keeping it simple *does* build success. Following are a few guidelines that can be used to make using laptops/tablets more successful for students:

- Go over directions using a computer projector and/or have them listed on Google Classroom or any other learning management system you are using. Model each step of the process that students will be replicating on their own device.
- Regularly remind students about online etiquette. For example, we will often have students use a common editable online document—to annotate an image, to write on an individual slide in a class Google Slideshow, etc. We have found that it is important to point out the expectations during this kind of activity, including respecting each other's work and not writing messages on another student's slide.
- Use computers more to *reinforce* key concepts, and less to teach them.
- Remember that students can be producers of online content and not just consumers.[40]

Supporting Research

In the article "Teaching English Language Learners: What the Research Does—and Does Not—Say," Claude Goldenberg explores extensive research on ELL instruction. He points to establishing routines as an effective learning support for all students in any classroom and explains "...predictable and consistent classroom management routines, aided by diagrams, lists, and easy to read schedules on the board or on charts, to which the teacher refers frequently" are a particularly important scaffold for English learners.[41]

It is also important to remember that research shows not only that routines and procedures can have a positive impact on student behavior and learning, but that involving *students* in the creation of these routines and procedures helps students feel empowered and more likely to follow them.[42]

By fostering relationships with students and parents, collecting and organizing resources, and establishing routines, teachers can lay the groundwork for powerful teaching and learning to occur. The following chapters contain instructional strategies and curriculum ideas that build upon this foundation of a positive and effective learning environment.

 Additional resources, including ones on building positive relationships with students and parents, research on the advantages of being bilingual, and successfully using technology with ELLs, can be found on our book's web site at www.wiley.com/go/eslsurvivalguide2.

PART TWO

Teaching Beginning English Language Learners

CHAPTER THREE

Key Elements of a Curriculum for Beginning ELLs

A traveling wise man and his friends passed through a town and asked to speak to a local scholar. He was brought to Nasreddin Hodja. The traveler didn't speak Turkish, and Hodja didn't speak any other languages, so they decided to communicate through signs.

The traveler used a stick to draw a large circle in the dirt. Hodja then divided the circle in two with his stick. The traveler followed by drawing a perpendicular line that divided the circle into four quarters and then pointed at the first three quarters and then lastly pointed to the fourth quarter. Hodja then swirled the stick around all four quarters. The traveler used his hands to make a bowl shape with his hands up and wiggled his fingers. Hodja then made a bowl shape with his hands down and wiggled his fingers.

When the meeting was over, the traveler's friends asked him what they had discussed. "Hodja is very intelligent," he said. "I showed him that the earth was round, and he said that there was an equator in the middle of it. I told him that three-quarters of the earth was water and one quarter of it was land. He said that there were undercurrents and winds. I told him that the waters warm up, vaporize, and move toward the sky. He said that they cool off and come down as rain." The townspeople surrounded Hodja and asked him the same thing.

"This stranger is hungry," Hodja started to explain. "He said that he hoped to have a large tray of baklava. I said that he could only have half of it. He said that the syrup should be made with three parts sugar and one part honey. I agreed, and said that they had to mix well. He then suggested that we should cook it on a blazing fire. I suggested that we should pour crushed nuts on top of it."[1]

Nasreddin Hodja was a Middle Eastern storyteller who lived in the thirteenth century. In this tale, we see both participants entirely focused on what they want to communicate, and absolutely convinced that they are communicating effectively. These assumptions lead to completely different understandings.

Perhaps we educators should be more concerned with what students hear and learn, and less focused on what we believe we are teaching. It could also be framed as the difference between being effective and being "right." The more we view learning as a process of guided self-discovery and less one of a "sage on stage"—more of a two-way conversation instead of a one-way communication— the better teachers we might be for our students. The activities described in this chapter and throughout this book use this perspective as a guide.

We conveyed a similar viewpoint in our first edition. One new development since its publication, though, has been the introduction of the Common Core Standards that, depending on your beliefs and experiences, helped, hindered or didn't make a difference to ELLs.

Fidelity to these standards vary from state-to-state (especially since many states don't use them and, instead, use their own), from district-to-district and from school-to-school (and, often, from classroom-to-classroom within those schools). Nevertheless, we felt that—at least in some portions of this book—it would be helpful to point readers in the right direction about which standards connect to our recommended strategies.

To make it manageable, and to not clutter our book with lengthy sections on standards that might be of questionable usefulness, we are focusing on the College and Career Readiness Anchor Standards for English Language Arts. These anchor standards represent broad standards in ELA for K-12 students, and are divided into four domains: Reading, Writing, Speaking and Listening, and Language. Each domain is divided into two to four smaller sections which, in turn, have even more specialized subsections.

We will list the *primary* domains and the sections (but not the subsections— those will be easy for readers to figure out when looking at the full Common Core Standards) for each major strategy we discuss in Chapters Three and Five. Of course, with minor modifications, most of our favorite strategies can meet *many* different standards.

Key Elements of a Curriculum

In this chapter, we present key learning and teaching activities that we regularly use in a beginning ELL classroom. They are divided into two sections—"Reading and Writing" and "Speaking and Listening"— though you will find that many of the activities incorporate all four of these language domains. We use each strategy either daily or weekly. Our plan for homework follows these two sections because it, too, is a weekly activity covering all four domains. A short section on assessment follows next, though we examine it more in-depth in Chapter Twenty-Two.

We have also included a final section called "Other Activities." These instructional strategies are ones we often use throughout the year, but just not as many times as the ones listed in the first sections.

An example of each strategy is included in this chapter. Chapter Four, "Daily Instruction For Beginning ELLs," however, includes *many* Figures and Exhibits for each of these strategies that are specific to themes/units that we teach throughout the year.

READING AND WRITING

The Picture Word Inductive Model

The Picture Word Inductive Model (PWIM) uses an inductive process (in which students seek patterns and use them to identify their broader meanings and significance), as opposed to a deductive process (where meanings or rules are given, and students have to then apply them). In the PWIM, an enlarged photo with white space around it (ideally laminated so it can be used again) is first placed in the classroom (see Figure 3.1); students and the teacher together label objects in the picture (the teacher says each word as he writes it on the image and students repeat it chorally); students categorize and add words to their categories; students use the words in sentences that are provided as clozes (fill-in-the-blank exercises; see Exhibit 3.1), which are then categorized. Students then write additional sentences about the image that fit into each category. They are then combined into paragraphs; and, finally, a title is chosen.

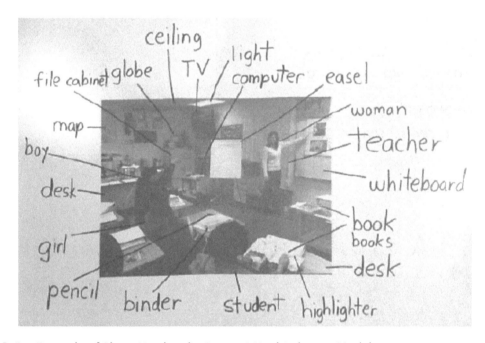

Figure 3.1 Example of Photo Used in the Picture Word Inductive Model

EXHIBIT 3.1. Classroom Picture Sentences

1. The _____ stands in _____ of the room.
   back   front   teacher   student

2. Three _____sit at _____.
   teacher   student   students   desks

3. There is a _____ near the _____.
   highlighter   globe   map   woman

4. The_____ is black and the_____ is yellow.
   highlighter   ceiling   map   computer

5. The _____points to a picture on the _____.
   book   computer   whiteboard   teacher

6. There are _____and _____on the desks.
   map   binders   books   easel

7. The _____is on the _____.
   student   desk   ceiling   light

8. A_____ is on top of the _____.
   file cabinet   boy   map   globe

9. We write with a_____ and a _____.
   binder   pencil   highlighter   girl

10. There are two girl _____and one_____ student.
    woman   students   student   boy

The PWIM process can easily be used as the centerpiece for many classroom activities during the year. Each week, a different photo can be connected to an appropriate theme (food, sports, house, and so on), and the instructional process can be made increasingly sophisticated and challenging for students—for example, later, the cloze sentences can have two blanks in each and not have words written below them for students to choose.

Verbs, written in a different color, can be added to the picture. For example, "points" could be written after "teacher"; "listens" after "student" and "raises his hand" after "boy."

The pictures themselves can be personalized. Local images and ones featuring students could be used. For example, in addition to using a house as the central photo for the class, each student can bring a picture of their own house that they can use for supplementary vocabulary instruction. Students can snap the photos with their cell phone for the teacher to print out or they can digitally label it (see the Tech Tool box for ideas). Photos can also easily be found on the Web. The best pictures to use in this activity contain one scene with many different objects and generally include people. Occasionally, though, there might be exceptions to these criteria, which are highlighted in the "Year-Long Schedule" section in Chapter Four.

Other ways to modify this strategy could include:

- If you have a multi-level class, you could create a more challenging "fill-in-the-blank" story about the picture, like in Exhibit 3.2 "Classroom Picture Story." Then, students could write their own.

- Have students say and write what they think happened before and after the picture was taken.

- Tape the picture on the class whiteboard and/or have students glue their own copies in the middle of a larger paper and invite students to draw and label what they imagine might be around it if the picture was bigger.

- Label two pictures about a similar topic (one inside a grocery store and the other an outdoor market) and introduce the concept of a Venn Diagram and a compare/contrast essay.

- Ask students to find a similar image online and annotate it on a Google Jamboard or similar tool. Students can then use it to teach their classmates.

Of course, some themes will take more than one week (especially if you use some of these modifications) and/or will require more than one picture. A unit on food, for example, could include separate subunits on healthy eating, eating at a restaurant, shopping at a store, farm life (both as a grower and as a laborer), fruit, vegetables, meat, and dairy.

A Picture Word Inductive Unit Plan describing in detail how to apply the strategy can be found in Chapter Four. The "Sample Week Schedule" in Chapter Four demonstrates how the PWIM might fit in with other class activities.

Using the PWIM correlates with the: Anchor Standards for Reading—Key Ideas and Details; Anchor Standards For Writing—Range of Writing; Anchor Standards for Language—Conventions of Standard English, Vocabulary Acquisition and Use.

Supporting Research. The PWIM is a literacy instructional strategy that was designed for early literacy instruction and has also been found to be exceptionally effective with both younger and older second-language learners.[2] It was developed by Emily Calhoun,[3] and some studies have found its use resulting in literacy gains of twice the average, and as great as eight times the average gain for previously low-performing students.[4] It takes advantage of student prior knowledge and visual clues and builds on the key strength of inductive learning—the brain's natural desire to seek out and remember patterns.[5] Substantial research also supports in general the value of associating new vocabulary with images which, of course, is a key element of the PWIM.

Studies reinforce the importance of having students repeat aloud new vocabulary, as is done using the PWIM. Researchers found that saying the word aloud helped learners develop an "encoding record" of the new word.[6]

EXHIBIT 3.2. Classroom Picture Story

The class is (before, after) lunch. The students' names are _____,

_____, _____, and

_____. They are feeling _____

(happy, sad) because they all got (good, bad) grades on a test. They (like, don't

like) the teacher because she is (very nice, not nice). _____

did not sleep very well last night, so he is (hungry, tired). _____

is (hungry, tired) because she did not eat (dinner, breakfast) in the morning.

Text Data Sets

Text Data Sets are very similar to the PWIM cloze sentences, and students use the same kind of categorization process done in that activity. Text Data Sets, however, are composed of sentences or short paragraphs. See Exhibit 3.3 for a Text Data Set that is appropriate for beginners. See Chapters Five, Six and Eight for examples of more advanced Text Data Sets. Students first classify them (individually or with partners), being sure to highlight or underline their evidence for determining that the example belonged in that specific category. They might use categories given to them by the teacher or ones they determine themselves. Then they might add new pieces of data they find and/or they may convert their categories into paragraphs and a simple essay. They might also just stop at the categorization process or, perhaps, create a poster listing the category names, the numbers that fit into each one, a sentence summarizing the concept/category, and a related drawing that they might share in small groups. These data sets are another scaffolding tool in the inductive teaching and learning process that can be used by students to develop increasingly sophisticated writing skills.

Using Text Data Sets correlates with the: Anchor Standards for Reading—Key Ideas and Details, Range of Reading and Level of Text Complexity; Anchor Standards For Writing—Research to Build and Present Knowledge, Range of Writing; Anchor Standards for Language—Conventions of Standard English, Vocabulary Acquisition and Use.

Supporting Research. As described in our book, *The ELL Teacher's Toolbox*, substantial research[7] finds that this kind of "guided discovery" or "enhanced discovery" teaching[8] not only enhances student autonomy and motivation, but also results in greater learning of content, retention,[9] and ability to "transfer" and apply knowledge to new situations.[10] The pattern-seeking that is supported by inductive learning has been found to be especially effective in acquiring both first[11] and new languages.[12] Interestingly enough, this ability to recognize patterns is also being sought more and more by employers, as well.[13]

Tech Tool

Photos on the Web

There are vast numbers of resources on the Web to support the use of photos with students. These sites include places where photos specifically designed for use with the PWIM can be seen and purchased, resources that have other lesson ideas and online literacy exercises connected to images, and sources of millions of photos that can be used in the classroom with few, if any, restrictions. You can find a regularly updated list of these links in "The Best Ways to Use Photos in Lessons" at http://larryferlazzo .edublogs.org/2012/10/19/the-best-online-tools-for-using-photos-in-lessons/.

Several free online tools are available for students (or teachers) to annotate images digitally. You can find them at "The Best Online Tools For Using Photos In Lessons" https://larryferlazzo.edublogs.org/2012/10/19/the-best-online-tools-for-using-photos-in-lessons/.

In addition, a related reinforcing lesson to the PWIM is having students create Picture Data Sets online. Using the categories they have chosen for that week's classroom picture, students can grab images from the Web or upload their own photos of items that fit into those same categories (for example, "words that begin with r," "vegetables," or "transportation"). These photos can either illustrate words they have already identified in class or new ones, and then students can label them with words or sentences. They can also mix up their images, list the names of categories, and challenge other students to organize them correctly. Several easy and free online tools allow students to easily mix and match images for these kinds of activities, and you can find them at "The Best Online Virtual 'Corkboards' (or 'Bulletin Boards')" https://larryferlazzo.edublogs.org/2011/03/ 30/the-best-online-virtual-corkboards-or-bulletin-boards/.

EXHIBIT 3.3. "Describing Things" Data Set

Categories: Numbers, Colors, Size, Age, Weather, and Temperature

1. There are 22 students in class.
2. Choua is wearing a black shirt.
3. Mr. Ferlazzo is an old teacher.
4. Walter is tall.
5. Luther Burbank is a big school.
6. Johanna has a blue pencil.
7. There are 26 desks in the classroom.
8. Ms. Smith has short hair.
9. Chue has a young sister.
10. Today is a sunny day.

11. The boy is wearing white shoes.

12. Tomorrow will be a rainy day.

13. The rice is very hot.

14. The ice cream is freezing.

15. Ms. Vue has a little baby.

16. There are 24 hours in a day.

17. There are three computers in our classroom.

18. Yesterday was a windy day.

19. Mr. Ferlazzo drives a gray car.

20. The students in our class are young.

21. The water is cold.

22. The ant is tiny.

Critical Pedagogy

Critical pedagogy is the term often used to describe a teaching approach whose most well-known practitioner was Brazilian educator Paulo Freire. Freire was critical of the "banking" approach towards education, where the teacher "deposits" information into her students. Instead, he wanted to help students learn by questioning and looking at real-world problems that they, their families, and their communities faced. Through this kind of dialogue, he felt that both students and the teacher could learn together.[14] Freire was careful to call his learning approach a "problem-posing" one, not a "problem-solving" exercise. He wanted to put the emphasis on teachers raising questions through this process and not giving solutions.[15]

There are many ways to use this strategy in the ELL classroom. One way is to first show a very short video clip, photo, cartoon, newspaper article, song, or comic strip or, if the English level of the class is advanced enough, students can act out a dialogue that represents a common problem faced by students (a teacher can also perform the dialogue on his/her own). Ideally, it should be connected to the thematic unit that is being studied at that time, and should reflect an actual problem that students or their families have faced or are facing. However, there is no need to be strictly limited to the thematic unit, and issues may arise in students' lives at any time that can provide learning opportunities. The problems can be identified by the teacher first modeling an example and then by eliciting ideas of problems from students. Students can also draw their own representations of the problems.

For example, if the thematic unit is "school," a short video clip from either the movie *My Bodyguard* or *The Karate Kid* can be shown to illustrate the problem of bullying. Students can then work in pairs and small groups in a five-step process responding to the following questions,[16] with a class discussion after each one (certain words may need to be simplified and/or defined, especially when done for the first time):

1. Describe what you see: Who is doing what? What do they look like? What objects do you see in the video? Summarize what they are saying.
2. What is the problem in the video?
3. Have you, your family, or friends ever experienced the problem? Describe what happened.
4. What do you think might be the causes of the problem?
5. What solutions could a person do on their own? What solutions could people do together? Would one be better than the other? Why or why not? (The teacher might have to caution students that the solution(s) they choose must also be realistic).

Students can create simple posters or slideshows and make presentations (including role-plays) illustrating the problem, sharing their personal connection to it, listing potential solutions, and choosing which one they think is best and why. A "writing frame" (an extended "fill-in-the-blank" form) like the one in Exhibit 3.4 "Problem/Solution Writing Frame" can also be shared with students.

As students become more advanced, they can develop this outline into a problem-solution essay using the same outline (see Chapter Six for more ideas on how to support students writing a problem-solution essay). Students can also take real-world actions to confront the problem, as one of our classes did by organizing a fair bringing ten different job training agencies to our school so they and their families could learn what services were available (see Chapter Six for more information on action projects).

This five-step outline can be used to approach multiple problems on a weekly or biweekly schedule for different thematic units—perhaps discussing the problem of unemployment when learning about jobs, not having health insurance when discussing a medical unit, or landlord issues during a week on "home." Each time, the problem can be demonstrated in a different form, and each time, students can be challenged to present their answers in an increasingly more sophisticated way.

As ELLs increase their language proficiency, an extra step can be inserted into the five-point outline to incorporate another level of inductive learning: It can be numbered 2.5 or later in the process. Students can be asked to make a list of questions they would need answered about the problem in order to solve it (during the first time using this strategy, teacher modeling might be necessary). For example, questions about the bullying video could include:

- How old are they?
- Are they in the same class?
- What is the school policy on bullying?
- Does the teacher know what is going on?
- How might the bully respond?
- Do their parents know each other?
- Was there a specific incident that started it?
- Are other students being bullied too?
- Are there other students the bully seems to listen to?

Students can then be asked to categorize the questions into the steps needed to solve most problems—researching information, identifying allies, and preparing for a reaction. They can then use similar questions and categories to develop their own specific action plan to solve the more personal problems they identify and present those plans with their solutions. Finally, students can perform short role-plays or draw a comic strip portraying how they would solve the problems.

Using critical pedagogy correlates with the: Anchor Standards for Reading—Key Ideas and Details; Anchor Standards For Writing—Range of Writing; Anchor Standards for Language—Conventions of Standard English, Vocabulary Acquisition and Use.

Supporting Research. Using the problem-based learning exemplified in these kinds of critical pedagogy lessons can bring many benefits to the ELL classroom. These include the more authentic issues represented in the process promoting enhanced language acquisition, compared to prepackaged dialogues and worksheets or role-plays. In addition, this kind of instruction has been found to increase the likelihood of learners applying the classroom content to their outside lives.[17]

EXHIBIT 3.4. Problem/Solution Writing Frame

Name _____

1. **What is the problem in the picture?**
   The problem in the picture is _____.

2. **Have you had that problem in the past?**
   Yes, I have had that problem in the past. When I was in _____,
   _____.

   OR

   No, I have not had that problem in the past.

3. **Do you know other people who had that problem?**
   Yes, I know other people who have had that problem. _____
   _____.

   OR

   No, I do not know people who have had that problem.

4. **What do you think is the cause of that problem?**
   I think _____ is the cause of
   the problem.

5. **What are solutions to that problem?**
   One solution is _____.
   Another solution is _____.

6. **What is the best solution to that problem?**
   The best solution to that problem is _____
   because _____.

Tech Tool
Digital Storytelling

Students can portray the problems, and their potential solutions, online through the use of video, animations, or slideshows. Smartphones make the creation of these digital stories even easier, and they can be created by even the least tech-savvy students and teachers. Multiple digital storytelling tools for smartphones and computer use can be found at "'Best' Lists Of The Week: Listening & Speaking Resources" https://larryferlazzo.edublogs.org/2018/08/04/best-lists-of-the-week-listening-speaking-resources/.

Free Voluntary Reading and Reading Strategies

Free Voluntary Reading, also called Extensive Reading, Silent Sustained Reading, and recreational reading, is the instructional strategy of letting students choose books or other reading material they want to read with minimal or no academic work connected to it. Its purpose is to promote the enjoyment of reading. It's expected that since students are choosing the books they will read, they will also feel more motivated to want to learn the new vocabulary that appears in them. Students are also encouraged to change books if they find the one they are reading to be uninteresting.

Though students are typically not assessed on what they are reading, students can be encouraged to interact with the text through the use of reading strategies. Without this kind of encouragement, students can more easily fall into the trap of learning to "decode" words without truly understanding their meaning. Teachers can model what good readers do through short and simple "think-alouds" (see Exhibit 3.5). Teacher comments are noted in the exhibit. (Read-alouds, where short passages are read to students without modeling reading strategies, are also an effective instructional method. See Chapters Five and Six for further information.)

A teacher can identify short, accessible passages and over a period of a few weeks use this sequence with students:

1. Teacher models a think-aloud (showing it on a document camera or overhead projector), focusing on one of several reading strategies—asking questions, making a connection, predicting what happens next, evaluating, visualizing, monitoring and repairing, and summarizing. Asking students to use these strategies can help in comprehension, and can enhance student engagement. In other words, they provide an explicit task and reason for students to engage with the text.

2. Small whiteboards with markers and erasers (or white sheets of paper) are distributed to students.

3. Teacher shows and reads another short passage and asks students to apply the previously modeled reading strategy. Students hold up their boards when they are ready for teacher feedback so all students can see many examples.

EXHIBIT 3.5. Think-Aloud

Note: The names used here should be changed to reflect you and your own students. Teacher think-aloud comments appear in italics.

The students were working very hard in class one day (*I wondered what they were doing?*). In the middle of a lesson, Jose screamed, "Look, there's a mouse!" (*This makes me see a picture of a little tiny mouse in my mind.*) All the students started yelling, and some jumped on their desks. Tou threw his pencil at it, and Chou threw his pen. The teacher was very afraid, too. Pang wasn't worried. (*I wonder why she wasn't afraid?*) She took two books and used them to push the mouse out the door. The mouse was free, and Pang was a hero. (*This makes me see a picture in my mind of the teacher and students cheering Pang. This story is about a mouse in the classroom and how Pang got rid of it.*)

Students can be given a simple form (see Exhibit 3.6) that asks them to show a few reading strategies each week. It is less important that students are using all the reading strategies correctly. It is more critical for them to recognize that genuinely understanding any text requires readers to be proactive and not passive. There is some debate among researchers about how much time students need to spend on explicitly applying reading strategies to texts. What many miss, however, is what many teachers experience in the classroom—having students read *and* apply these strategies can be a very effective engagement strategy that increases the odds of students actually reading the text![18]

Students can begin each class with 10–15 minutes of silent reading (this is a time when peer tutors can take students outside and listen to them read). An important consideration is what the teacher is doing during this period of time. Though some suggest that the teacher should also be a model and read during the same time, we feel strongly that it is more important to be walking around, asking students questions, having them read aloud short passages, and so forth. Not only does this kind of interaction serve as a good formative assessment, but at least one important study has also found it to be a good instructional strategy. In an article in the *Journal of Educational Psychology*, researchers found that teachers providing individual feedback to students during this kind of reading time was by far one of the most effective way to help improve students' reading ability. It primarily looked at students using their silent reading time to read class text (though not exclusively), but it seems close enough to the basic ideas of Free Voluntary Reading that we should carefully consider what they found.[19]

Students could also read the same book together—perhaps by going outside or sitting in the back and saying the words softly. In a multi-level class, we sometimes invite students to "pair-up," choose a book, complete Exhibit 3.7, and then verbally present what they wrote to the class or in small groups. This kind of "paired reading" has been shown to improve reading fluency and increase comprehension.[20]

Students could also be encouraged to read at home each night. The Tech Tool section discusses the countless online options where students can read have the text spoken aloud to them.

In addition, students can be encouraged to talk with their classmates using simple Book Talks, which are explained more in Chapter Five and in Exhibit 5.4.

An additional lesson to reinforce reading strategies is to have students complete—either on their own or in pairs—the Reading Strategies Data Set—Beginners in Exhibit 3.8. It's a simple Text Data Set, which is an instructional strategy introduced earlier in this chapter. Students categorize the examples while underlining their evidence (for example, the question-mark would be underlined if a student was going to put it in the "Ask Questions" category).

Using Free Voluntary Reading and reading strategies correlates with the Anchor Standards for Reading—Key Ideas and Details, Craft and Structure, Range of Reading and Level of Text Complexity; Anchor Standards for Language—Vocabulary Acquisition and Use.

Supporting Research. Numerous studies have shown the benefits of Free Voluntary Reading, particularly with English language learners.[21] A review of 23 studies showed that in all cases ELLs using Free Voluntary Reading had a higher gain in reading comprehension than those in classes not using the strategy. In addition, other research has demonstrated that ELLs using Free Voluntary Reading have greater gains in writing, grammar usage, and spelling.[22]

Research by Professor Jim Cummins also supports explicit teaching and learning of reading comprehension strategies.[23]

EXHIBIT 3.6. Reading Log

Name _____

Period _____

Date _____

Reading Log

Summarize: This book or story is about . . . □━▶□

Predict: I predict that . . . ⟶

Ask questions: Will . . . ? Why . . . ?

Evaluate: I agree (or disagree) with . . . I like (or do not like) . . . ☺ or ☹

Visualize: Reading this book or story makes me see a picture of . . . ☺❀

Connect: This makes me remember . . . Book · Movie · Personal Experience

Date	Book or Story Title	Reading Strategy Used

Extensive research supports using the "Think-Aloud" strategy to teach and reinforce students becoming skilled in applying reading strategies.[24] Think-alouds are an example of teacher modeling, which has been shown to be an effective instructional strategy in multiple areas, including in think-alouds.[25]

Helping ELLs develop oral fluency, one of the prime goals behind having students read the same book together, is a critical element of improving reading comprehension skills.[26]

EXHIBIT 3.7. Partner Reading

Name of Partner Students _____ and _____

1. What is the title of your book? _____

2. Three words in the book that are new to you and what do they mean? Include picture

      Word _____   Definition _____

              Picture:

      Word _____   Definition _____

              Picture:

      Word _____   Definition _____

              Picture:

3. A summary of what you have read so far in the book. This book is about _____ _____.

4. We liked this book because _____.
OR

We did not like this book because _____.

EXHIBIT 3.8. Reading Strategies Data Set -Beginners

Put these examples into these categories: **Summarize, Predict, Ask Questions, Evaluate, Visualize, and Connect**

1. This story is about a girl's first day in the United States.
2. Will Rocio go out with Miguel, Tou or John?
3. The girl was wrong for yelling at her little brother.
4. Reading "he was very tired" makes me see a picture of a man going to sleep.
5. This story makes me remember the movie I saw about monsters.
6. This story makes me remember another book I read about the coronavirus.
7. I predict that the lion will eat the rabbit because he is hungry.
8. I like this book about basketball because I like to play the game.
9. Will the boy get hit by a car?
10. Will the girl buy the truck or the small car?
11. I predict the girl will buy the small car because it is cheaper.
12. This book tells about the family's trip to Mexico.
13. The title of the book is "Asia." I predict it will tell about China, Vietnam, Thailand and other countries.
14. This makes me remember when my father died.
15. Will the boy live or die when the boat sinks?
16. Reading "it was raining" makes me see a picture of people getting wet.

Tech Tool

Online Books

Thousands of free online books are available and accessible to English language learners and provide audio and visual support for the text. These are particularly useful for older ELLs because they help students read higher-level texts, as opposed to simpler ones designed for young children. In addition, many free and easily printable short books are available online. Lists of these online resources can be found at

"'Best' Lists Of The Week: Resources For Reading Instruction" https://larryferlazzo .edublogs.org/2018/03/18/best-lists-of-the-week-resources-for-reading-instruction/. These lists include one sharing sites that offer "parallel texts"—sites where pages in English are translated side-by-side into the home language of the reader.

There are also many tools that allow users to "annotate" websites, texts, and even materials that teachers upload for students to read. Some even allow students to see the annotations made by their classmates and comment on them. These can be helpful when explicitly using reading strategies. You can find them at "Best Applications For Annotating Websites" https://larryferlazzo.edublogs.org/2008/12/18/best-applications-for-annotating-websites/.

Communicative Dictation Activities

These three dictation exercises combine reading and writing skills with developing listening and speaking skills.

Interactive Dictation. In interactive dictation, students are assigned a simple passage or a book the class has been using, so students are familiar with it. They are then divided into pairs or triads, and each student is given a small whiteboard, marker, and eraser (or blank sheets of paper). One student reads a few words while the other(s) write them down. The writers can look at their copy of the text as a kind of cheat sheet, but should be encouraged to work toward not using it. The reader can give feedback on the accuracy and errors of the writer.

Dictogloss. Dictogloss can be done a number of different ways but here is one variation. First, students divide their papers in half. Then the teacher reads a short text, often one students are familiar with. After the first time of just listening, the teacher reads it again and students write down notes on one-half of the paper about what they have heard. Next the teacher reads it a third time and again the students write down additional notes in the same space. Students then compare their notes with a partner and they work together to develop a reconstruction of the text on the other half of the paper one that is not the exact wording, but that demonstrates its meaning accurately. Finally, the teacher reads the selection again and students judge how well they did.

Picture Dictation. In picture dictation, the teacher can draw or find a simple image and, without showing it to the class, describe it while students draw ("There is a man on the lower-left with short hair. There is a car on the bottom right, and a bright sun above the car"). It can also be a partner activity where half of the class is given one picture and the other half a different one—it's even more fun when students are asked to draw their own pictures "in secret" so no one else sees it! Students with different pictures are made partners and stand up a book or folder between them. One student describes her picture while the other draws. When it's complete and the student is given feedback, the roles can be reversed. Students can also be asked to work together and write sentences describing each image.

Picture dictation is one of many exercises (and our favorite one) that fall under the broad category of "information gap" activities. They are generally designed as partner exercises where one student has to get information from the other, speaking the target language—in order to complete the assignment.

Delayed Dictation. We learned about Delayed Dictation from teacher Gianfranco Conti.[27] In our version, it can be a form of "Interactive Dictation" or "Dictogloss." The difference is that instead of having students immediately starting to copy down a sentence you are saying, they are told to wait ten seconds. You could even make it harder (and maybe more fun!) by singing a song or saying random words during that 10-second interval! This activity builds on the value of "retrieval practice," which we discuss later in this section.

Using Communicative Dictation Activities correlates with the: Anchor Standards For Speaking and Listening—Comprehension and Collaboration; Anchor Standards for Language—Knowledge of Language.

Supporting Research. Numerous studies have shown that communicative dictation activities can increase student engagement,[28] enhance English listening comprehension,[29] and improve grammar skills.[30] These communicative activities are different from the often deadly teacher-centered uses (passages repeated multiple times in a "drill-and-kill" fashion until students get it "right",) which can be particularly frustrating for beginning-level learners.

Tech Tool

Online Dictation Exercises

Many free online dictation exercises—using audio only or audio and video together—are available, providing automatic and immediate assessments. You can find them at "The Best Sites For ELLs To Practice Online Dictation" https://larryferlazzo .edublogs.org/2017/07/15/the-best-sites-for-ells-to-practice-online-dictation/.

Concept Attainment

Concept attainment, originally developed by Jerome Bruner and his colleagues,[31] is a form of inductive learning where the teacher identifies both "good" and "bad" examples (ideally, taken from student work—with the names removed, of course) of the intended learning objective. After developing a sheet like the one in Exhibit 3.9, which is designed to practice conjugating the verb "to be" correctly, the teacher would place it on a document camera or overhead projector. At first, everything would be covered except for the "Yes" and "No" titles, and the teacher would explain that he is going to give various examples and he wants students to identify why certain ones are under "Yes" and others are under"No."

EXHIBIT 3.9. Concept Attainment Example

Yes	No
Hmong food is good.	
	Many people is big and heavy.
The food is spicy.	
	Hmong foods is good.
It is a sort of soup that Hmong people eat.	
	Ginger and galangal is good.
The foods are spicy.	
	Hmong food are natural.
American foods are not spicy.	
	Papaya salad are good and spicy.

After the first "Yes" and "No" examples are shown, students are asked to think about them and share with a partner why they think one is a "Yes" and one is a "No." After the teacher calls on people, if no one can identify the reason, he continues uncovering one example at a time and continues the think-pair-share process with students until they identify the reasons. Then students are asked to correct the "No" examples and write their own "Yes" ones. Last, students can be asked to generate their own "Yes" examples and share them with a partner or the class. This inductive learning strategy can be used effectively to teach countless lessons, including ones on grammar, spelling, composition, and even speaking (using recorded audio).

We have even used this strategy to teach essay organization by taping parts of essays on the classroom wall under "Yes" and "No"—with names removed and after getting permission to do so from the student authors. This kind of exercise is much easier to do when there are positive relationships throughout the classroom.

Using concept attainment correlates with the: Anchor Standards for Reading—Key Ideas and Details; Anchor Standards For Writing—Range of Writing; Anchor Standards For Speaking and Listening—Comprehension and Collaboration; Anchor Standards for Language—Conventions of Standard English, Knowledge of Language.

Supporting Research. Concept attainment is another instructional strategy that builds on the brain's natural desire to seek out patterns. Judy Willis, neurologist, teacher, and author, writes: "Education is about increasing the patterns that students can use, recognize, and communicate. As the ability to see and work with patterns expands, the executive functions are enhanced. Whenever new material is presented in such a way that students see relationships, they generate greater brain cell activity (forming new neural connections) and achieve more successful long-term memory storage and retrieval."[32]

Numerous studies have shown that concept attainment has a positive effect on student achievement, including with second-language learners.[33]

Concept attainment, like the other forms of inductive teaching and learning discussed in this chapter (Picture Word Inductive Model and Text Data Sets) can also be described as an example of "enhanced discovery learning." As we mentioned earlier, in a recent meta-analysis of hundreds of studies, researchers found that "enhanced discovery learning" was a more effective form of teaching than either "direct instruction" or "unassisted discovery learning."[34]

Language Experience Approach

The Language Experience Approach involves the entire class doing an activity and then discussing and writing about it. The activity could be

- Watching a short video clip
- Taking a walk around the school
- Doing a science experiment
- Playing a game
- Just about anything else you can think of!

Immediately following the activity, students are given a short time to write down notes about what they did (very early beginners can draw). Then the teacher calls on students to share what the class did—usually, though not always, in chronological order. The teacher then writes down what is said on a document camera, overhead projector, or easel paper. It is sometimes debated whether the teacher should write down exactly what a student says if there are grammar or word errors *or* should say or write the correct version back to the student—without saying the student was wrong (known as "recasting"). We find the second strategy is more effective at maintaining a positive learning environment where students feel comfortable communicating in a new language. Students can then copy down the class-developed description. Since the text comes out of their own experience, it is much more accessible because they already know its meaning.

The text can subsequently be used for different follow-up activities, including as a cloze (removing certain words and leaving a blank which students have to complete); a sentence scramble (taking individual sentences and mixing up the words for learners to sequence correctly); or mixing up all the sentences in the text and having students put them back in order.

Using the Language Experience Approach correlates with the: Anchor Standards For Writing—Production and Distribution of Writing, Range of Writing; Anchor Standards for Speaking and Listening—Comprehension and Collaboration; Anchor Standards for Language—Conventions of Standard English, Knowledge of Language, Vocabulary Acquisition and Use.

Supporting Research. Respected ELL researchers Suzanne Peregoy and Owen Boyle have found that "the language-experience approach is one of the most frequently recommended approaches for beginning second-language readers. The beauty of the approach is that the student provides the text, through the dictation, that serves as the basis for reading instruction. As a result, language-experience reading is tailored to the learner's own interests, social, and cultural strengths and interest the student brings to school."[35]

Writing Collaborative Stories

Collaborative story writing can be done in a number of ways and bears some similarities to the Language Experience Approach.

One example is to start by dividing the class into groups of three. Within the small groups, each person is numbered either one, two, or three. Each group is given one sheet of paper, and at the top of each paper the group writes "Once Upon a Time..." (at times, it might make sense to provide some parameters for the story so it is connected to the thematic unit the class is studying—such as food or school—but as we discussed earlier, it's okay not to have all activities directly connected to the theme at all times).

Next, the teacher puts a piece of paper under the document camera and projects it on the screen and writes:

1. Who?

This means that the number ones in each group have to write one sentence describing who is going to be in the story. Students can be encouraged to have fun with it and pushed to write adjectives ("the ugly monster" and the "handsome boy").

Students are given no more than two minutes to write it, and their group members can help.

The teacher then writes:

2. Where?

The number ones in each group pass their paper to the nearby number twos, who then write their idea about where the story is taking place. Of course, everyone in their group can help! Students generally begin to get engaged in the exercise at this point.

Then, the teacher writes:

3. When?

The papers are passed to the number threes in each group, who write when the story is happening (time of day, season, time period/year).

The process continues with following prompts:

1. What is the problem?
2. Who said what? (indicating that someone in the story had to say something, which is a great time to reinforce quotation marks)
3. Who said what back to that person?
4. Something bad happens
5. Something good happens
6. Something funny happens

The entire small group then determines how the story ends.

Students can be given a big piece of easel paper to convert their sentences into a story with illustrations (or work on a shared Google Slides presentation or create an online book). Next, in a round-robin fashion, each group can tell and show their story to the other groups.

Follow-up activities with the texts can be similar to the ones suggested in the Language Experience Approach section. In addition, students can even convert their story into a short skit they perform for the class.

Writing collaborative stories correlates with the: Anchor Standards For Writing—Text Types and Purposes, Range of Writing; Anchor Standards for Speaking and Listening—Comprehension and Collaboration; Anchor Standards for Language—Conventions of Standard English, Knowledge of Language, Vocabulary Acquisition and Use.

Supporting Research. Working in small groups has consistently been found to develop second-language learner self-confidence and increase opportunities for language interaction. Specifically, it results in more student speaking practice and reduces future student errors because of those increased practice opportunities, along with students feeling more motivated and engaged in learning.[36] Studies have also shown that collaborative writing among English Language Learners can enhance the quality of the produced text, perhaps through the ongoing feedback the co-writers provide to each other.[37]

Tech Tool
Online Collaborative Storytelling

Numerous free online sites and tools enable students to easily create collaborative stories. You can find many of them at "The Best Sites For Collaborative Storytelling" https://larryferlazzo.edublogs.org/2010/12/29/the-best-sites-for-collaborative-storytelling/.

Phonics

Countless debates have taken place about the amount of time that should be spent on teaching phonics and which instructional method should be used to teach it. Extensive research supports the idea of spending limited time teaching what Stephen Krashen calls "basic phonics," the very basic consonant and vowel rules needed for students to comprehend text.[38] Some researchers suggest that English language development of ELLs can be harmed by an over-emphasis on phonics instruction.[39] To modify an old community organizing saying, we believe phonics instruction in the ELL classroom has its place, and also has to be kept in its place. Unfortunately, a fair amount of phonics instruction can be characterized as the "drill-and-kill" method of instruction. We believe that, instead, using an inductive process is the most effective and engaging way to teach basic phonics.

The easiest tool we've found to use in this process is the book *Sounds Easy* by Sharron Bassano.[40] A sample page from the book can be found in Exhibit 3.10. It is designed for use with beginning ELLs from grade five through adult education. The inductive method we recommend builds upon and adds to the instructional strategy suggested in the book.

First, copies of a page from the book are distributed to students. In the case of Exhibit 3.10, it is a page with a series of pictures that can be described by words with the long *a* sound. Each picture has one or more of the letters in the describing word missing. The teacher has the same sheet on the overhead or document camera. The teacher says the number of the picture, gives students a few seconds to complete the blanks with what they believe goes there, and then the teacher writes the correct letters (students correct their papers if they have made any mistakes).

EXHIBIT 3.10. Sounds Easy! Phonics, Spelling, and Pronunciation Practice

Sounds Easy! _____

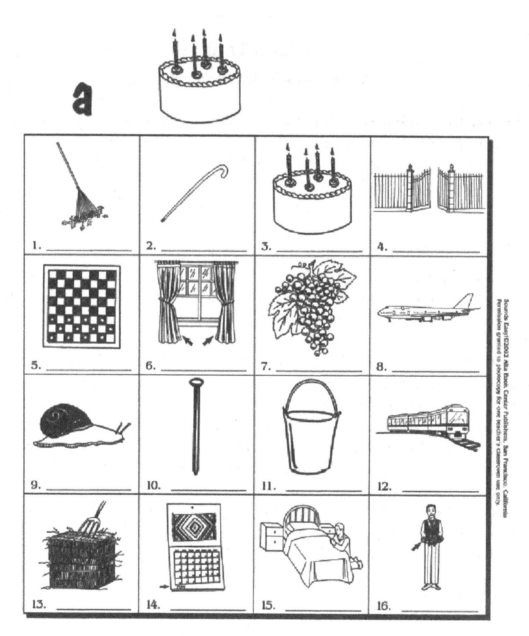

Source: S. Bassano (2002). *Sounds Easy! Phonics, Spelling, and Pronunciation Practice*. Provo, UT: Alta Book Center. Copyright © 2002 Alta Book Center Publishers. Reproduced by permission.

After the sheet is complete, it is reviewed again. The teacher can point rapidly to the different pictures and ask for a choral response, doing it faster and faster to make it a more fun activity. Then students work with partners to practice pronouncing the words. Next, they work together to put the words into two or three categories. They could be "words that have *ai*," "words that have an *a* with a silent *e* at the end," or categories that reflect how they are used—such as food, for example.

Pairs then become groups of four to compare and explain the reasoning behind their categories. The groups then choose which categories they think are best and add words to them using what they learned from the Picture Word Inductive Model activity, dictionaries, or other resources. They can create posters of the categories and share them with the class, along with one, two, or three phonics rules they might have learned.

More often than not, students themselves will identify the key phonics "rules" that apply—in this case, that the letter *a* would be pronounced with a "long" sound if it was the third letter from the end of a word that ended with an *e* or if it was the second from the last letter if the last letter was a *y*. In addition, the letter *a* would likely be pronounced with a "long" sound if it appeared as an *ai*.

To "switch things up" sometimes, students can be asked to write a simple story using the words from that day's phonics lesson as a form of "collaborative writing." In reading activities later that day or shortly thereafter, the teacher and students can also highlight instances where this rule applies.

Of course, it is not necessary to use this *entire* inductive process for every letter sound. Teachers should use their judgment about which sounds they think are the most important, how it fits into the other units they are teaching at the time, and the energy level displayed by their students on any given day.[41]

We need to point out that the "Sounds Easy" book now appears to be out-of-print. Even though it seems fairly easy to find a used copy online, we hope that it is reprinted at some point. Of course, this inductive instructional strategy can also be applied to the many textbook pages and other books that use similar images to teach phonics.

Teaching phonics inductively correlates with the Anchor Standards for Reading— Key Ideas and Details; Anchor Standards for Language—Conventions of Standard English, Vocabulary Acquisition and Use.

Supporting Research. Extensive research demonstrates that an intensive emphasis on explicit phonics instruction can lead students to focus on decoding instead of comprehension. Along with the previously cited studies by Krashen,[42] he has done further review of the confirming research (for a list of Krashen's publications see http://sdkrashen.com), as has Professor Brian Cambourne.[43] Additional research suggests that possible phonemic overlap between an ELL students' home language and English can reduce the amount of time needed for explicit phonics instruction.[44]

In addition to the support previously cited for inductive teaching and learning, studies have shown students in inductive learning classrooms scoring as much as 30 percent higher in assessments than those using deductive models.[45] In addition, ESL researcher H.D. Brown writes that "most of the evidence in communicative second language teaching points to the superiority of an inductive approach to rules and generalizations."[46]

Tech Tool

Phonics Practice

There are numerous free online sites where phonics can be reinforced in engaging ways through games and practice. You can find them at "The Best Articles & Sites For Teachers & Students To Learn About Phonics" https://larryferlazzo .edublogs.org/2011/03/01/the-best-articles-sites-for-teachers-students-to-learn-about-phonics/.

Reflection

Robert J. Marzano calls reflection "the final step in a comprehensive approach to actively processing information."[47] As such, it can also function as a useful formative assessment (see Chapter Nineteen).

We recommend having a short—five to seven minutes or so—reflection activity, usually a "think-write-pair-share," two or three times each week at the end of class. It could be useful to both student and teacher to collect these for monthly, bimonthly, or quarterly review, so keeping them in a separate folder or notebook is an option. We suggest that these activities fall into four different categories—summarize, self-assess, assess the class and teacher, and relevance—and that the reflection activity vary between them (and any other ideas you might want to try). Depending on the English level of the class, sentence starters to help students with their responses might be helpful in addition to asking the questions themselves. Students can verbally share with partners what they wrote and some could be asked to read it to the entire class.

Beginning the day with a reflection can also be a nice "opening bell" activity. You could quickly go through the room and have each student verbally share the answer they wrote to a question. This type of warm-up could function as a time for Social Emotional Learning, as well. For example, the sentence starters in Exhibit 3.11 "Warm-Up Sentence Frames" support students in writing about gratitude, kindness, self-affirmation, and personal vulnerability. Research shows that developing this kind of "pro-social behavior" can lead to greater academic achievement.[48]

Here are the four categories related to more academic reflection:

SUMMARIZE

There is a wealth of research documenting the effectiveness of having students summarize what they have been studying.[49] Students can respond to prompts like:

What are two things you learned today?

What is the most interesting thing you learned today?

What do you know now that you didn't know before today?

What will you tell your parents tonight if they ask what you learned?

Draw something that represents the most important thing you learned today or that summarizes the day. Please write a short description.

SELF-ASSESS

Robert J. Marzano recommends students share how well they think they did in class and what they believe they could have done better.[50] Using the metacognitive strategy of reviewing what they did that helped them learn, along with what they did that was not particularly effective, can assist students in developing a greater sense of self-efficacy.[51] Here are a few more questions students can answer:

What did you do that helped you the most today to learn English?

What did you do to help yourself understand something when you were not clear?

What, if anything, do you think you need more help in understanding?

What, if anything, are you having difficulty doing?

After students complete the lesson on the Qualities of a Successful Language Learner in Chapter Sixteen, they can periodically be asked to reflect on what they did to meet their goals or what they could have done differently to meet them.

ASSESS THE CLASS AND TEACHER

Asking students to share their perspectives on class activities and the teacher's style can help on a number of levels. This is best done anonymously to ensure candid responses. Questions can include

What was your favorite class activity today, and why did you like it?

What was your least favorite class activity today, and why was it your least favorite?

Was the pace of this class too slow, too fast, or just right?

These one-day quick check-ins should not be confused with the more extensive class evaluation suggestions in Chapter Two and in Chapter Nineteen..

RELEVANCE

Some studies have shown that having students write a few sentences explaining how they can *specifically* apply what they learned to their lives resulted in higher achievement.[52] ELL teachers can apply this same concept in their classes. Students might write, "I will be able to ask someone for directions" or "I can fill out a job application" and, in addition to refreshing their memory, they might feel more encouraged to actually do these things.

Using various types of reflection activities correlates with the Anchor Standards For Writing—Range of Writing; Anchor Standards for Speaking and Listening—Comprehension and Collaboration; Anchor Standards for Language—Conventions of Standard English, Knowledge of Language, Vocabulary Acquisition and Use.

Supporting Research. In addition to the specific research already cited under each category of reflection, there are a number of additional studies that reinforce the importance of reflection on learning, including but not limited to ones that specifically support the idea of writing them down in a "journal" form, as we mentioned at the beginning of the Reflection section.[53]

EXHIBIT 3.11. Warm-up Sentence Frames

1. The best thing that happened to me last week (or yesterday) was _____.

2. The most important thing I learned last week (or yesterday) was _____.

3. One thing I did well last week (or yesterday) was _____.

4. One thing I worry about is _____ because _____.

5. One thing I'm grateful for is _____ because _____.

6. A mistake I learned from last week was when I _____. I learned that I should _____.

7. I want to give a compliment to _____ because _____.

Retrieval Practice Notebook

Retrieval practice is the idea of trying to remember something that you've learned without having something in front of you to prompt your memory. This kind of practice makes it more likely to "stick." No surprise to teachers, right? Retrieval practice is what's behind quizzes, tests, and flashcards that many of us use in our classes all the time.

However, there are many other ways to implement retrieval practice, and we would like to highlight one in particular that we use in all of our ELL classes—no matter their English proficiency level.

We call it the "Retrieval Practice Notebook." Since we often have two class periods with ELL Beginners, we might have one warm-up be the SEL reflection questions described in the previous section, and then have this "notebook" as the way to begin the second period. Though we're placing it in its own section, you'll see from its description that it could also fall under the "Reflection" category.

We give each student a composition notebook and, every day when they enter the room, they take a few minutes to write in it what they learned in each of their classes the previous day (if they were absent or if they don't remember, they can talk to a seatmate). Students use two sheets of their notebook for each week—they write the date of the week and then divide the sheets into their class schedule so they can write under each class "heading." Once they complete writing their sentences, they can draw illustrations on the page representing things they learned. After five minutes, each student shares what they wrote with a classmate, sometimes in a very rapid Speed Dating process where they share with multiple classmates and have to move around. Then we call on some students to share one thing they wrote. The whole process takes less than ten minutes and can be shortened when necessary (it's also fine to just do it every other day). Of course, a physical notebook can be replaced by an online one, instead.

Doing this activity not only increases the likelihood that students will remember what they learned and apply it in different situations, but it also functions as a form of the "Language Experience Approach" that we discussed earlier in the chapter. Students practice writing in English about their own direct experience, talk about it in English, and it creates opportunities for us to give quick English lessons based on what students write and say. For example, we can restate a sentence in the correct form after a student has said it "incorrectly" (see Error Correction in Chapter Sixteen). On top of all that, their other teachers love it because it helps students learn *their* content.

Using the Retrieval Practice Notebook correlates with the: Anchor Standards For Writing - Range of Writing; Anchor Standards for Speaking and Listening—Comprehension and Collaboration; Anchor Standards for Language—Conventions of Standard English, Knowledge of Language, Vocabulary Acquisition and Use.

Supporting Research. There are more studies supporting retrieval practice than "you can shake a stick at".[54]

Tech Tool
Other Ideas For Retrieval Practice

There are many other creative ideas beyond the typical tests and flash cards for applying retrieval practice in your classroom (including just having a warm-up question asking students to write down one thing they learned the previous day). You can learn more very practical strategies at "The Best Resources For Learning About Retrieval Practice" https://larryferlazzo.edublogs.org/2017/10/22/the-best-resources-for-learning-about-retrieval-practice/.

Sequencing Activities

Sequencing activities have long been a staple in ELL classes, where teachers provide text or text and images, in the case of comic strips, out of order and then students have to put them in the correct sequence. Mixing up music lyrics and dialogues are also popular forms of sequencing lessons in the ELL classroom.

Though there are several types of these kinds of activities, we primarily use "strip stories" that are connected to the thematic units that our class is studying. Strip stories are several sentences placed out of order that tell a story.

After reading sentences as a class and making sure everyone understands the vocabulary involved, students cut-up the sentences and put them in the appropriate sequence as well as highlighting the "clue" words they are using to determine the sentence's place. We don't always have students cut them up, though sometimes it saves time to just have them number the sentences in order if there are not too many of them.

Exhibit 3.12 "Money Strip Story" is an example of one we use when we're studying the theme of "Money." You'll notice that the sentences are numbered, but not in the correct chronological order. Numbering each sentence makes it easier to discuss which sentence goes where and to quickly check student work. Often, after students have completed the lesson correctly, we'll ask students to create their own (usually of five sentences or less) and then have students exchange them with one another.

Even though "strip stories" are the main way we use the sequencing strategy, if we have a few extra minutes at the end of class, we might fill them in with a "sentence scramble" game and put the words of a sentence out of order on the board.

Sequencing activities correlate with the: Anchor Standards for Reading—Key Ideas and Details, Range of Reading and Level of Text Complexity; Anchor Standards For Writing—Text Types and Purposes, Range of Writing; Anchor Standards for Language—Conventions of Standard English, Vocabulary Acquisition and Use.

Supporting Research. As we described in our book *The ELL Teacher's Toolbox*, teachers can frame sequencing activities as "puzzles." Researcher Mihaly Csikszentmihalyi and others have found that looking at learning tasks and challenges as "puzzles," can promote the development of flow,[55] which is the highest state of intrinsic motivation. Csikszentmihalyi suggests that an even better flow activity would be having students create their own "puzzles" that others can then solve.[56]

There is a substantial amount of research demonstrating the positive impact strip stories can have on English language acquisition.[57] As far as we can tell, however, there have been no studies specifically done on sentence scrambles and reordering comic strips. However, since their process closely mirrors strip stories, we don't believe it's a stretch to say that research can also support these two versions of sequencing activities.

Research supports the benefits of students explaining their thinking to classmates and/or their teacher[58] as well as explaining it to themselves.[59]

EXHIBIT 3.12. Money Strip Story

1. He went home and gave his parents back the $10 he did not spend.

2. His parents gave him the money.

3. Juan woke up late on Saturday.

4. He took a bus to the store.

5. He wanted the money to buy a new shirt and to buy lunch.

6. After getting dressed, he decided to go to the store.

7. He spent $10 on two burritos and a soda.

8. He went to a restaurant after he bought the shirt.

9. He paid twenty dollars for a new shirt.

10. He asked his parents for $40.

Answer key: 3, 6, 10, 5, 2, 4, 9, 8, 7, 1

Tech Tool
Online Sequencing Activities

There are many free online tools where teachers *and* students can create different types of sequencing activities. They can be found at "The Best Sites For Creating Sentence Scrambles" https://larryferlazzo.edublogs.org/2010/03/29/the-best-sites-for-creating-sentence-scrambles/. Even though the title of the blog post specifically says "Sentence Scrambles," most of the tools listed can also be used for other activities.

Jigsaw

The Jigsaw strategy basically means that students become "experts" in a section of text or on a topic and then teach others about it.

We primarily use this strategy with Beginners by developing five sentences or short paragraphs about a nonfiction topic related to each thematic unit. For example, we use Exhibit 3.13 "Sacramento Jigsaw" when we are studying the theme "Community." You'll notice that each section of text is longer and more complex than the preceding one. Jigsaws work well for differentiation—the students least proficient in English can be assigned the easier sentences, while higher-English proficiency students can be assigned the longer ones.

Each student is assigned a sentence "number" and given a cut-out strip of their text only, along with several other copies of it. They then meet with the other students who have the same text (all the "number ones" meet together; all the "number twos" meet together, etc.) to review and practice reading it while the teacher moves around to assist students with comprehension and pronunciation. We'll also often assign a leader for each group and review the sentences with them in advance so that they can act as "teachers." Depending on class size, these four "expert groups" may range from two to six students in each one. Of course, there is nothing "magical" about keeping the text at only four sections. We, however, have found that it can get a little chaotic past that number.

The teacher then assigns the students in each expert group a letter (a,b,c,d, etc.). Then, after students are familiar with their text, they join their classmates who have the same letter. Sometimes it's easy to ensure an equal number of students in each group, and sometimes letter groups have more than one student saying the same numbered text—either way works out fine. The student with the first text distributes copies of it to everyone in their letter group, and then reads it to them. Each student in the letter group then repeats the same process.

Afterwards, each group works together to complete a follow-up activity, which is usually a cloze (fill-in-the-blank) and a writing question related to their personal goals, experiences, or preferences, such as Exhibit 3.14 "Sacramento Information." The teacher can review the cloze with the class afterwards, and ask one or two students to share their written response.

Jigsaw activities correlate with the: Anchor Standards for Reading—Key Ideas and Details, Range of Reading and Level of Text Complexity; Anchor Standards For Writing—Text Types and Purposes, Range of Writing; Anchor Standards for Speaking and Listening—Comprehension and Collaboration; Anchor Standards for Language—Conventions of Standard English, Vocabulary Acquisition and Use.

Supporting Research. As we described in our book *The ELL Teacher's Toolbox*, researchers share our enthusiasm for the jigsaw strategy. In fact, well-known education researcher John Hattie says that it is the *only* strategy that scores high in *all* sections of his newer four quadrant model of learning: acquiring surface learning, consolidating surface learning, acquiring deep learning, consolidating deep learning.[60]

Other researchers have also found a number of academic benefits attributable to the jigsaw strategy for mainstream[61] and ELL students.[62]

Several studies have specifically found that the expectation to teach material has a positive impact on learning.[63]

A jigsaw is also called an "information gap" activity, a broader strategy used in many ELL classrooms. The idea behind an "information gap" activity is that one student is required to obtain "information" from a classmate in order to complete an activity. In other words, he/she has to "bridge the gap." It utilizes what researchers identify as a primary lever of motivation—the "curiosity gap."[64]

EXHIBIT 3.13. Sacramento Jigsaw

1. Native Americans lived in the area of Sacramento for thousands of years.

2. People found gold near Sacramento in 1848. Thousands of people came to Sacramento to try to find gold.

3. Sacramento is on the American and Sacramento rivers. The city flooded several times in the downtown area. Because of all the water, they brought in a lot of dirt to raise the level of downtown. Now, there is an old downtown area underneath the newer buildings.

4. Sacramento is the capital of the state of California. The Governor of the state lives here. Sacramento has a professional basketball team called the Sacramento Kings. The city also has a professional soccer team called The Sacramento Republic Football Club. There is a minor league baseball team in the nearby city of West Sacramento.

EXHIBIT 3.14. Sacramento Information

Name _____ Date _____

Sacramento is a _____ in California. People found _____ near the city in 1848. Our school is in _____. Sacramento is the capital of _____. Water from rivers _____ downtown several times. Sacramento has _____ professional sports teams.

two   California   city   gold   flooded   Sacramento

What do you like about living in Sacramento?

_____

_____

_____

_____

_____

_____

Tech Tool

Online Jigsaw Resources

You only need to go to one site on the Web for additional resources for using the Jigsaw method in the manner we've described, and that's Nancy Callan's ESL Jigsaws site (https://esljigsaws.com/). She's been supporting ELL teachers for years, and has both free and very low-cost materials available.

Academic Vocabulary

Chapters Five and Six discuss developing academic vocabulary with intermediate ELLs, but that doesn't mean it can't start with beginners!

There are two ways we regularly and explicitly teach academic vocabulary to Beginners.

In one popular activity, we take two to four words from an academic word list categorized by grade-level (you can find many online—check out the Tech Tool box for more information). After defining a word through various means – gesture, translation, images, etc.—we write down a funny question and answer using that word. For example:

- *Would you **compare** Mr. Ferlazzo to this school building?*
- *Yes, I would **compare** Mr. Ferlazzo to this school building because they are both very old.*

Students practice asking and answering the question to each other, and also review ones they learned previously.

We use Brainpop—and, specifically, Brainpop, Jr.—in our other favorite academic vocabulary activity (however, the strategy itself can be used with any engaging video that uses at least a few academic words).

Each of the "Jr." videos offers a follow-up activity called "Word Play." It identifies five key words from the video along with their definitions, and then provides forms that students can either complete on print-outs or online where they can draw the image, write about it, or create a *very* short dialogue using it.

We prefer to use the dialogue activity, and have pre-printed Brainpop forms ready to be completed. Students can work in pairs, choose whichever of the words they want, and then act out the dialogue in small groups. As we mentioned earlier, teachers can do this with any video they want—if they don't use Brainpop, they just have to pre-identify the words and their definitions.

Teaching academic vocabulary correlates with the: Anchor Standards for Speaking and Listening—Comprehension and Collaboration; Anchor Standards for Language—Conventions of Standard English, Vocabulary Acquisition and Use.

Supporting Research: See the Academic Vocabulary section in Chapter Five for more extensive research support.

Tech Tool

Online Resources For Teaching & Learning Academic Vocabulary

There are many online activities where English Language Learners can learn and practice academic vocabulary. You can find links to many of these resources, along with a long list of other teaching ideas, at "The Best Websites For Developing Academic English Skills & Vocabulary" https://larryferlazzo.edublogs.org/2008/04/06/the-best-websites-for-developing-academic-english-skills-vocabulary/.

LISTENING AND SPEAKING

Total Physical Response

The purpose of Total Physical Response (TPR) is to have students physically act out the words and phrases being taught by the teacher. One way to implement TPR is by first asking all students to stand, and they can move to the front or stay where they are. Two students are brought to the front. The teacher models a verb or two—for example, "sit" and "stand." She then asks the two students in front to "sit," "stand," "sit," and "stand." The two students are asked to return to their regular places, and the teacher then tells the class to "sit" and "stand" several times. Students can then divide into partners or in small groups and take turns giving each other commands.

TPR can be an engaging activity by spending 10 minutes a day doing it and focusing on a few words each time. Once key verbs are learned, the commands can be made more complicated and even silly. More complicated play-acting scenes can eventually be used ("open the peanut butter jar, put some on your knife, and lick it"). One nice change of pace can be having a student give the commands to the class and creating opportunities where students can give commands to the teacher!

After teaching a few specific words, we also sometimes turn the TPR "commands" into a fun short story, like this:

> *Stand up and look to the right.*
>
> *Pretend you see a monster.*
>
> *Yell!*
>
> *Cry!*
>
> *Kill the monster*

Once students become familiar with the idea, we might have small groups use Exhibit 3.15 "TPR Story Planning Sheet" to create and then teach their own five sentence stories. Or, as a differentiation strategy, a group of students with a higher English proficiency level might just do it.

Using Total Physical Response correlates with the Anchor Standards for Speaking and Listening—Comprehension and Collaboration; Anchor Standards for Language—Conventions of Standard English, Knowledge of Language, Vocabulary Acquisition and Use.

Supporting Research. TPR was originally developed by Dr. James J. Asher and modeled from his analysis of how a child learns by doing more listening than speaking and by often responding to commands from his parents.[65]

Numerous studies have documented its effectiveness,[66] and TPR is used in English classes around the world.

EXHIBIT 3.15. TPR Story Planning Sheet

What is the problem? _____

How does the story end? _____

What are three verbs you can use in the story?

1. _____

2. _____

3. _____

What are the five lines of the story?

1. _____

2. _____

3. _____

4. _____

5. _____

Now that you have the five lines in the story, are there any other words you need to pre-teach? If, so, what are they?

_____

Who will teach each line of the story?

1. _____

2. _____

3. _____

4. _____

5. _____

Practice!

MODEL:

Stand up and look to the right.

Pretend you see a monster.

Yell!

Cry!

Kill the monster

Tech Tool
TPR

You can find many TPR resources, including lists of words easy to teach with the activity, at "The Best Resources For Learning About Total Physical Response (TPR)" https://larryferlazzo.edublogs.org/2016/09/10/the-best-resources-for-learning-about-total-physical-response-tpr/.

Music

Songs can be an all-purpose tool in the ELL classroom. Many students who are reluctant to speak feel more comfortable singing with a group. Music is a universal language that most people enjoy. In addition to speaking practice, songs provide multiple opportunities for listening, reading, and even writing practice. Using pop songs can be much more engaging for older students (our favorites for ELL Beginners included "Hello, Goodbye," "You Are So Beautiful," "The Lion Sleeps Tonight," and "Three Little Birds"). However, simple songs geared specifically to teaching children or ELL vocabulary can often be useful and enjoyed by everybody!

Here are just a few ways to use songs in the classroom:

- Give students copies of lyrics to a song connected to the thematic unit you're studying and first review them together. Then practice singing the chorus, followed by playing the music and singing at the same time. Next, do the same with verses though for some songs you might just want to teach the chorus or the chorus and one or two verses. Different halves or thirds of the class can sing different portions and then switch, creating a friendly competition to see which groups sing the "best."

- Provide copies of the lyrics with some of the words blanked out (clozes). Students fill in the blanks as the song is played. The missing words can either be listed out of order at the bottom of the sheet or not listed anywhere so that students must come up with the words and correct spelling on their own.

- Provide the lyrics cut into separate lines (or cut every two lines). Another option is to copy and paste the scrambled lines in an electronic document, print it out, and have students cut them out. As the song is playing, students have to put the lines in the correct sequence. This may require periodically replaying portions (depending on the levels of student outrage!). Students can work together in pairs.

- Students develop comprehension questions about the song, which they use to quiz other students.

- Students can be challenged to write their own lyrics for certain lines of a song and perform them in small groups. For example, if students are learning the Beatles song "Hello, Goodbye," they can be asked to replace "hello" and "goodbye" in the line "You say hello, and I say goodbye" with any other pair of opposites they have been learning (for example, "You say short, and I say tall").

Keep in mind that not everybody likes singing even if it's in a group. If you have that type of class—no worries! Just lead students in *saying* the words, not singing them.

Using music correlates with the: Anchor Standards for Reading—Craft and Structure; Anchor Standards for Speaking and Listening—Comprehension and Collaboration; Anchor Standards for Language—Conventions of Standard English, Knowledge of Language, Vocabulary Acquisition and Use.

Supporting Research. Extensive research has shown that using songs is an effective language-development strategy with English language learners.[67] They are often accessible because popular songs use the vocabulary of an 11-year-old, the rhythm and beat help students speak in phrases or sentences instead of words, and the word repetition assists retention.[68] Neuroscience has also found that music can increase dopamine release in the brain and generates positive emotions. This kind of emotional learning reinforces long-term memory.[69]

Tech Tool

Music Sites for ELLs

Many free online sites offer teacher resources for using songs in the classroom and online exercises similar to the classroom activities recommended in this section, such as clozes and sequencing. Karaoke is another activity that can be used either in the classroom or individually online. There are even sites designed to show music videos and have students complete clozes in the subtitles—individually or projected on a screen so the whole class can participate by writing their choices on mini-whiteboards. In addition, plenty of free sites provide online audio access to just about any song you might want to use in class. You can find links to all of these tools in "The Best Music Websites for Learning English" https://larryferlazzo.edublogs .org/2008/01/30/the-best-music-websites-for-learning-english/.

Chants

Carolyn Graham is well known for developing the concept of Jazz Chants to teach English. These are short, rhythmic chants that reinforce vocabulary and/or grammar lessons in a fun way.

She encourages teachers to create their own chants.[70] One of her recommendations is to start with three words—the first one having two syllables, the second three, and the third having one. For example, if your thematic unit is "school," a vocabulary chant could be

> whiteboard, eraser, pen
>
> whiteboard, eraser, pen
>
> whiteboard, eraser, pen

Having students clap and chant in unison for a minute or two, with the teacher or a student pointing to each item, could be a fun reinforcing activity.

Or, as Graham suggests, the same words could be turned into a grammar chant:

> He uses the whiteboard
>
> She uses the eraser
>
> They use pens
>
> They use pens

These can be chanted together or in rounds.

Of course, just about anything can be turned into a chant, and chants don't always have to meet these criteria. For example, a chant can be structured in a question-and-response format with students on different sides of the room saying one or the other. Advanced students can also create their own chants and teach them to the class.

Using chants correlates with the: Anchor Standards for Speaking and Listening—Comprehension and Collaboration; Anchor Standards for Language—Conventions of Standard English, Knowledge of Language, Vocabulary Acquisition and Use.

Supporting Research. These kinds of chants have the same advantages cited by research supporting songs in the classroom[71] and are particularly helpful for teaching stress and intonation.[72] A big benefit to chants is that it is far easier and quicker to compose a chant than a song!

Dialogues

Short dialogues, ideally related to the thematic unit that is being studied and that has practical use outside the classroom, can be a useful tool for oral language practice. After teacher modeling, students—in pairs, threes, or fours—can practice and perform in front of the class or for another small group. It's often helpful to inject some humor into the dialogue. We try to have a dialogue or two that correspond to each of our thematic units.

There are several ways to vary this activity:

- The dialogue can have different options for students to choose from (see Exhibit 3.16).
- Dialogue performers can develop a few questions to ask their listeners about what was said.
- Students can develop their own dialogues after being given certain parameters (should be related to a certain topic and a certain length). They can use teacher-prepared dialogues as models and possibly be asked to create just one line and build from there as they develop more confidence.
- Students can be given the dialogue with sentences mixed up and asked to put them in the correct sequence.
- Exhibit 3.20 Conversation "Cheat Sheet" in the Homework section could also easily be used during class time. The teacher could model several of the short "question/answers" and then students could practice them.

Using dialogues correlates with the Anchor Standards for Reading—Key Ideas and Details; Anchor Standards for Speaking and Listening—Comprehension and Collaboration; Anchor Standards for Language—Conventions of Standard English, Knowledge of Language, Vocabulary Acquisition and Use.

1-2-3

This is a modification of an exercise developed by Paul Nation called the 4–3–2 Fluency Activity.[74] In his original activity plan, students line up (standing or sitting) facing each other. Each one must be prepared to speak on something that they are already quite familiar with. First, they speak to their partner for four minutes about the topic. Then they move down the line and say the same thing for three minutes to a new partner. Next, they move again and speak for two minutes. Then the students on the other side do the same thing.

EXHIBIT 3.16. Dialogue Example

First Week of School Dialogue

Student One:

    a. I am so happy to be in Mr. Ferlazzo's class!

    b. I feel so sad that I'm in Mr. Ferlazzo's class.

    c. I hate being in Mr. Ferlazzo's class. I feel sick when I'm there!

Student Two:

    a. Me, too. I feel like my dream has come true.

    b. I don't agree with you. Mr. Ferlazzo is a wonderful teacher!

    c. Yes, I agree.

Student Three:

    a. Let's go buy Mr. Ferlazzo a big present to show him how much we like him as a teacher.

    b. Let's give him a chance. Let's tell him we don't understand something, and we can see if he's a good teacher and helps us or if he just gets angry.

    c. Let's go talk to the principal to see if we can get transferred to a different class.

(Choose one of the following options and act it out.)

Next:

    a. Go to the store to buy a present.

    b. Pretend not to understand something.

    c. Ask the principal to change classes.

(Choose one of the following options and act it out.)

Last:

    a. Give a present to a student pretending to be Mr. Ferlazzo.

    b. A student pretending to be Mr. Ferlazzo responds to students not understanding something.

    c. What does a student pretending to be the principal say?

Supporting Research. Dialogues have been found to be effective forms for language practice and confidence building. Students who have practiced within the relatively nonthreatening environment of the classroom will be more likely to actually use the language outside of school.[73]

Tech Tool
Online Dialogues & Pronunciation Practice

It's easy to record students saying a dialogue on a smartphone and, if they are doing it in front of class, immediately play the recording for them so they can hear themselves. The recording can be posted on a class website or blog (with student permission, of course). Students can also record dialogues privately. In addition, there are numerous free sites that allow users to listen to dialogues, practice them, and be quizzed. They can be found at "'Best' Lists Of The Week: Listening & Speaking Resources" https://larryferlazzo.edublogs.org/2018/08/04/best-lists-of-the-week-listening-speaking-resources/.

Some online tools (like Peaksay https://www.peaksay.com/home) will let students and teachers create conversations and then mix them up to create a puzzle or game. You can learn more at "The Best Sites For Developing English Conversational Skills" https://larryferlazzo.edublogs.org/2008/04/05/the-best-sites-for-developing-english-conversational-skills/.

Online tools (like Quizizz https://quizizz.com/) let you record a question, and then students can choose the correct answer. For example, the question could be "How are you?" and students have to choose from (1) Blue (2) I'm fine (3) It's a book. You could also reverse it, with the recording being the answer and the choices being questions. See "The Best Websites For Creating Online Learning Games" https://larryferlazzo.edublogs.org/2008/04/21/the-best-websites-for-creating-online-learning-games/ for links to other similar game sites.

When it comes to pronunciation, recent studies (https://www.sciencedaily.com/releases/2020/02/200207141658.htm) have found that individuals generally believe their pronunciation is the best—we're not able to be accurate judges. The research emphasizes the importance of receiving more objective feedback. Students can get that in the classroom, but what about when they are not in class? There are a few online tools that use Artificial Intelligence to provide immediate feedback on students' English pronunciation You can find them at "The Best Sites For Online Pronunciation Feedback" https://larryferlazzo.edublogs.org/2020/02/08/the-best-sites-for-online-pronunciation-feedback-do-you-know-more/.

We developed a major modification of this activity that could be called 1–2–3 or, even 30 seconds-60 seconds-90 seconds. In this exercise , students are told to pick any topic they know a lot about or have been studying in class (for example, Larry does it after every three chapters in his ELL World History class), and they are asked to talk about it to a partner for one minute (or 30 seconds, depending on the English level of the students), and then for two minutes and then for three. But they need to do some preparation prior to the speaking activity.

First, they should write down notes about what they might want to say. Next, students are asked to record themselves on their cellphones where they practice speaking by recording all or part of what they want to say (or practice with peer tutors). Afterward, students are told they have two minutes to review their notes before they have to be put away. Next, the teacher models questions that students who are listening can ask the speaker if they appear to be stuck. It is also useful to model characteristics of being a good listener (such as maintaining eye contact and not talking to other students). Then, students begin the speaking and switching process described earlier. Later, if feasible, students can go back to the computer lab and record their speaking again so they can compare and identify improvement.

When students are doing this around a topic they have all studied, they can get reminders and new information from listening to their partners. This kind of graduated speaking practice can increase student self-confidence and fluency.

Using the 1–2–3 activity correlates with the Anchor Standards for Speaking and Listening—Comprehension and Collaboration; Anchor Standards for Language—Conventions of Standard English, Knowledge of Language, Vocabulary Acquisition and Use.

Supporting Research. Regular use of the original 4–3–2 exercise has been shown to improve learners' fluency, producing natural and faster-flowing speech.[75]

Video

We've already described one way of using videos with the Language Experience Approach. Another technique called Back to the Screen is adapted from *Zero Prep: Ready-to-Go Activities for the Language Classroom* by Laurel Pollard, Natalie Hess, and Jan Herron.[76] The teacher picks a short clip from a movie (the famous highway chase scene from one of the *Matrix* movies, for example) and then divides the class into pairs, with one group facing the TV and the other with their backs to it. Then, after turning off the sound, the teacher begins playing the movie. The person who can see the screen tells the other person what is happening. Then, after a few minutes, the students reverse places. Afterward, the pairs write a chronological sequence of what happened, which is shared with another group and discussed in class. They could even include a prediction of what they think happens next! Finally, everyone watches the clip, with sound, together.

Another way to use videos is to have students watch short clips and create questions about what they saw and heard. The questions can then be exchanged with a classmate to answer. An example of this strategy can be found in Chapter Five and in Exhibit 5.15.

It's important to play videos at a slightly slower speed than normal and show subtitles when using videos in an ELL class. Showing English subtitles during English videos improves listening and reading comprehension among English language learners.[77]

Using video in the described ways correlates with the: Anchor Standards for Speaking and Listening—Comprehension and Collaboration; Anchor Standards for Language—Conventions of Standard English, Knowledge of Language, Vocabulary Acquisition and Use.

Supporting Research. Substantial evidence suggests that the visual clues offered by video have a positive effect on student listening comprehension.[78] In addition, video use has been shown to have a positive impact on student motivation to learn.[79]

Tech Tool

Online Videos

A number of free video support sites for English language learners are available. You can find recommendations and links to video clips and associated lesson plans at "'Best' Lists Of The Week: Teaching With Movies & Video Clips" https://larryferlazzo .edublogs.org/2018/06/13/best-lists-of-the-week-teaching-with-movies/.

Improvisation

Improvisation is an activity done without student preparation. Here is one way to incorporate it into the classroom.

Each student can be given a small whiteboard—these are versatile and inexpensive, and if you don't want to buy them you can make them easily, too—along with a marker and cloth eraser. The teacher can explain (the first time—after that, students will understand what to do) that he will start off a conversation and that students will write on their board what they might say in response and hold it up so everyone can see it. The teacher then chooses one of the responses they wrote and, in turn, responds to it, and so on.

Here is what happened in one of our classrooms when we first tried this activity:

I began by saying that I was holding onto a cliff with my fingers and ready to fall. I then yelled "Help!" and told students to write a response on their whiteboards. Students immediately got the idea and the fun began. Responses included "No" "Why should I?" "What do you need?" and "Goodbye." Some students just held up their boards and I asked others to share their responses aloud. I chose "Why should I?" to respond to and said "I'm going to die if you don't help, please!" The next responses, with much laughter, included "I will step on your fingers to help you fall!" "What will you pay me?" and "Have a good trip." In print, it may sound like I have a class of crazed students, but it was all done in fun, and everybody participated. I would also point at various people for them to say what they wrote, too.

I next asked them to imagine that I was an attractive girl or boy, and said, "Will you go on a date with me?" A similar process then began, including at one point my asking, "What restaurant will you take me to?" followed by "I don't want to go there." Many students came back with responses like "Too bad," but one wrote "Where do you want to go?" I pointed out that the student who came up with that response was likely to get far more dates than the rest of them.

Lastly, I said "You are getting an F in this class and will have to repeat it again next year." Needless to say, an energetic conversation followed.[80]

Very simple scenarios can be chosen that relate to the thematic unit being studied, and students can begin taking turns up front, developing a scenario, choosing which responses they want to pick, and responding to them.

Using improvisation correlates with the: Anchor Standards for Speaking and Listening—Comprehension and Collaboration; Anchor Standards for Language—Conventions of Standard English, Knowledge of Language, Vocabulary Acquisition and Use.

Supporting Research. Improvisation in music has been shown to deactivate parts of the brain that provide "conscious control, enabling freer, more spontaneous thoughts and actions," according to scientists.[81] These same researchers have discovered connections between music and language, suggesting that improvisation can lead to greater fluency in language as well as music.

Tech Tool

Online Improvisational Resources

For more ideas on using improvisation with English Language Learners, go to "The Best Resources On Using Improvisation In The ESL/EFL/ELL Classroom" https://larryferlazzo.edublogs.org/2012/07/23/the-best-resources-on-using-improvisation-in-the-esleflell-classroom/.

Thematic Personal Reports

At the beginning of each thematic unit, we give students a simple form to complete that includes "sentence frames" where students can write about their personal experiences connected to the theme, and a place to illustrate it. You can see an example of this "Thematic Personal Report" for "Sports" in Exhibit 3.17.

But that's not all.

After students complete the form, we have a peer tutor or an assigned student take a picture of each one with our cellphone and then take each student outside to record him/her reading the completed sentence frames. That recording serves as the narration for his/her picture, and we upload the short video to our YouTube channel where we can show the entire class.

There are many free and easy-to-use apps that allow you to provide audio narration to an image, though our favorite is Adobe Spark.[82]

Using Thematic Personal Reports correlate with the: Anchor Standards for Writing—Text Types and Purposes, Production and Distribution of Writing, Range of Writing; Anchor Standards for Speaking and Listening—Comprehension and Collaboration; Anchor Standards for Language—Conventions of Standard English, Knowledge of Language, Vocabulary Acquisition and Use.

EXHIBIT 3.17. Personal Thematic Report

Name_____

My Favorite Sport

My favorite sport is _____. I like it because _____

_____.

My favorite player is _____ because_____

_____.

I (play/don't play) _____. My position is _____

_____.

Draw your favorite sport here:

Giving Instructions, Wait Time, Using Gestures, and Checking for Understanding

All these important points were described in Chapter One, but they can't be repeated too many times!

- Give verbal *and* written instructions.
- After asking a question, wait a few seconds before calling on someone to respond.
- Don't speak fast, do use gestures to help reinforce what you are saying, and if a student says he/she didn't understand what you said, never, ever, repeat the same thing in a louder voice!
- Regularly check for understanding through the use of thumbs-up or thumbs-down, sticky notes, and whiteboards.

HOMEWORK

This section presents the homework that we *sometimes* give our beginning and early intermediate English language learners. Some years, we assign it all; other years, not much of it. Our choices depend on whether we have students for one period or two, what level of intrinsic motivation many of our students appear to have (see Chapter Sixteen "Addressing Additional Opportunities and Challenges" for ideas on how to encourage its development), what the political and economic situation is like (expecting to be deported or to be evicted can impact a student's level of concentration), and if they have access to technology at home. Homework covers all four domains: reading, writing, listening, and speaking. It is shared and turned in on Fridays, and 20 minutes of class time is sometimes provided to students during the week to work on it:

- Read a book in English at home for at least 10 minutes each night and demonstrate the use of at least three reading strategies during the week (see the

Reading Log in Exhibit 3.6). In addition, students must complete a Weekly Reading Sheet (see Exhibit 5.17 in Chapter Five).

- Write a journal sharing two or three good events that occurred that week and one event that was not necessarily positive. In the last instance, share if there was something that the student could have done differently to improve the outcome. If the student is an early beginner, he or she can draw or paste pictures representing the same events. In class, students share what they wrote with a partner, and the partner should ask at least one question.

- Complete a Four Words sheet with new words they learned that week in or out of class that they think are important (see Exhibit 3.18 in this section). In class, students share the words they chose with a partner.

- Spend at least 10 minutes each day "talking to themselves" (while riding a bicycle or walking to school, for example) or to someone else in English (this could sometimes happen during reading time at the beginning of class), and complete the Conversation Log in Exhibit 3.19. Note that the log is set up to also include a 10 minute conversation each day with an in-class tutor or another classmate, and uses a conversation "cheat sheet" (Exhibit 3.20). Teachers may or may not be working in schools that can provide other students who can act as peer tutors. Students can also practice with the "cheat sheet" in partners in class.

- Watch a movie or television program in English for at least 10 minutes each night.

- Depending on whether students have computers and internet access at home, online practice can substitute for the last two assignments (see the Tech Tool box later in this section).

Supporting Research. Cathy Vatterott, the author of *Rethinking Homework: Best Practices That Support Diverse Needs*, recommends these guidelines for homework:

"The best homework tasks exhibit five characteristics. First, the task has a clear academic purpose, such as practice, checking for understanding, or applying knowledge or skills. Second, the task efficiently demonstrates student learning. Third, the task promotes ownership by offering choices and being personally relevant. Fourth, the task instills a sense of competence—the student can successfully complete it without help. Last, the task is aesthetically pleasing—it appears enjoyable and interesting."[83]

We feel confident that the homework we assign meets these guidelines.

In addition, research supports the particulars of these assignments. For example, in addition to the journals facilitating writing practice, the sharing of positive events can develop trust,[84] which is an important quality to cultivate in an ELL classroom.

EXHIBIT 3.18. Four Words Sheet

Name _____ **Period** _____ **Date** _____

Word and Definition in English
_____

_____

Definition in Primary Language
_____

Picture

Sentence
_____
_____
_____

Word and Definition in English
_____

_____

Definition in Primary Language
_____

Picture

Sentence
_____
_____
_____

Word and Definition in English
_____

Definition in Primary Language
_____

Picture

Sentence
_____
_____
_____

Word and Definition in English
_____

Definition in Primary Language
_____

Picture

Sentence
_____
_____
_____

EXHIBIT 3.19. Conversation Log

Date	I talked to my tutor about. . .	I talked to myself about. . .	Tutor Signature and Student Signature
Oct. 17, 2021	1. What is your favorite fruit? 13. What is your name? 19. What did you eat for lunch yesterday?	What I saw on the street My lunch	

EXHIBIT 3.20. Conversation "Cheat Sheet"

1. Q: What is your favorite fruit?
   A: My favorite fruit is (a banana, an apple, a peach, a melon, a nectarine).

2. Q: How are you?
   A: I am fine.

3. Q: How do you feel?
   A: I feel (happy, sad, tired, angry, hungry, sick).

4. Q: Did you have a good weekend?
   A: Yes, I did. (No, I did not.)

5. Q: What did you do over the weekend?
   A: I (read, slept, played soccer, went to the park, watched TV, went to Fresno, played with my baby).

6. Q: Can I use the phone please?
   A: Yes, you can. (No, you cannot.)

7. Q: How old are you?
   A: I am _____ years old.

8. Q: What grade are you in?
   A: I am in _____ grade.

9. Q: I'm cold. Can you turn the air conditioner off?
   A: Yes, I can. (No, I cannot.)

10. Q: I don't understand. Can you repeat that?
    A: Yes, I can. (No, I cannot.)

11. Q: What are you going to do this weekend?
    A: I am going to (read, sleep, do homework, go to the park, watch TV, play with my baby).

12. Q: What is your address?
    A: My address is _____.
    Q: Is it close or far away?
    A: It is _____ _____.

13. Q: What is your name?
    A: My name is _____ _____.

14. Q: What is the word for this in English?
    A: The word in English is _____ _____.

15. Q: What do you buy at the store?

A: I buy (food, clothes, vegetables, fruit, bananas, rice).

16. Q: Where do you buy food?

A: I buy food at (Main Street Grocery).

17. Q: What is your phone number?

A: My phone number is _____ _____.

18. Q: What did you eat for lunch yesterday?

A: I ate (rice, a burrito, a hamburger, a sandwich).

19. Q: What did you eat for breakfast today?

A: I ate (rice, cereal, bananas, toast).

20. Q: Who is your favorite teacher?

A: My favorite teacher is _____ _____.

21. Q: What is your favorite website for studying English?

A: My favorite website is _____ _____.

22. Q: What is your favorite meal?

A: My favorite meal is _____ _____.

23. Q: What was your favorite field trip?

A: My favorite field trip was when we went to _____.

24. Q: How do you get to school?

A: I (drive, walk, ride my bike, run).

25. Q: Do you have any brothers or sisters?

A: Yes, I have _____ brothers and _____ sisters. (No, I don't have any brothers or sisters.)

26. Q: When is your birthday?

A: My birthday is on _____.

27. Q: What is today's date?

A: Today's date is _____.

28. Q: Are you feeling okay?

A: I'm fine. (No, I'm feeling sick.)

29. Q: Excuse me, I can't see. Can you move please?

A: Sure, I can.

30. Q: What time is it?

A: It is _____.

31. Q: Was the (homework, test) easy or hard?

A: It was _____.

32. Q: How long until we get to (San Francisco, Thailand, New York, St. Paul)?

A: We will get there in _____ (minutes, hours, days, weeks).

33. Q: How far is (downtown, the restaurant, San Francisco, New York, St. Paul)?

A: It is _____ (blocks, miles) away.

34. Q: How do you get to (San Francisco, Burbank, the grocery store, downtown)?

A: You drive to the (first, second, third) stoplight, then make a (left, right) turn, then go to _____ (street, road) and make a (left, right) turn. It will be on your (left, right).

35. Q: What size is this (jacket, shirt, pair of pants)?

A: It is (small, medium, large, extra-large).

36. Q: How much does this (shirt, TV, jacket) cost?

A: It costs _____ (cents, dollars).

37. Q: First Person: I (love, like, hate) you.

A: Second Person: I (love, like, hate) you, too.

38. Q: What time does the movie start?

A: The movie starts at (1:00, 7:30).

39. Q: What are you going to do this weekend?

A: I am going to (read, play soccer, sleep).

40. Q: What are you going to do tonight?

A: I am going to (study, read, eat).

41. Q: What are you going to eat for dinner tonight?

A: I am going to eat (rice, papaya salad).

42. Q: What do you usually eat for breakfast?

A: I usually eat (cereal, rice, toast) for breakfast.

43. Q: What time do you usually go to sleep?

A: I usually go to sleep at (9:30, 10:00).

44. Q: What time do you usually get up?

A: I usually get up at (7:00, 7:30).

45. Q: Can I use the restroom (bathroom)?

A: Yes, you can. (No, you cannot right now; please wait five minutes.)

46. Q: Can I borrow that book?

A: Yes, you can. (No, you cannot.)

47. Q: How is your (father, mother, baby, brother)?

A: (He, She) is (okay, sick, fine, tired).

48. Q: Would you like to go to dinner (tonight, this weekend, next Friday)?

A: Yes, that would be nice.

49. Q: What kind of work would you like to do when you graduate from high school (college)?

A: I would like to be a (doctor, teacher, cook).

50. Q: I would like to go home now. Is that okay?

A: Sure it is. I'll take you home.

51. Q: I have a headache. Do you have an aspirin?

A: Yes, here's one. I hope you feel better.

52. Q: I have a stomachache. Can I call home?

A: Sure, you can. (No, you cannot.)

53. Q: Can I listen to music now?

A: Sure, you can. (No, you cannot.)

54. Q: Can you give me a ride home?

A: Sure, I can. (No, I cannot.)

55. Q: What is that?

A: That is a _____.

56. Q: What is this?

A: This is a _____.

57. Q: I'm hungry. What time is (breakfast, lunch, dinner)?

A: We'll eat at (7:30, 12:00).

58. Q: Where does it hurt?

A: My (nose, arm, leg) hurts here.

59. Q: Can you call the police?

A: Sure, I can. (No, I cannot.)

60. Q: I'm sorry, I don't understand. Can you repeat that and speak slowly?

A: Yes, I can. (No, I cannot.)

61. Q: Can I keep this pencil?

A: Yes, you can. (No, you cannot.)

62. Q: Can you get a teacher to help?

A: Sure, I can. (No I cannot.)

Tech Tool
Online Homework

A number of free or low-cost engaging sites—many of which are very accessible to English language learners—let teachers register entire classes so that students can sign in to the site and the teacher can see the work of individual students. Many of these tool can be integrated into Google Classroom. These sites can be used as homework or during school time. You can find our favorites at "The Best Online Homework Sites For English Language Learners—Please Offer Your Own Suggestions" https://larryferlazzo.edublogs.org/2017/07/30/the-best-online-homework-sites-for-english-language-learners-please-offer-your-own-suggestions/.

ASSESSMENT

Chapter Nineteen will cover assessment—formative and summative—in depth. Since the "typical week" section in this chapter will refer to one formative assessment in particular, however, we wanted to explain it a little further here.

Each Friday, at the end of a Picture Word Inductive unit, a teacher might want to give a quiz. For a very early beginners' class, the picture can remain on the wall, but in most cases you will want to remove it.

The first 20 questions could be a basic spelling test with the teacher saying the word, using it in a sentence, and then saying the word again. The next 10 questions could be a combination of other exercises reflecting the texts and vocabulary studied during the week (see Exhibit 3.21). They include sentences that do not have the words separated and that require students to write them correctly; short cloze sentences where students need to write the correct word (any word that makes sense would be correct); sentence scrambles, where students have to put the words and punctuation in the correct order; a question that students have to answer; and a sentence that has a mistake in it that students have to correct.

In addition, after students have developed initial English writing skills, a second part of the test—at least for those with slightly more advanced proficiency—could be a short writing prompt. The prompts that we use are typically connected to the Personal Thematic Report that we used that week. For example, if we used the one found in Exhibit 3.17 where students had written about their favorite sport and players, the prompt might be "What sports do you like and why do you like them?" We would ask students to try responding to it without looking at what they had written earlier in the week.

An easy way to assess the first part of the test (we usually have the writing prompt on a separate sheet that we collect) is to have students give it to the person behind them, who will put a check mark next to the correct responses, while having two students take the lead in front writing the correct answers on the board or overhead and pointing to the picture (with the teacher monitoring, of course, to ensure the answers are indeed correct). Students can score the test by writing a fraction—the number of correct answers above the total number of test questions. Students return the papers, and any scoring disputes can be discussed among students and the teacher.

EXHIBIT 3.21. Sample Friday Test

1. Thewheelrollsthroughthebarn.

2. Pigeonsliveincities.

3. Juanhadarottenday.

4. Squirrels _____ nests in trees.

5. Juan _____ a giant hug.

6. The wheel _____ toward the river.

7. in live cities . dogs

8. had . day Rosie horrible a

9. What are you going to do this weekend?

10. Bee and Jose hits the teacher.

OTHER ACTIVITIES

There are hundreds, if not thousands, of lesson ideas that have been used in ELL classes over the years. We believe the ones we have discussed so far are the ones that can regularly offer superior opportunities for language learning. However, there are a few others that we have also found useful as lessons to use periodically throughout the year.

Tongue Twisters

Tongue twisters are short phrases that use alliteration, like "Sally sells sea shells by the sea shore." They are easy to create at various levels of difficulty using vocabulary being taught in the classroom. It is also fun to have students try saying them—chorally or in pairs. Teaching one to students, and then having them say it three times quickly can help develop accurate pronunciation skills and bring some levity into the classroom—especially when the teacher makes a mistake! Students can create their own tongue twisters, make a poster illustrating them, and then perform and teach them to the entire class.

Idioms

Countless idioms are used in the English language. Teaching some of them when they are at least peripherally connected to a thematic unit ("It's raining cats and dogs" with the animal theme, for example) might be a good strategy to help students remember them. However, they are good to teach at any time. Having students write them, practice them, and draw a representational picture can be a quick and useful activity.

Tech Tool

Online Idiom Practice

There are many free sites designed to help English language learners become familiar with idioms. Check out our favorites at "The Best Sites To Help ELL's Learn Idioms & Slang" https://larryferlazzo.edublogs.org/2009/07/03/the-best-sites-to-help-ells-learn-idioms-slang/.

Dialogue Journals

Dialogue journals have often been used in ELL classes. Typically, students write a journal entry and then a teacher writes a response—not pointing out errors in grammar or spelling, but instead correctly reflecting back what the student wrote (as we mentioned earlier, this is called "recasting"). For example, the student might write "I go to the piknik yesterday and have fun" and the teacher might respond, "That's great that you went to the picnic yesterday and had fun." ELL teachers can choose to let their students know in advance about these "recasts" or let them figure it out on their own.

Realistically, however, we feel it's not very practical for many teachers to write these responses—there is just not enough time in the day for teachers with multiple classes to take on this responsibility. However, it can still be done—and we believe it can be done more effectively—by developing a sister class relationship with English-proficient speakers, either in the same school or another school. Students generally will feel more engaged with their peers than with their teacher, and other English teachers may welcome the opportunity to have their students become grammar and spelling tutors. Of course, such a relationship does not have to be limited to a journal—we have had sister classes come in and teach lessons in small groups to our English language learners and our ELLs have taught a lesson about their culture to them, as well as having joint celebrations. This kind of social engagement has been found to be critical to language learning.[85]

Supporting Research. Numerous studies have documented the positive effect that dialogue journals have had on improving writing and how that improvement transfers to better essay writing, increased fluency, and enhanced learner motivation by providing a low-stress opportunity to write for an authentic audience.[86]

Tech Tool

Online Sister Classes

There are many free sites that help classes from around the world make connections with others. You can find links to them at "The Best Ways To Find Other Classes For Joint Online Projects" https://larryferlazzo.edublogs.org/2009/05/30/the-best-ways-to-find-other-classes-for-joint-online-projects/.

Puppets

Puppets are often used in ELL classes with students of all ages. They often remove inhibitions to speaking a new language and can provide an opportunity to develop writing skills, especially if a full-fledged story will be performed. Sometimes, the show can be performed not only in the classroom but also at a nearby elementary school. Puppets can be made out of paper bags, regular paper, or papier-mâché.

Supporting Research. Studies have shown that using puppets is an effective tool for helping English language learners enhance reading, writing, speaking, listening, and especially oral skills.[87]

Readers Theater

Readers Theater typically entails having a group of students dramatically perform a short story only using their voices and directly reading from a script. There are hundreds of Readers Theater scripts available online that are accessible to English language learners. We prefer, after sufficient teacher modeling, to have students write their own scripts and then perform them.

Supporting Research. ELL researchers have found that performing Readers Theater improves fluency and comprehension. It also enhances learner motivation.[88]

"Clines" (Spectrum)

Teaching words within a spectrum (also called a cline)—such as "always, usually, sometimes, seldom, never" or "very sad, sad, okay, feeling good, happy" or "I can't do it, it's hard; I can do it, it's easy"—can be an engaging learning activity. The teacher can write the words across the whiteboard and ask students questions that can be answered by one of the words. Students can then stand underneath the word they chose. If it's done in a fun way ("Can you jump 30 feet in the air?" or "How would you feel if you got an F in this class?"), students can enjoy and learn from this type of exercise.

The teacher can also just draw a horizontal or vertical line on an overhead and list the words in sequence while teaching them. Students can copy them down while drawing illustrations and/or writing the words in their home languages.

Past, Present, and Future Chart

As students learn new vocabulary, having a three-column Past, Present, and Future chart on the wall can function as a helpful reminder. Teachers can display one chart for regular verbs and one for irregular ones. When teaching the tenses, don't forget to have students use gestures—have them stand, point, and look backward when using the past tense, point down when using the present tense, and point and take a step forward when using the future tense. Connecting words to physical action enhances student learning.[89] Even more research supporting physical movement and gestures in learning can be found in Chapter Five.

Venn Diagrams

A Venn Diagram is a useful graphic organizer with two or more circles that partially overlap. It is a very accessible scaffolding tool for students to compare one or two events, people, planets, holidays, or ethnic foods, for example, and can be a first step toward writing a simple compare-and-contrast essay. (See Chapters Five and Six for information on other useful graphic organizers.)

Tech Tool
Online Compare-and-Contrast Tools

Many free interactive tools are available online to help students understand and use Venn Diagrams and write a compare-and-contrast essay. You can find them at "The Best Resources For Teaching/Learning About How To Write Compare/ Contrast Essays" https://larryferlazzo.edublogs.org/2015/08/01/the-best-resources-for-teachinglearning-about-how-to-write-comparecontrast-essays/.

K-W-L Charts

A K-W-L chart—a three-column sheet that stands for *What do you know? What do you want to know?* and *What have you learned?*— can sometimes be a good tool for activating students' prior knowledge on a topic at the beginning of a unit. In addition, it can help them track new information they have learned and look for patterns. Finally, it can be used to support reflective activities.

It is important to note that there are many ways to activate student prior knowledge. The Picture Word Inductive Model, for example, always begins by asking students to identify words that they know and describe items they see. K-W-L charts are just one more tool to occasionally use. K-W-L charts are discussed more in Chapters Six and Eight.

Supporting Research. Advance organizers like the K-W-L chart and other questioning strategies have long been found to be effective in increasing student achievement.[90]

"Words You Want To Know"

Periodically giving students time to identify 10 words they want to learn can be a nice change of pace (especially if they are going to have a substitute that day). They can identify a picture or concept that they want to know the word for by drawing a representation or cutting out a picture from a newspaper or magazine.

With teacher and/or tutor assistance, students can learn the words, make an illustrated poster of all 10, and teach them to other classmates in pairs or in slightly larger groups.

Teaching Others

Having students teach their classmates can be an effective and fun learning activity. Exhibit 3.22 leads students through the process we use (there are similarities to the Picture Word Inductive Model, so it's not entirely new to students):

First, in groups of two, students find a picture online that relates to the theme we are studying as a class. They print-out three copies - one to use as a teaching tool and one each for the students they will be teaching so they can annotate the image.

Next, the "teachers" have to identify six words in the picture they are going to "teach," learn their definitions, and decide who is going to teach each one and how they are going to do it (through gestures, use of home language, pantomime, etc.).

Then, they write six sentences using each of those words, but leaving the space for the word blank. In other words, they are writing clozes, or "fill-in-the-blank" sentences.

Next, they teach their "students." After they have introduced the image and "students" have labeled it, taught the words, and had "students" complete the clozes, it is time for the final element of the teaching process. Their "students" have to write their own sentences about the picture.

It usually takes less than a class period in the computer lab for students to prepare their lessons. The following day, one pair of students teaches another pair, and then they do it in reverse. It's important to do a quick class evaluation after each "teaching day." The first time will be a bit rough, but it gets a lot smoother the second time. It is best to do this activity later in the year when everyone has developed more English proficiency. If you do it closer to the beginning of the year, it would be better to have the more English-proficient students teach Newcomers and not expect it to be a reciprocal activity.

Supporting Research. There is extensive research finding that students teaching their classmates improves the academic achievement of *both*. You can read about these studies, along with learning about other ways we implement this strategy in our classroom, at "The Best Posts On Helping Students Teach Their Classmates."[91]

EXHIBIT 3.22. Student-Led Lesson Plan

Student-Led Lesson Plan

Names of Teachers _____

Lesson Topic _____

Choose a picture online related to your topic. Print out three copies:

- One copy you will give to your student
- One copy you will use to teach
- One copy you will use to test your student after the lesson

Six Words Your Students Need to Know—Write words, definition & how you will teach it (gesture, picture, acting, translation, etc.). The words will need to be connected to the picture.

1.
2.
3.
4.
5.
6.

What are the clozes you will use to help teach the words. Don't write them in the same order as the words. You will need to write one sentence using each of your six words, but you will leave a blank (_____) where that word would go.

1.
2.
3.
4.
5.
6.

Next, have your students write their own sentences about the picture on a paper. They can use those six words, or not use them.

Field Trips

Simple field trips, including lessons to prepare for them and classroom follow-up activities, can be excellent learning opportunities, especially when they are connected to thematic units being studied.

Scavenger hunts can be engaging and reinforcing. For example, when studying clothes in the classroom, a class can visit the mall or a thrift store and students can be given a list of different kinds of clothes (such as a blue skirt or a large boot) and asked to take photos of each item with a cellphone. Students can later create slideshows or posters with them. Similar hunts can be done in food stores, around a school, looking for signs, or the like. When visiting some of these places, though, it's courteous to let staff know ahead of time and schedule the visit during times when the business is not crowded.

Other field trips can include ordering a soda at a fast food restaurant, asking a local bank for a tour, or just playing a sports game. The list is really endless! They also make great fodder for using the Language Experience Approach.

Logistically, we recommend that students be organized ahead of time in groups of two or three (with a student leader) to take advantage of the learning benefits inherent in small groups, to help ensure student safety, and to help maintain teacher sanity.

Supporting Research. ELL researcher Heide Spruck Wrigley, in a study for the US Department of Education, emphasized the importance of field trips with English language learners and called it "bringing in the outside."[92] She particularly recommends trips and minitrips that relate to language and situations students have to regularly deal with in their lives.

Tech Tool
Virtual Field Trips

Though they do not offer anywhere near the kind of personal interaction and direct experience of a real, physical field trip, virtual field trips can offer a change of pace and an opportunity to see places that cannot realistically be seen in person. Some of our favorite sources for virtual field trips can be found at "Great Resources For Creating & Going On Virtual Field Trips" https://larryferlazzo.edublogs .org/2020/03/28/great-resources-for-creating-going-on-virtual-field-trips/.

Links to all the online activities listed in the chapter, as well as to the downloadable student hand-outs, can be found at www.wiley.com/go/ eslsurvivalguide2.

CHAPTER FOUR

Daily Instruction
for Beginning ELLs

*N*obody thought Juan was very capable. People didn't take him seriously when he said he wanted some land to farm. Finally, he was given a small plot, but everyone laughed because they believed it was poor soil and Juan wouldn't be successful. Juan, though, was a hard worker, and he had the knowledge that his friends, the Zanate birds, shared with him. Following their advice, he planted what are known as the "three sisters": corn, beans, and squash. The birds—and the indigenous people of Mexico—know that these three plants complement one another during the growing season. The townspeople were shocked to see the success of Juan's harvest. From that day forward, he was known as Juan Zanate.[1]

In this Mexican folktale, people had a low opinion of Juan's ability. However, through his determination and his use of inner gifts—which most people didn't see he had—Juan succeeded beyond his neighbors' imaginations.

The suggestions in this chapter for daily instructional activities, as well as the ideas found in every chapter in this book, are designed to help the gifts and assets carried by our ELL students shine as bright as those that were inside of Juan Zanate.

Chapter Three provided an overview of different elements to include in a beginning ELL classroom. This chapter will describe what the application of these elements might look like on a day-to-day basis. Please note that several of the Exhibits and Figures listed in this chapter can be found in Chapter Three.

The Picture Word Inductive Model Unit Plan discusses one of those strategies in more detail because we believe it can be the centerpiece of a beginning ELL curriculum. The unit plan is followed by a sample week schedule, which is in turn followed by a list of specific ways to implement our recommended strategies in many units throughout the entire school year.

Picture Word Inductive Model Unit Plan

INSTRUCTIONAL OBJECTIVES

Students will:

1. Learn at least 20 new theme-related vocabulary words.
2. Develop categorization skills.
3. Write an essay.

DURATION

Five approximately 20 to 30-minute lessons over a five-day period.

Using the PWIM correlates with the Anchor Standards for Reading—Key Ideas and Details; Anchor Standards For Writing—Range of Writing; Anchor Standards for Language—Conventions of Standard English, Vocabulary Acquisition and Use.

MATERIALS

1. Enlarged laminated photo representative of a thematic unit (such as food, sports, or school) mounted on poster board with border space around the image. The photo should reflect a real-life incident and should show a variety of objects. See Figure 3.1 for a sample photo.
2. A photocopy of the photo for each student
3. A Text Data Set composed of a list of sentences about the picture with blanks in them (see Exhibit 3.1). Potential answers should appear below each sentence. Provide enough copies for each student.

PROCEDURE

First Day

1. Teacher asks all students to come to the front of the room and stand in front of the laminated picture. He asks if students can say some of the things that they see in English. As students say a word and point to it in the picture, the teacher writes each letter and asks students to repeat it, and then says

the word, again asking students to repeat. He then draws an arrow from the word to the object. Along with identifying nouns, the teacher could add verbs labeling actions taking place in the image (it's best for verbs to be written in a different color). This process should continue until there are approximately 20 words on the photo, including new words that the teacher has added.

2. Students then return to their seats and copy the words in the same way on their individual photos.

3. Teacher reviews the words again.

4. After class, the teacher develops a data set of cloze sentences (see Exhibit 3.1 for an example) about the picture using all the words that were labeled.

Second Day

1. Teacher reviews the words on the image, asking students to repeat.

2. Students are asked to put the words into three or four categories on a sheet of paper, leaving space for additions. Then, they can work individually or in pairs. The teacher might want to encourage students to look at particular word qualities during their categorization, including word endings or plural versus singular forms.

3. After a few minutes, the teacher asks students to share a few of the category names they have identified and writes them on the board (words that start with *p,* people-related words, things that are red). This is to help students who are having a difficult time categorizing. A few minutes later, the teacher asks one or two students he has identified to share one list of words they have categorized—without saying the name of the category. He will then ask students to think for a moment—without saying anything— about which category might work for those words. He next asks students to share their answer with a partner and then calls on students to share their guesses. After each time a student says what they think it is, the teacher will ask the student who originally gave the words if it is correct or not.

4. Next, the teacher will ask students to use their dictionaries, cellphones, and prior knowledge to add three or four new words to their categories.

5. Students share their completed work orally and in writing with a partner.

Third Day

1. Teacher reviews the words on the image, asking students to repeat.

2. Teacher distributes a data set composed of a list of sentences with blanks in them. Potential answers appear below each sentence.

3. Students fill in the blanks and then share—both orally and in writing—their answers with a partner.

4. Teacher reviews the answers with the class.

5. Teacher asks the students to put the sentences into at least three categories (either by cutting and pasting each sentence under the name of a category or by writing the name of a category and underneath writing the numbers of the sentences that belong there). The teacher can provide the categories or ask students to develop their own. Students then categorize and are asked to share (similar to step 3 from the previous day). Students must also underline the clue words they used to place each sentence in a particular category.

6. Students then write three additional sentences about the picture under each category, either in class or as homework.

Fourth Day

1. Teacher reviews the words on the image, asking students to repeat them.

2. Teacher asks students to rewrite their categories as paragraphs and explains some structures of an essay (such as indents for paragraphs and a single line separating them).

Fifth Day

1. Teacher reviews the words on the image.

2. Teacher asks students to develop a title for their essay. Students share their titles, which are recorded by the teacher or students on easel paper next to the laminated photo (this can also be done on the fourth day, if desired).

3. Essays are turned in, and student writing is used for lessons using concept attainment (discussed in Chapter Three) in the following days.

ASSESSMENT

1. Teacher gives a test that includes all 20 words. Teacher says the word, uses it in a sentence, then says the word again. The test also includes completing sentences with blanks, sentence scrambles (mixing up the words in a sentence and having students reorder them correctly), and other items covered during the week, along with a short writing prompt.

2. Students exchange papers with each other for checking as the teacher says the correct answer or asks students to contribute them. Students are told to put check marks next to the answers that are correct. Papers are returned to students and then given to teacher for review.

POSSIBLE EXTENSIONS AND MODIFICATIONS

1. After the second day, the teacher can have students lead the class in reviewing the words at the beginning of the lesson.

2. Depending on the class level, more sophisticated writing elements (such as topic sentences and thesis statements) can be taught and used.

3. Depending on the class level, students can label the laminated photo with sentences they generate the first day, which can also be used in the data set.

4. If you have a multilevel class, you could create a more challenging "fill-in-the-blank" story about the picture, like in Exhibit 3.2 "Classroom Picture Story." Then, students could write their own.

5. Have students say and write what they think happened before and after the picture was taken.

6. Tape the picture on the class whiteboard and/or have students glue their own copies in the middle of a larger paper and invite students to draw and label what they imagine might be around it if the picture was bigger.

7. Label two pictures about a similar topic (one inside a grocery store and the other an outdoor market) and introduce the concept of a Venn Diagram and a compare/contrast essay.

Source: Ferlazzo, L. (2009). *English Language Learners: Teaching Strategies That Work.* Columbus, OH: Linworth. Copyright © 2010 by ABC-CLIO, LLC. Reproduced with permission of ABC-CLIO, LLC.

A Sample Week in a Two-Period Beginning ELL Class

This sample schedule is not designed to be scripted curriculum—it's a sample, that's all. It's designed to provide a general snapshot of an effective ELL classroom, one that balances reading, writing, listening, and speaking; one that provides a flexible routine and time for reflection; one that incorporates music and movement; and one that includes fun and higher-order thinking skills.

It does not use all the strategies discussed in Chapter Three—it's only one week, after all. If you want to include more writing one week, you can replace Total Physical Response lessons with one on critical pedagogy. One week you might use improvisation instead of a dialogue. If you have three periods with your students instead of two, then you can incorporate more of the key elements more often.

If your students have slightly more advanced English proficiency, you can begin to include some of the activities discussed in Chapters Five and Six. If you have a mixed-level class, you can incorporate activities from Chapters Three through Six (see the section on multilevel classes in Chapter Sixteen for more ideas). If you have to, or want to, integrate a standard textbook into this routine, please see the section on that topic in Chapter Sixteen.

Again, this is not a scripted curriculum. It is a compass, not a road map.

MONDAY

1. **Reading and writing.** Students enter the classroom and immediately begin copying down a short and simple plan for the day that is written on the board. Bridging words will vary, such as "*First,* we are going to. . . ." and *then* and *next* and the like. When the bell rings, the teacher asks students to stop writing and she reads what is on the board while pointing to the words. Students then finish writing and begin reading a book of their choice alone or quietly with another person. After students develop some English proficiency, the round robin could be replaced with the Retrieval Practice Notebook activity described in Chapter Three (15 minutes).

2. **Listening and speaking.** A short round-robin dialogue takes place. For example, the teacher first models "What did you do on the weekend?" and then lists potential responses on the board with student brainstorming assistance. The teacher asks the question of the first student who then answers. That student quickly asks the next person, and so on. Many other questions can be used, including "What did you learn yesterday?" and "What do you remember from yesterday?" This could also be a time to practice the "Warm-Up Sentence Frames" in Exhibit 3.11 (5 minutes).

3. **Reading and writing.** A picture on the theme of school is introduced. Students are asked to come close to the wall where the picture is hung, and the first stage of the Picture Word Inductive Model process begins (labeling the picture) (20 minutes).

4. **Reading and writing.** Individual whiteboards are distributed to each student, along with markers and an eraser. Each student also gets a hard copy or an online version of a common book the class is reading (ideally, though not necessarily, connected to the thematic unit the class is studying). The teacher reads short phrases to the class, with students repeating them chorally. The teacher stops periodically to help the class understand words that are new to them. Occasionally, the teacher models a reading strategy and asks students to demonstrate it on their whiteboards (such as writing a question or visualizing). Students are then divided into pairs and read those same pages to each other (20 minutes).

5. **Listening and speaking.** A Total Physical Response lesson is done (15 minutes).

6. **Listening and speaking.** The song of the week is introduced. The song is played with the lyrics shown on a class screen. Students then practice the chorus (led by the teacher) and are given copies of the lyrics. As the song is played, the teacher points out the lines on the screen and encourages students to sing all of them or at least the chorus. Next, each half of the room is assigned certain lines of the chorus in a friendly competition (20 minutes).

7. **Reading and writing or listening and speaking.** Game (see Chapter Eighteen) (15 minutes).

8. **Reading and writing.** Reflection activity (see Chapter Three) (5 minutes).

TUESDAY

1. **Reading and writing.** Students enter the classroom and immediately begin copying down a short and simple plan for the day that is written on the board. Bridging words will vary, such as "*First,* we are going to. . . ." and *then* and *next* and so on. When the bell rings, the teacher asks students to stop writing and she reads what is on the board while pointing to the words. Students then finish writing and begin reading a book of their choice alone or quietly with another person. After students develop some English proficiency, the round robin could be replaced with the Retrieval Practice Notebook activity described in Chapter Three (15 minutes)

2. **Listening and speaking.** A short round-robin dialogue begins. For example, the teacher first models "What did you eat for breakfast today?" and then, with student brainstorming help, lists potential responses on the board. The teacher asks the question of the first student, who then answers, and that first student then quickly asks the next one, and so on. This could also be a time to practice the "Warm-Up Sentence Frames" in Exhibit 3.11(5 minutes).

3. **Reading and writing.** Students do the second stage of the Picture Word Inductive Model process (categorizing words) (15 minutes; students can complete as homework if not done).

4. **Listening and speaking.** Students sing the song of the week again, working on additional verses. Students complete a cloze of the song (15 minutes).

5. **Listening and speaking.** A Total Physical Response lesson is done (10 minutes)

6. **Reading and writing.** An inductive phonics lesson is done (see Chapter Three) (20 minutes).

7. **Reading and writing.** Individual whiteboards are distributed to each student along with markers and an eraser. Each student also gets a hard copy or

online version of a common book the class is reading (ideally, though not necessarily, connected to the thematic unit the class is studying). The teacher reads short phrases to the class, with students repeating them chorally, though probably adding only one or two new pages. Afterward, students are divided into pairs or threes to do interactive dictation with the whiteboards (20 minutes).

8. **Listening and speaking.** A short video lesson or other Language Experience Approach lesson is done (20 minutes).

WEDNESDAY

1. **Reading and writing.** Students enter the classroom and immediately begin copying down a short and simple plan for the day that is written on the board. Bridging words will vary, such as "*First,* we are going to. . ." and *then* and *next* and the like. When the bell rings, the teacher asks students to stop writing and he reads what is on the board while pointing to the words. Students then finish writing and begin reading a book of their choice alone or quietly with another person. After students develop some English proficiency, the round robin could be replaced with the Retrieval Practice Notebook activity described in Chapter Three (15 minutes).

2. **Listening and speaking.** A short round-robin dialogue begins. For example, the teacher first models "What did you learn in math class yesterday?" and then, with student brainstorming help, lists potential responses on the board. The teacher asks the question of the first student, who then answers, and that first student then quickly asks the next one, and so on. This could also be a time to practice the "Warm-Up Sentence Frames" in Exhibit 3.11 (5 minutes).

3. **Reading and writing.** Students do the third stage of the Picture Word Inductive Model process (completing cloze sentences about the picture, categorizing them, and adding additional sentences) (20 minutes).

4. **Listening and speaking.** Students practice and perform a short dialogue (20 minutes).

5. **Listening and speaking or reading and writing.** Students spend an hour working at an online site of their choice (Duolingo, Raz-Kids, English Central, etc.) or doing a Sequencing activity described in Chapter Three (55 minutes).

6. **Reading and writing**. Reflection activity (5 minutes).

THURSDAY

1. **Reading and writing.** Students enter the classroom and immediately begin copying down a short and simple plan for the day that is written on the board. Bridging words will vary, such as "*First,* we are going to. . ." and *then* and *next* and the like. When the bell rings, the teacher asks students to stop writing and he reads what is on the board while pointing to the words. Students then finish writing and begin reading a book of their choice alone or quietly with another person. After students develop some English proficiency, the round robin could be replaced with the Retrieval Practice Notebook activity described in Chapter Three (15 minutes).

2. **Listening and speaking.** A short round-robin dialogue begins. For example, the teacher might first model "What are you going to eat for lunch today?" and then, with student brainstorming help, list potential responses on the board. The teacher asks the question of the first student, who then answers, and that first student then quickly asks the next one, and so on. This could also be a time to practice the "Warm-Up Sentence Frames" in Exhibit 3.11 (5 minutes).

3. **Reading and writing.** Students do the fourth stage of the Picture Word Inductive Model process (putting categorized sentences into paragraphs and writing titles; 20 minutes).

4. **Listening and speaking.** Students sing the song of the week again, working on additional verses. Students have to complete a sequencing activity with the lines of the song cut out (15 minutes).

5. **Listening and speaking.** A Total Physical Response lesson is done (10 minutes).

6. **Reading and writing.** An inductive phonics lesson is done (20 minutes).

7. **Reading and writing.** Individual whiteboards are distributed to each student along with markers and an eraser. Each student also gets a hard copy or online version of a common book the class is reading (ideally, though not necessarily, connected to the thematic unit the class is studying). The teacher reads short phrases to the class, with students repeating them chorally, though probably adds only one or two new pages. The teacher stops periodically to help the class understand words that are new to them. Occasionally, the teacher models a reading strategy and asks students to demonstrate it on their whiteboards (such as writing a question or visualizing) (15 minutes).

8. **Listening and speaking or reading and writing.** Game (20 minutes).

FRIDAY

1. **Reading and writing.** Students enter the classroom and immediately begin copying down a short and simple plan for the day that is written on the board. Bridging words will vary, such as "First, we are going to. . . ." and *then* and *next* and so on. When the bell rings, the teacher asks students to stop writing and she reads what is on the board while pointing to the words. Students then finish writing and begin reading a book of their choice alone or quietly with another person. After students develop some English proficiency, the round robin could be replaced with the Retrieval Practice Notebook activity described in Chapter Three (15 minutes).

2. **Listening and speaking.** Students share their vocabulary homework and part of their weekly journal with a partner, and then homework is collected (10 minutes).

3. **Reading and writing.** Concept attainment grammar lesson (20 minutes).

4. **Reading and writing.** Weekly test (see Exhibit 3.21) (20 minutes).

5. **Listening and speaking or reading and writing.** Students spend an hour working at an online site of their choice (Duolingo, Raz-Kids, English Central, etc.) or doing a Jigsaw activity described in Chapter Three (50 minutes).

6. **Reading and writing.** Reflection activity (5 minutes).

Year-Long Schedule

Teaching English language learners through the use of thematic units is a long-used, research-based, and effective instructional practice. As Suzanne Peregoy and Owen Boyle write in *Reading, Writing, and Learning in ESL*, "thematic instruction creates a meaningful conceptual framework within which students are invited to use both oral and written language for learning content. The meaningful context established by the theme supports the comprehensibility of instruction, thereby increasing both content learning and second language acquisition. In addition, theme-based collaborative projects create student interest, motivation, involvement and purpose."[2]

This section contains some suggested thematic units for a beginning or early intermediate ELL class. These themes are also covered in many beginning ELL textbooks, which facilitate integrating them into these activities. Though this chronology works well for us, it also offers a great deal of flexibility. Beginning with the theme of "school" is generally going to work well, which is why the activities listed under it also include a number of introductory and early phonetic exercises, as well as simple and inspiring songs. However, as the year goes on, intrinsic motivation will tend to be generated if students can have a voice in deciding when specific themes are studied. People are more confident and motivated if they feel they have control over their environment.[3] This is especially important for students who have had little choice in being moved to a new country and culture where a different language is spoken.

The ideas listed in each unit are not meant to be an exhaustive list. It's assumed that each thematic unit will include the Picture Word Inductive Model, so that strategy is not listed here. There are also many options for incorporating technology in all these units in addition to those mentioned in this section. Ideas on how students can easily create online content are discussed throughout this book. This section is designed to provide a few helpful ideas in addition to the ones already shared in this chapter, and it is likely that a creative teacher can develop countless more ideas that are as good or better than the ones here.

In the first two thematic units—"School" and "Describing People and Things"—we include ideas and student-handouts for most of the key activities we discussed in Chapter Three. The subsequent units are not as exhaustive, but it's easy to add your own!

We will highlight only a few Tech Tools in this section, and you can find links to multiple reinforcing online activities at our book's web site.

1. School

- Topics covered: school vocabulary, building relationships, and self-confidence
- Introductory activities (see Chapter Two)
- Personal Thematic Report (see Exhibit 4.1 "Schools Report") Chapter Three discusses how to use this activity in class.
- Introduction Dialogue (see Exhibit 4.2)
- Greetings Dialogue (see Exhibit 4.3) This Exhibit has two versions—one for Newcomers, and one for Beginners.
- Address Dialogue (see Exhibit 4.4) This Exhibit also has two versions
- Introduce the alphabet and make an A-B-C book.
- Teach computer vocabulary, perhaps through Total Physical Response
- If there are other subjects that beginners might not be able to take right now because they have to spend extra time in English, arrange short sample lessons by the relevant teachers (art, physical education, music, science, and so forth).
- School scavenger hunt

- Make two collages: one of words illustrated by pictures that they know and the other of 10 words they do not know that they can learn through dictionaries and other sources; then they need to teach them to the rest of the class.

- School objects jazz chant

- Various songs, including:

  Sam Cooke's "Wonderful World"

  "You Can Get It If You Really Want"

  "Hello, Good-bye"

  "Tutti Frutti," "Doo Wah Diddy," and "A Ram Sam" are excellent songs for students to work on letter sounds; in addition to singing the lyrics as written, they can change them (Butti Lutti).

  "The Vowel Song" (sung to the tune of "Bingo Was His Name," it goes "AEIOU, AEIOU, AEIOU, I won't forget my vowels, will you? These vowels are short, These vowels are long, I won't forget my vowels, will you?").

  "Happy Birthday" song: a student's birthday is always a good opportunity for practice.

  "Twist and Shout" is a great song to get students feeling more comfortable singing, and it's like Total Physical Response for verbs.

- Mr. Bean clips are very accessible to ELLs, and his "Back to School" episode works well for this theme; you can find most of the episodes online.

- Education data set (see Exhibit 4.5)

- Read the book *Teacher from the Black Lagoon* by Mike Thaler (Cartwheel Books, 2008).

- "College Jigsaw" (see Exhibit 4.6) and "College Information" (see Exhibit 4.7). These student handouts would obviously have to be modified for your local situation, but we offer it as an example. See the explanation in Chapter Three about how to use jigsaws.

- School Sequencing Activity (see "School Strip Story" Exhibit 4.8). See the explanation in Chapter Three for how to use sequencing activities.

- Critical pedagogy lesson on school bullying (see Chapter Three for the steps in a critical pedagogy lesson plan)

EXHIBIT 4.1. Schools Report

The name of the school in my home country was _____. It was in the town or city of _____. We would start school at _____ and end school at _____. My favorite class there was _____ because _____. My favorite teacher was _____ because _____. We would eat _____ for lunch.

Draw your old school here:

EXHIBIT 4.2. Three-Person Introduction Dialogue

Juan: Hi, my name is Juan. What's your name?

Li: My name is Li.

Juan: What's your name?

Elizabeth: My name is Elizabeth. I'm from Mexico. Where are you from?

Juan: I'm from El Salvador.

Elizabeth: Where are you from?

Li: I'm from China. I've been in the United States for _____ months. How long have you been here?

Elizabeth: I've been here for _____ months.

Li: How long have you been here?

Juan: I've been here for _____ months. I'm in tenth grade. What grade are you in?

Li: I'm in tenth grade.

Juan: What grade are you in?

Elizabeth: I'm in tenth grade. Mr. Ferlazzo is my English teacher. Isn't he a great teacher?

Li and Juan: Yes!

Mr. Ferlazzo: All of you are getting 10,000 extra credit points!

EXHIBIT 4.3. Greetings & Good-bye Dialogue

First Dialogue

STUDENT ONE: Hi, _____! How are you?

STUDENT TWO: Hello, _____! I'm fine.

STUDENT ONE: I have to go to class. Have a nice day!

STUDENT TWO: Okay. See you later!

Second Dialogue

STUDENT ONE: Good morning, _____! Good to see you!

STUDENT TWO: Good morning, _____! Did you have a nice weekend?

STUDENT ONE: It was great! I _____. What did you do?

STUDENT TWO: I did homework for Mr. Ferlazzo's class. English is crazy!

STUDENT ONE: Oh, no! I forgot to do the homework!

STUDENT TWO: You are a bad student! I don't want to talk to you anymore!

STUDENT ONE: (cries)

EXHIBIT 4.4. Address Dialogue

First Dialogue

STUDENT ONE: Hi, _____. Let's study at my house after school.

STUDENT TWO: Sounds good. What's your address?

STUDENT ONE: My address is _____

STUDENT TWO: Can you tell me your phone number, too?

STUDENT ONE _____.

STUDENT TWO: Cool! Studying English will be fun!

Second Dialogue

STUDENT ONE: Hi, _____, how are you doing?

STUDENT TWO: I'm doing fine. How about you?

STUDENT ONE: Good. Thanks for asking. Want to come over to my house after school?

STUDENT TWO: Maybe. What do you want to do?

STUDENT ONE: We can listen to music, eat pizza and play video games.

STUDENT TWO: We could do English homework, too.

STUDENT ONE: No! English is too crazy!

STUDENT TWO: Okay. What's your address?

STUDENT ONE: _____

STUDENT TWO: See you then. Let's party!

EXHIBIT 4.5. Education Data Set

Categories: Schools; Classes; Times

1. Most students go to high school for four years.

2. Students learn about the world in geography class.

3. First period starts at 8:15 in the morning.

4. Students can go to high school for free until they are 18 years old.

5. Some students can go to high school for free after they are 18 years old.

6. Students paint pictures in art class.

7. Most students go to elementary school for six years.

8. Most students go to middle school for two years.

9. Students use numbers in math class.

10. Sixth period ends at 3:15 in the afternoon.

11. Students play sports in physical education (PE) class.

12. Seventh period starts at 3:30 in the afternoon and ends at 4:30 in the afternoon.

EXHIBIT 4.6. College Jigsaw

1. You can go to college after you graduate from high school.

2. One kind of college is called a community college. You can go to community college for two years.

3. There are four community colleges in the Sacramento area. You can take many different kinds of classes. You can learn how to fix cars, cut hair, fix airplanes, and how to become a police officer. You can also take classes that prepare you to go to a four-year university.

4. You do not have to pay a lot to go to community college. It costs about $500 every semester. The college gives many scholarships to students. A scholarship means it is free for you to go to the college. You can get a scholarship even if you are undocumented. Being undocumented means you don't have papers.

EXHIBIT 4.7. College Information

Name _____ Date _____

You can go to a community college for _____ years. There are

_____ community colleges in our area. It does_____

cost a lot to go to community college. You can get a _____ to help pay
for it. You can learn about _____, _____, and

_____ at community colleges.

Do you want to go to college? Why? What do you want to study?

_____

_____

_____

_____

_____

_____

EXHIBIT 4.8. School Strip Story

1. She went to the bathroom, took a shower and brushed her teeth.

2. After eating, she walked to school.

3. She talked with her friend before school began.

4. The bell rang and she went to class.

5. Maria was sleeping.

6. She put on her clothes.

7. Then, she ate breakfast with her family.

8. The alarm on her phone woke her up.

Answer Key: 5, 8, 1, 6, 7, 2, 3, 4

Tech Tool

Vocabulary Reinforcement

There are plenty of free online sites where ELLs can reinforce new vocabulary, including words related to school and every other theme in this curriculum. Find links to our favorite tools at "'Best' Lists Of The Week: Resources For Vocabulary Instruction" https://larryferlazzo.edublogs.org/2018/04/02/best-lists-of-the-week-resources-for-vocabulary-instruction/. You can also find individual lists for each of the themes in this chapter at "'Best' Lists Of The Week: Thematic Lists For Beginner ELLs" https://larryferlazzo.edublogs.org/2018/05/28/best-lists-of-the-week-thematic-lists-for-beginner-ells/.

2. **Describing people and things**

- Topics covered: parts of body, clothes, colors, numbers, weather (including temperature), and other adjectives (such as size, age, and attractiveness)
- Personal Thematic Report (see Exhibit 4.9 "Describing Myself Report")
- Weather and Temperature Dialogue (see Exhibit 4.10)
- Clothing Dialogue (see Exhibit 4.11)
- Clothing store scavenger hunt (provide a list of twenty to thirty items, like "blue skirt" and "red shoes"). Take a field trip to a store after receiving permission from its manager.
- Various songs, including:
  "What a Wonderful World"
  "You Are So Beautiful"
  "Heads, Shoulders, Knees, and Toes"
- "Hair by Mr. Bean of London" video
- Cut out pictures from magazines and describe them on a poster
- Describing things data set (see Exhibit 3.3); the categories are age, color, size, temperature, weather, and numbers. Sometimes, students can be given the categories, and sometimes they can develop them on their own
- "Guess The Person Game": Display pictures of different people on the walls of the classroom; the teacher will describe one of them, and students have to identify which person the teacher is describing (small whiteboards can be used) (see Chapter Eighteen). A similar activity could be used with a "lost" cat or dog.
- Cline (Spectrum) exercise (explained in Chapter Three): "roasting, hot, warm, just right, cool, cold, freezing," "tiny, small, average, big, bigger, huge" etc.
- "Natural Disasters" Jigsaw (see Exhibit 4.12) and "Natural Disasters Information" (see Exhibit 4.13)
- Exercise Sequencing Activity (see "Exercise Strip Story" Exhibit 4.14). This activity would be a great one to act out.
- Critical pedagogy lesson: someone doesn't understand something or is lost

EXHIBIT 4.9. "Describing Myself" Report

I am a _____(young man, young woman). I am from _____
My eyes are _____ and my hair is _____. I am _____
tall. I am _____ years old. For fun, I like to _____ and
_____. My favorite class in school is _____.

Draw Yourself:

EXHIBIT 4.10. Weather and Temperature Dialogue

Dialogue One
STUDENT ONE: What is the weather like today?
STUDENT TWO: It is very cold! Brrrrrrrrrrrr!
STUDENT ONE: I hate the cold!
STUDENT TWO: I hate it, too!

Dialogue Two
STUDENT ONE: It's so hot today!
STUDENT TWO: It's so hot that I feel like I'm going to die!
STUDENT ONE: I need to drink some water! (Gulp, gulp, gulp)
STUDENT TWO: Don't drink it all! I want to drink, too. (Tries to grab the water bottle)
STUDENT ONE: Go away! There is only enough water for me!
STUDENT TWO: I am going to die! (pretends to die)

EXHIBIT 4.11. Clothing Dialogue

Dialogue One

Student One: Your (dress/shirt) is (beautiful/handsome/ugly).
Student Two: Thank you. I like yours, too. **OR** That is a rude thing to say!

Student One: That's a nice thing to say. We both have nice clothes! **OR** Let's go outside and fight!

Student Two: I agree! I'm sure many people think we dress nicely! **OR** Okay! Let's do this!

Dialogue Two

Student One: I have a big date tonight. What do you think I should wear?

Student Two: I think you should wear your _____ (color) _____ (clothes item) and your _____ (color) _____ (clothes item).

Student One: I don't agree. I think I should wear my _____ (color) _____ (clothes) and my _____ (color) _____ (clothes item).

Student Two: I think you'll look great in anything you wear!

Student One: Thank you! You are very nice!

EXHIBIT 4.12. Natural Disasters Jigsaw

1. We call something a "natural disaster" when nature causes something bad to happen and there is a lot of damage.

2. A flood is a natural disaster. In a flood, a lot of water comes and can go into houses and buildings. Many times floods happen when there is a lot of rain.

3. An earthquake is a natural disaster. The ground shakes during an earthquake, and buildings and bridges can fall down when it is a very bad one. Many earthquakes happen in California, but most of them do not cause a lot of damage. Sometimes, though, big earthquakes happen and people die.

4. Hurricanes are a natural disaster. In hurricanes, it is very, very wet and windy. The wind blows many things over, like signs, trees and telephone poles. The wind can also blow people over if they are outside. Tornados are another natural disaster. They are also very windy, but most of the time it is not raining when tornadoes happen.

EXHIBIT 4.13. Natural Disasters Information

Name _____ Date _____

Floods, earthquakes, hurricanes and tornadoes are called _____ _____.

A lot of water can go into buildings during a _____. The ground shakes

during an _____. It is very windy during _____ and

_____.

Tell about a natural disaster you were in. If you weren't in a natural disaster, tell about
   a time you were in a bad storm. When did it happen? Who was with you? What
   did you see? How did you feel?

_____

_____

_____

_____

_____

_____

EXHIBIT 4.14. Exercise Strip Story

1. He finished by running around the track.

2. Next, he bent over and touched his toes with his hands.

3. Alberto was tired after he was done, and was happy to go home.

4. He wanted to exercise to get in shape for playing soccer.

5. After squats, he did pull-ups by getting his chin above a bar.

6. School ended, and it was time for Alberto to exercise.

7. First, he did a warm-up and swung his legs back and forth.

8. Third, he squatted by bending his knees

Answer key: 6, 4, 7, 2, 8, 5, 1, 3

3. **Data (or information)**

- Topics covered: telling time, filling out forms, calendars and seasons, and days of the week
- Personal Thematic Report (see Exhibit 4.15 "Seasons in My Home Country–Summer, Fall, Winter, Spring")
- Time Dialogue (see Exhibit 4.16)
- Getting around school or classroom (giving directions); Giving Directions Game (tie a blindfold around a student, and a partner has to give him or her directions around obstacles)
- Library field trip: getting a library card
- Various songs:
   "You've Got a Friend"
   "Happy Days"
   "Rock Around the Clock"
- Simple science experiments where students complete a simple lab report
- Time data set (see Exhibit 4.17)
- Calendar data set (see Exhibit 4.18)
- Reading strategies data set (see Exhibit 3.8)

EXHIBIT 4.15. Seasons in My Home Country (Summer, Fall, Winter, Spring)

In my home country, _____, the _____ season happens during the months of _____.

The weather during the _____ is _____.

Some of the things we do during the _____ are _____.

I like/don't like the _____ because _____

Draw what your country looks like during one of the seasons:

My picture shows _____

_____

_____

_____

_____.

EXHIBIT 4.16. Time Dialogue

First Dialogue

Student One: Hurry up! We will be late for class!

Student Two: Don't worry! Class does not start until 8:05, and it's 7:55.

Student One: You're wrong! It's 8:02!

Student Two: Oops! You're right! I made a mistake. If we are late, Mr. Ferlazzo will give us an F! He's so mean!

Student One: He's a bad teacher! I am always happy when his class ends at 9:07!

Second Dialogue

Child: I want to eat right now!

Parent: You have to wait until _____.

Child: I've been hungry since _____. I want my food now!

Parent: I did not get home from work until _____. You have to wait!

Child: You are a bad parent! If you were a good parent, my food would have been ready at _____.

Parent: You made me feel sad. I am going to cry!

Child: I am sorry. I love you!

EXHIBIT 4.17. Time Data Set

Categories: Morning, Afternoon, Evening/Night

1. First period starts at 8:15 A.M.
2. Students eat lunch at 12:25 P.M.
3. School ends at 3:15 P.M.
4. Seventh period starts at 3:30 P.M.
5. Mr. Ferlazzo goes to sleep at 10:00 P.M.
6. Zero period begins at 7:15 A.M.
7. Mr. Ferlazzo plays basketball at 7:00 P.M.
8. Second period ends at 10:15 A.M.
9. School starts at 9:30 A.M. on Wednesdays.
10. Families eat dinner after 5:00 P.M.

EXHIBIT 4.18. Calendar Data Set

Categories: Summer, Fall, Winter, Spring

1. School starts in September.
2. It is cold in December.
3. We plant our garden in late April.
4. It is hot in July.
5. Christmas is on December 25th.
6. School ends in June.
7. It rains a lot in January.
8. Students get a one-week vacation in early April.
9. The weather begins to get cooler in late September.
10. Thanksgiving is a holiday in November.
11. It begins to snow in the mountains in late October.
12. There are 31 days in March.
13. There are 31 days in May.
14. Mr. Ferlazzo's birthday is in December.
15. The new year begins in January.

4. Family

- Topics covered: family members
- Personal Thematic Report (see Exhibit 4.19 "Writing About Family")
- Make a family tree including the work that each member does or did and project what they would like to see their future family tree look like.
- Various songs:
    "We Are Family"
    "Are You Sleeping?" lullaby (good to sing in a round)
- Mr. Bean "Christmas Dinner" video
- *Funniest Home Videos* has plenty of good family scenes
- Scene in *My Big Fat Greek Wedding* film where everyone is going crazy getting ready for the wedding
- Mr. Ferlazzo's Family cloze example (see Exhibit 4.20)
- Critical pedagogy lesson: "A Family Is Poor" (use the beginning few minutes of the movie *Les Miserables*)

EXHIBIT 4.19. Writing About Family (father, mother, sister, brother, grandmother, grandfather, cousin—pick TWO)

My _____ is _____ years old. He/She lives in

_____. He/She likes _____ and

_____. During the day, he/she _____

_____ and _____.

He/she _____

_____

_____

_____.

Draw a picture of your family member here:

EXHIBIT 4.20. Mr. Ferlazzo's Family Cloze

Mr. Ferlazzo has an interesting family. His father is from Italy. _____ mother is from Trinidad. They met in New York City.

Mr. Ferlazzo's aunts and uncles live in New York and in Florida. He has many cousins. His _____ live in many different places in the United States.

He is married. His wife is a nurse. She also teaches other nurses. _____ came to our classroom on Mr. Ferlazzo's birthday.

Mr. Ferlazzo has three children. One of his _____ is married. Two of his _____ go to high school. _____ also has two grandchildren.

Mr. Ferlazzo also has a dog and a cat that are part of his family. His dog is named Bella. His cat is named Josie.

His wife has two _____. They are Mr. Ferlazzo's brothers-in-law. One lives in West Sacramento. His other brother-in-law _____ near Los Angeles.

His wife's parents live in Davis. Her father, Charles, is Mr. Ferlazzo's father-in-law. Her mother, Marilyn, is Mr. Ferlazzo's_____ -in-law.

Mr. Ferlazzo loves his family. They love him, too.

5. **Friends and fun activities**

- Topics covered: sports, hobbies, nature, and anything students consider fun!
- Personal Thematic Report (see "My Favorite Sport" Exhibit 3.17)
- Students make a collage on what they do for fun and describe them with sentences
- Various songs:
  "The Bowling Song" by Raffi
  "Take Me Out to the Ballgame"
  "Under the Boardwalk"
- Field trips to a local park, shopping mall, bowling alley, museum, local amusement park, school playground, and so on
- There are many Mr. Bean episodes that would fit this unit
- Sports blooper videos
- Great Moments in Sports videos
- John Turturro's scene in the movie *The Big Lebowski* where he licks a bowling ball is always a big hit with students
- Critical pedagogy lesson on trash or pollution in the park

6. **Holidays**

- Topics covered: many different holidays
- Personal Thematic Report (see "Holiday" Exhibit 4.21)
- New Year's resolutions
- Various songs:
    "Jingle Bells"
    "We Wish You a Merry Christmas"
    "White Christmas"
    "The Marvelous Toy"
    "Rudolph the Red-Nosed Reindeer"
    "Monster Mash"
    "Feliz Navidad"
- Students can go around caroling to different classrooms.
- Holiday data set (Exhibit 4.22) Note: This data set should be expanded to include other holidays celebrated by your students.
- Halloween data set (Exhibit 4.23)
- Mr. Bean Christmas video
- *National Lampoon's Christmas Vacation* has a scene of Chevy Chase setting up Christmas lights.
- Clips from *Dracula, Frankenstein,* or other monster movies are great for teaching about Halloween.
- Video clips with movies having love stories are good to relate to Valentine's Day.
- Students create a Venn Diagram and a short compare-and-contrast essay using the different holidays
- Santa Claus dialogue (see Exhibit 4.24)
- Halloween dialogue (see Exhibit 4.25)
- Students can make a Big Book about all the holidays—including ones from their home country—using large poster board: each student, or each pair, can make a page about one holiday.
- Students make posters sharing holiday traditions from their home countries.

EXHIBIT 4.21. Holiday

Name _____ Date _____

HOLIDAY

A holiday we celebrate in my home country is _____. We celebrate it in (month) _____. We do many activities during this holiday, including _____, _____, and _____. We eat _____. The purpose of our holiday is _____.

Draw your holiday celebration:

EXHIBIT 4.22. Holiday Data Set

Categories: Christmas, Valentine's Day, Thanksgiving, Martin Luther King, Jr., Day, Presidents' Day, Halloween, The Day of the Dead, Ramadan, Hanukkah, Indigenous Peoples' Day

1. Christmas is on December 25th.

2. People often give candy or roses as gifts on Valentine's Day.

3. Thanksgiving is on the fourth Thursday in November.

4. Indigenous Peoples' Day is celebrated instead of Columbus Day in some communities.

5. Martin Luther King, Jr., fought for African Americans to have equal rights.

6. Presidents' Day is on the third Monday in February.

7. Children wear costumes on Halloween.

8. During Ramadan, Muslims do not eat or drink during the day.

9. Presidents' Day celebrates George Washington and Abraham Lincoln. They were both presidents of the United States.

10. Many people eat turkey on Thanksgiving.

11. Many people celebrate the birth of Jesus Christ on Christmas. People who believe that Jesus Christ is the son of God are called Christians.

12. The Day of The Dead is celebrated in Mexico, and by Mexicans who live in other countries.

13. On Thanksgiving, some families travel to other family member's homes to share a meal together.

14. Martin Luther King, Jr., Day is on the third Monday in January.

15. During The Day of The Dead, people remember people they love who have died.

16. People eat a lot of candy on Halloween.

17. Valentine's Day is on February 14th.

18. People celebrate love on Valentine's Day.

19. In the United States, Indigenous Peoples' Day honors Native American history and culture.

20. Ramadan is a holiday observed by Muslims.

21. People celebrate the fight for equality on Martin Luther King, Jr., Day.

22. A heart is a symbol for Valentine's Day.

23. Hanukkah is celebrated for eight days and nights.

24. People often decorate a Christmas tree in their house.

25. Jewish people celebrate Hanukkah at around the same time Christians celebrate Christmas.

EXHIBIT 4.23. Halloween Data Set

Categories: Pumpkins, Imaginary Monsters, Children

1. A ghost is a person who died but is still here.
2. Children say "trick or treat!" when they go to homes on Halloween.
3. When children say "trick or treat!" they mean "Give me a treat or I will play a trick on you."
4. A vampire is a monster who drinks blood at night.
5. Children are given candy on Halloween.
6. Frankenstein is a monster made from parts of different dead people.
7. Carved pumpkins are called *jack-o'-lanterns*.
8. Pumpkins are vegetables.
9. Children wear costumes and visit homes on October 31st.
10. People can make pies using the inside of pumpkins.
11. Monsters can be scary.
12. A mummy is a dead person wrapped with cloth. A mummy is a monster when it is alive.

EXHIBIT 4.24. Santa Claus Dialogue

Santa Claus: Ho, ho, ho! Merry Christmas! Have you been a good (boy or girl)?

Boy or Girl: Yes, Santa, I have been a good (boy or girl).

Santa Claus: Great! What would you like for Christmas?

Boy or Girl: I would like a _____, a _____, and a _____.

Santa Claus: I will see what I can do for you. Is this your (mother or father)?

Boy or Girl: Yes.

Santa Claus: What would you like for Christmas?

Mother or Father: I would like a_____ and a _____.

Santa Claus: Okay. Merry Christmas and Happy New Year!

EXHIBIT 4.25. Halloween Dialogue

Student One and Student Two: Trick or treat!

Adult: You scared me! What do you want?

Student One: We want a treat!

Adult: I only have one piece of candy left, and there are two of you. Will you share?

Student Two: No, I want it!

Student One: No, I want it!

Student Two: *I want it!*

Student One: *I want it!*

Adult: Since you can't share, I'll eat it.

Student One and Student Two: We don't like you!

Tech Tool

Learning About Holidays Online

There are many free sites where ELL students can deepen their understanding of different holidays. You can find our favorites at "'Best' Lists Of The Week: Holidays, Anniversaries & Special Days" https://larryferlazzo.edublogs.org/2018/06/17/best-lists-of-the-week-holidays-anniversaries-special-days/.

7. **Home**

- Topics covered: types of homes, rooms, items found in them
- A scavenger hunt in a large store for items used or found in a home
- *Pink Panther* movies with Peter Sellers have many funny scenes with Sellers and Burt Kwock (who portrayed his valet) fighting in his apartment and wreaking havoc in the process; these scenes are excellent to use with the Language Experience Approach to identify items in the house—usually getting destroyed!
- Several Buster Keaton and Charlie Chaplin movies have funny home scenes in them; some refugee students will be familiar with Chaplin, since his movies appear to be shown often in refugee camps.

- *The Money Pit* and Home Alone movies also have a number of good scenes for this unit.
- Sound Effects Game (see Chapter Eighteen)
- Draw and write about their childhood home
- Students do a Door Poster Project that opens to their room or their ideal room: They label the items and on the inside flap describe what's inside and why it's their ideal room. Students draw and write about their future home.
- "Homeward Bound" song
- Critical pedagogy lesson on living in poor conditions

8. **Community**

- Topics covered: This unit could begin with the solar system and planets, then move to the Earth and continents, next to the state you live, followed by your town or city, and ending with your neighborhood; this unit also includes signs and transportation.
- Personal Thematic Report (see "My Neighborhood" Exhibit 4.26)
- Personal Thematic Report (see "Visiting A City" Exhibit 4.27)
- In this unit, in addition to using the Picture Word Inductive Model with a photo of an authentic community or activity, you might want to have a picture of the different planets in the solar system as well as world, state, and city maps.
- Students can draw and/or create papier-mâché representations of the planets; they can also make a Big Book on the solar system by working in pairs to make a page on a planet from poster board.
- A field trip with a scavenger hunt to identify different signs: Students and teacher take photos to create a photo data set; then students place the images in categories (such as warnings, names, instructions and informational).
- Transportation (auto museum field trip or auto show if available)
- Students can draw and label a map of their neighborhood
- Various songs:
    "This Land Is Your Land"
    "Leaving on a Jet Plane"
    "It's a Small World"
    "What a Wonderful World"
- Songs about your local area or state
- Students make a poster about places they would like to visit

- "Sacramento" Jigsaw (see Exhibit 3.13) and "Sacramento Information" (see Exhibit 3.14)
- Travel Sequencing Activity (see "Going to San Francisco Strip Story" Exhibit 4.28)
- Critical pedagogy lesson on problems in neighborhoods

EXHIBIT 4.26. My Neighborhood

Name _____ Date _____

My neighborhood

There are several things I like about the neighborhood where I live. I like _____

because _____. I like _____

because _____. And I like _____

because _____.

One thing I don't like my neighborhood is _____ because

_____.

Draw your neighborhood here:

EXHIBIT 4.27. Visiting a City

I would like to visit the city of _____. One reason I would like to visit it is because _____. Another reason I would like to visit it is because_____.

Draw what you think this city looks like:

EXHIBIT 4.28. Going To San Francisco Strip Story - Answer Sheet

1. He got in his car and drove to the first stop sign.

2. He saw a sign saying that the speed limit was 55 miles per hour (mph).

3. Edgar decided he wanted to visit San Francisco.

4. He drove for an hour and a half.

5. He saw an exit sign for San Francisco and got off the freeway.

6. He saw an entrance sign for the freeway going west and drove on it.

7. Edgar returned to Sacramento.

8. He had fun in San Francisco!

Answer Key: 3, 1, 6, 2,4,5,8, 7

9. Food

- Topics covered: food, menus, nutrition
- Personal Thematic Report (see "My Favorite Meal" Exhibit 4.29)
- Scavenger hunt at a local food store (provide a grocery list of 20 to 30 items like "gallon of nonfat milk," "tomato," and so on)
- Various songs:
    "On Top of Spaghetti"
    "Crazy over Vegetables"
    "The Corner Grocery Store"
    "Lollipop" by the Chordettes
- Students write a recipe
- There are many easy food-related science experiments that can be done.
- The movie *Cheaper by the Dozen* has a scene where chaos reigns during breakfast.
- Food-related Mr. Bean video clips
- Venn Diagram and short compare/contrast essay comparing typical American food with food from another culture
- Food Sequencing Activity (see "Maria's Day" Strip Story Exhibit 4.30).
- Critical pedagogy lesson: a person or family is hungry (similar to the lesson in the unit on family earlier in this chapter)

EXHIBIT 4.29. My Favorite Meal

My Favorite Meal—Use adjectives: color, size, temperature, number

I eat my favorite meal for (breakfast, lunch, dinner).

The main dish is _____. It is made of

_____.

Let me tell you how it looks. It _____

_____.

Let me tell you how it smells. It _____

_____.

Let me tell you how it tastes. It _____

_____.

In addition to _____, my favorite meal includes _____

_____ and _____.

My favorite drink is _____.

DRAW YOUR FAVORITE MEAL:

EXHIBIT 4.30. "Maria's Day" Strip Story

1. She went home and cooked her dinner.

2. After work, she went to the store to buy food.

3. Then she went to sleep.

4. Maria left work at 5:00 PM.

5. After dinner, she watched TV.

6. She ate a chicken burrito for lunch.

7. Maria ate a breakfast of eggs and tortillas.

8. Maria went to work after she ate.

Answer Key: 7, 8, 6, 4, 2, 1, 5, 3

10. Money

- Topics covered: money and financial transactions
- Personal Thematic Report (see "Money" Exhibit 4.31)
- In this unit, in addition to using the Picture Word Inductive Model with a photo of an authentic activity related to money, teachers might want to display a picture showing the different kinds of coins and currency used in the United States.
- Field trip to a bank, ideally with a tour
- Students imagine that they have $500 (or whatever amount you choose), and they make a poster of how they would spend or donate it and why
- "Money, Money, Money" song
- Money cloze and data set. (See Exhibit 4.32. Note that this is both a cloze and a data set. The cloze is a little different—there is no blank, and the missing word is after the sentence in parentheses. Students have to determine where the word correctly belongs without the clue of a blank space.)
- Money Sequencing Activity (see "Borrowing Money Strip Story" Exhibit 4.33)
- Critical pedagogy lesson: someone earns a very low salary at their job and can't support their family

EXHIBIT 4.31. Money

Name_____Date_____

Money

When I graduate from college, I hope to get a job as a _____.

When I get enough money, I want to buy a _____because

_____.

I also want to give money to _____ because

_____.

Draw what you will do with your money here:

Tech Tool

Learning About Money Online

There are many free sites that allow students to deepen their understanding of money. You can find links to many of them at "'Best' Lists Of The Week: Tools For Teaching About Economics & Jobs " https://larryferlazzo.edublogs.org/2018/02/11/best-lists-of-the-week-tools-for-teaching-about-economics-jobs/.

EXHIBIT 4.32. Money Cloze and Data Set

1. One is equal to one hundred pennies. (dollar)
2. You can save your money a bank. (in)
3. One quarter equal to two dimes and one nickel. (is)
4. Can pay for things with cash, a credit card, a debit card, or a check. (you)
5. A will pay you interest on money you save in it. (bank)
6. A cashier give you change if you pay them more than the price of the item. (will)
7. You can take money out of a bank with an ATM card. An ATM card also called a debit card. (is)
8. A bank open an account for you if you save money there. (will)
9. One dollar is to four quarters. (equal)
10. Fifty is equal to .50. (cents)
11. A bank almost the same as a credit union. (is)
12. Many people borrow from a bank to pay for a house or a car. (money)
13. Two quarters is to five dimes. (equal)

EXHIBIT 4.33. Borrowing Money Strip Story

1. Juan decided to first ask to borrow the money from Maria.

2. Edgar said, "Yes," and gave Juan ten dollars to buy lunch.

3. He was still hungry, so he next asked Edgar for money.

4. Juan went to the restaurant and bought a tamale and a burrito.

5. Maria told Juan she didn't have any money.

6. Juan was sad after Maria said, "No."

7. Juan needed money to buy lunch.

8. Juan paid the 10 dollars back to Edgar the next day.

9. He also bought a soda.

Answer Key: 7, 1, 5, 6,3,2, 4, 9, 8

11. Jobs and careers

- Topics covered: occupations, job training, college
- Personal Thematic Report (see "Jobs" Exhibit 4.34)
- In this unit, in addition to using the Picture Word Inductive Model with a photo of an activity related to work, teachers might want to display a picture showing images of many different kinds of occupations.
- Students can go on a field trip and take a tour of a local college and job training agency.
- The class can have various guest speakers talk about their jobs (and it's especially helpful when guests are of the same ethnicities as students).
- Students can create a photo collage showing different occupations they are interested in and why.
- Students can make a poster describing their family's work history
- Students can research careers of their choice
- Jobs Jigsaw Activity ("Fast-Growing Jobs in California" Exhibit 4.35 and "California Jobs" Exhibit 4.36)
- Jobs Search Sequencing Activity ("Jobs Search Strip Story" Exhibit 4.37)
- Jobs Interview Sequencing Activity ("Jobs Interview Strip Story" Exhibit 4.38)
- Critical pedagogy lesson: someone telling you you're not smart enough to go to college

EXHIBIT 4.34. Jobs

Name_____ DATE_____

Jobs

My father (or mother or guardian) works as a _____. My

Grandfather (or Grandmother) worked as a _____.

I want to work as a _____ because

_____. I might also

work as a _____ because _____

_____.

Draw yourself doing the two jobs you chose:

EXHIBIT 4.35. Fast-Growing Jobs in California

1. Taking care of people who are sick will be a fast growing job.
2. You can get electricity from the sun. Putting panels on roofs to get power from the sun will be a fast-growing job.
3. Nurse practitioners are another fast-growing job. Nurse practitioners are between a nurse and a doctor. They can do most of the things a doctor can do.
4. Construction work is another area where they are looking for many workers. Roofers, electricians, and people who can do dry wall are some of the construction jobs that will need workers in California.

EXHIBIT 4.36. California Jobs

Name _____ Date _____

JOBS

There are many fast-growing jobs in California. Taking care of _____ will be one job. That could mean taking care of people in their homes or apartments, or in hospitals.

Putting panels on _____ to get electricity is another job. The panels are called solar panels.

These panels are like mirrors that "drink" the sun's rays and turn them into electricity. _____ practitioners are another job that will need many new workers. Mr. Ferlazzo's wife is a nurse practitioner. Construction is another area that will need workers. Roofers, _____, and people who can do dry wall will be needed. Dry wall is put on walls and then it's painted.

Instruction: Pick one of the jobs listed in the paragraph and say why you are interested or are not interested in doing it:

_____

_____

_____

_____

_____

EXHIBIT 4.37. Job Search Strip Story

1. First, she read about what doctors do.

2. Rosa became a great doctor.

3. Then, she talked to doctors about their job.

4. Rosa wanted to be a doctor.

5. Third, she volunteered in a clinic that helped sick people who were poor.

6. After she became a doctor, Rose helped other young people who had the same dream.

7. Next, she applied to colleges and worked hard so she could get into medical school.

Answer Key: 4, 1, 3, 5, 7, 2, 6

EXHIBIT 4.38. Job Interview Strip Story

1. He saw a "help wanted" ad for a job.

2. Fernando applied for the job.

3. The ad said a business needed someone to help work with customers.

4. Fernando wanted to own a business.

5. He was asked to come in for an interview.

6. First, he needed to learn how to run a business.

7. Fernando was very happy he got the job.

8. The owner of the business liked Fernando and hired him.

Answer Key: 4, 6, 1, 3, 2, 5, 8, 7

Tech Tool

Learning About Jobs and Careers Online

There are many free sites where students can learn more about jobs and careers. We've linked to the ones we think are the best at "'Best' Lists Of The Week: Tools For Teaching About Economics & Jobs" https://larryferlazzo.edublogs.org/2018/02/11/best-lists-of-the-week-tools-for-teaching-about-economics-jobs/.

12. Animals

- Topic covered: animals
- Personal Thematic Report (see "Pets" Exhibit 4.39)
- Various songs:
   "Going to the Zoo"
   "The Lion Sleeps Tonight"
   "Old McDonald Had a Farm"
- Field trip to zoo

- Many Funniest Animals or Funniest Pets videos are available.
- *The Bear* movie is very accessible to ELLs.
- The *Free Willy* movies are accessible to ELLs and, combined with a trip to the zoo, can lead to a discussion on the ethics of animal captivity.
- Sound effects game with animal sounds (see Chapter Eighteen for details)
- Students can use a graphic organizer to write about an animal (see Figure 4.1 and Exhibit 4.40).

EXHIBIT 4.39. Pets

Name _____ Date _____

Pets

I have had different pets in my life. One pet was_____.

He/she was a _____. I liked him/her

because _____.

Another pet I have/had was/is _____.

He/she was a _____.

I liked him/her because _____.

In the future, I would like to get a _____

as a pet because _____.

Draw the pets here:

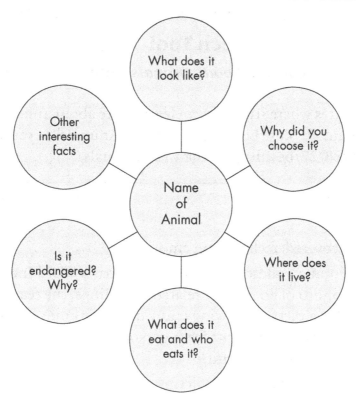

Figure 4.1. Graphic Organizer

EXHIBIT 4.40. Animal Report Example: Parrots

Parrots are beautiful birds and live in rain forests around the world. Most live in the jungles of South America. They are many different colors, though many are green.

They can be between four and forty inches long. They are very smart. They can talk and have been kept as pets for 2,000 years. Parrots can live to be 75 years old.

Parrots eat seeds, berries, nuts, and fruit. They hang upside down when they search for food.

Parrots are popular pets. They are endangered because they don't give birth to many baby parrots, and so many people want them as pets. Bigger birds, like hawks, also attack and eat them.

I chose to write about parrots because I saw a movie about a group of them living in San Francisco.

Tech Tool

Learning About Animals Online

There are many free sites where students can learn more about animals. A few of the best sites can be found at "Best Lists Of The Week: Animals" https://larryferlazzo .edublogs.org/2018/08/27/best-lists-of-the-week-animals/.

13. **Feelings**

   - Topics covered: feelings and emotions
   - In this unit, in addition to using the Picture Word Inductive Model with a photo of an activity related to feelings, the teacher might want to display a picture showing many different kinds of facial expressions communicating different feelings, such as the well-known "How Are You Feeling Today?" print.
   - Students create posters depicting experiences when they felt different emotions.
   - Students cut out pictures from magazines of people and make posters describing how they feel and why.
   - Various songs:
       "Feelings"
       "I Feel Good"
       "I Just Called to Say I Love You"
       "Don't Worry, Be Happy"
       "Happy and You Know It"
       "Stand by Me"
       "Happy Together"
       "Sing" by the Carpenters
   - Critical pedagogy lesson: You're angry because someone broke into your home
   - Critical pedagogy lesson: someone calls you an ethnic slur

14. **Art and music**

   - Topics covered: art and music
   - Students can make simple musical instruments (see the next Tech Tool for further information).
   - Ask the school's art teacher to give the class a lesson, or arrange to go to his classroom and ask his students to teach the ELL students.

- Ask the school's music teacher to give the class a lesson or arrange to go to her classroom and ask her students to teach music to the ELL students.
- Do some of the many easy classroom science experiments related to sound.
- Field trip to a local museum
- Students can write, design, and create a puppet show to perform at a local elementary school.
- "I'm Your Puppet" song
- Any of the STOMP videos
- Watch the Mr. Bean video about him and a saxophone.

Tech Tool

Learning Music and Art Online

There are many online sites that provide instructions on how to create simple musical instruments, and that let users easily create art and music online. You can find them at "'Best' Lists Of The Week: Music" https://larryferlazzo.edublogs.org/2018/07/25/best-lists-of-the-week-music/ and at "'Best' Lists Of The Week: Tools For Learning About Art & Creating It" https://larryferlazzo.edublogs.org/2018/02/08/best-lists-of-the-week-tools-for-learning-about-art-creating-it/.

15. Health

- Topic covered: health
- Have guest speakers, such as nurses, nurse practitioners, or physicians come to class.
- Take a field trip to a local clinic
- "Moonshadow" song (the lyrics are a bit "dark," but older students might like it for that reason)
- Watch the video of Mr. Bean going to the dentist
- Students make a collage of healthy habits
- Critical pedagogy lesson: An ill or injured person cannot be treated because they do not have insurance.

Tech Tool

Learning About Health Online

There are many free sites where students can learn more about health issues. You can find our recommendations at "'Best' Lists Of The Week: Resources For Teaching About Health" https://larryferlazzo.edublogs.org/2018/02/18/best-lists-of-the-week-resources-for-teaching-about-health/.

Other Potential Units

- End the year with small groups of students making units on topics of their own choice using the common teaching strategies (such as the Picture Word Inductive Model, text data sets, songs, clozes, and video clips). Groups can teach portions of their units to other small groups.

- A unit on heroes, including examination of the qualities of good leaders, studying leaders from student home cultures and from the United States, and doing compare/contrast work on them

- A unit on preparing for the United States Citizenship exam

- A unit on continuous verbs and opposites

- A unit on tools, which could include a scavenger hunt at a hardware store

Links to all the online activities listed in the chapter, as well as to the downloadable student hand-outs, can be found at www.wiley.com/go/eslsurvivalguide2.

PART THREE

Teaching Intermediate English Language Learners

CHAPTER FIVE

Key Elements of a Curriculum for Intermediate ELLs

One day, a poor man visited his wealthy friend. The friends ate and talked well into the night. When the poor man went to bed, he fell into a deep sleep. In the middle of the night, the rich man was summoned by a messenger to travel to a distant land. Before he left, he wanted to do something for his poor friend to show how much he cared for him. Because he didn't want to disturb his sleeping friend, the rich man sewed a beautiful colored gem inside the hem of his poor friend's robe. This jewel had the power to satisfy all of one's desires.

The poor man awoke to find himself all alone in his wealthy friend's house. He left and wandered from place to place, looking for work. All the while, he was completely unaware that he possessed a priceless jewel in the hem of his robe.

A long time passed until one day, the wealthy friend came upon the poor man in the street. Seeing the man's impoverished condition, the wealthy friend asked him: "Why have you allowed yourself to become so poor? You could have used the jewel that I gave you to live your life in comfort. You must still have it, yet you are living so miserably. Why don't you use the gem to get what you need? You can have anything you want!"

Confused, the poor man fumbled through the inside of his robe and, with the help of his friend, found the gem. Ashamed of his ignorance yet overcome with joy, he realized for the first time the depth of his friend's compassion. From then on, the poor man was able to live comfortably and happily.[1]

In this Buddhist parable, a man is completely unaware of the amazing jewel he is carrying around inside of his robe. He suffers many hardships until he sees his friend again, who helps him discover the priceless gem within the robe.

As educators, it is easy to feel overwhelmed by what our students "don't know." However, every student comes to the classroom with a wealth of experiences and knowledge. It is the teacher's job to remind students of the treasures they already possess, the "gems within their robes," and to use them as a foundation upon which to build new knowledge and skills.

English language learners sometimes view themselves and are viewed by others as "deficient" or "lacking" because they are not proficient in English. This "deficit" attitude hinders learning and can have long-term negative effects on students. Teachers must recognize the assets their students bring to the classroom in order to promote a healthy and effective learning experience. The activities in our book reflect this philosophy.

At the beginning level, students need to learn key "survival" language to begin interacting in a new school, community, and country. Many of our students arrive without a formal education in their home language. As they progress to the intermediate level, students need continued language development. They also need to learn the academic language necessary for the reading, writing, and speaking they will do in their secondary classes, in college, and in the workplace. A sense of urgency exists when working with English learners at the secondary level because they face the challenge of developing their proficiency in English while also striving toward the looming deadline of graduation and navigating their way through adolescence.

As adolescents, they deserve a curriculum that directly connects to their lives and is intellectually challenging. For this reason, when teaching intermediates, it is important to focus on developing students' analytical and academic writing skills. This chapter will present several research-based and highly effective instructional strategies for use with intermediate English learners. You will notice a shift from themes more relevant to beginners (such as school, family, or feelings) to thematic teaching based on academic topics and writing genres. The sample unit plan in Chapter Six models how to integrate these reading, writing, and oral language activities in order to connect to students' lives, build new background knowledge, and strengthen their academic English skills.

As we explained in Chapter Three, many of the College and Career Readiness Anchor Standards for English Language Arts can be met by using the strategies presented in this book. In this chapter, we will again list the primary domains and sections of the Anchor Standards which correspond with the strategies being discussed.

Key Elements of a Curriculum

This section presents key learning and teaching activities that we regularly use in an intermediate ELL classroom. Though these strategies are divided into two sections for organization purposes—"Reading and Writing" and "Speaking and Listening"—you will find that many of them incorporate all four of these domains. These are strategies we use either daily or weekly. We also include our plan for homework because it is a daily or weekly activity covering all four domains. Assessment ideas for intermediate students are discussed in Chapter Nineteen.

As we did in Chapter Three, we have also included a section called "Other Activities." These activities are ones we often use throughout the year, but not always on a daily or weekly basis.

Chapter Six will discuss how these individual strategies fit into a broader curriculum for intermediate students.

READING AND WRITING

Free Voluntary Reading and Reading Strategies

As previously described, Free Voluntary Reading, also called Extensive Reading, Silent Sustained Reading, and recreational reading, is an effective way to elevate the level of student interest in reading while increasing literacy skills at the same time. Students are allowed to choose whatever reading material they are interested in and are given time to read each day (10 to 15 minutes has worked well with our students. At the beginning of each semester, students can set reading goals for themselves that they can periodically reflect on and revise throughout the school year (see Exhibit 5.1). Setting goals increases intrinsic motivation and gives students ownership of their learning. By setting goals for their reading, students also learn what readers can do to improve their skills.

EXHIBIT 5.1. Reading Goals

1. What do you want to learn about through reading? What topics are you interested in? What genres (types of books) would you like to try?

2. What is your reading time goal for this quarter? How many minutes? How many days? Where will you do your reading?

3. Which reading strategies do you want to practice more this quarter?

4. How will you help yourself accomplish these goals? List three things you need to do in order to accomplish your goals.

Helping students realize the importance of practice can be a great way to keep them engaged. In our classroom, we emphasize that reading is like a sport or anything else—if you want to improve, you have to practice. However, it is much easier to practice something you enjoy, hence our classroom rule for free voluntary reading, "You must be reading a book you like!" See Chapter Sixteen for ideas on helping students select interesting and challenging books. Also, sharing research with students on the benefits of reading (see the Supporting Research section on Free Voluntary Reading in Chapter Three) can help students develop intrinsic motivation for reading.

Visiting the school library and developing a relationship with the school librarian is an important strategy for promoting literacy in the classroom. Taking students to the library on a regular basis helps keep engagement levels high. Having students fill out a Library Goal Sheet each time they go to the library can promote a positive and productive experience (see Exhibit 5.2).

EXHIBIT 5.2. Library Goal Sheet

Name _____

Date _____

My goal(s) for the library today is/are_____

_____

_____.

I _____ (did or did not) accomplish my goal today because

_____

_____.

Today in the library, I was_____ (very focused, mostly focused, somewhat focused, not focused) because _____

_____.

As discussed in Chapter Three, Free Voluntary Reading serves to generate student motivation for reading and is typically not formally assessed. However, the teacher may use free reading time to learn about students' reading strengths and challenges in English. Spending one-on-one time with students—listening to them read, talking about new words, and discussing their books—is critical to their progress.

During this daily Free Reading Time, students begin to apply the strategies they see modeled and practiced in class to their personal reading. One way to review these strategies at the beginning of the year is to have students do a Text Data Set on reading strategies to identify the characteristics of each strategy (see Exhibit 5.3). As literacy researcher Timothy Shanahan suggests these strategies "have all been found to be beneficial because they prescribe actions that encourage students to spend more time thinking about the ideas in texts."[2] Text Data Sets were explained in Chapter Three and will be described in more detail later in this one.

The teacher can assess how well students are using these reading strategies in their personal reading by asking students periodically to respond in Reading Logs (see Exhibit 3.5 in Chapter Three). Intermediate students should be moving toward using higher-order thinking in their reading log responses. One way to practice this is by teaching students about the Revised Bloom's Taxonomy and having them practice asking and responding to higher-level questions—focusing more on analysis and evaluation as opposed to recall and comprehension (see the Other Activities section at the end of this chapter for more on Bloom's Taxonomy). Concept attainment is one way for students to see the difference between lower and higher-level questions (see Chapter Three for more explanation of concept attainment).

Warning: Reading Logs can become a tedious task if they are assigned too often (one or two times a week works well for our students), so students should be invited to respond to their reading in other ways as well.

Book Talks are a way for students to interact with their reading and gain valuable speaking practice. Students answer questions about a book they are reading or have recently finished and turn these answers into a Book Talk where they discuss their book with a partner, in a small group, or with the whole class. Books Talks can be modeled by the teacher and can be done "live" or can be recorded and shared (see the Tech Tool following this section for ideas). This activity promotes speaking and listening practice and builds interest for reading as students learn about interesting books from their classmates (see Exhibit 5.4).

Using Free Voluntary Reading and reading strategies correlates with the: Anchor Standards for Reading - Key Ideas and Details, Craft and Structure, Range of Reading and Level of Text Complexity; Anchor Standards for Language - Vocabulary Acquisition and Use.

Supporting Research. As stated in Chapter Three, numerous studies show the effectiveness of Free Voluntary reading with English learners. In addition, this practice has been found to have a stronger effect on student comprehension and vocabulary than other reading interventions.[3]

There are also many studies showing the benefits of goal setting for students, especially when students set "learning goals" (to read more challenging books, to take more leadership in small groups, to be more organized, for example) as opposed to "academic performance goals" (higher test scores or a higher GPA, for example). Research shows that when students focus on learning goals, they actually raise their GPA more than students who had emphasized performance goals related to improving their grades.[4]

EXHIBIT 5.3. Reading Strategies Data Set

Predict, Ask Questions, Make Connections, Visualize, Summarize, Evaluate

1. This book reminds me of another book I read titled *A Child Called It*. Both authors experienced horrific child abuse and survived to tell about it. They both wrote books in order to help others in similar situations.

2. Why did the girl lie to her mother about where she was? Was she scared she would get in trouble?

3. As I read the last chapter of the book, I visualized the look of fear on Victor's face and felt his thumping heart as he was being chased by the dogs. I could imagine what it looked like as he tried to climb the chain-link fence and kept turning his head to see if the dogs were getting closer.

4. I predict that Justin will break up with Karina because she has been lying to him. He will probably find out about her lies when he reads her texts on her phone.

5. This chapter was about DeShawn's decision not to join the basketball team. He decided that he didn't want to give up his part-time job, which he needed to help his family. He felt sad about the decision and wished things could be different.

6. The problem in this book is similar to a problem I have been experiencing with my best friend who would rather spend time with her boyfriend than with her friends. I also feel frustrated and hurt by my friend.

7. While reading this section of my book I can picture how beautiful the mountains looked covered with sparkling snow. I can picture how the sunrise gave them a pink and orange glow.

8. I predict that Sundara's family will not be happy about her relationship with Jonathan because they don't want her to date anyone outside of her own culture. They want her to date a Cambodian young man.

9. I think that the friends will go inside the haunted house because they are curious and want to see if ghosts are real or not. Maybe they will run out if they get too scared.

10. The main character, Billie, decided to run away from home. She left during the middle of the night and went to her best friend's house. Billie's mom was worried and kept calling her phone, but Billie wouldn't answer it because she was so mad.

11. I think the ending of this book was too short. I want to know more about what happened to Johnny and Susan after high school. I don't like that it ended on their graduation day because I want to know if they decided to attend different colleges and if they stayed together or not.

12. I predict the next chapter of this book will describe what happened to Cesar Chavez as a teenager because the previous chapter was about his childhood.

13. What does the word "arrogant" mean? Is it similar to bragging?

14. As I read this sentence, I see many students bumping into each other in a crowded hallway, making lots of noise. I can see Johnny and Maureen holding hands, looking at each other, and ignoring everybody else around them.

15. I wonder why many teenagers don't like to talk about their problems with their parents. I also wonder why many parents feel uncomfortable talking to teenagers about important issues such as drug abuse or sexual activity.

16. I don't agree with Billie's decision to run away. I think she needed to take some time and calm down before making any decisions.

17. I can relate to Maria because she feels so sad and powerless because her parents are getting a divorce and that is how I felt when my parents got a divorce. I felt like I had no choice about what was happening to our family.

18. Why did the author of this book decide to write about the problem of bullying in schools? Did he ever experience being bullied by someone?

19. This character reminds me of my aunt because she is also very determined to reach her goals no matter what obstacles get in her way.

20. The first chapter of the book focused on Cesar Chavez's childhood. His parents were migrant farm workers who moved a lot to find work. Cesar attended many different schools but had to drop out after eighth grade in order to go to work to help his family.

21. If I were the author, I would have added more of DeShawn's thoughts so the reader could know more about his feelings. I also would have added more description of what his school was like so I could really visualize what it looked like.

EXHIBIT 5.4. Book Talk

1. Say the title of your book and show it to the other person.

2. Say the name of the book's author.

3. Explain why you picked the book.

4. Explain what the book is about.

5. Share what you like about the book. (You shouldn't be reading it if you don't like it!)

6. Share a quote from the book and why you picked it.

Tech Tool
Online Book Responses

Book Trailers are a fun way to engage students and encourage speaking practice. Students write a script in which they review a favorite book (see Exhibit 5.5). They then practice aloud several times before recording on a laptop or smartphone. These trailers can easily be posted on YouTube or on a class blog. They can also simply be presented in front of the class or in small groups.

#BookSnaps, introduced to us by educator and author Tara Martin http://www.tarammartin.com/booksnaps/ are another way to get students thinking and talking about their reading. This activity involves students selecting an excerpt of text, "snapping" a photo of it using a phone or device, and using an app to create a visual representation of their thinking which they then can share with others. In other words, students "snap" a section of text and add an annotation along with any other visual elements to represent their thinking (Emojis, stickers, Bitmojis, drawings, colors, etc.). We also require our students to include the title and author of the book. Many teachers and students use the Snapchat app, but Google Slides and Flipgrid, along with other apps can be used to create BookSnaps.

There are many ways to have students record and share their book responses online. While we most frequently use Adobe Spark https://spark.adobe.com/sp/ and Flipgrid https://flipgrid.com/ with our students, there are a variety of resources available and can be found at "The Best Sites to Practice Speaking English" https://

larryferlazzo.edublogs.org/2008/03/17/the-best-sites-to-practice-speaking-english. For more resources specifically related to digital book trailers and reviews see "The Best Posts On Books: Why They're Important & How To Help Students Select, Read, Write & Discuss Them" https://larryferlazzo.edublogs.org/2010/05/30/my-best-posts-on-books-why-theyre-important-how-to-help-students-select-read-write-discuss-them/. For multiple examples of BookSnaps and how-to-guides for using different applications to create them see Tara Martin's website at http://www.tarammartin.com/.

EXHIBIT 5.5. Book Review Trailer

You will prepare a short "trailer" about your favorite book that you read this year. It will be recorded and posted on YouTube and will be used next year to help students find good books.

Your book review trailer must include:

- Book title and author
- A brief summary of the book (you want to make someone interested in the book without giving away the good parts!)
- Give two specific reasons why you liked this book and explain why someone else should read it

Remember—a trailer is like a commercial—you are trying to "sell" this book to someone. Be convincing and support your opinions with specific reasons. You will need to show the book while you are talking about it. Be creative and *practice, practice, practice*!

Academic Vocabulary Instruction

As described in Chapter Three, we regularly teach academic vocabulary to beginners. In this section, we will describe academic vocabulary instruction for intermediates and specifically highlight two effective tools we regularly use: Word Charts and Word Webs.

When selecting academic words to focus on with intermediate students, we keep in mind the categories of vocabulary known as Tiers One, Two, and Three based on the work of Isabel Beck, Margaret McKeown, and Linda Kucan.[5] In short, Tier One words are the words of everyday speech (e.g. words we practice daily with newcomers like hungry, pencil, or clock). Tier Two are general academic words that can be found in a variety of texts (e.g. sustained, essential, relevant). Tier Three are domain-specific words that are closely tied to content knowledge (e.g. legislature, cerebellum, circumference). In our experience with intermediates, focusing on Tier Two words gives us more "bang for our teaching buck" because they are found in a wide variety of complex texts and, therefore, can help to make those texts more accessible to our students.

Along with considering which words to teach, we are also mindful of *when* to teach them. In general, we *pre* teach words when they embody two elements: 1) they are key to understanding the main ideas in a text and 2) they may be difficult for students to independently learn through the use of reading and word learning strategies. In other words, it makes sense to pre teach words that students will need to know in order to access the key concepts in the text, but only if students likely can't figure them out on their own using context clues or other reading strategies.

Word Charts are critical tools that can be used to pre teach or to reinforce vocabulary that students will encounter in academic reading, writing, listening, and speaking. Before starting a unit, the teacher can identify words students will need to know in order to understand the reading and writing assignments (many of these will be Tier Two words).

Exhibit 5.6 shows an example of a Word Chart from an argument writing unit. It contains key words students will need to know in order to understand the features of argument writing. Students first make connections and guesses for the words they've heard. Students may translate the words into their native language. After students have time to share in partners and as a class, the teacher builds upon this knowledge and guides students toward an accurate definition of each word, which they write in the Meaning column of the Word Chart. Students can then list any related words or synonyms in the Related Words column (they can also write the word in their native language in this space). Students next draw a sketch or image to represent each word. Finally, a body movement or gesture is taught to go with each word. First the teacher models the movement, and then students repeat it. For example, with the word *fact* the teacher could point to the ground, stomping her foot, and with the word *opinion* the teacher could point to her mind. The teacher should look for opportunities to repeat the gesture and reinforce student understanding throughout the unit. Students enjoy collaborating to come up with the best movement for each word.

Students can also be asked to create their own versions of Word Charts when reading a text. They can then identify and define words that are new to them. Students could then share their individual Word Charts in partners or small groups and add new words learned from their classmates to their charts.

EXHIBIT 5.6. Argument Word Chart

Word	Meaning	Related Words	Picture
Fact			
Opinion			
Claim			
Evidence			
Reason			
Persuade			
Argument			
Convince			
Opposing opinion			
Counterargument			
Audience			

Students can keep individual Word Charts in their binders or folders and can staple their Word Charts to the front of their folders for easy reference. It is important to post the words on the classroom wall as well. The key to making Word Charts and word walls effective tools is to use them! In other words, they are living documents that should be added to, revised, and referred to on a daily basis.

Words Webs, also known as Semantic Maps and Word Maps, involve using graphic organizers that in some way visualize connections between words and help students understand them. We often use Word Webs in preparation for a writing assignment to review words/concepts that will be useful for students when formulating and composing their ideas on a topic. In this case, we organize them with one key word/concept in the middle and other related words/phrases "branching off" on the sides. Other times, we create Word Webs to build background knowledge prior to reading complex text or when brainstorming synonyms for a word. See Figure 5.1 Immigration Word Web for an example of a Word Web we use with a thematic unit on immigration.

Teaching academic vocabulary correlates with the: Anchor Standards for Speaking and Listening—Comprehension and Collaboration; Anchor Standards for Language—Conventions of Standard English, Vocabulary Acquisition and Use.

Supporting Research. Research supports the explicit instruction of academic vocabulary words for English Language Learners—by using definitions, visuals,

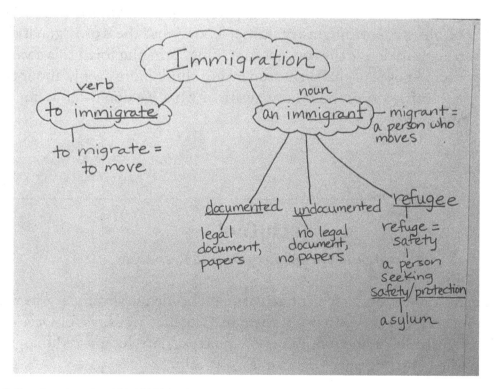

Figure 5.1. Immigration Word Web

examples and non-examples—as well as the explicit instruction of word-learning strategies—using context clues, identifying cognates, utilizing a dictionary, etc.[6]

Many researchers have also focused on the benefits of using drawing and movement to increase vocabulary development.[7] In the book *Building Background Knowledge for Academic Achievement: Research on What Works in Schools*, Robert J. Marzano states that academic vocabulary development involves students being able to express their knowledge of the words through both "linguistic and nonlinguistic representations."[8] He describes nonlinguistic representations as "drawings, pictures, graphic organizers, acting the word out, etc."[9] Also, studies of adolescent learners indicate that nearly 75 percent of those studied were better learners when movement was incorporated into their classroom environment.[10]

It is important to clarify that word charts can be an effective way to pre-teach and reinforce vocabulary but only if they contain a limited amount of key words.[11] We are not suggesting that teachers have students create an endless chart or glossary of a zillion new words. In fact, researchers have suggested that providing students with lengthy vocabulary lists or glossaries to use while reading can create a "cognitive load that splits the learner's attention" as he/she goes back and forth between text and glossary, and that it is more effective to have students write down a word's meaning right next to the difficult word on the text itself.[12]

In addition, asking students to write and talk with classmates about words and concepts they think they might already know, but that are actually hard for them to define, can be one of the most motivating types of curiosity for learning.[13] For example, many of our students might think they know what the word "gravity" means, but then struggle to define the concept in writing. Bringing forth this awareness of what they don't know can challenge students to think more deeply about the word or concept. In other words, becoming aware of what we don't know can make us want to know more!

Tech Tool

Academic Vocabulary Online Resources

There are many online reinforcement activities for academic vocabulary, as well as teaching resources. You can see a list of them in "The Best Websites for Developing Academic English Skills and Vocabulary" at https://larryferlazzo.edublogs.org/2009/07/15/the-best-sites-where-ells-can-learn-vocabulary/.

Read-Alouds and Think-Alouds

A read-aloud is used to model fluent reading for students. The teacher selects a short piece of text related to the unit of study and reads it aloud with prosody (intonation, rhythm, and expression). The teacher does not stop during the reading to share his or her ideas. Sometimes, it is necessary to supply easier synonyms for difficult vocabulary, but the teacher shouldn't spend a lot of time defining the words. In order to help students understand the concept of prosody, the teacher can read a passage twice—one time in a robotic tone and then again with feeling and intonation. Students can instantly hear the difference between the two styles. Students should have copies of the text in front of them or be able to see it projected on a screen with a document camera. Read-alouds can be followed by writing or speaking prompts ("What would you have done in this situation?" or "What does the author mean by _____?"). The teacher can quickly check for understanding by asking students to use whiteboards to share their responses.

A think-aloud (sometimes known as an interactive read-aloud) also models fluent, prosodic reading for students, but additionally models interacting with text through the use of reading strategies. As mentioned in Chapter Three, teachers can model their thinking while reading a short piece of text. Students can then replicate the think-aloud process on their own by writing their own thoughts in the margins of a different piece of text. Next, students can share their think-alouds with a partner.

Doing this kind of guided and independent practice with the class gives students more exposure to the reading strategies they employ during free voluntary reading. As researchers Roger Farr and Jenny Conner explain: "We are encouraging them to think about why and when to use certain strategies, and providing them with the tools they need to successfully monitor their own comprehension. With enough modeling and coached practice, students will be on their way to becoming independent users of strategies. Eventually, they will become their own coaches. Ultimately, using the strategies will become more automatic for them, so that activities they have practiced will be happening automatically in their heads."[14]

Reading in pairs in a positive learning environment and with familiar text is one way to help students build fluency. However, doing round-robin reading or popcorn reading, where individual students are called on to read aloud for the class without any prior practice, is an ineffective practice that can be harmful to students. We never recommend having students do these "cold reads" because, as studies have shown, it can lead to embarrassment and frustration for the student who is called on to read. It also does not provide an engaging or valuable learning experience for the other students in the class.[15]

Read-alouds and think-alouds provide opportunities for students to expand background knowledge and vocabulary within a unit, which can lead to better writing.

Exhibit 5.7 shows a think-aloud used in our intermediate class as part of an argument writing unit.

Read-alouds and think-alouds correlate with the: Anchor Standards for Reading—Key Ideas and Details, Craft and Structure, Range of Reading and Level of Text Complexity; Anchor Standards for Language—Vocabulary Acquisition and Use.

EXHIBIT 5.7. Argument Think-Aloud

Note: Teacher think-aloud comments appear in italics.

Many middle schools and high schools have adopted school uniform policies in recent years. (*I wonder if our school has ever considered uniforms?*) Some proponents claim uniforms can increase school unity and promote a focus on academics rather than fashion. (*Yes, I've heard this argument before when I worked at a middle school.*) However, opponents of school uniform policies argue that uniforms inhibit individuality and prevent students from expressing themselves at an age when self-expression is very important. (*This makes sense to me. But I also wonder if students can express themselves in other ways?*) They also argue that many families may not be able to afford uniforms, which can be costly. Some schools have tried to compromise by not requiring students to purchase a specific uniform, but instead requiring they wear certain colors of clothing such as blue or khaki on the bottom and white on top. (*This is an interesting compromise—I wonder what students think of this?*)

Supporting Research. Recent research has found that explicit teaching of prosody to students can improve both fluency skills and reading comprehension.[16] Well-known researcher Dr. Timothy V. Rasinski further explains this link between prosody and reading comprehension: "When readers embed appropriate volume, tone, emphasis, phrasing, and other elements in oral expression, they are giving evidence of actively interpreting or constructing meaning from the passage. Just as fluent musicians interpret or construct meaning from a musical score through phrasing, emphasis, and variations in tone and volume, fluent readers use cognitive resources to construct meaning through expressive interpretation of the text."[17]

Reading aloud to students also promotes literacy development and generates interest in reading. In one study, children whose families were educated about the benefits of read-alouds and who were given free books showed consistent gains in vocabulary development.[18]

See the Supporting Research section under "Free Voluntary Reading and Reading Strategies" in Chapter Three for research supporting the use of think-alouds as an effective instructional strategy.

Scaffolding Complex Texts

Reading and comprehending complex literary and informational texts are skills embedded in the learning standards for students at all grade levels and across disciplines.[19] Intermediate students are often faced with reading and comprehending complex texts in their content classes *while* still learning a new language. In the ELL classroom, we want to provide our students with opportunities to access complex text with support so they can develop their comprehension strategies, communication skills, and confidence. This doesn't mean, however, that we rewrite complex texts to make them more "simple." As researcher Pauline Gibbons puts it, we need to "amplify" the text to make it more accessible without reducing its complexity.[20] In order to do this we use a process called "text engineering"[21] introduced to us by Elsa Billings and Aída Walqui at WestEd, which makes the process of reading challenging texts more accessible and supports students in learning how to approach these texts with success in the future.

Here are a few ways we might "engineer a text":

- Adding images to help students visualize the concepts they are reading about
- "Chunking" the text into smaller sections and adding headings
- Adding focus questions to guide reading
- Providing space in the margins for student annotations

We further assist students in accessing complex text by following what researchers suggest and using texts that are "brief, engaging, and have sufficient heft for thought-provoking discussions."[22] In addition, we often provide opportunities for students to build background knowledge prior to working with complex text. This sometimes involves students reading about a topic in their home language, reading short, accessible texts on the topic, viewing video clips or other images, and providing time for students to share their ideas with each other.

See Chapter Six for an example of how we scaffold complex texts for intermediate students.

Scaffolding complex texts correlates with the Anchor Standards for Reading—Key Ideas and Details, Craft and Structure, Range of Reading and Level of Text Complexity; Anchor Standards For Writing—Range of Writing; Anchor Standards for Speaking and Listening—Comprehension and Collaboration; Anchor Standards for Language—Conventions of Standard English, Vocabulary Acquisition and Use.

Supporting Research. Scaffolding complex texts for ELLs by employing strategies like text engineering and the study of supplementary texts, images, or video to build background knowledge are cited as best practices by researchers.[23]

Clozes

Clozes (also known as fill-in-the-blank or gap-fill) are another activity students can do to practice reading strategies and build background knowledge for writing. As explained in Chapter Three, a cloze is a piece of text from which several words have been removed and replaced with blanks. Students must use higher-level thinking skills in order to choose words to fill in the blanks.

Depending upon the cloze, students may be asked to demonstrate linguistic knowledge (for example, if the teacher replaces prepositions with blanks) or to demonstrate textual comprehension by using context clues to make guesses. Challenging texts can be made more accessible by offering a word bank of answers at the bottom of the cloze or by simplifying some of the language. When creating a cloze for students, it is important to carefully consider which words are removed and replaced with blanks. Students should be able to use contextual clues to make a guess and should circle those clues. In order to preserve meaning, blanks should not be put in the first or last sentence of the passage. Cloze passages should be relatively short (a few paragraphs) and generally should not contain more than fifteen blanks.

Teachers of intermediate-level students can use clozes to teach reading strategies like predicting and using context clues, while also teaching students about metacognition (or "thinking about their thinking"). After students complete the cloze, the teacher can ask them to explain *why* they chose the answers they did. Students could use the following sentence frame to explain their thinking: "I chose the word _____ because _____." The teacher should first model this process of explaining the clues he or she used when choosing a word for a specific blank; in other words, making his or her thinking transparent for students. This strategy of challenging students to explain their thinking in writing helps them become more conscious of the reading strategies they are using and reinforces the idea that good readers employ these tools while reading.

Another way for students to reinforce metacognitive skills is by creating their own clozes for classmates to complete. During the process of developing the clozes, students need to be very aware of ensuring that gap words have clues somewhere in the text. So that you can ensure accuracy, these clozes should use text from books or articles related to class lessons, not pieces of original student work.

Clozes can also be used to assess the reading progress students are making. They can be given to students several times throughout the year to measure growth in reading comprehension and vocabulary development.

Additionally, clozes can serve as models for the types of writing that students will be expected to produce. The teacher can have students do a cloze and then evaluate the features of the writing that he or she would like students to practice. Students can then do a mimic write and replicate the features on their own. Exhibit 5.8 is an example of a cloze designed to reinforce persuasive concepts along with a mimic writing scaffold. Figure 5.2 is the mimic write a student produced using that cloze as a model. Mimic writing will be explained in more detail later in this chapter.

EXHIBIT 5.8. Persuading My Parents Cloze and Mimic Write

Sometimes, I need to persuade my parents to let me do things that I want to do. Last week, when I wanted to _____ up late and watch a movie, I had to convince my parents that it was a good idea. First, I had to think of a convincing _____ and support this reason with facts. For example, I told them that the reason I _____ be able to watch a movie is because I already completed my homework and set my alarm clock. My parents disagreed with me and presented an _____ viewpoint. They argued that if I stayed up to watch a movie, then I would be too tired to _____ up on time and get ready for school in the morning. I reminded them that just last week I stayed up late finishing my homework and the next_____ when my alarm clock went off at 6:00 a.m., I got up and got ready for_____ on time. This was a great counterargument because they were convinced and they agreed to let me watch my movie!

Sometimes, I need to persuade_____ to let me do things that I want to do. Last week, when I wanted to _____, I had to convince_____ that it was a good idea. First, I had to think of a convincing reason and support this reason with facts. For example, I told them that the reason I should be able to_____ is because_____.
_____disagreed with me and presented an opposing viewpoint. _____argued that if I _____, then I _____.
I presented a counterargument when I said:_____
_____
_____

Persuade My Parents

> One time, I tried to persuade my parent to let me do things that I want to do. Last week, I wanted to wake up early to play basket in my brother school. I had to convince my parents that it was a good idea. One reason I used was it help me to get exercise and my body get stronger. Another reason was I already finished cleaning the house and I already did my homework.

Figure 5.2. Persuading My Parents Student Sample

EXHIBIT 5.9. Mammoths Cloze

Fill in the blanks with the correct form: **they** or **them**

Mammoths became extinct 4,000 years ago. Scientists think they went extinct because humans hunted _____ and the climate got warmer. When it got warmer, some of the plants _____ needed to eat died out. Mammoths only ate plants.

Now, scientists believe they can create a mammoth from genes they have discovered in mammoths who died long ago and were frozen. They think we can learn a lot about _____ if we bring the animals back to life.

Other scientists believe that it would be a bad idea to bring back animals who have gone extinct. If we do that, _____ think society will worry less about the environment. They say that people won't care about destroying the environment that animals need to live if they just think we can bring _____ back after they die.

Finally, one of the best ways we have found to apply clozes in an ELL classroom is by using them as an opportunity to merge content knowledge with language instruction *and* teach it inductively! For example, as part of a unit on prehistoric times, we read about woolly mammoths. Exhibit 5.9 is a cloze we used to reinforce the content while also learning a language "rule." We first read the passage aloud, saying "ummmm" where the blanks were located, and then we gave students time to complete it. We discussed the content as a class, and then asked students to work on their own to use the cloze to figure out the language rule about when to use "they" and when to use "them." Most students came up with something like "they comes before the verb and them comes after the verb" or "they comes at the beginning of a sentence and them later." Having students use an inductive process to "create" their own knowledge in this way not only results in greater learning, but also enhances student autonomy and motivation (see the Supporting Research section under Text Data Sets in Chapter Three).

The cloze strategy correlates with the: Anchor Standards for Reading—Key Ideas and Details, Range of Reading and Level of Text Complexity; Anchor Standards For Writing—Text Types and Purposes, Range of Writing; Anchor Standards for Speaking and Listening - Comprehension and Collaboration; Anchor Standards for Language—Conventions of Standard English, Vocabulary Acquisition and Use.

Supporting Research. Research indicates the cloze procedure to be an effective tool for helping students learn to monitor their reading comprehension and search for context clues to enhance understanding.[24] It is a strategy that can be varied by teachers according to their instructional goals and the levels of proficiency of their students. Studies have shown that the use of clozes specifically with ELLs can result in a significant increase in vocabulary and an increased use of that new vocabulary in other contexts.[25] The metacognitive aspect of cloze has many benefits for learners. Judy Willis, a neurologist and teacher, explains the importance of metacognition as "one of the distinct learning behaviors that enhances students' competence and confidence and helps them become optimal learners."[26]

Tech Tool

Creating Clozes Online

If teachers do a search on "interactive online clozes," they can find many versions that students can do online. However, many of these online interactive clozes do not appear to have blanks inserted strategically. In other words, they may have been placed there randomly. For that reason, we suggest you first review online interactive clozes prior to recommending them to your students. The safest and best way to ensure that students are getting the most learning they can from online interactive clozes is for teachers to create them. For both teacher and student resources on creating clozes see "The Best Tools for Creating Clozes (Gap-Fills)" at https://larryferlazzo.edublogs.org/2012/04/30/the-best-tools-for-creating-clozes-gap-fills/ .

Text Data Sets

The Picture Word Inductive Model (PWIM) and Text Data Sets are key strategies to use with beginners. With these strategies students seek patterns and use them to identify their broader meanings and significance. Inductive learning can also be powerful at the intermediate level through the use of more sophisticated Text Data Sets.

As previously explained, Text Data Sets can be composed of short examples of text which can be organized into categories. Each example may be a sentence or a paragraph in length, and the level of text can be adjusted depending upon the proficiency level of the students.

Students use their reading strategies to decode and comprehend the text first and then employ a higher level of thinking to recognize patterns in the text. They organize the examples into categories either given to them by the teacher or generated by the students themselves. For example, a data set on a country might include the categories of history, climate, and economy.

Students can then add to each category using information presented in further reading (read-alouds, think-alouds, and clozes) and from videos or online research. Students can organize their information using a graphic organizer or by simply folding their paper so they have a box for each category. This is an opportunity for the teacher to emphasize the note-taking skills students are practicing that will help them as they advance into mainstream classes.

Organizing information into categories can also serve as a scaffold for writing an essay. Once students have enough information, they can use their notes to write sentences in their own words about each category. As with the PWIM, the teacher can model how to structure each paragraph with a topic sentence and supporting details. Once students have written about a certain number of categories, these paragraphs can serve as body paragraphs. The students can then work on adding introductory and concluding paragraphs and they have an essay!

Having students create their own Text Data Sets is another writing opportunity. Students can first select a topic and then identify categories within it. After researching the categories, they can write their own examples (ranging from a sentence to a short paragraph) for each category. Students can also create online Text Data Sets. Their categories can be presented in different online formats, including online books or on an online "wall" with pictures. Students can then read each other's data sets and work to categorize them. See the Tech Tool for online writing practice in Chapter Three for resources on web tools that allow students to easily write online.

This type of inductive teaching and learning pushes students to develop both their reading and critical thinking skills and saturates them with language and ideas to use in their writing. Exhibit 5.10 "Describing Things" Intermediate Data Set is a

Text Data Set we use in our Intermediate class. It is similar to the Describing Things Data Set we use with Beginners (Exhibit 3.4 in Chapter Three), but contains more sophisticated language.

Further explanation of how to use inductive teaching with intermediate English language learners can be found in the Inductive Lesson Plan in Chapter Six.

Using Text Data Sets correlates with the: Anchor Standards for Reading—Key Ideas and Details, Range of Reading and Level of Text Complexity; Anchor Standards For Writing—Research to Build and Present Knowledge, Range of Writing; Anchor Standards for Language—Conventions of Standard English, Vocabulary Acquisition and Use.

Supporting Research. As discussed in Chapter Three, using the inductive process builds on the brain's natural desire to make connections and seek patterns. This can result in higher levels of literacy for English language learners.

Also see Supporting Research under Mentor Texts and Mimic Writing in the next section for additional research on inductive learning.

EXHIBIT 5.10. "Describing Things" Intermediate Data Set

Categories: Numbers, Colors, Size, Age, Weather, and Temperature

1. The frightened dog squeezed through a narrow hole in the fence to escape.

2. Students at LBHS currently attend school for seven hours a day, except for students who have a seventh period. Those students are in school for eight hours.

3. The steaming hot chocolate warmed my hands as I held the hot mug.

4. Mr. Ferlazzo is a healthy middle-aged man, but many of his students think he is old.

5. Juan's backpack is dark blue with grey straps, but Kenia's is white with black checkered straps.

6. The dim hallway with dark paint and no windows felt scary.

7. It was a beautiful, clear day. The sun glistened and there wasn't a cloud in the sky.

8. Most high school teachers enjoy working with adolescents because they are intelligent and funny.

9. I dipped my toe into the freezing water and quickly pulled it back out. I was not going to swim in a pool that felt as cold as ice.

10. The fiery sunset glowed like lava in the sky.

11. The Mayans built massive structures that were used for ceremonies and large gatherings.

12. I changed into shorts and a t-shirt because the air outside was hot and humid.

13. Twelve students in our class are female and there are 24 students overall. Therefore, 50 percent of the students are female.

14. During a heat wave, the temperature remains very high for days at a time.

15. I looked out the airplane window at the miniature towns and roads far below me.

16. My grandmother is the oldest person in my family at age 94, while my baby brother is the youngest at six months old.

17. The powerful wind scattered the leaves across the yard and knocked over a lawn chair.

18. The computer cart has 30 laptop computers and one printer.

19. We turned up the air conditioner in our car as we drove through the sizzling desert.

20. Mia hung festive lights and bright purple streamers from the walls as she decorated for the party.

Mentor Texts and Mimic Writing

The study of mentor texts, or models of good writing, in order to mimic their features can sometimes be confused with copying, and therefore, some teachers are hesitant to use the process with English learners. However, research shows that teaching students to analyze and mimic mentor texts is a key element of effective writing instruction for adolescents.[27]

Analyzing mentor texts (which have been identified or written by the teacher) can be used to practice numerous features of writing related to organization, style, and grammar.

Students first evaluate a mentor text and identify the features they will be mimicking. For example, students may explore how an author uses imagery and figurative language to describe a person. It can be helpful for students to participate in identifying both good and bad examples of the feature of writing they will be imitating. Concept attainment can be an effective way to do this (see Chapter Three). Writing techniques can also be examined using inductive learning. For example, students can read a Text Data Set containing multiple examples of figurative language and categorize them by type (such as simile or metaphor). See Exhibit 5.11 for a sample figurative language data set.

EXHIBIT 5.11. Figurative Language Data Set

1. I was as quiet as a mouse so I wouldn't wake up my little sister.

2. My alarm clock screamed at me to wake up.

3. The girl's soft voice was music to his ears.

4. The fog wrapped us in a blanket of cool mist.

5. Our car was a hot, dry desert when the air conditioner broke.

6. The medicine my mom gave me for my upset stomach was as pink as a flamingo.

7. The moon was playing hide-and-seek among the clouds in the night sky.

8. Juan's new shoes were as white as my grandma's hair.

9. Her eyes sparkled like diamonds when she looked at me.

10. Drew was a wall, deflecting every shot on goal made by the other team.

11. The tall trees shivered in the cold wind.

12. Sitting in my English class and listening to the teacher was as boring as watching paint dry.

13. My best friend was a potato chip about to be crushed by the group of boys approaching him.

14. The boys on the opposing basketball team were as tall as redwood trees!

15. The raindrops danced across the windowpane.

16. The frozen lake was a smooth glass mirror.

17. The warm sun greeted me as I stepped outside onto the front porch.

18. The trees were a huge, green umbrella shielding the road from the rain.

Note: The Answer Key is below. Teachers may or may not want to give it to students after they complete their own categories.

Categorized Similes

1. I was as quiet as a mouse so I wouldn't wake up my little sister.

6. The medicine my mom gave me for my upset stomach was as pink as a flamingo.

8. Juan's new shoes were as white as my grandma's hair.

9. Her eyes sparkled like diamonds when she looked at me.

12. Sitting in my English class and listening to the teacher was as boring as watching paint dry.

14. The boys on the opposing basketball team were as tall as redwood trees!

Categorized Metaphors

3. The girl's soft voice was music to his ears.

5. Our car was a hot, dry desert when the air conditioner broke.

10. Drew was a wall, deflecting every shot on goal made by the other team.

13. My best friend was a potato chip about to be crushed by the group of boys approaching him.

16. The frozen lake was a smooth glass mirror.

18. The trees were a huge, green umbrella shielding the road from the rain.

Categorized Personification

2. My alarm clock screamed at me to wake up.

4. The fog wrapped us in a blanket of cool mist.

7. The moon was playing hide-and-seek among the clouds in the night sky.

11. The tall trees shivered in the cold wind.

15. The raindrops danced across the windowpane.

17. The warm sun greeted me as I stepped outside onto the front porch.

After viewing multiple examples, students then mimic the features they have just studied by generating their own examples of figurative language. Or, for the model text containing a description of a person, students can then write a description of a different person or a place using their own examples of imagery.

Using mentor texts and mimic writing correlates with the: Anchor Standards for Reading—Key Ideas and Details, Craft and Structure; Anchor Standards For Writing—Text Types and Purposes, Production and Distribution of Writing, Range of Writing; Anchor Standards for Speaking and Listening—Comprehension and

Collaboration; Anchor Standards for Language—Conventions of Standard English, Knowledge of Language, Vocabulary Acquisition and Use.

Supporting Research. In addition to the research identifying the use of mentor texts as a key element of adolescent writing instruction, researchers also cite the use of mentor texts as effective scaffolds for ELLs. Using texts that highlight specific elements of well-structured responses can help students understand assignment expectations and better meet them.[28] Recent studies have found that using student work as models can often be more effective than using rubrics as a primary planning and assessment tool.[29]

Writing Frames and Writing Structures

The terms "writing frames" and "writing structures" are sometimes used interchangeably. However, we tend to view them as a continuum along which students can use their experience to apply the writing strategies they are learning with less support needed over time. When students are given a frame to structure the academic language and organization of their writing, it often frees them up to focus on the ideas they want to communicate in their writing. As they use these frames, they begin to internalize the structures and language, eventually becoming less dependent on that support over time.

In general, we view writing frames as templates that include sentence starters, connecting words, and an overall structure to assist students in responding to a question or writing prompt.[30] In other words, they provide words and phrases that students can use as an assist in their writing. On a continuum, the most simple frames would be single-sentence starters (also called stems) progressing to writing frames that are basically fill-in-the-blank sentences. Writing structures generally do not contain sentence starters or frames, but can be described as a "series of instructional prompts" designed to scaffold student thinking as they generate their own sentences in response to a question or prompt.[31] Writing structures are further along the continuum—scaffolding is still being provided, but sentences are student-created. The farthest end of the continuum, of course, involves students using the skills they've gained to write without teacher-generated scaffolds.

One of our favorite writing frames we use with intermediate students is the A-B-C—or Answer, Back it up, and Comment or connect—strategy for helping students formulate higher-level responses to questions. This strategy, introduced to us by educator Kelly Young, is a great way to scaffold analytical writing and thinking processes with ELLs. This strategy can be modified in various ways, but generally involves the following sequence: students are presented with a question related to a topic of study (e.g. How should smartphones be used in the classroom?), they answer the question, back it up with evidence (from a text or texts, personal experience, and/or observation), and then they make a comment or connection about the evidence (generally explaining how that evidence directly supports their position). Note this last section also contains the option of using less sophisticated comments and connections. Exhibit 5.12 A-B-C Writing Frame: Smartphones in the Classroom is an A-B-C writing frame we use with students during a unit on teens and technology. For other examples of using the A-B-C strategy, see Chapter Eight and the lesson plans in Chapter Sixteen.

The Sample Unit in Chapter Six shows how we use writing frames and structures to scaffold essay writing. Also see The Best Scaffolded Writing Frames for Students at https://larryferlazzo.edublogs.org/2016/12/01/the-best-scaffolded-writing-frames-for-students/ for more examples of effective writing frames and structures we use with students.[32]

Using writing frames correlates with the: Anchor Standards For Writing—Text Types and Purposes, Range of Writing; Anchor Standards for Language—Conventions of Standard English, Knowledge of Language, Vocabulary Acquisition and Use.

Supporting Research. Both Writing Frames and Writing Structures have been found to support greater writing fluency among English-proficient students.[33] In addition, they have also been shown to be effective when used with English Language Learners.[34]

Using Images to Generate Writing

Using images is a key strategy in an ELL classroom. Pictures are immediately engaging and often less daunting for students than texts. Images can be used to push language development and thinking skills within a unit by asking students to look at an image posted on the wall, on a document camera, or individual student copy. The image may be related to a thematic unit or may reflect a problem (similar to the critical pedagogy example in Chapter Three).

First, students describe in writing what they observe, trying to record as many details as possible. Then the teacher asks students to write as many questions they can think of about the image and the details they have listed. Once students have shared their questions with a classmate, the teacher asks them to use the inductive process to organize these questions into categories. These questions could serve as writing entry points for students to develop a longer writing piece based on the image.

We also use images to build students' argument thinking and writing skills. This activity was inspired by Claudia Leon, Margaret Montemagno and *The New York Times'* The Learning Network[35] and involves students developing claims and evidence based on an image. Students are first shown a picture and asked to write words describing what they see. Then, the teacher asks students to write a *claim* about what they think is happening in the picture. Students are then asked to provide at least

EXHIBIT 5.12. A-B-C Writing Frame: Smartphones in the Classroom

QUESTION: How should smartphones be used in the classroom?

Answer the Question

Smartphones should be used in the classroom to _____.

Back it Up with Evidence to Support Your Answer

The author says that _____.

OR

The author states, "_____"

This means _____.

Make a Comment or Connection

The evidence supports my answer because_____.

This is interesting because_____.

It reminds me of _____.

Now put it all together!

Put all your sentences together into one or two short paragraphs and write them below.

two pieces of *evidence* to support the claim (what they specifically see that supports their idea about what is happening in the image). Exhibit 5.13 Claim and Evidence Image Analysis is an example of this activity used with our intermediate students.

See the Tech Tool on photos on the web in Chapter Three for a collection of web sites and lessons related to using images in the ELL classroom.

Using images to generate writing correlates with the Anchor Standards for Reading—Key Ideas and Details; Anchor Standards For Writing—Text Types and Purposes, Range of Writing; Anchor Standards for Language—Conventions of Standard English, Vocabulary Acquisition and Use.

Supporting Research. Research has shown that these types of inquiry activities—where students are asked to analyze a piece of concrete data such as a picture or an object in order to generate ideas for writing—are an effective instructional practice for improving the writing of adolescent learners.[36]

Tech Tool

Images and Making Inferences

Online images can be used to help students make inferences. We especially like the inference collection at "Once Upon a Picture" https://www.onceuponapicture. co.uk/the-collections/the-inference-collection/ . Teachers can also search "inference photos" online for lots of other collections.

Also see the Tech Tool for Photos on the Web in Chapter Three for more resources on using images in the classroom.

EXHIBIT 5.13. Claim and Evidence Image Analysis

What Is Going On In This Picture?

1. First, write words for what you see:

https://unsplash.com/photos/aZVpxRydiJk

2. **What do you think is happening in the picture? In other words, what is the story behind the picture? This is called a Claim.**

3. **What do you see that makes you say that? This is called Evidence. Give at least two pieces of evidence.**

4. **What do you think happened next? This is called a Claim.**

5. **What do you know or what do you see that makes you say that? This is called Evidence.**

6. **Write a question that you have about the picture:**

7. **Put all your answers together in one paragraph:**

_____

_____

_____

_____

_____

_____

_____

_____

_____

_____

_____

What Is Going On In This Picture?

1. First, write words for what you see:

https://pixabay.com/photos/homeless-man-beggars-homeless-2653445/

2. **What do you think is happening in the picture? In other words, what is the story behind the picture? This is called a Claim.**

   I think the man is very poor and is living in the street.

3. **What do you see that makes you say that? This is called Evidence. Give at least two pieces of evidence.**

   I think this is correct because the man is sitting on the ground with his dog.

   I also think this is true because it looks like he is trying to make a home on the street with blankets, a mattress, and some chairs.

4. **What do you think happened next? This is called a Claim.**

   I think he asked people walking by for some money or for some food or a drink.

5. **What do you know or what do you see that makes you say that? This is called Evidence.**

   I think this is true because he has a cup in front of him.

6. Write a question that you have about the picture:

I wonder if anyone will help him.

7. Put all your answers together in one paragraph:

I think the man is very poor and is living in the street. I think this is correct because the man is sitting on the ground with his dog. I also think this is true because it looks like he is trying to make a home on the street with blankets, a mattress, and some chairs. I think he asked people walking by for some money or for some food or a drink. I wonder if anyone will help him.

Framework developed by Claudia Leon. Permission granted to modify and publish it here.

Micro-writing

Providing students with frequent opportunities to produce short bursts of writing, known as "micro-writing" or "quickwrites," can help them practice important writing skills and improve their confidence. These short writing opportunities (generally lasting 3–10 minutes) can be followed up by students sharing their writing in partners or small groups.

We incorporate micro-writing in our intermediate class in different ways, but the most common include:

- *To activate prior knowledge*: We often ask students to write to a prompt related to a new topic of study (e.g. "What do you think of when you hear the term *climate change?*"). Sharing these responses can be helpful in creating a class list of what is known and what questions students are curious about.

- *To prepare for longer writing pieces*: We provide multiple opportunities for students to capture their thinking on a topic before producing a longer essay. These quickwrites can give students practice using the unit vocabulary we are studying and can be referenced later as students begin drafting a longer writing piece. See the lesson sequence in Chapter Six for a detailed explanation of how we use quickwrites to scaffold essay writing.

- *To reflect:* We often use micro-writing to help students reflect on their learning. This can involve responding to short prompts about their reading (e.g. Choose a part of the book you have read and explain how you would change the story. Why would you make this change?), prompting students to summarize or explain a concept we've studied in class (e.g. How would you explain the idea of a *food desert* to your younger brother or sister?), asking them to connect what they are learning to their lives outside the classroom (How could what you learned in today's lesson help you in the future?), or assessing student understanding ("What are you still confused about?").

Micro-writing correlates with the: Anchor Standards For Writing—Range of Writing; Anchor Standards for Speaking and Listening—Comprehension and Collaboration; Anchor Standards for Language—Conventions of Standard English, Knowledge of Language, Vocabulary Acquisition and Use.

Supporting Research. One key benefit of providing students frequent opportunities to write in short bursts includes the application of what researchers have dubbed The Progress Principle—the finding that people are most motivated by experiencing everyday progress, no matter how small.[37]

Retrieval Practice

As we explained in Chapter Three, we use a retrieval practice notebook with beginners on a daily basis. We do the same with intermediate students, but we first use a read-aloud to promote the concept of retrieval practice and its importance. We share Exhibit 5.14 with students and the teacher reads the text aloud. Students are then given the prompt at the end of the text. Students can be given sentence stems to scaffold their answers to the prompt. Once students have written their ideas, they can be asked to share with a partner or in small groups.

See Chapter Six for an example of how we scaffold this type of prompt response for our students.

Using the Retrieval Practice Notebook correlates with the: Anchor Standards For Writing—Range of Writing; Anchor Standards for Speaking and Listening—Comprehension and Collaboration; Anchor Standards for Language—Conventions of Standard English, Knowledge of Language, Vocabulary Acquisition and Use.

EXHIBIT 5.14. Read-aloud and Prompt: Retrieval Practice

Scientists have discovered that without any reinforcement, information is quickly forgotten, roughly 56 percent in one hour, 66 percent after a day, and 75 percent after six days.*

They have also found that the best kind of reinforcement is called "retrieval practice." This means that you are pushed to remember something you have previously learned. Retrieval practice can be taking tests and quizzes, using flash cards, or teachers asking students at the end of class to share the most important thing they learned that day.

When you are pushed to "retrieve" that information, it then gets put into what is called long-term memory.

You may or may not think it's important to remember a lot of what you learn in your classes.

However, it is important for three reasons:

One, of course, there will be tests in your classes (called "summative") where you need to use the information you learned to answer questions or do projects way-past six days after you originally learned it.

Secondly, much of what you learn this year will help you do well in future classes you will take here and in college. If you forget the writing skills you learn in ninth grade English, you are going to have a lot of problems in 10th-grade English; not remembering what you learn in Geography is going to make your World History class much harder next year.

Thirdly, when we're young, even though we tend to think we know all the answers, we don't necessarily know what knowledge will help us in the future. That doesn't mean we need to try to remember *everything* we learn. It just means that we need to be aware that some things we don't think are important may be important in the future. It may not be wise to just dismiss a great deal of information from classes as not very useful to us.

*https://www.edutopia.org/article/why-students-forget-and-what-you-can-do-about-it

What does this read-aloud say about the importance of memory and retrieval practice. Do you agree with it? Please support your position with examples from the article, other texts you've read, and/or your observations and personal experiences.

LISTENING AND SPEAKING

Video

Chapter Three explained how to use video with beginners in the Language Experience Approach and the Back to the Screen activity. Another technique that can be used with intermediate learners involves students watching a short video clip and generating questions. Students divide into pairs, exchange their papers, and answer their partner's questions. Students then exchange papers again and "grade" their partner's answers.

Using the concept attainment strategy, the teacher can show student samples that illustrate "yes" and "no" examples of good questions and good answers to questions. The fact that students are writing questions for a real audience (a classmate) tends to lead to better questions. Students may also take more time answering the questions because they know a classmate will be "grading" them.

Our students have enjoyed watching the *Connect with English* video series by Annenberg Media. It is a bit outdated but is available for free on a variety of YouTube channels. Exhibit 5.15 can be used with the *Connect with English* series or with any video.

How-to videos (also called tutorials), in particular, can be another way to build listening and speaking skills. We choose simple how-to videos that only have five or six steps. Prior to viewing, we ask students to pay close attention to the different steps and to listen for signal words (transitions, ordinal numbers, etc.) indicating a new step in the process. Then, after watching the video, we give students time to write down the steps in order (either individually or in pairs). This activity can be further scaffolded by providing a graphic organizer where students can note the signal words and/or take brief notes on each step in the process. After studying several how-to videos, students can then create their own versions about something they know how to do. Students can record them on their phones or they can be recorded in class by the teacher and shared, with permission, on a class blog or YouTube channel.

Using video in the described ways correlates with the: Anchor Standards for Speaking and Listening—Comprehension and Collaboration; Anchor Standards for Language—Conventions of Standard English, Knowledge of Language, Vocabulary Acquisition and Use.

Supporting Research. Research shows the practice of using video in ELL instruction can enhance students' comprehension, language skills, and motivation.[38]

See the Tech Tool on online videos in Chapter Three for research and resources related to using videos in the ELL classroom.

Dialogues

Dialogues can be written by the teacher or by students on any topic and can be performed in numerous ways. They can be frequently used to reinforce the concepts and vocabulary within a unit. Students can be given a list of unit-related words and work together to produce a dialogue or skit using the words. Not only does this provide oral language practice, it also serves to assess student understanding of the vocabulary words and incorporates writing practice.

Students can also generate a list of real-life "speaking situations" that they would like to practice (such as going to the doctor, asking a teacher for help, dealing with a landlord, or asking for directions). The teacher can then lead students in developing key words and phrases for these situations that can be turned into dialogues by the teacher or by students.

Students at the intermediate level need to practice saying, and listening to, the academic language they are learning. For example, students can discuss a topic of study using academic phrases such as "I understand your point; however, I disagree because _____", "I partially agree with your point because _____," "Based on my experience, _____." These academic sentence frames can be posted on a classroom wall. Dialogues that incorporate academic language can be acted out in front of class, in a group, or even recorded online.

Also, see the section Critical Thinking Dialogues in Chapter 8 for a more rigorous twist on dialogues that we use in Social Studies. The advanced activity described there can be applied to all content areas.

Using dialogues correlates with the: Anchor Standards for Reading—Key Ideas and Details; Anchor Standards for Speaking and Listening—Comprehension and Collaboration; Anchor Standards for Language—Conventions of Standard English, Knowledge of Language, Vocabulary Acquisition and Use.

Supporting Research. Communicative opportunities, such as dialogues, have been found to be an effective way to promote speaking skills.[39]

See the Tech Tool *Online Dialogues and Pronunciation Practice* in the Dialogues section of Chapter Three for resources related to online listening and speaking practice.

EXHIBIT 5.15. Practicing English Video Sheet

Name_____ My partner_____

Before watching:

The title of today's video is _____.

Write two predictions about this video based on the title:

1.

2.

While you watch the video, write three questions about this video for a classmate to answer. After the video, give your paper to a classmate so that he or she can write answers to your questions.

Question 1:
Answer:

Question 2:
Answer:

Question 3:
Answer:

After watching:

Were your predictions correct? Explain why or why not.
1.

2.

1-2-3

As mentioned in Chapter Three, we use a highly modified version of the fluency activity called 4–3–2 created by Paul Nation.[40] In our version, students choose a familiar topic or one that the entire class has been studying and talk about it for one minute, then two minutes, and then three minutes. Students can first write down notes about the topic to help generate ideas for speaking. After studying their notes, students put them away and form two rows facing each other. Students then talk about their topics for one minute with a partner, and then one row moves to the right and students talk for two minutes with a new partner. The process is repeated one more time, with students talking to a new partner for three minutes.

See Chapter Three for a more detailed explanation of this activity.

Using the 1-2-3 activity correlates with the: Anchor Standards for Speaking and Listening - Comprehension and Collaboration; Anchor Standards for Language—Conventions of Standard English, Knowledge of Language, Vocabulary Acquisition and Use.

Presentations: "Speed Dating"

Similar to 1-2-3, Speed Dating is a quick way for students to gain speaking practice while presenting their work to classmates. Students divide into two rows and stand facing each other or remain seated and turn their desks to face each other. The teacher assigns one row to be the "movers" and then announces that each pair will have a certain amount of time to speak. When the teacher says "Switch," everyone in the "movers" row stands and moves to the right (or to the left). The idea is for students to share with several different partners. Students can share their work in numerous ways (by explaining or reading something they have written, for example). The teacher may also encourage students to ask their partners questions.

Using the Speed Dating activity correlates with the: Anchor Standards for Speaking and Listening—Comprehension and Collaboration; Anchor Standards for Language—Conventions of Standard English, Knowledge of Language, Vocabulary Acquisition and Use.

Supporting Research. As discussed in Chapter Three, research supports the use of activities like 1-2-3 and Speed Dating for improving students' fluency.

Listening Strategies Practice

While our students practice listening on a daily basis both inside and outside of school (and we remind them of this!), we also facilitate listening practice sessions where students can learn, use, and reflect on different listening strategies. These listening sessions can use a variety of "listening texts" such as videos, dialogues, or shorter excerpts from TED Talks or podcasts.

Exhibit 5.16 is a tool we use to help students improve their listening skills and understand metacognition (being aware of how and when to use different learning processes). We write the title of the "text" (e.g. "14-Year-Old Girl Earns a College Degree") and type of text (e.g. a podcast) on the board for students to fill in at the top of the sheet. Then we ask students to write in the "Before Listening" section anything they already know about the topic (e.g. What do they know about the words "earn," "college," or "degree"? What do they know from their own experience or from friends/family? From anything else they've read?) and the type of "text" (e.g. What kinds of information does it have? How is this information presented?).

After students individually list some ideas, we provide time to share in partners or small groups to generate more ideas. Students then write predictions based on these ideas about the content (e.g. "I predict the podcast will tell us about the girl and how she got to go to college at such a young age") and how it will be delivered (e.g. "I predict the podcast will have an interview with the girl and her parents.") If students are new to this kind of listening activity, we model the above process and do it together as a class.

Next, we remind students of the listening strategies they can employ to aid their understanding which are similar to the reading strategies they use to help them comprehend written texts—visualizing, making predictions, asking questions, using context clues to determine word meanings, activating prior knowledge, summarizing, and monitoring your attention and focus. Just as we discussed earlier how the use of reading strategies challenges students to pay closer attention to texts, listening strategies can do the same. It can be helpful to work on just one or two listening strategies at a time when first doing this kind of listening activity. Students can be asked to consider which strategies might be more or less helpful based on the type of listening "text" (e.g. activating prior knowledge might be helpful before listening to a news report or visualizing might not be necessary when watching a video) and based on their prior experience (e.g. Summarizing helped me a lot the last time I listened to a podcast).

If the listening task is being conducted with the whole class (and students are not able to be on individual computers with headphones) it is important to pause and replay the listening text several times. After listening, we ask students to use the "After Listening" section to reflect on which strategies they used, how they were helpful, and to set goals for improvement. This process can also be modeled by the teacher when students are new to the activity or more language support is needed.

Of course, this type of listening task and focus on metacognition is much easier to do in a classroom setting where the teacher and students can pause the task. Students aren't able to hit pause during a conversation with their doctor or at a job interview. However, practicing these listening and metacognitive strategies in the classroom regularly can make these processes more automatic and boost students' confidence as listeners.

Listening strategies practice correlates with the: Anchor Standards for Speaking and Listening - Comprehension and Collaboration; Anchor Standards for Language—Conventions of Standard English, Knowledge of Language, Vocabulary Acquisition and Use.

Supporting Research. Research shows that ELLs can make more progress if they are aware of how listening processes work and how to apply them in their own listening.[41]

Tech Tool
Listening Practice Sites

There are several sites we frequently use with students that provide engaging opportunities for listening practice.

We use two online game sites: Quizizz https://quizizz.com/ and FluentKey https://fluentkey.com/. Both let all students in an entire class compete against each other. As we described in Chapter Three, teachers can record a question that students listen to and then they choose the correct answer. FluentKey lets teachers show videos with questions interspersed, along with real-time game results.

ISL Collective https://en.islcollective.com/video-lessons/ and Lyrics Training https://lyricstraining.com/ are sites teachers can "gamify" by displaying videos on a projector and having students answer questions on mini-whiteboards.

EdPuzzle https://edpuzzle.com/ and Nearpod https://nearpod.com/ can be used to create interactive listening tasks with videos and all student responses are completed on the platform.

There are, and we're sure will be in the future, additional sites. The ones we listed here are our present favorites and ones likely to be around for a while.

EXHIBIT 5.16. Listening Strategies Practice Sheet

Title of listening text:
Type of text:

Before listening:

What do I **already know** about this topic and this type of text?

What **predictions** can I make based on the title and the type of text?

Listening strategies I can use:

> visualizing
>
> making predictions
>
> asking questions
>
> using context clues to determine word meanings
>
> activating prior knowledge
>
> summarizing
>
> monitoring your attention and focus during the listening task

---

After listening:

> Which strategy did I use to help me? How did it help?
>
> Which strategy will I focus on next time?

HOMEWORK

The homework we give our intermediate students covers the four domains of reading, writing, listening, and speaking and is similar to the homework we assign our beginners and early intermediates, with a few variations:

- Read a book in English at home for at least twenty minutes each night and have a parent or guardian sign a Weekly Reading Sheet (see Exhibit 5.17).

- Complete one Reading Log and demonstrate the use of at least three reading strategies (see Exhibit 3.6 in Chapter Three).

- Write a journal entry sharing two or three good events that occurred that week and one event that was not necessarily positive. In the last instance, explain what they learned from this event or share whether there was something that they could have done differently to improve the outcome.

- In class, students share what they wrote with a partner, and the partner should ask at least one question.

- Complete a Four Words sheet with new words learned that week—in or out of class—that students think are important (see Exhibit 3.18 in Chapter Three). In class, students share the words they chose with a partner.

- Spend at least 10 minutes each day talking to someone else in English (for example, with a teacher, another student, or a coworker) and complete the Conversation Log (see Exhibit 3.19 in Chapter Three).

- Extra credit: Read a book aloud to a child and complete the Read a Children's Book sheet (see Exhibit 5.18).

Please see the Homework section in Chapter Three for the research support behind effective homework activities and for Tech Tools on homework.

EXHIBIT 5.17. Weekly Reading Sheet

Name _____

Date	Book Title	Minutes Read	Student Signature	Parent Signature

EXHIBIT 5.18. Read a Children's Book

Student name_____

1. What is the name of the child you read the book to?

2. What is this child's relationship to you?

3. What is the title of the book you read?

4. Why did you pick that book?

5. Did the child enjoy having you read the book to him or her? How could you tell?

6. How did you feel about reading the book to him or her? Why?

ASSESSMENT

Please see Chapter 19 for an in-depth explanation of the different types of assessments that can be used with intermediate-level students.

OTHER ACTIVITIES

This chapter contains research-based instructional strategies that we believe are key to an intermediate-level ELL curriculum and can in fact work well with many classes. While the following activities didn't make the list of key strategies for language instruction, we have found them to be effective with our intermediate-level students.

Gallery Walks

Gallery walks are a way for students to get out of their seats and move around the room to view student work or other learning materials (such as images, texts, and maps) posted on the classroom walls and to interact with them in various ways. Students can take notes or use graphic organizers to note observations, questions, and responses. It can also be useful to give students sticky notes and have them leave questions and/or comments on the walls as they walk around the room. If you have a large class, it can be helpful to divide students into small groups. Each group can start in a different part of the room and then move together to the next area after a few minutes to prevent traffic jams.

Sequencing Activities

As mentioned in Chapter Three, sequencing activities work well with simple texts, comic strips, songs, and dialogues. With intermediates, sequencing activities can work with more complex text. The teacher can select a multiple-paragraph text on a topic of study and give it to students with the paragraphs mixed up. Students can then cut out the paragraphs and use reading strategies like predicting and context clues to put the text strips in the correct order. It is important to choose a text that contains enough contextual and chronological clues for students to be able to sequence it.

Sentence Modeling

Having students practice writing more complex sentences is a valuable activity in an intermediate-level class. High school teacher Martin Brandt has developed several sentence structures to help students write more advanced sentences. Brandt has created multiple charts to help teachers scaffold this kind of practice for their students. See Exhibit 5.19 for a sample that uses a sentence from *Into Thin Air* by John Krakauer[42] to model complex sentence construction.

EXHIBIT 5.19. Sentence Modeling: The North Face

Doing What?	Description	Who	Action	Action	Action	What
Straddling the top of the world	one foot in Tibet and one in Nepal	I	chipped the ice from my oxygen mask,	hunched a shoulder against the wind,	and stared absently	at the vast sweep of earth below.

This table allows students to see the different parts of a sentence along with a model of a well-written and complex sentence before trying out their own sentence. This type of sentence modeling chart can be used for a variety of other sentence structures to help students write in more advanced forms.

An image or photograph can serve as an additional scaffold to a sentence chart. Students can view the image, write about what they see, and then be shown a model sentence related to the image. Then when students take a turn at writing their own sentence, they have some writing and thinking to draw from.

Graphic Organizers

Numerous graphic organizers are available to help English learners organize their thinking before writing and after reading. Research has shown that the use of graphic organizers and other "...nonlinguistic representations...stimulates and increases activity in the brain."[43] Many graphic organizers, like Venn Diagrams, K-W-L charts, and Word Charts, encourage higher-order thinking. It is helpful to offer students multiple opportunities to use graphic organizers, to teach students the purpose behind them, and to encourage students to develop their own graphic organizers. As students gain practice organizing information and ideas in various ways, they can be encouraged to apply these skills as they read and learn in other content classes.

We have found foldable graphic organizers to be particularly engaging and useful for our students. Foldables are basically three-dimensional graphic organizers that provide more space for content and are fun for students to make.

Tech Tool

Graphic Organizer Resources

Numerous web sites offer free, printable graphic organizers and online tools for creating graphic organizers .For some of the best we've found see "The Best List of Mindmapping, Flow Chart Tools & Graphic Organizers" at https://larryferlazzo. edublogs.org/2009/02/09/not-the-best-but-a-list-of-mindmapping-flow-chart-tools-graphic-organizers/ . For specific information on foldable graphic organizers see "The Best Teacher Resources for 'Foldables'" at https://larryferlazzo.edublogs. org/2009/06/07/the-best-teacher-resources-for-foldables/ .

Revised Bloom's Taxonomy

Using the Revised Bloom's Taxonomy is one way to teach students about higher-order thinking. It is important for students to see the different levels of thinking and how they can be applied in their lives. One way for students to use the Revised Bloom's levels to make their writing more sophisticated is through question writing. Students can practice writing questions (preferably related to a theme being studied in class) for each level of thinking. Question stems and teacher modeling can serve as scaffolds.

Tech Tool

Online Resources for Bloom's Taxonomy

Lists of sample Revised Bloom's Taxonomy question stems can easily be found online by searching "Revised Bloom's question stems." Links to these question stems, as well as other online resources on Bloom's, including some great video clips to help students understand the different levels of Bloom's, can be found in "The Best Resources for Helping Teachers Use Bloom's Taxonomy in the Classroom" at https:// larryferlazzo.edublogs.org/2009/05/25/the-best-resources-for-helping-teachers-use-blooms-taxonomy-in-the-classroom/ .

Thinking Routines

Thinking routines, introduced to us by Harvard's Project Zero,[44] are simple steps or processes that help guide and deepen student thinking. They become "routines" when they are used frequently to encourage active processing and to make thinking processes visible to students.

The thinking routine we use most frequently is *Think-Pair-Share* where students *Think* about their response (to a question, a problem, etc.), form a *Pair* with a classmate and discuss their responses, and then *Share* their ideas with the class or another group.

Another thinking routine called *See-Think-Wonder* works well with an image or video clip. First, students are asked "What do you *see*?" and they note what they are observing without any interpretation. Then, they are asked "What do you *think* is happening? Why do you think this?" and note the opinions they are forming based on their observations. Finally, they are asked "What does this make you wonder?" as they note questions they now have based on their observations. This thinking routine can be used with a simple graphic organizer listing the three sections (*See-Think-Wonder*) and providing space underneath each section for student notes.

Tech Tool
Thinking Routines Resources

For many more examples of thinking routines see Project Zero's Thinking Routine Toolbox at https://pz.harvard.edu/thinking-routines. To see other ways that teachers have applied thinking routines in their classrooms see "Project Zero's 'Thinking Routines Tool' is an Excellent Resource" at https://larryferlazzo.edublogs.org/2020/01/18/project-zeros-thinking-routines-tool-is-an-excellent-resource/.

Field Trips

As discussed in Chapter Three, field trips can be a way to extend the classroom learning that students are doing within a thematic unit. For intermediate students, the activities students do in preparation for the trip and as a follow-up can involve more writing and higher-level analysis than for beginners.

For example, as part of a unit on argument writing, we have students research, visit, and critically evaluate two different neighborhoods according to various criteria such as public transportation access, housing costs, diversity, and overall livability. Afterward, students write a persuasive essay choosing the best neighborhood. For more explanation of this project and a lesson plan, see *Helping Students Motivate Themselves: Practical Answers to Classroom Challenges* by Larry Ferlazzo.[45]

Links to all the online activities listed in the chapter, as well as to the downloadable student handouts, can be found at www.wiley.com/go/eslsurvivalguide2.

CHAPTER SIX

Daily Instruction
for Intermediate ELLs

One day a large buck went to drink at a spring. As he bent down, he noticed his own reflection in the clear water. He admired his great, strong horns, but as he looked at his legs and feet, he suddenly felt angry and thought "Why are they so thin and weak?" While the buck was immersed in his negative thoughts, a lion approached the spring, ready to hunt his prey. The buck immediately turned and shot off into the distance, his strong legs carrying him far across the plains to safety. "It was my legs, not my mighty horns, which saved me from death," the buck said to himself.[1]

In this story the buck wasn't able to see his most valuable strength until he was faced with a challenging situation. In the classroom, our students sometimes have a hard time seeing their valuable qualities. The strategies and lesson ideas presented in this chapter are designed to build upon students' strengths and experiences and help students see the value both in their learning and in themselves.

Chapter Five provided an overview of different elements to include in an intermediate ELL classroom. This chapter will describe what the application of these elements might look like on a day-to-day basis in a sample unit plan, followed by two lesson plans on scaffolding extended writing tasks for intermediate ELLs, and, lastly, a sample week schedule.

Designing Thematic Genre Units

Thematic instruction (where an instructional unit focuses on a certain topic, theme, or genre) can be an effective way to build vocabulary and provide students with many opportunities for rich reading and writing experiences. At the intermediate level, students are moving further toward proficiency in academic literacy in English. Therefore, it can be helpful to organize thematic instruction around academic writing genres they will likely be exposed to in secondary education and beyond. In other words, examining the ways people write for different purposes, such as arguing, explaining, reporting, narrating, reflecting, and so forth. This type of instruction means helping ELLs learn about the structure and language features of a variety of genres in order to apply these features in their own writing.[2]

When designing a thematic genre-based unit of study, there are several elements that can be particularly helpful to keep in mind. In order to promote "language development, critical thinking, independence, and interpersonal collaboration," Suzanne Peregoy and Owen Boyle describe these six criteria for organizing thematic instruction for English learners:[3]

1. *Meaning and purpose:* connecting topics of study to students' lives and offering students choice in topics studied

2. *Building on prior knowledge:* making connections to students' life experiences

3. *Integrated opportunities to use oral and written language for learning purposes:* promoting a variety of oral language and literacy experiences that are aligned with student interests

4. *Scaffolding for support:* using multiple scaffolds to support students who are at various levels of language proficiency

5. *Collaboration:* providing opportunities for students to work together in pairs and small groups for learning tasks

6. *Variety:* creating a dynamic learning environment that emphasizes variety and flexibility in all aspects of the classroom

These criteria have guided the development of the genre units we use with our intermediate-level students throughout the year. If students are scheduled into a two-hour block, it is possible to teach several genres a year. Problem-solution, argument, and autobiographical or narrative writing are three types of writing commonly taught and assessed in high school, and also exist in college and in real-world writing. Of course, these are not the only genres that students need to be exposed to, but they each contain critical thinking and writing techniques that students will use both in and outside of school. During a genre unit, students are not limited to just that genre, but continue to write daily for many different purposes.

When selecting genres for study, the following questions may be important to consider: *Is this type of writing commonly used in secondary courses? Is this a genre students will need to know to be successful on district and state assessments? Is this a genre students will frequently be required to use at the postsecondary level? Does this genre exist outside of academics in real-world writing?*

This last question is especially important in terms of student motivation--both student learning and intrinsic motivation are enhanced when students can see how the writing skills they are practicing in class can be applied outside of school. We point out to students how writing in the real world often blurs the lines of genre. For example, an online news article might blend elements of narrative and explanation in order to make it more engaging and relevant for readers. This ability to blend genres is not just for professional writers, however. With the proper support, intermediate students can practice this skill while building English proficiency.

A Sample Unit: Problem-Solution

This section will explain the key components of a problem-solution unit for intermediate students. Problem-solution is a powerful genre for students to practice because it can include elements of narrative and argument writing. Students can incorporate anecdotes and personal experiences as part of their argument for why a problem needs to be addressed and how to best solve it.

The following sections describe ways to both develop student knowledge of the problem-solution genre *and* provide opportunities for valuable listening, speaking, reading, and writing practice. The learning process is one of guided discovery using inductive learning as a key component (see Chapters Three and Five for more information on this concept). Near the end of the unit, students choose their own problem to research and produce a problem-solution essay of their own. We think the steps in this process can be applied to studying many other genres. This unit takes six to eight weeks, depending upon the level of the class and whether the students take the class for one or two periods.

This unit contains some elements of argument writing, a heavily emphasized genre in secondary and post-secondary education. We have written more extensively about scaffolding argument writing in our book *Navigating the Common Core with English Language Learners*. See the next Tech Tool for additional resources on how to support students' argument skills.

Tech Tool

Argument Writing Resources

There are many online activities for developing argument skills, as well as teaching resources. You can see a list of them at "The Best Online Resources For Helping Students Learn to Write Argument Essays"

https://larryferlazzo.edublogs.org/2009/11/14/the-best-online-resources-for-helping-students-learn-to-write-persuasive-essays/.

Exhibit 6.1 lays out the typical sequence we follow when teaching a genre-based unit. In the previous chapter, we discussed most of these activities and will now explain in further detail how we apply them throughout a unit.

EXHIBIT 6.1. Key Elements of a Writing Genre Unit

Student Connections and Prior Knowledge

Drawing

Talking

Writing

Building Background Knowledge and Academic Language

Word Charts

Read-alouds and think-alouds

Clozes

Text Data Sets

Mimic writing

Mini-themes or practice essays

Dialogues

Scaffolding the Writing Process

Choosing a Topic

Research

Mentor Texts

Oral outlining

Drafting: writing frames and structures

Revising and editing

Publishing or presenting

Assessing

Extensions

Action projects

On-demand writing practice

STUDENT CONNECTIONS AND PRIOR KNOWLEDGE

Our students come to us with a wealth of knowledge and experiences that they can build on when they start a new unit of study. Research has shown that activating prior knowledge is a crucial step in the learning process,[4] and research on the brain confirms that learning something new is easier when we can attach it to something we already know.[5]

There are many ways to activate prior knowledge: students may draw, write, or talk in response to a question or series of questions relating to the unit topic. The key is to validate what students know and what they have experienced so they are able to make new connections and new learnings, and so they can see the relevance of a unit of study to their own lives.

Exhibit 6.2 shows a quickwrite called Problems All Around that we use at the beginning of the problem-solution unit. Students are asked to think about a problem in their lives (at school, at home, or with friends) and a problem in the community or in the world. Then students are asked to sketch each problem, write a few sentences about each problem, and then share with a partner. This activity helps students immediately see the connections between the problem-solution unit and their daily lives. The section on critical pedagogy in Chapter Three describes another powerful activity that challenges students to think critically about problems and make connections to their experiences and beliefs.

This type of quick-write can be used at the beginning of any genre unit. For example, with a unit on argument writing, students can respond to a prompt like "Write about a time when you wanted something or wanted someone to do something. How did you convince that person to do what you wanted?"

EXHIBIT 6.2. Problems All Around Quickwrite

Think about a problem in your life (at home, at school, or with friends, for example). Quickly sketch the problem below:

Now write a few sentences describing this problem:

Think about a problem in your community or in the world. Quickly sketch the problem below:

Now write a few sentences describing this problem:

At the beginning of a genre unit, students can quickly demonstrate what they've previously learned about a type of writing by responding to prompts like "Write down anything you know about writing stories" or "What do you think of when you see or hear the word *argument*?" The teacher can ask students to think even more broadly and ask, "Write down anything you know about writing essays" or "What does school writing look like to you?" We are not looking for a formula. Instead, this can be an opportunity for the teacher to validate what students already know and for both teacher and students to discover areas to be further explored.

BUILDING BACKGROUND KNOWLEDGE AND ACADEMIC LANGUAGE

Along with students making connections to their own lives, it is important for them to begin building the academic language related to the problem-solution genre. Students need to practice the language structures of cause and effect when describing the problem and of argument when evaluating solutions. The following strategies can help students develop the academic language necessary to talk and write about problems and solutions while building additional critical English literacy skills:

- *Reading the prompt.* Exhibit 6.3 shows the prompt we give our students for this unit. We provide it at the beginning of the unit so they can visualize what the unit's end goal will be. It also gives us an opportunity to "cheerlead" and reinforce students' belief that "they got this."

- *Word Chart.* At the beginning of the unit, students are given a Problem-Solution Word Chart (see Exhibit 6.4; also see Exhibits 6.5, 6.6, and Exhibit 5.6 in Chapter Five for Word Charts for other genres). Students can access this chart on a daily basis as a tool for writing and speaking. The Word Charts serve as a key way to reinforce the features of the problem-solution genre—describing a problem, stating the causes and effects of the problem, proposing realistic solutions to the problem, evaluating both the benefits and potential problems of each solution, formulating counterarguments to anticipate the arguments against a solution, and identifying the best solution and presenting reasons why it is the best.

- *Read-alouds and think-alouds.* Finding texts to make into read-alouds or think-alouds is fairly easy in a problem-solution unit. One can find numerous articles about current problems. Some articles may need to be scaffolded to fit the language proficiency level of students (see the section "Scaffolding Complex Texts" in Chapter Five for suggestions on how to make texts more accessible without reducing their complexity). There are countless stories about problems and solutions. The book *I Felt Like I Was from Another Planet: Writing from Personal Experience* by Norine Dresser is an old favorite of ours and contains 15 multicultural student-written stories about issues of immigration and cultural differences.[6] Each one is accompanied by pre-teaching ideas and follow-up writing activities. A story from this anthology is used in the Using Text to Generate Analytical Writing Lesson Plan later in this chapter.

- *Clozes.* A text about a problem can easily be turned into a cloze and then be used as a read-aloud or think-aloud (see Exhibit 6.7).

- *Text Data Sets.* Text Data Sets can be used for different reasons within the unit. If the class is focusing on a particular problem (such as gun violence or climate change), students can learn new information about the problem while practicing their reading and thinking skills. Students can also practice identifying the different features of problem-solution writing by doing a data set (see Exhibit 6.8). The Inductive Lesson Plan later in this chapter explains how to use this type of Text Data Set.

EXHIBIT 6.3. Problem-Solution Writing Prompt

We all experience problems or challenges in life. Sometimes, we face problems at home, at school, or in our communities.

Choose a problem you see at home, at your school, or in your community and describe it. Think about and explain the causes of the problem. Describe the effects of this problem. Propose two or three solutions to this problem. Analyze the pros and cons of each solution. Choose the solution you feel is the best and support your position with reasons and examples.

EXHIBIT 6.4. Problem-Solution Word Chart

Word	Meaning	Related Words	Picture
Problem			
Solution			
Fact			
Opinion			
Cause			
Effect			
Convince			
Opposing argument			
Counterargument			

EXHIBIT 6.5. Autobiographical Incident Word Chart

Word	Meaning	Related Words	Picture
Incident			
Hook			
Context			
Dialogue			
Sensory details			
Interior monologue			
Significance			
Narrative			

EXHIBIT 6.6. Literary Response Word Chart

Word	Meaning	Related Words	Picture
Plot			
Character			
Setting			
Imagery			
Figurative language			
Historical context			
Theme			
Symbol			
Tone			

EXHIBIT 6.7. Problem-Solution Cloze

As you've probably heard, more people are overweight today than ever before. Obesity is a medical term for carrying unhealthy weight on your body which can lead to other health problems. Obesity can affect kids and teens as well as _____. So, younger people are now getting health problems that used to affect only adults, like high blood pressure, high cholesterol, and type 2 diabetes.

There are many causes of obesity. Some people have a genetic tendency to gain _____ more easily than others. Although genes strongly influence body type and size, the environment also plays a role. Some people are gaining weight because of unhealthy _____ choices (like fast food) and a lack of exercise. People can be tricked or pressured to make these choices by online advertising and TV commercials. Other people may experience obesity because of other health problems or medications they are taking.

Obesity can lead to many negative health effects. Being overweight increases the risk of developing diabetes, heart disease, high blood pressure, and other serious health conditions. Obesity can also affect a person's overall health and well-being. For example, it _____ affect energy levels, sleep, and self-esteem.

While obesity is a major problem in our society, there are steps we can _____ in order to address it. Making an effort to get more exercise each day can help. Even simple things like taking the stairs or walking to school can have a positive effect. Cutting down on fast food and sugary drinks is _____ way to lead a healthier lifestyle. Learning about the _____ and effects of this problem and sharing this information with others are big steps toward promoting a healthy lifestyle.

It is also important to remember that bodies come in all shapes and sizes and there isn't a "right" weight for someone to be. What is most important is that your body is at a healthy weight for you and that you feel good about yourself.

Source: Adapted from Mary L. Gavin, "Review of 'When Being Overweight Is a Health Problem.'" Retrieved from http://kidshealth.org. https://kidshealth.org/en/teens/obesity.html[7]

Completed Problem-Solution Cloze

Note: This portion of the exhibit should not be reproduced for student use.

As you've probably heard, more people are overweight today than ever before. Obesity is a medical term for carrying unhealthy weight on your body which can lead to other health problems. Obesity can affect kids and teens as well as **adults**. So, younger people are now getting health problems that used to affect only adults, like high blood pressure, high cholesterol, and type 2 diabetes.

There are many causes of obesity. Some people have a genetic tendency to gain **weight** more easily than others. Although genes strongly influence body type and size, the environment also plays a role. Some people are gaining weight because of unhealthy **food** choices (like fast food) and a lack of exercise. People can be tricked or pressured to make these choices by online advertising and TV commercials. Other people may experience obesity because of other health problems or medications they are taking.

Obesity can lead to many negative health effects. Being overweight increases the risk of developing diabetes, heart disease, high blood pressure, and other serious health conditions. Obesity can also affect a person's overall health and well-being. For example, it **can** affect energy levels, sleep, and self-esteem.

While obesity is a major problem in our society, there are steps we can **take** in order to address it. Making an effort to get more exercise each day can help. Even simple things like taking the stairs or walking to school can have a positive effect. Cutting down on fast food and sugary drinks is **another** way to lead a healthier lifestyle. Learning about the **causes** and effects of this problem and sharing this information with others are big steps toward promoting a healthy lifestyle.

It is also important to remember that bodies come in all shapes and sizes and there isn't a "right" weight for someone to be. What is most important is that your body is at a healthy weight for you and that you feel good about yourself.

Source: Adapted from "When Being Overweight Is a Health Problem," (2018). Reviewed by Mary L. Gavin, June. Retrieved from http://kidshealth.org. https://kidshealth.org/en/teens/obesity.html[8]

EXHIBIT 6.8. Problem-Solution Features Data Set

Categories: Hooks, Thesis, Causes, Effects, Solutions

1. Obesity is a widespread problem in our country that needs to be addressed immediately.

2. Many food companies make food that is bad for us and addictive. They advertise these foods to kids and teens which can cause unhealthy weight gain among those who eat these foods.

3. A real solution to the growing problem of obesity is to teach teens about the ways food companies are trying to manipulate (trick) them.

4. Another cause of obesity is that many people don't get enough exercise and spend a lot of time sitting at school or at their jobs.

5. Only allowing fresh, healthy foods at school is another way to reduce obesity among kids and teens.

6. Imagine if schools only served fresh fruits and vegetables and other healthy foods to students. What would be the effect? Would obesity among children go down?

7. In my opinion, obesity is a growing problem that must be addressed so people can live long and healthy lives.

8. Every day, I see advertisements for fast food or sugary drinks on TV. Usually, the people in the ads are smiling and full of energy. Unfortunately, this is not how I feel after I eat junk food!

9. Childhood obesity can affect how children perform in school. If they are eating unhealthy foods and aren't getting much exercise, then they may have less energy for their schoolwork.

10. When you drive through your neighborhood, do you see markets selling fresh food or do you see mostly fast food restaurants? Does this have an impact on the health of the people living in your neighborhood?

11. A serious challenge facing my community is obesity, and something must be done.

12. Obesity can result in devastating health effects like diabetes or heart disease.

13. I believe a big problem in our society is the mass marketing of unhealthy food and drinks to teens. Corporations choose to make money by making people sick and it has to stop.

14. A lack of affordable, healthy food options in the community can lead to unhealthy eating and weight gain.

15. In order to reduce childhood obesity rates, we must make it easier and more affordable for parents to buy fresh fruits and vegetables.

16. One effect of being overweight as a child or teen is being at a higher risk of developing diabetes and asthma.

Categorized Hooks, Thesis, Causes, Effects, Solutions

Note: This portion of the exhibit should not be reproduced for student use.

Hooks

6. Imagine if schools only served fresh fruits and vegetables and other healthy foods to students. What would be the effect? Would obesity among children go down?

8. Every day, I see advertisements for fast food or sugary drinks on TV. Usually, the people in the ads are smiling and full of energy. Unfortunately, this is not how I feel after I eat junk food!

10. When you drive through your neighborhood, do you see markets selling fresh food or do you see mostly fast food restaurants? Does this have an impact on the health of the people living in your neighborhood?

Thesis

1. Obesity is a widespread problem in our country that needs to be addressed immediately.

7. In my opinion, obesity is a growing problem that must be addressed so people can live long and healthy lives.

11. A serious challenge facing my community is obesity, and something must be done.

13. I believe a big problem in our society is the mass marketing of unhealthy food and drinks to teens. Corporations choose to make money by making people sick and it has to stop.

Causes

1. Many food companies make food that is bad for us and addictive. They advertise these foods to kids and teens which can cause unhealthy weight gain among teens who eat these foods.

4. Another cause of obesity is that many people don't get enough exercise and spend a lot of time sitting at school or at their jobs.

14. A lack of affordable, healthy food options in the community can lead to unhealthy eating and weight gain.

Effects

9. Childhood obesity can affect how children perform in school. If they are eating unhealthy foods and aren't getting much exercise, then they may have less energy for their schoolwork.

12. Obesity can result in devastating health effects like diabetes or heart disease.

16. One effect of being overweight as a child or teen is being at a higher risk of developing diabetes and asthma.

Solutions

1. A real solution to the growing problem of obesity is to teach teens about the ways food companies are trying to manipulate (trick) them.

5. Only allowing fresh, healthy foods at school is another way to reduce obesity among kids and teens.

15. In order to reduce childhood obesity rates, we must make it easier and more affordable for parents to buy fresh fruits and vegetables.

- *Mimic writing.* Students can examine multiple examples of certain writing features through strategies like concept attainment, Text Data Sets, and teacher modeling. Then students can mimic these writing features by creating their own examples. For example, students can examine several Yes and No examples of topic sentences and identify the features of a good topic sentence. Then students can write their own topic sentences and evaluate them according to these features. See Exhibit 6.9 for a data set that can be used to teach effective openers or "hooks" through the mimic writing process. We use examples about the topics of obesity, smoking, and unfair grading practices. Since the purpose is to teach the qualities of effective hooks, this data set can be used when teaching any topic and can apply to many genres of writing.

- *Mini-themes and practice essays.* Within a larger problem-solution unit, various mini-themes based on problems chosen by the teacher, or preferably by students, can be explored using many of the strategies in this sample unit plan. For example, we have focused on problems like gun violence, climate change, gangs, immigration laws, and many other current issues within the larger problem-solution unit. After students have been exposed to enough text and information on one of these mini-themes, they can write a practice problem-solution essay on that theme. It can work well for the class to do one together first, with the teacher modeling some sentence frames.

- *Micro-writing.* As we explained in Chapter 5, providing students an opportunity to capture their thinking and practice unit vocabulary through short bursts of writing can serve as a scaffold during the essay writing process. Students can be asked to share their thinking on the problems the class is reading about or the problem they are researching for their final essay by responding to prompts like:

  - What have you learned so far about the problem of _____?
  - Why should people care about solving the problem of _____?
  - What do you think is the biggest cause of _____?
  - If you could solve the problem of _____ tomorrow, what would be the first thing you would do?

  The teacher can model their own responses to these prompts and provide sentence stems if more support is necessary.

- *Dialogues.* Students need a lot of practice with the academic vocabulary required for a problem-solution essay. They need to see it, write it, and *say* it! Students can write dialogues depicting various problems and solutions (see Exhibit 6.10). Another activity we've used to build speaking and writing skills is Exhibit 6.11. This sheet asks students to match several examples of problems with their possible solutions. Then students choose one of the problem-solution scenarios to develop into a "scene" with several lines of dialogue. Students can perform these dialogues for the class or record them for class viewing. See Chapter Eight's discussion on Critical Thinking Dialogues for other ideas.

EXHIBIT 6.9. Types of Hooks Data Set

Categories: Critical Thinking Questions, Anecdotes and Observations, Interesting Facts and Statistics

1. Imagine if schools only served fresh fruits and vegetables and other healthy foods to students. What would be the effect? Would obesity among children go down?

2. In my English language development class, 40 percent of my classmates have at least one F grade in a course even though they are working very hard and attending class each day.

3. There is a problem I see every day in my neighborhood. It affects the old, the young, and teenagers. When you live with someone who smokes, then there is no way to escape the effects of second-hand smoke.

4. How would you feel if you attended class each day and worked your hardest to learn a new language, but the teacher gave you an F?

5. My aunt was diagnosed with lung cancer last year. Did she smoke a pack a day? No. Did she smoke earlier in her life and then quit? No. Did she live with my uncle who has smoked for the last 30 years? Yes.

6. The food industry spends $1.6 billion a year on ads for kids promoting foods that are high in calories and low in nutrition. In fact, teens between the ages of 13–17 see on average 17 food ads a day.

7. My friend Malal never missed a day of school last quarter. He took an extra English class every morning. However, one of his teachers gave him an F because he couldn't complete his test in time and couldn't write all of his answers in English.

8. When you drive through your neighborhood, do you see markets selling fresh food or do you see mostly fast food restaurants? Does this have an impact on the health of the people living in your neighborhood?

9. Second-hand smoke kills tens of thousands of people every year in the United States and causes life-threatening illnesses for thousands more.

10. Every day, I see advertisements for fast food or sugary drinks on TV. Usually, the people in the ads are smiling and full of energy. Unfortunately, this is not how I feel after I eat junk food!

11. What if you were diagnosed with lung cancer when you had never even smoked a cigarette before? Is that even possible? How would you react? Unfortunately, this situation can happen to nonsmokers who have been exposed to second-hand smoke.

12. Childhood obesity has more than tripled in the past 30 years. Almost 20 percent of children and adolescents in the United States are overweight.

Note: This portion of the exhibit should not be reproduced for student use.

Critical Thinking Questions

1. Imagine if schools only served fresh fruits and vegetables and other healthy foods to students. What would be the effect? Would obesity among children go down?

4. How would you feel if you attended class each day and worked your hardest to learn a new language, but the teacher gave you an F?

8. When you drive through your neighborhood, do you see markets selling fresh food or do you see mostly fast food restaurants? Does this have an impact on the health of the people living in your neighborhood?

11. What if you were diagnosed with lung cancer when you had never even smoked a cigarette before? Is that even possible? How would you react? Unfortunately, this situation can happen to nonsmokers who have been exposed to second-hand smoke.

Anecdotes and Observations

3. There is a problem I see every day in my neighborhood. It affects the old, the young, and teenagers. When you live with someone who smokes, then there is no way to escape the effects of second-hand smoke.

5. My aunt was diagnosed with lung cancer last year. Did she smoke a pack a day? No. Did she smoke earlier in her life and then quit? No. Did she live with my uncle who has smoked for the last thirty years? Yes.

7. My friend Malal never missed a day of school last quarter. He took an extra English class every morning. However, one of his teachers gave him an F because he couldn't complete his test in time and couldn't write all of his answers in English.

10. Every day, I see advertisements for fast food or sugary drinks on TV. Usually, the people in the ads are smiling and full of energy. Unfortunately, this is not how I feel after I eat junk food!

Interesting Facts and Statistics

1. In my English Language Development class, 40 percent of my classmates have at least one F grade in a course even though they are working very hard and attending class each day.

6. The food industry spends $1.6 billion a year on ads for kids promoting foods that are high in calories and low in nutrition. In fact, teens between the ages of 13–17 see on average seventeen food ads a day.

9. Second-hand smoke kills tens of thousands of people every year in the United States and causes life-threatening illnesses for thousands more.

12. Childhood obesity has more than tripled in the past 30 years. Almost 20 percent of children and adolescents in the United States are overweight.

EXHIBIT 6.10. Problem Dialogue

Student 1: I hate going to the bathrooms at school. They are so dirty!

Student 2: I know—the floors are disgusting and the sinks look like they haven't been cleaned in a long time.

Student 1: The soap dispenser is empty, and there aren't any paper towels.

Student 2: How are we supposed to wash our hands and stop the spread of germs if we don't have any soap?

Student 1: What can we do about it? Should we tell our teacher?

Student 2: I think we should talk to our teacher and the principal. This is a big problem and we need help.

Student 1: You're right. We have to do something if we want to make a change.

Student 2: Come on—let's go talk to the teacher.

Student 1: Okay, maybe she can tell us how to meet with the principal.

Student 2: Good idea! Let's go!

EXHIBIT 6.11. Problem-Solution Matching and Dialogue

Match the problem with the solution.

Problems:

I don't have any money. Will you give me some money?

It's raining and I don't want to walk home.

Help! I'm drowning!

I have a date tonight! What should I wear?

The bear is going to eat you!

I feel nervous speaking English.

I didn't do my homework. Can I copy yours?

I'm hungry.

Solutions:

No you cannot. You need to do your own work.

A black shirt and a pair of jeans.

Practice speaking with your friends in this class.

Run!

Here is five dollars.

Call your parents for a ride.

Here is a sandwich.

I'll save you!

Choose one of the problem-solution situations above and work with a partner to write a 7–10 line dialogue about this situation. You can use the phrases above to help you get started. Write your dialogue here:

SCAFFOLDING THE WRITING PROCESS

Research shows the fluency, accuracy, and complexity of ELL writing increases when they are given time and support for planning before writing.[8] In the activities on building background knowledge, students did a variety of reading, thinking, speaking, and writing about problems and solutions. They also learned and practiced the academic language needed for a problem-solution essay. They are now ready to begin the process of planning and drafting their essay.

- *Revisiting and dissecting the prompt.* We redistribute Exhibit 6.3 and teach students how to carefully read and "dissect" the prompt. The first step is to read it carefully and underline any key words or phrases, especially words that are telling them to do something. Then, we have students number the specific tasks (what they must do first, second, third, and so on). We also have them draw a box for each number that they can use as a graphic organizer to list ideas and words. Sometimes, with more complicated prompts, we have students rewrite the key tasks in their own words. For more on this process and an illustrated example, see the Using Text to Generate Analytical Writing Lesson Plan later in this chapter.

- *Choosing a Topic.* Students can then choose a problem that they would like to write about for their final problem-solution essay. The topic can be a problem in their lives, at their school, or in the larger community or world. The teacher can lead students in a brainstorming process to select their topic using criteria such as, "Is it interesting to you? Would it have an impact on others?" We have also asked students to make a list of problems they might be interested in writing about. Then for each one, asking them to answer the question "How would this being solved make the world a better place?"

- *Research.* Part of their research can involve interviewing students, family, and teachers (see Exhibit 6.12). This activity allows students to practice their interviewing and speaking skills while also collecting more ideas for their writing.

Students can also research their problem online. They can use a simple graphic organizer divided into sections for notes on causes, effects, and solutions to their problem. This kind of tool helps them categorize the information, allows them to keep all their research notes in one spot, and provides a graphic organizer for their use while drafting the essay. While it may be easier for students to use a digital graphic organizer where they can copy and paste information, we like to encourage them to take notes on paper so they can practice culling and transcribing key information. Of course, it helps to model this process for students and it works best when students are visiting sites where the text is accessible for their proficiency level. See the Tech Tool on search engines for resources on making research more accessible for ELLs.

Tech Tool

Search Engines for English Language Learners

Doing research online can be especially challenging for ELL students as they try to navigate through all the clutter of search engine results. For a list of search engines that we have found particularly accessible for English language learners see "The Best Search Engines for ESL/EFL Learners" at

https://larryferlazzo.edublogs.org/2009/11/13/the-best-search-engines-for-eslefl-learners-%e2%80%94-2009/.

EXHIBIT 6.12. Problem-Solution Interview

My name _____

Your assignment is to ask two students, one adult who works at our school, and one family member, the following questions about the problem you have chosen as the topic of your problem-solution essay. You will write their answers in the space below the questions.

Name of student interviewed: _____

What do you think are the causes of _____?

_____

_____

_____

What do you think are the consequences (effects) of _____?

_____

_____

_____

What do you think are possible solutions to this problem?

_____

_____

_____

Name of student interviewed: _____

What do you think are the causes of _____?

_____

_____

_____

What do you think are the consequences (effects) of _____?

_____

_____

_____

What do you think are possible solutions to this problem?

_____

_____

_____

Name of staff member:

What do you think are the causes of _____?

_____

_____

_____

What do you think are the consequences (effects) of _____?

_____

_____

_____

What do you think are possible solutions to this problem?

_____

_____

_____

Name of family member: _____

What do you think are the causes of _____?

_____

_____

_____

What do you think are the consequences (effects) of _____?

_____

_____

_____

What do you think are possible solutions to this problem?

_____

_____

_____

- *Mentor texts/models.* It is important for students to see good models of problem-solution writing. Many examples can be found online (see the upcoming Tech Tool on online writing resources). These samples can also be written by the teacher or be student examples from previous years. Students can read the sample essays and identify the organizational and language features of problem-solution writing. See Exhibit 6.16 in the Inductive Lesson Plan later in this chapter for one of the sample essays we use with students as part of our problem-solution unit.

- *Oral outlining.* Having students do an oral outline of their essay can reinforce the essay structure in a metacognitive way. Students can explain aloud step-by-step how they will write their essay: "In my introduction, I will start with an interesting hook. Then, I will describe the problem." The teacher can provide students with a cloze to complete (see next example) or ask students to write out the steps on their own. Then students can practice reciting their oral outline aloud with a partner or even record themselves. They could then share their recordings with the class or with their families.

Here is an example of a cloze our students completed before writing their problem-solution drafts:

> Tomorrow, I will begin writing my problem- _____ essay. I will start my essay with a _____ and I will state the problem. Then I will describe the _____ of the problem and the effects of the _____. In each of my body paragraphs, I will present a _____ to the problem and will explain how it will work. Then I will describe the pros and _____ of each solution. In my conclusion, I will restate the _____ and explain which solution is the _____. I will give specific _____ to support why I believe it is the best solution.

- *Drafting—Writing Frames and Structures.* Before students begin the drafting process, they can consult all of the activities in their problem-solution folder (including the problem-solution writing prompt) and use this prewriting to complete an outline of their essay.

Depending upon the range of proficiency levels within a class, the teacher can decide whether some students need the additional support of sentence stems or frames to help with the drafting process (see the section "Writing Frames and Writing Structures" in Chapter Five). For example, the teacher and students can develop topic sentences together, or the teacher can give students several examples of transition words. The teacher can also give students who need more support a copy of Exhibit 6.13, which contains writing frames for each section of the essay. Students who need less support can complete the outline in Exhibit 6.14 which contains a writing structure for students to follow. Some of the scaffolds in this outline can be removed for students with higher English proficiency.

Note: We emphasize to students that writing does not follow a certain "formula," and essays aren't a certain number of paragraphs. Writing frames and structures can serve as guides or maps, especially when writing in a new language. But once students become familiar with the "roads and directions" on the map, then they can start to navigate on their own with less direct guidance.

EXHIBIT 6.13. Problem-Solution Writing Frames

Use some or all of these sentence frames to help you write your draft of your Problem-Solution Essay.

Introduction

My thesis (What is wrong and why I care) :

In my opinion,_____ is a widespread problem.

A serious challenge facing my community is _____

I believe a very large problem is _____

_____ is a growing problem that must be addressed.

Causes of problem (Why is this happening?):

One of the main causes of _____is _____

Another cause is _____

_____ is also caused by _____.

Effects of problem (What is happening because of this problem?):

_____ can result in _____

One effect of _____is _____

_____ can affect _____.

So what? (What are the consequences if the problem isn't solved? Why should we care?)

If this problem is not solved, then _____

Not addressing this problem could result in _____.

Body Paragraph

One solution to this problem is _____.

How it will work:

The first step to make this solution happen is _____. The second step is _____. The third step is _____.

Pros:

One advantage to this solution is _____. Another benefit of this solution is _____.

Cons:

One disadvantage to this solution is _____

Counterargument(s) to address cons:

This disadvantage can be overcome by _____

Body Paragraph

Another solution to this problem is _____

How it will work:

The first step to make this solution happen is _____. The second step is _____. The third step is _____.

Pros:

One advantage to this solution is _____. Another benefit of this solution is _____.

Cons:

One disadvantage to this solution is _____

Counterargument(s) to address cons:

This disadvantage can be overcome by _____

Conclusion

Restate problem and its consequences:

As I stated earlier, _____

Best solution:

I think the best solution is _____

Reasons why it is best:

This is the best solution because _____. Another reason is _____.

EXHIBIT 6.14. Problem-Solution Writing Structure

Use this outline to organize your thinking before writing your essay. You don't need to write complete sentences. Instead, write key words and ideas that will help you as you begin to draft your essay.

Introduction

Hook:

_____

_____

My thesis (What is wrong and why I care):

_____

_____

Causes of problem (Why is this happening?):

_____

_____

Effects of problem (What is happening because of this problem?):

_____

_____

So what? (What are the consequences if the problem isn't solved? Why should we care?):

_____

_____

Body Paragraph 1

Solution:

_____

_____

How it will work:

_____

_____

Pros:

_____

_____

Cons:

_____

_____

Counterargument(s) to address cons:

_____

_____

Body Paragraph 2

Solution:

How it will work:

_____

_____

Pros:

_____

_____

Cons:

_____

_____

Counterargument(s) to address cons:

_____

_____

Conclusion

Restate problem and its consequences:

_____

_____

Best solution:

_____

_____

Reasons why it is best:

_____

_____

_____

_____

- *Revising.*

  Teacher Feedback. Once students have produced a draft, it is important that they receive immediate feedback in order to make revisions. Research shows that the quality of student work increases when students are expecting to receive "rapid" feedback from the teacher—a teacher's verbal or written response shortly after the work or test is completed.[9] This can be done effectively by circulating around the room as students are drafting and offering verbal feedback. Conferencing one-on-one with students after they have finished a draft is also a good way to give both verbal and written feedback. To make the process go more smoothly, it is important for all students to be engaged in an activity while the teacher is conferring with individual students. Having students identify one or two parts of the draft they want the teacher to help them with can make these conferences more effective.

  Peer Feedback. Research shows that peer review can result in improved student writing and can increase the ability of ELL students to self-edit and revise their future writing.[10] One way we facilitate peer review is by having students exchange papers and complete a peer review sheet like the Problem-Solution Peer Checklist (see Exhibit 6.15). It is most effective to first model its use with the whole class using a sample essay. Then students can be divided into pairs, exchange their papers, complete the checklist, discuss it with each other, and then make needed changes to their own drafts. Another strategy we use builds on the work of educator Ron Berger's approach to feedback focusing on three guidelines: Be Kind, Be Specific, Be Helpful.[11] We provide our students with sentence frames to support these three types of responses. We often have students write their feedback on sticky notes after modeling the process first. Search "Be Kind, Be Specific, Be Helpful sentence starters" online for many examples to use with students or you can create your own.

- *Editing.*

  Teacher Feedback. Error correction is best addressed through concept attainment and games—activities that teach students grammar in context and without a red pen! See Chapter Three for a description of using concept attainment for error correction. Chapter 16 describes other error correction strategies and the research behind them. Chapter 18 shares examples of error correction learning games.

  Peer Feedback. A simple, but effective way for students to assist one another in the editing process is by reading their writing aloud to a partner. We have found this activity helps the reader to more easily catch errors than by just silently reading over their essay on their own. They also get the added bonus of a second set of ears by reading to a partner!

EXHIBIT 6.15. Problem-Solution Peer Checklist

My name: _____ **My partner's name:** _____

1. Is there a **hook** at the beginning of the essay?
   Yes   No
   What kind of **hook** is it?

2. Does the writer include a thesis stating the problem?
   Yes   No

3. Does the writer explain the **causes** of the problem?
   Yes   No
   Copy the **causes** here:

4. Does the writer explain the **effects** of the problem?
   Yes   No
   Copy the **effects** here:

5. Does the writer propose **two solutions** to the problem?
   Yes   No
   Copy each **solution** here:

   1.

   2.

   Is there a separate **body paragraph** for each solution?
   Yes   No
   Does each paragraph have a **clear topic sentence**?
   Yes   No
   (Highlight each topic sentence.)
   Does the writer explain how the **solution** will work?
   Yes   No

6. Is there a **conclusion** where the problem is restated?
   Yes   No
   Does the writer explain which solution is **best** and give reasons **why**?
   Yes   No

7. Did your partner read his or her essay **aloud** to you in order to catch errors?
   Yes   No

- *Publishing or presenting.* As mentioned earlier in Chapter Five, Speed Dating is a way for students to share their work. When sharing an essay, students can read their whole essay or just choose specific parts. Another way to share their final products is to post them online. This can be done on an individual class blog or through creating a sister class relationship where students from different schools post their work on a shared blog and can read and comment on each other's writing. Students can also share their writing with peers the old-fashioned way by exchanging essays with another class and writing comments on sticky notes.

Writing for an authentic audience of their peers is motivating for most students. As educator Anne Rodier powerfully states, "Students have to believe that what they have to say is important enough to bother writing. They have to experience writing for real audiences before they will know that writing can bring them power."[12]

Tech Tool
Online Writing Resources

A variety of activities available online reinforce the thinking and language required for problem-solution writing and many other genres of writing. For a list of resources related to writing instruction for many different genres see "The Best Websites for K–12 Writing Instruction Reinforcement" at https://larryferlazzo.edublogs .org/2008/01/11/the-best-websites-for-k-12-writing-instructionreinforcment/. For links to sites containing online reinforcement activities where students can write for an authentic audience, see "The Best Online Tools That Can Help Students Write an Essay" at https://larryferlazzo.edublogs.org/2015/06/29/am-i-missing-something-or-are-there-very-few-online-tools-than-can-help-students-write-an-essay/. For ideas on peer review see "The Best Ideas on Peer Review of Student Writing" at https:// larryferlazzo.edublogs.org/2019/05/12/the-best-ideas-on-peer-review-of-student-writing/ and for resources on revision see "The Best Resources on Getting Student Writers to 'Buy-Into' Revision" at https://larryferlazzo.edublogs.org/2015/07/23/ the-best-resources-on-getting-student-writers-to-buy-into-revision-help-me-find-more/. Finally, for a comprehensive collection of resources on writing instruction, see "My Best Posts on Writing Instruction" at https://larryferlazzo.edublogs.org/ 2013/06/13/my-best-posts-on-writing-instruction/.

- *Assessment.* If they wish, teachers can create a rubric appropriate for their classroom situation. For more on using rubrics and other forms of assessments with student writing, see Chapter Nineteen. Also, see the Tech Tool on Online Rubrics.

  Note: We usually teach this genre in the sequence we've just described. Taking substantial time to build background knowledge and academic language before students complete a culminating problem-solution essay on a problem of their choice works well for many intermediate level students. However, for students with less English proficiency, we sometimes have them identify their own problem for research at the beginning of the unit and support them in writing their essay in sections after each individual lesson. For example, after completing the Hooks Data Set, we may have students write the hook for their own essay. Or, after the Problem-Solution Features Data Set, students can identify the specific causes and effects for their problem.

EXTENSIONS

- *Action projects.* The problem-solution unit provides students with the opportunity to extend their writing into action projects. For example, one of our ELL classes was studying the issue of getting a good job and the problems involved with this pursuit. The class decided to take action by organizing a meeting focused on job training opportunities. They organized, planned, and led a multilingual meeting of area job training providers that was attended by 150 parents and students![13]

Tech Tool

Online Rubrics

There are many free online sites where teachers can find premade rubrics or create their own. For a list of resources, see "The Best Rubric Sites and a Beginning Discussion About Their Use" at https://larryferlazzo.edublogs.org/2010/09/18/the-best-rubric-sites-and-a-beginning-discussion-about-their-use/.

- *On-demand writing practice.* The above activities are designed to support students as they move through the writing process over the course of several weeks. However, English language learners also need practice with on-demand writing assessments (writing to a prompt in a timed situation). See the lesson plan on Using Text to Generate Analytical Writing later in this chapter for ways to help students practice this type of writing and thinking.

Sample Lesson Plans

Inductive Lesson Plan

This lesson is used during a unit on problem-solution writing after students have done a number of activities to build knowledge and vocabulary related to this genre. See the sample problem-solution unit earlier in this chapter for the sequence of activities students would do prior to the lesson and afterwards. This lesson was designed around the topics of obesity, corporate manipulation of teens by the food industry, and the lack of access to healthy food in the community, which were concerns of our students at the time. However, the activities described in this lesson can work with any problem that your students are experiencing or are interested in learning about.

INSTRUCTIONAL OBJECTIVES

Students will:

1. Read text and demonstrate use of reading strategies.
2. Identify different features of a problem-solution essay through categorization.
3. Apply knowledge of features of an essay by labeling them on a sample essay.

DURATION

Two 120-minute class sessions or four to five 60-minute class sessions.

This inductive lesson correlates with the: Anchor Standards for Reading—Key Ideas and Details, Craft and Structure, Integration of Knowledge and Ideas; Anchor Standards For Writing—Text Types and Purposes, Production and Distribution of Writing, Research to Build and Present Knowledge, Range of Writing; Anchor Standards for Speaking and Listening—Comprehension and Collaboration; Anchor Standards for Language—Conventions of Standard English, Knowledge of Language, Vocabulary Acquisition and Use.

MATERIALS

1. Copies of Problem-Solution Features Data Set (Exhibit 6.8) for students and teacher.
2. Copies of Problem-Solution Sample Essay (Exhibit 6.16) for students and teacher.

PROCEDURE

First Day

1. Teacher writes "Problem-Solution Essay" on the board and asks students to quickly brainstorm everything they have learned so far about problem-solution writing. Students list their ideas on a piece of paper and then share in pairs. Teacher facilitates a class discussion of what students have learned. The teacher then explains that students will be expanding upon this knowledge by reading a Text Data Set that contains several important features of a problem-solution essay: hooks, thesis, causes, effects, and solutions. Students can use their Problem-Solution Word Charts (see Exhibit 6.4) to review the meanings of these words.

2. Teacher explains that students will be doing a data set next with two goals in mind: to learn new information about this topic, but more important, to identify the key features in a problem-solution essay. Teacher distributes the Problem-Solution Features Data Set (Exhibit 6.8) and models reading the first three examples, thinking aloud while highlighting key words (in this case, any problem or solution words) and writing questions and/or connections in the margin.

3. Teacher posts written directions for students to continue reading individually, to highlight any problem-solution words, and to write at least two more questions and make at least two more connections. Teacher circulates as students are working to check highlighting and to look for evidence of reading strategies. When finished, students share their highlighting and comments with a partner and add one new question from their partner's paper.

4. Teacher explains to students that next they will be putting the examples into categories. Students cut out all of the 16 examples (being careful not to cut off the numbers) and spread the strips out on their desks. Depending on the class, the teacher may display the categories up front (Hooks, Thesis, Causes, Effects, and Solutions) or lead students in coming to some conclusions on their own by asking questions such as these: Are any of these examples similar? Why? Which examples would you group together? Why? What would you call that group? The teacher reads an example and models thinking aloud about why they think that example goes in a certain category and circles the clue words.

5. Teacher posts written directions: "Put each example into a category and circle any clue words that make you think it belongs in that category." Students begin to group the examples into categories, working side-by-side with a partner. Teacher circulates and offers assistance and praises good thinking. The inductive process works best when *students* are doing the thinking, so it is important that the teacher remain neutral and not tell students where to put the examples. The teacher can respond to student questions with

responses like, "Which category do *you* think it belongs in? What is your reasoning? Which category does that example *not* belong in? How can that help you figure this out?"

6. Once students have arranged the examples into categories on their desks, they compare their work with a partner. The teacher asks partners to share with the class which examples were difficult or placed in different categories. Teacher facilitates a class discussion about these examples and guides students to correct category placement by prompting *them* to do the thinking. Once all the examples are correctly placed, students make a category poster by writing the five category titles on a large piece of paper and then gluing or taping the examples underneath (see the student sample of a category poster in Figure 6.1).

Figure 6.1.   Student Sample of Category Poster for Data Set (Photo)

Second Day

1. The teacher asks students to take out their category posters and review their categories from the previous day. Teacher explains that now that the data set is categorized, students will examine the features, or characteristics, of each category. The teacher asks students questions like "What do all the *hooks* have in common? How are all the *causes* similar?"

2. Students work in pairs to make a list of common features underneath each category on their poster. Teacher explains that they will call on different pairs to share about one category.

3. Students take a few minutes to discuss their answers to the questions and then the teacher leads a whole-class conversation by calling on pairs to share what they talked about. Teacher records the features or characteristics of each category on the board, and students add any new ideas to their posters.

4. Teacher distributes a problem-solution sample essay (Exhibit 6.16) and explains that students will use their knowledge of the features of problem-solution writing to label them on the sample essay. Teacher reads the essay aloud for students. Teacher posts directions: "Reread the sample essay. Label the following features: *hook, thesis, causes, effects,* and *solutions.* Circle any clue words that help you, and remember the common features of each category."

5. Students work individually to reread the sample essay and to label the hook, thesis, causes, effects, and solutions on the sample essay. Students circle clues that help them figure out a certain feature. When finished, students share their work with a partner and discuss any differences. The teacher circulates and encourages students to share their thinking about why they labeled certain features.

6. Teacher calls on partners to share their findings and facilitates a whole-class discussion on where each feature can be found in the sample essay. Students make notes and revise their previous guesses as needed.

ASSESSMENT

Teachers can assess student understanding of problem-solution features by reviewing students' categories and the students' labeling of the sample essay.

POSSIBLE EXTENSIONS AND MODIFICATIONS

- *Concept attainment.* The teacher can show students Yes and No examples of hooks and theses and have students evaluate *why* each example is a Yes or a No.

- *Mimic writing.* After examining the characteristics of each category, students can create their own examples for each category.

- *Jigsaw.* Students can be divided into groups and each group given a different sample problem-solution essay. Each group can label the features on their sample essay and then share with another group. See Chapter Three and Chapter Eight for more details on how to use this strategy.

- *Synthesis.* Each group receives three different sample essays and creates a large chart, writing the five features—hook, thesis, causes, effects, and solutions—along the top and the three essay titles down the left-hand side. The group reads all three essays and identifies the different features by cutting them out and gluing them underneath the correct category on the large chart (see the student sample of synthesis in Figure 6.2).

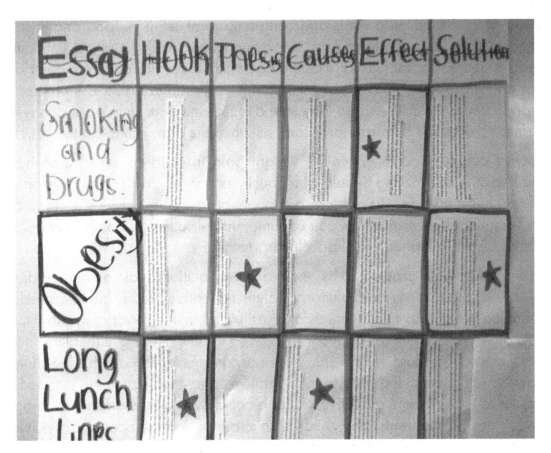

Figure 6.2. Student Sample of Synthesis Chart Poster (Photo)

EXHIBIT 6.16. Problem-Solution Sample Essay

Every day, I see advertisements for fast food or sugary drinks on TV. Usually, the people in the ads are smiling and full of energy. Unfortunately, this is not how I feel after I eat junk food!

Many teenagers and children in our country are targeted by food companies who want them to keep buying and eating food and drinks that are highly unhealthy and very addictive. When teens eat unhealthy food and don't get enough physical activity, they are at a higher risk of obesity and the health issues that come with it. Obesity among young people is a growing problem that must be stopped. If this challenge is not addressed, then many youth will be at risk of experiencing dangerous health effects in the future.

There are different causes of obesity in young people. Many kids don't have access to healthy food choices at school and in their homes. Some communities have plenty of fast food restaurants, but not many Farmers Markets, fresh food stands, or even grocery stores. Fast food restaurants and companies that sell junk food and sugary treats often directly market their products to young people. So, making unhealthy food cheaper and easier for kids to access than healthier options can be a contributing factor to rising obesity rates among the young. Children are also less physically active than in decades past because they spend more time watching TV and playing video games. They don't burn as many calories when they are sitting on the couch.

These factors can all lead to unhealthy weight gain in children, which can have numerous health effects. Young people with obesity are at a higher risk of developing diabetes and heart disease. They can also experience low energy levels, sleep problems, and emotional effects like low self-esteem. Another effect of being overweight as a child or teen is a higher risk of developing asthma.

While this is not an easy problem to fix, there are two solutions that can help address the challenge of obesity. My first solution involves education. Young people need to learn about the dangerous health effects of obesity and, more importantly, how they are being directly targeted with advertising by companies selling unhealthy food. This type of education could involve students analyzing junk food ads for false information as well as researching the types of additives and chemicals being added to food in order to make it more addictive. Schools could even offer workshops throughout the year for both parents and children in order to learn about healthy living choices. The main advantage of this solution is that it addresses the problem at its core and can have long-term effects if it is sustained over time. Some may argue that this solution would be too expensive for schools to implement. However, this initiative could be funded by government grants or even sponsored by health care agencies. This kind of education would even reduce health care costs in the future.

A second solution to the problem of rising obesity rates among young people is to make school food healthier and more appealing. If schools provided a variety of fresh foods including fruits and vegetables, then many students would have access to a healthy breakfast and lunch five days a week. Over time, this could really have an impact on the health of millions of children across the country. Others may argue it is too difficult for schools to prepare and serve fresh foods. However, many schools already have gardens or land that could be turned into areas for growing fruits and vegetables. Students could participate in growing and even cooking the food that is then served to them in the school cafeteria.

What is the best way to solve this growing problem of obesity? I believe that educating young people is the best way to solve the problem in the long run. This solution is most powerful because people can always make better, healthier choices in their lives if they have access to information. Using schools to spread this information is the best way to reach millions of children and teens in our country. If we can address this problem with young people now, we will see healthier, happier adults in our future.

Using Text to Generate Analytical Writing
Lesson Plan

The following lesson plan uses the story "Monsy and Michelle" (see Exhibit 6.17) from the book *I Felt Like I Was from Another Planet: Writing from Personal Experience*, which contains 15 personal stories written by adolescent English Language Learners. While the book is quite old, the still relevant stories touch on racism, stereotypes, and biases. "Monsy and Michelle" engages students, spurs them to think more about problems and solutions, and challenges them to develop their analytical thinking and writing skills. We have used this lesson both as an extension of the problem-solution genre unit and as a stand-alone lesson. While some of the activities described here are specifically tailored to this story, they can easily be adapted to work with other stories and be applied in multiple ways.

The writing prompt in this lesson is based on the style of prompts used in the Analytical Writing Placement Examination (AWPE), the entry-level writing assessment that many incoming University of California freshmen are required to take. Every AWPE assessment contains a piece of text and a multiple-step prompt that requires students to analyze the author's ideas and generate their own response or claim, supported by examples. In this lesson, intermediate students can produce a multi-paragraph response to a college-level style prompt using summarization and argument skills!

INSTRUCTIONAL OBJECTIVES

Students will:

1. Read a student-written story and demonstrate their understanding by completing a summarization chart.
2. Learn new vocabulary words.
3. Practice reading and dissecting an on-demand writing prompt.
4. Use the prompt to develop an outline and to write an analytical, multi-paragraph response.

DURATION

Two 120-minute class sessions or four sixty-minute class sessions.

Using text to generate analytical writing correlates with the: Anchor Standards for Reading—Key Ideas and Details, Craft and Structure; Anchor Standards For Writing—Text Types and Purposes, Production and Distribution of Writing, Range of Writing; Anchor Standards for Language—Conventions of Standard English, Vocabulary Acquisition and Use.

MATERIALS

1. Copies of the book *I Felt Like I Was from Another Planet: Writing from Personal Experience* by Norine Dresser (1994) or copies of the story "Monsy and Michelle" (Exhibit 6.17) for students and teacher
2. Copies of pre reading strategies (Exhibit 6.18) for students and teacher
3. Copies of the summarization sheet (Exhibit 6.19) for students and teacher
4. Copies of the writing prompt (Exhibit 6.20) for students and teacher

EXHIBIT 6.17. Monsy and Michelle

I am Mexican American and my friends call me Monsy. In the seventh grade, I met Michelle, an African American. From the beginning of that year, I had always felt scared of African Americans, so when I first saw Michelle in my history class I did not want to sit close to her. Many of the other students did not want to sit close to her either. The boys always made fun of her. They laughed at her because of the way she dressed, how she combed her hair, and because of her skin color. Although the teacher always told the class to be quiet when we laughed at jokes about Michelle, sometimes we got so carried away we made her cry.

At first, I made fun of her, too, but only because I didn't want other students to make fun of me. Since I have a brownish complexion, I thought they would probably make bad jokes about me, too. After two weeks I got tired and sad that some students still continued to make fun of her. The following week, I began to sit next to her.

Michelle was surprised and smiled at me. Everyone in the class was shocked. They began making fun of me. They told me that I was dirty like her, that we were black because we didn't take showers. I felt very bad and I began to cry. I got so angry that one day, I stood up in class and shouted at the other students. They all stood quiet. I told them that it wasn't fair to make fun of people because of their appearance and culture. In fact, Michelle was the smartest student in class. Michelle was so happy I stood up for her that we became very good friends.

Through this experience I learned that all people are the same no matter what they look like. I learned that because of the different cultures we have in this country we can learn many new things that help us have a more interesting life. By speaking out and proving to others what you are able to do, you can make a difference. Michelle and I found out that each human being is unique in appearance, but many feel the same inside. As a result of this experience I learned not to be scared of...those from different cultures.

Source: Dresser, N. (1994). *I Felt Like I Was from Another Planet: Writing from Personal Experience.* Boston: Addison Wesley. Pearson Education.

EXHIBIT 6.18. "Monsy and Michelle" Pre Reading Strategies

Talk with a partner and write anything you know about these words:

complexion:

appearance:

prejudice:

ethnicity:

Pre Reading Question

Have you or someone you know ever experienced prejudice because of your physical appearance, age, religion, or ethnicity? Explain what happened.

EXHIBIT 6.19. "Monsy and Michelle" Summarization Sheet

Work with a partner to complete this chart.

Problem:

Causes:

Effects:

Solutions:

EXHIBIT 6.20. "Monsy and Michelle" Writing Prompt

In the story "Monsy and Michelle," Monsy tells of her experience with prejudice and explains what she learned from this experience. In your essay, describe Monsy's views on prejudice. To what extent do you agree with Monsy's opinions? To develop your position, be sure to write specific examples from your own experiences, your observations of others, or any of your reading, including this story.

PROCEDURE

First Day

1. Teacher distributes the "Monsy and Michelle" pre-reading strategies (Exhibit 6.18). The teacher reads the new vocabulary words and gives students a few minutes to write down what they already know about them. They then share in pairs. The teacher asks students to share their guesses and guides students toward a correct definition of each word. Students revise their guesses as needed and write down the correct meanings. Then, students write a response to the pre reading question: "Have you or someone you know ever experienced prejudice because of your physical appearance, age, religion, or ethnicity? Explain what happened."

2. Teacher distributes copies of the story "Monsy and Michelle" (Exhibit 6.17). Teacher begins by asking students to write two predictions they have about the story using the pre reading strategies and the title of the story.

3. Teacher reads the story aloud, stopping after each paragraph and asking students to use one reading strategy of their choice by writing a question, a prediction, a connection, a summary statement, or the like in the margin. Students can also write their comments on sticky notes and stick them on the page. (After they have finished the lesson, students can attach all these responses to a piece of paper and turn them in for the teacher to review.)

4. Students work in pairs for ten minutes to complete the summarization sheet (Exhibit 6.19). Teacher asks students to share and records their ideas on a copy of the chart displayed using a document camera. Teacher and students discuss differences in student responses, and the teacher guides students toward correct responses.

5. Teacher distributes copies of the writing prompt (Exhibit 6.20) and reads it aloud to students. Teacher asks students to reflect on what they've learned about reading and responding to prompts. Teacher asks students to share and then reviews how to "dissect" a prompt:

   - Read the prompt once all the way through
   - Underline words that are unfamiliar and use context clues to make a guess about what the word means
   - Reread the prompt and circle key words (words that are telling you to do something and/or key words that are repeated more than once)
   - Write a number next to each place you are asked to do something (like numbering the steps in directions)
   - Draw boxes around each number so you can brainstorm your ideas for each step of the prompt

Students write these down on a sheet of paper and staple the sheet to their writing prompt.

Second Day

1. The teacher asks students to think about the previous day's lesson and to work in partners to write down all the steps of "dissecting" a prompt. Teacher circulates, and when most students have finished, the teacher calls on several pairs to share what they remembered. Teacher asks students to take out all their materials from the previous day, including the writing prompt and the steps for dissecting a prompt. The teacher tells students that now that they have reviewed how to dissect a prompt, they will use this strategy with the "Monsy and Michelle" writing prompt (Exhibit 6.20). Teacher gives students five minutes to dissect the prompt on their own. If students need more support, this activity can be done together, with the teacher modeling and then students trying it out. Teacher circulates, checking for understanding and offering assistance.

2. The teacher then models drawing three boxes numbered 1, 2, and 3 underneath the prompt and explains that students will use the boxes to brainstorm ideas for responding to each section of the prompt. The teacher models this process and provides a sentence starter in each box (see the sample in Figure 6.3). Students use the sentence frames as springboards to add ideas to each box. Teacher circulates and chooses a few good examples to quickly post on the document camera or reads them aloud.

3. After students have completed their boxes, the teacher models how to use this pre-writing exercise to develop a longer response to the prompt. The teacher models how to cite the title and author when responding to a prompt linked to a piece of text. As a class, the teacher and students develop a few different hooks that can be used to engage the reader. They can also develop a thesis statement (or claim) that students can use or modify. Then the teacher models how the ideas in each box can be organized into a separate body paragraph with a topic sentence and supporting details. Last, the teacher models how to write a concluding paragraph that summarizes the thesis and includes a reflection.

4. Students then use this graphic organizer to write a multiple-paragraph response. Teacher circulates, offering verbal feedback on organization and content.

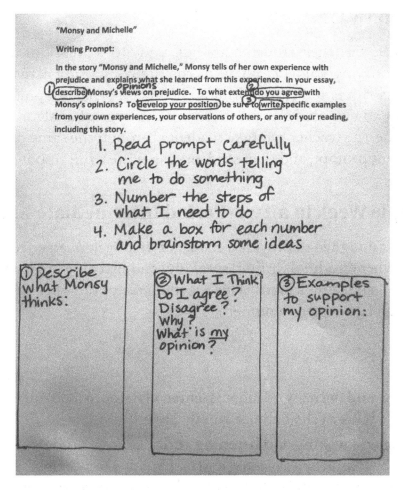

"Monsy and Michelle"

Writing Prompt:

In the story "Monsy and Michelle," Monsy tells of her own experience with prejudice and explains what she learned from this experience. In your essay, describe Monsy's views on prejudice. To what extent do you agree with Monsy's opinions? To develop your position be sure to write specific examples from your own experiences, your observations of others, or any of your reading, including this story.

1. Read prompt carefully
2. Circle the words telling me to do something
3. Number the steps of what I need to do
4. Make a box for each number and brainstorm some ideas

① Describe what Monsy thinks:

② What I Think
Do I agree?
Disagree?
Why?
What is *my* opinion?

③ Examples to support my opinion:

Figure 6.3. Teacher Sample of Dissecting the Prompt

ASSESSMENT

1. The teacher should assess student understanding of prompt analysis by circulating and reviewing students' work. This will let the teacher know whether further instruction or practice is required.

2. The purpose of this lesson is to teach students tools they can employ in on-demand writing situations and to expose them to the analytical thinking required in college-level writing. Therefore, scoring the final product using a detailed rubric is not necessary. Through observation during the lesson and quickly reviewing the student writing, the teacher will get a good picture of student successes and challenges with this type of writing. The following questions represent the key skills: "Did students understand the prompt? Were they able to summarize the author's views? Did they write the extent to which they agreed with the author and why? Did they use examples to support their position?" The teacher can use the answers to these questions to plan further instruction and practice opportunities for students.

POSSIBLE MODIFICATION

1. If teachers feel their students are not ready to write a full response to the prompt, having students do all of the pre composing activities (including prompt analysis and brainstorming their ideas on the graphic organizer) can be a way to give students practice with this type of analytical prompt. At a later time, the teacher can take students through the same process but with a different prompt, and then students can write a full response.

A Sample Week in a Two-Period Intermediate ELL Class

This schedule is designed to provide a snapshot of a week in an effective intermediate level class where reading, writing, speaking, and listening are incorporated into challenging and engaging lessons. This schedule is not designed as a scripted curriculum and can be adapted in numerous ways.

MONDAY

1. **Reading and writing.** Students enter classroom and immediately begin reading a book of their choice quietly (20 minutes).

2. **Reading and writing and listening and speaking.** Students respond to their reading by completing a reading log (see Exhibit 3.6 in Chapter Three). Students share what they wrote in their reading log with a partner (five minutes).

3. **Shortened critical pedagogy lesson.** See Chapter Three for an example (30 minutes).

4. **Reading and writing and listening and speaking.** Teacher distributes a Word Chart for the problem-solution unit to students. Teacher reads each word aloud. Then students take a few minutes to write down the meanings of any words they might already know and share them with partners. Teacher begins a discussion of each word by asking students what they think it means and why: Where have they heard or seen this word before? Teacher guides students toward a correct definition of each word and writes on a teacher copy of the Word Chart which is projected for all students to see using a document camera. For each word, the teacher models a gesture or body movement, and students practice it. Students can participate in developing gestures by working in pairs to come up with ideas. After all the words are defined and have an accompanying gesture, students "quiz" each other and the teacher takes volunteers to demonstrate for the class (40 minutes).

5. **Reading and writing or listening and speaking.** Game to review problem-solution words (see Chapter Eighteen) (20 minutes).

6. **Reading and writing.** Reflection activity (see Chapter Three) (five minutes).

TUESDAY

1. **Reading and writing.** Students enter classroom and immediately begin reading a book of their choice quietly (15 minutes).

2. **Reading and writing.** Students work on Four Words homework sheet (see Exhibit 3.18) (five minutes).

3. **Reading and writing.** After brainstorming possible problems to explore as a class the previous week, the teacher tells students they will be studying the problem of vaping/smoking in depth this week and then writing a practice problem-solution essay on the topic. Teacher distributes a K-W-L chart. Students fill in the K section, what they already know about vaping/smoking, and then the W section, listing questions of what they want to learn. Students share with each other and as a class (20 minutes).

4. **Listening and speaking and reading and writing.** Teacher conducts a read-aloud using a piece of text about smoking. Students have a copy of the text in front of them and follow along as the teacher reads with prosody. The teacher posts a question related to the read-aloud and students write their responses. Students share their responses with each other. Students add new learnings to the L section of their K-W-L chart. (30 minutes).

5. **Listening and speaking.** Teacher passes out a dialogue (a conversation between two friends about vaping) and reads it aloud. Teacher quickly models reading in a monotone voice and then reads again, but this time with feeling. Teacher asks students which way is better and why. In pairs, students take turns performing the dialogue with prosody in preparation for recording themselves (20 minutes).

6. **Listening and speaking.** Students use a phone or computer to record their dialogues and share them with the teacher (30 minutes).

WEDNESDAY

1. **Reading and writing.** Students enter classroom and immediately begin reading a book of their choice quietly (20 minutes).

2. **Reading and writing and listening and speaking.** Students respond to their reading by completing a reading log. Students share what they wrote in their reading log with a partner (five minutes).

3. **Listening and speaking.** Teacher uses speakers to play the recordings from the previous day. Students listen to the dialogue and the teacher elicits student comments on good examples of reading with expression and clear pronunciation (five minutes).

4. **Reading and writing.** Teacher distributes a cloze passage on vaping and reads it aloud to students. Then students work to complete the cloze on their own. Teacher asks students to share their guesses and clues for each blank and writes down all the possible answers on a copy of the cloze displayed using a document camera. Teacher and students go back through and discuss which word fits best in each blank and why (identifying the context clues). Students will have circled the clue words they used to make each guess. The teacher posts written directions for students to select one of their guesses and to explain their thinking behind that guess ("I chose the word _____ because _____ .") (30 minutes).

5. **Listening and speaking.** Students quickly practice saying the words and doing the gestures they learned on Monday for the problem-solution words. Students spend a few minutes "quizzing" each other (one student calls out a word and the other student says the meaning and does the gesture) (five minutes).

6. **Reading and writing.** Teacher distributes a Text Data Set on vaping. The teacher reads the first three examples and models highlighting key words and using a reading strategy (asking a question, making a connection, or summarizing, for example). Students take turns reading the rest of the data set with a partner, stopping every three examples to compare their highlighting. Teacher specifies that students must demonstrate three reading strategies on each page (40 minutes).

7. **Reading and writing or listening and speaking.** Game (see Chapter Eighteen) (15 minutes).

8. **Reading and writing.** Reflection activity (five minutes)

THURSDAY

1. **Reading and writing.** Students enter classroom and immediately begin reading a book of their choice quietly (15 minutes)

2. **Listening and speaking and reading and writing.** Students respond to their reading by preparing a Book Talk (see Exhibit 5.4) to share with a class-

mate the following day. Students write down what they will say and then practice giving their Book Talk (10 minutes).

3. **Reading and writing.** Students take out the Vaping Data Set from the previous day and review their highlighting and annotations. Students begin to organize the data set into categories (such as health effects, quitting, cost) on a sheet of paper, writing the title of the category and the numbers that go in that category underneath. The teacher may give the categories to students, or students can be challenged to come up with them on their own. As students place each example in a category, they circle any clue words that make them believe it fits in that category. Students can work individually at first and then check their work with a partner (30 minutes).

4. **Reading and writing.** Students use computers and their category sheets to capture new information by doing online research. Students add two to three new facts to each category (30 minutes).

5. **Listening and speaking.** Students come back to class and share their new information with a partner (5 minutes).

6. **Reading and writing.** Students add new information to their K-W-L charts. The teacher gives them a few minutes to review the category they find most interesting. Then students put away their notes and write a paragraph about that category with a topic sentence and supporting details. The teacher should model this process by first reviewing the information in one category. The teacher should then create a topic sentence for that category and select key facts to rewrite in his or her own words for supporting sentences. Teacher circulates and checks for understanding while students are writing their own paragraphs (30 minutes).

FRIDAY

1. **Reading and writing.** Students enter classroom and immediately begin reading a book of their choice quietly (20 minutes).

2. **Listening and speaking.** Students take out their Book Talk notes and share with a partner. The teacher takes a volunteer to do his or her Book Talk for the whole class (15 minutes).

3. **Reading and writing and listening and speaking.** Students have time to work on their weekly journal to reflect on the week, sharing one or two positive events that occurred that week and one event that was not necessarily positive and what they could have done differently to improve the outcome or what they learned from the experience. Students share what they wrote with a partner, and the partner should ask at least one question (20 minutes).

4. **Reading and writing or listening and speaking.** Game to quiz students on problem-solution words and gestures (see Chapter Eighteen) (20 minutes).

5. **Reading and writing or listening and speaking.** Students use computers to visit interactive sites on problem-solution writing and vocabulary (40 minutes).

6. **Reading and writing.** Reflection activity (five minutes).

Links to all the online activities listed in the chapter, as well as to the downloadable student handouts, can be found at www.wiley.com/go/eslsurvivalguide2.

PART FOUR

Teaching English Language Learners in the Content Areas

CHAPTER SEVEN

English Language Learners in the Mainstream Classroom

The Mulla Nasrudin was crawling around in the dust. A man stopped and asked, "What are you doing?" Mulla answered, "I've lost a key to a treasure and am trying to find it." The man offered to help and joined Mulla on the ground. More and more people saw them and also began to help. Finally, one person asked Mulla if he was sure this was the place where he had lost the key. Mulla answered, "No, I lost it inside my house. But it is too dark there. There is far more light out here."[1]

In this Middle Eastern story, the solution to the problem was in one place, but it was easier to look elsewhere.

Teaching any class can be a challenge, and needing to differentiate for English language learners does not make it any easier. It can sometimes be tempting to use a lesson that has a few crumbs of ELL modifications thrown into it—there is "more light" there. Another option is to consider developing unique learning opportunities that are not only particularly accessible to English language learners, but can also offer a superior experience to *all* students. With this strategy, we can see ELLs through a lens of *assets*, not *deficits*.

In fact, we believe that viewing *all* students from that perspective benefits both them and teachers alike. That mindset is the cornerstone of successful "accelerated learning," a phrase that has been used a great deal in education as schools try to "bounce back" from the COVID-19 pandemic. "Accelerated learning" refers to a strategy of *not* "starting from the beginning" in the name of "remediation" to help students "make up" for what they might have allegedly missed in previous years.

Instead, in "accelerated learning," teachers try to determine what students don't know at the time of the lesson but need to know in order to access the grade level content that is going to be taught *now*. Then, through various strategies (like the ones listed in this chapter and throughout this book), teachers help students learn what's needed when they need it.

"Accelerated learning" is, in fact, what teachers of English Language Learners (and many other educators) have been doing for years. As we've often said, good ELL teaching is good teaching for everybody!

When teaching ELLs, educators are challenged to simultaneously make grade-level content accessible in English *and* help students gain English Language Proficiency. Many ELLs come from countries where the education system may be limited or subpar, or have had to miss years of education because of economic challenges, gang violence, or military conflict. There often just isn't enough time available for ELLs, especially for those who enter the United States at an older age, to review everything they might have missed.

We believe that there are certain universal principles for making learning more accessible to ELLs and, in fact, make it more accessible to all learners. Research cited throughout this book supports our belief. We can call these universal principles the Organizing Cycle (based upon successful strategies used by community organizers): building student relationships, accessing prior knowledge (particularly through student stories), developing student leadership potential, learning by doing, and reflection. We think it is also a particularly helpful framework to use when talking about modifications that mainstream teachers who have ELLs in their classroom can use to create a more fruitful learning environment for *all* their students, including ELLs. All of the strategies discussed in the preceding chapters fall into these five categories, and using this Organizing Cycle can work as a simple outline for a conversation with any content subject teacher.

This chapter will first provide a short summary of the different elements of the Organizing Cycle, along with the supporting research (and a much more complete discussion can be found in *English Language Learners: Teaching Strategies That Work*, by Larry Ferlazzo).[2] In this summary, we will also include a few specific suggestions on how to apply it in a mainstream English classroom that includes ELLs. Then, we'll provide specific suggestions for applying these modifications in social studies, science, and math classes in Chapters Eight, Nine, and Ten.

This book is primarily for ELL teachers and not mainstream teachers with ELLs in their classrooms. We are not suggesting that this chapter will function as a complete guide for mainstream classroom teachers who seek to differentiate instruction. There are many other books dedicated to this topic, including *Differentiating Instruction and Assessment for English Language Learners: A Guide for K–12 Teachers* (by Fairbairn and Jones-Vo) and *Teaching English Language Learners: Across the Content Areas* (by Haynes and Zacarian).[3] We also discuss it further in our book, *The ELL Teacher's Toolbox*.

The ideas in this chapter, however, can function as a beginning point for suggestions that ELL teachers might offer to their colleagues. You may notice that we repeat a few points that have already been made earlier in this book. We do so intentionally, since we see this section as more of a stand-alone chapter that an ELL teacher can either use as a quasi-script for a conversation or actually give to a content teacher to read.

What Is the Organizing Cycle?

The framework for the Organizing Cycle is similar to one used by successful community organizers to encourage people to participate in public life, particularly those who have not previously participated in community improvement efforts. It is used to help people learn a new language and new thinking about how to engage with each other and with the world. The concepts behind it can apply equally well to English language learners who are developing competence and confidence in a new language, a new academic environment, and a new culture.

Next, we will briefly discuss each of the five steps and how to apply them in a mainstream class that includes English language learners—and why.

BUILDING STRONG RELATIONSHIPS WITH STUDENTS

Creating a supportive environment in a "low-anxiety" classroom is critical in order for ELLs to get "comprehensible input."[4] In Chapter Two, we shared other research highlighting the importance of this kind of atmosphere for ELLs developing self-confidence and intrinsic motivation.

In addition to the specific suggestions in Chapter Two about ways to develop and maintain positive teacher-student and student-student connections, Robert J. Marzano recommends four simple strategies teachers can keep in mind and implement:[5]

1. Showing interest in students' lives by asking them questions about events in the world and in their lives
2. Advocating for students by making time for individual conversations and communicating that teachers want to go the extra mile to help students succeed
3. Not giving up on students, and positively reinforcing student effort
4. Being friendly through smiles, a light and quick supportive touch on the shoulder, and/or sharing an appropriate joke

You or your colleagues might ask, "How am I supposed to have conversations with students when their English proficiency is not high and I don't speak their home language?"

It's a good question and, fortunately, there are answers—thanks to technology. At the time we're writing this book, there are two tools we like that facilitate two-way conversations in different languages, though we're sure there are more on the way—and some may already be out by the time you are reading this book!

One is the "Interpreter Mode" in the mobile Google Assistant app. Download the free app, say something similar to "Be my Spanish translator," and it will automatically translate in writing and in audio what you say in English to Spanish and then what the other person says in Spanish into English. It can do this in 44 languages. Obviously, the translation is not even near perfect, but it's workable.

Microsoft Translator (https://translator.microsoft.com/) is an intriguing audio-and-text-based chat tool. Multiple people can log-in to it, choose their preferred language, speak their home language, and what they say will appear on everyone's screens in the language they each selected.

Tech Tool
Translation Tools

To keep up-to-date on the latest simultaneous translation tools, go to "The Best Sites For Learning About Google Translate & Other Forms Of Machine Translation" https://larryferlazzo.edublogs.org/2012/06/04/the-best-sites-for-learning-about-google-translate/.

ACCESSING PRIOR KNOWLEDGE (ESPECIALLY THROUGH STORIES)

We all learn best by connecting new information to what we already know. This personal linkage makes it more likely that new content will be moved into our brain's long-term memory.[6] Research shows that this process is just as important with English language learners as with any other learner.[7]

ELLs may not have extensive prior knowledge about what exactly is going to be covered in a lesson in a mainstream class, such as one studying *Romeo and Juliet* in English. But ELLs do have years of life experience and have likely either been in a relationship, seen a family member or friend in one, or watched one on television or in the movies. Some ELLs may also have knowledge of gangs in their home countries that they can apply to the study of *Romeo and Juliet*. Making those connections, either through the use of a K-W-L chart (These charts help students differentiate what students already "know about a lesson, want to know, and will learn") or embedded in other ways in the lesson, can spark student curiosity and interest and make the entire lesson more accessible.

In the *Romeo and Juliet* example, it's one thing to have students share that yes, they know about gangs and leave it at that, and another to have them share a brief narrative about the experience. Cultivating the expression of our students' prior knowledge through their sharing of personal stories can have a particularly strong learning impact. Neuroscientists like Renate Nummela Caine and Geoffrey Caine have found that the brain is particularly receptive to learning in the context of stories,[8] and Jerome Bruner writes that this can be especially important in the context of language acquisition.[9]

It is important, however, to also be very aware of potential past student trauma when activating prior knowledge. In the case of discussing gangs, for example, it would be important to check in with ELLs prior to the lesson to explore their comfort level in sharing their experiences. We discuss this issue more in Chapter Sixteen.

Some ELLs might not know specifically about Mardi Gras if you are teaching about New Orleans, but they will know about cultural celebrations they have experienced in their home countries; they may not know about the American Civil War, but they will know about conflicts in their country/region of origin; they may not know about the specific details of climate change, but they may know that one of the reasons their families emigrated could have been due to worsening drought conditions.

We are not suggesting that teachers need to spend hours upon hours eliciting student stories to activate their background knowledge. We are suggesting, however, that teachers consider broadening their perspective about what qualifies as prior knowledge whenever possible. We also encourage teachers to tease out a few more words and sentences from students when they are sharing background knowledge that can be linked to lessons.

We do particularly like K-W-L charts because they are a tool that can hit "a lot of birds with one stone." After students have completed them, they can provide critical data to teachers about what students know and don't know so we can plan our lessons accordingly. They are also excellent opportunities for students to act as co-teachers—those who have more knowledge on a topic can share with those who have less (which supports the next step in the Organizing Cycle—leadership development). Finally, the questions that students ask can help teachers identify student interests, which can then be used to make lessons more accessible and relevant.

The importance of activating student prior knowledge is summed up by long-time second-language researcher, author, and Professor Jim Cummins, who wrote: "Activating prior knowledge is like preparing the soil before sowing the seeds of knowledge."[10]

IDENTIFYING AND MENTORING STUDENTS' LEADERSHIP POTENTIAL

As we've mentioned, the Organizing Cycle concept is adapted from the work of successful community organizers. In this type of organizing for social change, some of the key elements of a good leader include being intrinsically motivated, a sense of self-efficacy (or self-confidence or self-esteem), a willingness to take risks and learn from mistakes, and a desire to teach others. Researchers, coincidentally, have found that successful language learners share similar attributes.[11] The Qualities of a Successful Language Learner Lesson Plan in Chapter Sixteen is designed to help students learn about this research and evaluate their own progress toward developing these qualities.

There are several ways that content teachers can foster these characteristics among their English language learner students (and their non-ELL students, too) and, through their development, make their class content more accessible to them.

Intrinsic Motivation   Researchers, have identified four elements[12] that can help create the conditions where student intrinsic motivation can flourish:

1. Autonomy, where students feel like they have some control over what they are being taught and how they are learning. Providing student choice[13] is one way for teachers to incorporate this quality, including writing instruments to use (laptop or pen), homework options ("answer any two of these seven questions"), seating arrangements, topics, or chronology of study. Offering opportunities to choose can be particularly important to ELLs who likely had little or no voice in the process of moving to a new country.

2. Competence, where students feel like they are capable of successfully learning and completing assigned tasks. Research says that, no matter how much we like to say that people learn a lot from failure, many do not,[14] and that may include our students. Sharing student work examples as models,[15] providing graphic organizers to scaffold instruction,[16] and offering specific supportive and critical feedback[17] are all steps we can take to provide opportunities for success.

3. Relatedness, where students feel like the work they are being asked to do brings them into relationship with people they like and respect. Research highlights the pedagogical effectiveness of small group work,[18] as well as the previously mentioned importance of the teacher/student relationship.[19] Learning about students' lives, regularly showing concern and interest, and demonstrating overall flexibility can solidify teachers' relationships with students, as well as provide a way to gain important information that can inform instruction.

4. Relevance, where students feel that what they are studying is either aligned with their interests or can clearly help them achieve their goals and dreams. Getting to know students can help teachers tailor lessons that connect with student goals and interests.[20] An example Larry often shares is when his 9th grade class was writing an argument essay about what they thought was the worst natural disaster. One student had his head down on the desk. Larry knew his student was a football fan, and he asked him if he would rather write one on which NFL team he thought was the best. The student's eyes lit up, and he produced an essay using all the appropriate argument conventions. As the civil rights ballad says, we have to "keep our eyes on the prize." In this case, the "prize" was learning how to write an argument essay, not writing about natural disasters.

Self-Confidence and Willingness to Take Risks   Teachers can help ELLs develop self-confidence and a willingness to take risks by developing a supportive classroom community—and using the previously suggested relationship-building activities can play a key role in making that happen. Another way to strengthen student belief in their own competence is by regularly assisting them to develop learning strategies they can use to handle challenges. This assistance could include encouraging student use of previously mentioned reflective activities to help them monitor when they have been successful or unsuccessful and why, reinforcing reading comprehension strategies, including summarizing and "monitor and repair," and using inductive learning techniques to help refine student skills at detecting patterns—all tools they can use more and more on their own.[21] Finally, Carol Dweck has done extensive research and writing on the long-term positive impact on student self-confidence of praising effort ("That was impressive today, Zhao, when you really worked hard on understanding that passage—highlighting key words, summarizing, and asking classmates for help"), as opposed to praising intelligence ("You are a really smart kid, Zhao").[22]

Teaching Others   The Roman philosopher Seneca reportedly said: "While we teach, we learn." Creating opportunities for all students to teach—especially for ELLs who might feel that they are in constant learning mode (both language *and* content) with less to contribute than their classmates—is another way teachers can help develop leadership skills. Using the jigsaw method—where small groups of students prepare presentations on different aspects of a chapter or topic—is one way for ELLs to work in a supportive group and gain self-confidence.[23]

Extensive research also shows that students learn content better when they know they are expected to teach it to others.[24]

Jigsaws also happen to be an exceptional differentiation tool. If students are reading an article, for example, some groups can be given shorter passages and others longer ones. If they are researching a figure's life, one group could be assigned to research an easier part, like the person's family, while others are asked to learn about challenges or legacies.

Exhibit 7.1 "Jigsaw Instructions" is a student hand-out we use when we are working on a chapter in a textbook, and groups are assigned different pages. As you can see, the student handout itself is differentiated—some groups might be given only the first page, while others who need more scaffolding might get both page one and page two, "Presentation Sentence Starters."

One of our favorite strategies for student leadership development is by creating "Leadership Teams" in our classes. We notice students who have demonstrated some of the elements of a good leader discussed in this section and invite them to become members of a "Leadership Team." Team members are often responsible for leading small group discussions (with training we provide), regularly meet with us to evaluate what seems to be working and not working in class, help identify new students who they will mentor, and complete weekly "self-assessments" on their work as leaders (see the Reflection section later in this chapter for an example of the self-assessment questions). ELL and non-ELL students can participate in these roles, and we can say with certainty that class participation, student self-confidence, and the overall quality of our classes have all increased since we began these teams.

The origin of the word *leadership* means "to go, to travel." By mentoring our students' leadership potential, we are better equipping them to choose their own life destinations and how they will get there. Since we are not going to be there for the rest of their journey, we have the responsibility to do this intentionally and strategically.

EXHIBIT 7.1. Jigsaw Instructions

Your group is responsible for preparing a one-to-two minute presentation about your page in the book.

You must create a poster, and use index cards. Everyone must speak in the presentation.

Only put key words and draw a picture on the poster to help you in your presentation. Do not put everything you are going to say on the poster! You can use your index cards to remind you of what to say.

Your presentation must include:

- Three important words from the page and what they mean - in your own words.
- A one-sentence summary of the page.
- Three other important facts from the page.
- A picture you draw that helps people understand the page.

You must choose at least one of these additional options. You will receive extra credit if you do more than one:

- Use your phone to look up more information about events or people talked about on your page and add them to your presentation and poster.
- Act out an event from the page.
- Connect something from the page to another thing we learned in a previous chapter.

LEARNING BY DOING

Learning by doing is a phrase popularized by education theorist John Dewey. He believed that we learn better by actually participating in an experience rather than by just being told about it, particularly if we do the work with others.[25] Much subsequent research has borne him out, finding that interactive teaching methods, including various forms of cooperative learning, tend to generate far more effective learning results than lectures.[26]

Well-structured cooperative learning activities (ones that have clear instructions and goals) are especially effective for English language learners, whether they use the Jigsaw (mentioned in the previous section), project-based or problem-based learning, think-pair-share, or partner assignments. Grouping, especially with proficient English-speaking classmates, creates countless opportunities for ELLs to be naturally encouraged to speak and participate, as well as creating an atmosphere where they will feel more comfortable asking questions in order to understand content.[27]

In other parts of this book, we have shared numerous examples of another kind of learning by doing—inductive teaching and learning. Providing students examples from which they can create a pattern and form a concept or rule can work in any content class. Text Data Sets are a key tool to use in this kind of inductive methodology. Examples of these data sets, and explanations of how to use them can be found in earlier chapters, as well as the upcoming one on Social Studies. In addition, many of the scaffolded writing strategies discussed in Chapter Six will also fit into this stage of the Organizing Cycle.

We would also include oral reading and, particularly, partner reading, in this "learning by doing" category. Substantial research finds that reading aloud leads to the "production effect" that enhances memory of the reading content for everybody and improves general comprehension.[28] In our experience, it also promotes accountability because we can see and hear students doing it, working in partners tends to be more engaging for many, students can practice prosody (reading with expression and intonation), and it prompts students to ask for help in pronouncing words that are new to them.

"One-Pagers" are a relatively new term for a strategy many teachers have had students "do" for years to demonstrate understanding of a text or concept. They are basically graphic organizers with questions or guides (sometimes similar to the ones found in Exhibit 7.1 Jigsaw Instructions with differentiated instructions and scaffolds) where students write and draw to demonstrate their understanding of a book, article, video, podcast, etc. We particularly like having students use a "3-2-1" guide we learned about from educator Ekuwah Moses. In one case, after students read a chapter in a History textbook, we had them choose three words they thought were important and explain *why* they thought each one was important; then had them pick phrases of three to six words each; choose a quote, and then draw a picture. Students then shared their creations in small groups.

See the Tech Tool for sources and ideas of many templates and ideas for using One-Pagers—there is no need to reinvent the wheel!

Keeping the perspective of learning by doing in mind when planning class lessons can be an asset to ELLs and non-ELLs alike.

Tech Tool

One-Pagers

You can find many templates and student guides to One-Pagers at "The Best Resources (& Templates) For 'One-Pagers' That Students Can Use To Show Their Learning"   https://larryferlazzo.edublogs.org/2021/06/24/the-best-resources-templates-for-one-pagers-that-students-can-use-to-show-their-learning/.

REFLECTION

In Chapter Three, we discussed in detail four different categories of reflection: summarize, self-assess, assess the class and teacher, and relevance. All of these can be useful in a content class, especially for the metacognitive value of self-assessing successful learning strategies and for memory reinforcement.

Here are some examples of questions on the weekly self-assessment form that members of the class Leadership Team answer (rating is on a 1-5 scale):

1. How would you rate how you've done helping lead small groups this past week?

2. How would you rate how you did in small groups to get everyone participating?

3. How would you rate how you did in modeling being kind, welcoming, and friendly to others in our class this past week?

4. How would you rate yourself in contributing to whole class discussions by sharing your thoughts or asking questions?

5. How would you rate yourself this past week in acting as a co-teacher when we're in the whole class by answering questions other students have, respectfully pointing out to Mr. Ferlazzo when he's making a mistake, or clarifying any confusion?

6. We have students in our class who are still learning English. How would you rate yourself as trying to be welcoming and helpful to those particular students?

7. Is there anyone else in this class you think you could encourage and mentor to eventually also join the leadership team? If so, who do you think it could be?

8. What are your suggestions about what Mr. Ferlazzo can do to make the class better for everyone?

9. How would you like to improve as a leader over the next week? What do you want to work on?

ORGANIZING CYCLE ADD-ONS

Content teachers can use several other instructional strategies that are particularly helpful to ELLs. These may not fit precisely into the Organizing Cycle, but are nonetheless important.

Giving Instructions. The simple act of giving verbal *and* written instructions can help all learners, especially ELLs. In addition, it is far easier for a teacher to point to the board in response to the inevitable repeated question, "What are we supposed to do?"[29]

Preview-View-Review. This is an effective instructional strategy that involves the teacher giving a brief overview of the lesson in the student's native language prior to the lesson, followed by the lesson in English, which is then followed by a review in the native language again.[30]

Even though it is probably unrealistic for most content teachers to directly use this technique, the Web offers an alternative. Many textbooks now offer online multilingual translations or summaries of covered topics. If the text you are using does not, the ones that do probably offer coverage of comparable study units. Students can be given a heads-up about upcoming topics and asked to visit the online home language summaries either at home (if they have Web access) or at school (either during class or at other times in the school day).

Tech Tool

Online Multilingual Support

If your own textbook does not offer multilingual summaries and glossaries, you can find others that do in "The Best Multilingual and Bilingual Sites for Math, Social Studies, and Science" at https://larryferlazzo.edublogs.org/2008/10/03/the-best-multilingual-bilingual-sites-for-math-social-studies-science/.

In addition, there are extensive interactive online resources for all content classes. Many of these sites are very accessible to English language learners, though they are in English, because of the audio and visual support they provide. We will provide specific recommendations on teaching social studies, science, and math in Chapters Eight, Nine, and Ten.

Wait Time, Speaking Rate, and Gestures. Though this has been mentioned several times already throughout the book, it can never be stated too often—after asking a question, wait for a few seconds before calling on someone to respond (and, even better, give your ELL student advance warning that you are going to call on them); don't talk fast, do use gestures, and, if an ELL student tells you she didn't understand what you said, never, ever repeat the same thing in a louder voice!

Word Charts. ELLs are more likely to learn vocabulary if it is directly taught and then reinforced in various contexts.[31] Using the kind of word charts recommended in Chapter Six could be useful for preteaching key vocabulary prior to some lessons.

Visuals. Teaching with pictures and other visuals (such as short video clips) can be huge assets to ELLs.[32] Specific suggestions for teaching social studies, science, and math appear in Chapters Eight, Nine, and Ten.

Bilingual Dictionaries or Online Access to Translation Sites. An ELL classroom should not be the only place where a bilingual dictionary can be found. Identify the native languages of your ELL students and make sure you have the appropriate dictionaries around. Another option, of course, is to just give your ELL students permission to use their phone or other device to translate when needed. Important note: When students are using Google Translate to help write, encourage them to use it for *words*, not *sentences*.

Learning Transfer. If English language learner students in some content classes are also taking an ELL class during the day, the ELL teacher can create related student homework assignments. For example, the ELL teacher can ask the student to create a word chart of new social studies terms.

More of these kinds of "transfer" assignments, where the ELL teacher helps to explicitly transfer what is being taught in his class to a content class, can also be developed in coordination with content area teachers.

Note-Taking Strategies. For ELLs in content classes, academic listening is a critical skill that places the heaviest processing demands on students.[33] Providing note-taking scaffolds is a key accommodation teachers can offer their ELLs to help students process new vocabulary. A note-taking scaffold can look similar to a cloze passage and include the most important content with blanks for students to fill in as they listen throughout the lesson. For example, a social studies scaffold sheet might have several lines similar to "_____ was the primary cause of the American Civil War." As students gain more experience with academic listening and note taking, teachers can gradually remove the scaffold or adjust it to include only a few key words.

Graphic Organizers. Graphic organizers can help all students[34] and particularly help ELLs[35] organize what they are learning and/or help them make connections between new pieces of information. See the Tech Tool under Graphic Organizers in Chapter Six for online resources.

Making Texts More Accessible. "Engineering the text" means making existing text more accessible—not by changing the words to "simplify" it, but by modifying the layout to "amplify" it.[36] For example, creating more white space, adding subheadings, vocabulary definitions, visual supports, and guiding questions are just a few ways to make texts more accessible to all students.

Making Tests Accessible. If we are not careful, assessment in content classes can turn into language assessments and not provide accurate measures of what English Language Learners have actually learned. Including word banks, visuals, and sentence starters, as well as limiting the use of multi-part questions, are just a few modifications that could help ELLs more clearly demonstrate their content knowledge.

Closed Captioning. Extensive research has found that closed captioning supports increased comprehension for ELLs and non-ELLs alike.[38] But use of this strategy need not be limited to videos alone. Google Slides provides automatic closed captioning in the language being spoken, and PowerPoint will do it in whatever language you choose, including one different from what you are speaking (see the Tech Tool for more information). Depending on the English proficiency level of the ELLs in your class, teachers who are showing slides in their class can show captions in English or in rough translations of the home language of their students.

Peer Tutors: Having peer tutors to assist ELLs can be helpful in mainstream classes. See Chapter Two for additional information.

Tech Tool
Closed Captioning Support

To learn more about how to use closed captioning in your presentations, go to "Automatic Captioning Tools For Presentations" at https://larryferlazzo.edublogs.org/2018/10/08/google-slides-gets-automated-captions-huge-help-to-online-teachers-of-english-could-maybe-help-in-regular-classroom/.

The Content Areas. We believe that the Organizing Cycle—building strong relationships with students, accessing prior knowledge through stories, identifying and mentoring students' leadership potential, learning by doing, and reflection—provides an effective framework for effectively differentiating instruction for *all* learners, including ELLs. We feel that using this kind of research-based model can help maximize student achievement for everyone in the classroom.

In Chapters, Eight, Nine, and Ten we will share specific lesson ideas that teachers can use in social studies, science, and math classes. As we've already mentioned, the brief overview in this chapter is not meant to be a definitive guide for the content teacher. Instead, we hope that the lessons will put a little "meat on the bone" of the Organizing Cycle and help get the creative juices flowing so that teachers can adapt these instructional strategies in ways that work best for their students and for them. We see this chapter as a source of recommendations that ELL teachers can offer their colleagues.

Before we begin discussing each of these three content areas, though, we want to make a point about the first and last elements of the Organizing Cycle: relationship building and reflection.

We discussed in Chapter Two the importance of building a trusting atmosphere in the classroom where students feel safe to take learning risks. This is a critical quality for any successful classroom and is even more critical in a class with English language learners whose risks are often magnified by the questions circulating in their mind: Am I correctly understanding what she is saying? Am I making sense? Are people making fun of me? Why is everything so hard?

Relationship building is a critical element of developing this sense of trust, both when school begins in the fall and through the rest of the year. The basics—a teacher making a point of taking a minute to check in with three or four students each day, not just on the subject that is being studied, but on what is happening in the student's life—can hold true for any teacher in any class. There is often a little time to chat with students arriving in the classroom early and as they are leaving, and while students are working at their desks.

In addition, as we mentioned, well-designed cooperative learning projects where students have been strategically divided by the teacher (often, though not always, with student input) can offer excellent opportunities for strengthening student-to-student relationships.

There are additional relationship-building activities that can be organized periodically in class. Chapter Two shared a number of introductory exercises (such as the All About Me activity, the "I Am" project, or a class scavenger hunt) that can be used throughout the year as student interests change and as they gain new life experiences. If you are teaching in a large school where few students share the same classes, then all classes can do these same exercises, since there will be little student overlap. However, if your students are staying with each other most of the day, doing the same introduction projects in several classes might not be the most energizing experience for them.

An option is to add elements to the standard introductory exercises to customize them for your course of study. In math class, for example, students could be invited to share something about themselves using numbers, or discussing a time when they have previously felt successful when learning about, or doing, math.

For reflection, the four categories and their representative examples that were shared in Chapter Three can be used in all classes.

It's not possible to create a usable infographic including *all* of our recommendations, but English teacher Wendi Pillars has created a nice "cheat sheet" with several common differentiation tips for ELLs, and she and her colleagues have graciously given us permission to publish it here as Figure 7.1 "Differentiation Tips."

Figure 7.1. Differentiation Tips
Published with permission of Wendi Pillars, Leslie Wilkie and Mirian Vasquez
https://mswendisworld.blogspot.com/2020/10/differentiating-your-instruction-six.html

Tech Tool
Additional Resources

For even more ideas on how to support ELLs in Content classes, please see "The Best Advice To Content Teachers About Supporting English Language Learners" at https://larryferlazzo.edublogs.org/2017/09/08/the-best-advice-to-content-teachers-about-supporting-english-language-learners/.

This chapter opened with a Middle Eastern folktale about a person looking for a key outside his house even though he had lost it inside. He was doing this because the light made it easier to look outside. In the chapters that follow, you'll find some ideas on how to find the key *inside* the house.

Links to all the online activities listed in the chapter, as well as to the downloadable student hand-outs, can be found at www.wiley.com/go/eslsurvivalguide2.

Portions of this chapter originally appeared in *The Washington Post* https://www.washingtonpost.com/education/2021/06/02/the-kind-of-teaching-kids-need-right-now/.[37] Reprinted with permission.

CHAPTER EIGHT

Teaching Social Studies

*N*asreddin Hodja was traveling with a companion. They came to a place that had extremely tall minarets—much taller than the Hodja's friend had ever seen. He asked the Hodja, "How do you think they could have built them so tall?"

"Simple," he explained. "They just go to a well and turn it inside out."[1]

In many ways, Nasreddin Hodja's explanation is similar to the teaching practice that we're suggesting in this chapter and in this book—we are "turning inside out" many traditional teaching assumptions. We are suggesting that, instead of educators using the "sage-on-stage" model, a focus on the relationships, stories, and leadership abilities of our English language learners can result in huge learning strides.

This chapter will discuss how to build these "tall minarets" in social studies classes using The Organizing Cycle. In addition to the strategies in this chapter, all of the suggestions listed in Chapter Seven are also applicable to classes in this content area.

It is not an exaggeration to say that, depending on the exact ways teachers implement these strategies, they all can meet most of the Common Core History/ Social Studies secondary standards under Key Ideas and Details, Craft and Structure, Integration of Knowledge and Ideas, Range of Reading and Level of Text Complexity.[2]

Building Relationships with Students

Along with, or instead of, some of the questions included in previously mentioned introductory activities, social studies teachers can ask ones like these periodically during the year (of course, as with most assignments, teacher modeling is important, as well as creating a relationship-building opportunity through an exchange of stories):

Describe a geographic feature (such as a hill, mountain, river, jungle, or forest) that you have a fond memory of from your younger days. Draw it and explain why it is such a nice memory.

Think of times when you have been on a hill or mountain, in a forest or jungle, in an ocean or river, on a different continent, or in a different time zone (teachers can add more here if they wish). Draw and describe in writing what it was like and why you were there.

What is the most historic moment you remember? In other words, which moment do you think will be in history books for a long time to come? Draw it and answer these questions: Where were you, what happened, what did you think, and how did you feel? And why do you think it will be remembered in the history books? Ask your parents the same questions, and write down their responses.

We will be learning about the biographies of many historic figures and the most important moments in their lives—in other words, what shaped them into the kind of people they are. Think of two or three key moments in your life that made you the person you are today. Draw them, write about them, and explain why and how you think they have shaped you.

We will be studying economics—money—in this class. Write about and draw three important times in your life when money mattered.

The only limitation to these kinds of questions is your own imagination!

Tech Tool

Making Online Maps and Timelines

Though these kinds of introductory questions can easily be answered with pen, markers, and paper, there are also plenty of free and easy online tools where students can make their own individual multimedia presentations describing important moments and showing them by grabbing images from the Web. In addition to Google Slides, these presentations can include making personalized maps and timelines. You can find our favorites at "The Best Map-Making Sites On The Web" https://larryferlazzo.edublogs.org/2008/12/03/the-best-map-making-sites-on-the-web/ and "The Best Tools For Making Online Timelines" https://larryferlazzo.edub logs.org/2008/08/06/the-best-tools-for-making-online-timelines/.

ACCESSING PRIOR KNOWLEDGE THROUGH STORIES

The importance of connecting new information to existing student prior knowledge was explained earlier in Chapter Seven.

The questions in the relationship-building sections of Chapter Seven and in this chapter, in addition to providing opportunities to build personal connections, can also help students access related prior knowledge. Following are a few more ways of integrating this idea into the social studies classroom.

K-W-L Charts and Presentations

K-W-L charts (what do you *know*, what do you *want* to learn, and what have you *learned*) were discussed in earlier chapters. Using these charts can be an excellent way to introduce new lessons and in ongoing classroom use, as students organize newly learned information and connect it to what they already know. K-W-L charts also informally assess the quality and quantity of student background knowledge, which in turn can help inform a teacher's instructional plan.

It is very possible that ELL student prior knowledge about many social studies topics covered in class will be more limited than that of other students. So how do you turn that challenge into an opportunity? Their knowledge about particular United States–related topics may be narrow, but their overall knowledge of social studies topics may be broad. With all students, and especially ELLs, we also want to look for ways to connect their prior knowledge and the new content we are teaching to current events. Making these kinds of connections can enhance student interest and motivation.

For example, before beginning a unit on the American Civil War, in addition to having all students list what they know about that war, the teacher can also invite them to share what they know about *any* civil war. There are few countries in the world that have not experienced these tragedies, and the stories from immigrant students can add to the learning experience of *all* students.

Interestingly, students in Larry's ELL US History class were beginning to present slide presentations on civil wars in their home countries the same day of the January 6th, 2021, Insurrection at the US Capitol. The insurrection itself, including the well-known photo of the insurrectionist carrying a Confederate flag into the building, certainly created the conditions for countless student questions and an opportunity to connect the past with the present.

There are other opportunities, too. Before discussing the Mexican-American War, for example, immigrant students from Mexico can be asked to report the very different perspective on that conflict that is taught in their home country (this kind of activity can also help develop the important language learner quality of teaching others). When a world history class is going to start a unit on Chinese history, who better for the class to hear from than a student from that country? And when discussing natural disasters in geography class, the long history of these tragedies extends across all borders.

It doesn't have to stop with K-W-L charts, either. ELL presentations on these topics can be an excellent language-development experience for them and a fruitful learning opportunity for the entire class.

Connecting Personal Stories in Other Ways

Student stories can also be used to engage additional higher-order levels of thinking. All students, including ELLs, can share stories of how and why their families moved to the local community, the risks they took, and how it changed their lives. This information, along with the stories of explorers and immigrants throughout history, can easily be used to develop Venn Diagrams, followed by compare-and-contrast essays.

Another example might take place prior to discussing the Protestant Reformation (or other rebellions and revolutions). Students can be asked to think about a change they would like to see happen in the school, why they would like to see it happen, who they might need to help them make that change, why they think they need that help, and what might happen if they do not get that assistance. This activity can be followed by a discussion of Martin Luther's plan of not moving ahead publicly with his Ninety-Five Theses until after he had support from the public and among German princes. Making the connection between the student's thinking process and Luther's strategy can make the lesson more accessible *and*, perhaps even more importantly, teach broader concepts of change and the dangers of recklessness that can be related to many other historical—and personal—events. In other words, good ideas are great, but you want to do what you can to increase their odds of success before you move forward with them.

IDENTIFYING AND MENTORING STUDENTS' LEADERSHIP POTENTIAL

The increasingly difficult tandem of learning a second language and learning content knowledge can grow frustrating for English language learners as they move from the beginning level to higher levels.[3] As the levels of intrinsic motivation decrease during this time, it is important for teachers to use the methods discussed previously in Chapter Seven that have been shown to assist students to "motivate themselves," including encouraging student autonomy, praising effort, creating opportunities for students to teach, and helping students master learning strategies they can use when facing obstacles.

LEARNING BY DOING

We have discussed the value and effectiveness of inductive learning with students—both with English language learners and with those proficient in the language. The roots of the word *inductive* mean "to lead into" and "to lead." This section describes a scenario for leading students through this kind of guided discovery process in a social studies classroom.

K-W-L charts were mentioned earlier in this chapter, under Accessing Prior Knowledge. However, there are a number of historical eras where it is obvious to the teacher that prior knowledge on a topic may be very limited. In those situations, a teacher may want to use an introductory lesson like this one.

A few days prior to starting a unit on ancient China, a teacher can display three pictures on the classroom wall (ideally they should be oversized, but 8 1/2-inch by 11-inch images will work and can be shown using a document camera for students to see an enlarged image; an online image could also be projected): one showing the ancient Chinese use of gunpowder, another an image of Confucius teaching, and the third an image of the recently discovered terra cotta warriors (an internet search will turn up many photos of all these items).

On the day the unit is to begin, students are given a K-W-L chart and asked to write down what they see in each picture: when they think it took place or was produced, and what clues lead them to that conclusion. Then students write questions they have about each picture. Students can work individually or, better yet, in pairs.

Next, the teacher should explicitly teach a few key vocabulary words, such as *archeology, philosophy,* and *terra cotta,* which students can use to make a small Word Chart. In addition, a teacher can give a short read-aloud using some of the newly taught words.

Then students can be given a Text Data Set like the one in Exhibit 8.1 (which can easily be expanded if desired). They can read them in pairs and categorize them. Afterward, they can revisit their K-W-L chart about the photos to write down answers to some of the questions they might have found from the data set. Students can later be asked to add new information to the categories as they learn more about the topics. They can prepare posters or online presentations highlighting what they feel are the most important points in each category, along with illustrating them. And, as demonstrated in both Chapters Four and Five, data set categories can be extended into essays.

EXHIBIT 8.1. Ancient China Data Set

Categories: Inventions, Archeological Sites, Philosophers

1. Chinese scientists invented gunpowder in the eighth century and began using it in weapons.

2. The Great Wall of China is four thousand miles long and protected the Chinese border.

3. Nearly 2,000 years ago, the Chinese invented paper by combining tree bark, rope, old rags, and fish nets.

4. Confucius was a philosopher who believed that there should be strict rules in society and that people should follow those rules.

5. It took one million workers to build hundreds of buildings in the Forbidden City. It was the center of government, and construction on it started over five hundred years ago.

6. The Chinese invented the abacus, which was an ancient calculator. It is still used in some places.

7. Even though Buddhism started in India, it became very popular in China. It was started by an Indian prince named Siddhartha Gautama Buddha.

8. Even though many Chinese eat using chopsticks, they also invented the fork over four thousand years ago.

9. The remains of Peking Man (sometimes called Beijing Man), a creature that lived 750,000 years ago, before humans, have been found in China.

10. Thousands of large clay soldiers made over 2,000 years ago were found in 1974.

11. Lao Tsu was a philosopher who believed that the government should not make a lot of rules. He also believed that everything had a dark side and a light side, which he called yin and yang. His philosophy was called Taoism.

12. The Chinese invented the compass thousands of years ago to show in what direction they were traveling.

A lesson like this incorporates visual clues, cooperative learning, inductive teaching, read-alouds, and explicit vocabulary instruction, including Word Charts and all instructional methods that have been found to help both ELLs and non-ELLs. We are not suggesting that a teacher needs to incorporate all these elements in every introductory lesson—at times, just doing a K-W-L chart with the photos is workable, as is using visuals (including a video clip) in some other way. Cooperative learning can be used in any number of circumstances. And a Text Data Set (and its optional extension into essays) can be used at any time. We lay out this teaching and learning sequence, though, to offer a practical idea of how these instructional strategies can be effectively used in a social studies class.

More "Learning By Doing" Examples:

Writing Inductively

We've discussed how students can turn Text Data Sets into essays. We've also encouraged students to use a similar mode when writing an essay from "scratch." This is how we explain it:

First, choose your overall topic. We sometimes use the topic of "cars" as an example to illustrate the process. Obviously, social studies topics could be biographies, eras, wars, inventions, etc.

Second, identify three or four major categories within your overall topic. For cars, it could be companies, parts, and prices. In biographies, it could be family, younger life, accomplishments, and legacy.

Third, research to identify four to eight key points in each category.

Fourth, turn your categories into paragraphs by writing a topic sentence and putting the main points into your own words (we usually include doing a lesson on paraphrasing and summarizing here).

Fifth, write an introduction.

Sixth, write a conclusion.

No, it's not an extraordinarily sophisticated writing lesson. But, yes, it's a simple and accessible strategy for ELLs and others to use and begin to develop more extensive writing skills which they can apply in other classes, too.

A-B-C Writing Frames

We discussed the value of using writing frames for shorter student writing projects, especially in lessons when we use the A-B-C strategy (Answer the question, Back it up with evidence, Comment or Connect).

Exhibits 8.2, 8.3 and 8.4 are examples of how we use this strategy in Social Studies classes.

EXHIBIT 8.2. Metric System Argument A-B-C Paragraph

State your opinion

I think OR **I don't think** everyone in the world should use the metric system.

Give a reason from the video to back up your opinion:

The video said _____.

Say how the reason you gave supports your opinion:

This fact supports my opinion because_____.

EXHIBIT 8.3. Sacramento A-B-C Paragraph

What is the most interesting thing you learned about Sacramento?

First fill in the blanks, and then turn it into a paragraph on a lined sheet of paper.

***A**nswer The Question*

The most interesting thing I learned about Sacramento was _____.

***B**ack It Up With Evidence*

The list of facts (or the videos) said that _____.

*Make a **C**omment*

This is interesting to me because _____.

Here is an example:

The most interesting thing I learned about San Francisco was that the 1906 earthquake and fire destroyed most of the city. I read that the earthquake only lasted one minute, but that the fires it caused burned for days. This is interesting to me because I live in Sacramento, and we're not that far from San Francisco. I wonder if it could happen again and cause damage here.

EXHIBIT 8.4. American Revolution A-B-C

What would you do if you were an American living in the 13 colonies in 1775? Would you help the Americans or the British?

Answer the Question

Back it up with Evidence

Make a comment explaining how your evidence backs up your answer
I would help the _____ if I were an American living in the 13 colonies in 1775. The textbook says, "_____
_____."

This quotation supports my answer because _____
_____.

Critical Thinking Dialogues

The ability to formulate an argument, as we've discussed in earlier chapters, is an important skill to foster among students. Writing an essay is one way to develop that skill. However, we've found that a prelude to that often challenging task can be promoting student talk through what we call "Critical Thinking Dialogues" that are helpful to ELLs and others.

After we've studied a topic, we'll introduce a dialogue where students have to take a position on a question and explain their reasons. We also inject a bit of humor in them, and students practice them in small groups and then perform them for the entire class or for another small group.

Exhibit 8.5 and Exhibit 8.6 are examples of the dialogues we use after learning about the Great Depression and the atomic bombings of Japan.

They function as good opportunities for critical thinking and for speaking practice!

EXHIBIT 8.5. Critical Thinking Dialogue "Great Depression"

Student One: It was pretty interesting learning about the Great Depression.

Student Two: Yes, it was interesting. I didn't know so many people didn't have jobs for such a long time.

Student One: It lasted 10 years!

Student Two: And so many people didn't have enough food to eat!

Student One: If you lived back then, do you think you would have left school and tried to get a job to help your family?

Student Two: I think _____ because _____. What do you think you would have done?

Student One: I think _____ because _____. What do you think you would have done, _____?

Student Three: I think _____ because _____. If I left school one good thing would be that I wouldn't have to take Mr. Ferlazzo's class. It's so boring!

Student One and Two - together: BORING!!!!!

EXHIBIT 8.6. Critical Thinking Dialogue "Hiroshima"

Student One: Did you know that 160,000 people were killed in the atomic bombings in Japan, and most of them were civilians?

Student Two: I didn't know that until we learned it in class. It is sad and terrible!

Student One: The United States said it had to bomb those cities to end the war. The government said if they did not drop the bombs, American troops would have had to invade Japan.

Student Two: A lot of people would have died if that had happened.

Student One: Some said that the United States could have dropped the bomb on an island where people didn't live. They thought that might have scared Japan into surrendering instead of killing 160,000 people. What do you think?

Student Two: I think the United States _____ because _____. What do you think, _____?

Student Three: I think the United States _____ because _____. What do you think, _____?

Student One: I think the United States _____ because
_____.

Student Two: Mr. Ferlazzo is old and bald, but he does sometimes teach us important things.

Student One and Three Together: You are right - he is old and bald!

Analyzing Images

After we've begun teaching about a subject, like the Transcontinental Railroad or early twentieth century immigration to the United States, we'll sometimes show three related photographs/paintings. We'll then ask small student groups to choose one and complete the Photo Analysis Sheet in Exhibit 8.7. They then will share what they wrote with another small group and some will report to the entire class. This kind of activity "meets students where they are"—students with different levels of English proficiency can answer the questions appropriate to their level.

There are many versions of image analysis sheets available online including from The National Archives. Check them out and create a version that works best for you and your students.

EXHIBIT 8.7. Image Analysis Sheet

Student Name or Names _____

Image Analysis: Which photo did you choose (one, two or three): _____

A. OBSERVATION: Describe what you see in this picture (people, objects, buildings, landscape, etc.)

B. KNOWLEDGE: Summarize what you already know about the situation in the image and that time in history.

C. INTERPRETATION: Describe what you think is happening in the picture and predict what will happen in the future. If you already think you *know* what happened in history after the situation pictured in the image, write what you think you *know*.

D. List three questions you have about the picture:

1.

2.

3.

Creating Audio/Visual Summaries

Having students create summaries of units is not unusual in Social Studies and other subject classes. We like to have students create these kinds of summaries in a recorded audio-visual form. It not only creates a low-risk way for ELLs to practice speaking, but it also allows for student creativity.

For example, after having completed a three-chapter unit on the American Civil War in our textbook, we had students use the Unit Summary Outline in Exhibit 8.8 to create a narrated slideshow. See the Tech Tool Box to learn about the many free online tools that students can use for such a project.

EXHIBIT 8.8. Unit Summary Outline

Audio Slideshow Unit Report

The first slide should show the name of the unit and your name:

Record:

SLIDE ONE: *The name of the unit is* _____ *and my name is* _____
_____.

Note: **Do not write everything you say on the slides – only key words! And include images!**

SLIDE TWO: *The most important thing I learned in Chapter* _____ *was* _____. *This is important because* _____
_____.

SLIDE THREE: *The most important thing I learned in Chapter* _____ *was* _____. *This is important because* _____
_____.

SLIDE FOUR: *The most important thing I learned in Chapter* _____ *was* _____. *This is important because* _____
_____.

After you have completed a slide for each chapter, make a slide saying:

SLIDE FIVE: *The most important thing I learned in this unit was* _____
_____. *This was the most important thing because* _____
_____.

Your final slide should say:

Of all the things I learned in this unit, the one thing I want to learn more about is

_____.

I want to learn more about this because _____.

Note: Do not write everything you say on the slides – only key words! And include images!

Tech Tool

Audio/Visual Resources

There are many free tools students can use to create audio-narrated slideshows. Find a list at "The Best Sites To Practice Speaking English" https://larryferlazzo .edublogs.org/2008/03/17/the-best-sites-to-practice-speaking-english/. Adobe Spark (https://spark.adobe.com/sp/) is our favorite at the time of our writing this, but that could easily change in the future as new tools become available. If your school has a Brainpop subscription, it's "Make a Movie" tool is also very easy for students to use.

Current Events

There are countless ways to incorporate high-interest current events in a Social Studies class, and you can access many of them in the next Tech Tool Box. After learning about them, we like to incorporate Critical Thinking Dialogues like the one in Exhibit 8.9 on Ethnic Studies.

We do have one other favorite activity we like to use when discussing current events—after reviewing the usual aspects of a topic in the news (who, what, when, where, why), we like to have students think about and discuss *what they think will come next and why they think that will happen.* In fact, that's where we find the energy and thinking to be at its highest.

EXHIBIT 8.9. Critical Thinking Dialogue "Ethnic Studies"

Student One: Have you taken an Ethnic Studies class yet? Do you know what it is about?

Student Two: (Yes, I have/No I have not). It teaches about how different groups have contributed to make the United States what it is today, and talks about the challenges they have faced, including racism.

Student One: That sounds interesting. I've heard that some people don't like it. They say it makes people not like each other, and makes them feel less like a part of this country. What do you think?

Student Two: I think it is a (good/bad) idea because _____. What do you think?

Student One: I think it is a (good/bad) idea because _____. What do you think, _____?

Student Three: I think it is a (good/bad) idea because _____.

Student One: It does sound more interesting than what Mr. Ferlazzo teaches us.

Student Two: You should be nice to Mr. Ferlazzo. He tries his best.

Student Three: Yes, just because he is old and makes lots of mistakes, we should still be nice to him.

Tech Tool

Current Events

Many different ways to approach current events in accessible ways can be found at "The Best Resources & Ideas For Teaching About Current Events" https://larry ferlazzo.edublogs.org/2016/10/16/the-best-resources-ideas-for-teaching-about-current-events/.

Clozes

We discuss clozes (also called "gap-fills") in Chapter Five. They are fill-in-the-blank "puzzles" where students act as "detectives" searching for "clues" that assist them in identifying the words that belong in the blanks (we also generally ask students to highlight those "clue" words or write reasons for their choosing the words).

One example of a cloze with a word bank can be seen in Exhibit 8.10. There are many possible variations, including having students create their own that classmates can complete. See the Tech Tool box for additional resources

Tech Tool

Clozes

- There are many different versions of clozes, and there are a number of free online tools available to use when creating them. Learn about these ideas and sites at "The Best Tools For Creating Clozes (Gap-Fills)" https://larryferlazzo.edublogs .org/2012/04/30/the-best-tools-for-creating-clozes-gap-fills/.

EXHIBIT 8.10. Slavery Cloze

The trip that enslaved people were forced to take from Africa after they were kidnapped was called the Middle Passage. Many _____ people died during this trip. They were imprisoned in areas below the deck of the ship and kept in chains. The trip could last eighty days. The enslaved people might be given small amounts of food and _____ twice a day. The areas where enslaved people were forced to stay were _____. Many _____ of disease on the voyage.

water

enslaved

died

dirty

REFLECTION

Any of the reflection activities discussed in Chapter Three can be incorporated in a social studies class. We especially like utilizing retrieval practice by asking students to write in "warm-ups" the most important content they learned—and why they think it's important—from the previous day or week, and then share (in pairs, in Speed Dating where students quickly share with their classmates one after another, or in small groups).

OTHER SUPPORT

Chapter Seven listed a number of useful instructional strategies that can be used by content area teachers to help their ELL students (and other students), including wait time, talking speed, the use of gestures, and Word Charts to assist vocabulary acquisition, bilingual dictionaries, preview-view-review, providing instructions verbally and in writing, and "transfer" assignments from ELL classes. These are all applicable to social studies classes, and in the next subsections we highlight a few more.

Simplified Texts. Both the value of text "previews" in students' home languages and the importance of "amplifying" texts instead of "simplifying" them were discussed in Chapter Seven. However, prioritizing those strategies does not mean teachers should *never* use more simplified texts. In many situations, ELLs can gain greater comprehension of content lessons if they have specific prior knowledge. For example, knowing about slavery in the United States is important prior to studying the American Civil War. In those cases, providing "simplified" text containing the needed prior knowledge could be a very useful instructional strategy. In fact, there are numerous free online resources where teachers can obtain or create the "same" text at different lexile levels so that it's easy to provide all students with the same resource. See the Tech Tool Box for these kinds of online resources.

Tech Tool
Simplified Text Resources

There are many free sites providing thousands of accessible text at different lexile levels, as well as tools that let you do the same for any text of your choosing. See "The Best Places To Get The 'Same' Text Written For Different 'Levels'" https://larry ferlazzo.edublogs.org/2014/11/16/the-best-places-to-get-the-same-text-written-for-different-levels/ for more information.

Graphic Organizers. In our description of the Organizing Cycle, we provided information and resources on graphic organizers. One organizer we have found particularly useful in social studies is called the Historical Head. This sheet, which is just a simple outline of a large empty head, can be labeled as a specific historical figure or a group of people the class is studying. Of course, when using this activity, it is important to view it as a tool for understanding and not for re-enactment—we don't want students to try to "walk in someone's shoes" if it can create trauma for them. Students can draw or paste five images inside the head representing the "thoughts, ideas, visions, and motivations" of the person or people. Each image is numbered and then a brief written description explaining how the image connects to the person can be written on the back.[4]

Reviews and Summaries. Holding a brief review at the beginning of class and a brief summary at the end (with students actively participating in both) can be particularly helpful to ELLs in a social studies class.[5]

Tech Tool
Interactive Content Class Resources

In addition to the many primary language online resources available to help ELLs in content areas, including in Social Studies, that were mentioned in Chapter Seven, there are numerous free sites offering engaging social studies resources in English that are accessible to all students, and especially to English language learners. Sites for all content-area classes can be found in "My Best of Series" at https://larry ferlazzo.edublogs.org/best-of-week/ .

Links to all the online activities listed in the chapter, as well as to the downloadable student handouts, can be found at www.wiley.com/go/ eslsurvivalguide2.

CHAPTER NINE

Teaching Science

The Buddha was born as a bird, and he lived together with a flock of birds in a mighty tree; the Buddha was the king of these birds. The branches of the tree where the birds lived began to grind one against the other, producing sparks and smoke. The Buddha realized that these sparks and smoke were the signs of a fire that was coming, so he warned all the other birds. "I have seen the sparks," he told them, "and I have seen the smoke. To save ourselves, we must fly away now, before it is too late." The wise birds listened, but the foolish birds ignored the Buddha's warning. The whole tree eventually caught on fire, and the foolish birds perished in the flames.[1]

In this Buddhist parable, the wise bird is a kind of scientist: he studies the natural world, and he shares what he has learned with others. In the science classroom, students learn both about scientific discovery and about scientific communication, which gives English Language Learners (ELLs) many new opportunities to develop their language skills.

This chapter was written by Stephen Fleenor, PhD. He is an educational consultant in San Antonio, Texas with Seidlitz Education (www.seidlitzeducation.com). Stephen earned a PhD in Developmental Neurobiology from the University of Oxford before teaching high school science in San Antonio. His pedagogy developed out of a passion to serve English language learners and other students while spreading his love for science. As a facilitator of professional development and developer of educational materials, he advocates for a growth-minded approach to teaching and learning that encourages and strengthens learners' academic expression.

Introduction: Science and Language

Learning science is as much a process of acquiring language as it is that of conceptualizing the natural world. In addition to being able to master a large and conceptually complex lexicon, science students must also master the intricacies of spoken and written science language to become successful professionals[2] in STEM (science, technology, engineering, math) fields. For that reason, language-rich pedagogy is simply the most effective method of teaching science.

In fact, science instruction that specifically focuses on the English language development of English Language Learners (ELLs) has been shown to result in dramatically enhanced performance on science assessments. In Texas, for example, former ELLs (who were determined to have achieved English language proficiency) substantially outperformed the general population in all three statewide science assessments during the 2017–2018 school year (see Figure 9.1). Similarly, current and former ELLs dramatically outperformed the general population on the 2015 statewide science assessments in several California school districts. According to a report from The Education Trust-West, what set these districts apart from other districts was that they were "engaged in innovative initiatives to advance science learning for EL students."[3]

This data suggests that (a) increasing English-language development of ELLs results in better science learning, and that (b) English-only students comprising the general population are not as proficient with science language as their former-ELL peers. Therefore, language-rich approaches are not only good for ELLs but necessary for *all* science students.

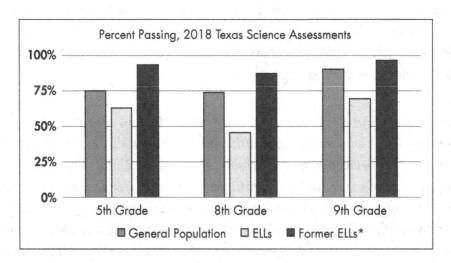

Figure 9.1. Percentage of general population (gray), ELL (light green), or former ELL (dark green) students on the Spring 2018 STAAR assessments in Texas. *Former ELLs were in the second year after exiting ELL services at the time of testing.

Source: Texas Education Agency, 2018.

Such language-rich approaches go hand-in-hand with the innovations in teaching since the release of the Next Generation Science Standards (NGSS) in 2013. These standards, which have either been adopted or used as a model in 44 US states, focus on a more student-centered approach to learning science: less passive listening, more doing; less memorizing facts, more asking questions; less learning units or modules in isolation, more connection building across science. This a dramatic, exciting, and challenging shift in teaching science for K-12 science teachers.

In this chapter, I describe specific pedagogical practices and strategies which support all domains of the science language. It is my belief that these practices form a fundamental model to deliver the student-centered ideals of the NGSS. In a language-rich science lesson, we are not simply teaching words but rather the connections between words. And students do not just hear the words but practice using words in varied contexts. Thus, teaching the science language is truly the next-generation standard for science instruction.

CHALLENGES TOWARDS FOSTERING A LANGUAGE-RICH SCIENCE CLASSROOM

Acquiring a new language—be it English, Mandarin Chinese, or, in this case, the science academic language—is conceptually very simple: make input (new content) comprehensible, and provide low-stress opportunities for output.

Many teachers have expressed to me (and indeed, I initially felt myself) that they would love to adopt these practices if only they had the time. Giving a few extra seconds of wait time or allowing students to talk out questions with their partners before calling on them, as two of many examples, adds up to precious minutes every day that could be spent teaching new content. In many teachers' perspectives, the science curriculum is so fast-paced and so deep that there is not a moment to spare away from directly delivering new content to their students. In other words, there is only time for *input* (and hardly time to even scaffold the input to make it comprehensible), and no time for *output*.

And yet, science curriculum is so complex that a model of direct-teach-only almost guarantees that students will, even in the best case, only reach the recall level of science understanding. For students to engage at a deeper level with science curriculum, they need opportunities to master the complexities of science language. In addition to understanding the large number of vocabulary words, Stanford University researcher Jeff Zwiers points out key language processes successful science students need to use.[4] For example, students need to:

- Describe relationships between concepts (e.g. force and acceleration).
- Speak/write objectively with third-person perspective.
- Use nominalizations of words (e.g. *evaporation* as the process of *evaporating*).

These kinds of processes are often less emphasized in students' English language arts classes. Therefore, there is actually no time to *not* teach science as a language. For students to truly begin to describe relationships between abstract concepts and learn to read and write like scientists, they must have just as many opportunities for low-stress output as they do for comprehensible input. Instead of being seen as a distraction from content delivery, taking the time to allow students to think and interact with their peers in a structured way should be seen as an investment in science language development.

QUESTIONING IN THE SCIENCE CLASSROOM

The thinking and peer-to-peer interaction that is so critical for science language development is best mediated through structured questioning. Importantly, these questions should come from both teachers *and* students.

Teacher-Led Questions

For teachers, open-ended questions are always more effective at promoting deep thought and discussion than closed-ended questions. For example, the teacher could show the class a force diagram showing several objects and several forces acting on objects. The teacher could ask the closed-ended question *"Which object is at rest?"* or the open-ended question *"How do you know object B is at rest?"* The closed-ended question has one—and only one—correct response: *object B*. This automatically raises the affective filter (in other words, increases anxiety and decreases motivation) for many students because it raises the stakes: You're either right or wrong. The question also does not provide any structure for discussion about forces acting on objects. The thinking opportunity is limited to the few moments students have between the question and the first volunteer's raised hand.

The open-ended question, by contrast, has many possible correct answers. It allows all students the time and structure to think if the question is posed with ample think time and given to students as a discussion prompt (see "Facilitating Student Conversations" below). Most importantly, there are a million different ways to answer an open-ended question correctly, so the stakes of potential embarrassment in front of the class are kept low. The importance of crafting open-ended questions cannot be understated. The challenge of crafting open-ended questions can also not be understated, and teachers should make sure to plan out key open-ended questions in advance. Exhibit 9.1 outlines several example closed-ended questions with corresponding open-ended questions.

EXHIBIT 9.1. Examples of Closed-Ended Questions with Corresponding Open-Ended Questions

Examples of Closed-Ended Questions	Examples of Open-Ended Questions
If temperature increases, does pressure increase or decrease?	How does increasing temperature cause pressure to increase?
What is a mutation?	Why is it important that DNA can change?
What are the causes for hypertension?	Why is chronic stress more likely to cause hypertension than old age?

Adapted from Fleenor and Beene (2019), p. 66.[4]

It is important to note that sentence stems accompanying questions are tremendously beneficial for ELLs and non-ELLs at all levels of English language proficiency. This is because sentence stems structure student responses using academic language. Sentence stems also give students the opportunity to practice using Tier Two (general academic words) and Tier Three (content-specific vocabulary words) in context. For example, consider the scenario below in which a teacher posts a sentence stem on the board and encourages her students to use it:

Teacher: Jasmine, what is the evidence that a chemical reaction has occurred?

Jasmine: The beaker got hot.

Teacher: (*points to the sentence stem on the board*: "One piece of evidence that a chemical reaction has occurred is _____.") Could you say that again in a complete sentence please?

Jasmine: One piece of evidence that a chemical reaction has occurred is that the beaker got hot.

In using the sentence stem, Jasmine was able to practice using the Tier Three words *beaker* and *chemical reaction* in context with the Tier Two words *evidence* and *occurred*. Sentence stems also help to lower students' affective filter by providing the structure to begin their response in a way that sets them up to "sound smart."

Though open-ended questions are essential to structure deep thinking and discussion, ELLs at early stages of English language development often require closed-ended (fill-in-the-blank-style) sentence stems. These sentence stems can be particularly effective when paired with a word bank and/or labeled visual. For classes with a broad range of English language proficiency, I recommend providing tiered stems (one fill-in-the-blank, one open-ended). Alternatively, the teacher can provide a written closed-ended sentence stem but verbally require students to justify their reasoning in their response. Either method provides scaffolding that beginning ELLs need to succeed as they acquire more fundamental aspects of the English language. See Chapter Five for more background information on Tier One, Two, and Three categorization.

Student-Led Questions

For ELLs and non-ELLs of all English language proficiency levels, encouraging students to be the askers of questions is particularly powerful in the science classroom. But as I explain in *Teaching Science to ELs*, asking the class if they have any questions often results in a room full of blank stares, because the perception for students is:

that the only way to be inquisitive is to ask eloquent, thought-provoking questions which extend the content. This is reinforced by the fact that the askers of these questions are usually the high-performing, highly engaged students of the class who are also first to raise their hands and volunteer an answer. The perception becomes that unless the question is a 'good' question, it should not be asked.[5]

It is important, therefore, to encourage students to ask simple clarifying questions, such as "Can you explain that again please?" (In my own classroom, for example, I had that question on a poster and would pre-select one or two students to ask me the question at any time during the lesson.) This process provides a structure for students to connect with content and their own metacognition in a safe and supportive way. Contrary to the perception that clarifying questions might be "dumb" questions, clarifying questions are in fact at the heart of the scientific process, driving follow-up experimentation and formation of scientific theories. We need to teach our students that asking for clarification is actually one of the smartest things they can do.

VISUALS AND INFERENCING IN THE SCIENCE CLASSROOM

Science is the study of the natural world, which means every lesson is a new opportunity for students to make inferences about a different piece of the natural world. This is best facilitated through the use of visuals. Visuals promote both critical thinking and language development of ELLs by allowing students to connect to the semantic, pragmatic, and sociolinguistic meanings of the vocabulary and concepts the visuals depict.[6] In fact, one analysis of a middle-school science assessment showed that ELLs outperformed non-ELLs on a question which provided a visual even though that question was open-ended and was the most vocabulary-dense question of the entire test.[7]

This kind of success often results from that fact that visuals are both highly accessible and constructivist in nature. Visuals can be understood better because they often contain vocabulary words (many times seen as labels) which are explicitly taught in the science class. In visuals, words like *somehow*, *at least*, or *immediately* are not a filter or barrier in understanding of the science concept. Without the visual, a beginning-level ELL might see the word *immediately* in a text, writing prompt, or discussion stem and have no linguistic framework to understand its meaning. However, the same ELL could infer from a visual that one event occurs very soon after another event; when presented the text, writing prompt, or discussion stem with the word *immediately*, the student now has a context to which he or she can apply meaning (see, for example, Figure 9.2).

Visuals are also highly supportive of ELLs and non-ELLs alike because they drive a constructivist process of learning science. Constructivism is an education theory that suggests learners actively create their knowledge in the context of their perceptions and experiences.[8] It is, of course, necessary in the science classroom for students to learn absolute facts (such as the fact that species evolve over time or that the atom is the fundamental unit of matter) which have complete consensus in the scientific community and which are ingrained into the curriculum. However, it is equally important that students draw meaning in the relationships between these facts and the relationship between these facts and their lives through a constructivist approach to learning.

Figure 9.2. Constructivist Visuals
Example Text
"Prophase, in which dense bodies called chromosomes can be first seen under a microscope, marks the beginning of mitosis and occurs immediately after Interphase."
Example Visual

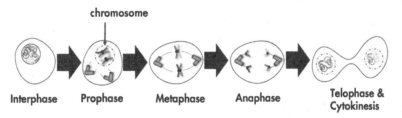

Figure 9.2. If only provided the visual, a student can infer that Prophase occurs as the next step after Interphase without prior knowledge of the word *immediately*. If only provided the text, the student depends on prior knowledge of the word *immediately* to understand that Prophase occurs as the next step after Interphase. If provided the visual with the text, the student can acquire *immediately* into his/her vocabulary, understanding that *immediately* refers to the next step after an event.

Visuals play an enormous role in constructivist learning by allowing students to understand and express concepts in their own words. According to Martina A. Rau at the University of Wisconsin-Madison, visuals can be thought of as "thinking tools for individuals and groups, communication tools, as well as problem-solving tools."[9] When students engage in structured conversations about their understanding from visuals, they are engaging in critical thinking. Think of facts that students need to learn as dots, and critical thinking as the lines connecting the dots. Having a visual as a reference point in a structured conversation between students is an ideal scaffold for helping students to connect the dots.

Activities Using Visuals

There are many excellent examples of activities science teachers can provide that promote inferencing and language through visuals. What they have in common is: one or more visuals, possibly with labeled vocabulary; opportunities for peer-to-peer discussion of the visuals; and structure (such as sentence stems) for using and thinking about relationships in vocabulary. One example activity is *Tap and Talk*,[10] in which students are given several different visuals and a word bank with several different vocabulary words (see Figure 9.3). Students take turns in groups or with partners discussing which word each picture represents (using, for example, the sentence stem *I think this picture represents _____ because. . .*). The pictures can be scientific models, such as a cartoon of molecules dissolved in a beaker, or metaphorical representations, such as a sponge soaked with water (either picture could justifiably represent the word *saturated*). Another activity, *Vocab Connection Web*,[11] requires students to create a web of vocabulary words with lines drawn between them and relationships between the words written along the lines. For example, students might write the words *tissue* and *cell* on the paper, and along the line between the words, write "a *tissue* is a group of *cells*."

A note of caution: Visuals should not be meant to replace text entirely from the science classroom. Language development depends on the practice of reading text with contextualized understanding as well as the practice of writing text. Visuals should be presented as scaffolds before and/or during reading passages, and during structured conversations and writing. With visuals as a guide, the science language development of all learners is enhanced.

Facilitating Structured Conversations

A common thread between questioning strategies, using visuals, and any other strategies designed to support ELLs in content areas, is the absolute need for structured peer-to-peer conversations. Structured conversations are the "low-stress output"

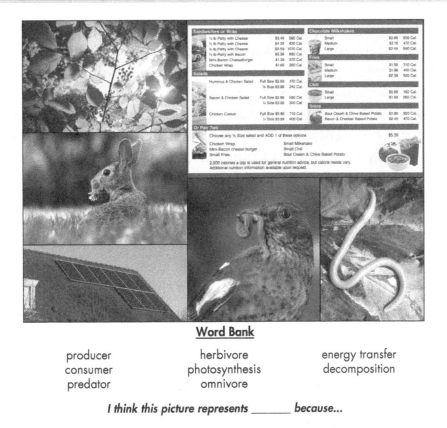

Word Bank

producer	herbivore	energy transfer
consumer	photosynthesis	decomposition
predator	omnivore	

I think this picture represents _____ because...

Figure 9.3. Example set of visuals and word bank for *Tap and Talk* activity. Each picture justifiably represents multiple vocabulary words. For image attribution, see Reference List.

Figure 9.3 Image Attribution

"Animals Nature Bird" by Gellinger [CC0] (*no alterations*) via Pixabay https://pixabay.com/photos/animals-nature-bird-blackbird-worm-3329900/

"Leaves Flora Tree" by valiunic [CC0] (*cropped*) via Pixabay https://pixabay.com/photos/leaves-flora-tree-branch-park-3089991/

"Letter S Earthworm" by Eukalyptus [CC0] (*rotated*) via Pixabay https://pixabay.com/photos/letter-s-earthworm-lumbricidae-202404/

"Menu or Menu Board Offering Standard items for a Special Price" by U.S. Food and Drug Administration [Public Domain] (*no alterations*) via Flickr https://www.flickr.com/photos/fdaphotos/40968303264

"Rabbit Hare Animal" by 12019 [CC0] (*no alterations*) via Pixabay https://pixabay.com/photos/rabbit-hare-animal-cute-adorable-1903016/

"Solar Panel Array Roof Home" by skeeze [CC0] (*no alterations*) via Pixabay https://pixabay.com/photos/solar-panel-array-roof-home-house-1591358/

"Animals Nature Bird" by Gellinger [CC0] (*no alterations*) via Pixabay https://pixabay.com/photos/animals-nature-bird-blackbird-worm-3329900/

half of the second-language acquisition equation. The "structure" of these conversations includes scaffolds for student participation and success. This could mean using sentence stems, specifying who speaks to whom, providing wait time, repetition of instructions or the question, or all of the above.

All of these scaffolds are embedded within the QSSSA ("Q-triple S-A") strategy.[12] QSSSA has been shown to be significantly effective at encouraging 100 percent participation, promoting depth of student discussions, and improving student learning outcomes.[13] I personally used QSSSA as a matter of practice in teaching high school as well as currently in adult learning settings. It is as simple as this: As a teacher, if I want my students to be engaged in a structured conversation about content (which is usually at least half of the time), I use QSSSA. QSSSA is an acronym that represents each step of the process:

Question: Open-ended and posed slowly. The expectation should be clear that students should not respond immediately.

Signal: A gesture the students make to indicate readiness. The teacher should not proceed until all students have given the signal.

Stem: The sentence stem students should use in their response, directly based on the question.

Share: The instructions for which students will speak to whom, and who will speak first (for example, speak in your groups, with the tallest person speaking first).

Assess: Randomly calling on students, either through randomization strategies or selecting a random member from each group to share.

The first three steps of this process (Question, Signal, and Stem) set up the structure for thinking and academic speaking. Wait time is built into the thinking signal, and the stem makes it clear to all students how they should begin their responses. A common and effective variation is to provide the sentence stem first, then instruct the students to give the thinking signal when they are ready to finish the stem. The latter two steps (Share and Assess) ensure total participation and lower the affective filter: Students know they will be accountable to their peers and possibly the entire class (if randomly called upon in the Assess step), but they also know they can discuss and get ideas from their peers.

Below is an example of how a science teacher might employ QSSSA:

"Okay class, I want you to think about how the revolution of the Earth causes seasons. Will everyone please raise their hands?" *(All students raise their hands.)* **"Take a look at the 'Revolution and Rotation' anchor chart. When you are ready to describe how the revolution of the Earth causes seasons, go ahead and lower your hand."** *(The teacher waits approximately 10 seconds for all students to lower their hands, then continues.)* **"I want you to use the stem, "The revolution of the Earth causes seasons by. . . ."** *(The teacher* *points to the board, where the sentence stem is written.)* **"Turn to your partner, and the partner closest to the window speaks first. Remember to use the sentence stem."** *(Students discuss with their partners as the teacher walks around the room, listening to the discussions. When about half of the students have finished discussing, the teacher reaches into a cup and pulls out two popsicle sticks.)* **"Let's all come back together, class. Okay, I want to hear from two people. First, Araceli. Araceli, in a complete sentence, tell us, please, how does the revolution of the Earth cause seasons?"**

In this example, the teacher created a safe environment for students to think about and discuss science content while setting them up for success. It was completely clear to the class who they should be talking to, how they should be talking, and what they should be talking about. Importantly, the teacher put the power in the students' hands to determine how much thinking time they needed by asking them to lower their hand when ready. In my experience, the thinking signal is the most important component of QSSSA in ensuring successful participation, but ironically also tends to be the easiest for a teacher to forget when beginning to implement QSSSA. For the first few instances of implementing QSSSA, I recommend teachers write out and post each step ahead of time, including the signal. The step-by-step structure becomes less necessary and the process becomes more fluid when teachers use QSSSA on a regular basis. Also, student responses to the process of engaging in structured conversations becomes similarly more fluid. This is truly when a classroom becomes language-rich and when students feel completely confident with science language. When QSSSA is used on a regular basis, the words "I don't know" are almost never uttered.

Evidence-Based Reasoning

A hallmark of next-generation science instruction is inquiry-driven evidence collection and reasoning. To be successful in science classes and STEM professions (as well as many other subjects and careers), students must be able to ask questions related to their work, collect relevant evidence to support the questions, and justify answers to the questions from the evidence. This process, known sometimes as inquiry science or evidence-based reasoning, has increased in popularity in science curricula and instruction in recent years due to the increasing demand of critical reasoning skills in the STEM workforce. Following some controversy about whether evidence-based reasoning is accessible and beneficial to ELLs, a 2018 meta-analysis of 26 studies found a significant gain in science achievement scores for ELLs who were exposed to evidence-based reasoning in their instruction.[14]

In their analysis, the researchers cited contextual factors to explain the variation in success of evidence-based reasoning on ELL performance, including how much professional development the teachers implementing evidence-based reasoning instruction received. In general, effective implementers of evidence-based reasoning organize their teaching in a way that is beneficial to ELLs and non-ELLs alike. In this process, teachers use strategies like sentence stems to break up the process of inquiry into manageable chunks. For example, following presentation of a central question, students could have structured conversations using the sentence stem "_____ is a piece of evidence related to the question because. . . ." Following this structured conversation, students could discuss and write structured justifications of their reasoning based on their evidence.

Structured evidence-based reasoning is equally effective in the laboratory setting.[15] An initial collection of evidence could include students' background knowledge about a topic, followed by a hypothesis based on the evidence. Then a second round of evidence can be collected as the observations or measurements from the laboratory experiment.

For example, when assigned the question "Why do objects float?" students can first brainstorm what they know about flotation: weight, density, which objects from their personal lives they've seen float or not float, etc. Then students can form a hypothesis based on the evidence from their prior knowledge about why objects float. A student's hypothesis might be, "I think light objects float because they do not have enough force of gravity to push through the surface of the water." Students then make measurements of the masses of different objects and whether or not they float, then discuss the evidence in a second round of reasoning to draw a conclusion.

Written between the lines of this example are abundant opportunities for students to discuss their thinking in structured ways. Evidence-based reasoning is a powerful approach to engage science students in deep thinking. The science teacher of ELLs must ensure this approach is accessible to all students, by making the process comprehensible and providing numerous opportunities for low-stress output.

For the ELL Teacher Supporting Science Students

Increasing proficiency in the science language is essential for all science students. For ELLs, growing science language proficiency also accompanies growing English language proficiency. The ELL teacher, whether in a pull-out, push-in, or whole-class role, is uniquely poised to support ELLs' English-language development through supplemental science instruction.

In fact, one study showed that when ELL teachers used inquiry-based science experiences as the platform to promote English-language development, the testing performance on both science and English tests significantly improved.[16] While science instruction is typically shortened in favor of expanded English language arts instruction for ELLs, the study's concluding remarks actually recommended lengthening language-rich science instruction *as a means* to improving English language skills of ELLs.

One advantage science instruction has among other content areas is the abundance of engaging inquiry-based experiences like those highlighted in the study above. ELL teachers (particularly those who teach ELLs in a whole-class ELL setting) can capitalize on many fun, simple experiments to encourage students to listen, speak, read, and write about science content. ELL teachers should communicate with ELLs' mainstream science teachers so that ELL lessons can preview upcoming content from mainstream lessons, such that ELLs will have more comprehension and practice when they enter the mainstream class.

In all units of study, an aspect of science content on which ELL teachers should focus intently is building vocabulary. Vocabulary, of course, is paramount to science instruction for all learners, but repetition and practicing of vocabulary for ELLs is doubly important as they learn English structures and struggle to comprehend at the same pace as non-ELLs. An emphasis on the form (pronunciation, spelling, and prefixes, roots, and suffixes) in addition to meaning of technical science vocabulary words in ELL classes has been shown to significantly increase retention of science vocabulary words and resulting performance.[17]

ELL teachers can also support ELLs by explicitly teaching Tier Two words in addition to Tier Three vocabulary words. In the mainstream instructional setting which all ELLs and non-ELLs receive, only Tier 3 words are often taught; Tier Two words are assumed to be known previously and are refined in the context of lessons. This assumption of course is often invalid for ELLs (particularly those at the beginning stages of English language proficiency), and the ELL teacher's role is vital in supporting acquisition of those words. A study on the effects of instructional emphasis of Tier Two and Tier Three vocabulary words showed a significant gain in reading comprehension for ELLs and non-ELLs alike.[18] Thus, while the content of mainstream science classes might be centered around Tier Three vocabulary words only, the content of ELL lessons can and should include emphasis on Tier Two words as well as Tier Three words.

Finally, ELL teachers can help science teachers in planning to make their lessons more language-rich. Great questions for discussion during planning meetings include:

- What opportunities do students have for structured conversations in this lesson?
- What language do you want to see in your students' verbal/written responses to the questions/prompts?

- What sentence stem(s) or other structures will help set students up to use that language?

With a dedicated team of ELL and mainstream science teachers crafting language-rich science instruction, ELLs will be set up to master both the English language and the science language.

CONCLUDING REMARKS

Science is the study of the world around us. That, in and of itself, is completely amazing! Science is a daily interaction with the big and small, the beautiful and strange, and the infinitely complex and interesting. Whenever I hear of a person who says, "I don't like science," or, "I'm not a science person," I always believe that person simply hasn't yet learned to speak and comprehend the language of science. But we can change that! Structured science lessons which emphasize listening, speaking, reading, and writing, with deep critical reasoning opportunities about natural phenomena, can lead to that comprehension of science language for *all* learners.

Tech Tool

Science Resources

For additional Science resources, please see "The Best Resources For Teaching The Next Generation Science Standards To English Language Learners" https://larryferlazzo.edublogs.org/2014/11/22/the-best-resources-for-teaching-the-next-generation-science-standards-to-english-language-learners/.

Links to all the online activities listed in the chapter, as well as to the downloadable student handouts, can be found at www.wiley.com/go/eslsurvivalguide2.

CHAPTER TEN

Teaching Math

Tenalirama was the court poet, and also the court jester, of King Krishnadevaraya, a ruler of the Vijayanagara Empire in southern India during the 16th century. This is a famous legend about the king and his jester:

"Your new poem pleases me, Tenalirama," said the king. "Name your reward!"

Tenalirama pointed to the king's chessboard. "Just put one sesame seed here," Tenalirama told the king, "and then put two seeds on this next square; four seeds here; then eight, then sixteen, and so on, until the board is covered with sesame seeds. That will satisfy me!"

The king laughed. "That's too small a reward!"

"Not at all!" Tenalirama replied, smiling.

The king quickly discovered that Tenalirama was correct: he put one sesame seed on the first square, and then two, four, eight, sixteen, and so on. But by the time he started the second row he needed 256 sesame seeds. . . and over 30,000 sesame seeds would be needed on the last square of the second row. And there were still six more rows to go.

The royal treasurer performed the calculations nervously. "This will bankrupt the kingdom!" he exclaimed. "Billions upon billions of sesame seeds will be needed, Your Highness. The whole world does not contain enough sesame seeds to satisfy Tenalirama's request."

Then Tenalirama laughed, and the king also laughed.

"I knew you were a skilled poet," said the king. "I had no idea you were also a mathematician!"[1]

As this story from India shows, mathematics can be full of surprises. If you're curious, the number of sesame seeds that would need to go on the final square of the chessboard would be 9,223,372,036,854,775,808! It's not always obvious where a mathematics problem may lead, and students might need to learn new ways of thinking, along with new ways of reading and writing, as they develop their mathematical skills and awareness.

This chapter was written by Cindy Garcia. Cindy has been a bilingual educator for 15 years and is currently a districtwide specialist for P-6 bilingual/ESL mathematics. She is active on Twitter at @CindyGarciaTX and on her blog (https://teachingelementaryels.weebly.com/)

Introduction

Mathematics is considered by many to be the "universal language" because regardless of the different symbols, notations, units of measurement, and words used, the mathematical principles of mathematics remain the same. While that statement is true, in order for our English Language Learners to fully comprehend those mathematical principles and explore how mathematics works, they need to be able to communicate effectively about mathematics.

The Common Core Standards are composed of Standards for Mathematical Practice and Standards for Mathematics Content. The eight Standards for Mathematical Practice describe ways in which all students are expected to engage with mathematics across levels in such a way that they develop deep understanding of mathematical concepts from elementary through high school.

CCSS.MATH.PRACTICE.MP1 Make sense of problems and persevere in solving them.

CCSS.MATH.PRACTICE.MP2 Reason abstractly and quantitatively.

CCSS.MATH.PRACTICE.MP3 Construct viable arguments and critique the reasoning of others.

CCSS.MATH.PRACTICE.MP4 Model with mathematics.

CCSS.MATH.PRACTICE.MP5 Use appropriate tools strategically.

CCSS.MATH.PRACTICE.MP6 Attend to precision.

CCSS.MATH.PRACTICE.MP7 Look for and make use of structures.

CCSS.MATH.PRACTICE.MP8 Look for and express regularity in repeated reasoning.

There are four main challenges that English Language Learners encounter in the mathematics classroom as they engage with the eight Standards for Mathematical Practice:

1. Reading mathematics texts
2. Knowledge of appropriate academic vocabulary
3. Participating in mathematical conversations
4. Understanding abstract concepts

Challenge: Reading Mathematics Texts

EXPLANATION OF THE CHALLENGE

Mathematics is its own reading genre and students' reading skills can support or hinder their understanding of mathematics embedded in math context. In order for mathematics to be more accessible to English Language Learners it is critical for students to be explicitly taught how to read mathematics and how it differs from reading in other situations and content areas.

INSTRUCTIONAL STRATEGIES TO SUPPORT ENGLISH LEARNERS

Mathematics is much more than good computational skills. Students' reading skills can support or hinder their understanding of mathematics embedded in context. In order for mathematics to be more accessible to English Language Learners (ELLs) it is critical for students to be explicitly taught how to read mathematics and how that differs from reading in other situations. Math researcher Joan M. Kenney writes: "Mathematics teachers do not need to become reading specialists in order to help students read mathematics texts, but they do need their help in reading in mathematical contexts."[2] We can help students build their math literacy by taking the time to analyze how a mathematics text is structured and how to approach reading it.

In English language arts students read left to right and top to bottom. There might be a picture or a graphic that they can look at any time during the reading to clarify meaning. How should students read a mathematics text that contains a graph or chart? How should students approach a mathematics text that contains various types of representations, charts, tables, math symbols, word labels, short phrases, and sentences. In mathematics, text is not just words read left to right and top to bottom. For example, when analyzing graphs, it is common to read a combination of words, numbers, and symbols from bottom to top and right to left in order to understand all of the data presented. Assumed directionality when reading could lead to students committing an error that breaks down their understanding of a foundation concept. For example, 21<57> 13 could be read by a student as 21 is less than 57 greater than 13 rather than 21 is less than 57, 57 is greater than 13. The second statement is precise and supports students understanding of the meaning of the comparison symbols.

It is important for math teachers to include short grammar mini-lessons in their classes. This instruction can make connections to what ELLs have learned in their language arts classes and see how that is applicable in math. Prepositions such as on, after, for, below, at, to, over, and in can lead to student misconceptions when reading because they might not understand that these small words can change the implied meaning of another word or add precision to a phrase. Think about the following problem: *Sam saved a total of $6 over 3 weeks.* In this example the meaning of over refers to extended periods of time. Without spotlighting prepositions, students might not understand that the $6 must last all 3 weeks.

In mathematics, proper nouns rarely make a big impact on a mathematical concept. Students should spend their time grappling with the concept rather than trying to read the name of a store in a word problem like *Shioban's Sundae Shop*. Students can practice locating proper nouns and renaming them with easier names to read and pronounce or just use the initials of the proper nouns. Ideally, of course, teachers can find the time to rewrite word problems to make them more accessible and reflective of their student population.

Cognates can be a powerful tool to use with vocabulary previously learned in Spanish or other Romance languages. Students need to be aware that they may already know the meaning of words such as *angle, perimeter, area, volume, minute* and *decimals* because they appear similar to the words *ángulo, perímetro, área, volumen, minuto, and decimales*. Realizing that there are cognates in mathematical terms can make them more accessible.

In mathematics, we encounter words that have various meanings in math, other subject areas, and everyday life. Students need the opportunity to find these polysemous terms in order to make sense of their meaning in mathematics. Sometimes, if students do not fully understand a concept, they define important terms with definitions or examples unrelated to the concept being taught. For example, the word "degree" can refer to a unit of measurement of an angle (mathematics), a unit of measurement for temperature (science), or an academic rank (everyday life).

Practicing the strategies of visualization, chunking the text, and summarizing will support students to make sense of what they have read. Educator Laney Sammons writes: "Educators must teach students to draw upon their own inner resources to generate mental images of what they read and the mathematics with which they work to strengthen their abilities to construct meaning."[3] Students must practice using previous learning and daily life to generate mental images while they are reading. Students can also access classroom anchor charts, manipulatives, and physical objects as references to form their mental images. After students generate the mental images, they can draw a representation of what they see in their mind. As they continue reading, they can revise their representation as needed. The purpose of visualization is to help students make an abstract idea more concrete and then use the representation to make sense of the mathematics.

Some students can feel overwhelmed by just looking at a piece of text that mixes words, numbers, symbols, and graphics. To reduce this kind of stress, students can practice reorganizing and chunking text by creating bullet points (obviously, a teacher would need to model this process first). Bulleting mathematics text makes it easier to understand the math because each action, step, question, and piece of data is its own line of text. Students can routinely determine and share the most important information or ideas from a text. One way to have students practice summarizing is by asking them to work in partners to read a math problem and identify the three most important pieces of information necessary to complete the task.

The complexity of the English language when students are reading independently can increase the difficulty level of mathematics. Students can feel defeated by the words before they are able to dig deep into the math. Providing them with these reading comprehension strategies will make mathematics more accessible to all students regardless of language proficiency level. The standards of "make sense of problems" (CCSS) and "reason abstractly and quantitatively" (CCSS) can be met if teachers show students how math texts are organized, facilitate grammar mini-lessons, and promote the use of reading strategies .

Challenge: Knowledge of Appropriate Academic Vocabulary

EXPLANATION OF THE CHALLENGE

Tier One, Tier Two, or Tier Three vocabulary[4] strongly affects students' ability to master the following standards because limited vocabulary makes it difficult to craft descriptive and in-depth explanations. Tier One vocabulary consists of everyday and daily life words such as container and patio. Tier Two vocabulary consists of general cross-curricular words, such as explain, analyze, and justify. Tier Three vocabulary consists of mathematics specific words such as denominator and numerator. ELLs need to learn all three in order to access grade-level mathematics content.

INSTRUCTIONAL STRATEGIES TO SUPPORT ENGLISH LEARNERS

It is imperative when lesson planning that the teacher select the most important Tier One, Tier Two, and Tier Three words to focus on during the lesson. The words selected should be those that have the greatest impact in students understanding the concept and will have a high impact on subsequent lessons. Educator John Hattie suggests: "In addition to identifying words that students need to know, the timing for providing instruction of those words is important. In too many cases, students are exposed to new words before they need to use them."[5] Instead of front-loading all important vocabulary prior to starting a new unit of study, it is more effective to decide which words should be taught before, during, or after the lesson. Here are some examples:

Before the Lesson:

- Consider what students should have previously learned. For example, reviewing the names of two-dimensional figures before the lesson is appropriate for most fourth-grade students because they probably learned most of those terms in third grade. Previewing the names of angles is not appropriate because this was not part of the third-grade standards and students do not have prior knowledge of this information.

- Explain and explore the context before working on math tasks. Use pictures, videos, or real-life items to activate student schema and make connections to the Tier 1 vocabulary they will encounter. For example, if the context is attending a summer camp some possible Tier One vocabulary could be *camp, cabins, counselor, campers, woods,* and *canoes.*

- Review Tier Two vocabulary that they will encounter during the unit of study. Are students able to explain the meaning of each word based on previous lessons or work in other content areas? Do students know what actions they are supposed to take when they see those words?

During the Lesson:

- Teachers can choose not to preview or review vocabulary. Instead, teachers can strategically choose stopping points during the lesson to explore the meaning of the vocabulary as the students engage and use the words to work on math tasks successfully.

After the Lesson:

- If a concept is new to students or if a large number of students have not had instruction related to the math concept in more than one school year, then Tier Three vocabulary should be reviewed at the end of the lesson. After the lesson has concluded and students have an experience to connect to that vocabulary, teachers can spend time reviewing the vocabulary. Teachers can use this time to clarify misunderstandings and check student comprehension.

Whether vocabulary instruction takes place before, during, or after the lesson, there are specific steps to support student understanding and use of the vocabulary.

Steps for Vocabulary Instruction:
1. Post each word clearly written for all students to see.
2. Choral read or echo read each word as a whole group.
3. Prompt students to generate and share the meaning or an example of the word.
4. Reach a consensus for the classroom definition or example of the word.
5. Prompt students to generate non-linguistic representations or real-life example of the word.
6. Reach a consensus for the classroom representation or pictorial example. Add the representation or example to the posted word.
7. Create a word bank for each mathematics concept.
8. Create a math word wall. Each math concept should have its own Tier Three word bank that the teacher and students build together.

The focus on Tier One, Tier Two, and Tier Three vocabulary instruction helps students as they "construct viable arguments" (CCSS) and "express regularity in repeated learning" (CCSS).

Challenge: Participating in Mathematics Conversations

EXPLANATION OF THE CHALLENGE

English Learners need multiple opportunities every day to talk and reason about mathematics with their peers and teachers. As math educators, Suzanne H. Chapin, Catherine O'Connor and Nancy Canavan Anderson state: "Classroom dialogue may provide direct access to ideas, relationships among those ideas, strategies, procedures, facts, mathematical history, and more. Classroom dialogue supports student learning indirectly through the building of a social environment a community that encourages learning."[6] However, due to the varying levels of language proficiency of English Language Learners not all students will be able to participate in conversations to the depth expected of the standards. Not all students have had the opportunity to be active participants in two-way conversations in their mathematics classrooms. Furthermore, when taking part in conversations it is not guaranteed that students will use appropriate Tier Two and Tier Three academic vocabulary.

INSTRUCTIONAL STRATEGIES TO SUPPORT ENGLISH LEARNERS

Mathematics is not always the "universal language" and may pose challenges for English Language Learners because people don't always speak in their daily life the way that they speak in the mathematics classroom. It is important that students' affective filters[7] are lowered (so students feel safe and confident) to allow them to be able to produce output in English. English Language Learners can benefit from having scaffolded classroom conversations that help them learn how to take part in productive math conversations.

Talk Moves   Using "Talk Moves" can help teachers build a classroom culture that encourages students to share their thinking in a risk-free environment. Talk Moves are specific strategies and prompts that provide students "think time" and a way to organize their thoughts before speaking. They can include:

- Revoicing: The teacher or another student restates the thought shared by a student. Then the student is asked to verify the paraphrased statement. Revoicing allows students to practice expressing themselves succinctly and in a way that others will understand.
    - Possible revoicing prompts include:
        - I heard you say. . . .
        - You're thinking that . . . .
        - You said that . . . .
        - So, did you mean . . . .?
- Paraphrasing: The students paraphrase what another student has said and use their own words. In order to paraphrase ideas that have been shared, students must listen carefully and can use their classmates' and teacher's language as models.
    - A possible paraphrasing prompt could be:
        - Paraphrase what your classmate said in your own words.
- Reasoning: Students listen to ideas shared and figure out if they agree with them. Reasoning prompts students to listen critically to what is being said because they will need to share their opinion using their prior knowledge. Reasoning also provides students the opportunity to change or modify their solution or response because they have heard important information from their peers.

- Possible reasoning prompts include:
  - Do you agree or disagree with your classmate's thinking? Why?
  - How is your idea different?
- Adding On: A student shares an idea and another student is encouraged to add on and extend the idea. This process can support students who are having difficulties expressing their thinking because they do not have to come up with a completely new response. However, they are still able to contribute to the conversation. Adding on encourages students to actively listen to various perspectives because they will need to extend a thought and not just paraphrase it.
  - Possible adding on prompts include:
    - How can you add on to what your classmate shared?
    - What else can you say to make the response more clear?
- Wait Time: After a question is posed or a problem is presented the teacher provides students with think time to organize their thoughts and consider how they will explain their thinking.
  - Possible wait time prompts include:
    - Think carefully about what you will share.
    - Take your time, we are not in a hurry.

Math Routines Short five-to-ten-minute "math routines" can prompt students to share what they are thinking. These routines can vary greatly and can range from asking students to estimate the number of jelly beans in a bottle to discussing a common error made by students. They can include Talk Moves to facilitate math conversations.

Below is a list of sites that can be used for math routine discussions:

- www.estimation180.com
- www.stevewyborney.com
- http://wodb.ca/

Language Frames Targeted language frames are tools that can be used to scaffold classroom conversations. Language frames support students in using specific vocabulary while speaking in complete sentences. They can use increasingly complex language structures. One advantage with language frames in the mathematics classroom is that similar ones are used in K-12. The vocabulary is different, but the language structure remains the same. Language frames can be differentiated based on language proficiency in order to support students' language development. Exhibit 10.1 shows an example of how to differentiate a common language frame.

EXHIBIT 10.1. Language Frames

Most Common Language Frame:

- The _____ is _____.
  - The angle is obtuse.

Differentiated Language Frames:

- I determined the _____ is _____ because it measures _____.
  - I determined the <u>angle</u> is <u>obtuse</u> because it measures <u>100 degrees</u>.
- I think the _____ is _____ since _____.
  - I think the angle is obtuse since it measures more than 90 degrees.
- Based on the _____ measurement of the angle, the given angle is _____.
  - Based on the 100-degree measurement of the angle, the given angle is obtuse.

Using Talk Moves and language frames as scaffolds during math conversations can support students in developing their abilities to "construct viable arguments and critique the reasoning of others" and "express regularity in repeated reasoning" (CCSS).

Challenge: Understanding Abstract Concepts

EXPLANATION OF THE CHALLENGE

Explanations of abstract mathematics concepts may be difficult for our English Language Learners to understand if they have not been in US schools and following the usually US progression. In order to make math concepts comprehensible, ELLs need to be able to see, touch and apply the mathematics in a such a way that will allow them to make sense of it.

Instructional Strategies to Support English Learners

Manipulatives and visual representations are effective strategies that can provide hands on practice to make abstract math concepts more concrete. As math educator Margie Pearse writes:

> *The very act of generating a concrete representation establishes an image of the knowledge in students' minds. The use of manipulatives stimulates the learning environment for the tactile learner. Manipulatives give students a conceptual frame of reference, a physical proof that the mathematical concept makes sense.*[8]

Students can advance their thinking by using their experiences with manipulatives to create visual representations. A few key manipulatives in the mathematics classroom include: base 10 blocks, fraction circles, decimal squares, algebra tiles, and Cuisenaire Rods. Visual representations (tables, graphs, diagrams, etc.) help students see relationships and connections. The visual representations they create support ELLs as they take part in meaningful mathematics conversations because they can reference their visual as they explain their reasoning to others. When students consistently use manipulatives and create visual representations, they are meeting the standards of "model with mathematics" and "use appropriate tools strategically" (CCSS).

Tech Tool
Math Resources

For more resources on supporting ELLs in math instruction, visit "The Best Resources For Teaching Common Core Math To English Language Learners" https://larryferlazzo.edublogs.org/2014/11/22/the-best-resources-for-teaching-common-core-math-to-english-language-learners/ .

Links to all the online activities listed in the chapter, as well as to the downloadable student handouts, can be found at www.wiley.com/go/eslsurvivalguide2.

PART FIVE

Working with Specific Groups of English Language Learners

CHAPTER ELEVEN

Supporting Long-Term English Language Learners

Once upon a time, there was a woman named Dolores who had two children: a girl named Chabelita and a baby boy named Joaquín. Her husband, Pancho, had disappeared one day. No one knew what happened to him, and now Dolores was raising the children on her own.

One day Chabelita took her baby brother to play by the ocean, but a wave pulled him under. As she stood there weeping, she heard a voice. She turned around: their cow was speaking to her!

"Take your knife," said the cow. "Kill me, and then skin me. Leave my bones here, and spread my hide on the water. Use the hairs from my tail to help you, and use my eyes to see where you need to go."

Chabelita did what the cow ordered and then sailed away on the hide, far away. When icebergs blocked her path, she threw a hair from the cow's tail at the icebergs; they melted, and she kept on sailing.

Using the cow's eye like a spyglass, she saw an island in the distance. She landed on the island, and then she saw a castle. Using the cow's other eye, she peered through the wall of the castle. She saw her baby brother there. . . and she saw her father too, locked up in a dungeon filled with gold and jewels.

Chabelita approached the castle. She threw another hair at the wall and it became a ladder that she climbed. Another hair became a sword that she used to kill the guards. The third hair became a key that unlocked the door to the dungeon. She took baby Joaquín in her arms while her father stuffed his pockets with gold and jewels, and then they sailed back home on the cow-hide.

When they arrived at the beach, Dolores was there waiting for them, and she wept with joy to see them. Then Chabelita wrapped the cow's bones inside the hide and returned the eyes to their sockets. Next, she waved one last hair from the cow's tail over the bundle, and the cow came back to life. So, they all lived happily ever after, including the cow.[1]

In this fairy tale from Chile, Chabelita needed a lot of support to accomplish an extremely challenging task. But with the right kind of support, she discovered that nothing is impossible.

How to adequately support Long-Term English Language Learners (LTELLs) is a challenge facing schools and teachers throughout the country.

In this chapter, we'll discuss who LTELLs are, how researchers suggest they can best be supported, and how Larry and his school have tried to implement those recommendations and their results. Finally, we'll end with sharing some reflections and questions, and by providing resources for additional information.

Who Are Long-Term English Language Learners?

As we discussed in Chapter One, there are nearly five million English Language Learners in US schools today[2] and it's estimated that between one-quarter and one-half of them are considered Long-Term ELLs[3]—students who have been classified as ELLs for six years or more. In some states, like California, LTELLs are an even higher percentage.[4] Six years is nearing the estimated *longest* amount of time it should take—assuming students receive adequate support—to acquire both social and academic English proficiency.[5]

The key phrase in that last sentence is "assuming students receive adequate support." Lack of specialized English language development classes, limited access to standard curriculum because teachers have not received adequate professional development in ELL support, and socioeconomic issues such as poverty are just a few of the many reasons behind this language acquisition delay. In addition, family mobility for economic reasons or fear of immigration enforcement can also result in a lack of stable school attendance for some.[6]

LTELLs may appear to function reasonably well verbally in English, but may not have the oral or literacy skills needed for academic success. These challenges can often result in setbacks at school, including a higher likelihood of dropping out.[7]

How Can We Best Support LTELLs?

Researchers have identified a number of interventions to provide the extra support LTELLs need to be academically successful, including—but not limited to:

- Enrolling them in a support class that supplements, but does not replace, a core academic class such as English.
- "Cohorting" LTELLs in academic classes, though not exclusively. In other words, they might stay together in the same classes, but there would also be non-LTELLs enrolled in the classes, as well.
- Regular monitoring of student progress and providing support and intervention when needed.
- Creating an inclusive school climate and implementing culturally responsive-sustaining teaching.
- Providing support for home language development.[8]

The federal Every Student Succeeds Act (ESSA) "ups the ante" for schools to develop strategies to successfully move LTELLs towards English proficiency, since successful "reclassification" of ELLs is now an ESSA accountability standard.

How Did Larry and His School Try to Put These Recommendations into Action?

Approximately 35 percent of the student population at Larry's school, Luther Burbank High School, are ELLs and, like many California schools, a sizable number are LTELLs. It has a long institutional commitment towards supporting ELLs. This effort included welcoming ELLs during the No Child Left Behind years when others discouraged their attendance because of potentially being a "drag" on test scores. The administration and faculty have believed that inviting large numbers of ELLs into their student population challenges them to be better teachers for *all* students.

In the spirit of innovation to support students *and* to support teacher initiatives, Larry's school decided in 2018 to do a pilot class and program to support Long Term English Language Learners. Larry and his colleagues studied what researchers recommended as actions to take, and reflected on education researcher Dylan Wiliam's comment that:

In education, "What works?" is rarely the right question, because everything works somewhere, and nothing works everywhere, which is why in education, the right question is, "Under what conditions does this work?"[9]

So, in addition to past research, Larry and his colleagues examined the local situation, their students, and their own experiences, and developed a plan of support for LTELLs that did not cost the school or district any extra funds.

This plan of action included:

1. **Support Class:** Following the recommendations of researchers, they would create a support class, taught by Larry—for 20 ninth graders who were Long Term English Language Learners. Researchers recommended that this type of class should be focused on academic literacy. They agreed with that focus, though decided to target it more specifically. All the teachers of their other academic classes would send Larry a weekly email composed of a few sentences explaining what they planned to teach the following week and what prior knowledge would be helpful for students to know. Larry, in turn, would prepare and teach lessons supporting those topics. Offering this kind of support was less challenging than it might seem since Larry had taught the regular English and Social Studies curriculum for years, and had long included Science instruction in his ELL classes.

   Through these introductory lessons, not only would students be in a better position to learn, they would also come into the classes knowing more about the subject than most of their non-LTELL classmates! Since a lack of self-confidence resulting from a history of academic challenges is a characteristic of many LTELLs, this strategy could put them in a very different position than they had been in previous years.

2. **Cohort:** Following research recommendations, the school would "cohort" those 20 LTELL students so that they each attended all the same academic classes. Ten to fifteen other non LTELLs (not the same in each class) would be their classmates in every class except their period with Larry. The school was already divided into Small Learning Communities (approximately 300 students and 20 teachers each) where students would take most of their classes together so it wouldn't be very difficult to make that kind of scheduling happen.

3. **Regular monitoring:** The school decided to apply that recommended intervention in two ways:

   A. **Turbo charged advisory:** The support class would function as an "advisory" on steroids (or home room). Larry would be in regular contact with parents (it helped that Larry speaks Spanish), and periodically pull students out of their academic class during his "prep period" to have short check-in conversations. These kinds of "walk-and-talks" are strongly encouraged at the school.

   B. **Peer Mentors:** Older students (ELLs and non-ELLs) in Larry's International Baccalaureate Theory of Knowledge (TOK) classes would act as peer mentors and pull the LTELLs out of one of their classes for 15 minutes each week to check in and discuss different topics (goals, challenges, and sometimes just what they're doing for fun).

4. **Social and Emotional Learning:** In terms of the research recommendation on school climate and culturally responsive teaching, as the author of several books on Social Emotional Learning, Larry would have ready-to-use SEL lessons and strategies to emphasize in the classroom, and most of the school's teachers were already active practitioners of culturally responsive-sustaining teaching. In fact, Ethnic Studies was one of the academic classes students would be taking.

5. **Brainpop:** The animated educational video site had been an engaging tool in Larry's past ELL English and Social Studies classes. He thought their videos and related activities would be particularly helpful in this support class—he could use them in class to supplement his limited Science knowledge and his minimal Math experience, and students could use it at home to gain "extra credit" in all their academic classes. Brainpop agreed to let Larry and the school use their program for no-cost during the year of the pilot class.

   Note: As mentioned earlier, support for LTELL's home language was another primary support recommendation. Because of scheduling challenges, the school was not able to have LTELL students enroll in home language classes (for example, Spanish for Spanish speakers) during their ninth-grade year. However, they did so in tenth grade, and the next year's LTELL support group (composed of new ninth graders) was able to participate in those classes. This subsequent class is discussed later in the chapter.

After identifying a similar gender and language-level mix of 20 other ninth-grade LTELLs throughout the school who would function as our control group, Larry, his colleagues and school administrators met with staff from the District office. They helped develop measurable goals and determined a variety of pre- and- post assessments. District staff also agreed to help in quantitative data collection.

WHAT HAPPENED WITH THE CLASS?

All the plans were implemented, though writing that one sentence does not accurately portray the amount of work that went into making it happen.

In addition, more supportive measures were added along the way, including:

- Having students do a daily warm-up activity in the LTELL support class where they wrote about important knowledge they gained in each of their classes during the previous day. Students shared with classmates what they wrote in a "Retrieval Practice Notebook" and then with the entire class. See Chapter Three for more information on this activity.

- Larry's classroom "suite" includes an adjoining room that functions as a support center for ELLs and is often empty. Responsible members of the cohort would come down there regularly to do work their other teachers felt they could complete independently. Many of them loved having the freedom (and knowing they were trusted) to work on their own or with other cohort members semi-independently. This space was also often used for meetings with their mentors.

WHAT WERE THE RESULTS?

Quantitative Data (What students actually did)

Based on quantitative reporting from the District, the cohorted students outperformed the control group in every assessed area, including in writing and "cloze" measurements. While the differences were generally small, they were an encouraging sign that the pilot was working.

Larry and his colleagues also recognized that the numbers were based on a small sample size, as well as being based on averages, which doesn't necessarily provide an accurate measurement—outliers on the high or low end can influence the measurements.

The lowest gain—where the cohort had a .53 percent greater gain than the control group—was in what was arguably the most important assessment, the ELPAC test (English Language Proficiency Assessment for California). This is a key test for determining if ELLs can be "reclassified" as English-proficient and is a required test for ELLs in the state of California (other states have similar tests).

In "non-tested" measurements that were used to help assess student "engagement," cohorted students had a nine percent higher rate of attendance; an eight percent lower rate of behavior referrals, and a nine percent lower rate of suspensions.

EXHIBIT 11.1. Quantitative Results

	Pilot Group (N = 19)	Control Group (N = 20)
Average point increase	22.37	14.2
Average starting score	1,526.9	1,522.6
Average ending score	1,549.3	1536.8

Note: the pilot group had a .53% greater increase over the control group

Qualitative Data (What students—and teachers—were thinking)

Students anonymously ranked how well each of the specific interventions "helped them learn."

Having peer mentors was rated the highest. Here are some student comments about them:

> *I do like having a mentor because they are fun and cool to be with, they are also very*
>   *supportive.*
> *They help me by giving advice and guiding me to do well in class and school.*
> *They help me become a better student by talking to me.*

Interestingly, in comparing the first and second semester GPAs of the students in Larry's TOK classes who were mentors with those who were not, the grades of those who were mentors went up and those who were not went down.[10] This element of our project might have had an unexpected positive benefit for the mentors, too!

The LTELL students said the second highest-ranked intervention was their being able to come to the ELL support center during the day to work independently.

Next came taking classes together as a cohort, followed by being able to use the Brainpop site, and then getting the "previews" of lessons they would be having in their academic classes.

Coming up in the rear were "writing essays in class" (though, interestingly, the writing assessment was where they showed the greatest improvement); using the Retrieval Practice Notebook, and the private "walk-and-talk" conversations they had with Larry during his prep period (Larry didn't take that personally).

Students rated the class overall very positively and gave Larry an A minus as a teacher (though one student "thought out of the box" by saying Larry deserved "a 19 out of 30.")

Most of the participating teachers felt very positive about the experience, and particularly appreciated students coming to class with prior knowledge, having the opportunity to send students to the ELL Center to work independently when appropriate, and receiving Larry's help in supporting individual students and communicating their parents.

WHAT WERE REFLECTIONS & QUESTIONS?

Larry and his colleagues *did not* enter into this pilot program planning to evaluate it through a rigorous data analysis. They knew there would be too many variables (in addition to the previously mentioned small sample size and "averaging" of scores).

They also knew that they were going to apply several specific interventions, and that they wouldn't be able to be sure which ones might contribute to the quantitative data—positively or negatively—though they would have the student self-reports. Of course, they were also aware of the possibility that none of those interventions might actually have an impact on student performance. Perhaps something else might— quality of instruction always varies, and perhaps it might be the quality of the day-to-day teaching that would have the greatest effect (the teachers who participated were volunteers, and may have been particularly motivated to help ELLs).

They *did* enter into the effort knowing:

- that they needed to try *something* to support a group of students who faced particular challenges—LTELLs.
- that they were informed by what researchers had suggested might be effective interventions to use.
- and that they believed they could successfully adapt those strategies—and develop other ones—based on their many years of supporting English Language Learners.

After the class was completed, *they did know* that:

- Students liked the class—very much so.
- Teachers like the class—very much so.
- It may not stand up to rigorous data scrutiny, but it appeared to them that it was likely to be more than just coincidence that students in the class had a greater rate of improvement in *every* data point that they, along with district staff, had determined as a measurement during the summer prior to the class.

And they had questions to ponder, including:

- Since peer mentors were rated so highly by the LTELLs, should that group be expanded to the greater ELL population—and beyond?
- If they did something like this again, how big did the sample size need to be, and what kind of data collection would be required in order to be able to "generalize" from the results?
- If more support classes were done by different teachers, how could they be made more feasible for those who may not have previous experience (like Larry did) in teaching the other academic classes?

- Would there be value to doing these types of support classes for more than just LTELLs? For all ninth graders? For students in other grades facing challenges?

- Would anything be learned from continuing to follow the cohort and the control group in subsequent years? What measurements could be used in that process?

At the end of that year, it appeared that their district's financial crisis would mean the end of the experiment, so many of those questions were put on the backburner. However, at the last moment, the school was able to provide a LTELL class for a new group of ninth graders and include similar supports, as well as adding a home language class to each of the new students' schedules. Pre-assessments were completed, but the school year was cut short by the COVID-19 pandemic, and final assessments, including the state English test, were not done. Though there is not hard data documenting the second year's success, they believe that it would have shown positive results though likely not as positive because of the pandemic.

We're not sure how many schools have the drive and the capacity to do something similar. We are sure, however, that millions of LTELLs need additional support, and we don't know of any better way to provide it to them.

Tech Tool

Additional Resources

Many other resources on supporting Long-Term English Language Learners can be found at "The Best Resources On Supporting Long-Term English Language Learners" https://larryferlazzo.edublogs.org/2016/12/03/the-best-resources-on-supporting-long-term-english-language-learners/.

Portions of this chapter originally appeared in ASCD Educational Leadership http://www.ascd.org/publications/educational_leadership/dec19/vol77/num04/Research_in_Action@_Ramping_Up_Support_for_Long-Term_ELLs.aspx. *Reprinted with permission.*

Links to all the online resources listed in the chapter can be found at www.wiley.com/go/eslsurvivalguide2.

CHAPTER TWELVE

Working with Elementary ELLs

*A*nansi found a pea lying in the road. Just one little pea. "I wish I had more," said Anansi sadly, but he planted his pea, and then he waited to see what would happen.

The pea-plant grew and grew.

Then one day Goat wandered by, and he ate Anansi's pea-plant.

"Hey!" shouted Anansi. "That was my pea-plant. You must give me something in exchange."

"Okay," said Goat, and he gave Anansi one of his horns.

Anansi took the horn down to the river to wash it, but the River grabbed the horn and took it away from Anansi.

"Hey!" shouted Anansi. "That was my horn. You must give me something in exchange."

"Okay," said River, and she gave Anansi a fish.

Walking home, Anansi met a woman. "I'm hungry!" the woman said, and she grabbed Anansi's fish.

"Hey!" shouted Anansi. "That was my fish. You must give me something in exchange."

"Okay," said the woman, and she gave Anansi a shirt.

Next, Anansi met a little boy who had no clothes on. "I need clothes!" he said, and he grabbed Anansi's shirt.

"Hey!" shouted Anansi. "That was my shirt. You must give me something in exchange."

"Okay," said the boy, and he gave Anansi his whip.

Then Anansi met a cowherd. "I need that whip to herd my cows!" said the cowherd, and he grabbed Anansi's whip.

"Hey!" shouted Anansi. "That was my whip. I want something in exchange. Give me one of your cows!"

So, the cowherd gave Anansi one of his cows.

From the cow, Anansi got milk, and from the milk Anansi got cheese.

Anansi sold the cheese and bought more cows.

Soon, Anansi had a herd of cows all his own.

And he started with just one pea![1]

Elementary English learners (ELLs) are just at the beginning of their journey, a journey that happens one step at a time, just like Anansi started with a pea and ended up with a herd of cows in this folktale from Jamaica.

> This chapter was written by Valentina Gonzalez. Valentina has more than 20 years of experience teaching and working with multilingual students from around the globe. Her personal experience as an immigrant from Yugoslavia and language learner fuel her desire to advocate for English learners and support teachers with the best research-based teaching methods. Her work's primary focuses have been on literacy, culture, and language. Valentina is the coauthor of Reading & Writing with English Learners: A Framework for K-5.

Who Are Elementary English Learners?

Elementary students who speak or hear a language other than English at home have different academic needs than secondary students in the same situation. Recognizing who our English Language Learners are will help us to determine their instructional path.

ELLs are undeniably one of the fastest growing populations. The National Center for Education Statistics reported that, in 2018, 10.2 percent or five million public school students in the United States were English language learners.[2] The majority of English learners sit in elementary classrooms across the United States because many students who are identified as English language learners when they enter elementary school meet exit criteria by the time they graduate to secondary school. Sixty-seven percent of English language learners are served in elementary classrooms kindergarten through fifth grade based on 2015 data from the National Center for Educational Statistics.[3] The Migration Policy Reported that 85 percent of

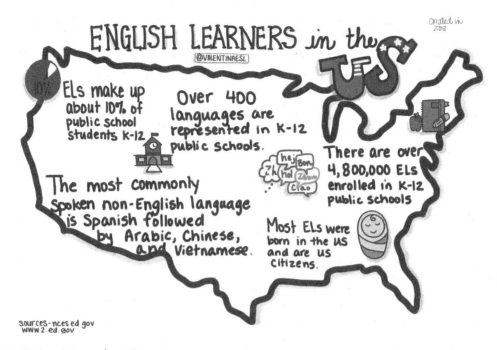

FIGURE 12.1. ELLs in the US

elementary English language learners were born in the United States and are US citizens as opposed to 62 percent of secondary ELLs.[4] A few details on ELLs in the US are visualized in Figure 12.1.

These are statistics and merely numbers. We see students in our classrooms who are unique individuals with different backgrounds and needs. It is likely that you have one or more English language learners in your elementary classroom at this moment and, if not, they may soon join you. We have to regularly check on the needs of our students in order to plan effective lessons and instruction.

English language learners are initially identified by a home language survey filled out by parents upon registration at school. Testing for services is generated when parents indicate a language other than English on the home language survey. A student who may benefit from linguistic support and accommodations may not receive them when parents do not indicate a language other than English. Often parents misunderstand the home language survey or have preconceived notions regarding English Language Learner (ELL) programs. Some parents fear their child will be placed in a less appropriate classroom or that they will have a negative label. Others fear their child will be excluded from gifted and talented services or other enrichment opportunities. There may be students in your classroom who are unidentified ELLs. They—and *all* students—will benefit from the accommodations and scaffolds that you put in place for language development.

Do Elementary English Language Learners Have Different Needs? Does Their Instruction Need to be Different from that of Older English Learners?

Acquiring two or more languages at the same time is called simultaneous language acquisition. Children born in the United States to families who speak English and a language other than English may be simultaneous bilinguals. Simultaneous bilinguals learn both languages at the same time.

Sequential language acquisition is the process of acquiring one language and then another at a later time. Newcomer or immigrant students are often sequential language learners. These students began life learning one language, started school in one country, and then moved to a new country (such as the United States) and began learning an additional language.

There are benefits to knowing if a student is a simultaneous bilingual or a sequential learner. Simultaneous learners have the opportunity to hear and speak both languages for the same or similar amounts of time. They have similar exposures to text and to oral expression in both languages. They have opportunities to hear and speak using language structures of both languages.

Sequential learners, on the other hand, will have exposure to their primary language and then later to a new language. Typically, students who have a strong foundation in their primary language can use that as a leverage when adding a new language. See Chapter Seventeen on the benefits of home language use.

These are the guiding questions to help us learn more about English language learners:

- Does the student have literacy in another language? If so, how much? Can they speak, comprehend, read, and write in another language?
- How long has the student been in US schools?
- How long has the student been learning English?
- Is English similar to the student's primary language?
- How do the two languages differ?
- What are the student's hobbies, passions, goals?
- Is there anything significant in their personal or academic life you should be aware of?

Program Types in Elementary

Elementary students who qualify as ELLs can either participate in an ELL Program or in a Bilingual Program. Many variations or models exist within each of the programs. It is important to know which program type(s) your school and/or district offers. This information will help you better advocate for the students and families that you serve.

ELL PROGRAM MODELS

ELL Program Models are based on English as a medium for instruction. However this does not mean that students should not receive primary language support. One component of an effective ELL Program Model is primary language support. A common characteristic of ELL Programs is that they have students with multiple home languages. It is unlikely that the teacher speaks all of them. Providing home language support in an ELL Program means using the students' home languages to make instruction comprehensible. One way to do this is by using the Preview-View-Review technique. See Instructional Strategies later in this chapter for more on preview-view-review and see Chapter Seven for ideas on how to implement it even if you don't speak your students' home language(s).

ELL Program Models are sometimes referred to as English Immersion Models and sometimes are called English Language Development (ELD) or English as a Second Language (ESL).

Pull-out is one method for serving ELLs on campuses where students are spread out in mainstream classrooms. An ELL/ELD certified teacher gathers ELLs for regularly planned daily/weekly instruction. Some schools use pull-out instruction for ELLs at the beginning English proficiency level only. Students at higher proficiency levels either receive instruction through push-in or content-based models. A benefit of the Pull-Out method is that students can get more individual instruction and potentially a greater sense of belonging. On the other hand, the Pull-Out model can sometimes result in ELLs being seen as the ELL teacher's responsibility. In addition, ELLs at higher English proficiency levels may continue to need specialized support but not receive it. This shortcoming can lead to language and academic gaps that may hinder students from exiting or reclassifying out of the program.

Push-in is another ELL Program Model and involves an ELL/ELD teacher coming into, or "pushing in" to a mainstream classroom to offer support and/or co-teach with the classroom teacher. Co-teaching holds many benefits for students and teachers alike. It can provide a lower student to teacher ratio which allows for more student interaction. Teachers are able to work closely with students to personalize instruction. While there are many benefits to co-teaching, it also requires taking time to co-plan lessons. Finding this time is a common struggle for co-teachers. Teachers who plan, reflect, and assess together can be successful in the push-in method.

A Content-Based ELL program or Sheltered English is typically delivered by a mainstream teacher that is ELL certified. The classroom teacher designates a special block of time for ELL/ELD instruction. It is highly important that teachers who deliver instruction be adequately trained to serve all English language learners.

Some schools offer Newcomer programs for newly arrived immigrants. These programs are specialized environments for students who are in their first or second year in US schools. Though they are more often seen in secondary, some elementary campuses offer them as well. Teachers who have training and certification in working with newly arrived ELLs provide students with language and academic instruction. Students transition into general education classrooms. Newcomer programs offer immigrants a safe, comfortable environment as they begin their learning journey in the United States.

BILINGUAL PROGRAM MODELS

Transitional Bilingual Education

Transitional Bilingual Education (TBE) programs are characterized by instruction delivered primarily in the students' home language for one to four years. Students gradually transition to English instruction overtime. Generally, TBE is from pre-kindergarten to third grade. TBE is one of the most common bilingual programs found in elementary schools in the United States. This type of program is often preferred over English-only models whenever possible because it supports students' literacy in their home language. However, because of its short term, some argue that the TBE program views home language through a deficit lens rather than from an assets-based view. Research shows that TBE programs are less effective than other bilingual education models in ensuring ELLs reach parity with their English-speaking peers.[5]

Developmental Bilingual Education

Developmental Bilingual Education (DBE), otherwise known as late exit or maintenance bilingual education, is similar to TBE. However, with DBE students stay in the program longer in an effort to create a stronger primary language foundation. The goal of DBE is for students to develop both English and their home language and to become biliterate and bilingual. DBE programs are often from pre kindergarten to fifth or sixth grade and are less common than TBE programs due to less funding access. However, many believe that DBE programs are stronger and create more successful students because they take more time to develop students' language and academic proficiency.

Dual Language Bilingual Education

Dual Language Bilingual Education or Two-Way Immersion programs include both native English speakers and English language learners. The most common Dual Language program offered in the United States is Spanish, however, districts offer Dual Language in languages such as Mandarin, Arabic, Cantonese, Korean, etc. depending on student demographics and available resources. Dual Language programs aim to develop students who are bilingual, biliterate, and academically successful in both languages. Typically, these programs are offered pre-kindergarten through fifth grade. Instruction is delivered in both languages by teachers who are bilingually certified. Sheltered instruction methods are provided in both languages to make content comprehensible to students. The amount of instruction in each language varies greatly within Dual Language programs. Some are 50/50 providing 50 percent of instruction in English and 50 percent in the ELLs' home language. Others may start as a 90/10 or 80/20 model (the larger percentage representing the ELLs' L1) and then gradually moving towards 50/50 as students get older.

The Core Elements of Supportive Instruction for Elementary English Language Learners

No matter the program type our English language learners are in, creating an environment where language and academics flourish is important work. We want students to feel safe, comfortable, supported, and valued. The environment created for students can either help language flourish and accelerate development, or it can stifle it and slow down the process.

When it comes to supportive instruction for elementary English language learners, three core elements come to mind: what the learning environment looks like, what it sounds like, and how it feels. Let's explore how to maximize the growth and progress of ELLs using these three elements as a framework.

What Does a Model Classroom that is Highly Supportive of Elementary English Learners Look Like?

Let's take a look inside a classroom that supports elementary English language learners. First let's explore what is easily *seen* (See Exhibit 12.1 for a visualization).

Wall space is carefully categorized by content areas (Reading, Writing, Social Studies, Math, Science). This helps young English language learners easily find information and resources that they need. It is clear and easy to find the subjects being studied in this classroom. If a student needs to find math information, words or support in that subject area they would know exactly where to look.

EXHIBIT 12.1. The Do's and Don'ts of Highly Supportive Classrooms of Elementary ELLs

Classrooms that are highly supportive of elementary ELLs	Classrooms that do not support elementary ELLs
• Are highly inclusive	• Segregate English learners
• Feel welcoming	• Feel unacceptable
• Encourage collaboration	• Work in isolation
• Set high expectations for all students	• Lower expectations for some students

Beneath each categorized content area are two or three anchor charts featuring the current learning and objectives for the content area. Anchor charts are neatly written and placed at students' eye level so everyone can see them. Text is visually supported with graphics or pictures and word choices are concise. There is not a great deal of writing on each chart. Some anchor charts tell a step-by-step process while others show labeled visuals. The anchor charts are not laminated. Instead they look freshly made using information like students' names from the current classroom.

The classroom has a few word walls that support academic vocabulary in content areas. The science word wall, for instance, is a "tree map" of the types of energy, while the reading word wall is a Venn Diagram of fiction and nonfiction books. Both word walls include images of real objects and student writing and drawing. The word walls have complementary sentence stems that can be used for structured, academic, peer-to-peer discourse and to support writing.

Students showcase their progress and growth by prominently displaying their work on the walls of the classroom. A map of the world hangs on the wall and includes student family photos. It is framed by the word "hello" in multiple languages. A partner chart can be found near the map. The chart has moveable names for Partner A and Partner B. All students' pictures and names are on the chart and the teacher has thoughtfully selected pairs to maximize learning growth for every child. The room itself is labeled in teacher and student writing. For example, the door is labeled "door" in teacher writing but also in student writing in English and in students' home languages with visual supports. This room belongs to the students and the teacher--and it shows.

Everything on the walls and in the room has a purpose and is used for learning.

Inside the walls are resources and books that support all learners too. The resources in this room are just as carefully selected as what is placed on the walls. There are picture

> ### *Characteristics of a Language Rich Elementary Classroom: What it LOOKS Like*
>
> - DISTINCT WALL AREAS FOR EACH CONTENT
> - CLEARLY POSTED LEARNING OBJECTIVES
> - ANCHOR CHARTS WITH VISUALS
> - UNIT BASED, THEMATIC WORD WALLS
> - STUDENT WORK DISPLAYED
> - BOOKS THAT REFLECT STUDENTS
> - SEATING THAT SUPPORTS COLLABORATION

FIGURE 12.2.   What an Elementary Classroom Should Look Like

books that showcase students of all cultures, non-fiction books that highlight places around the globe, and some books that are in languages other than English.

The tables and chairs are purposefully placed to foster cooperative learning and positive interdependence. Students sit in groups of three to four and are facing one another. This allows students to feel included and to be part of a learning group.

What Does a Model Classroom that Is Highly Supportive of Elementary English Learners Sound Like?

Now, let's explore what a supportive classroom for elementary ELLs sounds like. Who is talking? What language is used? Let's pretend that we walk into the classroom blindfolded. We can't see but we can hear. What do we hear in this language rich environment (see Figure 12.3 for a visualization)?

This classroom is alive in every way. There is little room for silence. Student voice is amplified and empowered. The teacher has fostered a classroom of talk and collaboration. Student-to-student academic conversations that are rich in academic and content vocabulary can be heard throughout the room. The teacher recognizes that students need to verbalize ideas and thoughts in order to internalize and own them. The teacher intentionally plans for opportunities and creates space for student-to-student talk.

We hear the teacher explicitly modeling for students how to hold a conversation. "This is what it will look like. Partner A will stand like this and talk first. And Partner B will face Partner A and listen. When we listen, we sometimes nod like this and look at the speaker with our eyes. Now, read with me, 'One way the book____is like the book____ is because.... What you said was that. . . Another way that the book ____ is like the book ____ is because....' Partner A, you will start by using this sentence stem. Then Partner B, you will respond to B using this one. Remember that you can use the word wall if you need it."

We hear students talking to partners using complete sentences, referring to the word wall, and using sentence stems. Later, we hear the teacher asking a question and then providing wait time for students to think about their response. The teacher does not call on a single student, rather she asks students to share with a partner. All students are engaged and participating in the conversation.

We hear groups of students collaborating on a problem during math. Each student has a role and brings value to the activity. One student asks another for clarification in Spanish. The partner responds first in English and then in Spanish. Primary language is valued and used as a support for learning English and the content.

In the afternoon, students are reading independently. The teacher walks around the room and confers with students. We hear the teacher ask a student to read to her. The student reads from his independent reading book. The teacher listens and coaches the student. Then the teacher asks the student to read from another book, any book the child would like to read to her. The student picks a book in his primary language. The teacher listens. The student is able to read fluently in his primary language. The teacher asks about the story and the student responds with a good retelling. The student smiles widely and the teacher acknowledges his skills. This child is an emerging bilingual. Finally, the teacher gathers a group of students for explicit instruction. She takes them through a lesson and guides them as they try out the skill under her watchful eye. They are all abuzz.

Throughout the day, students can be heard singing and chanting songs. There are songs about the water cycle, about vowels, and songs that teach students content and language structures. Later, we hear students humming and silently singing the songs to themselves. Music is part of their instructional day in every content area. Students are clearly having fun and learning at the same time.

Students are heard playing during the day. The play time is instructional as well as any other part of the day. Peer-to-peer interaction teaches students to communicate with one another. Students are discussing how to share building blocks in one corner of the room, in another we hear bakers working together to make a recipe, and in a third area we hear artists talking about their clay creations.

> *Characteristics of a Language Rich Elementary Classroom: What it SOUNDS Like*
>
> - MORE STUDENT TALK THAN TEACHER
> - STUDENT TO STUDENT ACADEMIC CONVERSATIONS
> - EXPLICIT MODELING OF EXPECTATIONS
> - USE OF SENTENCE STEMS
> - WAIT TIME
> - INDEPENDENT READING WITH SUPPORT
> - DIRECT INSTRUCTION
> - SINGING, CHANTING, PLAYING

FIGURE 12.3. What an Elementary Classroom Should Sound Like

What Does a Model Classroom that Is Highly Supportive of Elementary ELLs Feel Like?

The affective filter can change everything. It's often said that children don't care about what we know until they know how much we care about them. A caring supportive classroom can increase the degree and progress of language and content learning. The opposite is also true.

Dr. Michelle Yzquierdo describes the affective filter as "...the matrix of emotional and motivational factors that may interfere with language acquisition."[6] To ensure that our young language learners build language and content at appropriate rates, we employ many instructional techniques in our classrooms that lower the affective filter so students feel safe and supported.

In contrast, when students feel afraid or anxious at school, language acquisition may take longer. Let's look at two scenarios.

SCENARIO 1

In this second grade classroom there are 22 students. Four students are English language learners. One beginner, two intermediate, one advanced.

During the math lesson, students are working with groups to solve a problem. English language learners are mixed within the groups.

> *Teacher:* Work together to solve the problem. Remember that each of you has a job within your group. I am listening for you to use the sentence stems we have posted on the wall. Let's read them together. (Class chorally reads the stems.) We will share in 10 minutes.

Teacher walks around and listens as groups work together to solve the problem. Teacher smiles and leans into each group.

> *Teacher:* I like how I'm hearing all of you share your ideas in this group. Hmmm. Tell me more. Why do you think that? Can you explain your idea? You got this! Keep trying.

SCENARIO 2

In this second-grade classroom there are 22 students. Four students are English language learners. One beginner, two intermediate, one advanced.

During the math lesson, students are working independently to solve problems.

> *Teacher:* We will check the answers in 10 minutes.

The teacher pulls all of the English learners and works with them in a small group.

The teacher gives the beginner a coloring sheet and crayons and motions to her to start coloring, which she does.

> *Teacher:* These are the steps to solve the problem.
>
> *Advanced Student:* I solved it this way. (Student shows an alternate way to solve the problem).
>
> *Teacher:* No, you can't do it that way. This is the way I want you to do it. Now let's do another example.

The intermediate student followed directions and solved it the way he was asked but got the answer wrong.

> *Teacher:* That's wrong. You can't do it.

After 10 minutes, the teacher calls on one student at a time to give the answer to each question.

Teacher: Ray, what is the answer to number 1?

Ray: 110

Teacher: Correct. Jessica, what is the answer to number 2?

Jessica: 55

Teacher: No, Kevin, what did you get for number 2?

Kevin: 65

Teacher: Correct. (And this process continued until all answers were checked).

If you were an English language learner, which of these two classrooms would you feel most comfortable learning in? Which would you feel safest in? Probably in the first one. The first classroom made everyone feel included.

Looking at Scenario 2, students worked alone and not all English language learners were part of the learning experience. Even though it looked as if they were working in a small group setting with the teacher, they were not receiving differentiated instruction. The beginner student was not given an activity that supported her cognitive level in mathematics. This practice can negatively affect students' beliefs about themselves and how they are viewed in class, thus raising their affective filter (see Figure 12.4 for a visualization).

Characteristics of a Language Rich Elementary Classroom: What it FEELS Like

- ENCOURAGE COLLABORATION
- HIGHLY INCLUSIVE
- A SENSE OF BELONGING IS NURTURED
- FOSTER COMMUNITY
- VALUE & SUPPORTS PRIMARY LANGUAGE

FIGURE 12.4. What an Elementary Classroom Should Feel Like

Instructional Strategies that Support Elementary ELLs

SMALL GROUPS

Small groups range from two to five students. The lower teacher-to-student ratio allows teachers and students to work more closely and build relationships. In small groups, English language learners have more frequent opportunities to interact and engage with peers and the teacher.

GRAPHIC ORGANIZERS

Graphic organizers such as story maps, Venn Diagrams, timelines, Word Webs, and flow charts are visual scaffolds that help clarify concepts. See several other chapters for details.

CHANTS AND SONGS

Chants and songs that include academic vocabulary can support English language learners as they acquire English language structures. Many chants and songs can tie into units of study or thematic units. Using chants and songs as shared reading can help ELLs with reading fluency and prosody. See Chapter Three for more detailed ideas.

VISUALS AND LABELING

Pictures, images, and multimedia such as videos impact learning. These visual supports function as accommodations that increase comprehension during instruction. To maximize the use of visuals during instruction, teachers can label them with students. Labeling visuals as well as the classroom environment and reading the labels frequently as a class can build vocabulary, phonemic awareness, and letter sound relationships.

COOPERATIVE LEARNING

English language learners benefit from listening to their peers speak English and by speaking with their peers. During cooperative learning, small groups of students work together to accomplish a task.

STRUCTURED CONVERSATIONS

Structured conversations are partner or group talking opportunities which have a clear purpose and goal. Structured conversations are akin to the "turn and talk" technique, however, they clarify more directly what students will do and discuss, setting students up for success. One specific example of a structured conversation is the QSSSA.[7] QSSSA is discussed in more detail in Chapter Nine.

PREVIEW-VIEW-REVIEW

This technique taps into students' funds of knowledge using their primary language before and after a lesson in English. The teacher begins by previewing the lesson with the student in the student's home language. Following the preview, the teacher presents the lesson in English while using sheltered instruction methods (the "view"). Finally, a short review is done in the student's home language to clear up misconceptions. See Chapter Seven for modifications if teachers do not speak the students' home languages.

Tech Tool

Supporting Elementary ELLs

There are many ways that elementary teachers are using technology to enhance language development while ELLs are learning content simultaneously.

Listening & Speaking

Flipgrid is an app that is easy for both teachers and young students to navigate. It allows students to record themselves speaking. The benefits are many. For students, this platform helps to build confidence in speaking while practicing the English language. They can view their peers' videos, too, and practice listening skills. Allowing access to families increases family involvement and connects families with learning.

Listening & Reading

Epic! for Educators. Getepic.com offers free educator accounts with unlimited access to libraries with thousands of high-quality online books for students.

Students can read and listen to the books. Some books are offered in multiple languages. The program allows teachers to create student profiles and track student progress.

Writing

Book Creator app or BookCreator.com allows students to create digital books. Students can type text, draw, add, or import images, and video or voice record! The possibilities are endless with Book Creator. Once students publish, they can share with one another in their classroom, with families and beyond the school walls.

 Links to all the online activities listed in the chapter can be found at www .wiley.com/go/eslsurvivalguide2.

CHAPTER THIRTEEN

Teaching Adult ELLs

A fierce young Eagle sat on the branch of a tall tree by the lakeside. Down in the water, he saw an old Beaver-woman chopping wood.

"Look at you, chopping wood," scoffed the Eagle. "Gnawing and chopping, gnawing and chopping." He laughed.

The old Beaver-woman ignored the young Eagle's laughter and kept on working.

"Did you hear me, Beaver-woman?"

"I heard you, Eagle," she said. "But as you can see, I have work to do."

"You're ALWAYS working!" shrieked the Eagle.

The Beaver-woman looked up at the Eagle and shook her head. "Perhaps you should get to work, too, Eagle."

"I don't have time for that," said Eagle. "All that chopping wood, all that lifting, all that hauling."

"That's how we build our dam," explained the Beaver-woman. "We do this for the whole Beaver family, and the dam also deepens the stream for the other animals who make their home here."

The Beaver-woman then dove down into the water, while the young Eagle sat there, pondering her words. He had to admit: The old Beaver-woman was strong, and from high up in the tree he could see that her hard work was making the world a better place.[1]

The beaver in this story by the Dakota storyteller Ohíye S'a (Charles Eastman) exemplifies the practical persistence that is characteristic of many adult learners, who are often working hard to support their families at the same time they are learning a new language.

This chapter has been written by Antoinette Perez. Antoinette has more than ten years of experience working with English Language Learners of all levels, including extensive experience with international and adult learners. She has worked in California and Georgia at schools with high percentages of ELLs, which motivated her to obtain TEFL certification to teach English abroad. She currently serves as the English Co-Department Chair at Buena High School in Ventura, California, where she runs the ELD program and teaches honors and AP English. In another capacity, she instructs online English classes for children and adults. Her dedication to students and ESL instruction has taken her around the world to enrich her ability to connect with students and enhance her professional practice.

In the United States, the need for ELL instruction continues to increase for both children and adults, and instructors must be able to differentiate instruction for all levels of learners. Teaching English to adults can be similar to teaching young learners, but there are key differences, such as learning patterns, that influence how we should approach adult ELLs. It takes time, patience, training, and extensive research to successfully meet the needs of any English Language Learner. It might seem that we could make a few adjustments from teaching children to teaching adults, namely when it comes to the content we teach, but as ELL instructors, we cannot take a "one-size fits all" approach.

Adults generally seek English classes for three main reasons: continued education, business, and/or personal. Depending on someone's purpose for learning English, instructional approaches have to cater to a learner's needs, expectations, and goals. Those will also influence the structure of English classes, the content taught, and the tasks implemented. Classes for someone learning English to prepare them for the TOEFL exam, for example, are going to be geared toward specific skills, such as test-taking, that are necessary for academic environments. Classes for someone learning English for personal purposes, on the other hand, might be more casual and include more interactive tasks. Consider the purposes behind learning English for your students, and tailor instruction to be immediately applicable to their lives. Adults are relevancy-oriented, so they must be able to see the utility value of learning and find it relevant.

The ideas presented in this chapter are based on experience and research and are recommended for instructors of all levels of adult ELL instruction.

The Differences in Teaching English to Adults Versus Children

Adult learners are far different from young learners, especially when it comes to learning another language. Other than the obvious lack of behavioral issues in most adult classes, theories suggest that adult learners are generally more practical and self-directed than young learners. Adults have longer attention spans, are more independent, and have more advanced problem-solving skills than children. Based on experience and input from other teachers, these are the general characteristics that set K-12 education and adult education apart. Understanding how these differences influence instructional practices is critical for success with adult learners.

Malcolm Knowles, who coined the term andragogy and defined it as "the art and science of helping adults learn,"[2] suggests that four principles guide andragogy. While there are other factors that differentiate young learners from adult learners, these key differences determine the way we approach adult education and can be used to guide instructional planning. With these in mind, instructors can tailor lessons that reflect these key understandings to best meet the learning needs of adult learners. The four principles are:

1. Adults desire explanations of why specific concepts are being taught in the first place.

2. They typically respond best to learning that is centered around performing common tasks.

3. Adult learning materials should take into account different levels of prior experience.

4. Adult students prefer a self-directed approach that allows for discovery on their own.

STRUCTURING ADULT ELL CLASSES

The content, materials, and tasks utilized in adult ELL instruction can influence the environment of the class. Some classes contain more direct instruction, some require more student interaction and collaboration, and some are a mix of both. These environments can affect the way learners respond to the language. Some may engage in one environment better than in another, and it's important to be aware of the ways our learners respond so we can assess the effectiveness of our instruction. Some learners come from cultures where learning is a high-status, academic endeavor, [so] they may expect a more academically oriented environment[3], in which case a structured and professional environment is favored over a more casual or fun one. It will take a bit of work to get to know your adult learners, but it's an important step to take to help structure adult ELL classes.

WHY ADULTS SEEK ENGLISH INSTRUCTION

As previously mentioned, adults seek English instruction for various reasons, and the motivation behind that learning differs from person to person. While the demand for ELL instruction continues to increase, the majority of adults still seek English instruction for educational purposes, specifically to prepare for academic environments.[4] Others simply need to master the language for business purposes or for personal reasons. While some institutions offer specific courses for Business English or TOEFL preparation, most ELL classes are mixed. This tends to happen with most entry-level ELL courses. In any case, be mindful that there is a good balance of academic, business, and social content.

One way to balance content is to regularly group students based on their learning needs. Begin with a whole-class discussion or lesson that all learners will benefit from and move into groups for the remainder of class. This also gets students moving and collaborating, something adult learners appreciate. For groups, depending on classroom resources, direct instruction could be provided via audio or video recordings. If this is an option, the instructor could work or facilitate instruction with one group at a time while the other group(s) work collaboratively. If technology is not accessible, grouping is still possible with clear written instructions accompanied by visuals, samples, and verbal instruction. The tasks completed in groups are not a substitute for whole class instruction, but rather are used to supplement lessons or activities.

The following sample activities in Exhibit 13.1 are broken down by purpose for learning and reflect the general needs and interests of each group. Tasks will vary by instructor and learners, so answers will also vary. For beginning levels, instructors should provide possible responses/answers. For intermediate or advanced, teacher-supplied answers/responses may not be necessary. Each activity is a suggestion and may be modified to meet students' individual needs, and can be done in small or large classes. Additionally, some tasks may be modified to be completed individually, but most work best when completed with partners or in groups.

HOW A PERSON'S BACKGROUND CAN AFFECT LEARNING

A person's motivation for learning is generally influenced by their background—who they are, where they come from, what they have experienced. Adults have lived longer than children and have more life experiences. Teachers can use this wealth of experience to make connections that promote engagement.

Adults can bring their experiences to the classroom and it aids in their learning as suggested by Knowles' andragogy method. They can compare, contrast, and build on what they already know. Each adult has his/her own experiences, providing the opportunity to share their diverse perspectives on topics and have meaningful connections with other adults. Some adults come to class with little to no formal educational background, so it's important for us as educators to provide the environment where they can develop more confidence as learners.

Someone's motivation, desire for learning, and aptitude can be reflective of their background and experiences. The motivation of someone with limited educational opportunities is likely to differ from someone who has already earned a degree. This is why getting to know our students and learning about their background and experiences should guide our instruction. We want to tap into their prior knowledge and build on it. We want to make content relatable and relative to them. Most importantly, we want our students to feel like their learning is valuable, and we can do that better if we know how to connect our instruction to their past experiences and personal lives.

EXHIBIT 13.1. Example Group Activities by Purpose

Language Attainment Purpose	Activity Suggestions
Business	**A. Job Interview Questions** • Provide learners with a list of questions for practice. Ask students to read through the questions and formulate a response to each question separately. Consider including a handout on "Interview Tips/Reminders" with sample responses to questions for guidance. • Ask students to work with a partner to practice interviewing each other using their prepared responses. **B. Email Writing** • Provide email samples for reference and ask students to write an email to a coworker. Consider including a handout on "Email Etiquette" that highlights the difference between professional and social writing. • Several samples, activities, and tips for these activities are available at busyteacher.org. **C. Workplace Language/Needs** • Provide scripts of general workplace conversations. Ask students to work with a partner to choose from a series of questions, statements, and responses that reflect general workplace communication. These can be verbal or written activities or a combination of both. • Provide scenarios for the workplace and ask students to consider necessary action based on each scenario. It would be helpful to provide possible solutions for guidance that students can refer to after they participate in the activity.

Academic	**A. Collaborative Discussions** • As a group or whole class, pose a question for discussion and let students facilitate. The instructor should still moderate when needed but allow the group to do most of the talking. Encourage all members to participate, but do not force it. This is great exposure to multiple perspectives, conversational language, and culture. Consider providing a handout on respectful language to use and appropriate discussion etiquette (*Note*: this should be a review of etiquette, not an introduction to it). **B. Partner Questions** • Create a series of questions on various academic topics for pairs to discuss. Provide sentence frames, starters, or sample responses to questions for guidance. This will give each person a chance to talk and listen in a low-stress environment. **C. Article Reading** • Provide an article on an academic topic that introduces new vocabulary or concepts. Sometimes, front-loading vocabulary or background on topics is necessary, so consider a handout or short presentation that covers this. • Ask students to read individually or with a partner and discuss the reading. Then, offer after-reading questions for students to discuss or answer in writing. They should share their ideas to obtain different perspectives on the topic.
Personal	**A. Phone Call** • Provide scripts for students to practice phone conversations about various topics. Once students are more comfortable with phone calls, provide topics and ask them to create their own conversations (written or verbal). **B. Ordering at a Restaurant** • Provide menus from various local restaurants and guided scripts (sentence starters or just sample responses) for students to practice communicating at restaurants to become familiar with the process and etiquette of ordering. **C. Casual Conversation** • Create a series of questions on various topics (personal, cultural, or general) for pairs to discuss. Provide sample responses for more difficult topics, or provide sentence frames for guidance. This will give each person a chance to talk and listen in a low-stress environment. **D. Story Sharing** • Allow students to share a story with the group and ask for feedback, advice, or input. This is a great way to build relationships.

HOW L1 AND LITERACY SKILLS INFLUENCE LANGUAGE ACQUISITION

A common concern adults have when learning a second language is their ability to learn a new language after many years away from the classroom. The good news is that studies show adults are as capable as children in second language fluency. Some argue that children learn faster and with better fluency than adults as a result of their exposure to English and limited L1 fluency, which is often true. Interestingly, research shows that adults can obtain native-like mastery of a second language, and in some cases adult learners can even outperform native speakers.[5] That is not to say this will always be the case, but it's encouraging to share with our adult learners that although difficult, native-like mastery is attainable. This level of fluency is obviously influenced by factors such as prior schooling (in a person's L1 and English), cognitive abilities, motivation, and practice. Ultimately, understanding and learning about our students' language backgrounds is crucial for planning instruction because it can help us pinpoint areas of strength and weakness in relation to language needs.

As previously mentioned, it is believed that a person's L1 influences their second language acquisition. Research shows that the level of language fluency in a person's first language can both positively and negatively affect their acquisition of a second or third language. Essentially, if someone has a base knowledge of their L1, they can excel in a second language. Someone might take more time to acquire English fluency depending on L1 fluency levels, but it is possible. Someone with advanced L1 fluency on the other hand, is more likely to acquire second language mastery in a shorter period of time.

Most people know that the fastest way to learn a language is to become fully immersed in it. However, making this happen is not realistic for most adults seeking ELL instruction. Adults who enroll in ELL classes often have families with whom they communicate in their L1 at home, or they remain in constant contact with family and friends who only speak their native language. In addition, many can use their L1 regularly in their workplace. This is not a criticism—it just recognizes a reality that can represent one of the many challenges in acquiring a new language.

We want to support adult learners to take risks in using the English language even when it's uncomfortable. In addition to obvious classroom activities, one way would be by encouraging students to seek ways to use English at home or with friends. Teachers could also have a Community Board in the classroom with flyers or announcements about upcoming events in the neighborhood, or by passing out event flyers to the class and encouraging everyone to participate as a whole team. From experience, beach clean-ups and awareness walks are quite popular.

Beginning learners are more likely to rely on L1 use than advanced learners, so the goal is to lessen L1 support over time. Ultimately, the more exposure someone has to English, the better their chances are of acquiring it at a faster pace. Learning a language takes practice, and we must stress the value in both meaningful use and natural communication in English as much as possible in order to acquire fluency. One way to do this is to encourage learners to challenge themselves by reading texts or listening to conversations that are just above their fluency or comprehension level without L1 support; research shows this positively influences second language acquisition.[6]

How to Foster Success with Adult Learners

The fundamental best practices of teaching English Language Learners are fairly uniform. There are, however, a few factors to consider when teaching adult learners.

Use adult-appropriate content and materials and avoid lessons or activities that might seem childish for academic and professional environments. Create a balance of hands-on learning with direct instruction, and gauge student interest to determine when it's appropriate to implement fun or interactive tasks. Much like young learners, some adults learn best by watching, but many learn best by doing. Determine the types of learning activities that best speak to your students' needs and interests in order to maintain adult-appropriate instruction.

Because of the maturity of many older learners, adult education instructors tend to have less conflict in the classroom than in the K-12 setting. From experience, the conflicts that arise tend to be resolved with little to no serious consequences. The majority of issues are attendance related or are occasional differences that can be talked through. The following strategies are suggestions for success with adult learners and promote a positive learning environment with minimal issues.

STRATEGIES FOR SUCCESS

Set Clear Expectations

Adult learners like structure and organization, so be prepared. Come to class with the appropriate materials and resources needed for the day's lessons. Anticipate technology failures, interruptions, and possible lesson plan fails.

As adults, we expect to be treated a certain way, so modeling that to our students goes a long way. We must set clear expectations of our students, and we must lead by example. Model your own expectations and be consistent in them. A common practice among fellow adult ELL instructors is the use of a class contract. At the beginning of the course, we provide a thorough overview of the expectations for the course which include norms for behavior, responsibilities, and attendance. In doing this, students know exactly what is expected of them to be successful in the course, and they are front-loaded with the consequences of not living up to those expectations—a setback in second language acquisition. Attendance in any class is key, especially in the ELL classroom, and that goes for students and teachers. Every institution has a policy for attendance, so it's important to review it with students. Ask students to sign a contract outlining the course expectations stating they understand their responsibilities and commitment to the course. This agreement tends to minimize attendance issues and promote good classroom management.

Set Goals and Revisit Them Often

Goal-setting and creating a plan to reach those goals are two important tasks to tackle early on in adult ELL instruction. We must set goals for ourselves as instructors, but more importantly, our students need to set short-term and long-term goals for learning. Individual student goals are the driving force of instruction and the learning that happens both in and out of the classroom. Setting clear goals will promote self-discipline and foster motivation. Adult learners generally have more self-discipline, so setting clear goals and developing a plan to reach those goals will influence the overall success of second language acquisition. We can do this by helping learners create a plan for goal attainment.

Provide the opportunity for learners to set their own short-term and long-term goals— personal and professional, for self-growth and language growth. This can be done with an Initial Needs Assessment[7] or more informally with self-assessments. In either case, it is important for instructors to discuss these goals with students and use them as anchors for planning. Provide feedback for student goals to help them understand how and if those goals are attainable and in what time frame. Reviewing student goals is a critical factor in tailoring instruction to meet the needs of learners. It also sets clear objectives for students and helps them understand the purpose behind new learnings.

Instructors should keep each individual student's goals on record and revisit them regularly to assess if instruction is reflective of those goals. We also need to embed goal-setting into on-going lessons[8] because it enhances academic performance in language learning and helps us track student progress. Thus, goals need to be revisited by both students and instructors multiple times throughout language instruction. To monitor progress, there are specific questions we can ask students. See the progress check questions outlined below for suggestions.

The goals students set, both big and small, should not only be practical and realistic but should also encourage challenge and difficulty. These goals should enable adults to stay focused and be more self-directed in their learning; they should promote self-efficacy and the confidence necessary to successfully obtain acquisition. When creating objectives and goals for instruction, consider the S.M.A.R.T goal-setting framework—Specific, Measurable, Assignable, Realistic, Time-based.[9] While it's not necessary to cover all five criteria for each goal, it's a good idea to provide questions and examples that guide students in setting goals that are reflective of the S.M.A.R.T framework. One way to do this is to encourage students to create affirmative goal statements. This can be done at the beginning of the course or multiple times throughout the course for each unit. Revisit those goals to track progress and create instruction that supports goal attainment.

See the Tech Tool Box for additional goal-setting resources, and other supportive materials for adult ELL instruction.

Tech Tool

Online Resources to Support Adult ELLs

For more information on goal-setting and lesson plan ideas for goal-setting in the adult ELL classroom, as well as for other resources to support Adult ELL, see "The Best Resources for Teaching Adult English Language Learners" https://larryferlazzo.edublogs.org/2021/07/12/the-best-resources-for-teaching-adult-english-language-learners/.

BUILD RELATIONSHIPS AND RAPPORT

The rapport we create with our adult learners should be that of respect and acceptance so that we maintain professionalism while developing strong bonds. Get to know your students as much as they will allow you. It's likely to have a class made up of adults from varying backgrounds, ages, and levels, so avoid making assumptions about someone's background and encourage all students to welcome the differences among the group to support learning. Based on personal experience as well as input from fellow adult educators, this helps build trust among students as well.

1. How to Build Relationships and Rapport with Adult Learners   Take time to learn about the cultural makeup of your class. It's important to understand where our students come from and promote diversity among students by allowing them to understand each other's cultures. This helps build positive rapport, create a safe and comfortable classroom environment, and further develop respect.

   a. Encourage students to present to the class about their home cultures. These presentations can include to consist of visuals, food, stories, clothing, and audience participation.

   b. Facilitate whole group discussions or compare/contrast aspects of culture.

   c. Pair or group students and assign tasks for students to discuss and/or write about cultural similarities or differences (keep topics neutral and avoid controversy).

2. If possible, make the effort to become familiar with words or phrases in students' L1 that support learning. This is easiest in small group classes, one-on-one instruction, or classes with three or less languages among students. This can be difficult, but learning simple phrases like greetings and verbal praise can go a long way.

3. Show interest in what students "bring to the table." Don't be afraid to share stories or anecdotes that build on student comments, input, or questions. Make every effort to build connections during lessons to what students have asked about in past discussions.

4. Respect everyone's views, experience, and knowledge even if you disagree. We must set an example of what it's like to agree to disagree and to acknowledge everyone's ideas.

5. Always be professional, and avoid being intrusive, condescending, or judgmental. This is one of the most important aspects of building relationships because it builds trust and respect. If someone is not comfortable sharing information or ideas, leave it be; it's the best way to avoid conflict.

BE FLEXIBLE AND PATIENT

Like children, adults struggle, too, and learning a new language is not easy. Understand that life happens, so sometimes lessons will not go as planned. We need to expect to make changes as learners adjust to life in a new country and roles as students in a new environment. A few simple ways to demonstrate patience and flexibility include how we present instruction and how we respond to students.

Be prepared to provide multiple ways for learners to access concepts or complex ideas. Everyone responds differently to learning, and we know that no classroom is filled with one type of learner. When someone says, "I don't understand," it warrants rephrasing or finding a new approach to teaching. We must have visuals, examples, demonstrations, etc. to complement our instruction to help students fully grasp ideas.

Sometimes, asking other students to explain their understanding helps, too, so encourage assistance from all learners. That might even mean making connections to someone's L1, which is highly encouraged with adult learners. Most importantly, if students are not responsive or are slow to respond, don't panic. Wait time is a staple of ELL instruction with both children and adults. Sometimes, it takes longer to process information and really grasp it. Don't mistake silence for confusion. Give ample wait time for processing and understanding, and reiterate ideas to aid in comprehension as needed.

KEEP IT ENGAGING

Adults can lose focus and interest in anything just like children, so it's important to plan engaging lessons that foster ownership of learning. The more engaged students are, the more inclined they are to retain what they learn. Visuals, demonstrations, and hands-on learning are some ways to create engaging lessons. A class focused on academic English might entail more reading and writing than a class geared towards learning English for personal purposes. In these cases, the level of engagement in both situations will look different, so it can be difficult to compare. Engagement sometimes comes in the form of participation and other times comes in the form of performance.

One of the best ways to know if students are engaged is to ask for student feedback on lessons and learnings; this could be done daily, weekly, or monthly. This gives students a chance to take ownership of what they are learning because they have a say in how they learn it. Find out what is working and what is not working for students, and make changes to accommodate their needs. Applying this kind of flexibility is one of the best ways to engage adults in academic or professional settings because the content may not always be exciting. However, there are still ways to make learning *engaging*. For some students, that might come in the form of allowing them to choose discussion topics or giving them the chance to present something new to the class. Again, engagement comes in many forms, so knowing your audience will help you plan lessons accordingly.

BE MINDFUL OF HOMEWORK

Homework is a controversial issue in education, but those who see the value in it are not afraid to assign it. This is not to say all homework is valuable because it definitely is not. As instructors, we know that adults have other responsibilities like children or jobs. Any homework assigned should be for practice and needs to be valuable, not busy work. The homework assigned is not meant to create stress or be burdensome; it should be for meaningful and purposeful use. Homework should come in the form of practical tasks like speaking English for 20 minutes per evening or attempting a phone conversation in English. Sometimes, it's studying vocabulary and attempting to use words in a sentence. Students will often ask for worksheets and extra grammar practice, and there is no harm in providing these types of tasks. The important takeaway is that students are *learning* and not just *doing*.

For worksheets, conversation practice, or skills-based homework, demonstrate the value of this work by going over the homework together and discussing it. Sometimes, students like to share their experiences—what was easy, what was challenging, and what they learned. This is often an engaging way to assess the value of extra at-home practice because many adults practice with their children who are also learning English at school. It's great to hear stories of how adults are learning from their children, and it often sparks great questions and conversation amongst the group. It is not always necessary to review homework exercises that are simply for practice, but be sure to provide answer keys to students because it will encourage ownership of learning and self-discipline.

ENCOURAGE RECIPROCAL TEACHING

Adult learners can take more ownership of their learning through reciprocal teaching. In other words, they can teach each other. This is not to say instructors are off the hook with planning and facilitating, but it provides adults with the chance to share what they know, ask questions, or teach others. Ask them to come to class with questions, observations, or interests in new learnings, such as something they overheard in conversation or something they read about recently. Often, students know more than we think they do, so let them show off what they know and use this to assess what they need. This can be as simple as students choosing a current event to discuss and bringing an article to look at, or it can be as complex as students planning a presentation on new learnings to share with the class. Remember to provide clear guidelines and expectations, namely to avoid conflict or misunderstandings.

BUILD CONFIDENCE

Learning a new language requires having the confidence to take risks. From personal experience, students claim their biggest takeaway from ELL classes is the confidence they gain along the way. That is due in part to the students themselves, but it starts with educators. We can create the conditions so students can build a greater belief in their own abilities. With this confidence, students become more engaged, more motivated to learn, and more self-aware of their progress. Listed below are some simple ways to boost confidence with ELLs:

- Be positive and complimentary
- Encourage mistakes or going outside comfort zone
- Be constructive, not critical
- Highlight successes
- Rewards (verbal praise, high-fives, celebrations)
- Revisit goals and milestones

SIMPLE WAYS TO SUPPORT ADULT LEARNERS IN ELL INSTRUCTION

While some of these tips and strategies seem obvious, they are meant to serve as suggestions and a quick reference to the fundamental practice of ELL instruction that promote success with adult learners:

- Encourage L1 use to support learning in and out of the classroom when appropriate
- Build background and tap into prior knowledge as frequently as possible
  - Frontload vocabulary
  - Provide contextual background
  - Compare student knowledge (ask students to share what they know)
- Read out loud as much as possible (instructors and students)
  - Stop for comprehension checks
  - Model pronunciation, inflections, stress, tone, etc.
  - Allow students to hear and apply new learnings
- Spend time talking (class discussions, one-on-one, recordings)
  - Encourage authentic language use in and out of the classroom
  - Utilize the skills learned (the key to proficiency)
    - Record conversations and readings
    - Practice speaking with family/friends
    - Listen to recordings and self-assess
  - Encourage risk-taking in conversation
    - Make a phone call without help
    - Order at a restaurant
    - Talk to a friend solely in English
  - Don't be afraid to correct mistakes, but be respectful (constructive)
    - Restate a sentence to model correct English language use and explain the correction when necessary (it is not always needed)
    - Use mistakes as a guide for new lessons or review
    - Make discussions about students, their knowledge, or interests
- Offer reading materials or resources to encourage extra practice and practical application
  - Books, articles, journals, magazines, web sites, etc.
  - Grammar or writing workbooks
  - Phone apps (i.e. Hello English or Duolingo)

- Model and use resources to support learning
  - Model correct English language use
  - Use visual aids as often as possible
  - Encourage use of translation to L1 when needed (apps, dictionaries, pictures, etc.)
  - Encourage students to keep a journal or notebook
    - Notebooks can include lesson notes, personal notes, or vocabulary terms with L1 and English translation, definitions, examples, and possibly images

What Could Go Wrong in the Adult ELL Classroom?

Our hot topic discussion elevates to a heated debate between students. Someone gets offended by another person's opinion. Students don't see the relevance of a particular lesson that we spent hours preparing. No matter what we do, we can't avoid these issues, but we can do our best to minimize conflict. The best way to avoid conflict is to be consistent with expectations in the classroom. Before discussions, remind everyone that with sharing comes respect. If someone says something we disagree with, we must learn to listen and try to understand their perspective. In any case, it is never acceptable to intentionally disrespect or put someone down. Remind the class of the expected behaviors, attitudes, and responsibility of each individual in the course.

In some cases, it may be appropriate to request that someone remove themselves from the class to abate an issue. It would be wise to speak to them in private and welcome them back to the room or discussion after some time away (a few minutes or the remainder of the day). Based on input from other adult educators, this tends to be the most effective solution for individual issues though these instances seldom happen when clear expectations are set.

Essentially, always have a backup plan in the event something goes wrong or doesn't go as planned. If a topic is making students uncomfortable, be prepared to shift gears. If students aren't engaged, don't hesitate to move on or find a new approach. Try another strategy or make modifications. If an issue continues to present itself, consider the source and create a plan for resolution.

By implementing the various strategies presented in this chapter, instructors can create a positive learning environment that fosters success with adult English Language Learners. All of the strategies outlined support the valuable practice of reflective teaching, promoting the student-centered learning adults require. Try to anticipate what could go wrong in any given lesson, and prepare a plan for resolution based on the strategies provided. In addition, use any classroom conflicts as learning experiences for future planning. A benefit to education is that we learn a lot about our students, ourselves, and our instructional practices that provide us with the ongoing opportunity to do better.

Links to all the online activities listed in the chapter can be found at www.wiley.com/go/eslsurvivalguide2.

CHAPTER FOURTEEN

Teaching ELLs with Learning Differences

There was a young boy who worked in the fields with his father every day. The boy could understand the songs and messages of the birds, who would come each day to speak to the boy. The boy's father could not interpret these messages and became increasingly frustrated with the young boy. One day, he demanded to know what the birds were saying, and the young man told his father that the birds said that one day he would salute the young man. The father didn't believe him, and continued to be frustrated and treat him harshly, eventually sending the boy away. The young man wandered for a long time. He heard of a great chief who decreed that his daughter would marry someone who could tell him what the birds who visited each day were trying to tell him. The young boy was able to relate the crows' message to the chief, who kept his word. The young man married the chief's daughter and became the new chief. People from neighboring villages came from all around to salute the young chief and his wife, including the young man's parents. The father asked for forgiveness, and they were reunited.[1]

In this Mayan tale, a young man with an exceptional gift of communication struggles before finding a place where he is welcomed and he feels valued. His gift isn't immediately apparent or understood by others, just as the case may be for many English Language Learner students with exceptional needs. Through communication and teamwork, teachers can find the best fit for each student, allowing him/her to feel like they belong and are valued, just like the young man in the story.

This chapter was written by Jessica Bell M.Ed. Jessica taught English and English as a New Language (ENL) for 19 years, serving students from a diverse mix of backgrounds. A SIOP practitioner while in the classroom, she believes all students deserve equitable access to rigorous academic instruction. Jessica has transitioned from the classroom to the EdTech space, helping provide teachers with digital tools to enhance instruction.

If you work with children, or work in education, you're familiar with acronyms and labels. Labels and acronyms are tricky, because they're used to describe people—and we know people are very complex. A question that invariably comes up when you work with unique populations, like English Language Learners and students with special needs, is what do you do when these separate labels are used to describe the same person? In an educational context, a "label" is used to describe students who qualify to receive specific services and instructional support. This kind of assistance is needed for them to be successful in the least restrictive educational setting. A student may be an English Language learner, but may also qualify for special education, speech, or services due to being deaf/hard of hearing. Children, and all people, are more than their labels, so we must understand that the process of identifying the special education needs of ELLs is complex.

This chapter will consider the issue through several steps. The first part is what an ELL teacher should look for to prompt a more serious investigation. These indicators may or may not demonstrate that a student requires additional special services and, in fact, many times may show that they are not needed.

The following section looks at the process that might come next if the teacher concludes that a further investigation is needed to determine if and what kind of additional services would be best for the student.

The final piece considers the actual placement and scheduling of those needed services.

Considerations for Further Investigation

Teachers who work with ELLs know that each student develops language skills at their own rate, and that just as native English speakers have linguistic strengths and weaknesses, so do English Language Learners. Some students pick up a new language more quickly than others, but some may have an undiagnosed learning disability that has not been documented in school records. So, when is it appropriate to look deeper? What are some "red flags" that tell you a student may need more services? Answering yes to the following questions doesn't always mean a student may need special education services, but the answers *may* help you determine if further investigation is needed. Some of the questions I ask are:

- Has the student received formal education in a previous language, but seems to be acquiring English at a slower rate than his/her ELL peers?
- Does the student seem to be demonstrating high degrees of frustration in the classroom?
- Is one language domain progressing at a vastly slower rate than others?
- Has the student been in US schools for longer than three years and is still testing at the beginning level on ELP (state English Language Proficiency) Assessments?

Considerations for Determining Services

If your answers to the above questions are "yes," here are other indicators that a student might need to be evaluated for special education services. A student could have moved to the United States one or two years earlier, and testing had been deliberately put off until it could be determined if the issue was due to a lack of proficiency in English or a learning disability.

The student could also be a Long-Term English Language Learner, an LTELL, who has experienced past challenges that have been attributed by teachers only to language proficiency issues.

Occasionally a SLIFE (student with limited or interrupted formal education) is mislabeled because gaps in knowledge or application can be confused for a disability when the reality is that they have not had adequate schooling. For more information about determining if a student could be labeled SLIFE, I recommend *Boosting Achievement* by Carol Salva.[2] Speech-Language Pathologists are also an informative resource about distinguishing between language delays, disorders, and differences, and most districts have SLPs on staff.

At many schools, teams of specialists and teachers work together to determine what services may be best for students. Some places call this process RTI, or Response to Intervention, or MTSS, Multi-Tiered System of Support. If a school district or school uses one of these processes, they will meet over a period of time to evaluate data, suggest and enact interventions, review them, and finally make a determination of services and recommend placement. Teams may look at data from classroom teachers, English language proficiency testing, standardized tests, and whatever other information is available. A useful resource on this topic is the book *Supporting English Learners in the Classroom: Best Practices for Distinguishing Language Acquisition from Learning Disabilities* by Eric Haas and Julie Esparza Brown.[3] It is important to note that individual states and school districts have their own protocols about this process, so be sure to inquire about the process in your location.

In my experience, the more data, even anecdotal, the better. Parents must be involved along the way—not only are they a valuable resource, but they are also legally allowed to provide input about how schools should meet their child's educational needs. Some of the questions I might ask (recognizing that they might not be able to answer all of them) are:

- Based on reports from your child's teachers, are there any major changes in behavior between school and home?
- Is your child successful in sports or hobbies?
- Is there a marked difference between your child's spoken and written communication in L1?
- How is your child's personality when faced with a challenging task?
- Did your child attend a school where L1 was the primary language of instruction and is he/she literate in that language?
- Did your child receive special education services in L1?
- What kind of print environment is at home? Are their books in L1 and L2?
- How does your child interact with you and other members of the family?
- What tasks at home do they excel at or struggle with?
- How many schools (and in how many countries) has the student been enrolled in?
- Are you concerned about your student's academic performance?
- What are your goals for your child?

In addition to parents, I talk with content teachers (or grade-level teachers), a special education teacher of record, and a guidance counselor, if available. If a student also appears to have social challenges with peers, or seems to struggle with tasks that don't involve language (sports, hobbies, home tasks, etc.), then it is possible they may need more assistance than only ELL services. A decision about the kind of services a student requires must obviously be made by qualified and experienced staff. Additional information needed by those staff to make an informed decision could be obtained by asking other colleagues these questions:

- If the student is fluent in L1, are the issues the same as in L2?
- What data points are available to disaggregate?
- How much historical data is available?

- How does the student interact with their peers?
- How does the student interact with teachers?

*Please note that tests given in L1 may be skewed if the student isn't literate in L1.

Considerations for Placement/Scheduling

Once a recommendation for additional services is made, continuing to involve parents is imperative. Because services offered can vary from country to country, state to state, and school to school, it is important to ensure that parents understand the options and the long-term effects of choosing programs.

Determining services should be a team effort, even if your school doesn't use the RTI/MTSS system. I do recommend that the special education teacher and the ELL teacher confer prior to a formal placement/scheduling meeting. School staff need to all be on the "same page." Once the ELL and Sped teachers have developed a common recommendation on placement and scheduling, it is critical to involve the parents and the student in finalizing decisions. It is very possible that, based on new information, these conversations could result in a different recommendation than the ELL and Sped teachers had originally projected.

Always remember to ask parents if they have questions and explain any school acronyms or programs that they may not be aware of. It is necessary to have information printed in both English and the family's L1 so parents may refer back to it if needed.

Some additional questions to consider when determining placement and scheduling include:

- What is the student's disability?
- What classes should the student be taking?
- What are the student's strengths?
- What is their score in each language domain?
- Does the student have one domain that is very different than the rest?
- How long have they had English language services?
- Have their ELP (the state English language proficiency test) scores plateaued or does the student show improvement?
- What does the student want to do after high school?
- In what ways can the school support the student's goal for after high school?
- What additional services or supports does the student need so they can achieve their goals?

Resources

Throughout this process it is important to be aware of all locally available resources. In smaller districts, some services like ELL, Special Education, Speech, or Behavioral Therapists may not be provided daily at each school, but on a rotating schedule or by appointment only. You may or may not be fully aware of what kind of services are provided at the district level. In some rural areas, multiple school districts form consortiums for services.

There are often many community resources available to help parents and students. **However, always ask permission from the family to recommend them for outside services. Remember that some families may not have the necessary documentation and you do not want to put those families at risk.** Check with your individual state and county health department, churches, or children's bureau for more information.

See the Tech Tool for additional resources.

Tech Tool

Additional Resources

For additional resources, see "The Best Resources On Assisting ELLs With Special Needs" https://larryferlazzo.edublogs.org/2015/07/26/the-best-resources-on-assisting-ells-with-special-needs-help-me-find-more/.

Links to all the online resources can be found at www.wiley.com/go/eslsurvivalguide2.

PART SIX

Further Strategies to Ensure Success

CHAPTER FIFTEEN

Culturally Responsive and Sustaining Teaching

There was a family that lived on the Cavalla River in Liberia: a hunter, his wife, and their three sons; the mother was expecting another child soon. One morning, the hunter went into the forest. Night came; the hunter didn't come home.

A week passed. A month. The boys started hunting on their own; they did not speak about their absent father. Then, the mother gave birth to a daughter. Time passed. The baby girl learned to crawl, to stand up, to walk, and then to speak.

Her first words were "Where is my father?"

"Yes," said the first brother. "Where is he?"

"We should find out what happened to him," said the second brother.

"Let's go!" said the third brother.

The first son had a sixth sense that allowed him to find their father's body in the forest; a wild animal had killed him. Only his bones were left. The second son knew a magic spell to put flesh back on their father's bones. The third son had the power to breathe life back into their father's body. Their father rose up, thanked his sons, and they all went home together. The whole village celebrated the hunter's return.

"Whom shall we honor? Who rescued this man?" the chief asked.

The sons began arguing. "I found him!" "I put flesh on his bones!" "I breathed life into his body!"

The villagers also began arguing. The chief could not decide which son to honor.

Then the mother stepped forward. "Our daughter deserves the honor," the mother proclaimed, "because she noticed that her father was missing and asked: Where is my father?"

Everyone agreed with the mother's verdict, and they honored the wise little girl.[1]

As this folktale teaches, each person has a valuable contribution to make, and sometimes the most important contribution is to notice what is missing. What is often missing from instruction in our schools is acknowledgement and celebration of our students' identities and cultures.

While the majority of students in US public schools are students of color from linguistically and culturally diverse backgrounds, the vast majority of educators (around 80 percent) in K-12 public schools are white.[2] Many students have been harmed by pedagogy that has not acknowledged systemic racism[3] and educators play an important role in either addressing or not addressing these harms.[4] In light of increased public attention to police violence against people of color and a counter-reaction by conservatives opposing anti-racism teaching in schools,[5] educators should be intentional in addressing their own biases and practicing culturally responsive and sustaining teaching.

While we are including this as a separate chapter, we in no way want to imply that culturally sustaining teaching is optional or that it occurs only on certain days or in certain activities. As this chapter will describe, culturally responsive and sustaining pedagogy is an approach or mindset that underlies and guides *everyday* classroom practices. It focuses on validating the cultural learning tools that diverse learners bring to the classroom and leveraging them to effect positive learning outcomes for *all* students.

What Is Culturally Responsive and Sustaining Teaching?

Culturally responsive teaching (CRT) and culturally sustaining pedagogy (CSP) are two of the most common philosophies guiding how teachers of all races can be better teachers to students of color. These approaches are built on the foundational work of educator and researcher Dr. Gloria Ladson-Billings. She introduced the term *culturally relevant pedagogy* to describe a teaching approach centered on engaging learners whose experiences and cultures were often viewed through a "deficit" lens and traditionally excluded in mainstream educational settings.[6]

Geneva Gay expanded on the work of Ladson-Billings and identified the term *culturally responsive teaching* to describe pedagogy that uses "the cultural knowledge, prior experiences, frames of reference, and performance styles of ethnically diverse students to make learning encounters more relevant to and effective for them."[7]

Culturally sustaining pedagogy is a more recent perspective that builds on the tenets of culturally responsive and relevant teaching. This approach was first proposed by professor Django Paris,[8] who defines it as a pedagogy that "seeks to perpetuate and foster—to sustain—linguistic, literate, and cultural pluralism as part of schooling for positive social transformation and revitalization."[9] In other words, this approach prioritizes making sure that our educational practices not only *respond* to the diversity of languages and cultures in our classroom, but also that they aim to *sustain* these elements at the center of teaching and learning. As Zaretta Hammond, educator and author of the book *Culturally Responsive Teaching and the Brain,* points out: all of us are doing culturally responsive teaching at all times. The question posed by Hammond is, "Whose culture?"[10] What we want to do is to lift up the cultures of students who have been traditionally ignored or marginalized.

Viewing English Language Learners through an asset, not deficit, based lens guides all that we do in the classroom. Instruction that is culturally responsive and sustaining explicitly challenges the deficit perspective. We believe that recognizing, validating, and using the many linguistic and cultural tools that ELLs possess ultimately provides the best learning experiences for our students *and for us.*

The Organizing Cycle

In Chapters Seven and Eight, we discussed how the Organizing Cycle (based upon successful strategies used by community organizers) can be applied as a helpful framework for making learning more accessible to ELLs and to all learners. The research-based principles of building student relationships, accessing prior knowledge (particularly through student stories), developing student leadership potential, learning by doing, and reflection can also work as a frame for discussing culturally responsive and sustaining pedagogy in the ELL classroom.

In the following section, we offer ideas and practices for each principle of the Organizing Cycle. While these elements don't cover every aspect of culturally responsive teaching, they do represent foundational best practices we use in our classrooms. We hope our discussion in this chapter can spur continued research and deepen learning in your own practice. And again, we want to emphasize culturally responsive and sustaining teaching is not a "program" or list of strategies. It is a mindset that influences everything we do in the classroom.

BUILDING STRONG RELATIONSHIPS

Many educators view positive relationships with students as a classroom management tool. However, a culturally responsive-sustaining educator views these relationships as a critical foundation of *learning.* Zaretta Hammond explains the connection between our brain's ability to learn and positive relationships: "The oxytocin positive relationships trigger helps the amygdala stay calm so the prefrontal cortex can focus on higher order thinking and learning."[11] To put it simply, positive relationships in the classroom help students to feel safe. When they feel safe, they can better learn. In an ELL classroom that is culturally responsive sustaining, building positive relationships can involve:

- Taking the time to *listen* and to *learn* about our students through the relationship-building and sustaining activities shared in Chapter Two.

- Gathering information about students from the school (English Proficiency Level, home language survey, health information, transcripts, assessments, and so on). This data can provide context for conversations with students and their families. However, it's important to be *data-informed* (recognizing that numbers do not necessarily provide all the needed information or even the most important information that teachers want to know about their students). Sometimes being *data-driven* can result in teachers having too narrow of a focus on numbers and statistics, which don't provide a complete picture of students' lives, goals, strengths, and challenges.[12]

- Learning about students' home countries—current conflicts/issues, specific information on the city or region they come from, language(s) they speak, etc.—from students, their families, and your own research.

- Becoming familiar with the neighborhoods students currently live in can make it easier for teachers to connect students' daily experiences to the classroom and develop deeper relationships with students and their families.[13]

- Gathering information on students' academic strengths and challenges through discussions with students and their families (We like to ask parents: "What is something that has helped your child learn best?" "When has your child been most successful in school and what contributed to that success?"), regular check-ins, and close observations of students and their work.

- Giving surveys to students asking about their interests, goals, and feedback on the class can strengthen relationships *if* the teacher acts on this information. Asking students to fill out a Google form and then not acting on any of the feedback from students can be perceived as "performative" and can lead students to believe that the teacher doesn't really care about them or what they think.

- Using the *establish, maintain, restore* framework, which has been found by researchers to be one of the most effective techniques for positive relationship building.[14] This relationship framework involves first *establishing* positive relationships at the beginning of the year using strategies like the ones described in Chapter Two.

Positive, trusting relationships must then be *maintained* throughout the year by continuing to implement those strategies and being mindful of positive and negative interactions with students (research shows teachers should aim for a five-to-one ratio).[15]

When negative interactions do happen, then relationships must be repaired or *restored*. Some of the ways teachers can help restore positive relationships include admitting their own mistakes, taking responsibility for their actions, apologizing when needed, not blaming students when things go wrong, allowing students to have a "fresh start" each day, asking students what they need to move forward, and showing empathy. It can also be important to remember that when we are apologizing to students, we want the focus to be on the student—how *they* are feeling, how the mistake affected *them*, or what *they* need to move forward.[16]

- We can't say it enough times: taking the time to learn how to pronounce each of your student's names is essential to relationship building, and if you get it wrong, keep trying until you get it right!

Note: We understand that many of these relationship-building activities can be challenging when the teacher doesn't share the same home language as the student. We encourage you to revisit the Tech Tool in Chapter Two "Online Resources: Translating" for translation resources.

ACCESSING PRIOR KNOWLEDGE (ESPECIALLY THROUGH STORIES)

Research on the brain confirms it is easier to learn something new when we can attach it to something we already know.[17] For ELLs in particular, activating prior knowledge, also known as *activating schema*, plays a big role in promoting their academic literacy.[18]

In an ELL classroom, students possess varying levels of prior knowledge in English and academic content. They also bring with them valuable "funds of knowledge" created through their cultural, family, and general life experiences outside of school.[19] Culturally responsive-sustaining teachers of ELLs honor their students' experiences and understandings. They help students draw on their prior knowledge, including these funds of knowledge, in order to make connections to new learning. Once teachers elicit from students what they already know and have experienced about a topic or concept, they can then decide how much additional background knowledge is needed for students to understand new content.

Chapter Seven contains specific examples of eliciting and building background knowledge with ELLs. Here are a few more ways we support students to share and build upon their knowledge and experiences in culturally sustaining ways:

- *Listening, listening, and more listening!* Teachers can't help *students* access and expand prior knowledge if the *teacher* is doing all the talking. Sometimes, teachers leave out the "accessing prior knowledge" stage and move straight to "building background knowledge" by explaining every word, concept, or topic to their students. Not only can this be confusing and overwhelming for students, but it devalues students' prior knowledge and experiences.

  In addition, teachers should remember that students may possess an understanding of a concept that is "different" from the teacher's prior knowledge as opposed to "incorrect." For example, asking students from different cultural backgrounds to write what they know about healthcare and medicine may elicit very different responses from one written by the teacher.

- *Using what we call "brain sparks" to get students thinking, talking, writing, and sharing about a topic or concept we will be teaching.* When starting a new unit, text, or concept, we often show students a related video (possibly at a reduced speed and certainly with English subtitles), an image, a slideshow, or other visual and ask them questions like "What do you notice?"; "What do you find interesting?"; or "What does this remind you of?" Simply asking students to write or talk about it with a partner can gauge prior knowledge, build background, and generate interest. Newcomers can respond in their home language or even through drawing pictures of what they already know about the topic.

- *Validating and encouraging students' use of their home language when activating and building prior knowledge* (including providing texts in their home language on the topic of study). This perspective is also known as *translanguaging* where students are encouraged to leverage the linguistics tools of all the languages they know in order to develop their home and second (in some cases maybe their third, fourth, or even fifth) language, content, academic, and social skills.[20] See Chapter Seventeen for more on supporting students' use of home language.

- *Encouraging students to frequently share their cultural and linguistic knowledge with each other.* This sharing can happen more formally through projects or student presentations where students teach each other about their home cultures and their home languages. Even simple, informal practices like asking students to come to the board and translate a key vocabulary word into their different home languages (followed by the teacher attempting to say the word in each language) can instantly be affirming and inject some humor (at the teacher's expense!) into the lesson.

  Providing space and time for students to consider and share the different ways they solve problems, how they might approach an activity, what works/doesn't work best for them when learning, the similarities and differences of their home languages, and many other forms of knowledge and experience, can help teachers create what Zaretta Hammond calls "cognitive hooks" between students' valuable funds of knowledge and academic content.[21]

- *Asking students to share the problems and challenges they and their families have faced and discussing strategies for dealing with them.* The Paulo Freire-based Critical Pedagogy strategy discussed in Chapter Three is one example of this kind of activity.

IDENTIFYING AND MENTORING STUDENTS' LEADERSHIP POTENTIAL

As we mentioned in Chapter Seven when discussing the Organizing Cycle, researchers have found that good leaders and successful language learners share similar attributes including being intrinsically motivated, possessing a sense of self-efficacy (a belief in one's ability to succeed), a willingness to take risks and learn from mistakes, and a desire to teach others. We have heard many educators talk about wanting to "empower" their English language learners to develop these qualities. If you look up the definition of "empower," it is generally defined as: *to give (someone) the authority or power to do something.* In a culturally responsive-sustaining classroom, however, power is not something to be "given," just as self-efficacy or motivation are not "given" to students by the teacher. Instead, we as teachers can provide the *conditions* for these qualities to grow and flourish (an idea we have borrowed and modified from Sir Ken Robinson).[22]

When teaching ELLs through a lens of culturally responsive-sustaining pedagogy, in addition to building positive relationships and accessing prior knowledge, *centering a student voice* is another critical component of creating the *conditions* for student success. In other words, the teacher asks for, listens to, and *acts on* student ideas and feedback. Here are some practical ways we support students in "taking power" to co-construct the teaching and learning in our classrooms:

- *Engaging with students about **what** they want to learn, **how** they want to learn, and **when** they want to learn (in what chronological order).* Asking for student input on curriculum and instruction can be done in numerous ways—from simply asking them in conversation to eliciting their input through surveys or other writing activities. It is most important for teachers to *elicit student input on a regular basis* (we aim for once a week at a minimum) and *to act on this input* by using student feedback to improve instruction, increase engagement, and affirm students' voices. See Chapter Nineteen for examples of questions we use to gain this kind of student input.

- *Establishing Student Leadership Teams* in the ways we discussed in Chapters Two and Seven. We identify students who seem to be taking leadership in group or class activities and invite them to be part of a class leadership team. Team members are often responsible for leading small group activities, regularly meeting with us to evaluate what seems to be working and not working in class, helping to identify new students who they will mentor, and completing weekly reflections on their own work as leaders. Once the team is formed, we then extend an open invitation to *any* student who wants to develop their leadership skills.

- *Providing ELLs opportunities to teach others.* As we've stated, the ability to teach others is a key quality of a successful language learner and a good leader. We often incorporate strategies, like Jigsaw discussed in Chapter Three, where students are supported in teaching each other through literacy activities. These can be short and informal activities where students are teaching their ELL classmates, or may involve longer, scaffolded projects where ELLs and non-ELLs come together to teach and learn from each other. Many times the content of the jigsaws are based on student requests.

One project at our school that fits into this category, but is not a Jigsaw, is an annual event first organized by our colleague, Pam Buric, and named the Empathy Project. It involves intermediate-to-advanced ELLs writing stories about their lives which they then share with non-ELL students and their teachers in our school library. The non-ELL students arrive prepared with note-taking sheets to encourage active listening and empathetic responses. After writing and sharing their stories, the intermediate-advanced ELLs then "teach" students in the beginning ELL class how to write their own stories (with scaffolds like sentence starters), followed by a sharing day where both classes read their stories to each other. Every year, English proficient students and their teachers learn so much from our students, who, in turn, share with us the power they feel in having their voices heard. For more on this project, see the Tech Tool at the end of this chapter.

- *Having peer mentors, especially for ELL newcomers, enhances student-to-student relationships and centers students as leaders on campus.* Peer mentors are different from peer tutors because they are not asked to assist with daily academic tasks, but instead provide overall counsel on school and life. Older (though not always) trained student mentors who are ELL intermediates or advanced students meet weekly with their mentees (ELL newcomers or beginners) to build relationships and offer advice. Mentors regularly meet with teachers to discuss any problems the mentee may be dealing with and how the mentor can best be helpful.

- *Asking students to share with school staff what helps them learn*. Providing students with an opportunity to offer feedback on their classroom experiences can be powerful for students and teachers. One example of this kind of activity is asking our ELLs to complete a survey with questions focused on three key elements of ELL instruction—differentiation, student motivation, and affirming error correction. Here are examples of the questions we give to intermediate-advanced ELLs (beginners can be given a version that is simplified or translated into their home language):

- What do teachers do that helps you understand what they are teaching, even though you may not know English that well? For example, do they show pictures that help you understand the content? Please try to write about specific lessons and experiences.

- What are specific actions teachers have taken to help you become motivated to learn different subjects and the English language? Please try to write about specific lessons and experiences.

- What have teachers done to help you not feel bad about making mistakes and, instead, learn from them? In other words, what are the best actions teachers have taken to correct English errors you have made in writing or in speaking?

  The results of the survey can be shared in various ways, but we have found organizing a student panel (composed of student volunteers who meet together to practice and prepare ahead of time) to share their answers with teachers at staff or department meetings to be most powerful. In the past, we have recorded these sessions (with student and parent permission) and made them accessible to the whole school staff. See the Tech Tool for examples of these student panels and preparatory materials.

In community organizing, sometimes decision-makers feel that power is like a finite "pie"—if others get power, that can mean that the decision-makers have less power. In reality, organizers and others believe that the more power is distributed, the more possibilities are created. In other words, the pie itself gets bigger.

We would suggest the same is true in the classroom - the more power that is distributed to everyone in the class, the greater the motivation, the creativity, and the possibilities for everybody, including the teacher.

LEARNING BY DOING

As we discussed in Chapter Seven, the "Learning By Doing" element of the organizing cycle is rooted in the education theory of John Dewey who believed (and much research has since confirmed) that students learn better by actively participating in an experience, particularly if working with others, as opposed to just being told about it. [23]

Culturally responsive-sustaining teaching involves creating many opportunities for ELLs to "learn by doing." In earlier chapters, we've shared examples of "learning by doing" through cooperative learning activities and inductive teaching. Obviously, the activities described in the previous section on promoting student voice and leadership can also be categorized as "learning by doing." Here are some additional strategies for ELLs that promote active learning in culturally responsive-sustaining ways:

- *Creating lessons which directly connect to students' lives*. To ensure learning happens both inside and outside the classroom, teachers need to look to students, their families, and the community when planning learning activities. Asking students to identify and propose solutions to challenges they and their families are facing can result in greater learning and engagement. See the section on Critical Pedagogy in Chapter Three and the sample Problem-Solution Unit Plan in Chapter Six for how we structure these kinds of activities for beginner and intermediate ELLs.

  Another example of a lesson rooted directly in student experience happened when the neighborhood of our school was identified as a low response community for the US Census. Students decided to create bilingual posters and materials encouraging community members to complete the census forms so that their neighborhood would receive a fair share of public resources. Students then distributed those materials to friends, families, and neighbors. During the pandemic, we did a similar student-led project on vaccine awareness.

- *Providing students the opportunity to choose what they want to read from a diverse classroom library*. Dr. Rudine Sims Bishop has taught us that books can be "windows" for students (allowing them to see many different views of the world), they can also be "sliding glass doors" (that students can walk through, becoming part of a world created by the author), and when the lighting conditions are right, windows can also be "mirrors" (that students can see themselves and their experiences reflected in books and reading thus becomes a means of "self-affirmation").[24] Over the years, we have intentionally diversified our classroom libraries, along with the texts we share in class, so that our students are able see many mirrors.

- *Learning by doing from parents.* Inviting family members of our students to come and share their knowledge and experiences can be an especially meaningful learning activity. In our experience, once we have established positive relationships with parents (using the ideas described in Chapter Two), they have been very willing to share their skills and traditions in our classrooms (like the example in Chapter Two of a Hmong father sharing his expertise at making and repairing the traditional Hmong flute called the qeej).

REFLECTION

Though the ideas shared so far on the first four principles of the Organizing Cycle have focused on *students*, we are changing gears in this section to consider *teacher* reflection. Specific ideas on student reflection can be found throughout this book, especially in Chapter Three.

Chapter Twenty focuses on reflective teaching and professional development, but here we would like to share some questions that are particularly important for teachers to consider in the context of culturally responsive-sustaining teaching. These critical questions come from our book *The ELL Teacher's Toolbox*:[25]

- *How well do I know my students?*

    We try to ask ourselves this question on a regular basis and not just at the beginning of the year. Our students are growing young people who change on a daily basis and it's important we continue to seek out their interests, goals, challenges, and successes.

- *Do my words reflect a culturally responsive-sustaining mindset when I am talking to students and about students?*

    We try to stay mindful of the ways—both positive and negative—that our words can impact students. Pronouncing their names correctly and not characterizing students' beliefs as "right" or "wrong" through our words or even our facial expressions are two ways we honor students' cultural backgrounds and identities. We have found as teachers we can be far more effective in raising questions and being curious than in making judgements.

    We are also intentional in the way we speak about our students. Sometimes, well-meaning (or not) people ask us questions like "How do you do it?" or "How can those students learn when their lives are so crazy?" after learning that we work at a school located in a high-poverty area. While it can be tempting to tell stories of the trauma our students have faced in an attempt to demonstrate their resilience, doing so can often do more to perpetuate stereotypes than shatter them. Instead, we share about the rich cultural and linguistic contributions our students make each day to our school, their families, and the community.

- *How are my instructional practices culturally responsive and sustaining?*

  In our ELL classes, we use best practices, such as modeling, tapping prior knowledge, encouraging home language use, instructional scaffolding, and collaborative learning, just to name a few, to build the language, academic, and critical thinking skills students need to be successful lifelong learners. As we've described in this chapter and in many other parts of this book, building on students' cultural and linguistic experiences is critical to increasing learning outcomes for students.

- *How is the curriculum I am using culturally responsive and sustaining?*

  Curriculum doesn't have to incorporate texts and information about *every* student's culture in *every* lesson to be considered culturally responsive-sustaining. Nor should it include having a token "multicultural day" once a year to "celebrate" different cultures.

  Though we are continually learning how to make our curriculum more culturally responsive and sustaining, the following considerations have produced positive outcomes for our students:

  - materials representing diverse cultures and perspectives

  - curricular opportunities for students to share their cultural and linguistic knowledge with each other

  - allowing students to choose books to read from a diverse classroom library

  - inviting family and community members to share cultural knowledge in the classroom—using digital content to instantly connect students with a variety of cultural and linguistic resources

  - creating lessons on issues (like immigration policies) directly affecting students' lives

  - facilitating open classroom dialogues about the role of race, racism, and religious prejudice (e.g. Islamophobia) in our students' daily lives, including at school. See the Tech Tool for resources on having these kinds of discussions with students.

Tech Tool

Resources on Culturally Responsive and Sustaining Teaching

For many resources on culturally responsive and sustaining pedagogy, see "The Best Resources About 'Culturally Responsive Teaching' & 'Culturally Sustaining Pedagogy'" at https://larryferlazzo.edublogs.org/2016/06/10/the-best-resources-about-culturally-responsive-teaching-culturally-sustaining-pedagogy-please-share-more/.

More information on the value of correctly pronouncing student names can be found at "The Best Resources on the Importance of Correctly Pronouncing Student Names" at https://larryferlazzo.edublogs.org/2016/06/11/the-best-resources-on-the-importance-of-correctly-pronouncing-student-names/.

For more resources on helping students to teach others, see "The Best Posts on Helping Students Teach Their Classmates" at https://larryferlazzo.edublogs .org/2012/04/22/the-best-posts-on-helping-students-teach-their-classmates-help-me-find-more/.

A more detailed explanation of the Empathy Project, including downloadable handouts, can be found in the guest post on Larry's blog titled "What ELLs Taught Our School in a Week-Long Empathy Project" at https://larryferlazzo.edublogs. org/2017/04/21/guest-post-what-ells-taught-our-school-in-a-week-long-empathy-project/. For more on how we facilitated Student Panels, see "A New Student Panel of ELLs is Presenting at our Staff Training Tomorrow" at https://larryferlazzo. edublogs.org/2020/01/27/a-new-student-panel-of-ells-is-presenting-at-our-staff-training-tomorrow-here-are-videos-of-last-years-presentations/ .

For resources about the importance of diverse books for students, see "A Beginning Collection of Resources about Books as Windows, Mirrors, & Sliding Glass Doors" at https://larryferlazzo.edublogs.org/2019/06/21/a-beginning-collection-of-resources-about-books-as-windows-mirrors-sliding-glass-doors-please-suggest-more/ .

For information on facilitating classroom discussions on racism see "A Collection of Advice on Talking to Students about Race, Police, and Racism" at https:// larryferlazzo.edublogs.org/2016/07/14/a-collection-of-advice-on-talking-to-students-about-race-police-racism/ . In addition, you can find resources on teaching current issues related to students' lives at "The Best Posts and Articles on How to Teach 'Controversial' Topics" at https://larryferlazzo.edublogs.org/2014/10/04/the-best-posts-articles-on-how-to-teach-controversial-topics-suggest-more/ .

Links to all the online activities listed in the chapter can be found at www.
wiley.com/go/eslsurvivalguide2.

CHAPTER SIXTEEN

Addressing Additional Opportunities and Challenges

A king had a big tree near his palace, and he wanted it chopped down. The palace was built, and he also wanted a well dug near it. He offered great wealth to whomever could cut down the tree and dig a well.

Many people tried, but no one could make a dent in either the tree or the rock where the king wanted his well.

One day, a man named Boots and his brothers decided they would travel to the palace and try their luck at the tasks.

As they were walking, they heard something that sounded like hacking on top of a hill. "I wonder what is making that noise?" Boots said. "I think I'll go see what it is." His brothers scoffed at him, but Boots went and saw an axe that was chopping wood on its own and took it.

As the brothers continued to walk, they heard another sound in the forest. Boots said, "I wonder what the sound is?" And though his brothers were impatient again, Boots went and found a shovel that was digging on its own. He took it, too.

The brothers then came upon a stream, and Boots said, "I wonder where the water comes from?" Even though his brothers complained, he walked until he found the source of the water—it was a big walnut. He plugged it up with some grass and took it with him.

When they arrived at the palace, Boots' brothers tried chopping and digging first, but got nowhere. Then Boots set his axe to chopping and the tree came down. Then his shovel began digging, and when it reached a good depth he unplugged the walnut, put it in the ground, and the water came out. Boots was given great wealth, and his brothers afterwards always said to themselves, "Boots sure is smart—he kept wondering about questions and then went and found their answers."[1]

In this Norwegian folktale, Boots is facing the problems of how to cut down an "unchoppable" tree and to dig an "undiggable" well. He figures out solutions to these challenges by taking time to wonder about them, and his reflections lead him to think outside the box for answers. His thinking led him to solutions that made the work easier for him and got the king what he wanted, too.

Though we're not suggesting that thinking about problems will result in finding magical solutions that will do all the work for you, we do believe that schools don't have to be places where "young people go to watch older people work." We'll be offering a few suggestions here about how to approach common classroom challenges—student motivation, integrating Social Emotional Learning, textbook integration, error correction, limited access to technology, teaching in a classroom where all students have devices, multilevel classes, co-teacher and/or working with an aide/paraprofessional, student book selection, classroom management, supporting ELL students with Interrupted Formal Education (SIFEs), and evaluating international student transcripts—in ways that we hope will be energizing to both you and your students.

These suggestions are not meant to be thorough guides and, instead, are designed to provide some basic suggestions for teachers. We cover many of these challenges more extensively in our other books.

Student Motivation

Neither of us has ever motivated a student. As Edward Deci, the renowned researcher on motivation issues, wrote: "The proper question is not, 'how can people motivate others?' but rather, 'how can people create the conditions within which others will motivate themselves?'"[2]

There are many strategies ELL teachers can use to help foster students' sense of *intrinsic* motivation, which comes from within themselves, as opposed to *extrinsic* motivation, which comes from outside factors (such as grades).

We've previously written about this topic in Chapter Seven, but it's one of those things that it is not possible to talk too much about. . .

Teachers and researchers have found that positive teacher-student relationships, a supportive classroom atmosphere, enhancing students' sense of autonomy through providing choices (such as homework options and seating arrangements), and praising effort ("You pronounced the dialogue very clearly, Jose—all that time you spent practicing it paid off") instead of ability ("Your English is great, Jose") are a few strategies teachers can use to strengthen ELL student intrinsic motivation.[3]

ELL students setting their own goals has also been found to be an effective motivating strategy.[4] In addition to the goal-setting exercise in the second lesson plan in this section, Chapter Nineteen provides ideas and tools that can also be used to assist in this process.

Once students have identified their goals, substantial research has been done showing that student use of imagery[5]—particularly with those learning a second language—can result in both increased learning and increased student motivation.[6] We have certainly found that to be true in our own classrooms by having students take a minute or two at the beginning of each class to visualize in their mind successfully working toward achieving their specific language learning goals. After getting into the routine of playing meditative music with us providing some guiding narration, we've even had students who have volunteered to lead it!

We use the two following lessons in our classes to help students see how and why it is in their self-interest to do their best learning English inside and outside the classroom. The first lesson is on the economic, health, and neurological advantages of being bilingual. The other lesson discusses the qualities researchers have found important to being a successful language learner.

These lessons provide excellent language opportunities in themselves, and we are able to refer back to them constantly during the school year—both with the entire class and with individual students. We use pieces as mini-refresher lessons and are on the lookout for student actions and world news that can be used to reinforce their messages. In class evaluations, students regularly highlight these lessons as some of their most important learning activities during the year.

The Advantages of Being Bilingual or Multilingual Lesson Plan

INSTRUCTIONAL OBJECTIVES

Students will do the following:

1. Learn academic vocabulary, including the words *flexibility, gained, increased, disease, bilingual, multilingual,* and others of the teacher's choice.
2. Practice English reading, writing, speaking, and listening skills.
3. Develop critical thinking skills.
4. Strengthen their ability to write grammatically correct sentences.

DURATION

Three 60-minute class periods, including one double-block on the first day. The third 60-minute class period should occur one week later. In between these periods, though, the teacher should be checking in with students to see how they are doing in completing the assignment.

The activities in this lesson plan correlate with the: Anchor Standards for Reading—Key Ideas and Details; Anchor Standards For Writing—Range of Writing;

Anchor Standards for Language—Conventions of Standard English, Vocabulary Acquisition and Use.

MATERIALS

1. A computer, projector, document camera and internet access to YouTube (if YouTube is blocked, please see "The Best Ways to Access Educational YouTube Videos in School" at http://larryferlazzo.edublogs.org)

2. Student copies of the bilingual or multilingual advantages read-aloud (Exhibit 16.1)

3. Student copies of bilingual or multilingual surveys (Exhibit 16.2)—five copies for each student

4. Poster sheets of at least 11 by 14 inches—two for each student

5. Colored markers

Note: Some of the above materials may be able to be used online and not require physical copies *if* all students have laptops or tablets.

EXHIBIT 16.1. Bilingual or Multilingual Advantages Read-Aloud

Scientists and others have recently found that people get many benefits from learning English (and other languages):

Learning English can increase your income by 20 percent to 25 percent. It's a skill that employers want.

Learning another language "exercises" the brain as if it were a muscle. Because of that increased flexibility, bilingual people are better learners, have a better memory, and can do more things at once better than people who only speak one language. They are also better at solving problems.

People who are bilingual can delay the beginning of Alzheimer's disease by an average of four years over people who only speak one language. Being bilingual strengthens the part of the brain that gets attacked first by the disease.

Sources: M. de Lotbiniere (2011). "Research Backs English as Key to Development," *The Guardian,* July 5; "Why It Pays to Be Bilingual," (2011). Voxy, February 15, retrieved from http://voxy.com/blog; D. Marsh, "Languages Smarten up Your Brain," (2010). *The Guardian,* January 25; Dreifus, C. (2011). "The Bilingual Advantage," *New York Times,* May 30; Wang, S. S. (2010). "Building a More Resilient Brain," *Wall Street Journal,* October 12.

EXHIBIT 16.2. Bilingual or Multilingual Survey

Your name _____

Name of the person you're interviewing _____

1. How has speaking English and another language helped you? Please be specific and, if you can, share personal stories showing how it helped you. (Getting a better job? Easier to get a date? More friends?) Please share at least two ways.

2. How does speaking English and another language make you feel, and why? (More confident? Happier?)

3. What was the hardest thing about learning English, and how did you overcome it?

4. I'm learning English now. What advice would you give me?

PROCEDURE

First Day

1. The teacher tells students he is going to show a series of short video clips (the teacher can choose which ones and how many from "The Best Videos Showing the Importance of Being Bilingual" at http://larryferlazzo.edublogs.org). He explains that he wants students to write down what happens in each one.

2. After he shows the first video, he gives students a few minutes to write down their description and has them share what they wrote with a partner. The teacher then asks one or two students to share with the entire class. Depending on the English level of the class, the teacher may or may not want to write down a description on a document camera or the board.

3. After this process has been repeated a few times (with students sharing with a different partner after each clip), the teacher asks students to think about what the video clips might have in common. He tells the class he doesn't want anyone to say anything and instead just write it down. After a minute or two, he asks students to share what they wrote. Ideally, students say that the clips all show that it is important to speak more than one language. If not, the teacher can guide students to that conclusion.

4. The teacher then asks students to write down on a piece of paper all the reasons they can think of why it is important for them to learn English, if they think it is important. After a few minutes, students are asked to share with a partner. Then students share with the entire class, and the teacher compiles a list on easel paper or a document camera.

5. The teacher says that students have come up with some great reasons. He also wants to share what scientists and others have found are good reasons for people to speak two or more languages. But first, he wants to introduce a few words that might be new to students. He asks students to create a simple Word Chart (see Exhibit 6.4 in Chapter Six) and writes the words on his own version on the document camera: *flexibility, gained, increased, bilingual, disease, multilingual,* and any other words from the read-aloud that he thinks might be new to his students. The teacher works with students to understand each word and quickly completes the chart.

6. The teacher then passes out copies of the read-aloud (Exhibit 16.1) and asks students to look at his copy on the overhead. He explains he wants people to use their copy to make any notes that they want. The teacher reads the read-aloud.

7. The teacher then tell students he would like them to choose which reason (from the class list and from the read-aloud list) they think is the most

important one for learning English. He gives them a minute or two to think about it and then asks them to write it down.

8. Next the teacher writes these questions on the board: "Is it important to learn English? Why or why not?" He explains he wants students to respond to that question using the A-B-C format: answer the question, back it up, and make a connection or a comment. The teacher writes an example on the board:

Yes, I think it is important to learn English. One reason is because it will help me get a date. If I speak English, then there is a bigger number of people who might want to go out with me. (A little levity in the classroom can be helpful.)

9. Students write their A-B-C response with the teacher circulating around the classroom to help. Periodically he will ask students with good examples to share their paragraphs on the document camera with the rest of the class.

10. The teacher asks students to turn their response into a poster, writing it in larger letters and drawing a representative picture.

11. Students share their completed poster—either through the Speed Dating method described in Chapter Five or in small groups. The teacher might also want to tell students they need to ask a question of each person after they share. The teacher collects the posters and will place them on the classroom walls later that day.

12. The teacher explains that students are going to talk to five bilingual or multilingual people they know (English needs to be one of the languages), and no more than two of them can be high school students. They are going to ask them the questions on the Bilingual or Multilingual Survey in Exhibit 16.2. The teacher reviews the form, models an interview, gives each student five copies, and tells them they have one week to complete the assignment. The teacher can also give students time to practice with a partner in class.

13. Class ends with a reflection activity of the teacher's choice (see Chapter Three).

Second Day

(One week later, but in between these classes, the teacher should be checking in with students to see how the interviews are going.)

1. The teacher asks students to take out all their completed survey forms. He explains that he wants them to put a star next to the one answer to each question they think is most helpful. The answers can be on different forms.

2. The teacher explains that students are going to share with their classmates the responses they thought were most helpful. The teacher can either have students share in the Speed Dating style or in small groups. Students should make a note if they hear a response from another student they particularly like.

3. The teacher asks selected students to share their best response with the entire class.

4. The teacher announces that students are going to make another poster with the best response to the first question on the survey: "How has speaking English helped you?" The poster will include the response and a representative picture.

5. The teacher explains that students will be using the answers to the last few questions on the survey in another lesson (see the next lesson plan in this chapter). He then collects both the posters (which will be displayed on the wall) and the surveys, which he will hold onto for the upcoming lesson on the qualities of a successful language learner.

ASSESSMENT

The teacher can use the A-B-C assignment and the two posters as a formative assessment to identify student strengths and weaknesses and as a source for examples to use in a grammar lesson using concept attainment (see Chapter Three). If they wish, teachers can develop a more detailed rubric to evaluate student work. Please see the problem-solution unit plan in Chapter Six for links to rubric sites on the Web.

POSSIBLE EXTENSIONS AND MODIFICATIONS

1. Depending on the English level of the class, expectations and models for the A-B-C assignment can be simplified or made more challenging.

2. Students can convert their A-B-C responses or poster ideas to a digital format using any of the numerous Web 2.0 sites that are free and available (see the Tech Tool on digital storytelling in Chapter Three).

3. Students can prepare a simple teaching lesson on the advantages of being bilingual to present to another class.

4. Small groups of students can create a skit demonstrating the importance of knowing more than one language, using the video clips that were shown as

models. They can even be recorded and uploaded to the Web. These videos can be shown to the class (with student permission, of course) and/or students can show them to their families.

The Qualities of a Successful Language Learner Lesson Plan

INSTRUCTIONAL OBJECTIVES

Students will:

1. Learn academic vocabulary, including the words *qualities, risk, perseverance, assessment,* and other words of the teacher's or students' choice.

2. Practice English reading, writing, speaking, and listening skills.

3. Develop critical thinking skills.

4. Strengthen their ability to write grammatically correct sentences.

DURATION

Two 60-minute class periods, plus periodic check-ins on how students are doing toward achieving their goals.

The activities in this lesson plan correlate with the Anchor Standards for Reading—Key Ideas and Details; Anchor Standards For Writing—Range of Writing; Anchor Standards for Language—Conventions of Standard English, Vocabulary Acquisition and Use.

MATERIALS

1. A computer, projector, document camera and internet access to YouTube (if YouTube is blocked, please see "The Best Ways to Access Educational YouTube Videos in School" at http://larryferlazzo.edublogs.org)

2. Student copies of Exhibit 16.3: Successful Language Learner Assessment and Exhibit 16.4: Successful Language Learner Goal Sheet

3. Poster sheets of at least 11 by 14 inches, one for each student

4. Colored markers

5. Copies of the transcript to the Michael Jordan Nike commercial for all students and selected videos (available at "The Best Videos Illustrating Qualities of a Successful Language Learner" http://larryferlazzo.edublogs.org)

6. The completed surveys collected by the teacher during the previous lesson

PROCEDURE

First Day

1. The teacher explains that she is going to show a short video to the class and that she wants students to write a sentence or two afterward describing what they saw. The teacher then shows a video of a penguin getting courage to jump over a gap on a hill. This video, and all others used in this lesson plan, can be found at "The Best Videos Illustrating Qualities of a Successful Language Learner" (see preceding Materials section for URL address). The teacher gives students a minute to write and then asks them to share with a partner. The teacher circulates around the room and identifies good examples of sentences. She tells certain students she is going to ask them to come up to the document camera and share their work.

2. The teacher asks certain students to come up front and share their sentences. She explains that the penguin took a risk by making that leap (the teacher explains more fully what the word *risk* means) and asks "What would have happened to that penguin if it didn't take the risk of leaping?" Students might answer that it would have been stuck on the other side.

3. The teacher explains that they are going to spend some time today learning what researchers have discovered about the qualities of a successful language learner: "What does it take to be a successful learner?" (The teacher also explains more fully what the word *qualities* means.) She explains that a willingness to take risks is one of those qualities. She asks students to take a minute and write and/or draw about a time they took a risk—any kind of risk—and what happened. She says it's okay if the outcome was not positive. She gives an example from her own life.

Note: Research citations on the qualities described in this lesson plan can be found in Chapter Seven.

4. Students share what they wrote with a new partner. The teacher circulates around the room identifying students she will call on to share. After certain students share with the class, the teacher explains that sometimes risks don't work out, and sometimes we make mistakes. She says she is going to show a short video clip of Michael Jordan (she checks to see if students know who he is, and if not, she explains that he was a famous basketball player and maybe the best to ever play the game). She asks students to watch it once and then

watch it again with copies of what he is saying in front of them. The teacher then shows the video to students.

5. The teacher asks students to write down what they think Jordan meant when he said: "I've failed over and over and over again in my life. And that is why I succeed." Students share with a partner, and then the teacher asks certain students to share with the class. She explains that when you make mistakes, it's important that you learn from them, and the same thing is true if you take risks and they don't work out. She asks students to write down and/or draw about a time when they made a mistake and learned from it. She gives an example from her own life.

6. While students are working on their paper, she writes "Qualities of a Successful Language Learner" on the board and underneath it she writes "Taking Risks" and "Learning from Mistakes."

7. The teacher asks students to form groups of three and share what they wrote or drew. She then asks certain students to come up front and share with the class.

8. Next, the teacher says she is going to show another video (she can choose from several on the Edublogs web site—see "Materials") that demonstrate perseverance and an appetite for learning. She shows the video and asks students to think about what quality the person or animal in the video is showing. She asks students to share with a person they haven't talked with yet in class that day and then asks certain students to share with the entire class. Students might say that the video shows a person not giving up. The teacher explains what *perseverance* means, and what an *appetite for learning* means. She then writes both on the board.

9. The teacher asks students to think of a time they wanted to give up on doing something, but they didn't. She asks them to write what it was and why they didn't give up. She gives an example from her life. Students share with a partner and then with the class.

10. Next the teacher shows a video of someone teaching another person. She asks students to write down what they saw in the video and share with a partner. She asks certain students to share with the class and points out that being willing to teach others is another important quality of a successful language learner—we learn best what we teach. She asks students to write down or draw about a time they taught someone else (such as a little brother). She gives an example from her own life and writes "Teaching Others" on the board.

11. The teacher distributes the completed Bilingual or Multilingual Surveys (Exhibit 12.2) from the previous lesson. She asks students to review the answers from the last three questions and decide whether any of them illustrate or represent the qualities of a successful language learner. Students circle and label examples of these qualities and share them with a partner.

Note: This is the midpoint of the lesson. If the teacher wants to divide the lesson into two days, this would be a good place to stop.

1. The teacher then quickly reviews the qualities of a successful language learner that she wrote on the board. She reminds students that they have all demonstrated these qualities already and asks them to review their stories from the previous day. Now, she tells them, the class will focus on applying these qualities to learning English.

2. She explains that she is going to pass out a sheet that they are going to use to assess (she explains that *assessing* is like grading) themselves on if they are applying these qualities to learning English. She emphasizes that their grade is not going to count in the grade book—the important thing is that they are honest.

3. The teacher places a copy of the sheet (Exhibit 16.3: Successful Language Learner Assessment) on the document camera and reads it aloud, reviewing any new vocabulary. She stops at each of the four questions and asks students to answer each one before she moves on to the next.

4. The teacher then passes out the Successful Language Learner Goal Sheet (Exhibit 16.4). She explains that now that students know which areas they need to work harder on, they can make a plan on how to better develop those qualities. She says that students will review their goals and their progress toward accomplishing them each Friday. She reviews the sheet and asks students to complete the first question. She then asks students to share in groups of four, saying that students can change their answers if they hear ideas they like better. She encourages students to ask questions of their classmates to find out why they listed the plans they wrote.

5. The teacher repeats this same sequence for the rest of the sheet and has students share what they wrote in groups of four, but they must be four different (or mostly different) students each time. When they are in the groups, students can also take the opportunity to share what they wrote for the earlier questions, too.

6. After the sheet is completed, the teacher asks students to identify which goal they think is the most important one to them. She asks students to make a poster describing this goal, their plan to reach it, and why they chose it. This could be in the form of an A-B-C paragraph (described in the preceding lesson plan).

7. Students work on the poster and then share them in small groups or in Speed Dating style.

8. The teacher collects the sheets and posters from the students, explaining that she is going to make copies of the sheets (so both teacher and students have a copy) and return them the next day. She puts the posters on the classroom walls.

EVERY FRIDAY AFTERWARDS

The teacher asks students to review their goal sheet and write about their progress in their Retrieval Practice Notebook (see Chapter Three and Chapter Eleven for information on the notebook). At the end of a month, students can complete a new goal sheet.

ASSESSMENT

The teacher can use the student writings and the poster as a formative assessment to identify student strengths and weaknesses, and as a source of examples to use in a grammar lesson using concept attainment. If desired, teachers can develop a more detailed rubric to evaluate student work. Please see the problem-solution unit plan in Chapter Six for links to rubric sites on the Web.

POSSIBLE EXTENSIONS AND MODIFICATIONS

1. Students can write and perform short skits demonstrating their plans to accomplish their goals; the skits can be recorded and uploaded to the Web for student and family review.

2. Students can watch and sing along with the motivation music videos found on "The Best Videos Illustrating Qualities of a Successful Language Learne" (see preceding Materials section for URL address).

EXHIBIT 16.3. Successful Language Learner Assessment

Your name _____

Date _____

Circle the most accurate number: 1 means you don't try at all, and 10 means you try all the time.

1. I take a lot of risks to improve my English: I try speaking to people I don't know, I try to put myself in situations where I have to speak English, and I don't spend all my time with people who speak my home language.

      1   2   3   4   5   6   7   8   9   10

2. I am willing to make a lot of mistakes to improve my English, and I focus on learning from them—not feeling bad about making them. I figure if I don't make mistakes, then I'm not trying hard enough.

      1   2   3   4   5   6   7   8   9   10

3. I feel very motivated to learn English, and I will work and work until I get it right. I remember what we learned about the advantages of being bilingual or multilingual, and I want to make sure I gain all of those advantages.

      1   2   3   4   5   6   7   8   9   10

4. I always try to help my classmates and my family members learn English better. When I understand something better than they do, I try to help them because I know they will help me when I need it.

      1   2   3   4   5   6   7   8   9   10

EXHIBIT 16.4. Successful Language Learner Goal Sheet

Your name _____

Date _____

1. What are two risks I can take over the next month to improve my English? (for example, trying to talk to a native English speaker once each day or asking the teacher if I can read what I wrote to the class once a week)

- _____
- _____

2. What are two things I can do to learn from my mistakes? (for example, writing more in my weekly journal and not being so concerned about my grammar, or writing more in my Retrieval Practice Notebook about what I learn from my mistakes)

- _____
- _____

3. What are two things I can do to try harder to learn English over the next month? (for example, reading a more challenging book or reading ten minutes longer each night at home)

- _____
- _____

4. What are two things I can do to help teach what I know about English to someone else? (for example, reading a book to my little brother or sister once a week or asking the teacher if I can lead a small group in class)

- _____
- _____

Social Emotional Learning

Social Emotional Learning (SEL) Skills are commonly described as so-called "soft-skills" that help create the conditions for students to be successful in all aspects of their lives. In addition to the previously described essential element of intrinsic motivation, other aspects often include self-control, relationship skills, and others. As we pointed out in Chapter Fifteen, Culturally Responsive-Sustaining teaching is a mindset that needs to be integrated into daily instruction, the same can be said about Social Emotional Learning.

In addition to the motivation lessons and ideas we've already written about in this chapter, this section includes a few other SEL activities we regularly use with our ELL (and non-ELL) students. However, we always look for multiple opportunities to incorporate SEL including ones that can provide students with emotional support, enhance their sense of belonging, and further develop their self-confidence.

Starting Off the School Year: In addition to the introductory community-building activities described in Chapter Two, depending on the "chemistry" of the class (for example, if everyone is new to each other), we will spend additional time on "get-to-know-you" lessons. We especially like Facing History's "Activities For A Remote Or Hybrid Start" (https://www.facinghistory.org/resource-library/back-school-2020-building-community-connection-and-learning/activities-remote-hybrid-start).[7] We don't use all of them, and some require additional scaffolding for ELLs, depending on their language proficiency, but they are all high-quality activities and it's easy for teachers to pick and choose depending on their situation. We also like teacher Shana V. White's "Identity Through Self-Portraits" lesson where students first draw themselves and then draw a vertical line down the middle. On the left side, they literally draw what they look like. On the right side, they draw and label aspects of their identity that people would not know by looking at them (interests, goals, etc.). You can learn more about her lesson at Edutopia (https://www.edutopia.org/video/exploring-perceptions-about-identity-through-self-portraits).[8] ELL teachers can extend her lesson further by using the "self-portrait" as a graphic organizer to prepare students to write an essay about themselves.

Weekly "Check-Ins": We always make it a priority to verbally check in with students about how they are doing. In addition, we have students complete short weekly bilingual (some years, trilingual, depending on our class composition—we typically use Google Translate for the questions) Google Forms. We have learned an enormous amount of important information from these forms and, of course, surveys are only worth doing if you are ready to follow up on them. Here are some of the questions we ask (Several require a scaled answer that can be ranked from one to five):

How are you feeling about our class right now?

How are you feeling about school in general?

How are you feeling today about things in your personal life?

What is one goal you would like to accomplish this school week?

Please try to remember the goal you wrote down for last week. Did you accomplish it? Just click yes or no. But also take a few seconds to think: If you did accomplish it, what did you do that helped you be successful. If you did not accomplish it, what could you have done differently?

Is there anything else you think it would be helpful for (name of teacher) to know about how you or your family are doing?

Community Building Throughout the Year: In Chapter Seven, we discussed how an easy way to utilize retrieval practice was to ask a "Warm-Up" question at the beginning of class that asks students to write about something they learned the previous day. We often pair that question with a more personal one, like "Can you describe one member of your family?" or "What was your proudest moment?" Then, when students share their responses in partners, small groups or with the entire class, relationship building can continue throughout the year.

Dedicating Classes: As we mentioned in Chapter Two, we learned from teacher Henry Seton's *Edutopia* article[9] about his idea of having students take turns dedicating each class to someone who has inspired them (a family member, a friend, an historical figure, a fictional character, etc.) and why. We've had students display an image and briefly describe who they are and why they are inspiring. This kind of activity helps everyone focus on the task at hand, along with providing an opportunity for speaking practice.

Welcoming Students: A student can go an entire class day without hearing their name said by a teacher, and that experience definitely does not help create a sense of belonging.[10] Sometimes it's just a matter of calling out a student's name and saying "Good Morning" as they enter the room. Other times, while students are working on their warm-up, we make a point of walking around the room welcoming each student individually and pronouncing their first name correctly.[11]

Communicating affirmations and concerns: There are many tools that allow teachers to communicate easily through text with parents and students. One we use is called Remind (https://www.remind.com/). We are able to easily send group texts to entire classes (lots of students don't pay attention to Google Classroom email notifications) and individual texts to students complimenting them on something they've done (which they can easily show their parents) or checking in with students about their well-being if they've missed class.

"Everyone Is a Teacher": We've already discussed in more than one chapter how we develop Leadership Teams in each class. In addition to that strategy, we actively promote the important role that each student has in everyone's success. We make this happen through a multi-step process.

First, we build on research that finds that people's performance and commitment increases when they feel there is a broader purpose to what they are doing.[12] We start by having short individual conversations with some students asking the question that those researchers asked: "Who else (apart from myself) is going to benefit from what I'm doing?"

After "priming the pump" (so to speak), we initiate a class discussion on the same topic. During the discussion, we bring up the concept and phrase that "Everyone is a teacher." We discuss the fact that English is hard to learn, they only have a few years of high school left, and that it is going to take more than one teacher to help everybody learn—so we all have to be teachers! We share some ideas to illustrate the concept ("I'm a teacher when I speak English because I'm an example"; "I'm a teacher when I come to school because I'm a model for others") and then invite students to contribute other ideas ("when I sing the song we are learning"; "when I only use Google Translate for words and not sentences"; "when I am serious"). Students then create illustrated posters beginning "My name is _____ and I am a teacher" followed by their favorite ideas. We then put the posters on the wall and regularly refer to them, including by asking weekly reflection questions where students assess how they did as a teacher during the previous few days.

Textbook Integration

Textbooks can be a double-edged sword—they can be efficient, provide order, and save teachers time; they can provide good models; and they can provide a guide for effective language learning. There can be a danger, however, in teachers (and administrators and school districts) viewing them as being written in stone and insisting they be followed precisely.

We suggest that it is better to see textbooks as a sort of cookbook from which teachers can pick the right dishes for the appropriate occasions. The Latin root of the word *cook* means "to turn over in the mind." We believe that teachers using their experience, judgment, and skills to constantly turn things over in their mind is one of the main job requirements of effective educators.

The level of textbook flexibility provided to teachers varies however. Because of that potential challenge, we offer a few ideas on how to use a textbook most effectively in the context of the learning and teaching strategies that we have suggested throughout this book.

Textbooks for beginning and early intermediate English language learners are often divided into themes similar to the ones we discussed in Chapter Three on teaching beginning ELLs. In that case, it can be relatively simple to implement the suggestions we'll be making in this section. However, there tends to be a wider variance among textbooks for more advanced ELLs. For those classes, using our suggested instructional strategies is still eminently doable, but may require a little more work.

If you are obligated to follow the textbook closely, our recommendation is to try to use it as a framework for your class. In other words, first examine what the leaning goals are for each chapter and identify the places where you can most easily include more engaging teaching strategies. As Jason Renshaw, a longtime ELL/EFL teacher, puts it, "to innovate within concrete, start with the cracks."[13]

Incorporating more engaging teaching strategies could include any of the following:

- Convert textbook passages or dialogues into Text Data Sets, clozes, or sequencing activities to be completed by students (see Chapters Three through Six for more information on these strategies).

- If there are a lot of questions to answer in a textbook assignment, turn them into a Jigsaw exercise (see Chapters Seven and Eight), with each partner having a few questions to answer and being prepared to support their answer with reasons.

- Personalize textbook dialogues, and we're not talking about just the names! Often, these dialogues have little relationship to the everyday lives of students in a particular class.

- Convert dialogues and grammar lessons into Jazz Chants. See Chapter Three for more information.

- Turn textbook passages into read-alouds and think-alouds (see Chapters Three and Five for more information).

- Use pictures from the textbook for Picture Word Inductive Model (PWIM) or critical pedagogy lessons (see Chapter Three for more details).

- Most textbooks offer a large number of downloadable supplemental materials. These can be a great source of materials for use in the Stations Game, which is discussed in Chapter Eighteen.

- Many textbook publishers offer companion web sites for students with reinforcing interactive exercises. In our experience, often the online activities are superior to what's actually in the print version! If that's the case, by all means consider having students use them on their own devices or display them on a computer projector for the entire class.

- Phonics instruction in beginning textbooks can easily be modified into an inductive learning activity similar to the one described in Chapter Three.

- In our opinion, many textbooks lack sufficient scaffolding for teaching writing. Adding many of the writing strategies we suggest throughout the book can be particularly useful to students.

- Don't feel that you have to do all this on your own: you'd be surprised at the huge number of teachers from around the world who are facing similar challenges. By connecting with them as suggested in "The Best Ways ESL/EFL/ELL Teachers Can Develop Personal Learning Networks" (at http://larry ferlazzo.edublogs.org), teachers can share useful materials with others.

Error Correction

The issue of error correction, particularly focused on grammar, can be a controversial topic in ELL circles.[14] A number of studies suggest that correction—either through prompts that point out the error to a student and require an immediate attempt at a repair or through "recasts," when teachers rephrase correctly what the student said—can be a useful tool to assist language acquisition.[15]

Other research, however, suggests the opposite—that overt grammar correction can actually be harmful to English language learners. Some researchers suggest that oral grammar correction interrupts communicative activities and can generate a negative reaction from students when they are publicly corrected.[16] These studies point to similar hindrances resulting from correcting written grammatical errors, saying that it contributes to stress, which can inhibit language learning.[17]

These two points of view partially rely on varying perspectives on the difference between language "acquisition" and language "learning," which was described in Chapter One. To "acquire" language, according to many who question the use of error correction, it is important to have a greater emphasis on communication, rather than the correct form.[18] Researchers like Stephen Krashen would suggest that "learning" a language in schools can instead focus too much on the correct forms through grammar instruction and worksheets and not result in students actually being able to communicate effectively in the real world.

We share the concerns of those who question the advantages of error correction. However, we do believe that error correction does have a place in the ELL classroom.

Regular use of concept attainment (see Chapter Three) using both correct and incorrect grammar usage (which can include examples of oral and written language in the classroom and does not identify the student who committed the error); use of games that have students correct common grammar errors (this is discussed specifically in Chapter Eighteen); the use of "recasts" in dialogue journals, as described in Chapter Three, and collecting errors in writing and giving them to small groups to work together on correction are all teaching strategies we use frequently in our ELL classrooms. Dave Dodgson, an English teacher in Turkey, also suggests a modification on the last activity we do – his idea is that the teacher write a paragraph (instead of just giving a list of student-written sentences with errors) incorporating several common mistakes made by students and then have them make corrections in small groups.[19]

"Mistakes" and "errors" are terms often used interchangeably in ELL instruction, and in typical conversation related to just about everything. Some, however, consider "mistakes" to be something a learner has been taught but has forgotten in the moment or is unsure how to apply it. "Errors," on the other hand, could be something learners make because they haven't previously been taught the concept.[20]

As far as we're concerned, it's less important what you *label* the differences between the two and far more important that both teachers and students recognize that there *is* a difference.

This kind of understanding is critical, in our minds, for two reasons.

One, we have to be aware of it in order to practice one of our favorite, and what we think is one of the most effective, forms of correction: Pointing (or highlighting) to what is wrong (lack of punctuation, capitalization, verb tense, etc.) and asking the student or students to figure out what is wrong on their own and correct it. This activity, of course, can only work if we know that the student has already been taught the correct practice.

Two, as language teacher, researcher and author Dr. Gianfranco Conti writes: "Several studies. . .have shown the benefits of enhancing L2-learner ability to self-monitor through a synergy of awareness-raising (what mistakes do I make more often?), error-targeting (what mistakes am I going to eradicate?) and editing strategies (what strategies work best with this error type?)."[21]

As we promote this kind of metacognitive awareness among our students through reflective activities such as asking these questions, they, too, need to know the difference between errors and mistakes (or whatever you want to call them).[22]

In addition to the above ideas, instead of returning student-written papers where we point out numerous errors (which research has shown has little impact on student practice),[23] we might emphasize several positive aspects of an essay and only focus on one type of error. We never just hand back papers with comments. Instead, we always have a private conversation—albeit a brief one during the daily silent reading time—with the student. At times, instead of using this process or in addition to doing it, if we see a common error trend in the class (for example, subject-verb agreement), we might also do a short minilesson that provides more explicit instruction. This emphasis on a small number of issues is sometimes called Focus Correction.[24]

Limited Access to Educational Technology

We've discussed using a number of technology tools—document cameras, computer, computer projectors, internet access, and so forth. Most, but not all, readers of this book will probably have access to many of those resources. Some will not. What do you do if you're one of those without access (Of course, this is less of an issue for many after COVID-19, but still may be a challenge in some communities.)

First, it's important to remember that technology is just a tool. It can be an important tool that can have a major positive impact on language learning,[25] but great teaching and learning can certainly happen without it. In fact, like any tool, its effect depends on how it's used. Tech used in the ways we suggest throughout this book—as a way to reinforce what has already been learned and as a strategic vehicle through which to heighten student engagement—can result, and has resulted in significant student learning gains. If it is viewed as a babysitting device, as a time for teachers to do prep work instead of circulating throughout the room or as an opportunity to get by without thinking through a lesson plan, then it can actually result in a *negative* learning impact.

If you have limited access to tech, but want to maximize what you do have for student language learning, here are a few ideas:

- If you have access to only one computer and a projector, many of the web sites we recommend can still be used very effectively. Whether it is an online karaoke site designed for ELLs to fill in blank words from a song (see Chapter Three), online grammar games and activities, or an animated story, they can all be projected on the screen (and make sure you have good speakers.) Students can be divided into partners or groups and can write the correct answers on shared small whiteboards, or even pieces of paper, that they then hold up. These kinds of activities can be used as a game. We have regular access to a computer lab and still use these whole-class activities often.

- If you have a few computers in your classroom, have internet access, and if you are using a lot of cooperative learning activities (as we hope you are), then regularly assigning small groups or pairs to work on assignments using technology can be an option. They can also be used in the Stations Game (see Chapter Eighteen) as one or two of the stations.

- Again, if you have only a few computers, having students take turns using them during daily Free Voluntary Reading time to access the countless accessible reading opportunities on the Web is another option (see Chapter Three for recommended sites). Having headphones available is important.

- If you and your students don't have much access to educational technology, money may very well be a major reason behind it. If that is the case, you can find a growing list of inexpensive tech tools, where to get them, and places to seek grant funds for their purchase in "The Best Good, Inexpensive, and Simple Classroom Technology Tools" at http://larryferlazzo.edublogs.org.

Tech Tool

One-to-One Device Programs

Of course, because of the COVID-19 pandemic, most of us are more likely to be teaching in an environment where all our students have devices rather than a situation where we don't have enough educational technology. As of the writing of this manuscript, neither of us have actually yet taught in a classroom where all our students had devices all the time, except for a very limited period of concurrent/hybrid teaching. All of us will be gaining a great deal of experience in this new world though, of course, some schools had one-to-one programs prior to the pandemic. We have begun to collect what we consider the best advice at "The Best Resources On 'One-To-One' Laptop/Tablet Programs" https://larryferlazzo.edublogs.org/2014/02/12/the-best-resources-on-one-to-one-laptoptablet-programs-please-suggest-more/.

Multilevel Classes

Some schools, especially those with small ELL populations, do not create separate classes for beginners and intermediates. Though there are obviously different levels within those two categories of learners, the differences are much more pronounced when you combine both together. Those differences create opportunities and challenges.

A teacher might choose an overall strategy of dividing the class in two and, in effect, just using two entirely separate curriculums in a multilevel class.

At times in our careers, we have done exactly that in multilevel classes, primarily if we have had a student teacher, a teacher aide, or even one-to-two exceptional peer tutors working with us. In those situations, most of the time the two groups work on different assignments (often times in different sections of the classroom or, in Larry's case, in two separate rooms with an adjoining door) with us moving back and forth between groups and our "co-teachers" picking up the slack.

That kind of complete separation increases the workload of an ELL teacher who has to create two separate lessons plans each day, as well as lessens the sense of overall classroom community.

Another approach in such a class, and one that we have used on other occasions, is using more unified themes and strategies that have easily modifiable assignments across the beginner and intermediate spectrum. This approach also creates exceptional opportunities for all students, and particularly the higher-level students, to become more authentic teachers, one of the key qualities of an effective language learner and one of the best ways to learn (see the Qualities of a Successful Language Learner Lesson Plan earlier in this chapter). It is important for the teacher to ensure that these authentic peer teaching opportunities are beneficial to all students and not just to those being tutored. Another advantage to a unified approach is that it can expose progressing beginners to more challenging learning tasks more quickly.

A key part of making this kind of setting work is effective assessment—formative and summative. Chapter Nineteen covers how this might look in the ELL classroom, and ongoing assessment by both the teacher and the student will be critical in ensuring that a multilevel classroom meets the needs of everyone. Not only does it help teachers determine initial placement, but it also particularly helps to fine-tune placement throughout the year—it creates opportunities, for example, for someone who is a high early intermediate in writing but may be more advanced in speaking to participate in beginner-level writing and intermediate speaking partner work.

Next we discuss how a more coherent double-period multilevel class might look using many of the key elements of the curriculum discussed in Chapters Three and Five on teaching beginners and intermediates. Please remember that we are not proposing this plan as a scripted curriculum. Instead, this example is just one way a multilevel class could work effectively:

Whole Class. Begin the day with 15 minutes of Free Voluntary Reading. With a good classroom library or access to online materials (see the Free Voluntary Reading section in Chapter Three) this time can be equally effective for both beginners and intermediates. A teacher can easily model increasingly sophisticated uses of reading strategies for all levels. Book Talks—both face to face and online—can be shared with similar ability groups or pairs. In other words, group beginners with other beginners and intermediates with other intermediates.

Whole Class. An oral language activity can come next. For example, there can be a "question-of-the-day" ("What did you do during the weekend?") with sentence starters for Beginners and an expectation that Intermediates would share a more complex response. Depending on the size of the class, students can share their responses to the entire class or in smaller groups.

Whole Class. A photo, video, or cartoon can be used to introduce a Picture Word Inductive Model (PWIM) or critical pedagogy lesson, with beginners writing descriptive words and simple sentences and intermediates developing more sophisticated sentences and paragraphs.

Similar Ability Groups or Partners. Beginners can be using the Picture Word Inductive Model described in Chapter Three. Intermediates can use the elements of the inductive writing process described in Chapters Five and Six to write an argument, problem-solution, or autobiographical essay using the class visual as a prompt. For example, if the visual was about school, the intermediates' assignment could connect to a school-related problem or previous incident in the student's life. At times the teacher might want to bring all the intermediates or all the beginners together for a brief specific lesson while the other group works on their assignment.

Whole Class. The entire class is brought together, and the teacher explains that students will work in similar-ability groups or with similar-ability partners to complete one of the following assignments:

- Dialogue or role-play, where beginners are assigned to practice it as written or with small changes, and intermediates use it as a model to develop their own.

- Cloze (fill in the blank) of a short passage, where beginners would have a word/answer bank at the bottom of the page and intermediates would not. The teacher could be more strategic about using clozes that also serve as models for academic writing that intermediates are doing. Students could also create their own clozes by being strategic about where the blanks should be and making sure there are "clues" in the text that the reader can use to help determine the answers.

- Song, where both groups would listen, but beginners would again have a cloze with a word/answer bank at the bottom and intermediates would not have those clues.

- Jigsaw, where beginner groups review more simple text to prepare their presentations and intermediates use more challenging passages.

- Students are assigned work to do to from each of their textbooks (one for Beginners, one for Intermediates).

Similar Groups or Partners. Students do the assigned work related to the dialogue, cloze, song, Jigsaw or textbook and make presentations/share their work, if appropriate, to the entire class or to just another similar-ability partner. Or presentations/sharing can be made to all students at that same level with the teacher monitoring while the other group is working on their assignment or online activities.

Mixed-Ability Partner Groups. This could be a game, a time when intermediate students "teach" a prepared lesson to beginner groups, a picture dictation exercise (again where the intermediate student might be more of the teacher), or one of the other information gap activities described in Chapter Three where one student needs to get information from the other student by questioning him or her. In such a gap exercise, each partner's sheet could have the necessary information, but it could be made more difficult to find in the intermediate student's paper.

Whole Class. Student reflection (see Chapter Three).

In addition, here are other strategies that can be used to differentiate in a multi-level class:

Laptop Work. Of course, online work can be easily differentiated and actually personalized. In addition to the hundreds of thousands of different free activities on the Web, there are many free sites that enable student registration and let students and the teacher monitor progress. We have listed several of them in the Homework section of Chapter Three. Online games reinforcing lessons from the textbook (or any lessons) could be played, with Beginners and Intermediates playing different ones simultaneously.

Homework. Homework can certainly be modified for both beginners and intermediates to make it appropriate to their English level.

Peer Tutors. If, as we suggest in Chapter Two, you are able to get peer tutors, they can be used to further assist in differentiated instruction. For example, some days they can be assigned to work with the beginners during similar-ability group work while the teacher can concentrate on the intermediates. The reverse can also be true. Of course, a peer tutor can never be a replacement for a teacher, but can certainly be a positive force in helping students learn English.

Dialogue Journals. In Chapter Three we discussed the use of dialogue journals with "sister classes" composed of students who are fluent in English—either in your school or online with another school. Beginners and intermediates can easily be given different assignments for that task.

Graphic Organizers. Graphic organizers, discussed in many chapters of this book, can be modified to provide more support for beginning students and increased complexity for intermediates. For example, a K-W-L chart might contain pictures and words written by beginners, while intermediates can write in sentences.

Language Experience Approach (LEA). As discussed in Chapter Three, in the Language Experience Approach, all students do an activity and then talk/write about it afterwards. The whole class can do an activity together, and then Beginners and Intermediates can work together or separately to develop sentences about it, with different writing expectations for each group. The sentences could then be used for a myriad of other activities, ranging from grammar instruction through Concept Attainment, cloze activities, or sentence scrambles. LEA activities could include:

- Playing a soccer game
- Playing a basketball game
- Watching a funny movie
- Doing an art project
- Playing indoor games
- Taking a tour of the school
- Working in the garden
- Taking a walk around the neighborhood if you could arrange to do a field trip

Co-Teaching and/or Working with an Aide/Paraprofessional

Apart from a year when the two of us co-taught a class together, we have zero experience with co-teaching. Instead of trying to "fake it" here, we recommend you see the co-teaching resources in the Tech Tool below for helpful advice.

We do, however, have a great deal of experience working with classroom aides/paraprofessionals.

Here are some Do's and Don'ts for working with them:

DO'S

- Treat the aide as a co-teacher, and introduce her as one. Obviously, students will view you as the "senior" teacher, but she is a sister professional.
- Plan carefully how your aide can enhance each of your lessons. He should not be expected to do any planning outside of the classroom —it's your responsibility to determine how he can use his skills to benefit students.

- Invite your aide into your planning as a "co-conspirator." Even though she is not responsible for planning, she probably has good insights about particular students, what's working, and what's not working, with each one. Ask! Take a minute or two at the end of each period to ask her what she think worked well, what she thinks did not, and for any suggestions.

- Give specific praise to your aide when you see him do something particularly well. When giving critique, consider leading with inquiry, not judgment. In other words, consider asking him why he took a particular action before providing constructive criticism—something you don't know might be going on.

- Words of praise are nice, and so are other forms of acknowledgement. A Starbucks gift card during the holidays or a paid lunch at the school Food Faire will probably be appreciated. We teachers get paid a lot more than she does.

- Your aide is probably best used in working with an individual student or a small group of students who might be less proficient in English or more proficient in English than the rest of the class. Think about how she can help differentiate your lessons. She can also work with new students to help them get acquainted to a new environment and help them get "caught up."

- If your aide speaks the home language (L1) of some of your students, consider having him help implement the preview-view-review instructional strategy (preview the lesson briefly in the home language, teach the lesson in English, review it briefly in the home language).

- Have a specific plan for what your aide should be doing if you don't have a specific role for her in a lesson: She could be moving around and regularly checking for understanding with students (perhaps giving special attention to certain ones you have previously determined) or, perhaps, she could regularly take out students one at a time for a brief opportunity for relationship building and a check-in.

- Be very proactive dealing with any student behavior which may indicate students are not clear about personal and public boundaries. This can potentially be an issue especially if the aide is close in age to your students. Clearly communicate with the aide that you want to know immediately if any related issue arises—this is particularly important if you do not understand a language that might be shared by students and the aide, so you might not catch comments that are made.

- Go over sub plans with your aide if you know when you will not be there. Your aide can help ensure it is a day of productive learning and not a wasted one.

- Get to know your aide—what his future professional plans are, what skills he wants to improve. If possible, keep those in mind as you plan how he will work in your classroom—there may be opportunities where they can dovetail with work in the classroom. Support him in professional development opportunities.

DON'T'S

- Do not treat your aide as a "gopher." Emergencies may arise, but she should very seldom be used to make copies or retrieve school supplies. She's there to help students.

- Your aide is not responsible for classroom management. Do not assign a student or students to him because of behavior issues.

- Do not waste her time. If you do not want to put time into utilizing the aide in your instruction, let administrators know and they will find another class for the aide.

Tech Tool

Co-Teaching Resources

For advice on working as a co-teacher, please visit "The Best Resources On Co-Teaching With ELLs" https://larryferlazzo.edublogs.org/2017/07/07/the-best-resources-on-co-teaching-with-ells-please-suggest-more/.

Classroom Management

Many teachers, including us, would say that there are likely to be fewer classroom management problems in an ELL class than in a mainstream classroom for a number of reasons, including the fact that many ELLs have a high level of intrinsic motivation. If a good curriculum and engaging instructional strategies are used—like the ones we discuss in this book—few students will question the relevance or usefulness of what is happening in the classroom.

However, that does not mean an ELL classroom is immune from these challenges.

Besides good teaching, solid relationship building, and the suggestions we shared in the Motivation section earlier in this chapter, here are a few research-based tips to keep in mind. They are taken from the book *Helping Students Motivate Themselves: Practical Answers to Classroom Challenges*, by Larry Ferlazzo:[26]

Don't Use Incentives and Rewards. Plenty of research shows that the use of incentives and rewards ("If you do that, I will give you this") can, in the short term, increase compliance in tasks that require lower-level thinking skills. That same research, however, also shows that both in the short term and the long term, their use discourages and harms the development of higher-order thinking skills. We included the section on motivation in this chapter to provide practical ways to promote intrinsic desire among students.

This is not to say that, practically speaking, it is bad for a teacher to ever use incentives or rewards. Both of us have been teaching too long to have such an unrealistic perspective. Sometimes, you just need compliance *now*, and nothing else seems to be working. We are suggesting that it be used only when absolutely necessary.

Positively Framed Messages. By knowing students' goals through relationship building and introductory activities, teachers can use more "positively framed" messages ("Think of all the great things that can happen if you learn English—you can get the job you want as a nurse") than "loss-framed" messages ("If you don't do this, then I am sending you to the office and they'll call your parents").

Emphasizing What Students Can Do. Instead of regularly saying "Don't chew gum" or "You can't go to the bathroom," instead say "You can chew gum after class and you can drink water now" or "Yes, you can go the bathroom. Could you wait for a few minutes for a break in the lesson?"

Being Courteous. Saying "Please," "Thank you," and "I'm sorry" not only provides excellent role modeling, but is also far more likely to result in quicker compliance. Requests are always preferable to commands. This teacher attitude supports a student's need for autonomy, one of the key human needs identified by William Glasser.[27]

Calmness. Teachers reacting out of frustration or anger seldom leads to positive results—believe us, we can speak from plenty of experience! Taking a few deep breaths and speaking softly and respectfully—ideally privately to a student—will generally have far more success than losing one's temper.

Book Selection

Chapter Two discussed issues related to a classroom library. Access to books can be one challenge, and students selecting appropriate books can be another.

As we wrote earlier, we believe it makes things easier for students to have books divided into broadly leveled categories and at the same time encourage students not to be constrained by them. Challenging, high-interest books can be powerful intrinsic motivators to students. As we discussed in Chapter Fifteen on Culturally Responsive and Sustaining Teaching, it is also critical for students to see themselves in the available books.

There is a danger, however, in the ELL classroom of students regularly choosing very easy books to read and being hesitant to take the risk in challenging themselves. There is also the potential problem of students choosing books that are far beyond their English level because they want to show off or because they are very interested in the topic but don't have a realistic view of their reading abilities. In either case, teachers will want to help students come to their own conclusions about what kinds of books best serve their needs.

Teachers can approach this challenge by offering suggested guidelines: The book should be on a topic of genuine personal interest to the student, students should look through a book first to ensure that the vocabulary is not too hard or too easy, and if they decide they don't want to continue reading it, they should return it and find a replacement. Our first point can't be emphasized too much—*students must be interested in the book's content.*

One way that we illustrate how students can determine which "challenging" book might be right for them is with a simple teacher dramatization. We first ask students if they think we can reach the top of something easy in the classroom—for example, the top of a medium-tall bookcase or even the floor. They say "Yes," we go touch it, and then explain that it was easy. Then we ask them if they think we can touch something that is out of our reach in class—for example, the ceiling. They say "No," we try (to student laughter), and fail. We then explain that it was too hard. Finally, we identify something that we can reach with some effort—the top of the whiteboard, perhaps. We prepare with much drama, get a running start, touch its top, and explain that this is what we mean by choosing a "challenging" book—one that students are interested in and can understand with some effort. Teachers can explain this point further by asking students if they would always want to play sports opponents who were not as good or equal to them or only perform easy songs on musical instruments. This is another way to help students see the advantages to taking risks.

In addition, for highly motivated students who have a very strong desire to read certain popular books, we have loaned them two copies—one in English and one in their primary language. However, before we provide the students with those copies, we discuss the purpose of the class—to learn English—and ask for their commitment to focus on reading the English version and use the translated copy only sparingly to help them on occasion.

Supporting ELL Students with Limited or Interrupted Formal Education (SLIFEs)

As discussed in Chapter One, Students with Limited or Interrupted Formal Education are often called SLIFEs. These are students who, generally due to no fault of their own, have had gaps in their schooling. These extended absences from formal education could be due to economic hardships, war, or religious or political persecution. Many, though not all, of the young people called "unaccompanied minors" who enter the United States may fall into the SLIFE category, as do some refugees from other parts of the world.

Of course, a case can be made that a much larger number of students fall into this category because of schooling interrupted by the COVID-19 pandemic.[28] Indeed, as we discussed in Chapter Seven and elsewhere, good ELL teachers have been implementing the concept of "accelerated learning" (the term often used to describe how educators can support students post-pandemic) for many, many years, through emphasizing Social Emotional Learning, creating the conditions where intrinsic motivation can thrive, frequently using formative assessments, activating and providing prior knowledge, providing scaffolding to increase the odds of student success, and offering personalized instruction.[29]

However, as much as those strategies help, many SLIFEs experience so many challenges that these typical accelerated learning strategies are not enough to push them over the finish line to success.

Here are some additional supports we have found to be invaluable in supporting SLIFEs though, truth be told, apart from our work with Hmong refugees in the early 2000's, neither one of us have had an outstanding track record of success with SLIFEs, especially those who were unaccompanied minors:

Home Language Literacy: Extensive research has found that home language literacy assists in transferring phonological and comprehension skills to second language acquisition, as well as helping students acquire helpful background knowledge.[30] Some SLIFEs come to us not literate in their home language, which can be a particular challenge for older students. There are some online tools suitable for home language acquisition (see the next Tech Tool Box). We have also been able to recruit peer tutors, often supported by their World Language teacher, to provide personalized instruction, sometimes after school.

Trauma-Informed Instruction: Many experts recommend specific trauma-informed practices including, but not limited to (see the Tech Tool Box for addition resources):

- Really, and we mean *really*, working to develop trusting relationships with SLIFEs. Yes, yes, we want to do this with every student—of course. Research suggests, though, that a strong relationship with a caring teacher can "...negate harmful health effects caused by adverse childhood experiences."[31] Checking in with the student, listening, providing simple acts of support (like having the student choose a book on Amazon that we can buy for them) are all simple steps we can take to make a connection. We do not need to be, as educator Alex Shevrin Venet calls it, "trauma detectives."[32] Most of us teachers are not psychologists or trained counselors, and we could do damage trying to be someone who we are not. We are not the people who should help our students "process traumatic memories."[33] We can leverage these trusting relationships to help connect our students with others who can help, including school counselors.

- Working intentionally to connect SLIFE students to others and build a broader community of support. We discussed in Chapter Eleven how we had older students from other classes act as mentors to our ELL students. ELL students who have been in the United States for a longer period of time could do the same. If the SLIFE is interested, we work hard at connecting them with coaches of school athletic teams or student dance clubs. The "teacher as connector" is a critical role in effective trauma-informed education.[34]

- Collaborating with school counselors to help SLIFEs receive specialized mental health services if needed. Fortunately, our State of California will pay for mental health services for all young people through Medi-Cal (the state's name for Medicaid), including those who are undocumented[35] (a service offered by only five other states and the District of Columbia[36]). Another challenge, of course, is finding counselors who speak the home languages of students and who accept Medi-Cal reimbursement.

- Demonstrating flexibility and patience with SLIFEs who may experience behavior challenges in the classroom due to the stress in their personal lives and/or because of their lack of familiarity with the public conduct expected in a school classroom. Become particularly familiar with "de-escalation strategies," including active listening and providing choices.[37]

Tech Tool

Supporting SLIFEs

Additional resources to support SLIFEs can be found at "The Best Online Resources For Teachers of Pre-Literate ELL's & Those Not Literate In Their Home Language" https://larryferlazzo.edublogs.org/2008/12/06/the-best-online-resources-for-teachers-of-pre-literate-ells/ and at "'Best' Lists Of The Week: Responding To Student Trauma" https://larryferlazzo.edublogs.org/2018/06/14/best-lists-of-the-week-responding-to-student-trauma/ .

Tech Tool

Evaluating International Transcripts

Sometimes, evaluating K-12 transcripts from other countries can be challenging for schools in the United States. Support for that task can be found at "Resources For Helping K-12 Schools Evaluate International Transcripts" https://larryferlazzo.edublogs.org/2021/07/01/resources-for-helping-k-12-schools-evaluate-international-transcripts/ .

Many years ago, a man who worked with Mahatma Gandhi in India told one of us that the key to Gandhi's success was that he looked at every problem as an opportunity, not as a pain. That perspective has served us well over the years, and we hope that this chapter has provided some tools that might similarly help you.

Additional resources, including more ideas on incorporating mental imagery, teaching multilevel classes, using technology in the classroom, and dealing with error correction, can be found on our book's web site at www.wiley.com/go/eslsurvivalguide2.

CHAPTER SEVENTEEN

Home Language of ELLs

When the village chief died, his sons divided his property. The older sons took all the chief's prized possessions, and they gave the youngest son, named Koi, nothing but a kola-nut tree. Koi calmly picked the kola nuts from the tree, put them in his pocket, and went to seek his fortune elsewhere.

Along the way, Koi met a snake who needed some kola nuts as medicine; Koi shared his nuts with the snake.

Next, Koi met some ants who had stolen the devil's kola nuts and needed to pay him back; Koi shared his nuts with the ants.

Then, Koi met an alligator who had killed someone's dog and eaten it, and now he had to pay the owner for the dog; Koi gave the alligator the last of his nuts so that the alligator could pay his debt.

Finally, Koi arrived at a village. "I will marry your chief's daughter!" he proclaimed.

The people of the village all laughed at Koi.

"You don't look like you are a worthy suitor," the chief told him, but he gave Koi three tasks to complete. "If you can do all three," he said, "you can marry my daughter."

For the first task, Koi had to save the village from a tree that was leaning dangerously towards the village. "See this tree?" said the chief. "Start by chopping it down so that it falls towards the forest and spares the village."

The chief gave Koi an ax, but before Koi began chopping, he called to his snake-friend. "Summon all the snakes," he said, "and make yourselves into a chain to pull the tree towards the forest while I chop." With the help of the snakes, Koi brought down the tree so that it fell on the forest, not the village.

The chief was impressed. "For your next task, I will scatter five baskets of rice in the field. You must gather every single grain of rice and bring them to me."

This time, Koi called to his ant-friend. "Summon the ants," he says, "and help me to gather the rice into the baskets." With the help of the ants, Koi brought back all the baskets full of rice.

"For the last task," the chief said, "you must retrieve the royal ring from the depths of the river," and then he took off his ring and threw it into the river.

This time, Koi called to his alligator-friend. "Please bring me the ring," he said, and the alligator did exactly that: He plunged into the water, and then rose back up with the ring in his mouth, which he dropped into Koi's hand.

"Thank you, my friends!" Koi shouted.

"And I thank you too!" shouted the chief. "Please come to the wedding, all of you!"

So Koi married the chief's daughter, and when the chief died, Koi became chief of that village, and his fame is still alive even now since you also know his story![1]

In this folktale from Liberia, Koi surprises everyone. He starts out with assets that some did not necessarily value, but he makes good use of those assets to gain new assets, and in the end he is able to accomplish seemingly impossible tasks, enjoying a well-deserved happy ending.

In the ELL classroom, sometimes educators may not recognize the value of students' home languages and how it enhances their new language acquisition and brings greater value to everyone in class.

This chapter was written by Tan Huynh. Tan (@TanKHuynh) is a career teacher specializing in language acquisition. He nerds out on all things related to multilingual students and shares what he has learned from experts, scholars, and master teachers through his writings, podcast, courses, conference, and workshops.

To reject a child's language in school is to reject the child.

—*Jim Cummins, 2001*[2]

I gathered a group of fifth graders to guide them through a reading of *Hatchet* by Gary Paulsen.[3] My students, Stelina, Phong, Nhi and Misto, all come from families that speak a language other than English at home, but only three of the four are identified to receive language services. For all of them, though, the academic English used at school *is* an additional language.

After reading a page of Paulsen's novel, I tell them to stop and talk about what they have read with a partner. The three of them happen to be sitting next to students who also speak their home languages, Korean and Vietnamese. The grouping seemed like a wonderful opportunity for them to synthesize the content in their native languages, so I invited them to talk in Korean or Vietnamese with their partners.

Silence.

I was confused. Normally, after giving these instructions, there would be the chirping of students talking, but this group looked at me as if waiting to make sure I was serious. I asked, "Are you not comfortable speaking in your home language?"

Stelina responded, "Well, we weren't allowed to speak in Korean last year in Mr. Green's class."

Now I was the silent one.

"Every time we talked in Vietnamese, five minutes were taken off from my Friday-Choice Time," Phong added. "Nhi had to secretly whisper the instructions in Vietnamese when Mr. Green wasn't near."

With a sunken heart, I responded, "Ok! Well, that was last year. In fifth grade, we want you to use any language to help you learn. Let's talk to your partner in your home language about what happened on page 47."

This chapter is devoted to ensuring the above scenario does not happen in your classroom. It reviews the basic principles of language acquisition and visits examples that demonstrate a different approach to working in communities where English is not the dominant language (outside of the school setting, at least). This chapter is for teachers who are working in communities fortunate enough to have a diverse collection of home languages. Teaching experiences like the ones in these communities bring specific challenges that do not exist in other classrooms, and also offer unique and valuable opportunities.

Seeing Home Language as an Asset

Contrary to the philosophy of earlier English development programs, a **student's home language is a tremendous academic asset teachers can harness.**[4]

Think of the novel *Hatchet* by Gary Paulsen[5] as a metaphor for home language usage in the classroom. *Hatchet* is about a teenage boy who survives a crash landing in the Canadian forest. Brian, the protagonist, is without food, shelter, water, or any means to communicate with the outside world. The only thing that he has is a hatchet, which stayed securely on him through the crash.

With his hatchet, he is able to construct temporary shelter, fashion spears for fishing, and construct a bow and arrow to hunt small game. When Brian scrapes the hatchet against a rock wall that contains graphite, sparks rain down, which he uses to tease fire to life from dry kindling. Life and death depend on how well he uses this single tool.

Many language learners, like Brian, crash-land into their schools. They are lost in a forest where English is the language of instruction and the learning landscape resembles nothing of their former schools or communities. For many, they are deep in the wilderness of a new country.

Yet, just like Brian, they have one versatile, reassuring asset: their home language. It's not the fact that he has a hatchet that saves Brian from starvation. It's *how* he uses it to solve problems and interact with the wilderness that counts. Similarly, simply having a home language in your pocket is not enough to survive academically. It is how students *use* their home languages that counts.

But they can't hunt small game with a hatchet they're not allowed to use. It is the responsibility of their teachers to help language learners use their home languages *intentionally* to access content and engage in learning experiences.

A Mini Lesson on the Value of Home Languages

To have students experience the power of their home languages, I like to have them do a paper airplane challenge. Their job is to work with a partner to create a paper airplane that flies the farthest. There are two phases of the construction period. In the first phase, they are to work for five minutes without using any spoken language at all. Watch how inventive students are as they rush to sketch images, pantomime to communicate ideas, and model steps as they work to construct the plane. Remind students that they are not allowed to test their paper airplanes before the official testing period. In the second phase, remove the no-speaking restriction and allow them to collaborate freely. Once all the groups have finished, let them compete to see which design was the most successful.

The act of creating a paper airplane is not the point. You can easily substitute the airplane for another end product, such as the tallest spaghetti tower, an egg parachute, or a stand that holds a heavy book. It just needs to be something moderately complex that will require teamwork and communication to figure out.

After the task is completed, have students quickly write a reflection on what they noticed about these two different phases: *working without language* and *working with language*. Then, facilitate a whole-class discussion. Make sure to emphasize that English is not the only language we have as a tool, just like it is not really the only tool at all. Drawing, pantomiming, and modeling are all effective means of communication. Reiterate that you welcome students using any language to help them be successful at school.

For families that are resistant to anything but English-only classrooms, you might want to facilitate this activity for a group of interested parents, or to the Parent-Teacher Association. If you do facilitate this session with parents, group them by the same languages. Instead of the first phase where participants are not allowed to use spoken language, ask them to only use English. In the second phase, allow them to use their home languages to complete their design. Invite parents to reflect through this process as well to internalize the value of their own home languages.

Research on Home Languages in the Classroom

For students, this activity is enough for them to understand that home languages are learning tools. For adults and parents, however, they often require evidence-based research to support home-language usage in the classroom.

One of the main leaders in language acquisition research is Canadian educator Jim Cummins (2000, 2014).[6] He suggests that the processes developed while learning a home language actually support the learning of additional languages.

For example, when I was first learning colors in Lao, I noticed a particular pattern. A color always was preceded by the article ສີ (pronounced *si*), meaning *color*. To say the color *red* in Lao (ສີແດງ, pronounced *si daeng*), it is literally translated as *color red*. The *red house* in Lao (ເຮືອນສີແດງ, pronounced *huan si daeng*), literally translates as *house color red*, not *the red house* as is the language pattern in English.

I started comparing Lao language patterns to Vietnamese, which is my first language and noticed that Vietnamese has a similar grammar rule. All colors in Vietnamese are preceded by the article *màu* (pronounced *mao*), meaning *color*. If I was an English-only speaker, the concept of an article preceding a color would confuse me. We do not say, "I like the color black car." As a Vietnamese speaker, it made sense since both Lao and Vietnamese share the same grammatical concept. Consequently, it was relatively easy to learn Lao because I often used similar grammatical structures in Vietnamese.

Though not all languages share similar grammar patterns, one universal truth about language is that our most proficient language can help us learn another one. If students understand the concept of decoding, they can apply that skill as they are learning to decode English words. For example, if older students know how to write a sentence that starts with *if* in their home language, we can have them apply that skill when writing English sentences starting with *if*.

In addition to this ease of decoding, home language usage also reduces learning stress. When we become stressed, our amygdala withdraws all cognitive functions devoted to learning and creative thinking and reroutes them towards reaction and survival.[7] Students who are stressed, do not know the answer or are overwhelmed sometimes use their cognitive skills to create ways to avoid being called on or to act out and interrupt the lesson. What students fear the most is being embarrassed in front of their peers.

When we allow students to use their home languages, they feel less stressed because they can use the words and patterns they know to understand the instructions, find resources in their home language, and collaborate together. They retain a positive self-image, one of a competent and capable human being. We see this particularly in my student Ayaka's experience in sixth-grade science, taught by Mr. Eden with assistance from me. Mr. Eden wanted his students to understand the safe behaviors required when working in a science room, which sometimes contains many dangerous chemicals and equipment. He gave students a worksheet with pictures, each picture depicting either a safe or unsafe behavior. Go to this YouTube video (https://www.youtube.com/watch?v=VCLQZdxQ4a8)[8] and watch how I use comprehensible input strategies to help Ayaka understand the instructions.

Ayaka, being completely new to English, did not understand the instructions. We had her translate the unfamiliar English words—which were most of them—to help. She then successfully labeled the pictures in Japanese to show that she understood the rules of Mr. Eden's class. We allowed her to intentionally use Japanese, to engage in the activity because it was more important that she understood how to be safe in science class than it was that she spoke English perfectly. It did not matter what language she used to display her mastery of the content.

The second part of the instructions directed students to create a drawing that represented the most important safety behavior to follow. We translated the instructions, and Ayaka indicated that she understood by pointing to one of the behaviors on the sheet and began to work on her drawing. A few minutes later when it was time to share, Ayaka wowed the class with her detailed, whimsical interpretation of the rule *No Food in the Classroom* (see Figure 17.1).

Figure 17.1. No Food in the Classroom

When we read Ayaka's transcript and recommendation letter from her previous school, we learned that she was at the top of her class and scored in the 90th percentile in math, reading, and writing. She clearly saw herself as a high performing, capable, and competent student in Japan. We wanted her to keep that self-perception regardless of her English abilities. Ayaka's Japanese allowed her to understand the content and the instructions. Because Japanese empowered her to engage in the same task as the other students, she felt the same. When her classmates applauded her clever drawing, it validated her perception that she was indeed a capable and highly-performing student just like when she was in Japan.

This importance of a positive self-image cannot be overstated. John Hattie reminds us that a student's self-perception is one of the highest indicators of academic success.[9] If Mr. Eden and I demanded that Ayaka only use English, then she could have perceived herself as an incapable, limited, and underperforming student. Yet, when we allowed her to use Japanese, her self-perception remained positive.

This perspective around home language emphasizes that **recognizing home languages supports the students' need to feel safe, welcomed, and competent in our schools.** Acknowledging and approving the use of a home language is one way to create a nurturing, caring environment where learning can occur. Who among us can thrive when stressed or overwhelmed?

WHAT IF STUDENTS ARE NOT PROFICIENT IN THEIR HOME LANGUAGE?

Many of your language learners are like me: born outside the United States, immigrated to the United States (Canada, England, Australia, etc.), raised in a non-English speaking family, and not illiterate in their home language. When I first entered the American school system, Vietnamese was my dominant language.

As I grew older, my English strengthened and became the dominant language. If my high school teacher asked me to discuss *Romeo and Juliet* in Vietnamese with a Vietnamese friend after having read it in English first, I would produce more tears of frustration than meaningful sentences. In this situation, it is not effective to use students' home language.

My criteria for home-language integration is fluency. Whatever language is most fluent is the language I invite students to use in class to process information and understand instruction. See the diagram in Figure 17.2 to help visualize this concept.

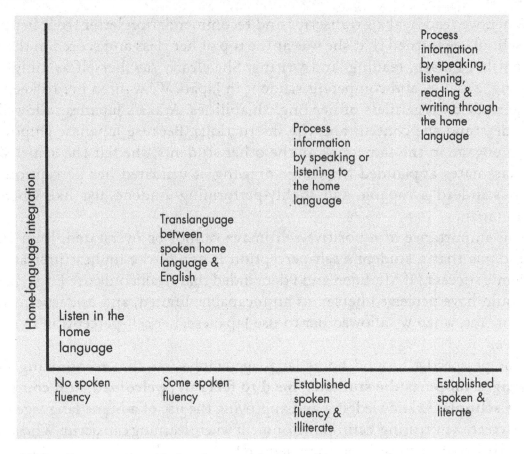

Figure 17.2. Diagram: How Much to Integrate the Home Language

For language learners who are not literate in their home language and only have some spoken fluency, they can incorporate English with their home language to process information and communicate. This jigsawing of languages is called translanguaging. When we allow students to translanguage, we allow them to move between worlds to borrow from different languages.[10] Students will translanguage less the more one language becomes dominant, and other times, students must translanguage because a word in one language does not exist in another.

Turning Bloom's Taxonomy into a Home-Language Framework

Most educators are familiar with Bloom's taxonomy as a framework for designing instruction. I also use Bloom's as a framework for home-language usage. Home languages can be used at each level of Bloom to support different tasks and types of thinking. We sometimes can fall into the trap of relegating home language usage in the classroom to simply translating words and instructions. However, as seen in the airplane mini-lesson and the following examples, home languages can be used as students move through Bloom's ladder to support them as they apply, analyze, evaluate, and create (see Exhibit 17.1).

EXHIBIT 17.1. Bloom's Taxonomy for Home-Language Integration

Create	● How can you use your home language while creating the product?
Evaluate	● In your home language, discuss the advantages and disadvantages of [topic].
Analyze	● In your home language, break down the parts/factors/reasons/steps of [topic].
Apply	● In your home language, explain the meaning of [topic] ● In your home language, explain what would happen if. . . . ● In your home language, describe what can happen when. . . .
Understand	● Can you translate this unfamiliar word into your home language? ● In your home language, restate the instructions. ● Can you watch the video with translated subtitles? ● Can you find an article related to the topic in your home language?
Remember	● What word or phrases in your home language means the same thing? ● In your home language, remind yourself what we talked about in the last lesson.

Home languages are valuable tools that make content more comprehensible. For example, try helping students establish comprehensible input with the aid of technology. For beginners, you can have students use the Google Translate Chrome extension to translate an entire page.

I know what you're going to say!

And you're right. Google Translate's algorithm does not produce accurate translations, but let me ask you this: Can students still develop an overall understanding of a concept with an imperfect translation? When we allow students to use their home languages, **we are seeking participation, not perfection.** An inaccurate translation still empowers students to participate, and engagement leads to learning and language development.

When reading an article online, students can open two tabs: one in English and the other translated into their home language (see example Figure 17.3).[11] Students can then cross-reference between articles while feeling like they are reading the same text. We are simply differentiating *how* they are reading while keeping the content and the resource the same.[12]

Auto-translating an article is helpful not only with text but also with YouTube videos. YouTube's algorithm can auto-translate spoken text into subtitles (see example in Figure 17.4).[13] I often have content teachers turn this function on just before they play a video for the whole class. With auto-translated subtitles, students can access the same resource and content that others are with a slight differentiation of the process.[14]

Figure 17.3. Two Tabs in Two Languages
(From Thornton and McKirdy (2018))

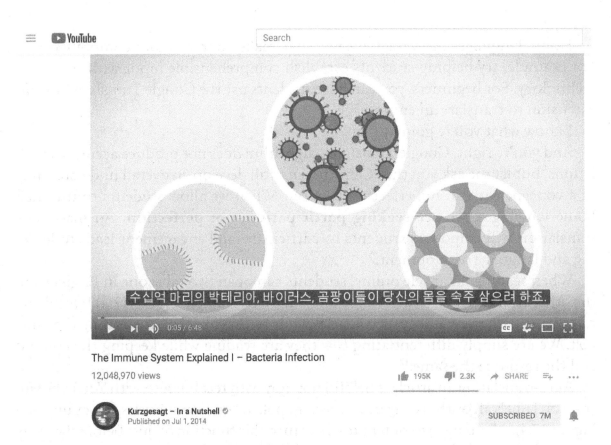

Figure 17.4. Example of Auto-Translated Subtitles

Another way that home languages can serve students is through the annotating of texts. For beginners, I have students annotate any unfamiliar words or phrases. They can translate the words and write them next to or above the English ones. The image in Figure 17.5 is a modified text about coral reefs. The original text from National Public Radio (NPR) was significantly more challenging for my group of students, so I modified the text to be more accessible while keeping the content the same. However, this is not a simplification because the modified version is still at their instructional reading level. As you can see, my student Yinou translated the unfamiliar words in the article and wrote them onto her text (you can't see it in this black-and-white image, but she also wrote them in a different color). We talked about each sentence, and I modeled how to summarize the sentence in my own words. She then copied my sentence, and I made sure she translated the summarized sentence into Google Translate to reinforce her comprehension.

I recommend that developing language learners annotate key parts of a longer text into their home languages. This chunks the text into manageable units, reducing the cognitive overload. Annotating is like eating a pizza slice by slice. Just like students would choke if we tried to shove an entire pizza down their mouths, students will figuratively choke if we ask them to comprehend a complex text without having mini-pauses to process the information.

> ## This Scientists Aims High To Save The World's Coral Reefs(Scientists Goal is save to coral Reefs)
>
> Richard Harris
>
> April 6, 2013
>
> http://www.npr.org/2013/04/22/176344300/this-scientist-aims-high-to-save-the-worlds-coral-reefs
>
> **The Scientist, the Problem, and His Experiment(实验)**
>
> Ken Caldeira is a famous(著名的) American scientist. He is conducting(进行) an experiment(实验) to measure(测量) how coral reefs are dealing(分配) with the increasing acidity(酸性) in the world's oceans.(Ken is doing an experiment to find out the coral reefs health when the acidity is increasing in the ocean) People are causing(成为...原因) this (increasing acidity in the ocean)change by burning(燃烧) fossil(化石) fuels and putting carbon dioxide into the air.(people are burning oil and the carbon dioxide go up to the air) Then the carbon(炭) dioxide(二氧化物) dissolves(溶解) into the oceans, making the ocean more acidic(酸的) . As a result(结果), the world's coral reefs are in big trouble. Actually(实际上), ocean waters can become so corrosive(腐蚀性) that reefs may start to dissolve faster than coral can grow(the acidic dissolves into the oceans, the ocean acidic increase, they impact the coral, the coral will be die.).

Figure 17.5. Online Annotated Text for Comprehension

The image in Figure 17.6 shows how Hyunseo annotated by hand and in Korean on a printed article. Notice how he is annotating sentence by sentence and how he annotated parts of sentences to better comprehend a highly complex idea.

Annotating falls under the Apply level of Bloom's because students are processing the text in a mixture of English and their home language but synthesizing it in *just* their own language. This extra step produces dividends much greater than the investment put into it. Hattie's research[15] suggests that annotating can produce more than one year of linguistic growth! The growth is likely due to the active nature of annotating. Students are working with content knowledge to twist and shape it into meaningful information in their own words rather than simply copying information.[16]

When I share these annotations with teachers during professional development training, they often ask: "How do I know what they're writing is on topic?" Well, I don't. But again, we are seeking participation, not perfection. If they are typing on a Google Doc, you can copy the sentence and translate it into English to make sure they are on track. However, I mostly just ask them to recall what they gleaned from the text. From my experience teaching annotations over the years, students really do want to understand the text, and they see annotations as a path towards comprehension.

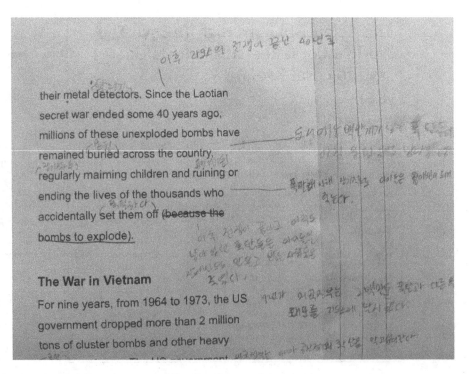

Figure 17.6. Handwritten Annotated Text for Comprehension

At the higher levels of Bloom's, have students use their home languages as they analyze a topic. For example, at the tail-end of an eighth-grade unit on the Renaissance, I had students analyze different Renaissance-related topics, such as philosophy, art, architecture, important inventions, and influential people. This was already a cognitively challenging task in any language, but I was more interested in their ability to analyze than their perfection of English, so I invited them to analyze in their home languages. Zheng Hong took up the invitation and created the mind map in Figure 17.7 with a mix of his two languages. He used his English when he could, and he switched to Chinese when it suited him more. In the end, he was able to complete the culminating task with the assistance of his home language.

Research suggests that when developing English literacy, we can and should incorporate their home languages.[17] I encourage you to use Bloom's language framework above when considering when to have students use their home languages. Wherever they are stuck on Bloom's, using their home language can actually help them become unstuck by giving them the confidence and differentiation they need. Maybe their developing English skills are simply preventing them from demonstrating their high-level thinking. **And when we take away English as a barrier, students can reveal their full potential.**

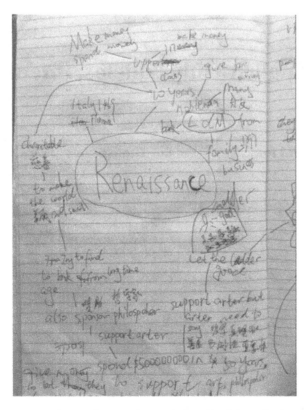

Figure 17.7. Handwritten Mind map for Analysis: Example of Translanguaging
Image: Student translanguaging in Chinese and English in a mind map.

Abandoning English-Only Policies

In the summer, I sometimes work at a New England boarding school in their language development program. Each summer, a particular teacher welcomes students with the following laminated sign that's posted in her classroom. Notice how it is ironically, grammatically incorrect (see Figure 17.8).

I see English-only policies like this one implemented in many international schools as well as in North American schools that have a student body consisting of mostly language learners. While these educators are well-intentioned, they are prizing the perceived benefits of English-only immersion over the research-based benefits of an additive, home language-friendly approach. **It is simply not necessary to impose a sink-or-swim immersion approach to learning language when there are other more identify-affirming models.**

Since **students' home languages are assets to learning and not impediments**, we need to seriously reconsider the value of English-only policies both for their effectiveness and for the impact they make on language learners' emotional stability. I completely understand the intention behind such subtractive models of teaching.[18] The following table (Exhibit 17.2) recognizes the good intentions of English-only policies but reveals the unintentional harmful effects they produce.

EXHIBIT 17.2. English-Only Policies: Intention Vs. Reality

English-only policies intend to. . . .	But English-only policies. . . .
help students learn language	discount the value of the home language as a tool for learning a new language and accessing content
create an English-rich environment	create an unwelcoming, exclusive environment where one language and culture is valued over others
promote English practice	prevent students from fully participating

English-only policies intend to promote English usage. However, an English-only environment has the unintentional consequence of alienating language learners from schools by making them feel unsuccessful and unwelcomed. There is explicit racism in English-only policies as they privilege those who can speak English

Figure 17.8. English Spoken Here Sign
Image: Recreated sign seen from a colleague's classroom.

and exclude those who cannot from participating. Furthermore, these are racist policies as they communicate that other languages have no place in school. Finally, English-only policies implicitly attempt to erase students' home language by not allowing students to use it in social settings or for academic purposes. If this occurs, students could have a reduced ability to communicate with their families in their home language and lose opportunities to develop literacy in their home language. To be an anti-racist teacher means to abandon English-only policies.

Instead, we must use an additive model where we invite students to ***add* their languages as a tool for learning.**[19] This does not mean that we expect all teachers to speak all the languages of their students. That is neither possible nor feasible. However, **we can encourage students to process the content in another language whenever they need to.** Researcher and author Michelle Yzquidero reminds us that the home language is used to clarify key concepts and not the main vehicle of instruction, especially for mono-lingual teachers or if you have a class where dozens of languages are represented.[20] For example, when I was working with Zheng Hong in a seventh-grade science class, he needed to know about the concept of *balanced* and *unbalanced* forces. I first translated these words for him using Google Translate on his laptop, and when he understood, I reinforced it by demonstrating with my hands. Once he demonstrated that he understood the science terms, he was able to participate in the science experiment. See a video of the actual lesson here: https://www.youtube.com/watch?v=G8tlzRe4WYk.[21]

With the additive model, students feel comfortable at school because they feel successful and competent. Their English might not be at the same level as others, but with the use of their home languages, they are still able to learn the same content and engage in the same tasks as their classmates. And when students feel comfortable at school, they might be more likely to attend class and engage in learning experiences. The additive model recognizes that **what we teach cannot be more important than how we make students feel.**

No matter where you are from, I'm glad you're my student.

Figure 17.9 No Matter Where You Are From, I'm Glad You're My Student

To counter my colleague's sign, I created this one and posted it on my door to welcome every student who walks into my class (see Figure 17.9). It speaks directly to Cummin's quote that when we value students' home language, we value them.

Conclusion

Dr. Jose Medina states, "*Serving language learners is NOT about using their home language(s) to transition students to English. Serving language learners IS about adding English to a student's linguistic repertoire but NOT at the expense of the home language(s) and culture(s).*"[22]

We cannot ignore the distinct challenges of working in a school setting where the community that the school serves speaks a language other than English. Likewise, we cannot ignore the rich opportunities that teachers can harness within students' cultures to motivate students to learn, to design instruction that meaningfully integrates their cultures, and home language to teach content and language development without having to sacrifice a language learner's culture or home language.

I close with this final quote from Barbara Chow (2018): **"Diversity is a number. Inclusion is a process; equity is an outcome."**[23]

It is not fair for us as teachers to ignore language learners' superpowers and simply nod at their cultures. Our work must move towards inclusion so that there is truly equity for all. Let's start with welcoming L1 usage in our classes.

Tech Tool

More Resources on Home Language Use

For more commentaries on students' using their home language in the ELL classroom, see "The Best Resources Explaining Why We Need To Support The Home Language Of ELLs" https://larryferlazzo.edublogs.org/2017/04/10/the-best-resources-explaining-why-we-need-to-support-the-home-language-of-ells/.

Links to all the online resources listed in the chapter can be found at www.wiley.com/go/eslsurvivalguide2.

Using Learning Games in the ELL Classroom

*I*n the Middle East long ago, Nasreddin Hodja crossed the border every day with bales of hay carried by a donkey. The guards were sure he was a smuggler, but could never find anything. Years later, one of the guards retired and saw Hodja at a market. "I'm retired, so you can tell me now, what were you smuggling?" Hodja replied, "Donkeys, only donkeys."[1]

It was very obvious to Hodja what was going on every day, but not so obvious to the guards. Teachers can use games in a similar way. "Trick them into thinking they aren't learning and they do," says Roland "Prez" Pryzbylewski, a teacher in the HBO television series *The Wire*. In the show, he gets a very challenging group of kids to learn math by showing them how to determine odds as they play dice for Monopoly money.

Learning another language can be a challenging and often frustrating experience for many of our students. No matter how motivated students are, a good teacher must have many instructional tools at his or her disposal to help students *engage* in the class and not have to *endure* it. Games are one of those tools.

Games can also serve as important formative assessments that inform both the teacher and student about what has and has not been learned. This knowledge can subsequently be used by both to prioritize instructional and studying time.

Research Support

Judy Willis, neurologist and teacher, writes that students, especially adolescents, are more likely to store information as part of their long-term memory and make it available for later retrieval by participating in activities they enjoy.[2] Researcher

Robert J. Marzano also endorses learning games as an "engagement activity" that can result in increased student academic achievement.[3]

Games have long been particularly popular in the ELL classroom, and research has borne out their effectiveness. Among their many benefits are creating meaningful and low-anxiety opportunities for learners to use all domains—speaking, listening, reading, and writing[4]—learning to remember things faster and better and developing greater fluency by "using" the language instead of "thinking" about making sure they use it correctly.[5]

Portions of this chapter were previously published in L. Ferlazzo, *English Language Learners: Teaching Strategies That Work.* Copyright © 2010 by ABC-CLIO, LLC. Reproduced with permission of ABC-CLIO, LLC. Other portions of this chapter were previously published in *Language Magazine* (December 2006). Reprinted with permission.

What Are the Qualities of a Good Learning Game?

We use six criteria to judge whether we want to use a game in our classroom:

1. It requires no or extremely minimal preparation on the teacher's part.
2. Any needed materials are developed by the students themselves—the preparation for the games is a language learning experience in itself.
3. In addition to not costing teachers much time, the game can also be done without costing any money.
4. The game is designed in a way to strongly encourage all students in the class to be engaged at all times.
5. The game, after being modeled by the teacher a number of times, can periodically also be led by a student.
6. All students, whether they are winning or losing, should be having fun. Games must be played in the spirit of friendly competition, and not result in those who lost feeling devalued or embarrassed.

CLASSROOM GAMES

The next sections present some games that meet these criteria and can be adapted to all levels of instruction (and to most other subjects in addition to language). Many are old standbys, with a few special modifications. All of these games can be used to reinforce whatever thematic unit is being studied in class at the time. A few of the games are probably most appropriate for beginners—for example, Slap, Spot the Difference, and the Labeling Game—but all the other games in this chapter can be modified to be useful and enjoyable in a beginning or an intermediate class and, in many instances, any class at all.

GAMES USING SMALL WHITEBOARDS

Having a few small, handheld whiteboards can make a number of games go smoothly, though pieces of scratch paper can act as substitutes. Keeping track of team scores is always a pain—we often will have students take turns or use a peer tutor to handle it though, in a pinch, we double as game Master of Ceremonies and scorekeeper.

Divide the class into small groups of two to four students. Research shows that the greatest individual gains come in groups of this size.[6] You can change the way groups are formed, sometimes allowing students to choose their own partners and at other times having them "number off." However, always reserve the right to move students around if you feel that one group is obviously too strong or weak in terms of language proficiency and/or you anticipate possible behavior issues.

One game is calling out a question to answer or a word or sentence to spell, giving the groups 20 or 30 seconds to write the answer (telling them not to raise their board until you say time is up), and then having each group show their answer at the same time. The groups with the correct answer get a point. This way everyone has an opportunity to score a point, not just the first one with the answer. Sometimes you can end this game, and others, with an opportunity for each team to bet all or part of their points on the last question (as in Final Jeopardy).

Another option is for the educator to make a list of common writing errors and write examples of them on the board (without indicating which student wrote the mistake) for groups to race to write them correctly. A variation for these games could be assigning a number to each group member. For example, if there are groups of three, each group would have a number one, a number two, and a number three. When it is time for groups to call out the answer or do the response, the teacher could call out "All number ones!" as a way to ensure everyone is participating. As in many of the games in this chapter, students can also develop a list of their own errors/questions and take turns being the game's leader.

A similar game with some different twists is having each group sit in a row from front to back, and rotate having one person from their group stand up in front with a small whiteboard. All other group members have to remain in their seats. The teacher asks questions that must be answered in writing by the person standing in front of each group. However, their group members can help them by calling out suggestions. The first group to get the answer correct scores a point. Needless to say, this game can get a little noisy.

Another game where whiteboards come in handy is one that has been commonly called "Hangman." In this version, though, you can dispense with the image of the hanged man—it has racist connotations, adds unneeded complexity, and creates an unnatural ending to the game. The goal is to have students guess entire sentences and not just words. To facilitate this process, the teacher should leave an obvious space between the word blanks, and the blanks can be further distinguished by using different colored markers. If you're studying food, for example, instead of having to guess the word *milk,* students have to guess the sentence "I drink milk in the morning." This way, students can learn sentence structure and the game can easily be made harder for students with a greater grasp of the language being taught.

In this version of the game, students are in groups. Each group gets a turn to guess a letter, and then the teacher either writes a correct letter in the appropriate blank or an incorrect letter below the blanks on the board. Groups get a point deducted if they incorrectly guess the sentence. The first group that writes the correct sentence on their whiteboard scores a point. Groups can guess the sentence at any time even if it is not their turn. However, if their guess is incorrect, they can either lose a point or lose a turn to guess a letter.

In what we call the "Sentence Addition" game, we'll write a simple sentence on the board, like "Mr. Ferlazzo is a teacher." Student groups get a point for every additional word they can add to the sentence while still making sense ("Mr. Ferlazzo is a very old teacher" or "Mr. Ferlazzo is a very old teacher, but he still plays basketball"). Apart from having to make sense, the only other rules are that new sentences have to begin the same way and be about the same topic. Other sentences could be similar to "I like burritos," "It is cold outside," or "The bird is flying." We were inspired by a similar game called "Expanding A Sentence" described by English teacher Svetlana Kandybovich.[7]

Playing sound effects and having student groups guess the source of the sound is another game that can be played with whiteboards. It is especially suitable for thematic units like animals and home. It's easy to find sound effects collections online or as phone apps.

Showing a funny photo and then challenging groups to come up with a good caption is a good game-playing opportunity. Endless photos can be found online by searching "funny photos," though you might want to double-check ahead of time that they are classroom appropriate. We determine the point total for each group, and tell them ahead of time it will be based on accuracy and creativity. This ambiguity sometimes results in good natured argument about our scores, but students enjoy playing it (adapted from Foreman).[8]

We also periodically play a very low-prep and low-tech activity in the format of the TV game "Jeopardy." In our version, we draw a Jeopardy-like game on the whiteboard and write the categories on top, with the appropriate increasing dollar amounts below each one. Each group takes turns picking a category and an amount. The two key differences between our version and the regular one are, one, students don't have to answer in the form of a question—we think that's just too confusing so students hear questions from us and have to give the answers; and, two, we don't do any preparation of the questions in advance—we're confident we can come up with questions "on the fly." Of course, it couldn't hurt to prepare the questions earlier or, even better, invite students to create them in advance.

"Odd One Out" is a game that has been used in ELL classrooms around the world for many years. The teacher says or writes down four words—three are somehow connected and one is not (dog, cat, hamster, bird). Small groups are given a few seconds to write down the "odd one out." Saying it without writing the words can obviously make it a little more challenging for students. Teachers can search online for "Odd One Out ESL" or "Odd Man Out ESL" and find countless lists of words that can be used, and many sheets have them divided by category. These groupings can make it an ideal game for vocabulary review after you've completed a thematic unit. You can make the game even harder, and promote metacognition, by requiring students to write down a short sentence explaining why the "odd one out" is, indeed, different from the others.

In "Dialogue Disorder," we display an out-of-order dialogue of five to seven lines. Each line is numbered (1,2,3,4,5,6,7), but the numbers don't indicate the correct order. Student groups are given a minute to write down the numbers in what they believe are the correct order. Another modification would be to give each group an envelope containing each line on a separate strip of paper. Then, groups can physically put the dialogue in order.

Teachers writing a phrase ("Juan is a student") or a word ("Sacramento") and then challenging individual students or groups to use the letters in that phrase or word to come up with as many new words as possible is an activity that has probably been used in every ELL classroom on the planet. However, ELL teacher Katherine Bilsborough created an interesting "twist" for her students that ours have enjoyed, too[9]. She shares a list of ways that students can also gain "bonus points," including by writing down the longest and shortest words, two words that rhyme, one that begins and ends with the same letter, a person's name, and more.

We learned about the "Question Word Listening" game from ELL teacher Claire Wilson.[10] In our slightly modified version, we play the audio of a short news story, and simply ask questions like "What is happening?" "Where is it taking place?" "When is it taking place?" Students are given 20 seconds or so to work in small groups and write the correct answers on their mini-whiteboards. The team with the most points wins the game.

Teacher Joe Dale[11] invented the "I'm Feeling Lucky" game. In this activity, open up Google Earth on the computer and project it to the class. Have a student click on the "I'm Feeling Lucky" icon, and then drag the "little person" that allows you to enter Street View to the new location. You can ask students in small groups to write on their mini-whiteboards responses to specific questions like "How many people are in the image?" "What is the man wearing?" and "What animals do you see?" or just give students one minute to write a description of the image. Teachers can then judge the number of points each group should receive based on their response. Then, another student can move Google Earth to a new location. There are several other online sites that can be used in this kind of game, too, including one that shows what different people around the world can see outside their windows. You can find those sites at "The Best Tools For Taking People Around The World" https://larryferlazzo.edublogs.org/2021/05/30/the-best-tools-for-taking-students-around-the-world/.[12]

Tech Tool

Using Online Video Sites in the Classroom

Having internet access and a computer projector in your classroom is another way to integrate games in your curriculum. There are free music sites that show a performer singing a line, immediately followed with that particular line converted into a cloze where students have to provide the correct word (these sites can be adjusted for various proficiency levels). Students—either on their own or in small groups—can complete answers on small whiteboards. You can find those sites at "The Best Music Websites For Learning English" https://larryferlazzo.edublogs.org/2008/01/30/the-best-music-websites-for-learning-english/.

Showing short online videos and asking comprehension questions afterward, with student groups again answering on whiteboards, can be a fun activity. You can find many individual videos and sources for more at "'Best' Lists Of The Week: Teaching With Movies & Video Clips" https://larryferlazzo.edublogs.org/2018/06/13/best-lists-of-the-week-teaching-with-movies/.

GAMES THAT FOCUS ON SPEAKING & LISTENING PRACTICE

One game that students enjoy has sometimes been called "Telephone." In this version, the teacher divides the class into two or three groups, depending on class size, and makes sure they are all seated. The teacher identifies who will go first in each group and whispers a sentence into each of their ears (also telling them to stay silent until she says "Go!"). They then each have to whisper it to the next person in their group who in turn has to whisper it to the person next to them. The last person in the group has to come up and whisper the sentence to the teacher. The first group who gets it correct gets a point. If their sentence is incorrect, they have to begin again, with the teacher whispering in the first person's ear. After each turn the second person becomes the one who starts off the next whisper, and the person who had begun the previous turn becomes the last.

"I Spy" is another old, but good, game. The teacher writes "Yes" and "No" on the board and mentally picks an object in the classroom. Students again are in small groups, and each group has a small whiteboard. Students have to formulate questions that call for yes-or-no answers. For example, "Is it brown?" or "Is it in the front of the class?" Groups take turns asking a question, and the teacher records it under "yes" or "no." For example, the teacher might record "Brown" under "Yes" and "In front" under "No." The first group to correctly guess the object wins. It's a particularly good game if you are teaching the "Describing Things" Unit in Chapter Four. Sentence starters could also come in handy, like:

Is it _____? (size: tiny, little, average, big, huge)

Is it _____? (color: blue, yellow, black, brown, green, blue)

"Messenger and Scribe" develops both speaking and writing skills.[13] The educator writes or types four sentences (or, depending on the class level, four short paragraphs) on four pieces of paper and tapes the four sheets in different sections of the room. You want to be careful that the letters are written or printed in regular size font so they can't be seen from a distance—and, ideally, they can be kept and used in future years. Students are then divided into pairs—one is the Messenger and one is the Scribe. One remains seated with a paper and pen, and the other has to run to the wall, read the sentence, and return to the Scribe. The Messenger then repeats what he or she read and the Scribe writes it down. The Messenger cannot stand by the sheet and yell to the Scribe, however. The first five or so teams to write all the sentences correctly, including spelling and punctuation, are the winners. The teacher can then remove the sentences from the wall and review them with students. We don't care who your students are—cheating will be rampant! Watch for them taking pictures with their phones of the sentences! The tekhnologic blog[14] gave us some ideas about how to make this game even more challenging, including by making the sentence strips lines of a dialogue that students have to put in the correct order or by making the sentences clozes (or gap fills) that students have to complete.

The old "stand-by" of "Two Truths and a Lie" is a fun short game that can be played in groups of four or five students. We discussed it in Chapter Two as a simple warm-up activity to strengthen relationships in the classroom. It can also be played as a game! Everyone has to think of two true things (we generally increase it to three to make it harder when we play it as a competitive game) about themselves and one falsehood. Every time a student says their "two (or three) truths and a lie," the others in their group have to write down (on a small whiteboard or a piece of paper) which one they think is a lie (it can be a shortened version). After everyone has written it down, they say what they wrote and a point is given to the student who correctly guessed the lie. The person with the most points at the end is declared the winner!

GAMES THAT REQUIRE STUDENTS TO CREATE MATERIALS

Students can create the classic game of bingo by making a board on a piece of paper with four squares down and four squares across (they can draw the squares or be given a pre-printed bingo sheet). They can write 16 words out of perhaps 25 or 30 the class has been studying and write one in each square. Students can use various items as bingo chips—from little pieces of paper to inexpensive tokens to dry beans. When one person wins, everyone clears their board and plays another game.

Students can also create their own word searches using graph paper and then exchange their creations with classmates. However, we think the typical kind of word search, where players are given a list of words and just have to find them, are not particularly effective language-learning tools. There *are* better alternatives. For example, word searches that, instead, have either lists of clozes (sentences with blanks in them) and students have to figure out what word belongs there and find it; or lists of vocabulary definitions and students have to search for the appropriate words. Having students create and complete these more challenging word searches maximizes the learning impact.

Sentence Scrambles are another popular game. Students are given blank index cards, or they can just cut up pieces of paper. Each student picks one sentence from a book they have been reading and writes the words and punctuation marks on the cards (one word or one punctuation mark per card). They mix up the cards and then paper-clip them together. (Depending on the class level, the teacher may want to check each card stack for accuracy before they are paper-clipped together). They then do the same for another sentence. Each student can create five of them. The teacher collects them all, divides the class into small groups, and gives each group a stack of the sentence scrambles to put into the correct order. The group that has the largest number of correct sentences in 10 or 15 minutes wins. After a group feels they have one sentence correct the teacher can check it and take the sentence scramble away after giving them a point.

In the game of Slap, students are divided into groups of four with their desks facing each other. Each group has to make cards with one word each written on them from the week's vocabulary list. They are all put face up throughout the four desks. The teacher calls out the word, and the first person to slap the card with their hand gets a point (one person in each group, who also plays the game, is designated the scorekeeper). We've never had a student experience an injury or even heard a yelp when playing this, but we guess there's always a first time!

ELL teacher John Carlson[15] gave us another idea for using the same kind of "flash cards" (you'll need enough cards to go around a few times). In his version, students are in small groups and the cards are face-down in a stack. One student picks up and shows the top card to the group. The first student who says the word correctly gets the card. People take turns showing the card. The student with the most cards in his/her hand after they've gone through the whole stack is the winner!

Only Connect was a BBC game show with a format easily adaptable for an English class. There are 16 squares with words on each one. The player needs to use the words to create four categories of four words each. It's a great game that helps develop the higher-order thinking skill of categorization. The online game is too difficult for all but advanced English Language Learners, plus you get only three minutes to complete it. However, the idea is a wonderful one for the ELL classroom (and even mainstream ones, too). Students first think of four different categories—for example, transportation, animals, fruits, and vegetables. Next, they create their own game sheets with 16 boxes. They think of four words for each of the four categories and write them in the boxes. Finally, they cut out the squares, mix them up, and then exchange their creations with a classmate. Their challenge is to then correctly group the 16 boxes into four categories. Of course, depending on the English level of the class, you might want to start with fewer boxes.

Headline Clues from Michigan State University fits into the category of an online game that might be difficult for students with a lower English proficiency, but could be adapted for classroom use with paper and pen.[16] In the game, you're shown the lead paragraph, but letters from two words in the headline are missing. Players have to use clues in the first paragraph to identify what the missing words should be. One of the great things about using this game in the classroom is that students can create their own and have classmates try to figure out the answers, as well as giving them clues if needed. Students and teachers can also have fun inventing their own imaginary stories.

Our students also enjoy "The Game of Cards." We learned about it from English teacher Cristina Cabal,[17] and she has given us permission to reprint her description of the game. Afterwards, we share some modifications we sometimes make in our classroom:

THE GAME OF CARDS

The game is SO simple. The only prep is to make sure you have enough pieces of paper cut up in advance.

Preparation:

Take a regular 8 ½' x 11' sheet of paper. Fold it in half and cut it along the crease. Fold the two pieces again and repeat procedure. Do it a third time and there you have your eight pieces of paper, each resembling the size of an average size of a card in a typical deck of cards.

- Ask students to sit in groups of three in a circle around a table.
- Write the topic you want to review on the board. For example, Education.
- Give each student in the group eight blank cards and tell them they will need to write on each card a word or expression related to the topic on the board. Explain that it does not matter if the words are repeated in the same deck of cards, in fact, if they get the same words twice, it will only help consolidate meaning and use. Challenge students to write newly acquired vocabulary. Allow them to have a look at their notes.

The game:

1. Ask a student in the group to take all the cards, shuffle them and deal three cards one at a time, face down, starting with the student to the dealer's left.
2. Place the rest of the cards face down on a pile in the center of the table.
3. Write on the board or call out a question for discussion. For example,

Are exams necessary or are they a waste of time?

1. Tell students they will all need to talk about the question in their groups trying to use the words on their cards. As they use them, they place them face up on the table and pick up another one from the pile. They always need to have three to choose from.
2. Allow five to six minutes per question. Once the time is up, ask students to count how many words they have used.
3. Repeat all the steps and write another question for discussion on the board.

Note:

- Every two or three questions, you can ask groups to swap cards and repeat steps 1–5. By swapping cards students get a new batch of cards with hopefully some new words to use.

Cristina's game is great, and we just sometimes make minor modifications. We might have students make more than eight cards each, and have groups of four or five students play together. We also always ask one person to be "in charge" of their group. After each round, we generally declare a "winner" and keep track of who wins each "round." We also sometimes have had a "tournament," where the winners of each small group game may move and play each other.

OTHER CLASSROOM GAMES

Most ELL classrooms have many word lists and pictures with words posted on the walls. Teachers can divide the class into small groups and give a yardstick to one person from each group (students can take turns). The yardstick holders start from the same point in the room and wait for the teacher to call out a word. The first person to correctly touch the word with their yardstick gets a point for their group. Other group members have to remain seated, but they can offer verbal assistance. This is also a noisy game. Another alternative is writing words on the board and giving students fly swatters instead of yardsticks.

Two other simple games are Pictionary, where either students or the educator draw something on the board and the first small group to write on their whiteboard the correct word symbolized by the drawing gets a point; and charades, where other students or the teacher act out verbs, again needing to be guessed by student groups.

Dividing students into groups, giving them a sheet of easel paper and a marker, and then calling out the name of a category (such as vegetables or sports) is another simple game. Give students a short period of time to see which groups can write down the biggest number of related words, and have groups check each other. They can call in the teacher when there's a question.

Having a student write a word on the whiteboard, and then having groups compete to see how many words they can write down that begin with the last letter of the word on the board, can be a fun activity.

In the Alphabet Game, students first write the alphabet down the side of their paper. The teacher, or student leader, then calls out the name of a category (such as animals or food) and small groups try to write at least one related word beginning with as many different letters as they can.

The Memory Game was inspired by the Exploratorium's "Memory Party Game"[1]. In the Exploratorium's version, players are given two minutes to try to memorize 20 objects, which are then covered with a towel. They then write down as many of the items as they can remember to determine the winner. We've had students play this object game in groups, as well as use the same idea by showing photographs and very short video clips. Many ELL teachers have boxes of image-based flash cards, which are also easy to tape on a whiteboard and students can be challenged to vmemorize them.

Another game for student review can be called Stations Game. Make five copies of five different worksheets related to the theme the class has been studying (this is one of the few good uses for worksheets). The class can then be divided into five groups of four or so students. One stack of each of the five worksheets will be placed in different sections of the room. Each student group is given a group number and begins at one of the five stations. They will be given three or four minutes (or longer) at each station to complete as many questions on the worksheet as they can and then told to stop. They write their group number on the worksheet, give it to the teacher, and then each group moves to the next station. After students have gone through all the Stations, each group is given another group's papers to correct and the answers are reviewed as a class. The number of correct answers is added up, and the group with the highest number wins.

Tech Tool
Online Worksheets

There are many online sources where free worksheets on many topics can be printed out for use in the Stations Game. You can find our favorites at "The Best Sites For Free ESL/EFL Hand-Outs & Worksheets" https://larryferlazzo.edublogs.org/2009/02/18/the-best-sites-for-free-eslefl-hand-outs-worksheets/.

One activity that requires a little teacher preparation time is called the Labeling Game. The teacher can write words describing various classroom objects on sticky notes, divide the classroom into four or five groups, and then each day during the week, one group will see how fast they can correctly label the classroom objects. The groups are timed, and the one with the fastest time wins. Additional labels are added each week.

Spot the Difference pictures can be a fun way to review vocabulary. Having students identify the differences and, more importantly, write a word that describes the difference, can provide an engaging competitive activity (in this game, and in all the ones listed in this chapter, you want to have multiple winners). You can find many Spot the Difference sheets to print out for free on the Web, but it's worth a few dollars to purchase Judy W. Olsen's *Look Again Pictures: For Language Development and Lifeskills* (it's out-of-print, but still available). This is a book of thematically organized Spot the Difference pictures that are specifically designed for English language learners.

One way to learn about new games to use in the classroom *and* to be more culturally responsive is to ask students about games they've played in their home countries. We learned about *Basta,* a children's game played in Mexico and in other countries, in this way. We make a short list of three to five categories (school, verbs, weather, etc.) and have students—in small groups—write them on a paper or larger mini-whiteboard. Then, we ask one student to start saying the alphabet, and choose another student to say "Basta" (Enough, Stop it) at a letter of their choice. Groups are given a minute to write as many words beginning with that letter that fit into each category.

ONLINE LEARNING GAMES

There are countless learning games on the Web that are accessible to English language learners. If you have microphones, in fact, these games can reinforce all the domains: speaking, listening, reading, and writing (though there are few good online writing games). They include building vocabulary development with I Spy hidden object games, generating excitement through games where you can create private online virtual rooms where students compete against each other and the score of all players is shown on the screen after each question and response, to—believe it or not—extraordinarily engaging games to practice grammar. Many games let you display the question and/or leaderboard on a screen and students can play it on their cellphones or other devices. Though often times students prefer to play as individuals, we also often encourage doing it in pairs to promote relationships and to ensure that the lowest English proficient students aren't always at the bottom of the rankings.

Check out the Tech Tool box for where you can find our favorites.

"Creating" is at the top of the Revised Bloom's Taxonomy, and the Web makes it easy for students to create their own online learning games. After they're made, they can be posted on a class blog (see Chapter Two) and other students can play them. You'll find a list of free game creation sites that are accessible to ELLs at the previously mentioned games list.

There are many "adventure," "escape the room," and "hidden object" online video games that at first glance might not appear to have much educational value. However, if you look a little closer, a number of them can be a gold mine for engaging language-development activities. Many gamers on the Web create "walkthroughs" for these games—written step-by-step instructions on how to beat them. For example, here's an excerpt from the walkthrough for Phantasy Quest, a student favorite (which, unfortunately, is no longer available because it was made with the now-defunct Adobe Flash software):

- Enter the cave. Go left, and take the skull.
- Go back once and go right, through the single door, through the top door, and through another single door to exit the cave.

Teachers can divide students into pairs and give them copies of walkthroughs; you're unlikely to find another English reading and speaking activity that inspires more engagement. Though class winners might be the first five pairs to get through the entire game, you'll find that students will love getting ahead of others and then will stop to help their classmates so they can show off their video game-playing prowess.

Links to many of these online games and their walkthroughs can be found in the Tech Tool box.

Tech Tool
Online Games

Quizizz https://quizizz.com/, Kahoot https://kahoot.com/, and Baamboozle (https://www.baamboozle.com/) are three of our favorite online games to play with students. Links to *all* our favorite online games to play *and* create, as well as to video games and "walkthroughs," can be found at "'Best Lists Of The Week: Learning Games" https://larryferlazzo.edublogs.org/2018/03/05/best-lists-of-the-week-online-learning-games/.

BOARD GAMES

Board games like Scrabble and Taboo have long been used in the ELL classroom. While these are good games, we prefer having students create their own board games. Not only does that process develop higher-order thinking skills, but it also lets students personalize, with teacher encouragement, the language learning areas where they might need the most reinforcement. There are many online sites that offer free ELL board game templates that students can use to create their own board games, or that teachers can use as models to show the class. Links to these sites can also be found in the "Online Games" Tech Tool box mentioned earlier in this chapter.

Though it isn't an actual board game, one game tool that we have found particularly engaging in the ELL classroom is a felt dartboard used with small Velcro balls. There are different dartboards—some with the consonants, some with vowels, some with phonic blends. Incorporating these with some of the previously mentioned games—for example, having a student throw a ball at the consonant board, and then having groups write as many words as they can that begin with that letter—can be a nice game addition.

A company named ESL Education Games used to manufacture these boards, which they called Phonicball. Unfortunately, they are no longer in business. It is, however, relatively simple to make your own, and you can search the Web for "Velcro Ball Dartboard." You can then either purchase a dartboard with numbers and just replace them with individual letters or consonant blends, or you can find directions on how to build one from scratch.

Of course, an even more simple plan is to just draw a very large version on your class whiteboard and have a student throw a crumpled piece of paper at it. The letters just have to be big enough so it's very obvious what letter was hit by the paper.

Along with games comes the issue of rewards for the winners and, often, the runner-ups. The rewards can cost the teacher little or nothing—an extra point on that week's test allows students to go to lunch two minutes early, or they don't have to do the required work of copying the plan for the day in their notebook. Sometimes it's a healthy snack.

But generally, after a short period of time you'll find that students forget about getting a reward and don't even ask about it. The game itself becomes the reward, and the enjoyment of the experience and the knowledge learned through playing it becomes the intrinsic motivator.

Additional resources, including links to useful video sites, online sources of sound effects, and more information on using online games, can be found on our book's web site at www.wiley.com/go/eslsurvivalguide2.

CHAPTER NINETEEN

Assessing English Language Learners

ong ago a prince set off on his horse seeking adventure. He came upon four animals in a forest—a tiger, a dog, an eagle, and an ant—who were arguing over the carcass of a deer. The lion asked the prince to help settle their argument by dividing the deer's carcass into four parts in exchange for a reward.

The prince gladly obliged and divided the carcass into four even sections. The animals were pleased and offered the prince a reward. The lion and the dog each gave him a piece of their hair, the eagle gave him a feather, and the ant gave him one of his antennae. They told the prince he could use each of these items to transform his human body into animal form by saying "tiger," "dog," and so on. When he wanted to return to human form he simply needed to say "man."

The prince continued on his way until he came to a large castle surrounded by a high wall. Thinking it would be impossible to gain entrance to the castle because of the high wall, he began to turn around until he remembered the feather in his pocket. He then used the feather to turn into an eagle and flew over the wall up to the highest tower, where he discovered a beautiful princess. He flew in the window and said "man" and turned back into a prince. The princess lamented that she was being held prisoner by an evil giant who would kill anyone who tried to rescue her. She further explained the only way to kill the giant was to find the secret egg that contained the giant's life within it and to destroy it.

At that moment, a booming voice sounded in the hall as the giant approached the tower. Just as he was about to barge into the room, the prince used the antenna and transformed into a tiny ant. The giant was confused as he had heard two voices, but searched the room and found no one but the princess.

The giant left the room, turned into a pigeon, and flew off. The prince, who was watching the giant the whole time, turned into an eagle and followed the pigeon to a cave, where he saw the pigeon with a box containing the secret egg. As soon as the pigeon saw the eagle land in the cave, he turned into a coyote and swallowed the egg. The prince then changed from an eagle to a tiger and chased the coyote. Unable to avoid the tiger, the coyote changed into a hare and hid under some bushes. The prince changed from a tiger to a dog and was able to dive under the bushes and capture the hare. The prince then broke the egg and the giant was destroyed.

He transformed into an eagle and flew to the castle. He then turned back into human form and freed the princess. They were married and lived happily together in the castle from that day forth.[1]

The prince in this folktale must constantly adapt and make adjustments to the rapidly changing circumstances he faces as he tries to slay the giant. Teachers and students face a similar challenge in today's world, where educational policies and assessments are constantly changing. ELL teachers face the additional challenge of assessing ELLs in an effective and equitable way in their own classrooms. They must also support their students as they face standardized tests that are not always equitable or designed with their needs in mind.

The prince in the story felt confident in his ability to slay the giant because of the tools at his disposal. It is our hope that this chapter will provide both knowledge and tools that teachers can use to navigate the challenge of assessing English Language Learners.

Assessing ELLs: Key Principles

Before sharing information on different types of assessments and ideas for implementing assessment in the ELL classroom, we feel it is first important to share a few key principles that can serve as a foundation for equitable and effective assessment of ELLs. We know many teachers may feel overwhelmed by the assessments at the state, district, and site level that they are required to implement but were created without their input. We also know how it feels to bombard students with multiple assessments that aren't directly connected to what they are learning and don't yield timely or valuable information on their progress. It is our hope that the following principles and assessment ideas will help teachers assess their ELL students in a meaningful way, one that yields value for both the student and the teacher.

- *Be data-informed, not data-driven.* As we discussed in Chapter Fifteen, when schools are *data-informed,* they use assessment data to make thoughtful decisions that directly benefit students.[2] When schools are *data-driven*, they may make decisions that do not help students. For example, they might keep students in an algebra class even though their skills are "borderline" between algebra and a higher level of math so that they do well on the algebra state test. Or, in English, teachers might focus a lot of energy on teaching a strand that is heavily represented on the tests, even though it might not help the student become a lifelong reader. In other words, the school may tend to focus on its institutional self-interest instead of what's best for the students. However, in schools that are *data-informed*, test results are just one more piece of information that can be helpful in determining future directions. Teachers who are data-informed will use assessment data to reflect on their practice, identify areas to modify and adjust, and seek out the resources and knowledge needed to enact those changes.

- *Assess knowledge and language separately.* Many ELL students may not be able to fully demonstrate what they know and what they can do because of their current levels of proficiency in English. It is not effective to measure a student's content knowledge by using an assessment that requires them to produce language beyond their level of proficiency. For example, asking beginning-level students to demonstrate their knowledge of a plant's life cycle by writing an essay is more a test of their English skills than their actual content knowledge. Researchers have recommended that teachers implement test modifications for their ELLs, such as simplifying test questions or allowing the use of bilingual dictionaries or translation apps, in order "to prevent language limitations from unnecessarily sacrificing ELLs' test performance."[3] We discuss additional testing modifications later in this chapter.

- *Assess students according to their* current *proficiency level.* As discussed in earlier chapters, it is important to get to know your students, identify their academic strengths and challenges, and know their current levels of English proficiency in speaking, reading, and writing. Having this information allows teachers to assess students according to their current level of English proficiency—not by the results of the last standardized test they took.

- *Involve students in self-assessment.* Involving students in the assessment process can be powerful and can result in increased motivation and learning.[4] When students are asked to evaluate their own progress, they feel more ownership of the learning process and are better able to identify specific learning goals for themselves. For examples of student self-evaluation, see the section on Reflection in Chapter Three and in the Student Self-Assessment discussion later in this chapter.

INITIAL, FORMATIVE, AND SUMMATIVE ASSESSMENT WITH ELLS

The following subsections describe three common assessment processes—initial, formative, and summative—that may be used to assess the progress of ELLs.

Initial or Diagnostic Assessments

When students enter a class, it can be helpful to assess their reading, writing, and speaking skills to get an idea of their current proficiency level. The purpose of these initial assessments is to gain information about students' levels of English in order to tailor future instruction to meet students' specific language needs. These types of assessments can also indicate whether a student has been placed in the appropriate class for their level of proficiency. Most schools and/or districts have protocols for assessing ELLs as they enter school. However, ELL teachers are the ones who interact with these students on a daily basis in a comfortable and safe environment, and therefore may be more capable of making accurate judgments about students' language abilities. Teachers can initially assess students' English abilities in a variety of ways, but here are a few we have found effective:

- *Writing.* Having students produce a piece of writing either in response to a prompt or on a certain topic is a way to get an idea of students' writing abilities. The teacher should think carefully about the prompt or topic and ensure that it is accessible. For example, after showing students a letter from the teacher (see Exhibit 2.1), students could be asked to write a letter to the teacher about themselves. Students can then use the teacher's letter as a model.

    Having students read a short piece of text and then write to a prompt can offer the teacher valuable information about students' reading comprehension skills and writing skills. Exhibit 19.1 is an example of an initial assessment we have used with our intermediate ELLs to gather information on students' reading, writing, and thinking skills. The teacher can select a piece of text that fits the level of the students and adjust the language of the prompt as needed. This initial assessment, as well as the next one for beginners, can also be used two or three other times during the year as a formative assessment so both students and teachers can see the progress that has been made. Students seeing their growth over time on three or four pieces of work can be a confidence booster.

    For beginners, we sometimes use Exhibit 19.2. If they have next-to-zero English proficiency, we tell them they can write a response in their home language (we use Google Translate for the instructions and to understand their response). Their ability (or inability) to write in their home language is important information for us to also know.

Of course, one piece of writing is not going to fully illustrate a student's English abilities, but it can be a quick snapshot that teachers can use to plan further assessments and conversations with students.

- *Cloze assessments.* Giving students cloze passages with fill-in-the-blanks (or gap-fills) can give the teacher useful information about students' vocabulary levels and reading comprehension skills. As students read a passage and consider possible words might go in the blanks, they must employ comprehension strategies like using context clues, as well as drawing on their own vocabulary knowledge.

This type of initial cloze assessment can be used to plan future reading instruction and can be done several times during the year to measure student progress. Clozes are a form of assessment that also serve to develop students' language skills each time they are assessed. In fact, research has shown that using clozes with students "led to significant gains in ESL students' receptive and productive vocabulary, and an increased ability to use the vocabulary in other contexts."[5]

When creating a cloze, it is important to carefully select the text and which words are omitted so that students can use contextual clues to make their guesses. The level of the passage can be adjusted according to the overall proficiency level of the class. For more on creating and using cloze passages, including where to find online cloze activities, see the Clozes section in Chapter Five.

EXHIBIT 19.1. Initial Assessment

Name _____

Date _____

Excerpt

The older you are, the younger you get when you move to the United States. Two years after my father and I moved here from Guatemala I could speak English. I learned it on the playground and by watching lots of TV. Don't believe what people say—cartoons make you smart. But my father, he worked all day in a kitchen with Mexicans and Salvadorans. His English was worse than a kindergartener's. He would only buy food at the bodega down the block. Outside of there he lowered his eyes and tried to get by on mumbles and smiles. He didn't want strangers to hear his mistakes. So he used me to make phone calls and to talk to the landlady and to buy things in stores where you had to use English. He got younger. I got older.

Source: Fleishman, P. (1997). "Gonzalo," in *Seedfolks*. New York: Harper Trophy, 17–18.

Writing Prompt

Read the paragraph above and write more than one paragraph responding to the following questions. Describe Gonzalo's experience of moving to the United States. Write your opinion about Gonzalo's experience: What do you think about his experience? How is his experience similar to or different from your own? Be sure to use specific examples from the paragraph above, anything else you've read, and/or your own life.

EXHIBIT 19.2. Beginners Assessment

Please write as much as you can about a close friend. Tell about how and where you met him or her, why he or she is your friend, what you do together, his or her family, etc.

Please try to write in English—without using Google Translate. This is not a test.

- *Fluency assessments.* Sitting down with each student and listening to them read aloud in English can be a useful practice at the beginning of the year to get an idea of students' reading abilities in English. This is also a valuable opportunity for the teacher to have a brief one-on-one conversation with each student, which also serves as an informal assessment of students' speaking and listening skills (and the teacher can ask a few questions about students' lives and interests).

  It is important that teachers choose an appropriate level of text for students to read aloud and that it is done in a sensitive, safe way so that students do not feel they are being tested. The teacher can casually ask students to read a little bit either from the teacher-selected text or from a student's free, voluntary reading book. If you wish, you can have students read for about a minute and discreetly keep track of the time, mark the errors made, and make notations about the students' reading behaviors (such as tracking with finger, sounding out words, or skipping word endings). There are many sources for a teacher-selected text—personally, we like the readings available from Edhelper (https://www.edhelper.com/).

  As with cloze assessments, this type of initial fluency assessment can be used to plan future reading instruction and can also be used throughout the year to measure student progress. It is important to use the same level of text or the same reading book in order to get an accurate measure of progress. Students can also record a beginning-of-the-year reading fluency sample, which can be maintained online indefinitely and used later on as a formative assessment. See the Tech Tool Box for suggestions of many free recording options.

Tech Tool
Audio Recording Tools

There are many free online tools available for audio recording. See "The Best Sites To Practice Speaking English" https://larryferlazzo.edublogs.org/2008/03/17/the-best-sites-to-practice-speaking-english/ for a list of them.

- *Speaking and listening assessments.* Teachers can initially assess their students' speaking and listening skills in a very simple way—by having brief, one-on-one conversations with students. As stated earlier, these can be part of the reading fluency assessment, as the teacher sits individually with each student. The teacher can informally ask students a similar set of questions (about their family, interests, or favorites). The teacher may want to wait to record her observations until after they have finished talking with the student, so she is able to give her full attention to the student. It can also be helpful for the teacher to briefly share a couple of things about her family, interests, and the like, in order for the conversation to feel natural and to promote relationship building and trust.

We also have had students use Exhibit 19.3 to assess speaking skills:

EXHIBIT 19.3. Speaking Fluency Assessment

Open the website called Vocaroo: https://vocaroo.com/

Record yourself reading these two paragraphs. Just try your best. This is not a test. It will help me be a better teacher for you.

Copy and paste the link on this page.

READ THIS

Learning a new language will be hard. But I will work hard and do a great job. I want to read. I want to learn. I want to write. I want to talk. I want to listen. I can do it!

I am going to do great in school this year! I am going to try hard and I'm sure my teachers will try hard, too. English can be hard sometimes, but I will do my best and study a lot. I will listen to my teacher and my classmates, and will tell my family what I am learning. I am sure they will all support me.

Formative Assessment Process

Formative assessment is not a type of test or assessment, but is a *process* that combines teaching, learning, and assessment. It is an ongoing process where teachers and students evaluate assessment evidence in order to make adjustments to their teaching and learning. Gathering this assessment evidence can be done in multiple ways—including more formal measures, such as written tests, and informal practices, such as student self-evaluation or observation.[6] The formative assessment process is an effective way for teachers to check students' understanding throughout the learning process and then use this information to guide instruction.

This type of on-going assessment process is critically important when teaching ELL students in order to identify when and how students need extra support. As WestEd researcher Robert Linquanti points out, "Formative assessment practices have enormous potential to strengthen teachers' capacities to developmentally stage or 'scaffold' ELLs' language and content learning."[7] As a WIDA Consortium document explains: "There should be a seamless transition between instruction and formative assessment. If its feedback truly shapes instruction, formative assessments do not need to be forced or complex to administer, but instead are a natural check for understanding that will be useful for planning the next lesson."[8]

The formative assessment process serves to strengthen students' abilities to assess their own progress, to set and evaluate their own learning goals, and to make adjustments accordingly. Formative assessment also elicits valuable feedback from students about what teachers are doing effectively and what they could do better.

The following activities can be used by teachers and students to collect evidence of student learning and progress. It is important to remember that *how* the teacher chooses to use this information ultimately determines whether it is "formative" in nature. Effective teaching and assessment involve using this evidence to make decisions about what students need and how best to meet those needs and encourage students to use this information in the same way.

- *Weekly "tests."* Assessing students on a weekly basis on what has been taught over the week can help the teacher check for student understanding. This information assists the teacher identify which students need more help and which concepts need to be further practiced. Both the teacher and the students can gain valuable information from these tests about what they need to do differently. In order for these "tests" to be helpful to students and the teacher, they need to be short and low stakes (not used as a "gotcha" or in a punitive way). It is also important that these assessments reflect what has already been taught and not be new concepts. When administered in a positive learning environment, these types of weekly tests can build students' confidence as they are able to demonstrate what they have learned. They can also be used as a teaching opportunity, as the teacher identifies questions or parts of the test that students struggled with and reteaches those concepts. Weekly tests can take various forms—labeling pictures, multiple choice, writing to a prompt, performing a role-play—depending on the level of the class and the concepts being assessed. For an example of a weekly assessment used with beginners, see the Sample Friday Test in Exhibit 3.21.

Using frequent low-stakes assessments—where students and teachers reflect on the results and make changes—is a key part of the formative assessment process and produces powerful results. As W. James Popham explains, "recent reviews of more than 4,000 research investigations show clearly that when this [formative] process is well implemented in the classroom, it can essentially double the speed of student learning."[9]

- *Writing prompts.* Teachers can assess student learning by having students write to a prompt. These prompts can take many forms, such as a question to answer, a statement with which to agree or disagree, a picture to describe, or a response to a text or video clip. It is important that writing prompts for ELLs contain clear directions and take into account the cultural and linguistic knowledge that students currently possess.[10] Asking students to write about content they have not yet learned or about cultural situations they are not familiar with will not yield valuable information about students' true abilities. For example, giving students a prompt asking them to describe their favorite carnival or fair ride might be confusing for students who haven't attended this type of event or aren't familiar with the term *carnival*.

When all our students have laptops, we will often (sometimes once each week) create a shared Google Slides presentation with a simple "personal" prompt and additional scaffolded instructions. Students write their responses on the slide that has their name on it. That night, we'll change the text color when appropriate to indicate important errors (not all of them!), give students time the next day to fix them, and then students will share their slide and present it to the entire class or in small groups. Not only do these responses function as important formative assessments to teacher and student alike, but they also provide grammatical teaching opportunities and the information shared can help build classroom community. Of course, students can also write out their responses on paper, too.

Here are some of the main prompts with scaffolded instructions that we have used:

A Typical Day:

Main prompt: Please go to the slide with your name and write as much as you can about a typical day in your life.

What time do you get up?

What do you do first?

What happens during the day?

Who do you see?

What do you eat?

What do you do at night?

What time do you go sleep?

Your Favorite Place:

Main prompt: Please go to the slide with your name and write as much as you can about your favorite place in the whole world.

What is it?

Where is it?

Why is it your favorite place?

What do you do there?

What else is there?

Who else is there?

Summer Plans:

Main Prompt: Please go to the slide with your name and write as much as you can about what you want your summer to look like.

What are the top three things you want to do this summer?

What will people around you be doing this summer?

Where do you want go?

Do you want to go to summer school? Why or why not? If you do, what do you want to learn?

Write about some of the favorite things you've done in past summers.

In addition, we sometimes use this same formative assessment process to help some students reduce dependence on Google Translate. We initiate a conversation with them comparing Google Translate to Siri or Google Maps voice directions: If you just mindlessly obey the instructions, you'll get to a destination, but won't necessarily learn anything about the community or neighborhood. But if you are aware of your surroundings as you follow the automated voice, you may learn to get to the place without using it. We follow up these talks by showing students an image, along with encouraging prompts, and ask them to write about it, either on Google Slides or on a paper—for ten minutes without using Google Translate. We then meet with them afterward to review what they wrote.

- *Student self-assessment and reflection.* Activities that promote metacognitive thinking and ask students to reflect on their learning processes are key to the formative assessment process. When students are asked to think about *what* they have learned and *how* they have learned it (the learning strategies they've used, like using graphic organizers, creating outlines in advance of writing, retrieval practice, etc.), they are better able to understand their own learning processes and can set new goals for themselves. Students can reflect on their learning in many ways: answering a set of questions, drawing a picture or set of pictures to represent their learning process, talking with a partner, or keeping a learning log or journal, for example. Students can be prompted to reflect on their learnings of academic concepts as well as life lessons and personal growth. Teachers can pause in the middle of a lesson—or at its end—and ask students to share the part of the lesson that was least clear to them. The teacher can use these responses to check for student understanding, but also to check the pulse of the class in terms of student motivation, confidence levels, and levels of metacognition.

  For more examples of student reflection, see the Reflection section in Chapter Three and the lesson plans in Chapter Sixteen.

- *Goal sheets.* As we explained in Chapter Five, having students set their own goals and evaluate progress toward achieving them is an effective part of the formative assessment process. It is important to help students distinguish between learning goals and performance goals. Research has shown the advantages of emphasizing learning goals ("I want to take more leadership in small groups") over performance goals ("I want to get an A in this class"). Both are important, but the issue is which one is given greater weight. Goal sheets are an effective way to help students set goals and track their progress. It can be helpful to identify specific goals. For example, "I will read in English for 20 minutes each night" is more specific than "I will read more." Also, goals need to be achievable in a short period of time and not impossibly difficult. The teacher can model how to set effective goals and also how to evaluate one's progress toward achieving them by asking students to periodically write or talk about what they have achieved, what they still would like to achieve, and *how* they will do it. An example of a goal sheet we use with our classes can be found in the lesson plan on the Qualities of a Successful Language Learner in Chapter Sixteen. The goal sheet for that lesson plan (Exhibit 16.4) can be modified in a variety of ways to promote student goal setting and evaluation.

- *Cloze or fluency.* As described previously, cloze and fluency assessments can be used to initially assess students' reading skills. They can also be used throughout the year as formative assessments that the teacher can use to design instruction and target areas students are struggling with. For example, a teacher who frequently listens to students read aloud on an individual basis might notice that her students are not pausing when they see a comma. She could then decide to model reading a passage aloud and pausing slightly at the commas, and then give her students time to practice in pairs. A teacher can continue this same process with different elements of reading fluency such as intonation, pronunciation, and appropriate reading rate.

- *Online audio recording.* Using an online audio recording site is a way for students and the teacher to assess student progress in speaking and reading fluency. Students can periodically record themselves (speaking or reading a text) and then can reflect on their improvement over time. See the previous Tech Tool Box for resources.

- *Observation.* A huge part of formative assessment takes place on a daily basis as the teacher observes his students. Teachers are constantly observing both the progress their students are making and the struggles they are encountering. This informal type of assessment should be formative, as the teacher changes and adapts both curriculum and instruction to meet students' current needs.

    We have found it helpful to jot down our observations during a lesson either on sticky notes or in a journal so that we can return to them later as we plan the next lesson. We also find it useful to create a folder for each of our students where we store their initial assessments and any written observational data (of course, this could also be done online). These can be easily accessed for parent meetings and at the end of a grading period. Teachers can also make a sheet for each student that contains a checklist of behaviors or skills they will be observing and space for additional comments.

- *Student conferences.* Meeting with students on an individual basis to discuss their learning progress can be hugely beneficial and informative. Asking students to share their goal sheets is one way to structure a conversation about student progress. During a conference, it can be helpful for the teacher to give students specific feedback such as "I've noticed that you are using more sensory details in your writing," as opposed to general comments like "Your writing is getting better." Robert J. Marzano explains that a key to formative assessment is providing students with "sound feedback," which means "it should be frequent, give students a clear picture of their progress and how they might improve, and provide encouragement."[11] It is also important to praise students' effort and not their intelligence. As mentioned earlier, research has shown that students who were praised for their effort instead of their intelligence worked harder, were more persistent, and scored higher on IQ tests compared to those who were praised for their intelligence.[12]

A student conference obviously isn't the only time to give feedback to students. There are many opportunities each day when teachers can provide this kind of "sound feedback." For more research and ideas on giving students feedback, see "The Best Resources for Learning How to Best Give Feedback to Students" at http://larryferlazzo.edublogs.org.

- *Rubrics.* Rubrics can be used as part of the formative assessment process and also can be used as a summative assessment after students have completed an essay or project. Teachers can develop rubrics for many types of assignments and projects and then create lessons that align with the assessment. It can be helpful to share the rubric with students before they even start a project. When students are shown a rubric at the beginning, they have the opportunity to better understand the criteria they must meet in order to be successful. It can also be useful to involve students in the creation of rubrics by asking them to select several criteria that they feel should be included on the rubric. This allows students to put the rubric criteria into their own words and to take more ownership of the assessment process.

Rubrics can be used as a guide for students to assess their work over the course of a project. If we are going to use a rubric to assess an essay, we first go over it together and then refer back to it often as they produce their drafts. Having a set of criteria can also help the students and the teacher focus on the specific areas that will be assessed, so that the revising process can be more targeted and effective.

Well-designed rubrics can be useful for students to understand the criteria of an assignment and to use as a tool for self-evaluation. However, not all rubrics are helpful all of the time. Rubrics with highly technical language or that don't align with the concepts students are being taught can be confusing and defeating for students. Creating different rubrics for every assignment can be confusing for students and time-consuming for the teacher. Also, using only one general rubric for different assignments and types of writing isn't beneficial because the criteria may be too vague. It can also be frustrating when rubrics are imposed on teachers and their students without their input, especially when they are being used as an assessment measure and are not aligned to the curriculum.

See Chapter Six for a list of online rubric sites.

With all this being said about using rubrics, we should also point out research suggesting that that sharing student examples from previous years[13]—both good and not-so-good—can be as effective—if not more effective—than rubrics in guiding students to create superior work. Though this recent evidence has not meant we have chosen to end using rubrics entirely, we have certainly reduced their use and used student work more. And when we do use them, we use what are called "improvement rubrics" that encourage students to evaluate their growth. These kinds of rubrics do not contain deficit language and, instead, emphasize what students *have done* instead of what they *have not done*. For example, instead of saying "Demonstrates little, if any, comprehension of the text," an improvement rubric could say, "Suggests partial understanding of the text."

Summative Assessment

Summative assessment differs from the formative assessment process in that it is mainly used at the end of an instructional sequence or grading period to measure student learning. Summative assessments often include midterm and final exams, benchmark tests, and state standardized tests. The typical goal of these types of assessments is to collect information about what students have and have not learned. Of course, many argue that most standardized tests do not accurately depict what ELLs have learned because many of the tests have not taken language proficiency into account. (High-stakes tests will be discussed in more detail later in this chapter.)

We question the usefulness of many large, high-stakes tests as they currently exist because they aren't always the best indicators of students' growth. However, some forms of summative assessment used in the classroom can be useful in measuring student progress. We use summative assessments with our ELL students at both the end of the semester and at the end of the year. The following are summative assessments we have used with our ELL students that we have found valuable.

- *Portfolios.* Portfolios can be an effective way for students to demonstrate their growth in reading, writing, and thinking throughout the semester or school year. Keeping portfolios "assists students in evaluating themselves and assists you in evaluating your own program."[14] We have found it beneficial for our students to create their own portfolios at the end of a semester. We give each student a folder and a set of directions for what kinds of "evidence" they must include to document their learning in writing, reading, speaking, and thinking (see Exhibit 19.4). Students then take time to look through their binders and pull out work samples that demonstrate their learning. They also write an explanation of how each piece of work shows their learning. This process can be modified depending upon the level of the class. For example, beginners can choose a "before" work sample from the beginning of the semester and an "after" work sample from the end of the semester to show their progress. These kinds of portfolios can also be created online.

EXHIBIT 19.4. Portfolio Directions

Semester Portfolio Project

Please answer these questions on a piece of lined paper. Write complete sentences.

1. Look through your portfolio at your evidence of reading. How many books did you finish this semester? How many pages are you reading each day? How have you improved as a reader this semester?

2. Look at your text logs. Choose two examples of your best text logs. Cut them out and glue them on your paper. Underneath each text log, explain why it is an example of your best work. Which reading strategies did you use? How does it show your understanding of the book?

3. What were the two books that you liked the most this semester? Please write at least two reasons why you liked each book.

4. Look at the writing you did this semester, especially your essays and longer writing pieces. Choose your best example and explain why it is your best. What did you learn by doing this piece of writing? What process did you use to complete this piece of writing? Please attach this writing piece to the back of your answers.

5. What would you like to improve (get better at) next semester and why?

6. Think about the kind of person, student, reader, and writer you were on the first day of school in September. Draw a picture of yourself then on one half of this paper. Then think about the kind of person, student, reader, and writer you are now. Draw a picture of yourself now on the other half of your paper. Write at least one sentence describing what your picture represents and why: I was _____ in September and now I'm _____ because _____.

Please attach your picture to the back of your answers.

- *End-of-semester or end-of-year exam.* Many of the formative assessments explained earlier can be used at the end of a semester or grading period to demonstrate learning over time. At the end of each semester, we give our students fluency and cloze assessments so we can compare the scores to their initial reading assessments from the beginning of the year. Students can also respond to a writing prompt similar to the initial prompt they wrote at the beginning of the year. Speaking and reading fluency progress can be measured using online audio recording web sites, or students can respond orally to a set of questions in a one-on-one conversation with the teacher (as described in the Initial Assessment section in this chapter).

ELLs and Standardized Testing

Currently many ELLs take two types of summative assessments each year: a standardized state test that measures content knowledge and skills and an English Language Proficiency test that measures proficiency in English listening, speaking, reading, and writing. Many, though not all, state standardized tests have been revised to reflect the Common Core standards.

One way for educators to help students feel less anxiety and to do their best on these tests is to make sure ELLs have access to testing accommodations. Depending upon the state, different accommodations are allowed to help ELLs access these tests. The most common accommodations include simplified instructions, providing instructions in their home language, extra time, small-group administration, and use of bilingual dictionaries or glossaries.[15] Research has indicated that "appropriate accommodations enable English learners to show what they know and can do on content tests administered in English (such as a math test) by reducing interference of English language demands on the test." Research has also found that for accommodations to be successful, they must also be used frequently during regular instructional time so students have experience with them.[16] Most important, accommodations must be matched to individual student needs, which can change over time as they gain proficiency. See the next Tech Tool Box for resources on permitted state test modifications.

Another way teachers can help make the testing process more comfortable and accessible for their students is by sharing some basic test-taking tips with them. Of course, we don't recommend that test prep ever take the place of language development instruction. Ultimately, the best way for students to raise their test scores is through the development of academic English literacy with the support of engaging classroom instruction. In other words, all the activities we have recommended in this book. However, the following ideas represent a few ways to help students feel more comfortable and do their best on standardized tests:[17]

- Familiarize students with the test format and types of questions. Most states provide sample tests online.
- Remind students that it is okay to skip hard questions and come back to them later (this helps avoid ELLs getting stuck on one question for a long period of time).
- Teach intermediate and advanced ELLs the difference between literal and inferential questions. This can help students identify when they should be able to find the answer on the page and when they must infer the answer in their mind.

Of course, these are not the only strategies to help ELLs feel more comfortable and prepared for standardized tests. Basic elements, like providing students with healthy snacks and explaining the importance of getting enough sleep the night before testing, can also decrease anxiety and boost energy.

Multiple states and groups have recently developed new English language proficiency tests. The development of this "next generation" of state testing was funded by federal grant money.[18]

The same "test-prep" advice we've given earlier works for these English language tests, as well. In addition to the obvious one of having students take a practice version of your state's English proficiency test prior to the official one, there are a number of specific actions we take with our students to help them become familiar with the English Language Proficiency Assessments for California (ELPAC). We've included a link to those resources in the next Tech Tool box—please take a look to see if any of those practices would be helpful in preparing ELLs to take your state's test.

The Every Student Succeeds Act places a high priority on ELLs making progress in language proficiency and, to a large extent, that progress will be determined by student results on these two tests. We are concerned that this structure is based more on being "data-driven" instead of being "data-informed" (see the Principles section near the beginning of this chapter), and may result in administrators making similar mistakes to the ones made under No Child Left Behind—that students may be pushed out of schools, not welcomed into them, or stuck in *many* hours of test-prep instead of real learning.

We've included resources in the State Testing Tech Tool Box related to these concerns.

Tech Tool
State Testing

For information on different types of permitted modification that can be made for ELLs in state testing, see "The Best Resources On ELL's & Standardized Tests" https://larryferlazzo.edublogs.org/2011/10/01/the-best-resources-on-ells-standardized-tests/.

For information on how we prepare our ELL students for California's language proficiency test, see "A Beginning List Of The Best 'Test-Prep' Ideas For California's English Language Assessment" https://larryferlazzo.edublogs.org/2019/12/13/a-beginning-list-of-the-best-test-prep-ideas-for-californias-english-language-assessment/.

For information on how The Every Student Succeeds Act may help, and hurt, ELLs, see "The Best Resources For Learning How The Every Student Succeeds Act Affects English Language Learners" https://larryferlazzo.edublogs.org/2015/12/29/the-best-resources-for-learning-how-the-every-student-succeeds-act-affects-english-language-learners/ and "The Best Resources For Learning About The Ins & Outs Of Reclassifying ELLs" https://larryferlazzo.edublogs.org/2016/03/23/the-best-resources-for-learning-about-the-ins-outs-of-reclassifying-ells/ .

Grading English Language Learners

Our overall perspective on grading   We must begin by saying that grades have seldom been an issue in our classes—whether they were ELD/ESL, mainstream, intervention, or advanced courses.

Because of that experience, we are often bewildered by the amount of energy, pressure and angst about them that we see among many teachers and administrators.

We view grades as information. They are one of many forms of communication we use with students and their parents, and definitely not the most important kind. As Rick Wormeli says,[19] they are not rewards or punishments.

Grades are, in many ways, the lowest level of communication between students, parents and ourselves. As its Latin word root suggests, they are "steps toward something."[20] Handled well, and with compassion, they can often provide directions for a student's learning journey—assisting them to adjust both their routes and their destinations. Handled badly, and with minimal flexibility, they can often demoralize students and lead them to dead-ends.

Grading ELLs in the Classroom

ELD CLASSES: Figuring out how to apply assessment information in the ELL classroom to the official grading process required by most schools can be challenging. It is important for grades of ELLs to reflect the effort put forth by the student and the growth each individual student has made throughout the grading period. The various assessments described earlier can all be used within an ELL classroom to determine how a student is progressing in the different areas of language development.

We base our grading structure in ELD classes (where students are all Beginner or Intermediate ELL students) on a Course Of Study that we helped our district develop a number of years ago.

Grading Guidelines (slightly modified from the work of Thomas Guskey[21] and others)

> *35%—**Product** Criteria (quality of student work and evidence of standards-based academic achievement)*

- Daily Assignments
- Essays
- Culminating Projects

> *35%—**Progress** Criteria (evidence that students are progressing—how much they have gained or improved)*

- Academic language development
- Demonstrated growth in speaking and listening
- Demonstrated growth in reading fluency and comprehension
- Demonstrated growth in writing proficiency

> *30%—**Process** Criteria (how students do their work—student actions that enable learning)*

- Self-Assessment and goal setting
- Collaboration/working with other students and teacher
- Participation and effort

GRADING ELLs IN THE MAINSTREAM CLASSROOM First, we must say that at this time, our own District offers little grading guidance to mainstream teachers who have ELLs in their classes. We hope that will change in the near future. To our best knowledge, our state of California also does not provide much guidance in that area.

In addition, our experience is in middle and secondary schools, and we will focus most of this section in those areas.

However, based on guidance from other states and districts—as well as the federal government—and based on our own experiences, we offer the following thoughts and advice:

Federal guidelines[22] make it clear that it is the responsibility of high schools to create a pathway for a student who enters high school as a Beginner to be able to graduate in four years (which is a particularly challenging timeline since it can take four to seven years to gain proficiency in academic English).[23] They must graduate with the prerequisites to enter college. They must be able to attain success in the school's "standard instructional program." We can't see how that is possible without a system of differentiated instruction[24] and differentiated grading[25] for ELLs in our schools.

The federal government[26] also provides clear instructions that accommodations on assessments must be made by states' Departments of Education on any assessments administered to ELLs. Though those guidelines only specify state assessments, it doesn't appear to us much of a stretch to believe that teachers should follow them in their own classes, too. We're not experts, but we wouldn't be surprised if a Civil Rights complaint to the Department of Education would result in the same opinion.

The districts and states that we have found to have specific grading policies for ELLs in mainstream classes appear—in various degrees[27]—to have some key points in common:

- It is the responsibility of the teacher to make content and assessments comprehensible to ELLs.
- No student should be retained because of English language challenges.

These policies point out the difference between being "equal" and being "fair" and make it clear that treating ELLs "equally" by treating them the same as English-proficient students is not "fair" and could even be unlawful.

Guidance from the state of Indiana[28] offers an example of a "fair" assessment for ELLs:

If a student is struggling with sequential vocabulary, they may not be able to write an essay on the water cycle. However, if given the opportunity to do a hands-on type of assessment through experimentation or pictures, the same student may be able to demonstrate knowledge of that content, confirming for the teacher their knowledge of science, not their limitations in English.

Content teachers can grade ELLs more equitably by offering alternative forms of assessment and providing modifications such as more time, visuals, bilingual dictionaries or access to cellphone translation, sentence starters, writing frames word banks and simplification of directions and questions.

Another option some districts use is to apply Pass/Fail grades to ELLs in content classes or to provide letter grades indicating accommodations were made (though those notations can appear on report cards, they may not be able to be added to formal transcripts).[29]

Larry spent 19 years as a community organizer prior to becoming a teacher. As an organizer, he recognized that "we live in the world as it is, not as we would like it to be." That doesn't mean we have to be cynical, but it does mean that as we continually strive towards how we should treat all ELLs, we also have to recognize that because of time pressures, lack of professional development, and just plain overwork, some "mainstream" teachers might not be able to provide the differentiated support needed by ELLs.

In those situations, we believe that it's critical for teachers to at least recognize that ELLs are faced with the sometimes overwhelming task of learning academic content and the English language simultaneously, and show compassion and support when it comes to giving them a letter grade.

We also want to highlight here, as we have throughout the book, the importance of student self-assessment and reflection. We strongly recommend that this concept be applied to grading as well in both ELL and content area classes. Students can be asked to suggest their own grades—and back their suggestions up with evidence—so that teachers can consider those recommendations. We have found that 90 percent of the time we agree with their suggested grade, five percent of the time we increase it, and 5 percent of the time we reduce it.

Tech Tool

Grading

For more resources on grading ELLs, see "The Best Resources On 'Differentiated Grading' For English Language Learners" https://larryferlazzo.edublogs.org/2018/01/05/the-best-resources-on-differentiated-grading-for-english-language-learners/ .

Assessing The Assessor

Though we have discussed student self-assessment a bit, most of this chapter has been about teachers assessing ELLs.

We also are strong believers in "turning the tables"—providing students with opportunities to assess *us*.

In previous chapters, we've discussed the role of Student Leadership Teams in our classes who, among other responsibilities, meet with us regularly to assess how the class is going. We've also shared how we use weekly "Check-In" forms that, among other things, inquire about how students are feeling about our class.

In addition, we have students complete anonymous classroom surveys, often bilingual or trilingual, at least three times each year inviting them to give specific feedback on activities we are doing and on our teaching skills. We have learned an enormous amount from these surveys, and become much, much better teachers as a result. Here is a sample of questions from one Larry recently did using Google Forms (students could use 1–5 on the ranking questions):

How did you generally feel about this class?

How interesting was the content of this class?

How organized was the Google Classroom for this class?

How fair was grading for this class?

How did you feel about the quantity of work that was required for this class?

How did you feel about Mr. Ferlazzo's teaching ability?

How much did you feel that Mr. Ferlazzo cared about you as a person?

What was the most interesting thing you learned in this class?

What was the best thing about this class?

What was the worst thing about this class and how do you think it could be improved?

Exhibit 19.5 shows a different example of an anonymous survey Larry has used.

Navigating the world of assessment of English language learners can be challenging for both teachers and students. It is easy to get caught up in its nuts and bolts, but ultimately in everything we do—whether it's grading, teaching lessons, or interacting with students—we need to ask ourselves, What will help this student move forward? In other words, what strategies will help this student develop intrinsic motivation and gain proficiency?

EXHIBIT 19.5. ELD Student Evaluation of Class

DO NOT WRITE YOUR NAME ON THIS FORM

ELD Student Evaluation Of Class

Please give a grade of A, B, C, D, or F on each. Grade it on how much the activity helps you learn English AND if you like doing it. Grade the teacher on how well you think he/she teaches you.

ACTIVITIES & TEACHERS IN FIRST PERIOD

1. Small Groups at the Beginning of Each Class _____
2. Recording What You Write For Videos _____
3. Picture Words, Sentences and Essays_____
4. Talking About Videos_____
5. Putting Sentences In The Right Order_____
6. Jigsaw (the driver's license activity we did)_____
7. Songs_____
8. Playing English games_____
9. Meeting With Mr. Ferlazzo in his "office" (at his desk)_____
10. Peer Tutors_____
11. Mr. Ferlazzo _____

ACTIVITIES & TEACHERS IN SECOND PERIOD - MS. P'S CLASS

1. Letter Sounds _____
2. Little Books_____
3. Textbook _____
4. Computers In The Library_____
5. Ms. P_____
6. Peer Tutors _____

ACTIVITIES & TEACHERS IN SECOND PERIOD - MR. FERLAZZO'S CLASS

1. Reading Books at Beginning Of Period _____

2. Reading and Writing Stories _____

3. Working in Textbook _____

4. Computers In The Library _____

5. Peer Tutors _____

6. Mr. Ferlazzo _____

ANYTHING ELSE YOU LIKE OR DO NOT LIKE ABOUT THIS CLASS?

I like _____ because _____

_____.

I do not like _____ because _____

_____.

WHAT WOULD YOU LIKE TO LEARN NEXT SEMESTER?

1. _____

2. _____

3. _____

4. _____

Tech Tool

Class Assessments

To see many more examples of student surveys we and other teachers have used, along with reviews of what we have learned from them, see "The Best Posts On Students Evaluating Classes (And Teachers)" https://larryferlazzo.edublogs.org/2010/05/08/my-best-posts-on-students-evaluating-classes-and-teachers/ .

The lives of many of our English Language Learners, who have been uprooted from their home, culture, and home language through no choice of their own, can be very difficult.

Let's not make it harder. Instead, let's demonstrate good sense, compassion and respect good educational practice. Let's treat them as we would like our own children to be treated if we had been uprooted to a new country, a new culture and a new language.

We hope you have gained (or been reminded of) some effective assessment practices and strategies that will promote learning and equitable assessment in the ELL classroom. We also hope you will use these ideas to reflect on your own assessment practices. Ultimately, ELL teachers must use their own judgment to determine what types of assessment techniques will work best with their students.

Additional resources, including ones on rubrics, formative assessment, test-taking strategies for students, up-to-date information on the new English Proficiency and Common Core standardized tests, and links to work being done connecting Common Core to ELLs can be found on our book's web site at www.wiley.com/go/eslsurvivalguide2.

CHAPTER TWENTY

Reflective Teaching/
Professional Development

The Bread in the Pond

Nasruddin's son was walking by the pond as he ate some bread. He leaned over to look in the water, and the bread fell out of his hand.

Then he saw that another boy in the pond had taken his bread, so he ran home crying and told his father what happened. "Someone in the pond stole my bread!" he sobbed.

Nasruddin then went to the pond and looked in the water. He saw a bearded man, about his own age. "Hey there, old man!" he shouted. "You ought to be ashamed of yourself, stealing bread from a little boy like that."[1]

Mulla Nasreddin is one of Islam's most famous trickster figures.[2] Nasreddin is considered a Holy Fool and stories about him are intentionally ridiculous so that we can more readily see a truth in them.[3]

In this tale, Nasreddin sees his reflection but he doesn't really reflect on what he is seeing. In this chapter, we will take a deep dive into the act of reflecting for our own professional development. Research is clear on its enormous impact on learning[4] and so we couple the practice of reflecting with considerations about risk taking. In the tale, Nasreddin wants to advocate for this child, but in his haste, he doesn't take time to see what he should see. We can appreciate the truths in this lighthearted Islamic folktale that helps us consider the clarity we can achieve if we take time for thoughtful, intentional reflection. Like Nasreddin, we want to advocate for the children in our care. But we can set our sights on using reflection to better our craft so that we are able to best support those learners.

This chapter was written by Carol Salva. Carol is an international education consultant with elementary, middle and high school teaching experience. She provides sheltered instruction workshops, coaching and modeling through Seidlitz Education. Carol is the co-author of Boosting Achievement; Reaching Students with Interrupted or Minimal Education.

I thank God for my failures. Maybe not at the time but after some reflection. I never feel like a failure just because something I tried has failed.

—Dolly Parton

Why Should We Have an Intentional, Formal Process for Reflecting?

Embrace failure! We say that to our students all the time. We ask them to take risks and to realize that failing is an important part of learning. Success isn't usually a straight line from attempt to accomplishment.

We want students to see that a big part of learning something new is to take a risk, struggle, perhaps fail, and then reflect on what happened. Consider how we learn to play an instrument, how we learn to ski, or how we learn to bake a cake. We know we will become more proficient at these things if we keep trying to do them correctly. If we want to become more proficient about any learning, we will take a moment to reflect on what is going well and what is not working for us.

Consider the cake baking example. What if our first cake comes out raw in the middle? If that's the case, we might consider how long we had that cake in the oven, the amount of liquid we used or the temperature of the oven while it was baking. Our first attempt may have not been successful, but we can look at what DID go well and hold on to those things while we tweak and adjust our approach for our next attempt. Eventually, we should get it right if we persevere. Imagine if we just kept baking cakes the same way without reflection. That would be ridiculous. As the saying goes (which appears to have originated from Al-Anon),[5] "The definition of insanity is doing the same thing over and over again, but expecting different results?"

So then why, for years, did I spend such little time reflecting on my teaching? And why does the thought of failure still feel so uncomfortable to me? I'd like to say that I embrace failure but if I am honest, my "needs improvement" ratings on observations and evaluations sting quite a bit! And we know that no one is perfect. We know that we can all improve. In fact, my evaluator is *supposed* to find something to help me grow. Knowing all that, I still get put off by constructive criticism until I make a conscious effort to use the information in some productive way.

If I'm not careful, I get defensive and begin to rationalize all the reasons I am doing things the way I'm doing them. But is that the best way to grow? Is that what we want to model for our students? Is that what we want for our own personal growth?

If we want to grow... if we really want to accelerate the process of improving our craft... we must not only take risks, we must make conscious efforts to reflect on our practice and then be vulnerable to the idea of failure.

Why I Began Filming Myself and Why I Continued

I always thought of myself as a pretty reflective person. I would think about what went well with a lesson on my way home in my car. When I was planning, I would consider what I might want to try again or what I felt didn't go well the last time I tried this lesson. I think reasonable people do that. But I became obsessed with reflection when my life as an educator changed drastically and I returned to the classroom after many years of being a specialist. I went back to teaching because our district received a large number of students with gaps in formal education. Many of these secondary students were coming from trauma and missing substantial amounts of formal education or lacking formal education entirely. I agreed to be part of the process of trying to figure out how to best serve them. I spent several weeks exasperated when many of my tried-and-true techniques were falling flat with this group of adolescents.

This was my worst fear. I worried that I would fail at being effective with this group. Here I was, a "specialist," and I felt that failures with them would reveal that I wasn't very special after all.

Thankfully, I remembered what gave me the most success as a new teacher. HELP! Asking for help has always been the key to my successes. I'm not too proud to ask for it. With the students' best interest in mind, I invited other teachers to come in, watch me teach and offer feedback. I also had a student teacher who collaborated with me regularly and challenged me to keep a high bar. The failures were not about the students' abilities or even my own. If something based on research wasn't working, we just needed to reflect more and try again with adjustments.

We were making progress but at one point, I couldn't understand why I was unable to have these kids learning in workstations while I pulled a small group. I received a lot of help and advice but I wasn't able to have colleagues observing me all the time to help me reflect.

Finally, a colleague suggested that I record myself. I could reflect on the video and try to pinpoint exactly where the center work would start to break down. I was able to see what triggered behavior from students and reflect on how much time they were able to work independently so that we could start to try to build that and address it specifically with the students.

It worked like magic! This was incredibly valuable information for me to see these things I was unable to see at the moment.

Thankfully, my instructional coach gave me some great advice. He said to focus on ONE thing when watching the video. He offered that we can be overly critical and tear a lesson apart. We might get so disheartened that we completely abandon the practice of recording for reflection. But if I blocked everything out and focused on where rotations were breaking down, I could tweak, record, tweak, record, and tweak until I was unable to make any further progress on my own. He suggested that then, and only then, should I share the video with him or someone else to get advice on that specific thing. This altered my thinking, my focus and my affective filter! Doing this allowed me to look at my craft with much more objectivity.

Adopting a Reflective Mindset

The improvement in the class surprised me but it shouldn't have. Taking time to watch my teaching on video, analyze my actions and plan for different outcomes is a highly personalized form of professional development.

The act of reflecting on my decisions is an act of metacognition. Nancy Chick, of the Center for Teaching at Vanderbilt University writes that metacognition is the act of thinking about our thinking. . . it is a critical awareness of a) one's thinking and learning and b) oneself as a thinker and learner. This is a powerful practice not only for our students but for our own growth as learners as well.[6]

The more I reflected with a focus on improving a particular technique, the more success I would have. This began to affect what I felt was possible for myself and for these under-schooled learners. They were learning so quickly! But wouldn't that make sense? Having a lack of formal education is not a cognitive issue. It is a lack of opportunity issue. Watching myself improve on video. . . and watching the students improve, began to have a positive impact on what I believed was possible for us. Carol Dweck has a good deal of research around the gains we make if we operate in a growth mindset.[7] The reflection was helping me change my mindset about failures. In alignment with Dweck's work, I found myself taking on challenges and learning from them, which generally leads to an increase in ability and in achievement. I was also getting better at thinking about my thinking and that helped me realize that the failures in the classroom really were just puzzles to be solved. The students could achieve literacy and the target language and I could improve at how I helped them do so. My belief in my abilities and theirs became stronger the more I reflected on what was happening in the videos. One of the biggest wins in this was that I was able to share all of this with the students. I was able to authentically model the advantages to adopting a growth mindset which helped many of them do the same.

In addition to how we teach, it can be worthwhile to reflect on exactly what we are able to teach. The following questions were adapted from a reflection activity Larry Ferlazzo conducts with student teachers.[8] I found the topics to be valuable for any ELL teacher to consider:

- What scaffolds were in place for the lesson/activity?
- What academic language, if any, was taught?
- Which domains (listening, speaking, writing, reading) were practiced and how often?
- Which higher order thinking skills were used? They might include, but are obviously not limited to:
  - categorizing
  - transfer – applying something learned previously to a new activity in a different context
  - critical thinking – making a judgment and providing evidence to support that judgment

METHODS OF REFLECTING

Using video, as described above, is by no means the only way to reflect on our practice. Consider the following extensive but not exhaustive list:

- Using Video
  - Using your phone or any device to record yourself and then reviewing that video to analyze your moves, consider what was successful and think about what you might change. Be sure to talk with your principal prior to doing this to clarify what kinds of permissions, if any, would be required if you will be the only person viewing the video. Even if you are told that no permission is required, it would be respectful to still let your students know what you are doing.
    - Advantages: Allows you to view, review and analyze your own actions and those of your students from a third-person point of view. You are able to keep this video private or share it with colleagues to help you reflect and take specific actions for improvement.
    - Possible Disadvantages: Being overly critical of one's own practice.
- Journaling
  - Using a paper or digital notebook to keep track of ideas, plans, lessons learned, and other reflections.

- Advantages: Easy or no hassle to start journaling. It can be private so a person can write freely without worry of criticism or scrutiny.
- Possible Disadvantages: No accountability. Not thinking with an audience in mind. Not open to input from others.

- Blogging
  - Free platforms exist for blogging but your blog can reside on any website. It can have a casual or formal tone. For the purposes of reflection, your blog is similar to a journal but when you create and publish a blog, you're opening your posts to a public audience. With some services, people can subscribe to your blog and receive newly published posts.
    - Advantages: Authentic audience has us reflecting on a different level. You also are able to get feedback from people who read your blog so it becomes an opportunity to collaborate with others.
    - Possible Disadvantages: Becoming proficient with a blogging platform. Not writing as freely or writing with a filter because others will be reading.

- Podcasting
  - Recording and posting audio shows. A podcaster records podcast episodes in the form of an audio file which is posted to the internet and made available to the public. The episodes can be downloaded and people can subscribe to a podcast to receive newly published shows.
    - Advantages: Much like blogging, an authentic audience changes how we reflect and you are able to invite collaboration from listeners. Recording apps, audio editing software and other technology needs can be found at low to no cost.
    - Possible Disadvantages: Becoming proficient with podcasting services, how to publish and use audio editing software.

- Vlogging
  - Recording and posting video shows. This is video version of a blog. A vlogger records episodes in the form of a video file which is posted to the internet and made available to the public. The episodes can be downloaded and people can subscribe to a video channel or to a web site to receive newly published shows.
    - Advantages: This is another medium that allows for an authentic audience. We reflect in a different way for an audience and you are able to invite collaboration from viewers. Recording apps, editing software and other technology needs can be found at low to no cost.
    - Possible Disadvantages: The need to become proficient with the technology.

A COMBINED APPROACH

You don't need to limit yourself to one form of reflection. I find that I'm growing the most when I'm in a constant state of reflection. To accomplish this, I am using a combination of the above methods.

I have used hours of my teaching on video to improve my practice. Initially, I reviewed that video on my own and I experienced significant improvement with specific challenges by reflecting on how I was teaching. Eventually, I began sharing the tape with the students so that we could reflect on our combined efforts. A colleague, Joseph Maurer, was using this technique to work with his class in different ways. Joseph would review video with students to preserve every instructional minute. He challenged his students to be efficient with class time and they would review classroom routines and norms. I began sharing video with my students in the same way. Later, with parent and student permission, we began using the video for teacher staff development. I have video with good and poor teaching examples that can help others reflect. This had the added benefit of giving the students an authentic audience for their efforts. I also began blogging during this time.

I have left the classroom and I am now an instructional coach and trainer full time. But I am still blogging and reflecting in multiple ways! I often embed video into my blogs to show examples of what I am writing about. Most of my video resides on YouTube, so people are able to subscribe to my blog or my YouTube channel to see videos that I upload. I now have an audio podcast where I try to record episodes at least twice a month. For the podcast, I am either reflecting on my own or with a guest. I write a blog post for every podcast that I publish. This allows me to provide links, video and other resources that go along with the show. I have to listen to the show, edit it and then type the blog version. This process is one of the most powerful things I do for reflection.

YOU ARE NOT ALONE. REFLECTING WITH OTHERS

Many schools have professional learning groups and collaboration time designated for teams. A team may decide to spend time reading, listening or watching what other team members are publishing. Co-teachers may find it natural to record, review and reflect on video of their combined class together.

Educators who do not have a team or a co-teacher can still offer their print, audio or video recordings to an instructional coach or colleague to help them review, reflect and refine their practice. The virtual professional learning network is another option for collaboration. Groups are forming on social media platforms and collaborating 24 hours a day, seven days a week. Teachers can now find like-minded virtual colleagues who often join with others for the specific goal of finding other educators with whom to collaborate. The reflection methods above offer us something to speak from as we ask others to help us reflect on our practice.

When I was teaching that first class of under-schooled students, I felt very alone. Like many ELL teachers, I was the only educator in my building serving this demographic for language acquisition and literacy. I was grateful for Kathryn Dierschke, the student teacher I mentioned, because she offered me the collaboration so many of us need to support deeper reflection than we might do on our own.

"The smartest person in the room is the room itself," says David Weinberger, in his book, *Too Big to Know*.[9] Weinberger writes about the Internet and its change on the way we share information. But I love this quote for what it says about working collectively with any group of people. If we are open to multiple perspectives, we allow the input of others to add to, grow or even change our thinking and how we reflect on our pedagogy. For these reasons, I find it an absolute must that I reflect in collaboration with others. I'm not alone in this thinking. Derek Rhodenizer, Director of Academics at Westboro Academy in Ontario, is a very important person in my professional learning network although we have never met in person. We have collaborated on several projects and our podcasts allow us to be transparent about the reflecting we are doing on our craft. Derek is such a strong advocate of public reflection that he speaks of it often on his show and, together with Peter Cameron, he founded #MADPD (Make A Difference Professional Development). This annual conference takes place on YouTube and offers any educator the opportunity to present something that is making a difference in their classroom. The sessions are live and encourage interaction and collaboration from viewers.

WHO SHOULD BE REFLECTING?

Have you heard the old saying "Do as I say, not as I do?" It refers to a person who is attempting to lead but not by example. When I left the classroom, for some reason, it didn't occur to me to continue filming myself. But why wouldn't I? A big part of my role is to offer staff development sessions to groups of teachers. If I found that reflecting on my teaching was so powerful, why wouldn't the same be true about reflecting on how I conduct staff development? I feel fortunate to work for an organization that designates time for us to observe each other and collaborate on ways to improve our craft. But I also appreciate the role that my blog and podcast play in helping me improve. My current role is as an ELL consultant, trainer and coach with Seidlitz Education. I push myself out of my comfort zone regularly by offering PD sessions on YouTube, creating blogs on breakout sessions I give at conferences and sometimes live streaming those sessions I'm doing in front of live audiences. If you are an instructional coach or even an administrator, I would ask you to consider modeling the act of intentional reflection. If you do it exactly the way you'd like your attendees to do it, you are modeling the process and also modeling vulnerability.

IDEAS FOR LEADERSHIP TO MODEL REFLECTING

- Video tape your staff development (with permission, of course), reflect on the video, and then share clips with your staff where you feel like you want to improve.

- Model a lesson in a teacher's classroom. Film a part of it and reflect with the teacher after the lesson. Ask for honest feedback on techniques and brainstorm best ways of supporting specific groups of students.

- Create a department blog, vlog, or podcast for teachers with modeled lessons and other supports. Include a section for how your department is growing and looking to improve on their craft.

REFLECTING ON REFLECTING

I begin every podcast by explaining that the episodes are a chronicle of my journey of learning. One of the most liberating and powerful things I've done for myself is to change my view on what my role is in supporting teachers. I used to think I was supposed to teach educators how to teach. Now I see that I can help teachers more by modeling how we continue to grow.

I don't want to pretend to know everything or pretend to be better than the next educator. I want to get really, really good at getting better.

Tech Tool

Professional Development Resources

For many more professional development resources, see "The Best Places For ESL/EFL/ELL Teachers To Get Online Professional Development" https://larryferlazzo.edublogs.org/2012/06/03/the-best-places-for-esleflell-teachers-to-get-online-professional-development/. You can also find videos there of ELL students helping lead professional development workshops for teachers.

Links to all the online activities listed in the chapter can be found at www.wiley.com/go/eslsurvivalguide2.

Afterword

*A*nansi the spider had all the world's wisdom in one pot and went to hide it at the top of a tree. He was having a hard time climbing with it, though, and his son suggested he tie it to his back. Anansi was tired and frustrated at hearing a young person trying to give him advice, so he threw the pot down. It hit the ground and all the wisdom spilt into a stream and washed out to sea. So, now, no one person has all the wisdom in the world, and everyone has some to share.[1]

This West African folktale emphasizes the message we would like to leave you with—though we feel that our book is an excellent resource for teachers of English Language Learners, we certainly don't feel we have a monopoly on the truth.

In this book, we have offered the best suggestions and advice we—and our nine guest contributors—can give about teaching English language learners. These recommendations come out of our classroom experience and well-documented research from multiple sources.

However, as we said in our Introduction, we also believe that it is important for schools to develop long-term relationships with high-quality professional development organizations that can provide on-site assistance for educators. While we have discussed the great advantages that professional connections developed through social media can provide, they are no substitute for hands-on support from experienced educators committed to developing long term and positive professional relationships with teachers and their schools.

We highly recommend:

The WRITE Institute is based at the San Diego County Office of Education and provides exceptional teacher training and curriculum for English language learners. (https://www.sdcoe.net/lls/MEGA/Pages/write-institute.aspx)

The California Writing Project and its national group, the National Writing Project, have provided important support to teachers at our schools, including those working with English language learners, on developing effective strategies to teach writing. (https://www.facebook.com/CaliforniaWriting Project/; http://www.nwp.org)

Seidlitz Education provides resources and technical assistance to districts, schools and educators serving English Language Learners. Several of the guest contributors to this book work very closely with them. (https://seidlitz education.com/)

It is also important to remember that online resources related to English language learners are constantly being changed and developed. Ferlazzo writes one of the most popular blogs on the Web for teachers of ELLs, and we encourage you to read it regularly and contribute your own comments, ideas, and experiences.

Our students are different every year, educators learn from experiences every year, new research is done every year, and new education policies are adopted by governing authorities every year.

For these reasons, we might want to keep in mind this quotation attributed to Mary Shelley: "The beginning is always today."[2]

Visit our book's web site at www.wiley.com/go/eslsurvivalguide2 for up-to-date information on Common Core standards for ELLs, language proficiency tests, and new teaching resources.

Notes

Introduction

1. The story of the hummingbird and the forest fire is from the book *Flight of the Hummingbird: A Parable for the Environment* by Michael Nicoll Yahgulanaas, published in 2008.

Chapter One

1. "Legend of the Mountain" is an inspirational story used in the Boy Scouts; see the US Scouting Service website: http://usscouts.org/usscouts/smminute/legend2.asp.
2. Csikszentmihalyi, M. (1990). *Flow: The Psychology of Optimal Experience* (New York: Harper Perennial).
3. Krashen, S. (2011). *The Compelling (Not Just Interesting) Input Hypothesis.* Retrieved from http://www.sdkrashen.com/content/articles/the_compelling_input_hypothesis.pdf
4. US Department of Education, Office of English Language Acquisition, *English Learners: Demographic Trends*, February 2020. Retrieved from https://ncela.ed.gov/files/fast_facts/19-0193_Del4.4_ELDemographicTrends_021220_508.pdf
5. National Center for Education Statistics, *English Language Learners in Public Schools*, May 2021. Retrieved from https://nces.ed.gov/programs/coe/indicator/cgf
6. US Department of Education, *Our Nation's English Learners: What are Their Characteristics?* n.d. Retrieved from https://www2.ed.gov/datastory/el-characteristics/index.html#intro.

7. Bialik, K., Scheller, A. and Walker, K. (2018). *6 Facts About English Learners in U.S. Public Schools*. Pew Research Center, October 25. Retrieved from https://www .pewresearch.org/fact-tank/2018/10/25/6-facts-about-english-language-learners-in-u-s-public-schools/.

8. National Center for Education Statistics, *English Language Learners*, 4.

9. National Center for Education Statistics, *English Language Learners*, 2.

10. Bialik, K., Schelloer, A. and Walker, K. *6 Facts About English Learners*.

11. Lewis, L., Gray, L. and Ralph, J. (2016). *Programs and Services for High School English Learners in Public School Districts: 2015–16*. National Center for Educational Statistics, September, p. 2. Retrieved from https://nces.ed.gov/pubs2016/2016150.pdf.

12. Garcia, A. (2021). "Words Matter—The Case for Shifting to 'Emergent Bilingual.'" *Language Magazine*, June 17. Retrieved from https://www.languagemagazine .com/2021/06/17/words-matter-the-case-for-shifting-to-emergent-bilingual/.

13. Kleyn, T. and Stern, N. (2018). "Labels as Limitations." *MinneTESOL Journal* 34(1). Retrieved from http://minnetesoljournal.org/journal-archive/mtj-2018-1/labels-as-limitations/#.WwmBhIIi6YE.twitter.

14. Baird, A. S. "Dual Language Learners Reader Post #2: Who Are Dual Language Learners?" New America. Retrieved from https://www.newamerica.org/education-policy/edcentral/dllreader2/.

15. US Department of Education, Office for Civil Rights, *Schools' Civil Rights Obligations to English Learner Students and Limited English Proficient Parents*, n.d. Retrieved from https://www2.ed.gov/about/offices/list/ocr/ellresources.html.

16. Fleischer, C. (2017). *ESL, ELL, Generation 1.5—Why Are These Terms Important?* National Council of Teachers of English, September 7. Retrieved from https://ncte.org/blog/2017/09/esl-ell-generation-1-5-why-are-these-terms-important/.

17. Saunders, W., Goldenberg, C. and Marcelletti, D. (n.d.). *English Language Development: Guidelines for Instruction*. American Federation of Teachers. Retrieved from https://www.aft.org/periodical/american-educator/summer-2013/english-language-development.

18. "Frequently Asked Questions About Careers in TESOL," n.d. Retrieved from https://www.tesol.org/docs/pdf/2466.pdf?sfvrsn=2.

19. Sugarman, J. (2017). *Beyond Teaching English: Supporting High School Completion by Immigrant and Refugee Students*. Migration Policy Institute, November, 2. Retrieved from https://www.migrationpolicy.org/sites/default/files/publications/Sugarman-BeyondTeachingEnglish_FINALWEB.pdf.

20. Kight, S. W. (2021). "Scoop: Biden Briefing Calls for 20,000 Child Migrant Beds." *Axios*, March 2. Retrieved from https://www.axios.com/biden-immigration-child-migrant-border-aeaf0231-02d3-4c96-b139-68069c0c1189.html?utm_campaign=organic&utm_medium=socialshare&utm_source=twitter.

21. Potochnick, S. (2018). "The Academic Adaptation of Immigrant Students with Interrupted Schooling." *American Educational Research Journal*, April 4, 23. Retrieved from https://journals.sagepub.com/doi/10.3102/00028312187 61026.

22. Sugarman, *Beyond Teaching English*, 1.

23. Sahakyan, N. and Ryan, S. (2018). *Exploring the Long-term English Learner Population Across 15 WIDA States*. Wisconsin Center for Education Research, October, 5. Retrieved from https://wida.wisc.edu/sites/default/files/resource/WIDA-Report-Long-Term-English-Learner-Population.pdf.

24. *Effective Interventions for Long-term English Learners*. (2017). Hanover Research, July, 3. Retrieved from https://portal.ct.gov/-/media/SDE/ESSA-Evidence-Guides/Effective_Interventions_for_Long-Term_English_Learners.

25. *Effective Interventions*, 7.

26. Olsen, L. (2010). "A Closer Look at Long-Term English Learners: A Focus on New Directions." *STARlight* no. 7, Dec.). Retrieved from https://californianstogether.org/a-closer-look-at-long-term-english-learners-a-focus-for-new-directions-in-the-starlight-issue-7/.

27. "Brain's Window for Language Learning Open Until Adulthood." (2018). *EurekAlert!*, May 1. https://www.eurekalert.org/news-releases/799453.

28. Byers-Heinlein, K. and Lew-Williams, C. (2013). "Bilingualism in the Early Years: What the Science Says." *Learning Landscapes* 7, 1, 95–112. Retrieved from https://www.ncbi.nlm.nih.gov/pmc/articles/PMC6168212/.

29. Cummins, J. (1979). "Cognitive/Academic Language Proficiency, Linguistic Interdependence, the Optimum Age Question and Some Other Matters." *Working Papers on Bilingualism*, 19, 121–119.

30. Scarcella, R. (2003). *Academic English: A Conceptual Framework* (Irvine: University of California Irvine, Linguistic Minority Research Institute). Retrieved from http://academics.utep.edu/LinkClick.aspx?link=Scarcella.pdf&tabid=63592&mid=143176.

31. Howard Research (2009). *Kindergarten to 12th Grade English as a Second Language Literature Review Update* (Calgary, Canada: Howard Research). Retrieved from http://education.alberta.ca/media/1182477/esl_lit_review.pdf.

32. Krashen, S. D. (1981). *Second Language Acquisition and Second Language Learning* (Oxford: Pergamon Press). Retrieved from http://sdkrashen.com/SL_Acquisition_and_Learning/SL_Acquisition_and_Learning.pdf.

33. Goldenberg, C. (2008). "Teaching English Language Learners: What the Research Does—and Does Not—Say." *American Educator* (Summer), 8–23, 42–4. Retrieved from https://www.aft.org/sites/default/files/periodicals/goldenberg.pdf.

34. Krashen, S. and Terrell, T. (1983). *The Natural Approach* (Englewood Cliffs, NJ: Alemany Press).

35. Hakuta, K., Butler, Y. G. and Witt, D. (2000). *How Long Does it Take Learners to Attain Proficiency?* The University of California Linguistic Minority Research Institute, Policy Report 2000–1, January, p. 13. Retrieved from https://eric.ed.gov/?ID=ED443275.

36. Ferlazzo, L. and Sypnieski K. H., (2016). *Navigating the Common Core with English Language Learners* (San Francisco: Jossey-Bass).

37. Goldenberg, "Teaching English Language Learners," 13.

38. Goldenberg, "Teaching English Language Learners."

39. Marzano, R. J. (2007). *The Art and Science of Teaching.* Alexandria, VA: ASCD.

40. Witt, D. and Soet, M. (2020). "5 Effective Modeling Strategies for English Learners." *Edutopia*, July 13. Retrieved from https://www.edutopia.org/article/5-effective-modeling-strategies-english-learners?utm_content=linkpos6&utm_campaign=weekly-2020-07-15&utm_source=edu-legacy&utm_medium=email.

41. Szpara, M. Y. and Ahmad, I. (2006). *Making Social Studies Meaningful for ELL Students: Content and Pedagogy in Mainstream Secondary School Classrooms* (Brookville, NY: Long Island University). Retrieved from https://www.semanticscholar.org/paper/Making-Social-Studies-Meaningful-for-ELL-Students%3A-Szpara-Ahmad/df0951142ef9c1f5caa3b4f68c568bbd72285b86?p2df.

42. Stahl, R. J. (1994)."Using 'Think-Time' and 'Wait-Time' Skillfully in the Classroom." *ERIC Digest*, May, 2. Retrieved from https://files.eric.ed.gov/fulltext/ED370885.pdf

43. Goldenberg, "Teaching English Language Learners."

44. Goldenberg, "Teaching English Language Learners."

45. Goldenberg, "Teaching English Language Learners."

46. *Understand Curriculum and Reshape Instruction: Checking for Understanding.* (n.d.). Retrieved from

47. Howard Research, *Kindergarten to 12th Grade English as a Second Language Literature Review Update.*

48. Figlio, D. N., Giuliano, P., Marchingiglio, R., Őzek, U. and Sapienza, P. (2021). *Diversity in Schools: Immigrants and the Educational Performance of U.S. Born Students.* National Bureau of Economic Research, March. Retrieved from https://www.nber.org/papers/w28596#fromrss.

Chapter Two

1. This is a retelling of an Aesop's fable: "The Farmer and his Sons" in The Aesop for Children, published in 1919. The book is online at Project Gutenberg: https://www.gutenberg.org/ebooks/19994.

2. Krashen, S. D. (2009). *Principles and Practice in Second Language Acquisition* (2nd ed.), 30–32. Retrieved from http://www.sdkrashen.com/content/books/principles_and_practice.pdf.

3. Vogel, S., Kluen, L. M., Fernández, G. and Schwabe, L. (2018). "Stress Affects the Neural Ensemble for Integrating New Information and Prior Knowledge." *Neuroimage*, 173, 176–187. Retrieved from https://pubmed.ncbi.nlm.nih.gov/29476913/.

4. Yatvin, J. (2011). "Letting Teachers Re-Invent Their Own Wheel." *Washington Post*, July 6. Retrieved from http://www.washingtonpost.com/blogs/answer-sheet/post/letting-teachers-re-invent-their-own-wheel/2011/07/06/gIQAM9lQ1H_blog.html?wprss=answer-sheet.

5. Marzano, R. J. (2007). *The Art and Science of Teaching.* (Alexandria, VA: ASCD), 150.

6. Ferlazzo, L. (2011). "How I Milked a Lesson for Every Last Ounce of Learning and Why I'm an Idiot for Not Thinking of It Earlier," Jan 22. Retrieved from http://larryferlazzo.edublogs.org.

7. Sethi, J. and Scales, P. C. (2020). "Developmental Relationships and School Success: How Teachers, Parents, and Friends Affect Educational Outcomes and What Actions Students Say Matter Most." *Contemporary Educational Psychology*, 63, 9. Retrieved from https://www.sciencedirect.com/science/article/abs/pii/S0361476X20300692?dgcid=author.

8. "Newcomer Immigrant and Refugee Students Are More Optimistic About the Future Than Their US-Born Peers." (2021). Teachers College, Columbia University, Newsroom, February. Retrieved from https://www.tc.columbia.edu/articles/2021/february/newcomer-immigrant--refugee-students-are-more-optimistic-than-us-born-peers/.

9. Suarez-Orozco, C., Pimental, A. and Martin, M. (2009). "The Significance of Relationships: Academic Engagement and Achievement among Newcomer Immigrant Youth." *Teachers College Record*, 111(3), 712–713.

10. Gregory, A. and Ripski, M. B. (2008). "Adolescent Trust in Teachers: Implications for Behavior in the High School Classroom." *School Psychology Review*, 37(3), 337–345.

11. Harvard Business School. (2018). "Collaborate, but Only Intermittently, Says New Study." *Science Daily*, August 13. Retrieved from https://www.sciencedaily.com/releases/2018/08/180813160528.htm.

12. Marzano, *The Art and Science of Teaching.*

13. California Department of Education. (2010). *Improving Education for English Learners: Research-Based Approaches.* Sacramento: California Department of Education. Retrieved from http://www.cal.org/resources/pubs/improving-education-for-english-learners.html, 195.

14. "Are You Happy for Me? How Sharing Positive Events with Others Provides Personal and Interpersonal Benefits." (2010). *Journal of Personal and Social Psychology,* 99(2), 311–329.

15. Gallardo, L. O., Barrasa, A. and Guevara-Viejo, F. (2016). "Positive Peer Relationships and Academic Achievement Across Early and Midadolescence." *Social Behavior and Personality,* 44(10), 1637–1648. Retrieved from https://www .sbp-journal.com/index.php/sbp/article/view/5581.

16. Southwest Educational Development Laboratory. (2002). *A New Wave of Evidence: The Impact of School, Family, and Community Connections on Achievement.* Austin, TX: Southwest Educational Development Laboratory.

17. Ferlazzo, L. and Hammond, L. (2009). *Building Parent Engagement in Schools.* (Santa Barbara, CA: Linworth).

18. Kraft, M. A. and Dougherty, S. M. (2013). "The Effect of Teacher-Family Communication on Student Engagement: Evidence from a Randomized Field Experiment." *Journal of Research on Educational Effectiveness,* 6(3), 199–222. Retrieved from https://www.tandfonline.com/doi/full/10.1080/19345747.201 2.743636?casa_token=V9MwQD5hJm4AAAAA%3AJvTD_9ysjqawinGDgBqb0 0onSIwyvLIzHeFLGPKwICTTlTToGMjnrWQfkFQUlSL__s7zXOsArUWM.

19. US Department of Justice, Civil Rights Division, and US Department of Education, Office for Civil Rights, *Information for Limited English Proficient (LEP) Parents and Guardians and for Schools and School Districts that Communicate with Them,* n.d. Retrieved from https://www2.ed.gov/about/offices/list/ocr/docs/ dcl-factsheet-lep-parents-201501.pdf.

20. Kratochvil, M. (2001). "Urban Tactics: Translating for Parents Means Growing up Fast." *New York Times* archives. Retrieved from http://www.nytimes .com/2001/08/26/nyregion/urban-tactics-translating-for-parents-means-growing-up-fast.html?pagewanted=1.

21. Ferlazzo and Hammond, *Building Parent Engagement.*

22. Ferlazzo, L. (2011). "The Best Resources for Learning the Advantages to Being Bilingual or Multilingual," February 16. Retrieved from https://larryferlazzo .edublogs.org/2011/02/16/the-best-resources-for-learning-the-advantages-to-being-bilingual/.

23. The Minneapolis Foundation. (2010). *Insights: Immigrant Experiences.* Saint Paul, MN: Wilder Research, May. Retrieved from "Parent involvement in school" https://files.eric.ed.gov/fulltext/ED511597.pdf.

24. Ho, P. and Cherng, H-Y. S. (2018). "How Far Can the Apple Fall? Differences in Teacher Perceptions of Minority and Immigrant Parents and Their Impact on Academic Outcomes." *Social Science Research,* 74(132–145), pp. 10–11. Retrieved from https://www.sciencedirect.com/science/article/abs/pii/S0049089X173 08281.

25. Ferlazzo, L. (2020). "Guest Post: 'All About Me' Activity to Begin the School Year," August 6. Retrieved from https://larryferlazzo.edublogs.org/2020/08/06/guest-post-all-about-me-activity-to-begin-the-school-year/.

26. Ferlazzo, L. (2010). *English Language Learners: Strategies That Work*. Columbus, OH: Linworth, 8.

27. "Activities for New Classes." (2020). The Hands Up Project, August 7. Retrieved from https://www.handsupproject.org/blog-impact-1/2020/08/07/activities-for-new-classes.

28. Seton, H. (2021). "A Daily Ritual that Builds Trust and Community Among Students." *Edutopia*, January 8. Retrieved from https://www.edutopia.org/article/daily-ritual-builds-trust-and-community-among-students.

29. Norwegian University of Science and Technology. (2020). "Why Writing by Hand Makes Kids Smarter." *Science Daily*, October 1. Retrieved from https://www.sciencedaily.com/releases/2020/10/201001113540.htm.

30. Almaliki, A. (2017). *The Impact of Using a Bilingual Dictionary (English-Arabic) for Reading and Writing*. Unpublished thesis, State University of New York, Fredonia. Retrieved from https://dspace.sunyconnect.suny.edu/handle/1951/70394.

31. Cummins, J. *Computer Assisted Text Scaffolding for Curriculum Access and Language Learning/Acquisition*. Retrieved from http://iteachilearn.org/cummins/comptext.html.

32. Goodman, G. (1999). *The Reading Renaissance/Accelerated Reader Program: Pinal County School-to-Work Evaluation Report*. ERIC document no. ED 427299.

33. Krashen, S. (2003). "The (Lack of) Experimental Evidence Supporting the Use of Accelerated Reader." *Journal of Children's Literature*, 29(2), 16–30.

34. "For Poor Families, Especially, Books at Home Propel Children to More Years in School." (2010). May 26. Retrieved from https://learningenglish.voanews.com/a/for-poor-especially-books-at-home-propel-children-in-school-94917694/113592.html.

35. Lyttle, L. A. (2011). *Do Peer Tutors Help Teach ESL Students to Learn English as a Second Language More Successfully?* April 7. ERIC document no. ED 518172. Retrieved from http://eric.ed.gov/PDFS/ED518172.pdf, 9.

36. Howard Research. (2009). *Kindergarten to 12th Grade English as a Second Language Literature Review Update*. Calgary, Canada: Howard Research, Oct. Retrieved from http://education.alberta.ca/media/1182477/esl_lit_review.pdf.

37. Ferlazzo and Hammond, *Building Parent Engagement*.

38. Howard Research, *Kindergarten to 12th Grade English*.

39. Ferlazzo, L. (2021). "Classroom Instruction Resources of the Week," July 216. Retrieved from https://larryferlazzo.edublogs.org/2021/07/16/classroom-instruction-resources-of-the-week-310/.

40. Ferlazzo, L. (2008). "What Are You Doing in that Computer Lab?". *Tech & Learning*, February 1. Retrieved from https://www.techlearning.com/news/what-are-you-doing-in-that-computer-lab

41. Goldenberg, C. (2008). "Teaching English Language Learners: What the Research Does—and Does Not—Say." *American Educator*, Summer, 8–23, 42–44. Retrieved from http://www.aft.org/pdfs/americaneducator/summer2008/goldenberg.pdf, 20.

42. Marzano, R. J. (2005). *A Handbook for Classroom Management That Works.* (Alexandria, VA: ASCD), 5–6.

Chapter Three

1. Ferlazzo, L. and Sypnieski, K. H. (2016). *Navigating the Common Core with English Language Learners.* San Francisco: Jossey-Bass.

2. Joyce, B., Hrycauk, M. and Calhoun, E. (2002). "A Second Chance for Struggling Readers." *Educational Leadership*, 58(6), Mar; Wood, K. D. and Tinajero, J. (2002). "Using Pictures to Teach Content to Second Language Learners." *Middle School Journal*, 33(5), 47–51. Retrieved from https://www.tandfonline.com/doi/abs/10.1080/00940771.2002.11495331?journalCode=umsj20

3. Calhoun, E. (1999). *Teaching Beginning Reading and Writing with the Picture Word Inductive Mode.* (Alexandria, VA: Association for Supervision and Curriculum Development).

4. Calhoun, E., Poirier, T., Simon, N. and Mueller, L. (2001). *Teacher (and District) Research: Three Inquiries into the Picture Word Inductive Model.* Paper presented at the Annual Meeting of the American Educational Research Association, Seattle, WA, April. Retrieved from http://www.eric.ed.gov/PDFS/ED456107.pdf.

5. Wilson, D. and Conyers, M. (2011). *60 Strategies for Increasing Student Learning.* (Orlando, FL: BrainSmart).

6. Ozubko, J. D. and Macleod, C. M. (2010). "The Production Effect in Memory: Evidence That Distinctiveness Underlies the Benefit." *Journal of Experimental Psychology: Learning, Memory, and Cognition*, 36(6), 1543–1549. Retrieved from http://www.ncbi.nlm.nih.gov/pubmed/20804284.

7. Prince, M. and Felder, R. "The Many Faces of Inductive Teaching and Learning." *NSTA WebNews Digest.* Retrieved from http://www.nsta.org/publications/news/story.aspx?id=53403.

8. Ferlazzo, L. (2016). "A Look Back: Is This the Most Important Research Study of the Year? Maybe," October 2. Retrieved from http://larryferlazzo.edublogs.org.

9. Stafford, T. (2011). "Make Study More Effective, the Easy Way." *Mind Hacks*, October 24. Retrieved from https://mindhacks.com/2011/10/24/make-study-more-effective-the-easy-way.

10. Ferlazzo, L. (2015). "Study: Inductive Learning Promotes 'Transfer of Knowledge' Better Than Direct Instruction," June 19. Retrieved from http://larryferlazzo.edublogs.org.

11. University of Sydney (2016). "Pattern Learning Key to Children's Language Development." *Science Daily*, May 5. Retrieved from https://www.sciencedaily.com/releases/2016/05/160505222938.htm.

12. Association for Psychological Science (2013). *Picking up a Second Language is Predicted by Ability to Learn Patterns*, May 28. Retrieved from http://www.psychologicalscience.org/news/releases/picking-up-a-second-language-is-predicted-by-the-ability-to-learn-statistical-patterns.html.

13. Wilson III, E. J. (2015). 5 skills employers want that you won't see in a job ad. *Fortune,* June 10. Retrieved from http://fortune.com/2015/06/10/5-skills-employers-want-that-you-wont-see-in-a-job-ad/?xid=timehp-popular.

14. Kabilan, M. K. (2000). "Developing the Critical ESL Learner: The Freire's Way." *ELT Newsletter*, June. Retrieved from http://www.eltnewsletter.com/back/June2000/art192000.shtml.

15. Shor, I. (1987). *Freire for the Classroom*. (Portsmouth, NH: Heinemann), 164.

16. Ferlazzo, L. (2011). "Freire's Learning Sequence." *Library Media Connection*, January/February. Retrieved from http://linworth.com/pdf/lmc/hot_stuff/LMC_JanFeb11_MediaMaven.pdf, 5

17. Mathews-Aydinli, J. (2007). *Problem-Based Learning and Adult English Language Learners*. CAELA Brief. Washington, DC: Center for Adult English Language Acquisition, April. Retrieved from http://www.cal.org/caela/esl_resources/briefs/Problem-based.pdf.

18. Ferlazzo, L. (2015). "The Best Posts on Reading Strategies & Comprehension—Help Me Find More!", March 19. Retrieved from http://larryferlazzo.edublogs.org.

19. Block, C. C., Parris, S. R., Reed, K. L., Whiteley, C. S. and Cleveland, M. D. (2009). "Instructional Approaches That Significantly Increase Reading Comprehension." *Journal of Educational Psychology*, 101(2), 262–281. Retrieved from http://bestpracticesweekly.com/wp-content/uploads/2011/07/Best-uses-of-independent-reading-time-Article.pdf.

20. Ferlazzo, L. (2020). "The Best Posts About Value of Oral Reading in Partners for ELLs and Others," April 13. Retrieved from http://larryferlazzo.edublogs.org.

21. Ferlazzo, L. (2011). "The Best Resources Documenting the Effectiveness of Free Voluntary Reading," February 26, 2011. Retrieved from http://larryferlazzo.edublogs.org.

22. Krashen, S. (2009). *81 Generalizations about Free Voluntary Reading*. IATEFL Young Learner and Teenager Special Interest Group Publication. Retrieved from http://

successfulenglish.com/wp-content/uploads/2010/01/81-Generalizations-about-FVR-2009.pdf.

23. Cummins, J. *Computer Assisted Text Scaffolding for Curriculum Access and Language Learning/Acquisition.* Retrieved from http://iteachilearn.org/cummins/comptext.html.

24. Gold, J. and Gibson, A. (n.d.). *Reading Aloud to Build Comprehension.* Reading Rockets. Retrieved from https://www.readingrockets.org/article/reading-aloud-build-comprehension; Sönmez, Y. and Sulak, S. E. (2018). "The Effect of the Thinking-aloud Strategy on the Reading Comprehension Skills of 4th Grade Primary School Students." *Universal Journal of Educational Research,* 6(1), 168–172. Retrieved from https://files.eric.ed.gov/fulltext/EJ1165440.pdf, p. 168; AlQahtani, M. (2015). *The Effects of Think-Aloud Strategy to Improve Reading Comprehension of 6th Grade Students in Saudi Arabia.* Semantic Scholar. Retrieved from https://pdfs.semanticscholar.org/ba0f/75cb434b23d1e416bf1c4cc12502bad0c678.pdf, p. 24.

25. Ferlazzo, L. (2020). "The Best Resources to Learn About the Importance of Teacher Modeling," January 6, 2020. Retrieved from http://larryferlazzo.edublogs.org.

26. Ferlazzo, L. (2020). "The Best Posts About Value of Oral Reading in Partners for ELLs and Others," April 13. Retrieved from https://larryferlazzo.edublogs.org/2020/04/13/the-value-of-oral-reading-in-partners-for-ells-others/.

27. Conti, G. (2019). *Beyond Transcription: Unlocking the Full Power of Dictation—My Favourite Dictation Tasks,* January 12, 2019. Retrieved from https://gianfrancoconti.com/2019/01/12/beyond-transcription-unlocking-the-full-power-of-dictation-my-favourite-dictation-tasks/.

28. Kit, C. O. (2004). "Report on the Action Research Project on English Dictation in a Local Primary School." *Hong Kong Teachers' CentreJournal,* 2, 1–10. Retrieved from http://edb.org.hk/hktc/download/journal/j2/P1-10.pdf.

29. Kiany, G. R. and Shiramiry, E. (2002). "The Effect of Frequent Dictation on the Listening Comprehension Ability of Elementary EFL Learners." *TESL Canada Journal,* 20(1), 57–63.

30. Kidd, R. (1992). "Teaching ESL Grammar through Dictation." *TESL Canada Journal* 10(1), 49–61.

31. Bruner, J., Goodnow, J. J. and Austin, G. A. (1967). *A Study of Thinking.* (New York: Science Editions).

32. Willis, J. (2006). *Research-Based Strategies to Ignite Student Learning.* (Alexandria, VA: ASCD), 15.

33. Shamnad, N. (2005). *Effectiveness of Concept Attainment Model on Achievement in Arabic Grammar of Standard IX Students.* Unpublished thesis, Mahatma Ghandi University, Kottayam, India.

34. Alfieri, L., Brooks, P. J., Aldrich, N. J. and Tenenbaum, H. R. (2011). "Does discovery-based instruction enhance learning?" [Abstract.] *Journal of Educational Psychology,* 103(1), 1–18. Retrieved from http://psycnet.apa.org/index.cfm?fa=buy.optionToBuy&id=2010-23599-001; Marzano, R. J. (2011). "The Perils and Promises of Discovery Learning." *Educational Leadership,* 69(1), 86–87. Retrieved from http://www.ascd.org/publications/educational-leadership/sept11/vol69/num01/The-Perils-and-Promises-of-Discovery-Learning.aspx.

35. Peregoy, S. F. and Boyle, O. (2008). *Reading, Writing, and Learning in ESL.* (Boston: Pearson Education), 279.

36. Liang, X., Mohan, B. A. and Early, M. (1998). "Issues of Cooperative Learning in ESL Classes: A Literature Review." *TESL Canada Journal,* 15(2), 13–23. Retrieved from http://www.teslcanadajournal.ca/index.php/tesl/article/view File/698/529; Polley, E. K. (2007). *Learner Perceptions of Small Group and Pair Work in the ESL Classroom: Implications for Conditions in Second Language Acquisition.* Unpublished thesis, University of Texas, Arlington. Retrieved from http://dspace.uta.edu/bitstream/handle/10106/315/umi-uta-1643.pdf?sequence=1.

37. Storch, N. (2005). "Collaborative Writing: Product, Process, and Students' Reflections." *Journal of Second Language Writing,* 14(3), 153–173, p. 153. Retrieved from https://www.sciencedirect.com/science/article/abs/pii/S1060374305000172.

38. Krashen, S. (2004). "Basic Phonics." *TexTESOL III Newsletter,* November, 2–4.

39. Robles, Y. (2020). *Colorado's Emphasis on Phonics in Reading Could Hurt English Language Learners, Advocates Say,* December 15. Retrieved from https://co.chalkbeat.org/2020/12/15/22174706/colorado-emphasis-phonics-reading-hurt-english-language-learners.

40. Bassano, S. (2002). *Sounds Easy! Phonics, Spelling, and Pronunciation Practice.* (Provo, UT: Alta Book Center). Retrieved from http://altaesl.com/Detail.cfm?CatalogID=1543.

41. Ferlazzo, L. (2010). *English Language Learners: Teaching Strategies That Work.* (Santa Barbara, CA: Linworth), an imprint of ABC-CLIO, 86.

42. Krashen, S. (2009). "Basic Phonics;" *81 Generalizations about Free Voluntary Reading,* IATEFL Young Learner and Teenager Special Interest Group Publication. Retrieved from http://successfulenglish.com/wp-content/uploads/2010/01/81-Generalizations-about-FVR-2009.pdf.

43. Cambourne, B. (2009). *The Drum Opinion,* October 13. Retrieved from http://www.abc.net.au/unleashed/29262.html.

44. Shanahan, T. (2017). *Phonics for English Learners? What do You Think?* July 15. Retrieved from https://www.shanahanonliteracy.com/blog/phonics-for-english-learners-what-do-you-think#sthash.fPSDXONq.cVGQi0J8.dpbs.

45. Ferlazzo, L. *English Language Learners: Teaching Strategies That Work,* 78.

46. Brown, H. D. (2007). *Principles of Language Learning and Teaching*, 5th ed. (White Plains, NY: Pearson Longman), 105.

47. Marzano, R. J. (2007). *The Art and Science of Teaching*. Alexandria, VA: ASCD, 57.

48. Beachboard, C. (2019). *Promoting Prosocial Behaviors in the Classroom*, December 11. Retrieved from https://www.edutopia.org/article/promoting-prosocial-behaviors-classroom?utm_source=Edutopia+Newsletter&utm_campaign=9ac08687e0-EMAIL_CAMPAIGN_012220_enews_promotingpro&utm_medium=email&utm_term=0_f72e8cc8c4-9ac08687e0-79377015.

49. Wormeli, R. (2004). *Summarization in Any Subject: 50 Techniques to Improve Student Learning*. (Alexandria, VA: ASCD), 2.

50. Marzano, *The Art and Science of Teaching*.

51. Schunk, D. H. (2003). "Self-Efficacy for Reading and Writing: Influence of Modeling, Goal Setting, and Self-Evaluation." *Reading and Writing Quarterly*, 19, 159–172. Retrieved from http://libres.uncg.edu/ir/uncg/f/D_Schunk_Self_2003.pdf.

52. Hulleman, C. S. and Harackiewicz, J. M. (2009). "Promoting Interest and Performance in High School Science Classes." *Science*, 326(5958), 1410–1412. Retrieved from http://www.sciencemag.org/content/326/5958/1410.full.pdf

53. Di Stefano, G., Pisano, G. P., Gino, F. and Staats, B. R. (2016). *Making Experience Count: The Role of Reflection in Individual Learning*. Retrieved from https://www.hbs.edu/faculty/Publication%20Files/14-093_defe8327-eeb6-40c3-aafe-26194181cfd2.pdf, 27; Lew, M. D. N. and Schmidt, H. G. (2011). "Self-Reflection and Academic Performance: Is There a Relationship?," *Advances in Health Sciences Education: Theory and Practice*, 16(4), 529–545. Retrieved from https://www.ncbi.nlm.nih.gov/pmc/articles/PMC3167369/.

54. Sumeracki, M. and Weinstein, Y. (2018). *Optimising Learning Using Retrieval Practice*, September 27. Retrieved from https://www.learningscientists.org/blog/2018/9/27-1.

55. Shernoff, D. J. (2013). *Optimal Learning Environments to Promote Student Engagement*. (New York: Springer).

56. Csikszentmihalyi, M. (2008). *Flow: The Psychology of Optimal Experience.*, New York: HarperCollins, 129.

57. Kiftiah, S. (n.d.). *Literature Review of Strip Story*. Retrieved from http://www.academia.edu/7741637/Literature_reviews_of_Strip_story.

58. Williams, J. J. and Lombrozo, T. (2010). "The Role of Explanation in Discovery and Generalization: Evidence From Category Learning". *Cognitive Science*, 34, 776–806. DOI: 10.1111/j.1551-6709.2010.01113.x.

59. Ferlazzo, L. (2017). "The best resources for learning about the value of 'self-explanation,'" May 5. Retrieved from http://larryferlazzo.edublogs.org.

60. Schwartz, K. (2017). How do you know when a teaching strategy is most effective? John Hattie has an idea. *KQED News*, June 14. Retrieved from https://ww2.kqed.org/mindshift/2017/06/14/how-do-you-know-when-a-teaching-strategy-is-most-effective-john-hattie-has-an-idea/.

61. National Association of Geoscience Teachers (n.d.). *Teaching Methods: A Collection of Pedagogic Techniques and Example Activities*. Retrieved from https://serc.carleton.edu/NAGTWorkshops/teaching_methods/jigsaws/why.html.

62. Sabbah, S. S. (2016). The effect of jigsaw strategy on ESL students' reading achievement. *Arab World English Journal*, 7(1), 445–458. Retrieved from http://www.academia.edu/25090010/The_Effect_of_Jigsaw_Strategy_on_ESL_Students_Reading_Achievement_The_Effect_of_Jigsaw_Strategy_on_ESL_Students_Reading_Achievement_Sabbah.

63. Ferlazzo, L. (2012). "The Best Posts on Helping Students Teach Their Classmates Help Me Find More," April 22. Retrieved from http://larryferlazzo.edublogs.org; Nestojko, J. F., Bui, D. C., Kornell, N. and Bjork, E. L. (2014). "Expecting to Teach Enhances Learning Recall," *EurekAlert!* August 8. Retrieved from https://www.eurekalert.org/pub_releases/2014-08/wuis-ett080814.php.

64. Dean, J. (n.d.). "The Emotion That Does Motivate Behaviour After All," *PsyBlog*. Retrieved from http://www.spring.org.uk/2017/06/emotion-change-behaviour.php

65. Dettenrieder, A. M. (2006).*Total Physical Response Storytelling and the Teaching of Grammar Rules in Second Language Instruction*. Unpublished research project, Regis University. Retrieved from http://adr.coalliance.org/codr/fez/eserv/codr:559/RUETD00307.pdf.

66. Asher, J. J. (2009). *The Total Physical Response* (TPR): *Review of the Evidence*, May. Retrieved from http://www.tpr-world.com/review_evidence.pdf.

67. Schoepp, K. (2001). "Reasons for Using Songs in the ESL/EFL classroom." *The Internet TESL Journal* VII(2). Retrieved from http://iteslj.org/Articles/Schoepp-Songs.html.

68. Li, X. and Brand, M. (2009). "Effectiveness of Music on Vocabulary Acquisition, Language Usage, and Meaning for Mainland Chinese ESL Learners." *Contributions to Music Education*, 36(1), 73–84. Retrieved from http://krpb.pbworks.com/f/music-esl.pdf.

69. Jensen, E. (2001). "Music Tickles the Reward Centers in the Brain," *Brain-Based Jensen Learning*, June 1. Retrieved from http://www.jensenlearning.com/news/music-tickles-the-reward-centers-in-the-brain/brain-based-learning.

70. Graham, C. (2010). "How to Create a Jazz Chant," *Teaching Village*, May 23. Retrieved from http://www.teachingvillage.org/2010/05/23/how-to-create-a-jazz-chant-by-carolyn-graham.

71. Ferlazzo, L. (2011). "The Best Sites (and Videos) for Learning about Jazz Chants," July 28. Retrieved from http://larryferlazzo.edublogs.org.

72. Tang, F. and Loyet, D. (2003). "Celebrating Twenty-Five Years of Jazz Chants," *Idiom*, Fall. Retrieved from http://www.nystesol.org/pub/idiom_archive/idiom_fall2003.html.

73. Wu, S.-Y. (2008). "Effective Activities for Teaching English Idioms to EFL Learners," *The Internet TESL Journal* XIV(3). Retrieved from http://iteslj.org/Techniques/Wu-TeachingIdioms.html.

74. Ferlazzo, L. (2011). "How We Made an Excellent Speaking Activity Even Better," April 11. Retrieved from http://larryferlazzo.edublogs.org.

75. Nation, P. (2007). "The Four Strands." *Innovation in Language Teaching*, 1(1), 1–12. Retrieved from http://www.victoria.ac.nz/lals/staff/Publications/paul-nation/2007-Four-strands.pdf.

76. Pollard, L., Hess, N. and Herron, J. (2001). *Zero Prep for Beginners: Ready-to-Go Activities for the Language Classroom*. (Provo, UT: Alta Book Center).

77. National Center for Technology Innovation and Center for Implementing Technology in Education (2010). "Captioned Media: Literacy Support for Diverse Learners." *Reading Rockets*. Retrieved from http://www.readingrockets.org/article/35793.

78. Canning-Wilson, C. (2000). "Practical Aspects of Using Video in the Foreign Language Classroom." *The Internet TESL Journal* VI(11). Retrieved from http://iteslj.org/Articles/Canning-Video.html.

79. Canning-Wilson (n.d.). "Practical Aspects of Using Video in the Foreign Language Classroom"; Williams, R. T. and Lutes, P. (n.d.). *Using Video in the ESL Classroom*. Retrieved from http://www.takamatsu-u.ac.jp/library/06_gakunaisyupan/kiyo/no48/001-013_williams.pdf.

80. Ferlazzo, L. (2009). "Improvisation in the ESL/EFL Classroom—at Least in Mine," December 2. Retrieved from http://larryferlazzo.edublogs.org.

81. Sherman, C. (2011). *The Neuroscience of Improvisation*. The Dana Foundation, June 13. Retrieved from https://dana.org/article/the-neuroscience-of-improvisation/.

82. Forta, B. (2018). *Go Back to School with AdobeSpark! What's New with Spark for Education*, August 20. Retrieved from https://blog.adobespark.com/2018/08/20/new-for-spark-for-education.

83. Vatterott, C. (2009). *Rethinking Homework: Best Practices That Support Diverse Needs*. Alexandria, VA: ASCD; Vatterott, C. (2010). "Five Hallmarks of Good Homework," *Educational Leadership*, 68(1), 10–15. Retrieved from http://www.ascd.org/publications/educational-leadership/sept10/vol68/num01/Five-Hallmarks-of-Good-Homework.aspx.

84. Barker, E. (2010). *Barking up the Wrong Tree*, August 2. Retrieved from http://www.bakadesuyo.com/whats-an-easy-way-to-strengthen-your-relation?utm_

source=feedburner&utm_medium=feed&utm_campaign=Feed:+bakade-suyo+
(Barking+up+the+wrong+tree.

85. Sparks, S. D. (2010). "Science Grows on Acquiring New Language," *Education Week*, October 22, 2010. Retrieved from http://www.edweek.org/ew/articles/ 2010/10/22/09window_ep.h30.html?tkn=TNPFqJBHpqUPsAmtxWv1RHBwsJ n%2BT WCr%2BbC9&cmp=clp-edweek.

86. Holmes, V. L. and Moulton, M. R. (1997). "Dialogue Journals as an ESL Learning Strategy," *Journal of Adolescent and Adult Literacy,* 40(8), 616–621; see also a list at http://www.gallaudet.edu/documents/clerc/dialogue-journal-and-writing-abstracts.pdf.

87. Summak, M. S. and others (1994) *Drama Behind the Curtain: Shadow Theatre in EFL/ESL classes.* Paper presented at the Annual Meeting of the Teachers of English to Speakers of Other Languages, Baltimore, MD, March.

88. Wu, S.-Y. (2003). "Effective Activities for Teaching English Idioms to EFL Learners," *The Internet TESL Journal* XIV(3). Retrieved from http://iteslj.org/ Techniques/Wu-TeachingIdioms.html.

89. Sparks, S. D. (2011). "Studies Find Students Learn More by 'Acting out' Text." *Education Week*, July 12. Retrieved from http://www.edweek.org/ew/ articles/2011/07/13/36read.h30.html?tkn=NPPFMxdzo%2Bnoreu2xBC70BS m2Vz2KWbb BWlk&cmp=ENL-EU-NEWS1.

90. Marzano, R. J. (2009). *Cues and Questions.* Marzano Research Laboratory. Retrieved from http://www.marzanoresearch.com/research/cues_and_questions.aspx.

91. Ferlazzo, L. (2010). "The Best Posts on Helping Students Teach Their Classmates–Help Me Find More," April 22.

92. "A Conversation with FOB: What Works for Adult ESL Students." Focus on Basics 6(C), September. Retrieved from http://www.ncsall.net/?id=189.

Chapter Four

1. The legend of Juan Zanate appears in *The Harvest Birds* by Blanca López de Mariscal, published in 1995. The book is online at the Internet Archive: https://archive.org/details/harvestbirds0000lope

2. Peregoy, S. F. and Boyle, O. (2008). *Reading, Writing, and Learning in ESL.* (Boston: Pearson Education), 93.

3. "Acquiring Power Inspires People to Take Risks, Act, According to Stanford Business School Research," (2009). January 23. Retrieved from http://www. reuters.com/article/2009/01/23/idUS128822+23-Jan-2009+BW20090123; Fast, N. J., Gruenfeld, D. H., Sivanathan, N. and Galinsky, A. D. (2008). "The Thought of Acquiring Power Motivates People to Act." December 1. Retrieved from http://www.hci.org/lib/thought-acquiring-power-motivates-people-act.

Chapter Five

1. "Parable of the Gem in the Robe." (n.d.). Retrieved from http://www.gakkaionline.net/kids/gem.html.

2. Shanahan, T. (2021). "What Does it Take to Teaching Inferencing?" Shanahan on Literacy, August 7. Retrieved from http://www.shanahanonliteracy.com/blog/what-does-it-take-to-teach-inferencing#sthash.hEk0e1AZ.4fCNDeGM.dpbs.

3. Krashen, S. and Mason, B. (2017). "Sustained Silent Reading in Foreign Language Education: An Update." *Turkish Online Journal of English Language Teaching*, 2(2), 70–73. Retrieved from http://www.benikomason.net/content/articles/sustained_silent_reading_in_foreign_language_edcucation_an_update.pdf; Swanson, E., Stevens, E. A., Scammacca, N. K., Capin, P., Stewart, A. A. and Austin, C. R. (2017). "The Impact of Tier 1 Reading Instruction on Reading Outcomes for Students in Grades 4–12: A Meta-analysis." *Reading and Writing*, 30, 1639–1665. Retrieved from https://link.springer.com/article/10.1007%2Fs11145-017-9743-3.

4. Latham, G. P. and Locke, E. A. (2006). "Enhancing the Benefits and Overcoming the Pitfalls of Goal Setting." *Organizational Dynamics*, 35(4), 332–340.

5. "Common Core State Standards for English Language Arts & Literacy in History/Social Studies, Science, and Technical Subjects": Appendix A (n.d.). p. 33. Retrieved from http://www.corestandards.org/assets/Appendix_A.pdf.

6. Gallagher, M., Barber, A. T., Beck, J. S. and Buehl, M. M. (2019). "Academic Vocabulary: Explicit and Incidental Instruction for Students of Diverse Language Backgrounds," *Reading & Writing Quarterly*, 35(2), 3. Retrieved from https://www.tandfonline.com/doi/abs/10.1080/10573569.2018.1510796?af=R&journalCode=urwl20.

7. Ferlazzo, L. (2011). "The Best Resources on Students Using Gestures and Physical Movement to Help with Learning," June 2. Retrieved from http://larryferlazzo.edublogs.org.

8. Marzano, R. J. (2004). *Building Background Knowledge for Academic Achievement: Research on What Works in Schools*. Alexandria, VA: ASCD.

9. Marzano. *Building Background Knowledge for Academic Achievement*, 97.

10. Jensen, E. (2000). *Brain-Based Learning*. (San Diego: Brain Store).

11. NSW Centre for Effective Reading, *Vocabulary—Pre-Teaching* (n.d.). Retrieved from https://cer.schools.nsw.gov.au/content/dam/doe/sws/schools/c/cer/localcontent/pre-teach_vocab.pdf.

12. Drucker, M. J. (2003). "What Reading Teachers Should Know about ESL Learners." *The Reading Teacher*, 57(1), 22–29. Retrieved from http://read4343.pbworks.com/f/Drucker.pdf, 27.

13. "What We Think We Know—but Might Not—Pushes Us to Learn More." *EurekAlert!* Retrieved from https://www.eurekalert.org/pub_releases/2019-05/uoc--wwt052319.php.

14. Farr, R. and Conner, J. (2004). "Using Think-Alouds to Improve Reading Comprehension." *Reading Rockets.* Retrieved from http://www.readingrockets.org/article/102.

15. Carrubba, C. (n.d.). *Round Robin Reading: Is There Justification for Its Use or Are There Better Alternatives Available for Oral Reading Instruction?* Williamsburg, VA: College of William and Mary, College of Education, Curriculum, and Instruction. Retrieved from http://tvo.wikispaces.com/file/view/justify+RRR.pdf.

16. Calet, N., Gutiérrez-Palma, N. and Defior, S. (2017). "Effects of Fluency Training on Reading Competence in Primary School Children: The Role of Prosody," *Learning and Instruction,* 52, 59–68. Retrieved from https://www.sciencedirect.com/science/article/abs/pii/S0959475217302530?via%3Dihub.

17. Rasinski, T. V. (2004). *Assessing Reading Fluency.* Honolulu: Pacific Resources for Education and Learning. Retrieved from http://www.prel.org/products/re _/assessing-fluency.pdf, 4.

18. Krashen, S. (2011). "Reach out and Read (Aloud)," *Language Magazine,* December. Retrieved from http://languagemagazine.com/?page_id=2688.

19. Billings, E. and Walqui, A. (n.d.). "De-Mystifying Complex Texts: What are 'Complex' Tasks and How Can We Ensure ELLs/MLLs Can Access Them?," 1. Retrieved from http://www.nysed.gov/common/nysed/files/programs/bilingual-ed/de-mystifying_complex_texts-2.pdf.

20. Mohr K. A. J. and Mohr, E. S. (n.d.). *Extending English Language Learners' Classroom Interactions Using the Response Protocol.* ¡Colorín Colorado! Retrieved from https://www.colorincolorado.org/article/extending-english-language-learners-classroom-interactions-using-response-protocol.

21. Heritage, M., Walqui, A. and Linquanti, R. (2015). *English Language Learners and the New Standards: Developing Language, Content Knowledge, and Analytic Practices in the Classroom.* (Cambridge: Harvard Education Press), 44.

22. Pimental, S. (2020). "The Immense Potential of English Learners and Their Realization of College and Career Readiness," in *The SAT® Suite and Classroom Practice: English Language Arts/Literacy,* Patterson, J. (ed.). (New York: College Board), 137.

23. "Selected Research on Providing English Language Learners Access to College-and Career-Ready, Grade-Level Instruction in Core Academic Classes," (n.d.). Retrieved from https://achievethecore.org/content/upload/Selected%20Research%20on%20Providing%20English%20Language%20Learners%20%20Access%20to%20College-%20and%20Career-Ready%20Grade-Level%20Instruction%20in%20Core%20Academic%20Classes.pdf.

24. Wright, T. S. and Cervetti, G. N. (2017). "A Systematic Review of the Research on Vocabulary Instruction That Impacts Text Comprehension," *Reading Research Quarterly*, 52(2), 203–226. Retrieved from https://ila.onlinelibrary.wiley.com/doi/abs/10.1002/rrq.163.

25. Lee, S. H. (2008). "Beyond Reading and Proficiency Assessment: The Rational Cloze Procedure as Stimulus for Integrated Reading, Writing, and Vocabulary Instruction and Teacher-Student Interaction in ESL," *System*, 36(4), 642–660. Retrieved from https://www.sciencedirect.com/science/article/abs/pii/S0346251X08000687?via%3Dihub.

26. Willis, J. (2006). *Research-Based Strategies to Ignite Student Learning*. (Alexandria, VA: ASCD), 33.

27. Graham, S. and Perin, D. (2007). *Writing Next: Effective Strategies to Improve Writing of Adolescents in Middle and High Schools—A Report to the Carnegie Corporation of New York*. Washington, DC: Alliance for Excellent Education, 20. Retrieved from https://media.carnegie.org/filer_public/3c/f5/3cf58727-34f4-4140-a014-723a00ac56f7/ccny_report_2007_writing.pdf.

28. Bunch, G. C., Kibler, A. and Pimentel, S. *Realizing Opportunities for English Learners in the Common Core English Language Arts and Disciplinary Literacy Standards*. Understanding Language, Stanford University, 6. Retrieved from https://www.semanticscholar.org/paper/Realizing-Opportunities-for-English-Learners-in-the-Bunch-Kibler/d14d3421edd41c6ccb6f33c7dfb44fece12021d0

29. Lemov, D. (2015). "Dylan Williams Advises: Forget the Rubric; Use Work Samples Instead," August 10. Retrieved from https://teachlikeachampion.com/blog/dylan-wiliam-advises-forget-rubric-use-work-samples-instead/.

30. Warwick, P., Stephenson, P., Webster, J. and Bourne, J. (2003). "Developing Pupils' Written Expression of Procedural Understanding Through the Use of Writing Frames in Science: Findings from a Case Study Approach." *International Journal of Science Education*, 25(2), 173–192. Retrieved from https://www.tandfonline.com/doi/abs/10.1080/09500690210163251.

31. Carthew, M. (2015). "An Investigation Into the Use of Writing Frames and Writing Structures to Overcome Boys' Reluctance to Write in Geography Lessons," *The STeP Journal*, 2(4), 17–37. Retrieved from https://ojs.cumbria.ac.uk/index.php/step/article/view/271/.

32. Ferlazzo, L. (2016). "The Best Scaffolded Writing Frames for Students," December 1. Retrieved from https://larryferlazzo.edublogs.org/2016/12/01/the-best-scaffolded-writing-frames-for-students/.

33. Warwick, Stephenson, Webster, and Bourne, "Developing Pupils' Written Expression"; Carthew, "An Investigation Into the Use."

34. George, S. G. K. (2011). *Academic Writing Strategies for Secondary ELLs in Social Studies*. Unpublished master's thesis, Hamline University, St. Paul,

Minnesota; Reyes, Jr., J. P. (2015). *The Impact of Sentence Frames on Student Readers Workshop Responses.* Unpublished master's thesis, Hamline University, St. Paul, Minnesota; Ferlazzo, L. and Hull Sypnieski, K. (2018). *The ELL Teacher's Toolbox: Hundreds of Practical Ideas to Support Your Students.* (San Francisco: Jossey-Bass), 152.

35. Leon, C., Montemagno, M. and The Learning Network (2018). "How to Use Interesting Photos to Help Students Become Better Writers," *The New York Times*, March 8. Retrieved from https://www.nytimes.com/2018/03/08/learning/lesson-plans/reader-idea-how-to-use-interesting-photos-to-help-students-become-better-writers.html.

36. Graham and Perin, *Writing Next.*

37. Amabile, T. M. and Kramer, S. J. (2011). "The Power of Small Wins," *Harvard Business Review*. Retrieved from https://hbr.org/2011/05/the-power-of-small-wins.

38. Almurashi, W. A. (2016). "The Effective Use of YouTube Videos for Teaching English Language in Classrooms as Supplementary Material at Taibah University in Alula." *International Journal of English Language and Linguistics Research*, 4(3), 32–47. Retrieved from https://www.eajournals.org/wp-content/uploads/The-Effective-Use-of-Youtube-Videos-for-Teaching-English-Language-in-Classrooms-as-Supplementary-Material-at-Taibah-University-in-Alula.pdf; Morat, B. N., Shaari, A. and Abidin, M. J. Z. *Facilitating ESL Learning Using YouTube: Learners' Motivational Experiences.* Retrieved from http://ijeisr.net/Journal/Vol-1-No-1-Isu-01.pdf.

39. Zúñiga, A. T. (2020). "Take English Learning Online," *Language Magazine*, June 22. Retrieved from https://www.languagemagazine.com/2020/06/22/taking-english-learning-online/?ref=eltbuzz.

40. Nation, P. (2007)."The Four Strands." *Innovation in Language Teaching*, 1(1), 1–12. Retrieved from http://www.victoria.ac.nz/lals/staff/Publications/paul-nation/2007-Four-strands.pdf.

41. Cubilo, J., Vandergrift, L. and Goh, C. C. M. (2014). "2012: Teaching and Learning Second Language Listening: Metacognition in Action," *Applied Linguistics*, 35(2), 224–226. Retrieved from https://academic.oup.com/applij/article-abstract/35/2/224/192218?redirectedFrom=fulltex t

42. Krakauer, J. (1999). *Into Thin Air: A Personal Account of the Mt. Everest Disaster.* (New York: Anchor Books/Doubleday).

43. Marzano, R. J. (2001). *Classroom Instruction That Works.* Denver: McREL, 73.

44. *Project Zero's Thinking Routine Box.* (n.d.). Harvard Graduate School of Education. Retrieved from https://pz.harvard.edu/thinking-routines.

45. Ferlazzo, L. (2011). *Helping Students Motivate Themselves: Practical Answers to Classroom Challenges.* (Larchmont, NY: Eye on Education).

Chapter Six

1. This is a retelling of "Antlers," a version of Aesop's fable as it appears in "Wisdom Tales" from *Around the World* by Heather Forest, published in 1996. The book is online at the Internet Archive: https://archive.org/details/wisdomtales froma0000fore.

2. Spycher, P., González-Howard, M. and August, D. (2020). "Content and Language Instruction in Middle and High School: Promoting Educational Equity and Achievement Through Access and Meaningful Engagement, in *Improving Education for Multilingual and English Learner Students*, California Department of Education, (eds). Sacramento, CA: California Department of Education, 364.

3. Peregoy, S. F. and Boyle, O. (2008). *Reading, Writing, and Learning in ESL.* (Boston: Pearson Education), 94–95.

4. Shanahan, T. (2013). "Letting the Text Take Center Stage: How the Common Core State Standards Will Transform English Language Arts Instruction." *American Educator,* Fall, 43.

5. Rea, S. (2015). "New Information is Easier to Learn When Composed of Familiar Elements." Carnegie Mellon News, August 13. Retrieved from https://www.cmu.edu/news/stories/archives/2015/august/reder-memory-learning.html.

6. Dresser, N. (1994). *I Felt Like I Was from Another Planet: Writing from Personal Experience.* (Boston: Addison Wesley).

7. Mary, M. L. and Gavin, L. (2018). "Review of 'When Being Overweight Is a Health Problem.'" Kids Health. Retrieved from http://kidshealth.org. https://kidshealth.org/en/teens/obesity.html.

8. Johnson, M. D. (2020). "Planning in L1 and L2 Writing: Working Memory, Process, and Product." *Language Teaching,* 53(4),3. Retrieved from https://www.cambridge.org/core/journals/language-teaching/article/abs/planning-in-l1-and-l2-writing-working-memory-process-and-product/BD24FCB72EE28CB57AC3EFB4BCFCC6D3.

9. DiSalvo, D. (2010). "When You Expect Rapid Feedback, the Fire to Perform Gets Hotter." *Neuronarrative*, March 11. Retrieved from http://neuronarrative.wordpress.com/2010/03/11/when-you-expect-rapid-feedback-the-fire-to-perform-gets-hotter.

10. Mulligan, C. and Garofalo, R. (2011). "A Collaborative Writing Approach: Methodology and Student Assessment." *The Language Teacher*, 35(3), 5–10. Retrieved from https://jalt-publications.org/files/pdf-article/art1_13.pdf.

11. "Learning from Peers' Strengths." (2016). *Edutopia*, November 1. Retrieved from https://www.edutopia.org/practice/critique-protocol-helping-students-produce-high-quality-work.

12. Rodier, A. (2000). "A Cure for Writer's Block: Writing for Real Audiences." *The Quarterly*, 22(2). Retrieved from http://www.nwp.org/cs/public/print/nwp_au /489.

13. Ferlazzo, L. and Hammond, L. (2009). *Building Parent Engagement in Schools*. (Santa Barbara, CA: Linworth).

Chapter Seven

1. The story of Nasruddin and his key appears in *Wisdom Tales from Around the World* by Heather Forest, published in 1996. The book is online at the Internet Archive: https://archive.org/details/wisdomtalesfroma0000fore

2. L. Ferlazzo, *English Language Learners: Strategies That Work* (Columbus, OH: Linworth, 2010).

3. Fairbairn S. and Jones-Vo, S. (2010). *Differentiating Instruction and Assessment for English Language Learners: A Guide for K–12 Teachers*. Philadelphia: Caslon; Haynes, J. and Zacarian, D. (2010). *Teaching English Language Learners: Across the Content Areas*. (Alexandria, VA: ASCD).

4. Krashen, S. D. (1981). *Principles and Practice in Second Language Acquisition*. (Upper Saddle River, NJ: Prentice-Hall), 6.

5. Marzano, R. J. (2001). "Relating to Students: It's What You Do That Counts." *Educational Leadership*, 68(6), 82–83. Retrieved from http://www.ascd.org/publications/educational-leadership/mar11/vol68/num06/Relating-to-Students@-It's-What-You-Do-That-Counts.aspx.

6. Willis, J. (2006). *Research-Based Strategies to Ignite Student Learning*. (Alexandria, VA: ASCD).

7. California Department of Education (2010). *Improving Education for English Learners: Research-Based Approaches*. Sacramento, CA: California Department of Education. Retrieved from http://www.cal.org/resources/pubs/improving-education-for-english-learners.html.

8. Caine, G. and Caine, R. N. (1992). *Making Connections: Teaching and the Human Brain*. (Menlo Park, CA: Addison Wesley).

9. Bruner, J. (1992). *Acts of Meaning*. (Cambridge, MA: Harvard College).

10. *Into the Book: Strategies for Learning* (n.d.). Retrieved from http://reading.ecb.org/teacher/priorknowledge/pk_research.html.

11. Ferlazzo, L. *English Language Learners*.

12. Ferlazzo, L. (2015). "Strategies for Helping Students Motivate Themselves." *Edutopia*, March 25. Retrieved from https://www.edutopia.org/blog/strategies-helping-students-motivate-themselves-larry-ferlazzo.

13. Deci, E. L. (1995). *Why We Do What We Do*. (New York: Penguin Books).

14. Eskreis-Winkler, L. (2021). "Oops! Why You Don't Learn from Failure." Character Lab. May 2. Retrieved from https://characterlab.org/tips-of-the-week/oops/.

15. Lemov, D. (2015). "Dylan Williams Advises: Forget the Rubric; Use Work Samples Instead," August 10. Retrieved from https://teachlikeachampion.com/blog/dylan-wiliam-advises-forget-rubric-use-work-samples-instead/.

16. Ferlazzo, L. (2017). "Here are the Ten Downloadable Graphic Organizers I Use with ELL Beginners to Write a Story," February 22. Retrieved from https://larryferlazzo.edublogs.org/2017/02/22/here-are-the-ten-downloadable-graphic-organizers-i-use-with-ell-beginners-to-write-a-story/.

17. Ferlazzo, L. (2010). "The Best Resources for Learning how to Give Feedback to Students," November 10. Retrieved from https://larryferlazzo.edublogs.org/2010/11/10/the-best-resources-for-learning-how-to-best-give-feedback-to-students/.

18. Ferlazzo, L. (2011). "The Best Posts on the Basics of Small Groups in the Classroom," September 18. Retrieved from https://larryferlazzo.edublogs.org/2011/09/18/my-best-posts-on-the-basics-of-small-groups-in-the-classroom/.

19. Ferlazzo, L. (2011). "The Best Resources on the Importance of Building Positive Relationships with Students," March 8. Retrieved from https://larryferlazzo.edublogs.org/2011/03/08/the-best-resources-on-the-importance-of-building-positive-relationships-with-students/.

20. Ferlazzo, L. (2017). "The Best Ideas for Helping Students Connect Lessons to Their Interests & the World," December 9. Retrieved from https://larryferlazzo.edublogs.org/2017/12/09/the-best-ideas-for-helping-students-connect-lessons-to-their-interests-the-world/.

21. Rausch, A. S. (2000). "Language Learning Strategies Instruction and Language Use Applied to Foreign Language Reading and Writing: A Simplified 'Menu' Approach." *Literacy Across Cultures*, 4(1). Retrieved from http://www2.aasa.ac.jp/~dcdycus/LAC2000/rausch.htm.

22. Glenn, D. (2010). "Carol Dweck's Attitude: It's Not about How Smart You Are." *The Chronicle of Higher Education*, May 9. Retrieved from http://chronicle.com/article/Carol-Dwecks-Attitude/65405.

23. Peregoy, S. F. and Boyle, O. (2008). *Reading, Writing, and Learning in ESL.* (Boston: Pearson Education), 357.

24. Ferlazzo, L. (2012). "The Best Posts on Helping Students Teach Their Classmates – Help Me Find More," April 22. Retrieved from https://larryferlazzo.edublogs.org/2012/04/22/the-best-posts-on-helping-students-teach-their-classmates-help-me-find-more/.

25. Fitzgerald, M. A., Orey, M. and Branch, R. M. (2004). *Educational Media and Technology Yearbook,* 29. Westport, CT: Libraries Unlimited. Retrieved from http://books.google.com, 132.

26. Marzano, R. J. (n.d.). *Cooperative Learning.* Retrieved from http://www.marzano research.com/research/strategy_cooperative_learning.aspx?utm_source= twitterfeed&utm_medium=twitter; Saville, B. K. (2000). "Using Evidence-Based Teaching Methods to Improve Education," October 21. Retrieved from https:// tle.wisc.edu/node/1045.

27. Peregoy and Boyle, *Reading, Writing, and Learning in ESL.*

28. Smith, M. (2020). "Why Reading Aloud Leads to Better Recall," January 31. Retrieved from https://theemotionallearner.com/2020/01/31/why-reading-aloud-leads-to-better-recall/; Ferlazzo, L. (2020). "The Best Posts About Value of Oral Reading in Partners for ELLs & Others," April 13. Retrieved from https:// larryferlazzo.edublogs.org/2020/04/13/the-value-of-oral-reading-in-partners-for-ells-others/.

29. Goldenberg, C. (2008). "Teaching English Language Learners: What the Research Does—and Does Not—Say." *American Educator*, Summer, 8–23, 42–44. Retrieved from http://www.aft.org/pdfs/americaneducator/summer2008/goldenberg.pdf.

30. Goldenberg, "Teaching English Language Learners."

31. Goldenberg, "Teaching English Language Learners."

32. Goldenberg, "Teaching English Language Learners."

33. California Department of Education (2010). *Improving Education for English Learners: Research-Based Approaches.* (Sacramento, CA: California Department of Education). Retrieved from http://www.cal.org/resources/pubs/improving-education-for-english-learners.html.

34. Billings, E. and Walqui, A. (n.d.). "Topic Brief 3: De-Mystifying Complex Texts: What are 'Complex' Texts and How Can We Ensure ELLs and MLs Can Access Them?". *Bilingual Education & English as a New Language*, New York State Education Department. Retrieved from http://www.nysed.gov/bilingual-ed/topic-brief-3-de-mystifying-complex-texts-what-are-complex-texts-and-how-can-we-ensure.

35. Bifield, J. (2019). "Message Abundancy—Amplify Don't Simplify the Curriculum." *EAL in the Daylight*, June 6. Retrieved from https://ealdaylight.com/2019/06/06/message-abundancy-amplify-dont-simplify-the-curriculum/.

36. Loftus, P. (2016). "More Research Concludes Nearly All Students Find Closed Captions Helpful for Learning." 3PlayMedia, December 20. Retrieved from https://www.3playmedia.com/blog/more-research-concludes-nearly-all-students-find-closed-captions-helpful-for-learning/; "Captions for Literacy," (n.d.). Retrieved from http://captionsforliteracy.org/learn.php; Kerr, P. (2020). "Questions About Subtitles and Language Learning." Adaptive Learning in ELT,

August 28. Retrieved from https://adaptivelearninginelt.wordpress.com/2020/08/28/questions-about-subtitles-and-language-learning/.

37. Strauss, V. (2021). "The Kind of Teaching Kids Need Right Now." *The Washington Post*, June 2. Retrieved from https://www.washingtonpost.com/education/2021/06/02/the-kind-of-teaching-kids-need-right-now/.

Chapter Eight

1. Eskicioglu, L. (2001). "Building a Minaret". Retrieved from http://www.read literature.com/h010512.htm.

2. "English Language Arts Standards >> History/Social Studies >> Grade 9-10." (n.d.). Common Core State Standards Initiative. Retrieved from http://www .corestandards.org/ELA-Literacy/RH/9-10/.

3. Griffiths, C. (2008). ed. *Lessons from Good Language Learners*. Cambridge: Cambridge University Press.

4. Percoco, J. (1998). *A Passion for the Past*. (Portsmouth, NH: Heinemann), 33.

5. Szpara, M. Y. and Ahmad, I. (2006).*Making Social Studies Meaningful for ELL Students: Content and Pedagogy in Mainstream Secondary School Classrooms*. Retrieved from http://www.usca.edu/essays/vol162006/ahmad.pdf.

Chapter Nine

1. This is a retelling of "The Birds in the Tree," a Buddhist jataka tale (birth story) that you can find in Tiny Tales from India by Laura Gibbs, online at India. LauraGibbs.net.

2. Seidlitz J. and Perryman, B. (2010). *7 Steps to a Language-Rich Interactive Classroom.* (San Clemente, CA: Canter Press).

3. Feldman S. and Flores Malagon, V.(2017). *Unlocking Learning: Science as a Level for English Learner Equity*. (Oakland, CA: The Education Trust-West).

4. Zwiers, J. (2008). *Building Academic Language: Essential Practices for Content Classrooms, Grades 5-12.* (San Francisco, CA: Jossey-Bass), 85–86.

5. Fleenor, S. and Beene, T. (2019). *Teaching Science to ELs*. (San Clemente, CA: Canterbury Press), 66.

6. Thakur V. S. and Al-Mahrooqi, R. (2015). "Orienting ESL/EFL Students Towards Critical Thinking Through Pictorial Inferences and Elucidation: A Fruitful Pedagogic Approach." *English Language Teaching*, 8(2),126–133.

7. Turkan S. and Liu, O. (2012). "Differential Performance by English Language Learners on an Inquiry-Based Science Assessment," *International Journal of Science Education,* 34(12), 2343–2369.

8. Nicholson, D. W. (2016). *Philosophy of Education in Action: An Inquiry-Based Approach.* (New York: Routledge).

9. Rau, M. A. (2017). "Conditions for the Effectiveness of Multiple Visual Representations in Enhancing STEM Learning," *Educational Psychology Review,* 29,723.

10. Fleenor and Beene, *Teaching Science,* 44.

11. Fleenor and Beene, *Teaching Science,* 53.

12. Seidlitz and Perryman, *7 Steps.*

13. Rogers, M. L. (2016). *The use of Reflective Practices in Applying Strategies Learned Through Professional Development in Social Studies Instruction.* Unpublished dissertation, Nova Southeastern University, Fort Lauderdale, FL.

14. Estrella, G., Au, J., Jaeggi, S. M. and Collins, P. (2018). "Is Inquiry Science Instruction Effective for English Language Learners? A Meta-Analytic Review," *AERA Open,* 4(2),1–23.

15. Fleenor and Beene, *Teaching Science,* 50.

16. Gomez Zwiep, S. and Straits, W. J. (2013). "Inquiry Science: The Gateway to English Language Proficiency." *Journal of Science Teacher Education,* 24(8), 1315–1331.

17. Ardasheva, Y. and Tretter, T. R. (2017). "Developing Science-Specific, Technical Vocabulary of High School Newcomer English Learners," *International Journal of Bilingual Education and Bilingualism,* 20(3), 252–271.

18. Ardasheva, Y., Newcomer, S. N., Firestone, J. B. and Lamb, R. L. (2017). "Mediation in the Relationship Among El Status, Vocabulary, and Science Reading Comprehension." *Journal of Educational Research,* 110(6), 665–674.

Chapter Ten

1. This is a retelling of "Tenalirama and the Chessboard" which appears in Tiny Tales from India by Laura Gibbs, online at India.LauraGibbs.net. You can also find the story referenced in the Wikipedia article about Power of Two: https://en.wikipedia.org/wiki/Power_of_two.

2. Kenney, J. M., Hancewicz, E., Heuer, L., Metsisto, D. and Tuttle, C. L. (2005). *Literacy Strategies for Improving Mathematics Instruction* (Alexandria, VA: Association for Supervision and Curriculum Development), 23.

3. Sammons, L. (2019). *Guided Math: A Framework for Mathematics Instruction for Elementary, Middle, and High Schools,* 147–148. Retrieved from https://www.guidedmath.org/.

4. Beck, I. L., McKeown, M. G. and Kucan, L. (2013). *Bringing Words to Life: Robust Vocabulary Instruction* (New York: Guilford Press).

5. Hattie, J., Fisher, D., Frey, N., Gojak, L. M., Moore, S. D. and Mellman, W. (2016). *Visible Learning for Mathematics, Grades K-12: What Works Best to Optimize Student Learning* (Thousand Oaks, CA: Corwin Press), 122.

6. Chapman S. H., O'Connor, C. and Anderson, N. C. *Classroom Discussions: Using Math Talk in Elementary Classrooms*. Math Solutions, 6. Retrieved from https://mathsolutions.com/uncategorized/classroom-discussions-using-math-talk-in-elementary-classrooms-pdf/.

7. Schütz, R. E. (2019). "Stephen Krashen's Theory of Second Language Acquisition," October. Retrieved from https://www.sk.com.br/sk-krash-english.html.

8. Pearse, M. and Walton, K. M. (2011). *Teaching Numeracy: 9 Critical Habits to Ignite Mathematical Thinking* (Thousand Oaks, CA: Corwin Press), 38.

Chapter Eleven

1. This is a retelling of "The Enchanted Cow," a folktale from Chile by Magdalena Muñoz, which you can find in John Bierhorst's Latin American Folktales, published in 2002. In that version, the protagonist is the little boy Joaquín instead of the girl Chabelita.

2. McFarland, J., Hussar, B., Zhang, J., Wang, X., Wang, K., Hein, S., Diliberti, M., Forrest Cataldi, E., Bullock Mann, F. and Barmer, A. (2019). *The Condition of Education 2019*. National Center for Education Statistics, May. Retrieved from https://nces.ed.gov/pubsearch/pubsinfo.asp?pubid=2019144.

3. Sahakyan, N. and Ryan, S. (2018). *Exploring the Long-term English Learner Population Across 15 WIDA States*. Wisconsin Center for Education Research, October. Retrieved from https://wida.wisc.edu/sites/default/files/resource/WIDA-Report-Long-Term-English-Learner-Population.pdf.

4. Hanover Research (2017). *Effective Interventions for Long-term English Learners*," July. Retrieved from https://portal.ct.gov/-/media/SDE/ESSA-Evidence-Guides/Effective_Interventions_for_Long-Term_English_Learners.

5. Hakuta, K., Butler, Y. G. and Witt, D. (2000). *How Long Does it Take Learners to Attain Proficiency?* The University of California Linguistic Minority Research Institute, Policy Report 2000–1, January. Retrieved from https://web.stanford.edu/~hakuta/Publications/(2000)%20-%20HOW%20LONG%20DOES%20IT%20TAKE%20ENGLISH%20LEARNERS%20TO%20ATTAIN%20PR.pdf.

6. American Educational Research Association, "Vanished Classmates: The Effects of Immigration Enforcement on School Enrollment." *EurekAlert!* Retrieved from https://www.eurekalert.org/news-releases/640939.

7. Haas, E. and Brown, J. E. (2019). *Supporting English Learners in the Classroom: Best Practices for Distinguishing Language Acquisition from Learning Disabilities.* (New York: Teachers College Press).

8. Olsen, L. *Meeting the Unique Needs of Long Term English Language Learners: A Guide for Educators*. National Education Association. Retrieved from https://www.laurieolsen.com/wp-content/uploads/2021/03/lo_nea_ltel_publication.pdf

9. Haesler, D. (n.d.). "Is John Talking Through His Hattie?" Retrieved from https://danhaesler.com/2014/11/17/is-john-talking-through-his-hattie/.

10. Ferlazzo, L. (2019). "Being a Mentor at Our School May Have Resulted in Improved Grades for the. . . Mentors," July 16. Retrieved from https://larryferlazzo.edublogs.org/2019/07/16/being-a-mentor-at-our-school-may-have-resulted-in-improved-grades-for-the-mentors/.

Chapter Twelve

1. This is a retelling of "Anansi and the Pea," a tale from Jamaica which you can find in Tiny Tales of Anansi, online at Anansi.LauraGibbs.net.

2. National Center for Education Statistics (2021). *English Language Learners in Public Schools*, May. Retrieved from https://nces.ed.gov/programs/coe/indicator/cgf.

3. Bialik, K., Scheller, A. and Walker, K. (2018). *6 Facts About English Learners in U.S. Public Schools*. Pew Research Center, October 25. Retrieved from https://www.pewresearch.org/fact-tank/2018/10/25/6-facts-about-english-language-learners-in-u-s-public-schools/.

4. Zong, J. and Batalova, J. (2015). *The Limited English Proficient Population in the United States in 2013*. Migration Policy Institute, July 8. Retrieved from https://www.migrationpolicy.org/article/limited-english-proficient-population-united-states.

5. Wright, W. E. (2015). *Foundations for Teaching English Language Learners: Research, Theory, Policy, and Practice*. (Philadelphia, PA: Calson, Inc).

6. Yzquierdo, M. L. (2017). *Pathways to Greatness for ELL Newcomers A Comprehensive Guide for Schools and Teachers*. (Irving, TX: Seidlitz Education, LLC), 79.

7. Seidlitz, J. and Perryman, B. (2011). *7 Steps to a Language-Rich Interactive Classroom: Research-Based Strategies for Engaging All Students*. (Irving, TX: Seidlitz Education, LLC).

Chapter Thirteen

1. This is a retelling of "The Eagle and the Beaver" from Wigwam Evenings: Sioux Folk Tales by Charles Alexander Eastman and Elaine Goodale Eastman, published in 1928. The book is online at Project Gutenberg: https://www.gutenberg.org/ebooks/28099.

2. "The Principles of Adult Learning Theory." Retrieved from https://online.rutgers.edu/blog/principles-of-adult-learning-theory/.

3. Hardman, J. C. (1999). "A Community of Learners: Cambodians in an Adult ESL Classroom". *Language Teaching Research*, 3, 145–166. Retrieved from https://journals.sagepub.com/doi/abs/10.1177/136216889900300204.

4. "Why Adults Are Learning English.

5. Chacon, S. (2018). "MIT Scientists Prove Adults Learn Language to Fluency Nearly as Well as Children." *Medium*. Retrieved from https://medium.com/@chacon/mit-scientists-Prove-adults-learn-language-to-fluency-nearly-as-well-as-children-1de888d1d45f.

6. Hardman, "A Community of Learners."

7. Magy, R. (2010). *Learner-Goal Setting*. Pearson Education. Retrieved from http://www.pearsonlongman.com/ae/emac/newsletters/RMagy_Monograph.pdf.

8. Magy, *Learner-Goal Setting*.

9. Meranus, J. (2009). "Writing SMART Goals for English Learners." *ELLevation*. Retrieved from https://ellevationeducation.com/blog/writing-smart-goals-english-learners.

Chapter Fourteen

1. "The Little Boy Who Talked to Birds" appears in The Bird Who Cleans the Wind and Other Mayan Fables by Victor Montejo, published in 1992. The English version is not available online, but the Spanish original, El Pajaro que Limpia el Mundo y Otras Fabulas Mayas, is online at the Internet Archive: https://archive.org/details/elpajaroquelimpi0000mont.

2. Salva, C. and Matis, A. (2017). *Boosting Achievement: Reaching Students with Interrupted or Minimal Education* (Irving, TX: Canter Press).

3. Haas, E. M. and Brown J. E. (2019). *Supporting English Learners in the Classroom: Best Practices for Distinguishing Language Acquisition from Learning Disabilities* (New York: Teachers College Press).

Chapter Fifteen

1. Adapted from the Liberian folktale "The Cow-Tail Switch" in The Cow-Tail Switch and Other West African Stories by Harold Courlander and George Herzog. In the original story, there are many more sons who each contribute to their father's rescue, and the youngest child is also a son. The book is available online at the Internet Archive: https://archive.org/details/cowtailswitchoth0000cour_a5o6.

2. Institute of Education Sciences, *Race and Ethnicity of Public School Teachers and Their Students* (2020). September. Retrieved from https://nces.ed.gov/pubs2020/2020103.pdf.

3. Valant, J. (2020). *The Banality of Racism in Education.* Brookings Brown Center Chalkboard, June 4. Retrieved from https://www.brookings.edu/blog/brown-center-chalkboard/2020/06/04/the-banality-of-racism-in-education/.

4. Will, M. (2020). "Teachers Are as Racially Biased as Everybody Else, Study Shows." *Education Week*, June 9. Retrieved from https://www.edweek.org/teaching-learning/teachers-are-as-racially-biased-as-everybody-else-study-shows/2020/06.

5. Ferlazzo,L. (2016). "The Best Resources About 'Culturally Responsive Teaching' & 'Culturally Sustaining Pedagogy'—Please Share More!" June 10. Retrieved from https://larryferlazzo.edublogs.org/2016/06/10/the-best-resources-about-culturally-responsive-teaching-culturally-sustaining-pedagogy-please-share-more/.

6. Ladson-Billings, G. (2014). "Culturally Relevant Pedagogy 2.0: a.k.a. the Remix." *Harvard Educational Review,* 84(1), 74–84. Retrieved from https://eric.ed.gov/?q=%22Ladson-Billings+Gloria%22&ff1=subCulturally+Relevant+Education&id=EJ1034303.

7. Gay, G. (2010). *Cultural Responsive Teaching Theory, Research, and Practice.* New York: Teachers College Press, 31.

8. Paris, D. (2012) "Culturally Sustaining Pedagogy: A Needed Change in Stance, Terminology, and Practice," *Educational Researcher,* 41(3), 93–97. Retrieved from https://journals.sagepub.com/doi/abs/10.3102/0013189x12441244.

9. Ferlazzo, L. (2017). "Author Interview: 'Culturally Sustaining Pedagogies," *Education Week*, July 6. Retrieved from https://www.edweek.org/teaching-learning/opinion-author-interview-culturally-sustaining-pedagogies/2017/07.

10. Hammond, Z. (2021). *The 180 Podcast: Zaretta Hammond: What is Culturally-Responsive Teaching?* July 15. Retrieved from https://turnaroundusa.org/the-180-podcast-zaretta-hammond-what-is-culturally-responsive-teaching/?utm_campaign=website&utm_source=twitter&utm_medium=site.

11. Hammond, L. (2014). *Culturally Responsive Teaching and the Brain: Promoting Authentic Engagement and Rigor Among Culturally and Linguistically Diverse Students.* (Thousand Oaks, CA: Corwin), 48.

12. Ferlazzo, L. (2011). "The Best Resources Showing Why We Need to be 'Data-Informed' & Not 'Data-Driven," January 28. Retrieved from https://larryferlazzo.edublogs.org/2011/01/28/the-best-resources-showing-why-we-need-to-be-data-informed-not-data-driven/.

13. Alicea, J. A. (n.d.). "Teachers in South Central LA Who Had Personal Ties to the Neighborhood Made Better Connections with Students." *The Conversation.*

Retrieved from https://theconversation.com/teachers-in-south-central-la-who-had-personal-ties-to-the-neighborhood-made-better-connections-with-students-157658.

14. Kincade, L., Cook, C. and Goerdt, A. (2020). "Meta-analysis and Common Practice Elements of Universal Approaches to Improving Student-Teacher Relationships," *Review of Educational Research,* 90(5), 710–748. Retrieved from https://journals.sagepub.com/doi/abs/10.3102/0034654320946836.

15. Terada, Y. (2019). "The Key to Effective Classroom Management," *Edutopia,* February 27. Retrieved from https://www.edutopia.org/article/key-effective-classroom-management?utm_medium=Email&utm_source=ExactTarget&utm_campaign=20190303MindShiftNewsletterSubscribers&mc_key=00Qi000001UhpKFEAZ.

16. Ferlazzo, L. (2013). "The Best Resources on the Importance of Saying 'I'm Sorry,'" October 8. Retrieved from https://larryferlazzo.edublogs.org/2013/10/08/the-best-resources-on-the-importance-of-saying-im-sorry/.

17. Rea, S. (2015). "New Information is Easier to Learn When Composed of Familiar Elements," Carnegie Mellon News, August 1. Retrieved from https://www.cmu.edu/news/stories/archives/2015/august/reder-memory-learning.html.

18. Eschevarría, J. (2005). *Teacher Skills to Support English Language Learners.* ASCD, July 1. Retrieved from https://www.ascd.org/el/articles/teacher-skills-to-support-english-language-learners.

19. Gonzalez, N., Moll, L. C. and Amanti, C. (Eds.) (2005). *Funds of Knowledge: Theorizing Practices in Households, Communities, and Classrooms.* (New York: Routledge).

20. Krastel, T. (2021). "Valuing Funds of Knowledge and Translanguaging in Emergent Bilingual Students," NWEA, May 11. Retrieved from https://www.nwea.org/blog/2021/valuing-funds-of-knowledge-and-translanguaging-in-emergent-bilingual-students/; "What is Translanguaging, Really?" May 16, 2017. Retrieved from https://www.youtube.com/watch?v=iNOtmn2UTzI.

21. Hammond, Z. (2021). "Integrating the Science of Learning and Culturally Responsive Practice," *American Educator,* Summer. Retrieved from https://www.aft.org/ae/summer2021/hammond.

22. Ferlazzo, L. (2012). "You Cannot Make a Plant Grow—You Can Provide the Conditions for Growth," June 4. Retrieved from https://larryferlazzo.edublogs.org/2012/06/04/you-cannot-make-a-plant-grow-you-can-provide-the-conditions-for-growth/.

23. Williams, M. K. (2017). "John Dewey in the 21st Century," *Journal of Inquiry & Action in Education,* 9(1), 91–102, p. 93. Retrieved from https://files.eric.ed.gov/fulltext/EJ1158258.pdf.

24. Harris, V. J. (2007). "In Praise of a Scholarly Force: Rudine Sims Bishop," *Language Arts,* 85(2), 153–159. Retrieved from https://library.ncte.org/journals/LA/issues/v85-2/6175.

25. Ferlazzo, L. and Hull Sypnieski, K. (2018). *The ELL Teacher's Toolbox: Hundreds of Practical Ideas to Support Your Students.* (San Francisco: Jossey-Bass), 152.

Chapter Sixteen

1. Heiner, H. A. (2005). "Boots and His Brothers," SurLaLune Fairy Tales. Retrieved from http://www.surlalunefairytales.com/books/norway/thornethomsen/boots brothers.html.

2. Deci, E. L. (1995). *Why We Do What We Do.* New York: Penguin Books, 10.

3. Thanasoulas, D. (2002). "Motivation and Motivating in the Foreign Language Classroom." *The Internet TESL Journal,* VIII(11). Retrieved from http://iteslj.org/Articles/Thanasoulas-Motivation.html.

4. Koda-Dallow, T. and Hobbs, M. (2005). "Personal Goal-Setting and Autonomy in Language Learning." *Supporting Independent English Language Learning in the 21st Century: Proceedings of the Independent Learning Association Conference Inaugural.* Retrieved from http://independentlearning.org/ILA/ila05/KOD 05058.pdf.

5. Ferlazzo, L. (2010). "My Best Posts on Helping Students 'Visualize Success,'" December 23, 2010. Retrieved from http://larryferlazzo.edublogs.org.

6. Dörnyei, Z. (2009). "Motivation and the Vision of Knowing a Second Language," in *IATEFL 2008: Exeter Conference Selections,* Beaven, B. (ed.). (Canterbury: IATEFL).

7. "Activities for the First Day of School," (n.d.). Facing History & Ourselves. Retrieved from https://www.facinghistory.org/resource-library/back-school-2021-building-community-connection-and-learning/activities-first-days-school.

8. White, S. V. (2010). "Exploring Perceptions About Identity Through Self-Portraits," *Edutopia,* June 24. Retrieved from https://www.edutopia.org/video/exploring-perceptions-about-identity-through-self-portraits.

9. Seton, H. (2021). "A Daily Ritual that Builds Trust and Community Among Students," *Edutopia,* January 8. Retrieved from https://www.edutopia.org/article/daily-ritual-builds-trust-and-community-among-students.

10. Ferlazzo, L. (2019). "The Best Resources for Learning How to Promote a Sense of 'Belonging' at School," August 15. Retrieved from https://larryferlazzo.edublogs.org/2019/08/15/the-best-resources-for-learning-how-to-promote-a-sense-of-belonging-at-school/.

11. Ferlazzo, L. (2016). "The Best Resources on the Importance of Correctly Pronouncing Student Names," June 11. Retrieved from https://larryferlazzo.edublogs.org/2016/06/11/the-best-resources-on-the-importance-of-correctly-pronouncing-student-names/.

12. Keller, V. and Webb, C. (2017). "Find Purpose Even in Your Most Mundane Tasks at Work," *Harvard Business Review*, March 8. Retrieved from https://hbr.org/2017/03/find-purpose-in-even-your-most-mundane-tasks-at-work?utm_campaign=hbr&utm_source=twitter&utm_medium=social.

13. Renshaw, J. (2010). "To Innovate within Concrete, Start with the Cracks," May 1. Retrieved from http://jasonrenshaw.typepad.com/jason_renshaws_web_log/2010/05/to-innovate-within-concrete-start-with-the-cracks.html.

14. Ferlazzo, L. (2011). "The Best Resources on ESL/EFL/ELL Error Correction," September 4. Retrieved from http://larryferlazzo.edublogs.org.

15. California Department of Education (2010). *Improving Education for English Learners: Research-Based Approaches*. (Sacramento, CA: California Department of Education). Retrieved from http://www.cal.org/resources/pubs/improving-education-for-english-learners.html.

16. Truscott, J. (2005). "The Continuing Problems of Oral Grammar Correcting," *The International Journal of Foreign Language Teaching*, 1(2), Spring 17–22.

17. Truscott, J. (1996). "The Case against Grammar Correction in L2 Writing Classes." *Language Learning*, 46(2), 327–369.

18. Krashen, S. D. (1981). *Second Language Acquisition and Second Language Learnin.g* Oxford: Pergamon Press. Retrieved from http://sdkrashen.com/SL_Acquisition_and_Learning/SL_Acquisition_and_Learning.pdf.

19. Dodgson, D. (2011). *Reflections of a Teacher and Learner: Tracking My Experiences as an EFL Teacher and an MA Student!* August 7. Retrieved from http://www.davedodgson.com/2011/08/rscon3-feeding-back-and-moving-forward.html.

20. Jeremy (2019). "Mistakes vs Errors—Know the Difference." The English Farm, September 28. Retrieved from https://theenglishfarm.com/blog/mistakes-vs-errors-know-difference.

21. Conti, G. (2018). "Focused Error Correctio—How You Can Make a Time-Consuming Necessity More Effective and Manageable." The Language Gym, May 17. Retrieved from https://gianfrancoconti.com/2018/05/17/focused-error-correction-how-you-can-make-a-time-consuming-necessity-more-effective-and-manageable/.

22. Conti, "Focused Error Correction."

23. Conti "Focused Error Correction"; McQuillan, J. (2019). "Error Correction is (Still) a Waste of Time," *The Backseat Linguist*, October 8. Retrieved from http://backseatlinguist.com/blog/error-correction-is-still-a-waste-of-time/.

24. Collins Writing (n.d.). "Focus Correction Areas," The Lions Share. Retrieved from https://sites.google.com/a/crfaculty.com/the-lions-share/collins-writing/focus-correction-areas; Conti, "Focused Error Correction."

25. Ferlazzo, L. (2011). "The Best Places to Find Research on Technology and Language Teaching/Learning," February 23. Retrieved from http://larry ferlazzo.edublogs.org.

26. Ferlazzo, L. (2011). *Helping Students Motivate Themselves: Practical Answers to Classroom Challenges*. (Larchmont, NY: Eye on Education).

27. "Quickstart Guide to Choice Theory,"(n.d.). Glasser Institute for Choice Theory. Retrieved from https://wglasser.com/quickstart-guide-to-choice-theory/#basic-needs.

28. Chang-Bacon, C. (2010). "Generation Interrupted: Rethinking 'Students with Interrupted Formal Education' in the Wake of a Pandemic," *Educational Researcher* 20(10), 1–10. Retrieved from https://www.academia.edu/45126448/Generation_Interrupted_Rethinking_Students_with_Interrupted_Formal_Education_SIFE_in_the_Wake_of_a_Pandemic.

29. Strauss, V. (2021). "The Kind of Teaching Kids Need Right Now," *The Washington Post*, June 2. Retrieved from https://www.washingtonpost.com/education/2021/06/02/the-kind-of-teaching-kids-need-right-now/.

30. Genesee, F.(n.d.). "The Home Language: An English Language Learner's Most Valuable Resource," *¡Colorín Colorado!* Retrieved from https://www.colorincolorado.org/article/home-language-english-language-learners-most-valuable-resource.

31. "For Kids Who Face Trauma, Good Neighbors or Teachers Can Save Their Longterm Health," (2019). *Science Daily*, September 16. Retrieved from https://www.sciencedaily.com/releases/2019/09/190916144004.htm.

32. Venet, A. S. (2019). "Role-Clarity and Boundaries for Trauma-Informed Teachers," *Educational Considerations*, 44(2), 2. Retrieved from https://newprairiepress.org/cgi/viewcontent.cgi?article=2175&context=edconsiderations.

33. Venet, "Role-Clarity and Boundaries," 4.

34. Venet, "Role-Clarity and Boundaries," 4.

35. California Department of Health Care Services (n.d.). "SB 75—Medi-Cal for All Children," Retrieved from https://www.dhcs.ca.gov/services/medi-cal/eligibility/Pages/SB75Children.aspx.

36. Artiga, S. and Diaz, M. (2019). "Health Coverage and Care of Undocumented Immigrants," July 15. Retrieved from https://www.kff.org/racial-equity-and-health-policy/issue-brief/health-coverage-and-care-of-undocumented-immigrants/.

37. Keels, M. (2018). "Support Students with Chronic Trauma," *Edutopia*, March 23. Retrieved from https://www.edutopia.org/article/supporting-students-chronic-trauma?utm_source=twitter&utm_medium=socialflow.

Chapter Seventeen

1. This is a retelling of "Koi and the Kola-Nuts," a folktale from Liberia that appears in Tales from the Story Hat by Verna Aardema, published in 1960. The book is online at the Internet Archive: https://archive.org/details/talesfrom storyha0000unse.

2. Cummins, J. (2019). "Bilingual Children's Mother Tongue: Why is it important for education?". *Sprogforum* 19,15–20. Retrieved February 12, 2019, from http://www.lavplu.eu/central/bibliografie/cummins_eng.pdf.

3. Paulsen, G. (2006). *Hatchet*. (New York: Simon & Schuster Books for Young Readers).

4. Cummins, J. and Early, M. (2015). *Big ideas for Expanding Minds: Teaching English Language Learners Across the Curriculum*. (Oakville, Ontario: Rubicon).

5. Paulsen, *Hatchet*.

6. Cummins, J. (2000). *Language, Power and Pedagogy: Bilingual Children in the Crossfire*. (Clevedon: Multilingual Matters).

7. Hammond, Z. and Jackson, Y. (2015). *Culturally Responsive Teaching and the Brain: Promoting Authentic Engagement and Rigor Among Culturally and Linguistically Diverse Students*. (Thousand Oaks, CA: Corwin).

8. Huynh, T. (2018). "Akaya in Science." *YouTube*, November 12. Retrieved from https://www.youtube.com/watch?v=VCLQZdxQ4a8.

9. Hattie, J. (2008). *Visible Learning: A Synthesis of Over 800 Meta-analyses Relating to Achievement*. (Abingdon: Routledge).

10. Garcia, O. and Kleyn, T. (2016). *Translanguaging with Multilingual Students: Learning from Classroom Moments*. (London: Taylor and Francis).

11. Thornton, C. and McKirdy, E. (201). "Japan Successfully Lands Robot Rovers on an Asteroid's Surface." CNN., September 23. Retrieved from https://edition. cnn.com/2018/09/22/asia/japan-rovers-asteroid/index.html

12. Tomlinson, C. A. (2016). *The Differentiated Classroom: Responding to the Needs of All Learners*. Boston: Pearson Education.

13. Kurzgesagt—In a Nutshell. (2014). "The Immune System Explained I—Bacteria Infection" [Video file]. *YouTube*, July 1. Retrieved from https://www.youtube. com/watch?v=zQGOcOUBi6s.

14. Tomlinson, *The Differentiated Classroom*.

15. Hattie, *Visible Learning*.

16. Mercer, N. (1995). *The Guided Construction of Knowledge: Talk Amongst Teachers and Learners*. (Clevedon: Multilingual Matters Ltd).

17. August, A., Branum-Martin, L., Cardenas-Hagan, E. and Francis, D. J. (2009). "The Impact of an Instructional Intervention on the Science and Language

Learning of Middle Grade English Language Learners." *Journal of Research on Educational Effectiveness* 2(4) 345–376; also Carlo, M. S., August, D., McLaughlin, B., Snow, C. E., Dressler, C., Lippman, D. N. and White, C. E. (2004). "Closing the Gap: Addressing the Vocabulary Needs for English Language Learners in Bilingual and Mainstream Classrooms." *Reading Research Quarterly*, 39(2), 188–215; also Liang, L. A., Peterson, C. A. and Graves, M. F. (2005). "Investigating Two Approaches to Fostering Children's Comprehension of Literature." *Reading Psychology*, 26(4–5), 387–400.

18. Cummins, J. (1994). "The Acquisition of English as a Second Language," in *Reading Instruction for ESL Students*, K. Spangenberg-Urbschat and R. Pritchard, eds. (Delaware: International Reading Association).

19. Cummins, J. "The Acquisition of English as a Second Language."

20. Yzquierdo, M. (2017). *Pathways to Greatness for ELL Newcomers: A comprehensive guide for schools and teachers.* (San Antonio: Canter Press).

21. Huynh, T. (2018). "Zheng Hong Unbalance Balance Top Subtitles." *YouTube*, November 1. Retrieved from https://www.youtube.com/watch?v=G8tlzRe4WYk.

22. Medina, J. [JoseMedinaJr89] (2018). "We must remember to be as additive as possible as we serve #emergentbilingual #students in #ESL, #EAL, #ESOL, and in #mainstream #classrooms! Every #teacher is a #language teacher! #ELL # ellchat #ELL #duallanguage #duallanguagerocks" [Tweet], October 21. Retrieved from https://twitter.com/JoseMedinaJr89/status/1054174884354551809.

23. Chow, B. (2018). *From Words to Action: A Practical Philanthropic Guide to Diversity, Equity, and Inclusion*, April 1. Retrieved from http://www.grantcraft.org/assets/content/resources/Words_to_Action-_Barbara_Chow.pdf.

Chapter Eighteen

1. "Smuggling" (n.d.). Retrieved from http://www.naqshbandi.ca/pages/print.php? id_article=403&language=English.

2. Willis, J. (2006). *Research-Based Strategies to Ignite Student Learning.* (Alexandria, VA: ASCD).

3. Marzano, R. J. (2007). *The Art and Science of Teaching.* Alexandria, VA: ASCD, 103.

4. Jacobs, G. M. and Cates, K. (1999). "Global Education in Second Language Teaching." *KATA* 1(1), 44–56. Retrieved from http://www.georgejacobs.net/EE/Global%20Issues%20in%20Second%20Language%20TeachingKATA.doc.

5. Uberman, A. (1998) "The Use of Games for Vocabulary Presentation and Revision." *English Teaching Forum*, 36(1). Retrieved from https://eric.ed.gov/?id=EJ595092

6. Marzano, *The Art and Science of Teaching*.

7. Kandybovich, S. (2018). "One-Sentence Games." *ELT-cation*, November 23. Retrieved from https://eltcation.wordpress.com/2018/11/23/one-sentence-games/.

8. Foreman, A. (n.d.). *Teaching English: Our Favourite Class Games*, Retrieved from https://padlet.com/TeachingEnglishJukebox/FavouriteClassGames.

9. Braddock, P. (n.d.). "A Five-Minute Game Where Everyone's a Winner," *Teaching English*. Retrieved from https://www.teachingenglish.org.uk/blogs/paul-braddock/a-five-minute-primary-game-where-everyones-a-winner.

10. "Quick Wins." Leo Languages, n.d. Retrieved from https://leolanguages.weebly.com/quick-wins.html.

11. Dale, J. and Geisel, N. (2019). "#EP 1—Mandarin Excellence Programme, Certifyem, Charlala, Chinese New Year and TechTalk Interview with Suzi Bewell" (podcast). #MFLTwitterati Podcast, November 13, 2019. Retrieved from https://mfltwitteratipodcast.com/.

12. Ferlazzo, L. (2021). "The Best Tools for Taking Students 'Around the World'", May 30. Retrieved from https://larryferlazzo.edublogs.org/2021/05/30/the-best-tools-for-taking-students-around-the-world/.

13. Wink, J. (2004). *Critical Pedagogy: Notes from the REAL WORLD,* 3rd ed. (Boston: Allyn & Bacon).

14. "Having Fun with Tearable Sentences." (2015). *Tecknologic*, June 14. Retrieved from https://tekhnologic.wordpress.com/2015/06/14/having-fun-with-tearable-sentences.

15. Carlson, J. (n.d.). "My #1 Ridiculously-Effective Vocab Flash Card Game for ELLs." Kid Inspired Classroom. Retrieved from https://kid-inspired.com/my-favorite-vocab-flash-card-activity/.

16. "Headline Clues." Michigan State University GEL Lab. Retrieved from http://gel.msu.edu/headlineclues/.

17. Cabal, C. (2018). "A Game of Cards to Revise Vocabulary in a Speaking Activity. Effective Engaging and No-Prep," October 8. Retrieved from https://www.cristinacabal.com/?p=9854&fbclid=IwAR1dPfJdPq9UDAt-7oPPs10yEHIjHFN5KsSGX7XDEctf1ui29wroxHs5zp0.

18. "Playing Games with Memory." (1998). *Exploratorium*. Retrieved from https://www.exploratorium.edu/memory/dont_forget/playing_games_4.html.

Chapter Nineteen

1. The story "El Secreto di Gigante" was told in Spanish by Don Genaro Fourzán, in Chihuahua, Mexico, and the English translation is by Gabriel Gabriel Cordova (master's thesis for UT Texas Western College, submitted in 1951). The stories

from Cordova's thesis are online here: http://www.g-world.org/magictales/secreto.html

2. Ferlazzo, L. (2011). "The Best Resources Showing Why We Need to Be 'Data-Informed' and Not 'Data-Driven,'" January 28. Retrieved from http://larry ferlazzo.edublogs.org.

3. Goldenberg, C. (2008). "Teaching English Language Learners: What the Research Does—and Does Not—Say." *American Educator* (Summer), 8–23, 42–4. Retrieved from http://www.aft.org/pdfs/americaneducator/summer2008/goldenberg.pdf, 20.

4. McMillan, J. H. and Hearn, J. "Assessment: The Key to Stronger Student Motivation and Higher Achievement." https://files.eric.ed.gov/fulltext/EJ815370 .pdf Student Self-

5. Howard Research. (2009). *Kindergarten to 12th Grade English as a Second Language Literature Review Update*. Calgary, Canada: Howard Research, Oct. Retrieved from http://education.alberta.ca/media/1182477/esl_lit_review.pdf, 41.

6. Popham, J. (2011). "Formative Assessment: A Process, Not a Test." *Education Week*, February22. Retrieved from http://www.edweek.org/ew/articles/2011/02/23/21 popham.h30.html?tkn=PSCCGmSb%2FB5QkuTaRS6t7BoT2I7Q%2 FQ9Ndg Ml&cmp=clp-sb-ascd.

7. Linquanti, R. (2011). *The Road Ahead for State Assessments*. May 16. Retrieved from http://renniecenter.issuelab.org/research/listing/road_ahead_for_state _ assessments.

8. Wisconsin Center for Education Research (2009). "IDEAL Formative Assessments Rating Tool." *WIDA Focus on Formative Assessment*, 1(2),5. Retrieved from www.wida.us/get.aspx?id=215, 5.

9. Popham, "Formative Assessment," para. 7.

10. "Ongoing Assessment of Language, Literacy, and Content Learning." (n.d.) *Teaching Diverse Learners: Equity and Excellence for All*. Retrieved from http://www .alliance.brown.edu/tdl/assessment/perfassess.shtml.

11. Marzano, R. J. (2006). *Classroom Assessment and Grading That Work*. Alexandria, VA: ASCD, 11.

12. Lehrer, J. (2009). *Learning from Mistakes*. October 22. Retrieved from http://scienceblogs.com/cortex/2009/10/learning_from_mistakes.php.

13. Lemov, D. (2015). "Dylan Williams Advises: Forget the Rubric; Use Work Samples Instead," August 10. Retrieved from https://teachlikeachampion.com/blog/dylan-wiliam-advises-forget-rubric-use-work-samples-instead/.

14. Peregoy, S. F. and Boyle, O. (2008). *Reading, Writing, and Learning in ESL*. (Boston: Pearson Education), 265.

15. Ferlazzo, L. (2011). "The Best Resources for Learning about the 'Next Generation' of State Testing," June 10. Retrieved from http://larryferlazzo.edublogs.org.

16. "No Child Left Behind (NCLB) and the Assessment of English Language Learners." (2008). Colorín Colorado. Retrieved from http://www.colorin colorado.org /article/22763/?utm_source=Twitter&utm_medium=Hootsuite& utm _campaign=CCSocialMedia.

17. Center for Public Education (n.d.). *What Research Says about Testing Accommodations for ELLs.* Alexandria, VA: Center for Public Education. Retrieved from http:// www.centerforpubliceducation.org/Main-Menu/Instruction/What-research-says-about-English-language-learners-At-a-glance/What-research-says-about-testing-accommodations-for-ELLs.html.

18. "No Child Left Behind (NCLB) and the Assessment of English Language Learners."

19. Ferlazzo, L. (2014). "Response: The Grading System We Need to Have." *Education Week,* May 2. Retrieved from https://www.edweek.org/teaching-learning/opinion-response-the-grading-system-we-need-to-have/2014/05.

20. "Grade." *Online Etymology Dictionary* (n.d.). Retrieved from https://www.ety monline.com/word/grade.

21. Guskey, T. R. (2020). "Breaking Up the Grade." *Educational Leadership,* 78(1), 40–46.

22. US Department of Justice (2015). Civil Rights Division, and US Department of Education, Office for Civil Rights, *Dear Colleague Letter: English Learner Students and Limited English Proficient Parents,* January 7. Retrieved from https://www2 .ed.gov/about/offices/list/ocr/letters/colleague-el-201501.pdf.

23. Hakuta, K., Butler, Y. G. and Witt, D. (2000). *How Long Does it Take Learners to Attain Proficiency?* The University of California Linguistic Minority Research Institute, Policy Report 2000-1, January. Retrieved from https://web.stanford. edu/~hakuta/Publications/(2000)%20-%20HOW%20LONG%20DOES%20 IT%20TAKE%20ENGLISH%20LEARNERS%20TO%20ATTAIN%20PR.pdf.

24. Ferlazzo, L. (2017). "The Best Advice to Content Teachers About Supporting English Language Learners," September 8. Retrieved from https://larryferlazzo. edublogs.org/2017/09/08/the-best-advice-to-content-teachers-about-supporting-english-language-learners/.

25. Ferlazzo, L. (2018). "The Best Resources on 'Differentiated Grading' for English Language Learners, January 5. Retrieved from https://larryferlazzo.edublogs. org/2018/01/05/the-best-resources-on-differentiated-grading-for-english-language-learners/.

26. US Department of Justice (2015). Civil Rights Division, and US Department of Education, Office for Civil Rights.

27. *Marking Practices and Procedures in Secondary Schools* (2005). Los Angeles Unified School District Policy Bulletin, December 23. Retrieved from https://grading forlearning.files.wordpress.com/2015/04/bul-1353-1-pdf.pdf.

28. *Authentic Assessment* (n.d.). Indiana Department of Education, Office of English Language Learning and Migrant Education. Retrieved from http://www.msdwt .k12.in.us/msd/wp-content/uploads/2011/10/authentic_assessment.pdf.

29. US Department of Justice (2015). Civil Rights Division, and US Department of Education, Office for Civil Rights.

Chapter Twenty

1. Inspired by: *Classic Tales of Mulla Nasreddin*, retold by Houman Farzad, and translated by Diane Wilcox. (2015). (Mazda Publications).

2. Ashliman, D. L. (2009). *Nasreddin Hodja: Tales of the Turkish Trickster*, May 16. Retrieved May 12, 2020, from https://sites.pitt.edu/~dash/hodja.html#contents.

3. Heffern, R. (2011). *Nasruddin and His Donkey: Tales of the Holy Fool.* EarthBeat, February 9. Retrieved from https://www.ncronline.org/blogs/earthbeat/eco-catholic/nasruddin-and-his-donkey-tales-holy-fool.

4. Hattie, J. (2009). *Visible Learning: A Synthesis of Over 800 Meta-analyses Relating to Achievement*, (New York: Routledge).

5. "Insanity is Doing the Same Thing Over and Over Again and Expecting Different Results." (n.d.). Quote Investigator Retrieved from https://quote investigator.com/2017/03/23/same/.

6. Chick, N. (2018). "Metacognition," May 7. Retrieved from https://cft.vanderbilt .edu/guides-sub-pages/metacognition/.

7. Dweck, C. S. (2006). *Mindset: The new psychology of success.* New York: Random House.

8. Ferlazzo, L. (2017). "Here's a Reflection Exercise I Did with My Student Teacher," October 7. Retrieved May 2, 2019, from https://larryferlazzo.edublogs. org/2017/10/07/heres-a-reflection-exercise-i-did-with-my-student-teacher/ comment-page-1/.

9. Weinberger, D. (2014). *Too Big to Know: Rethinking Knowledge Now that the Facts Aren't the Facts, Experts are Everywhere, and the Smartest Person in the Room is the Room.* (New York: Basic Books).

Afterword

1. "Anansi." (n.d.). Retrieved from http://en.wikipedia.org/wiki/Anansi.

2. Shelley, M. (2014). *The Short Stories of Mary Shelley—Volume 2: "The Beginning is Always Today"*. Miniature Masterpieces.

Index

1-2-3 activity, 91–94, 200–201
4-3-2 Fluency Activity, 91, 200

A

ABC. *See* Answer, Back it
    up, Comment
ABC Writing Frames, 190, 191e, 289
    American Revolution ABC, 291e
    Metric System Argument ABC
      paragraph, 290e
    Sacramento ABC paragraph, 290e
Abstract concepts, understanding
    (challenge), 324–325
Academic language,
    building, 218–219
Academic reflection, categories,
    77–79
Academic vocabulary, 84–85
    instruction, 172–176
    knowledge, challenge, 319–321
    learning, 401
    online resources (Tech Tool), 176
    teaching/learning academic
      vocabulary, online resources
      (Tech Tool), 85
Accelerated learning, 265–266, 424
Accelerated reading
    program, usage, 38
Acquisition, learning (contrast),
    9–10
Action projects, 244

Activating schema, 383
Active learning, promotion, 388
Activities
    types, 107–114, 207–211
    visuals, usage, 308
Adding on, usage, 323
Additive model, usage, 441
Address dialogue, 129e
Adolescent English language learners
    (adolescent ELLs), 7–8
Adult ELLs
    background, impact, 358–359
    classes
      engagement, 366
      structuring, 357
    classroom, problems, 369–370
    confidence, building, 367
    English instruction, seeking
      (reasons), 357–358
    expectations, setting, 362
    goals, setting/revisiting,
      363–364
    group activities, 359e–360e
    homework, controversy, 366–367
    language acquisition, L1/literacy
      skills (impact), 360–361
    reciprocal teaching,
      encouragement, 367
    relationships/rapport,
      building, 364–365
    success
      strategies, 362–364

      success, fostering
        (method), 362–370
    support
      ELL instruction, meth-
        ods, 368–370
      online resources (Tech
        Tool), 364
      teacher flexibility/patience, 365
    teaching, 355–356
      differences, 356–361
Advanced fluency/continued language
    development (language
    development stage), 11
Affective filter, raising, 18
Affirmations/concerns,
    communication, 409
Agendas, posting, 45
Aides/professionals,
    interaction, 419–421
All About Me (All About Me Bag),
    26–27, 279
Alphabet Game, 455
American Revolution ABC, 291e
Analytical writing lesson plan
    (generation), text (usage),
    251–252, 255–258
Analytical Writing Placement
    Examination
    (AWPE), 251–252
Analytical writing, scaffolding, 189
Ancient China data set, 288e
Andragogy, 357, 358

Anecdotes, 229, 230
Animals
 online learning (Tech Tool), 158
 report, example (parrots), 157e
Animals, topics, 155–156
Annotating, usage, 438
Annotation, example, 438f
Answer, Back it up, Comment (ABC)
 assignment, usage, 400
 format, usage, 399
 paragraph, usage, 405
 response
  conversion, 400
  writing, 399
 strategy, 289
Argument
 think-aloud, 178e
 word chart, 174
 writing resources (Tech Tool), 215
Art
 online learning (Tech Tool), 159
 topics, 158–159
Artificial intelligence, usage, 93
Asher, James J., 86
Assessment, 106–107, 207, 244, 400
 cloze assessment, 465, 466, 472
 diagnostic assessment, 464–465
 fluency assessments, 466, 472
 formative assessment, 106,
  416, 424, 464
  process, 468–474
 initial assessment, 464–465,
  465e, 472, 476
 speaking/listening
  assessments, 467, 467e
 student self-assessment,
  404, 463, 471
 summative assessment, 106, 416,
  464, 474–476
 writing, usage, 464–465
Assessors, assessment, 482
Audio recording tools (Tech Tool), 467
Audio/visual (A/V)
 resources (Tech Tool), 295
 summaries, creation, 294
Autobiographical Incident Word
 Chart, 221e
Autonomy (student intrinsic
 motivation element), 270
Auto-translated subtitles,
 example, 435, 436f

B

Background knowledge,
 building, 218–219
Back to the Screen
 activity, 198
 technique, 94
Basic art supplies, usage, 36
Basic interpersonal communicative
 skills (BICS), 9, 9f
Basic phonics, 73
Bassano, Sharron, 73
Basta (game), 457
Beck, Isabel, 173
Beginning ELLs, 307
 assessment, 466e
 daily instruction, 115
Beginning ELLs, curriculum
 elements, 49, 50
Bell, Jessica, 372
Berger, Ron, 241
Bilingual dictionaries, usage, 37, 277
Bilingual lesson plan,
 advantage, 395–405
Bilingual/Multilingual Advantages
 Read-Aloud, 396e
Bilingual/Multilingual
 Survey, 397e, 399
Billings, Elsa, 179
Bilsborough, Katherine, 449
Binders/folders, usage, 36
Blank words, completion, 414
Blogging, 492
Bloom's Taxonomy
 home-language
  framework, 434–439
 home-language integration,
  435e
 online resources (Tech Tool), 209
Board games, 458–459
Body paragraphs, 237e–240e
BookCreator, 354
Books
 content, student interest, 423
 review, trailer, 172
 selection, 422–423
 student selection, 388, 390
Booksource Classroom, 38–39
Book Talks, usage, 167, 171
Boosting Achievement (Salva), 373
Boyle, Owen, 71, 124, 214
Brainpop, impact, 85, 333

Brainpop, Jr., 85
Brain sparks, usage, 384
Brainstorming, 122, 259
Brown, H.D., 76
Bruner, Jerome, 69
*Building Background Knowledge for
 Academic Achievement*
 (Marzano), 176
Buric, Pam, 386

C

Caine, Renate Nummela/
 Geoffrey, 269
Calendar data set, 138e
California Writing Project, 498
Cambourne, Brian, 76
Cameron, Peter, 494
Canavan Anderson, Nancy, 321
Capitalization, sharing result, 22
Careers
 online learning, 155
 topics, 152
Caregivers, term (usage), 23
Carlson, John, 453
Causes, usage, 225–226, 246, 248
Chants, 90
 usage, 352
Chapin, Suzanne H., 321
Chaplin, Charlie, 146
Check-ins, usage, 420
Chick, Nancy, 490
Children's Book, reading
 exercise, 206e
Chow, Barbara, 442
Claim and Evidence Image
 Analysis, 192e–195e
Classes
 assessment (academic reflection
  category), 77–78, 274
 assessment (Tech Tool), 484
 dedications, 409
 discussion, initiation, 410
 ELD student
  evaluation, 483e–484e
 enhancement, Internet (usage),
  41
 leadership team, 22, 272, 410
 multilevel classes, 415–419
 whole classes, function, 416–418
Classmates, teaching others, 112

Classrooms. *See* Science
  courtesy/calmness, display, 422
  ELL grading, 479–481
  games, 446–447, 455–457
  home languages, research, 431–434
  incentives/rewards,
      avoidance, 421–422
  library
    access, 37–39
    books, student selec-
      tion, 388, 390
  management, 421–422
  No Food in the Classroom (visual
    interpretation), 432f
  online video sites, usage (Tech
    Tool), 450
  open classroom dialogues,
    facilitation, 390
  picture sentences, 52e
  picture story, 54e
  positive-framed messages,
    usage, 422
  smartphones, usage, 191e
  technology, usage (Tech Tool), 43
  walls, usage, 40–41
Class/teacher evaluations, 34
Clines (spectrum), 110
Closed captioning, usage/
  Tech Tool, 278
Closed-ended questions, usage, 304
Closed-ended sentence stems, 306
Clothing dialogue, 134e
Clozes (fill-in-the-blank) (gap-fill), 51,
  71, 180–183, 219, 417
  assessments, 465, 472
  example, 236
  family cloze exercise, 139e–140e
  mammoths cloze, 182e
  measurements, 334
  money cloze/data set, 151e
  online creation (Tech Tool),
    183
  Persuading My Parents Cloze and
    Mimic Write exercise/
    sample, 181e, 182e
  problem-solution cloze,
    223e–224e
  sentences, 189
  Slavery cloze, 297e
  story, 119
  Tech Tool, 297

textbook passages/dialogues,
  conversion, 411
  usage, 82, 296–297
Co-conspirator, aide invitation, 420
Cognates, power, 318
Cognitive academic language
  proficiency (CALP), 9, 9f
Cognitive hooks, 385
Cognitive load, creation, 176
Cohorting, 331, 332
Cold reads, 177
Collaborative learning, 21
Collaborative stories
  online collaborative storytelling
    (Tech Tool), 73
  writing, 71–73
Collaborative writing, 75
College and Career Readiness Anchor
  Standards for English
  Language Arts, 50
College information, 130e–131e
College jigsaw, 130e
Common Core State Standards
  (CCSS), 50, 316, 319,
  321, 324–325
Communicative dictation
  activities, 67–68
Community
  theme, study, 82
  topics, 146–147
Community Board, usage, 361
Community building, usage, 409
Compelling input, usage, 4
Competence (student intrinsic
  motivation element), 270
Complex texts, scaffolding, 179–180
Computer routines
  guidelines, 45–46
Concept attainment, 69–70,
  186, 227, 249
  example, 69e
  usage, 413
Concept map
  creation, 40
  sample, 41f
Confidence, boosting, 367
Connect with English video series, 198
Conner, Jenny, 177
Constructivist visuals, 307f
Content areas, impact, 278
Content-Based ELL program, 344

Conti, Gianfranco, 413
Conversation
  "Cheat Sheet," 91, 102e–105e
  log, 99, 101e
  structured conversations, 353
Cooperative learning, 21
  activities, usage, 273, 414–415
  usefulness, 352
Co-teachers
  actions, rating, 275
  audio/video recordings,
    review, 493
  challenges, 343
  impact, 269, 394, 416
  video usage, 493
Co-teaching, 343, 419–421
  resources (Tech Tool), 421
COVID-19
  impact, 414, 415
  masks, usage, 42
  schools
    interruption, 337, 424
    return, 265
Creating (learning game), 457
Critical Pedagogy (Freire), 57–59, 385
  lesson, 138, 147–148, 152, 158–159
  lesson plan, 126
Critical thinking
  dialogues, 228, 291,
    292e–293e, 295, 296e
  promotion, 214
  questions, 229–230
  skills, development, 401
Csikszentmihalyi, Mihaly, 81
Cultural knowledge
  family/community member
    sharing, 390
  usage, 384–385, 390
Culturally responsive-sustaining
  mindset, words
    (reflection), 389–390
Culturally responsive-sustaining
  pedagogy, impact, 385
Culturally responsive-sustaining
  teaching, opportunities, 388
Culturally responsive teaching
  (CRT), 379
  defining, 380–381
  resources (Tech Tool), 391–392
Culturally sustaining pedagogy (CSP)
  resources (Tech Tool), 391–392

Culturally sustaining pedagogy (CSP), defining, 380–381
Cultural pluralism, 380
Cultures, representation, 390
Cummins, Jim, 37, 63, 269, 428, 431, 442
Curiosity gap, 83
Current events
    Tech Tool, 296
    usage, 295
Curriculum
    beginning ELLs, curriculum elements, 49, 50
    cultural responsive/sustaining characteristics, 390
    intermediate ELLs, curriculum elements, 163, 164

D

Daily Dedications (activity), 33
Dale, Joe, 449
Data-informed/data-driven information, 382, 462–463, 477
Data sets
    Ancient China data set, 288e
    calendar data set, 138e
    category poster (student sample), 247f
    "Describing Things" data set, 56e–57e
    "Describing Things" Intermediate data set, 185e–186e
    education data set, 129e–130e
    examples, 273
    Figurative Language data set, 187e–188e
    Halloween data set, 144e
    holiday data set, 142e–143e
    Hooks data set, types, 229e–231e
    money cloze/data set, 151e
    Problem-Solution Features data set, 225e–227e
    reading strategies data set, 168e–170e
    Reading Strategies data set, 63
    text data sets, 55, 63, 184–185
    time data set, 137e
Deci, Edward, 394
Deep thinking, structuring, 305–306

De-escalation strategies, familiarization, 425
Delayed dictation, 68
"Describing Myself" report, 133e
"Describing Things" data set, 56e–57e
"Describing Things" Intermediate Data Set, 185e–186e
DeTommaso, Donna, 27
Developmental Bilingual Education (DBE), 344
Dewey, John, 273, 387
Diagnostic assessment, 464–465
Dialogue Disorder (game), 449
Dialogues, 91, 132, 199, 228, 417
    address dialogue, 129e
    clothing dialogue, 134e
    conversion, 411
    critical thinking dialogues, 291, 292e–293e
    dialogue journal, 108–109
    example, 92e
    greetings/good-bye dialogue, 128e
    Halloween dialogue, 145e
    journals, usage, 418
    online dialogues/pronunciation practice (Tech Tool), 93
    open classroom dialogues, facilitation, 390
    Problem Dialogue, 231e
    Problem-Solution Matching/ Dialogue, 232e
    round-robin dialogue, 123
    Santa Claus dialogue, 144e
    textbook dialogues, personalization, 411
    three-person introduction dialogue, 127e–128e
    time dialogue, 136, 137e
    weather/temperature dialogue, 133e
Dictogloss, 67
Differentiating Instruction and Assessment for English Language Learners (Fairbairn/Jones-Vo), 266
Differentiation (tips), 280f
Digital storytelling (Tech Tool), 61
Dodgson, Dave, 413
Door Poster Project, 146
Double-period multilevel class, appearance, 416–418
Dresser, Norine, 219

Drill-and-kill instruction method, 73
Dual Language Bilingual Education (Two-Way Immersion) programs, 345
Dual language learner (DLL), 6
Duolingo, 122, 124
Dweck, Carol, 271, 490

E

Early production (language development stage), 10
Editing, usage, 241
EDPuzzle, 203
Educational technology, access (limitation), 414–415
Education data set, 129e–130e
Education Trust-West report, 302
Elementary ELLs
    bilingual program models, 344–345
    Developmental Bilingual Education (DBE), 344
    Dual Language Bilingual Education (Two-Way Immersion) programs, 345
    interaction, 339
    model classroom
        appearance, 345–347, 347f
        feel, 349–351, 351f
        sound, 347–348, 349f
    needs, differences, 342
    program models, 343–344
    program types, 342–345
    support
        instructional strategies, 352–354
        Tech Tool, 353
    supportive classrooms, 346e
    supportive instruction, core elements, 345
    Transitional Bilingual Education (TBE) programs, 344
Elementary ELs, defining, 340–341
ELL Teacher's Toolbox, The (Ferlazzo/ Sypnieski), 55, 81, 83, 267, 389
Emergent bilingual, 5–6
Emergent Multilingual Learner (EMLL), 6
Empathy Project, 386, 391

Encoding record, development, 54
End-of-quarter evaluation, 34e–35e
End-of-semester/end-of-year exam,
        usage, 476
Engagement activity, 446
English as a second language (ESL),
        6, 343, 478
English Central, 122, 124
English Immersion Models, 343
English Language Development
        (ELD), 6, 343, 478
    classes, grading, 479
    student evaluation, 483e–484e
English language learner
        (ELL) classroom
    basics, 17
    learning games, usage, 445
    relationships, building/
        strengthening
        (activities), 26–34
            online resources (Tech Tool), 35
    resources, 36–43
English language learners (ELLs), 5
    adult ELLs, 355
    assessment, 461
        principles, 462
    assets, possession, 15–16
    beginning ELLs, 49, 50
    best practices, 12–16
    confidence, building, 367
    description process, 5–7
    development, 302
    elementary ELLs, 339
    grading, 478–481
    home language, 427
    instruction, 3
    intermediate ELLs, 163, 213
    mainstream classroom usage, 265
    music sites (Tech Tool), 89
    newcomer assistance, peer mentors
        (usage), 386
    population growth, 4–5
    search engines (Tech Tool), 233
    self-confidence/risk-taking,
        building, 271
    standardized testing, 476–477
    student goals, 394–395
    teacher support (science), 312–314
    teaching opportunities, 386
    three Rs, 18
    US presence/statistics, 341f

English Language Learners
        (Ferlazzo), 266
English language learner (ELL) with
        learning differences, 371
    considerations, 372–373
    placement/scheduling,
        considerations, 375
    resources/Tech Tool, 376
    services, determination
        (considerations), 373–374
English Language Proficiency
        (ELP), 373
    levels, 11–12
English Language Proficiency
        Assessment for California
        (ELPAC) test, 334, 477
English Language Proficiency
        Assessment for the 21st
        century (ELPA21), 11, 12f
English Learner (EL), 5
    elementary ELs, defining, 340–341
    support, instructional strategies
        (usage), 320–325
English-only policies
    abandonment, 440–442
    intention/reality, contrast, 440e
English proficiency level "labels," 12f
English Spoken Here (sign), 441f
English, teaching (year-long
        schedule), 124–126
English Video Sheet, practice, 200e
Enhanced discovery, 55
Epic! for Educators, 353
Error correction, 412–414
ESL Education Games, 459
Esparza Brown, Julie, 373
"Ethnic Studies" (critical thinking
        dialogue), 296e
Every Student Succeeds Act
        (ESSA), 331, 477
Evidence-based reasoning,
        usage, 311–312
Exercise strip story, 135e
Expanding A Sentence (game), 448
Extrinsic motivation, 394

F

Facts/statistics, usage, 229, 231
Family
    cloze exercise, 139e–140e

    term, usage, 23
    topics, 138
    writing exercise, 139e
Family Literacy Project, 24, 42
Farr, Roger, 177
Feedback, 363, 385, 492
    peer feedback, 241
    sound feedback, 473
    teacher feedback, 241
Feelings, topics, 158
Ferlazzo, Frank, 211, 266, 421, 491
    family cloze exercise, 139e–140e
    LTELL recommendations,
        implementation, 331–337
    reflection activity, 491
Field trips, value, 114, 146, 150,
        155, 210–211
Figurative Language Data
        Set, 187e–188e
Fill-in-the-blank. See Clozes
Final Jeopardy, 447
"Find Someone in This Class Who…"
        scavenger hunts, 29–30
Flash cards (usage/game), 453
Fleenor, Stephen, 301
Flipgrid app, usage, 171, 353
Fluency
    advanced fluency/continued
        language development
        (language development
        stage), 11
    assessments, 466, 472
FluentKey, 203
Food, sequencing activity/topics, 148
Formative assessment, 106,
        416, 424, 464
    observation, importance, 472
    process, 468–474
    rubrics, usage, 473–474
    student conferences,
        usage, 472–473
Four Squares activity, 31–32, 32f
Four Words sheet, 99, 100e
Free Reading Time, 166–167
Free Voluntary Reading (Extensive
        Reading) (Silent Sustained
        Reading) (recreational
        reading), 38–39, 44, 61–63,
        165, 167, 415
    time, computer usage, 415
Freire, Paulo, 57, 385

Friday test (sample), 107e
Friends/fun activities, 140
Friends of the Library Program, 39

G

Gallery walks, usefulness, 207
Game of Cards, The (game), 453–455
Games. *See* Learning games
Gandhi, Mahatma, 426
Garcia, Cindy, 316
Gestures, usage, 98, 276
Getepic.com, 353
Gibbons, Pauline, 179
Goal sheets, usage, 471–472
Goals, setting, 363–364
Going to San Francisco strip story,
    exercise, 148e
Goldenberg, Claude, 46
Gonzalez, Valentina, 340
Google Assistant, usage, 26, 268
Google Classroom, usage, 409
Google Doc, usage, 438
Google Forms, usage, 482
Google Slides, usage, 72, 171,
    285, 469, 471
Google Translate
    algorithm, limitation, 435
    avoidance, 471
    dependence, reduction, 470
    usage, 408, 410, 437, 441, 464
Grading, 478
    Pass/Fail grades, application, 481
    product/process criteria, 479
    Tech Tool, 481
Graham, Carolyn, 90
Grammar
    correction, impact, 412
    lessons, conversion, 411
    usage, 413
Graphic organizers, 157f, 208, 277
    providing, ELL best practice, 15
    resources (Tech Tool), 209
    usage, 156, 233, 352, 419
    usefulness, 298–299
"Great Depression" (critical thinking
    dialogue), 292e
Greetings/good-bye dialogue, 128e
Guardians, term (usage), 23
Guess the Person Game, 132
Guided discovery, 55
Guskey, Thomas, 479

H

Haas, Eric, 373
Halloween
    data set, 144e
    dialogue, 145e
Hammond, Zaretta, 381, 385
Hands-on learning, direct instruction
    (balance), 362
Hands Up Project, 31
Hangman (game), 448
Hatchet (Paulsen), 428–429
Hattie, John, 83, 433
"Hawthorne effect," 18–19
Headline Clues (game), 453
Health
    online learning (Tech Tool), 160
    topics, 159
Helping Students Motivate Themselves
    (Ferlazzo), 211, 421
Herron, Jam, 94
Hess, Natalie, 94
"Hiroshima" (critical thinking
    dialogue), 292e–293e
Historical Head, 298–299
Holidays
    data set, 142e–143e
    exercises, 141, 142e
    online learning (Tech Tool), 145
Home, exercises, 145–146
Home language. *See* L1
Homework, 98–99, 204–205, 418
    controversy, 366–367
    online homework (Tech Tool),
        106
    options, 270
Hooks, 225–226, 228, 246, 248
    cognitive hooks, 385
Hooks Data Set, 229e–231e, 244
How-to-videos (tutorials), 198
Huynh, Tan, 428

I

"I Am" project, 27–28, 279
Identify-affirming models, 440
Idioms, 108
    online idiom practice (Tech
        Tool), 108
I Felt Like I Was from Another Planet
    (Dresser), 219, 251
Images
    analysis, 293

black-and-white image, usage, 437
Claim and Evidence Image
    Analysis, 192e–195e
Image Analysis Sheet, 293e
inferences, making (Tech
    Tool), 192
usage, 190
I'm Feeling Lucky (game), 449–450
Immersion, approach, 440
Immigration word web, 175f
Improvisation, 95–97
    online improvisational resources
        (Tech Tool), 97
Incentives, avoidance, 421–422
Independence, promotion, 214
Inductive Lesson Plan, 219,
    236, 245–249
Inductive writing, 289
Inferences, making (Tech Tool), 192
Inferencing, usage, 306–314
Infographic, creation, 279
Information gap, 83
    activities, 68
Initial assessment, 464–465,
    465e, 472, 476
Initial Needs Assessment, 363
Instructions
    drill-and-kill method, 73
    giving (ELL best practice),
        14, 98, 275
    intermediate ELLs, daily
        instruction, 213
Interactive content class resources
    (Tech Tool), 299
Interactive dictation, 67
Intermediate ELLs, 8
    curriculum, elements, 163
    daily instruction, 213
Intermediate fluency (language
    development stage), 10
International transcripts,
    evaluation, 426
Internet
    access, 99, 396, 401, 414–415, 450
    audio/video files, posting, 492
    search, 287
    service, 24
    student access, 42
    usage, 41
Interpersonal collaboration,
    promotion, 214
Into Thin Air (Krakauer), 207

Intrinsic motivation, 215, 270–271,
    394, 424
    levels, decrease, 286–287
ISL Collective, 203
I Spy (game), 451

J

Jazz Chants, concept
        (development), 90
Jigsaw, 82–84, 249, 417
    activity, 124, 152
    college jigsaw, 130e
    instructions, 272, 272e–273e, 274
    natural disasters jigsaw, 134e
    online jigsaw resources
        (Tech Tool), 84
    Sacramento Jigsaw, 82, 83e, 147
Jobs
    exercises, 153e–154e
    interview strip story, 155e
    online learning (Tech Tool), 155
    search strip story, 154e
    topics, 152
Jordan, Michael (video), 401–405
Journaling, 491–492
Journal topic, usage, 44

K

Kahoots (game), 27
Kandybovich, Svetlana, 448
Karaoke, usage, 89
Keaton, Buster, 146
Kenney, Joan M., 317
Knowledge, assessment, 463
Knowles, Malcolm, 357, 358
Know-Want-Learn (K-W-L) charts,
        111, 259, 268–269, 285–287
Krakauer, John, 207
Krashen, Stephen, 4, 10, 73, 76
    affective filter, 18
Kucan, Linda, 173

L

L1 (home language) (first language)
        (native language) (heritage
        language), 8–9. See English
        language learners
    asset, perception, 429–430

classroom research, 431–434
development,
        encouragement, 14–15
    fluency, 360–361
    framework, Bloom's taxonomy
        (relationship), 434–439
    impact, 360–361
    integration
        amount, 434f
        Bloom's taxonomy, 435e
    language literacy, 424
    proficiency, absence
        (impact), 433–434
    resources (Tech Tool), 443
    usage, validation/
        encouragement, 384
    value, mini lesson, 430–431
L2 (acquiring language), 8–9
    learner ability, self-
        monitoring, 413
Labeling Game, 447, 456
Labeling, usage, 352
Ladson-Billings, Gloria, 380
Language Experience Approach
        (LEA), 24, 70–72, 79, 419
    usage, 114, 145
    video usage, 94, 198
Languages, 302–303
    acquisition, L1/literacy skills
        (impact), 360–361
    assessment, 463
    auto-translated subtitles,
        example, 435, 436f
    development
        promotion, 214
        stages, 10–11
    frames, 323, 324e
        providing (ELL best
        practice), 15
    grammar patterns, differences, 431
    language-rich science classroom,
        challenges, 303–304
    learner lesson plan,
        qualities, 401–405
    learning
        maximization, 414–415
        tools, 452
    processes, 303
    skills, development, 372–373
    student addition, additive model
        (usage), 441

tabs, display, 436f
    working with/without, 430
Laptop work, 418
"Leadership Teams," creation,
        272, 275, 386
Leadership teams, establishment, 22
Learning. See Cooperative learning
    acceleration, 39–40
    active learning, promotion, 388
    background, impact, 358–359
    collaborative learning/cooperative
        learning, 21
    environment, building, 17
    goals, setting, 167
    negative impact, 414
    ownership, 367
    Social Emotional Learning
        (SEL), 408–410
    student content/process/
        timing, 385
    transfer, 277
Learning by doing, 273–274,
        287, 387–389
    parents, impact, 389
Learning games
    board games, 458–459
    classroom games, 446–447
    engagement activity, 446
    online learning games, 457–458
    qualities, 446–459
    speaking/listening practice
        focus, 450–452
    usage, 445
    whiteboards, usage, 447–450
Leon, Claudia, 190
Lesson plans (sample), 245–249
Library goal sheet, 166e
Limited English proficiency (LEP), 6
Linguistic knowledge, sharing,
        384–385, 390
Listening, 86, 198–199, 258–262
    assessments, 467
    elementary ELL usage, 353–354
    importance, 384
    practice, games (focus), 450–452
    practice sites (Tech Tool), 203
    skills, practice, 401
    strategies practice, 201–202
        sheet, 203e–204e
    tasks, 202
    texts, 201–202

Literacy skills, impact, 360–361
Literary Response Word Chart, 222e
Long-Term English Language
        Learners (LTELLs), 7, 8
    advisory, support class
            function, 332
    Brainpop, impact, 333
    class reflections/questions,
            defining, 335–337
    cohorting, 331, 332
    defining, 330
    monitoring, regularity, 332
    peer mentors, role, 332
    qualitative data, 335
    quantitative data, 334
    quantitative results, 334e
    recommendations,
            implementation, 331–337
    resources (Tech Tool), 337
    results, 333–335
    social/emotional learning,
            usage, 333
    support, 329, 330–331
    support class, 332–333
    warm-up activities, 333
Look Again Pictures (Olsen), 456
Loss-framed messages, avoidance, 422
Low-anxiety classroom, support, 267
Luther Burbank High School (LBHS),
        24, 185, 331
Lyrics, usage, 88–89

M

Mainstream classroom, English
        language leaders
        (presence), 265
Make A Difference Professional
        Development
        (MADPD), 494
Mammoths cloze, 182e
"Maria's Day" strip story, 149e
Martin, Tara, 171
Marzano, Robert J., 19, 76–77,
        176, 267, 446
    formative assessment key, 473
    reflection, 76
Materials
    distribution, procedures, 44–45
    student creation (games), 452–455
Mathematics (math)

abstract concepts, understanding
        (challenge), 324–325
academic vocabulary, knowledge
        (challenge), 319–321
conversations, participation
        (challenge), 321–322
EL support, instructional
        strategies (usage), 320–321
resources (Tech Tool), 325
routines, 323
science, technology, engineering,
        math (STEM) fields,
        success, 302
teaching, 315
texts, reading (challenge), 317–319
universal language,
        perception, 316, 322
Maurer, Joseph, 493
McKeown, Margaret, 173
Medi-Cal/Medicaid, usage
Medina, Jose, 442
Memory Game, 455
Memory reinforcement, 274
Mentor models, 235
Mentor texts, 186–189, 235
Messenger and Scribe (games), 451
Metacognition, 471, 490
    connection, 306
    focus, 180, 202
    importance, explanation, 183
    promotion, 449
Metacognitive awareness, 413
Metacognitive reinforcement, 236
Metacognitive strategy, 77
Metaphors, 188
Metric System Argument ABC
        paragraph, 290e
Microsoft Translator, usage, 26, 268
Micro-writing (quickwrites),
        195–196, 228
    Problems All Around Quick-
            Write, 217, 217e
Mimic writing, 181, 186–
        189, 227, 249
Mindfulness, 389–390
Mind map, translanguaging
        (example), 439f
Mini-themes, basis, 228
Mistakes/errors, usage, 413
Mixed-ability partner groups,
        interaction, 418

Modeling (ELL best practice), 12–13
Money
    borrowing strip story, 152e
    cloze/data set, 150, 151e
    exercise, 150e
    online learning (Tech Tool), 151
    sequencing activity, 150
    topics, 150
Money Strip Story, 80, 81e
"Monsy and Michelle"
    analytical writing sample,
            251–252, 253e
    pre-reading strategies, 254e
    summarization, 254e
    teacher distribution, 255
    writing prompt, 254e, 256
Montemagno, Margaret, 190
Multilevel classes, 415–419
Multilingual Advantages Read-
        Aloud, 396e
Multilingual Learner (MLL), 5
Multilingual lesson plan,
        advantages, 395–405
Multilingual Survey, 397e, 399
Multi-Tiered System of Support
        (MTSS) process, 373, 375
Music
    ELL sites (Tech Tool), 89
    online learning (Tech Tool), 159
    topics, 158–159
    usage, 88–89
My Favorite Meal exercise, 149e
My Neighborhood (exercise), 147

N

National Center for Education
        Statistics report, 340
Nation, Paul, 91, 200
Natural disasters information,
        135e
Natural disasters jigsaw, 134e
*Navigating the Common Core with English
        Language Learners* (Ferlazzo/
        Sypnieski), 11, 215
Nearpod, 203
New York Times Learning
        Network, 190
Next Generation Science Standards
        (NGSS), release, 3032
No Child Left Behind, 331, 477

No Food in the Classroom (visual interpretation), 432f
No Matter Where You Are From, I'm Glad You're My Student (sign), 442f
Nonlinguistic cues, usage (ELL best practice), 13
Nonlinguistic representations, 208
Note-taking strategies, 277

O

Observations, 229, 230
O'Connor, Catherine, 321
Odd One Out (game), 449
Olsen, Judy W., 456
On-demand writing
    practice, 244
    situations, 257
"One-Pagers," strategy/Tech Tool, 274
One-to-one device programs (Tech Tool), 415
Online annotated text, example, 437f
Online audio recording site, usage, 472
Online books
    responses (Tech Tool), 171–172
    usage (Tech Tool), 66–67
Online compare-and-contrast tools (Tech Tool), 111
Online dictation exercises (Tech Tool), 68
Online games (Tech Tool), 458
Online learning games, 457–458
Online maps/timelines, making (Tech Tool), 284–285
Online multilingual support (Tech Tool), 276
Online resources, translating (Tech Tool), 26
Online rubrics (Tech Tool), 244
Online sister classes (Tech Tool), 109
Online worksheets (Tech Tool), 456
Only Connect (BBC game show), 453
Open classroom dialogues, facilitation, 390
Open-ended questions, usage, 304
Opening bell activity, 76
Opening/ending procedures, usage, 44

Oral outlining, creation, 236
Organizing Cycle, 266, 381–390
    add-ons, 275–281
    defining, 267

P

Paraphrasing, usage, 322
Parents, involvement/engagement, 23
Parent-Teacher Association (PTA), interaction, 430–431
Parent-Teacher Home Visit Project, 24
Paris, Django, 380
Parrots, animal report (example), 157e
Partner reading, 65e
Pass/Fail grades application, 481
Past, Present, and Future chart, 110
Pattern-seeking, support, 55
Paulsen, Gary, 428–429
Peaksay, 93
Pearse, Margie, 325
Peer feedback, 241
Peer mentors, assistance, 386
Peer tutors, 418
    training (Tech Tool), 40
    value, 39–40, 278
People/things, description, 132
Peregoy, Suzanne, 71, 124, 214
Perez, Antoinette, 356
Personal stories, connections, 286
Personal thematic report, 97e–98e
    usage, 132, 136, 140–141, 146
Personification, 188
Persuading My Parents Cloze and Mimic Write
    exercise, 181e
    sample, 182f
Pets, exercise, 156e
Phantasy Quest (game), 457–458
Phonicball (game), 459
Phonics, 73–76
    basic phonics, 73
    blends, 458
    instruction, modification, 412
    practice, 74e
    practice (Tech Tool), 76
Photos
    snapping, 171
    Web usage (Tech Tool), 55–56
Pictionary (game), 455
Picture dictation, 67–68

Picture Word Inductive Model (PWIM), 51–55, 112, 184, 411
    inclusion, 125
    photo, usage (example), 51f
    usage, 146
    web phots (Tech Tool), 55–56
Picture Word Inductive Model Unit Plan, 115–119
Picture Word Inductive unit, 106
Pillars, Wendi, 279
Podcasting, 492
Pollard, Laurel, 94
Popham, W. James, 469
Portfolios
    directions, 475e
    usage, 474–475
Positive-framed messages, usage, 422
Practice essays, 228
Prepositions, usage (challenge), 318
Preproduction (language development stage) (Silent/Receptive Stage), 10
Presentations, 285–286
    Sentence Starters, 272
    "Speed Dating" presentations, 201, 243
Preview-View-Review, 275, 343, 353
Prior knowledge
    access, 268–269, 383–385
    activation, 195, 217–218, 269, 424
    providing, 424
Problem-based learning, 273
Problem, causes/effects, 237e
Problem Dialogue, 231e
Problem-posing exercise/problem-solving exercise, 57
Problems All Around Quick-Write, 217, 217e
Problem-solution, 214
    cloze, 223e–224e
    drafts, 236
    essay, teacher introduction, 246
    sample unit, 215
Problem-Solution Essay, 246
Problem-Solution Features Data Set, 225e–227e, 244
Problem-Solution Interview, 234e–235e
Problem-Solution Matching/Dialogue, 232e

Problem-Solution Peer
    Checklist, 241, 242e
Problem-Solution Sample
    Essay, 250e–251e
Problem-Solution Word
    Chart, 218, 220e
Problem-Solution Writing Frame,
    60e, 237e–238e
Problem-Solution Writing
    Prompt, 219e
Problem-Solution Writing
    Structure, 239e–240e
Professional development, 487
    resources (Tech Tool), 495
Project-based learning, 273
Project Zero (Harvard), 210
Prompt
    dissect (teacher sample), 257f
    reading, 218
    revisiting/dissecting, 232–233
Pro-social behavior, 76
Prosody, reading comprehension
    (link), 178
Publishing/presenting, usage, 243
Pull-Out method/model, 343
Puppets, 109
Push-In method, 343

Q

Question Signal Stem Share Assess
    (QSSSA), 310–311, 353
Question Word Listening (game), 449
Quizziz, 93, 203

R

Rapport, building, 364–365
Rasinski, Timothy V., 178
Rate of speech (ELL best practice),
    13
Rau, Martina A., 308
Raz-Kids, 122, 124
Read-alouds, 184
    Bilingual/Multilingual Advantages
        Read-Aloud, 396e
    copies, usage, 398
    usage, 177–178, 218–219, 411
Readers Theater, usage, 110
Reading, 258–262
    assumed directionality, 318

Children's Book, reading
    exercise, 206
comprehension, prosody (link), 178
elementary ELL usage, 353–354
Free Voluntary Reading (Extensive
    Reading) (Silent Sustained
    Reading) (recreational
    reading), 61–62, 165–167
goals, 165e
logs, 64e, 167
partner reading, 65e
Picture Word Inductive Model, 51
skills, practice, 401
strategies data set, 168e–170e
student selection, classroom
    library (usage), 388
Weekly Reading Sheet, 205e
Reading Strategies Data Set, 63
beginners, usage, 66e
Reading, Writing, and Learning in ESL
    (Peregoy/Boyle), 124
Real Aloud and Prompt: Retrieval
    Practice, 197e
Reasoning, usage, 322–323
Recasting, 108
Reciprocal teaching,
    encouragement, 367
Reflection, 76–79, 196, 272, 297–298
    academic reflection, categories,
        77–79, 274–275
    intentional formal process,
        requirement
        (reasons), 488–489
    methods, 491–492
    modeling, leadership ideas, 495
    self-filming, 489–490
    self-reflection, 495
    sharing, 493–494
    student reflection, 389–390, 471
    teacher usage/
        identification, 494–495
Reflective mindset,
    adoption, 490–495
Reflective teaching, 487
Relatedness (student intrinsic
    motivation element), 270
Relationships
    activities, 26–34
    building, 279, 364–365, 381–385
        opportunity, 284, 420
    class/teacher evaluations, 34

daily dedications, 33
ELL class R, 18–35
end-of-quarter evaluation, 34e–35e
"Find Someone in This Class
    Who…" scavenger
    hunts, 29–30
Four Squares activity, 31–32, 32f
"I Am" project, 27–28
student-student
    relationships, 21–22
talking and walking activity, 33
teacher-parent relationships, 23–25
teacher-student letter exchange, 28
teacher-student
    relationships, 19–21
Tic Tac Toe activity, 31
Two Truths and Lie activity, 30–31
weekly reflections activity, 32–33
Relationships (ELL class R),
    strengthening
    (activities), 26–34
Relevance
    academic reflection
        category, 78, 274
    student intrinsic motivation
        element, 271
Remind, usage, 26, 409
Renshaw, Jason, 411
Research, activity, 233
Research-based instructional
    strategies/approaches,
    description, 4
Resources (ELL class R), 18, 36–43
    basic art supplies, usage, 36
    bilingual dictionaries, usage, 37
    binders/folders, usage, 36
    classroom library, access, 37–39
    classroom walls, usage, 40–41
    online reading resources
        (Tech Tool), 39
    peer tutors, value, 39–40
    technology, basics, 41–42
Response to Intervention (RTI)
    process, 373, 375
Rethinking Homework (Vatterott), 99
Retrieval practice, 196
    ideas (Tech Tool), 80
    Real Aloud and Prompt: Retrieval
        Practice, 197e
    usage, 409
    value, 68

Retrieval Practice Notebook,
    121, 196, 333
    activity, 122–124
    usage, 79–80, 335
Reviews, usage, 299
Revised Bloom's Taxonomy,
    167, 209, 457
Revising, usage, 241
Revoicing, usage, 322
Rewards, avoidance, 421–422
Rhodenizer, Derek, 494
Risk-taking, building, 271
Robinson, Ken, 385
Rodier, Anne, 243
Role playing, 417
Round-robin dialogue, 123
Routines
    agendas/schedules, posting, 45
    computer routines,
        guidelines, 45–46
    ELL class R, 18, 43–46
    materials distribution,
        procedures, 44–45
    math routines, 323
    modeling, 45
    opening/ending procedures, 44
    students, greeting, 43–44
Rubrics, usage, 473–474

S

Sacramento ABC paragraph, 290e
Sacramento Information, 84e, 147
Sacramento Jigsaw, 82, 83e, 147
Salva, Carol, 373, 488
Santa Claus dialogue, 144e
Scaffolding, 179, 309, 468
    providing, 424
    tool, 110–111
Scaffolds, usage, 386
Scales, Peter C., 20
Scavenger hunt, 145
Schedules
    posting, 45
    year-long schedule, 124–126
Schools
    online activities, 125–126
    report, 127e
    school year, starting, 408–410
    staff, student learning content
        (sharing), 387

School Strip Story, 126, 131e
Science, 302–303
    classroom
        visuals/inferencing,
            usage, 306–314
    classroom, questioning, 304–306
    closed-ended questions/
        open-ended
        questions, 304, 305e
    evidence-based reasoning,
        usage, 311–312
    language-rich science classroom,
        challenges, 303–304
    resources (Tech Tool), 314
    structured conversations,
        facilitation, 308–311
    student-led questions, 306
    students, ELL teacher
        support, 312–314
    Talk Moves, usage, 322–323
    teacher-led questions,
        usage, 304–305
    teaching, 301
    Texas Science Assessments,
        percentage passing, 302f
    word wall, 346
Science, technology, engineering,
        math (STEM)
    fields, success, 302
    professions, success, 311
Scrabble (game), 458
Seasons in My Home Country
    (exercise), 136e
See-Think-Wonder, 210
Seidlitz Education, 494, 498
Self-affirmation, 388
Self-assess (academic reflection
        category), 77, 274
Self-assessments, 272, 404
    student involvement, 463, 471
Self-confidence, building, 271
Self-editing ability, 241
Self-efficacy, sense, 270
Self-reflection, 495
Semantic Maps, 175
Sentence Addition (game), 448
Sentences
    chart, scaffolding, 208
    modeling, 207–208, 208e
    sentence scramble, 71
    starters, usage, 386

translation, Google Translate
    (usage), 437
writing, strengthening, 401
Sentence Scrambles (game), 452
Sequencing activities,
    80–81, 152, 207
    online sequencing activities
        (Tech Tool), 82
    textbook passages/dialogues,
        conversion, 411
Sequential bilinguals, 8
Sequential vocabulary,
    challenge, 481
Sethi, Jenna, 20
Seton, Henry, 409
Shanahan, Timothy, 167
Sheltered English, 344
Sheltered Instruction, 6
Similar ability groups/pairs/partners,
    interaction, 416–418
Similes, 188
Sims Bishop, Rudine, 388
Simultaneous bilinguals, 8
Sister classes, student
    composition, 418
Slap (game), 447, 453
Slavery cloze, 297e
Small groups, value, 352
Social Emotional Learning
    (SEL), 408–410
    emphasis, 424
    integration, 394
    lessons/strategies, usage, 333
Social studies, teaching, 283
Songs, usage, 352, 417
Sound feedback, 473
Sounds Easy (Bassano), 73
Sounds Easy! practice, 74e
Speaking, 86, 198–199, 258–262
    assessments, 467
    elementary ELL usage, 353
    fluency assessment, 467e
    practice, games (focus), 450–452
    rate, 276
    situations, generation, 199
    skills, practice, 401
Specific, Measurable, Assignable,
    Realistic, Time-based
    (SMART) goal-setting
    framework, 363
Sped teachers, 375

Speech emergence/production
    (language development
    stage), 10
Speed Dating, 298
    method, 399
    presentations, 201, 243
    process, 79
    style, 405
Spot the Difference (game), 447, 456
Spruck Wrigley, Heide, 114
Standardized testing, 476–477
    student comfort, 477
Standards for Mathematical
    Practice, 317
State testing (Tech Tool), 478
Stations Game, 411, 415, 456
Stories
    exchange, 284
    personal stories, connections, 286
    usage, 268–269, 383–385
Storytelling
    digital storytelling (Tech Tool), 61
    online collaborative storytelling
        (Tech Tool), 73
Strip stories, usage, 80
Structured conversations,
    facilitation, 308–311
Structured conversations, usage, 353
Student Leadership Teams
    establishment, 272, 275, 386
    role, 482
Students
    academic content, cognitive
        hooks, 385
    actions, emphasis, 422
    assessment, writing
        (usage), 464–465
    brainstorming, 122
    checking in, 425
    conferences, usage, 472–473
    cultural/linguistic knowledge,
        sharing, 384–385, 390
    data-informed/data-driven
        information, 382,
        462–463, 477
    extrinsic motivation, 394
    feedback, providing, 473
    funds of knowledge, 383
    goals, 394–395
    goal sheets, usage, 471–472
    greeting, 43–44

home language deficiency,
    impact, 433–434
interview, 234e
intrinsic motivation, 394
jobs, assigning, 44
knowledge, assessment, 463
L1 usage, validation/
    encouragement, 384
language assessment, 463
language learning,
    maximization, 414–415
leadership potential,
    identification/mentoring,
    270–272, 286–287, 385–387
learning, 215
    content/process/timing, 385
lives, lesson creation/
    connection, 388
materials (usage), games
    (focus), 452–455
metacognitive awareness, 413
motivation, 215, 394–395
prior knowledge, activation, 217
problems/challenges, sharing, 385
proficiency level assessment, 463
reflection, 389–390, 471
relationships, building,
    267–268, 284
science students, ELL teacher
    support, 312–314
self-assessment, 404, 471
    involvement, 463
student-led lesson plan, 113e
student-led questions, 306
student-to-student relationships,
    enhancement, 386
student-written sentences, error
    list (avoidance), 413
success, increase, 424
support, home language
    recognition
    (importance), 433
teacher knowledge, 389
teaching, 271–272
understanding, 382–383
    teacher assistance, 387
voice, centering, 385
weekly check-ins, usage, 408–409
welcoming, 409
writing, sharing, 402–403
Student-student relationships, 21–22

Students with Interrupted Formal
    Education (SIFEs), 394
Student with Limited or Interrupted
    Formal Education
    (SLIFE), 7, 373
    support, 424–425
    Tech Tools, 426
Successful Language Learner
    Assessment, 404, 406e
Successful Language Learner Goal
    Sheet, 404, 407e
Successful Language Learner Lesson
    Plan, qualities, 270,
    401–405, 416
Summaries, usage, 298
Summarize (academic reflection
    category), 77, 274
Summarizing, usage, 202
Summative assessment, 106, 416,
    464, 474–476
    end-of-semester/end-of-year exam,
        usage, 476
    portfolios, usage, 474–475, 475e
Support class, 332–333
*Supporting English Learners in the
    Classroom* (Haas/Brown),
    373
Survival language, learning, 164
Synthesis (sample), 249f

T

Taboo (game), 458
Talking and walking (activity), 33
TalkingPoints, usage, 26
Talk Moves, usage, 322–323
Tap and Talk Activity, visuals, 309f
Teacher from the Black Lagoon
    (Thaler), 126
Teacher-parent relationships, 23–25
Teachers
    affirmations/concerns,
        communication, 409–410
    assessment (academic reflection
        category), 78–79
    Community Board, usage, 361
    feedback, 241
    innovation, 411
    letter (sample), 29e
    model, 33f, 37
    modeling, 227

teacher-led questions (science), 304–305
Teacher-student letter exchange, 28
Teacher-student relationships, 19–21, 394
Teaching English as a foreign language (TEFL), 6
Teaching English Language Learners (Haynes/Zacarian), 266–267
Teaching English to speakers of other languages (TESOL), 6
Teaching/learning academic vocabulary, online resources (Tech Tool), 85
Technology, 41–42
    classroom usage (Tech Tool), 43
    educational technology, access (limitation), 414–415
TED Talks, 201
Telephone (game), 450–451
Terrell, Tracy, 10
Test Of English as a Foreign Language (TOEFL)
    exam, 356
    preparation, 358
Tests, accessibility, 277
Texas Science Assessments, percentage passing, 302f
Textbooks
    integration, 410–412
    passages/dialogues, conversion/ personalization, 411
Text Data Sets, 63, 184–185, 219, 227
    textbook passages/dialogues, conversion, 411
    usage, 55
Texts
    accessibility, increase, 277
    annotation, example, 438f
    online annotated text, example, 437f
    resources (Tech Tool), 298
    simplification, 298
Thaler, Mike, 126
Thematic genre units, designing, 213–215
Thematic personal reports, 97
Theory of Knowledge (TOK) classes, 332, 335

Thesis
    statement, development, 256
    usage, 225–226, 237e, 246
Think-alouds, 61, 177–178, 184, 218–219
    argument think-aloud, 178
    comments, usage, 62e
    usage, 411
Thinking aloud, 13
Thinking processes, scaffolding, 189
Thinking routines, 210
    resources (Tech Tool), 210
Thinking Routines Tool (Project Zero), 210
Think-Pair Share, 210, 273
Think-write-pair-share, 76
Three-person introduction dialogue, 127e–128e
Tic Tac Toe activity, 31
Time data set, 137e
Time dialogue, 136, 137e
Tongue twisters, alliteration (usage), 107–108
Too Big to Know (Weinberger), 494
Topics, selection, 233
Total Physical Response (TPR), 86, 123, 126
    resources (Tech Tool), 88
    story planning sheet, 87e
Transitional Bilingual Education (TBE) programs, 344
Translanguaging, 384, 434
    example, 439f
Translation sites, online access, 277
Translation tools (Tech Tool), 268
Trauma detectives, role, 425
Trauma-informed instruction, 425
Traumatic memories, student processing, 425
Travel sequencing activity, 147
Tree map, usage, 346
Trusting atmosphere, building (importance), 279
Tutorials, 198
Two-period beginning ELL class (sample), 119–124
Two-period intermediate ELL class (sample week), 258–262
Two Truths and a Lie activity/game, 30–31, 451–452
Two Truths and a Lie-Plus activity, 30

U
Unaccompanied minors, SLIFE category, 424
Understanding, checking (ELL best practice), 14, 98
Unit Summary Outline, 294e–295e

V
Vaping Data Set, 261
Vatterott, Cathy, 99
Venet, Alex Shevrin, 425
Venn diagrams, 110–111, 148, 286
    usage, 346
Video, 94–95, 198–199
    English Video Sheet, practice, 200e
    focus, 490
    online videos (Tech Tool), 95
    teacher usage, 402
    usage, 491
Virtual field trips (Tech Tool), 114
Visiting a City (exercise), 147
Visualization, strategies (practice), 318–319
Visuals, 309f
    activities usage, 308
    constructivist visuals, 307f
    usage, 276, 306–314, 352
Vlogging, 492
Vocab Connection Web (activity), 308
Vocabulary
    academic vocabulary, knowledge (challenge), 319–321
    importance, 313
    reinforcement (Tech Tool), 131
    sequential vocabulary, challenge, 481

W
Wait time (ELL best practice), 13, 98, 276
    usage, 323
Walkthroughs, web creation, 457–458
Walqui, Aida, 179
Warm-up question, usage, 44, 409
Warm-Up Sentence Frames, 76, 78e, 122
Weather/temperature dialogue, 133e

Web resources, photo usage (Tech Tool), 55–56
Weekly check-ins, usage, 408–409
Weekly Reading Sheet, 204, 205e
Weekly reflections (activity), 32–33
Weinberger, David, 494
Whiteboards
  distribution, 120
  usage, 447–450
White, Shana V., 408
Whole classes
  discussions, 248, 358
  function, 416–418
Wiliam, Dylan, 331
Willis, Judy, 70, 183, 445
Wilson, Claire, 449
Word
  bank, 297
  categorizing, 121
  decoding, 61
Word charts, 276
  Autobiographical Incident Word Chart, 221e
  Literary Response Word Chart, 222e
  Problem-Solution Word Chart, 220e
  usage, 218
Word Play activity, 85

Words Webs (Semantic Maps) (Word Maps), 175
"Words You Want to Know" activity, 111–112
World-class Instructional Design and Assessment (WIDA), 11, 12f, 468
Wormeli, Rick, 478
Wrigley, Heide Spruck, 114
WRITE Institute, The, 497
Writing, 258–262
  ABC Writing Frames, 289
    classroom smartphone usage, 191e
  analytical writing lesson plan (generation), text (usage), 251–252
  argument writing resources (Tech Tool), 215
  assessment usage, 464–465
  collaborative writing, 75
  elementary ELL usage, 355
  errors, list (correction game), 447
  frames/structures, 58, 189–190, 236, 289
  Free Voluntary Reading (Extensive Reading) (Silent Sustained Reading) (recreational reading), 165–167
  generation, images (usage), 190

  genre unit, elements, 216e
  inductive writing, 289
  micro-writing, 195–196
  mimic writing, 186–189, 227
  on-demand writing practice, 244
  online writing resources (Tech Tool), 243
  Picture Word Inductive Model (PWIM), 51
  pieces, preparation, 195
  Problem-Solution Writing Frame, 60e, 237e–238e
  Problem-Solution Writing Prompt, 219e
  Problem-Solution Writing Structure, 239e–240e
  process, scaffolding, 232–233
  prompts, usage, 466–467
  skills, practice, 401

Y

Year-Long Schedule, 53, 124–126
Yzquidero, Michelle, 441

Z

Zero Prep (Pollard/Hess/Herron), 94
Zwiers, Jeff, 303